CONSOLIDATED CANADA BUSINESS CORPORATIONS ACT AND REGULATIONS 2008

28TH EDITION

Contributing Editor

Rick Levinson

LL.B. (Ont.)

THOMSON

CARSWELL

D0227000

ISSN 1484-6640
ISBN 978-0-7798-1533-3 (28th edition)

**A cataloguing record for this publication is available from Library and Archives
Canada.**

One Corporate Plaza
2075 Kennedy Road
Toronto, Ontario
M1T 3V4

Customer Relations
Toronto 1-416-609-3800
Elsewhere in Canada/U.S. 1-800-387-5164
Fax 1-416-298-5082
World Wide Web: http://www.carswell.com
E-mail: carswell.orders@thomson.com

INTRODUCTION

The legislation in this 28th edition of the *Consolidated Canada Business Corporations Act and Regulations* is current to *March 19, 2008*.

This edition contains the full text of the *Canada Business Corporations Act*, R.S.C. 1985, c. C-44, Can. Reg. 2001-512 (*Canada Business Corporations Regulations, 2001*), Can. Reg. 427 (*Minister Designation Order*), Forms under the *Canada Business Corporations Act*, the *Winding-Up and Restructuring Act*, R.S.C. 1985, c. W-11, and Policy Statements issued by Corporations Canada with respect to the *Canada Business Corporations Act*.

The following amendments are included in this edition:

- *Canada Business Corporations Act* amended to S.C. 2007, c. 6, ss. 399–401.
- *Revised CBCA Forms*: Form 1 (*Articles of Incorporation*), Form 9 (*Articles of Amalgamation*).
- *Winding-Up and Restructuring Act* amended to S.C. 2007, c. 6, ss. 443–449 [ss. 445, 446(1), 447 not in force at date of publication.]; 2007, c. 29, ss. 113–116.
- *Revised Corporations Canada CBCA Policy Statements*:

  Policy Statement 6.1 — Canada Business Corporations Act Exemption Information Kits Overview

  Policy Statement 6.2 — Exemption Kit Application Under Subsection 2(6) of the CBCA for a Determination that a Corporation is not a Distributing Corporation

  Policy Statement 6.3 — Exemption Kit Application Under Subsection 82(3) of the CBCA to Exempt a Trust Indenture from Part VIII of the CBCA

  Policy Statement 6.5 — Exemption Kit Application Under Subsection 151(1) of the CBCA to Exempt a Dissident from the Proxy Solicitation Requirements

  Policy Statement 6.6 — Exemption Kit Application Under Subsection 151(1) of the CBCA to Exempt Management from the Proxy Solicitation Requirements

  Policy Statement 6.7 — Exemption Kit Application Under Section 156 to Exempt a Corporation from the Prescribed Financial Disclosure Requirements

  Policy Statement 6.8 — Exemption Kit Application Under Subsection 171(2) of the CBCA to Exempt a Distributing Corporation from Having an Audit Committee

  Policy Statement 9.3 — Policy regarding "Export" Transactions Under Section 188 of the CBCA

  Policy Statement 9.4 — Continuance (Export) Kit

  Policy Statement 10.5.1 — Changes concerning the taxation year-end

  Policy Statement 10.6 — Revival Policy

  Policy Statement 10.8 — Revival Kit

Proposed amendments to legislation which have not been proclaimed in force as of the publication date of this edition are in gray-shaded text.

This consolidation reproduces only the official English language version of the legislation.

Introduction

It is hoped that this consolidation will prove to be a useful desktop reference for all who study or have a special interest in this area of law.

SUMMARY TABLE OF CONTENTS

Introduction iii

Table of Contents vii

Table of Concordance xxv

Canada Business Corporations Act 1

    Canada Business Corporations Regulations, 2001 139

    Minister Designation Order (*Canada Business Corporations Act*) 183

    CBCA Forms 185

Winding-up and Restructuring Act 215

Corporations Canada Policy Statements 257

Fees 523

Index 525

Table of Contents

TABLE OF CONTENTS

CANADA BUSINESS CORPORATIONS ACT
SHORT TITLE

1	Short title	1

PART I — INTERPRETATION AND APPLICATION
Interpretation

2	Definitions	1

Application

3	Application of Act	5

Purposes of Act

4	Purposes	6

PART II — INCORPORATION

5	Incorporators	6
6	Articles of incorporation	6
7	Delivery of articles of incorporation	7
8	Certificate of incorporation	7
9	Effect of certificate	7
10	Name of corporation	7
11	Reserving name	8
12	Prohibited names	8
13	Certificate of amendment	8
14	Personal liability	9

PART III — CAPACITY AND POWERS

15	Capacity of a corporation	9
16	Powers of a corporation	9
17	No constructive notice	10
18	Authority of directors, officers and agents	10

PART IV — REGISTERED OFFICE AND RECORDS

19	Registered office	10
20	Corporate records	11
21	Access to corporate records	11
22	Form of records	13
23	Corporate seal	13

PART V — CORPORATE FINANCE

24	Shares	13
25	Issue of shares	14
26	Stated capital account	14
27	Shares in series	16
28	Pre-emptive right	16

Table of Contents

29	Options and rights	16
30	Corporation holding its own shares	17
31	Exception	17
32	Exception relating to Canadian ownership	18
33	Voting shares	18
34	Acquisition of corporation's own shares	19
35	Alternative acquisition of corporation's own shares	19
36	Redemption of shares	19
37	Donated shares	20
38	Other reduction of stated capital	20
39	Adjustment of stated capital account	21
40	Enforcement of contract to buy shares	22
41	Commission for sale of shares	22
42	Dividends	23
43	Form of dividend	23
44	[Repealed 2001, c. 14, s. 26.]	23
45	Shareholder immunity	23

PART VI — SALE OF CONSTRAINED SHARES

46	Sale of constrained shares by corporation	23
47	Proceeds of sale to be trust fund	24

PART VII — SECURITY CERTIFICATES, REGISTERS AND TRANSFERS

Interpretation and General

48	Application of Part	25
49	Rights of holder	26
50	Securities records	29
51	Dealings with registered holder	29
52	Overissue	31
53	Burden of proof	31
54	Securities fungible	32

Issue — Issuer

55	Notice of defect	32
56	Staleness as notice of defect	32
57	Unauthorized signature	32
58	Completion or alteration	33
59	Warranties of agents	33

Purchase

60	Title of purchaser	33
61	Deemed notice of adverse claim	33
62	Staleness as notice of adverse claim	34
63	Warranties to issuer	34
64	Right to compel endorsement	35
65	Definition of "appropriate person"	35
66	Effect of endorsement without delivery	36
67	Endorsement in bearer form	36
68	Effect of unauthorized endorsement	36
69	Warranties of guarantor of signature	36
70	Constructive delivery of a security	37
71	Delivery of security	37

Table of Contents

72 Right to reclaim possession 37
73 Right to requisites for registration 38
74 Seizure of security 38
75 No conversion if good faith delivery by agent 38

Registration

76 Duty to register transfer 38
77 Assurance that endorsement effective 38
78 Limited duty of inquiry 39
79 Limitation of issuer's liability 40
80 Notice of lost or stolen security 40
81 Agent's duties, rights, etc. 41

PART VIII — TRUST INDENTURES

82 Definitions 41
83 Conflict of interest 42
84 Qualification of trustee 42
85 List of security holders 42
86 Evidence of compliance 43
87 Contents of declaration, etc. 43
88 Further evidence of compliance 44
89 Trustee may require evidence of compliance 44
90 Notice of default 44
91 Duty of care 44
92 Reliance on statements 44
93 No exculpation 44

PART IX — RECEIVERS AND RECEIVER-MANAGERS

94 Functions of receiver 45
95 Functions of receiver-manager 45
96 Directors' powers cease 45
97 Duty to act 45
98 Duty under instrument 45
99 Duty of care 45
100 Directions given by court 45
101 Duties of receiver and receiver-manager 46

PART X — DIRECTORS AND OFFICERS

102 Duty to manage or supervise management 46
103 By-laws 46
104 Organization meeting 47
105 Qualifications of directors 47
106 Notice of directors 48
107 Cumulative voting 49
108 Ceasing to hold office 50
109 Removal of directors 50
110 Attendance at meeting 50
111 Filling vacancy 51
112 Number of directors 51
113 Notice of change of director or director's address 52
114 Meeting of directors 52
115 Delegation 53

ix

Table of Contents

116	Validity of acts of directors and officers	53
117	Resolution in lieu of meeting	54
118	Directors' liability	54
119	Liability of directors for wages	55
120	Disclosure of interest	55
121	Officers	57
122	Duty of care of directors and officers	57
123	Dissent	58
124	Indemnification	59
125	Remuneration	60

PART XI — INSIDER TRADING

126	Definitions	60
127–129	[Repealed 2001, c. 14, s. 53.]	61
130	Prohibition of short sale	61
131	Definitions	61

PART XII — SHAREHOLDERS

132	Place of meetings	63
133	Calling annual meetings	64
134	Fixing record date	64
135	Notice of meeting	65
136	Waiver of notice	66
137	Proposals	66
138	List of shareholders entitled to receive notice	68
139	Quorum	68
140	Right to vote	69
141	Voting	69
142	Resolution in lieu of meeting	69
143	Requisition of meeting	70
144	Meeting called by court	70
145	Court review of election	71
145.1	Pooling agreement	71
146	Unanimous shareholder agreement	71

PART XIII — PROXIES

147	Definitions	72
148	Appointing proxyholder	73
149	Mandatory solicitation	74
150	Soliciting proxies	74
151	Exemption	75
152	Attendance at meeting	75
153	Duty of intermediary	76
154	Restraining order	77

PART XIV — FINANCIAL DISCLOSURE

155	Annual financial statements	77
156	Exemption	77
157	Consolidated statements	78
158	Approval of financial statements	78
159	Copies to shareholders	78
160	Copies to Director	78

161	Qualification of auditor	79
162	Appointment of auditor	80
163	Dispensing with auditor	80
164	Ceasing to hold office	80
165	Removal of auditor	80
166	Filling vacancy	80
167	Court appointed auditor	81
168	Right to attend meeting	81
169	Examination	82
170	Right to information	82
171	Audit committee	83
172	Qualified privilege (defamation)	83

PART XV — FUNDAMENTAL CHANGES

173	Amendment of articles	84
174	Constraints on shares	84
175	Proposal to amend	86
176	Class vote	86
177	Delivery of articles	87
178	Certificate of amendment	87
179	Effect of certificate	87
180	Restated articles	87
181	Amalgamation	88
182	Amalgamation agreement	88
183	Shareholder approval	88
184	Vertical short-form amalgamation	89
185	Sending of articles	90
186	Effect of certificate	90
186.1	Amalgamation under other federal Acts	91
187	Continuance (import)	91
188	Continuance — other jurisdictions	92
189	Borrowing powers	94
190	Right to dissent	95
191	Definition of "reorganization"	98
192	Definition of "arrangement"	98

PART XVI — GOING-PRIVATE TRANSACTIONS AND SQUEEZE-OUT TRANSACTIONS

193	Going-private transactions	99
194	Squeeze-out transactions	100
195–205	[Repealed 2001, c. 14, s. 97.]	100

PART XVII — COMPULSORY AND COMPELLED ACQUISITIONS

206	Definitions	100
206.1	Obligation to acquire shares	104

PART XVIII — LIQUIDATION AND DISSOLUTION

207	Definition of "court"	104
208	Application of Part	104
209	Revival	104
210	Dissolution before commencing business	105
211	Proposing liquidation and dissolution	106
212	Dissolution by Director	107

Table of Contents

213 Grounds for dissolution 108
214 Further grounds 108
215 Application for supervision 109
216 Application to court 109
217 Powers of court 109
218 Effect of order 111
219 Cessation of business and powers 111
220 Appointment of liquidator 111
221 Duties of liquidator 111
222 Powers of liquidator 112
223 Costs of liquidation 112
224 Right to distribution in money 113
225 Custody of records 113
226 Definition of "shareholder" 113
227 Unknown claimants 114
228 Vesting in Crown 115

PART XIX — INVESTIGATION
229 Investigation 115
230 Powers of court 116
231 Power of inspector 116
232 Hearing *in camera* 116
233 Criminating statements 117
234 Absolute privilege (defamation) 117
235 Information respecting ownership and control 117
236 Solicitor-client privilege 118
237 Inquiries 118

PART XIX.1 — APPORTIONING AWARD OF DAMAGES
Interpretation and Application
237.1 Definitions 118
237.2 Application of Part 119

Apportionment of Damages
237.3 Degree of responsibility 119
237.4 Exception — fraud 119

Joint and Several, or Solidary, Liability
237.5 Individual or personal body corporate 120
237.6 Equitable grounds 120
237.7 Value of security 120
237.8 Court determines value 121
237.9 Application to determine value 121

PART XX — REMEDIES, OFFENCES AND PUNISHMENT
238 Definitions 121
239 Commencing derivative action 122
240 Powers of court 122
241 Application to court re oppression 122
242 Evidence of shareholder approval not decisive 123
243 Application to court to rectify records 124
244 Application for directions 124
245 Notice of refusal by Director 124

246	Appeal from Director's decision	125
247	Restraining or compliance order	125
248	Summary application to court	125
249	Appeal of final order	125
250	Offences with respect to reports	126
251	Offence	126
252	Order to comply	126

PART XX.1 — DOCUMENTS IN ELECTRONIC OR OTHER FORM

252.1	Definitions	126
252.2	Application	127
252.3	Use not mandatory	127
252.4	Creation and provision of information	127
252.5	Creation of information in writing	127
252.6	Statutory declarations and affidavits	128
252.7	Signatures	128

PART XXI — GENERAL

253	Notice to directors and shareholders	128
254	Notice to and service on a corporation	129
255	Waiver of notice	129
256	Certificate of Director	129
257	Certificate of corporation	129
258	Copies	130
258.1	Content and form of notices and documents	130
258.2	Exemption	130
259	Proof required by Director	130
260	Appointment of Director	130
261	Regulations	131
261.1	Fee to be paid before service performed	131
262	Definition of "statement"	132
262.1	Signature	132
263	Annual return	133
263.1	Certificate	133
264	Alteration	133
265	Corrections at request of Director	133
265.1	Cancellation of articles by Director	134
266	Inspection	134
267	Records of Director	135
267.1	Form of publication	135
268	Definition of "charter"	135

2001-512 — CANADA BUSINESS CORPORATIONS REGULATIONS, 2001

INTERPRETATION

1		139
2		139
3		139

Table of Contents

PART 1 — GENERAL

Forms

4 140
5 140

Electronic Documents

6 140
7 140
8 141
9 141
10 141
11 141
12 141

"Resident Canadian" Class of Persons Prescribed

13 141

Exemption Circumstances Prescribed

14 142

Retention of Records

15 142

Business Sectors

16 142

PART 2 — CORPORATE NAMES

Interpretation

17 142

Confusion of Names

18 143

Consideration of Whole Name

19 143

Prohibited Names

20 143
21 143
22 144
23 144
24 144
25 144
26 145
27 145
28 145
29 145
30 145
31 146

Deceptively Misdescriptive Names

32 146

Certain Names Not Prohibited

33 146

Criteria for English and French Forms

34 147

Table of Contents

PART 3 — CORPORATE INTERRELATIONSHIPS

Interpretation

35 147

Prescribed Conditions

36 147
37 147
38 148

PART 4 — INSIDER TRADING

39 148
40 148
41 148
42 148

PART 5 — MEETINGS OF SHAREHOLDERS

Record Date

43 149

Notice of Meetings

44 149

Communication Facilities

45 149

PART 6 — SHAREHOLDER PROPOSALS

46 149
47 150
48 150
49 150
50 150
51 150
52 150
53 150

PART 7 — PROXIES AND PROXY SOLICITATION

Form of Proxy

54 150
55 151
56 151

Contents of Management Proxy Circular

57 152
58 159
59 160

Dissident's Proxy Circular

60 160

Contents of Dissident's Proxy Circular

61 160
62 161
63 162
64 162

Table of Contents

Date of Proxy Circular and Information

65 162

Financial Statements in Proxy Circular

66 162

Proxy Circular Exemptions

67 162
68 162
69 163

PART 8 — FINANCIAL DISCLOSURE
Interpretation

70 164

Financial Statements

71 164

Auditor's Report

71.1 166

Contents of Financial Statements

72 166

PART 9 — CONSTRAINED SHARE CORPORATIONS
Interpretation

73 166

Disclosure Required

74 168

Powers and Duties of Directors

75 168
76 169

Limitation on Voting Rights

77 169
78 169
79 169

Sale of Constrained Shares

80 170
81 173
82 173
83 174
84 174

Disclosure of Beneficial Ownership

85 174
86 174

References and Definitions for the Purpose of Certain Provisions of the Act

87 175

PART 10 — RULES OF PROCEDURE FOR APPLICATIONS FOR EXEMPTIONS
Application

88 176

Table of Contents

Time of Filing Applications
89 176

Notice by Director of Decision
90 176

General
91 177
92 177
93 177
94 177

PART 11 — VALUE OF TOTAL FINANCIAL INTEREST
95 177

PART 12 — CANCELLATION OF ARTICLES AND CERTIFICATES
96 177

PART 13 — PRESCRIBED FEES
97 177

Repeal
98 178

Coming Into Force
99 178

SCHEDULE 1 — REPORTING ISSUER

SCHEDULE 2 — TAKE-OVER BIDS

SCHEDULE 3 — EXECUTIVE REMUNERATION

SCHEDULE 4 — INDEBTEDNESS OF DIRECTORS AND OFFICERS

SCHEDULE 5 — FEES

427 — MINISTER DESIGNATION ORDER (CANADA BUSINESS CORPORATIONS ACT)
SHORT TITLE
1 183

DESIGNATION
2 183

CBCA FORMS
Form 1   Articles of Incorporation 185
Form 2   Information Regarding the Registered Office and the Board of Directors . . . 187
Form 3   Change of Registered Office Address 188
Form 4   Articles of Amendment 189
Form 6   Changes Regarding Directors 190
Form 7   Restated Articles of Incorporation 191
Form 9   Articles of Amalgamation 193

Form 11 Articles of Continuance 195
Form 14 Articles of Reorganization 197
Form 14.1 Articles of Arrangement 199
Form 15 Articles of Revival 201
Form 17 Articles of Dissolution 202
Form 19 Statement of Intent to Dissolve or Revocation of Intent to Dissolve 204
Form 22 Annual Return 206
Form 22-A Change of Taxation Year-End 210
Form 26 Statement of Executive Remuneration 211
Form 27 Application for Exemption 213

WINDING-UP AND RESTRUCTURING ACT

SHORT TITLE

1   Short title 215

INTERPRETATION

2   Definitions 215
3   When company deemed insolvent 217
4   Company deemed unable to pay its debts 218
5   Commencement of winding-up 218

APPLICATION

6   Application 218
7   Certain corporations excepted 219

PART I — GENERAL

Limitation of Part

8   Subject to Part II 219
9   Subject to Part III 219

Winding-up Order

10   Cases where winding-up order may be made 219
10.1   Other winding-up circumstances 219

Application for Order

11   Application for winding-up order 220
12   How and where made 220
13   Power of court 221
14   Proceedings may be adjourned 221
15   Duty of company 221
16   Power of the court 221

Staying Proceedings

17   Actions against company may be stayed 221
18   Court may stay winding-up proceedings 221

Effect of Winding-up Order

19   Company to cease business 222
20   Transfer of shares void 222
21   Effect of winding-up order 222
22   Execution, etc. 222
22.1   Permitted actions 222
22.2   Aircraft objects 223

Table of Contents

Appointment of Liquidators

23	Liquidator	224
24	If more than one liquidator	224
25	Additional liquidators	224
26	Notice	224
27	Security	224
28	Provisional liquidator	224
29	Incorporated company	224
30	Trust company	224
31	Powers of directors	225
32	Resignation and removal	225

Powers and Duties of Liquidators

33	Duties after appointment	225
34	Liquidator to prepare statement	225
35	Powers	225
35.1	Liquidator not liable	226
36	Appointment of solicitor	226
37	Debts due to the company	226
38	Creditors may be compromised	226
39	Court may provide as to powers	226
40	[Repealed 1996, c. 6, s. 149.]	226

Appointment of Inspectors

41	Inspectors	227

Remuneration of Liquidators and Inspectors

42	Remuneration	227
43	Remuneration of inspectors	227
44–47	[Repealed 1996, c. 6, s. 150, together with previous headings.]	227

Court Discharging Functions of Liquidator

48	If no liquidator	227
49	Provision for discharge of liquidator	227

Contributories

50	List of contributories	228
51	Classes distinguished	228
52	Adding heirs to lists	228
53	Liability of shareholders	228
54	Liability after transfer of shares	228
55	Liability of contributory a debt	228
56	Provable against his estate	228
57	Handing over money and books	228
58	Payment by contributory	229
59	Calls on contributories	229
60	Consideration of possible failure to pay	229
61	Order for payment	229
62	Rights of contributories	229

Meetings of Creditors

63	Meetings	229
64	Votes according to amount of claim	229
65	Court may summon creditors to consider any proposed compromise	229
66	Sanction of compromise	230

Table of Contents

67   Chairman of meeting 230
68   Voting to be in person or by proxy 230
69   [Repealed 1996, c. 6, s. 152, together with previous headings.] 230
70   [Repealed 1996, c. 6, s. 152, together with previous headings.] 230

Creditors' Claims

71   What debts may be proved 230
72   Claims of clerks and employees privileged 230
73   Law of set-off to apply 231
74   Time for sending in claims 231
75   Creditors required to prove claims 231
76   Distribution of assets 231
77   Rank of claims sent in after distribution started 231

Secured Claims

78   Duty of creditor holding security 232
79   Option of liquidator 232
80   Ranking of secured creditor 232
81   Security by negotiable instrument 232
81.1   Authorized foreign bank 232
82   Security by mortgage or charge 232
83   In case of subsequent claims 233
84   Authority to retain 233

Dividend Sheet

85   Preparing dividend sheet 233

Liens

86   No lien by execution, etc., after commencement of winding-up 233

Contestation of Claims

87   Claims or dividend may be objected to 234
88   Objections in writing 234
89   Day to be fixed for hearing 234
90   Costs 234
91   Default in answer by claimant 234
92   Security for costs 234

Distribution of Assets

93   Distribution of property 235
94   Winding-up expenses 235
95   Distribution of surplus 235

Fraudulent Preferences

96   Gratuitous contracts 235
97   Contracts injuring or obstructing creditors 235
98   When contracts with consideration voidable 235
99   Contracts made with intent to defraud or delay creditors 236
100   Sale or transfer in contemplation of insolvency 236
101   Payments by company within thirty days 236
101.1 Definitions 236
102   Debts of company transferred to contributories 236
102.1 Inquiry into dividends and redemptions of shares 237

Appeals

103   Appeals 238

Table of Contents

104	Court of Appeal	238
105	Practice	238
106	Dismissing appeal	238
107	Appeal to Supreme Court of Canada	238

Procedure

108	Describing liquidator	238
109	Similar to ordinary suit	239
110	Powers exercised by a single judge	239
111	Court may refer matters	239
112	Service of process out of jurisdiction	239
113	Order of court deemed judgment	239
114	Ordinary practice in case of discovery	239
115	Attachment and garnishment	239
116	Witnesses attendance	239
117	Arrest of absconding contributory, etc.	239
118	Examination	240
119	Person summoned refusing to attend	240
120	Production of papers	240
121	Lien on documents	240
122	Examination on oath	240
123	Inspection of books and papers	240
124	Officer of company misapplying money	240
125	Dispensing with notice	241
126	Courts and judges auxiliary	241
127	Order of one court enforceable by another	241
128	Proceeding on order of another court	241
129	Rules with respect to amendments	241
130	Irregularity or default	241
131	Powers conferred are supplementary	241
132	Wishes of creditors	241
133	Solicitors and counsel representing classes of creditors	242
134	Liquidator subject to summary jurisdiction of court	242
135	Remedies obtained by summary order	242

Rules, Regulations and Forms

| 136 | Judges may make | 242 |
| 137 | Until rules are made, procedure of court to apply | 242 |

Unclaimed Deposits

| 138 | Unclaimed dividends | 243 |
| 139 | Money deposited not paid after three years | 243 |

Offences and Punishment

140	Court may direct criminal proceedings	243
141	Destruction of books or false entry therein	243
142	Failure to comply with order of court	243
143	Refusal by officers of company to give information	244
144	[Repealed 1996, c. 6, s. 158.]	244
145	Refusal of witness to answer or subscribe	244

Evidence

| 146 | Books to be proof of contents | 244 |
| 147 | Affidavits | 244 |

| 148 | Judicial notice of seals, stamp or signature | 244 |
| 149 | Copy of order | 244 |

PART II — AUTHORIZED FOREIGN BANKS

150	Application of Part	245
151	Notice	245
152	Duties after appointment	245
153	Authorized foreign bank to cease business	245
154	Effect of winding-up order	245
155	Execution, etc.	245
156	Liquidator to prepare statement	246
157	What debts may be proved	246
158	Law of set-off to apply	246
158.1	Distribution of property	246
158.2	Transfer to foreign liquidator	247
158.3	Right of action not debarred	247

PART III — RESTRUCTURING OF INSURANCE COMPANIES

159	Definitions	247
159.1	Application of Part	247
160	Protection of asset orders	247
161	Order of priority for payment of claims	247
162	Transfer and reinsurance of policies by liquidator	251
162.1	Partial payment or reinsurance	252
162.2	Modification of policies	252
163	Computation of claims	253
164	Transfer of funds and securities to the liquidator	253
165	Transfer to foreign liquidator	253
166	Liquidator to prepare statement of claimants and creditors	254
167	Right of action not debarred	254
168	Copy of statement filed in Office of the Superintendent	254
169	Notice of filing	254
170	Report to Superintendent	255
171	Publication of notice of proceedings	255
172	Priority of certain claims	255

CORPORATIONS CANADA

POLICY STATEMENTS

1.1	Name Granting Compendium	257
1.1a	Name Granting Guidelines	308
2.1	Bilingual Form and Bilingualization of Articles	342
2.6	Dating of CBCA Certificates Issued Pursuant to filing of Articles	343
2.7	Requests for Correction of CBCA Certificates	345
2.7.1	Requests for Correction of CBCA Forms 2, 3, 6 and 22	348
2.8	Cancellation of CBCA Certificates and Related Articles	350
3.1	Incorporation Kit	353
3.2	Registered Office of the Corporation	368
6.1	Canada Business Corporations Act Exemption Information Kits Overview	373

Table of Contents

6.2	Exemption Kit — Application Under Subsection 2(6) of the CBCA for a Determination that a Corporation is Not a Distributing Corporation	377
6.3	Exemption Kit — Application Under Subsection 82(3) of the CBCA to Exempt a Trust Indenture from Part VIII of the CBCA	387
6.5	Exemption Kit — Application Under Subsection 151(1) of the CBCA to Exempt a Dissident from the Proxy Solicitation Requirements	395
6.6	Exemption Kit — Application Under Subsection 151(1) of the CBCA to Exempt Management from the Proxy Solicitation Requirements	404
6.7	Exemption Kit — Application Under Section 156 to Exempt a Corporation from the Prescribed Financial Disclosure Requirements	413
6.8	Exemption Kit — Application Under Subsection 171(2) of the CBCA to Exempt a Distributing Corporation from Having an Audit Committee	420
7.1	Amendment Kit	426
8.1	Amalgamation Kit	437
9.1	Continuance (Import) Kit	450
9.2	Policy on Import Continuance	465
9.3	Export Policy	467
9.4	Steps to Follow for an Export Transaction	473
10.1	Canada Business Corporations Act Dissolution Kit	477
10.5	Annual Returns	482
10.5.1	Changes Concerning the Taxation Year-end	486
10.6	Revival Policy	488
10.8	Steps to Follow to Revive a Corporation	493
11.2	Policy Related to the Certificate of Existence and to the Certificate of Compliance	498
11.4	Notice of Acknowledgment for Forms Filed Under the Canada Business Corporations Act	503
11.20	Criteria for Complaints to be Considered by Corporations Canada	504
11.28.1	Exemption from the Filing of Certain Documents (Single Filing Exemption)	505
11.30	Oppression Remedy Guidelines	506
15.1	Policy of the Director concerning Arrangements Under Section 192 of the CBCA	509

2001-512 — CANADA BUSINESS CORPORATIONS REGULATIONS, 2001

SCHEDULE 5 — FEES

TABLE OF CONCORDANCE

This table concords the *Canada Business Corporations Act*, R.S.C. 1985, c. C-44 (CA) with the following:

Alberta *Business Corporations Act*, R.S.A. 2000, c. B.9	(AB)
Ontario *Business Corporations Act*, R.S.O. 1990, c. B.16	(ON)
British Columbia *Business Corporations Act*, S.B.C. 2002, c. 57	(BC)

Part 1 Interpretation and Application

	CA	AB	ON	BC
Definitions	2(1)	1	1(1)	1(1), 300
Relationship of corporations	2(2)–(5)	2	1(2)–(5)	2
Distribution to the public	2(6)–(8)	3	1(6)	—
Application and purpose	3–4	—	2	4–5

Part 2 Incorporation

	CA	AB	ON	BC
Incorporation	5	5	4(1)	10, 13
Articles of incorporation	6	6	5	11–12
Delivery of articles of incorporation	7	7	6	18
Certificate of incorporation	8	8	6, 7	13
Effect of certificate of incorporation	9	9	7	—
Corporate name	10	10	10, 11	23–26
Assignment of name	11	11	8	—
Prohibited names	12(1)	12	9	24
Direction to change corporate name	12(2), (4), (5)	13	12	28
Certificate of amendment	13	14	12	—
Pre-incorporation contracts	14	15	21	20

Part 3 Capacity and Powers

	CA	AB	ON	BC
Capacity of a corporation	15	16	15, 16	30–33
Restriction on powers	16	17	17	22
No constructive notice	17	18	18	421
Authority of directors, officers and agents	18	19	19	136, 137, 146

Part 4 Registered Office, Records and Seal

	CA	AB	ON	BC
Registered office, records, office, address for service by mail	19	20	14	34, 35
Corporate records	20	21	140	42, 196
Access to corporate records	21	23	145, 146, 258	46, 50, 426

	CA	AB	ON	BC
Form of records	22	24	139	44
Corporate seal	23	25	13	—

Part 5 Corporate Finance

	CA	AB	ON	BC
Shares and classes of shares	24	26	22	52
Issue of shares	25	27	23	62, 63, 65, 68
Stated capital accounts	26	28	24	—
Shares in series	27	29	25	60–61
Shareholder's pre-emptive right	28	30	26	—
Options and other rights to acquire securities	29	31	27	—
Prohibited share holdings	30	32	28	—
Exception	31	33	29	—
Exception relating to Canadian ownership	31	—	29	—
Voting shares	33	33(3)	29(8)	—
Acquisition by corporation of its own shares	34	34	30	76–82
Alternative acquisition by corporation of its own shares	35	35	31	78–79
Redemption of shares	36	36	32	79
Donated and escrowed shares	37	37	33	54(1)(i), 74
Other reduction of stated capital	38	38	34	74
Adjustment of stated capital account	39	39, 40	35	104
Enforceability of contract against corporation	40	41	36	—
Commission on sale of shares	41	42	37	67
Dividends	42	43	38(3)	70
Form of dividend	43	44	38(1), (2)	70–71
Financial assistance by corporation	—	45	20	195
Shareholder immunity	45	46	40, 92(1)	—

Part 6 Sale of Constrained Shares

	CA	AB	ON	BC
Sale of constrained shares by corporation	46	—	45	—
Proceeds of sale to be trust fund	47	—	45	—

Part 7 Security Certificates, Registers and Transfers

	CA	AB	ON	BC
Definitions and interpretation	48	47	53	—
Security certificates	49	48	54–57	57, 107, 110
Securities records	50	49	141–143	42
Dealings with registered holder and transmission on death	51	50	67	115–119
Overissue	52	51	58	—
Burden of proof in actions	53	—	—	—
Securities are fungible	54	—	—	—
Notice of defects	55	—	—	—

	CA	AB	ON	BC
Staleness is notice of defect	56	—	—	—
Unauthorized signature	57	—	—	—
Completion or alteration	58	—	—	—
Warranties of agents	59	—	—	—
Title of purchaser	60	—	—	—
Deemed notice of adverse claims	61	—	—	—
Staleness as notice of adverse claims	62	—	—	—
Warranties	63	—	—	—
Right to compel endorsement	64	—	—	—
Endorsement	65	—	53(1)	—
Effect of endorsement without delivery	66	—	—	—
Endorsement in bearer form	67	—	—	—
Effect of unauthorized endorsement	68	—	—	—
Warranties of guarantors of signatures or endorsements	69	—	—	—
Constructive delivery and constructive ownership	70	—	—	—
Delivery of security	71	—	—	—
Right to reclaim possession of security	72	—	—	—
Right to requisites of transfer	73	—	—	—
Seizure of security	74	—	—	—
No conversion if good faith delivery by agent	75	—	—	—
Duty to register transfer	76	—	—	—
Assurance that endorsement is effective	77	—	—	—
Limited duty of inquiry as to adverse claims	78	—	—	—
Limitation of issuer's liability	79	—	—	—
Rights and obligations on loss or theft	80	—	—	109
Rights, duties, etc. of issuer's agent	81	—	—	—

Part 8 Trust Indentures

	CA	AB	ON	BC
Interpretation and application	82	81	46(1), (2), (4)	91
Conflict of interest	83	82	48	92(2)–(5)
Qualification of trustee	84	83	46(3)	92(1)
List of security holders	85	84	52, 258	93, 94
Evidence of compliance	86	85	49(1)	95
Contents of declaration	87	86	49(2)	96
Further evidence of compliance	88	87	49(3)	96-97
Trustee may require evidence of compliance	89	88	49(4), (5)	97
Notice of default	90	89	51	98
Trustee's duty of care	91	90	47(1)	99
Trustee's reliance on statements	92	91	49(6)	100
No exculpation of trustee by agreement	93	92	47(2)	101

Part 9 Receivers and Receiver-Managers

	CA	AB	ON	BC
Functions of receiver	94	93	—	—
Functions of receiver-manager	95	94	—	—
Director's powers cease	96	95	—	105
Court-appointed receiver or receiver-manager	97	96	—	—
Duty under debt obligation	98	97	—	—
Duty of care	99	98	—	99
Powers of the court	100	99	—	—
Duties of receiver and receiver-manager	101	100	—	106

Part 10 Directors and Officers

	CA	AB	ON	BC
Directors	102	101	115(1), (2)	120, 136, 142
By-laws	103	102	116	140(3), 259
Organization meeting	104	104	117(1), (3), (4)	—
Qualifications of directors	105	105	118	121(2), 122(4), 124, 125
Election and appointment of directors	106	106	119, 124(2)	121, 122, 127, 128
Cumulative voting	107	107	120	—
Ceasing to hold office	108	108	121	128(1), (2)
Removal of directors	109	109	122	128(3)
Attendance at meetings	110	110	123	140
Filling vacancies	111	111	124	131, 132
Change in number of directors	112	112	125(1)	—
Notice of change of directors	113	113	—	127
Meetings of directors	114	114	126	140
Delegation to managing director or committee	115	115	127	—
Validity of acts of directors, officers and committees	116	116	128	143
Resolution in lieu of meeting	117	117	129	140(3)
Liability of directors and others	118	118	130	148, 154
Directors' liability for wages	119	119	131	—
Disclosure by directors and officers in relation to contracts	120	120	132	142, 147, 148
Officers	121	121	133	—
Duty of care of directors and officers	122	122	134	142
Dissent by director	123	123	135	154(5)–(8)
Indemnification by corporation	124	124	136	160
Remuneration	125	125	137	—

Part 11 Insider Trading

	CA	AB	ON	BC
Definitions	126	126–129	138	1, 192
First insider report	127	—	—	—
Notice of purchase of own shares	128	—	—	—
Publication	129	264	—	—

	CA	AB	ON	BC
Prohibition of short sale	130	—	—	—
Definition of "insider"	131	126–130	138	192

Part 12 Shareholders

	CA	AB	ON	BC
Place of shareholder's meetings	132	131	93	166
Calling meetings	133	132	94	189
Record dates	134	133	95	171
Notice of meeting, adjournment, business and notice of business	135	134	96	169
Waiver of notice	136	135	98	170
Shareholder proposals	137	136	99	187–191
Shareholder list	138	137	100	112
Quorum	139	138	101	172
Right to vote	140	139	102	173, 177, 181
Voting	141	140	103	173
Resolution in lieu of meetings	142	141	104	182
Meeting on requisition of shareholders	143	142	105	167
Meeting called by court	144	143	106	186(1), (2)
Court review of election	145	144	107	—
Pooling agreement	146	145, 146	108	—

Part 13 Proxies

	CA	AB	ON	BC
Definitions	147	147	109	1(1)
Appointing proxyholder	148	148	110	—
Mandatory solicitation	149	149	111, 258	—
Soliciting proxies	150	150	112, 258	—
Exemption orders	151	151	113	—
Rights and duties of proxyholder	152	152	114, 258	—
Duties of registrant	153	153	—	—
Court orders	154	154	—	—

Part 14 Financial Disclosure

	CA	AB	ON	BC
Annual financial statements	155	155	154(1)	185
Exemption	156	156	148	—
Consolidated statements	157	157	157	—
Approval of financial statements	158	158	159	199
Copies to shareholders	159	159	154(3)	198, 201
Copies to Chief of Securities Administration	160	160	156, 160	—
Qualification of the auditor	161	161	152	205, 221, 222, 208
Auditor's appointment and remuneration	162	162	149(1), (2), (7)	207
Dispensing with auditor	163	163	148	203
Auditor ceasing to hold office	164	164	150	—
Removal of auditor	165	165	149(4)	208, 209

	CA	AB	ON	BC
Filling vacancy	166	166	149(3)	204
Court-appointed auditor	167	167	149(8)	204(5)
Rights and liabilities of auditor and former auditor	168	168	149(5)–(7), 151	209, 210, 216–219
Auditor's duty to examine	169	169	153	212, 217, 218
Auditor's right to information	170	170	153(5), (6)	217, 218
Audit committee	171	171	153, 158	204, 216
Qualified privilege	172	172	151(7), 153(7)	220

Part 15 Fundamental Changes

	CA	AB	ON	BC
Amendment of articles	173	173	168	54, 60, 256, 259, 264(1)
Constrain shares	174	174	42(2)–(4)	264
Proposal for amendment	175	175	169	263
Class votes	176	176	170	61
Delivery of articles of amendments	177	177	171	263
Certificate of amendment	178	178	172	263
Effect of certificate	179	179	273(3)	256, 263
Restated articles of incorporation	180	180	173	—
Amalgamation	181	181	174	269, 279
Amalgamation agreement	182	182	175	270
Shareholder approval of amalgamation agreement	183	183	176	271, 272
Vertical and horizontal short form amalgamation	184	184	177	273, 274
Delivery of articles of amalgamation and statutory declaration to Registrar	185	185	178	—
Effect of certificate of amalgamation	186	186	179	282
Amalgamation under other federal Acts	186.1	—	—	—
Continuance (import)	187	188	180	302, 305
Continuance (other jurisdictions)	188	189	181	308
Borrowing powers	189	103, 190	184	—
Shareholder's right to dissent	190	191	185	238, 260
Definition of reorganization	191	192	186	—
Definition of arrangement	192	193	182, 183	288–291

Part 16 Going-Private Transactions and Squeeze-out Transactions

	CA	AB	ON	BC
Going-private transactions	193	—	—	—

Part 17 Take-over Bids

	CA	AB	ON	BC
Definitions	194	194	187	300
Bid for all shares	195	—	—	—
Bid for less than all shares	196	—	—	—
Every bid for shares	197	—	—	—
Sending bid	198	—	—	—

	CA	AB	ON	BC
Arrangements for funds	199	—	—	—
Share-for-share bids	200	—	—	—
Director's circular	201	—	—	—
Expert's consent	202	—	—	—
Approval of take-over bid	203	—	—	—
Exemption order	204	—	—	—
Offence	205	—	—	—
Definitions	206	194–205	187, 188	300

Part 18 Liquidation and Dissolution

	CA	AB	ON	BC
Definition of "court"	207	—	—	—
Application of Part	208	207	192, 206, 219	313
Revival	209	208–210	241(5)–(7)	354–368
Dissolution by directors or shareholders in special cases	210	211	237–239	324, 325
Voluntary liquidation and dissolution	211	212	192–205	314, 316
Dissolution by Registrar	212	213	240, 241	422, 424
Dissolution by court order	214	214	—	—
Other grounds for liquidation and dissolution	214	215	207, 208	324, 326
Application for court supervision	215	216	229	—
Show cause order	216	217	—	—
Powers of the court	217	218	209, 215, 229, 233	324–326
Commencement of liquidation	218	219	213	312, 340(2)
Effect of liquidation order	219	220	221	344
Appointment of liquidator	220	221	210	319, 322
Duties of liquidator	221	222	210(4), 221, 227	330, 331, 337, 338
Powers of liquidator	222	223	223, 224, 229	334–336, 320
Final accounts and discharge of liquidator	223	224	212, 218, 222, 229, 231	338, 341, 350
Shareholder's right to distribution in money	224	225	224, 229	336, 348
Custody of records after dissolution	225	226	217(2), 236	351
Continuation of actions after dissolution	226	227	242, 243	346
Unknown claimants	227	228	234, 235	331
Property not disposed of	228	229	244	368

Part 19 Investigation

	CA	AB	ON	BC
Court order for investigation	229	231	161	248–251
Powers of the court	230	232	162(6)	234, 236, 229, 230, 248(1), (3)
Powers of inspector	231	233	163	248, 251
Hearings by inspector	232	234	164	248
Compelling evidence	233	235	—	254

	CA	AB	ON	BC
Absolute privilege	234	236	165	255
Information respecting ownership and control	235	—	—	—
Solicitor-client privilege	236	237	166	252
Inquiries	237	—	167	—

Part 19.1 Apportioning Award of Damages

	CA	AB	ON	BC
Definitions	237.1	—	—	—
Applications	237.2	—	—	—
Apportionment	237.3, 237.4	—	—	—
Liability	237.5–237.9	—	—	—

Part 20 Remedies, Offences and Penalties

	CA	AB	ON	BC
Definitions	238	239	245	232
Commencing derivative action	239	240	246	232
Powers of the court	240	241	247	233, 236
Relief by court on the ground of oppression or unfairness	241	242	248	227
Court approval of stay, dismissal, discontinuance or settlement	242	243	249	233
Court order to rectify records	243	244	250	—
Court order for directions	244	245	—	—
Refusal by registrar to file	245	246	251	408(2)
Appeal from decision of Registrar or Board	246	247	252	28, 406
Compliance or restraining order	247	248	253	228
Summary application to court	248	249	254	235(1)
Appeals from court order	249	250	255	—
Offences relating to reports, returns, etc.	250	251	256, 257	427
General offence	251	252	258	—
Order to comply	252	253	259, 261	430

Part 20.1 Documents in Electronic or Other Form

	CA	AB	ON	BC
Definitions	252.1	—	—	—
Application	252.1	—	—	—
Use and consent	252.3	—	—	—
Creation and provision of information	252.4, 252.5	—	—	—
Statutory declarations and affidavits	252.6	—	—	—
Signatures	252.7	—	—	—

Part 21 General

	CA	AB	ON	BC
Sending of notices and documents to shareholders and directors	253	255	262	181
Notice to and service on a corporation	254	256	263	235(2)
Waiver of notice	255	258	264	—
Certificate of Registrar as evidence	256	259	265	416, 419
Certificate of corporation as evidence	257	260	266	—
Copies	258, 258.1, 258.2, 261.1	261	267	—
Proof required by Director	259	262	268	—
Appointment of Director	260	263	278	400
Regulations, publication of proposed regulation	261	266	272	432
Issuing of certificates	262, 262.1, 263.1	267	273	18
Annual return	263	268	—	51
Alteration of documents	264	269	—	—
Errors in certificates	265	270	275	414, 420
Inspection and copies	266, 261.1	271	270	416
Records of director	267	272	276	194, 198–200
Form of publication	267.1	264	—	—
Definition of "charity"	268	—	—	—

CANADA BUSINESS CORPORATIONS ACT

An act respecting Canadian business corporations

R.S.C. 1985, c. C-44, as am. R.S.C. 1985, c. 27 (1st Supp.), s. 187 (Sched. V, item 3); R.S.C. 1985, c. 27 (2nd Supp.), s. 10 (Sched., item 5); R.S.C. 1985, c. 1 (4th Supp.), s. 45 (Sched. III, item 5) (Fr.); S.C. 1988, c. 2, s. 19 [1988, c. 2, s. 19 repealed ss. 263 and 264 of 1974-75-76, c. 33, which had been neither consolidated nor repealed by R.S.C. 1985, c. C-44.]; 1990, c. 17, s. 6; 1991, c. 45, ss. 551–556; 1991, c. 46, ss. 595–597; 1991, c. 47, ss. 719–724; 1992, c. 1, ss. 53–57, 142 (Sched. V, items 11, 12); 1992, c. 27, s. 90(1)(h); 1992, c. 51, s. 30; 1993, c. 28, s. 78 (Sched. III, item 24) [Repealed 1999, c. 3 (Sched., item 4).]; 1994, c. 21, s. 125; 1994, c. 24, ss. 1–32, 34(c) [ss. 1, 2(1), (2), 4, 5(2), 8(1), 9, 13–15, 22(4), 34(c): (Fr.)]; 1996, c. 6, s. 167(g); 1996, c. 10, ss. 212–214; 1998, c. 1, ss. 380, 381; 1998, c. 30, s. 15(b); 1999, c. 3, s. 16; 1999, c. 31, ss. 63–65; 2000, c. 12, s. 27; 2001, c. 14, ss. 1–136, Sched. [ss. 1(2), (6), 2, 11(4), 16, 17(1), 18(1), 20, 21(1), 22(1), (2), 24, 28(2), 33, 34, 36, 47(2), 49, 65, 73, 78(2), 83(2), 91(2), 94(1), 96(2), 99(9), 103(1), 107, 113, 114(1), 117, 118, 123, 134: (Fr.)]; 2001, c. 27, s. 209; 2002, c. 7, s. 88; 2004, c. 25, s. 187; 2005, c. 33, s. 5; 2007, c. 6, ss. 399–401.

SHORT TITLE

1. Short title — This Act may be cited as the *Canada Business Corporations Act.*

PART I — INTERPRETATION AND APPLICATION

Interpretation

2. (1) Definitions — In this Act,

"affairs" means the relationships among a corporation, its affiliates and the shareholders, directors and officers of such bodies corporate but does not include the business carried on by such bodies corporate; *("affaires")*

"affiliate" means an affiliated body corporate within the meaning of subsection (2); *("groupe")*

"articles" means the original or restated articles of incorporation, articles of amendment, articles of amalgamation, articles of continuance, articles of reorganization, articles of arrangement, articles of dissolution, articles of revival and includes any amendments thereto; *("statuts")*

"associate", in respect of a relationship with a person, means

(a) a body corporate of which that person beneficially owns or controls, directly or indirectly, shares or securities currently convertible into shares carrying more than ten per cent of the voting rights under all circumstances or by reason of the occurrence of

1

an event that has occurred and is continuing, or a currently exercisable option or right to purchase such shares or such convertible securities,

(b) a partner of that person acting on behalf of the partnership of which they are partners,

(c) a trust or estate in which that person has a substantial beneficial interest or in respect of which that person serves as a trustee or liquidator of the succession or in a similar capacity,

(d) a spouse of that person or an individual who is cohabiting with that person in a conjugal relationship, having so cohabited for a period of at least one year,

(e) a child of that person or of the spouse or individual referred to in paragraph (d), and

(f) a relative of that person or of the spouse or individual referred to in paragraph (d), if that relative has the same residence as that person;

("liens")

"auditor" includes a partnership of auditors or an auditor that is incorporated; *("vérificateur")*

"beneficial interest" means an interest arising out of the beneficial ownership of securities; *("véritable propriétaire")*

"beneficial ownership" includes ownership through any trustee, legal representative, agent or other intermediary; *("véritable propriétaire")*

"body corporate" includes a company or other body corporate wherever or however incorporated; *("personne morale")*

"call" means an option transferable by delivery to demand delivery of a specified number or amount of securities at a fixed price within a specified time but does not include an option or right to acquire securities of the corporation that granted the option or right to acquire; *("option d'achat")*

"corporation" means a body corporate incorporated or continued under this Act and not discontinued under this Act; *("société par actions")*

"court" means

(a) in the Provinces of Newfoundland and Prince Edward Island, the trial division of the Supreme Court of the Province,

(a.1) in the Province of Ontario, the Superior Court of Justice,

(b) in the Provinces of Nova Scotia and British Columbia, the Supreme Court of the Province,

(c) in the Provinces of Manitoba, Saskatchewan, Alberta and New Brunswick, the Court of Queen's Bench for the Province,

(d) in the Province of Quebec, the Superior Court of the Province, and

(e) the Supreme Court of Yukon, the Supreme Court of the Northwest Territories and the Nunavut Court of Justice;

("tribunal")

"court of appeal" means the court to which an appeal lies from an order of a court; *("Cour d'appel")*

"debt obligation" means a bond, debenture, note or other evidence of indebtedness or guarantee of a corporation, whether secured or unsecured; *("titre de créance")*

"Director" means the Director appointed under section 260; *("directeur")*

"director" means a person occupying the position of director by whatever name called and "directors" and "board of directors" includes a single director; *("administrateur")*

"distributing corporation" means, subject to subsections (6) and (7), a distributing corporation as defined in the regulations; *("société ayant fait appel au public")*

"entity" means a body corporate, a partnership, a trust, a joint venture or an unincorporated association or organization; *("entité")*

"going-private transaction" means a going-private transaction as defined in the regulations; *("opération de fermeture")*

"incorporator" means a person who signs articles of incorporation; *("fondateur")*

"individual" means a natural person; *("particulier")*

"liability" includes a debt of a corporation arising under section 40, subsection 190(25) and paragraphs 241(3)(f) and (g); *("passif")*

"Minister" means such member of the Queen's Privy Council for Canada as is designated by the Governor in Council as the Minister for the purposes of this Act; *("ministre")*

"officer" means an individual appointed as an officer under section 121, the chairperson of the board of directors, the president, a vice-president, the secretary, the treasurer, the comptroller, the general counsel, the general manager, a managing director, of a corporation, or any other individual who performs functions for a corporation similar to those normally performed by an individual occupying any of those offices; *("dirigeant")*

"ordinary resolution" means a resolution passed by a majority of the votes cast by the shareholders who voted in respect of that resolution; *("résolution ordinaire")*

"person" means an individual, partnership, association, body corporate, or personal representative; *("personne")*

"personal representative" means a person who stands in place of and represents another person including, but not limited to, a trustee, an executor, an administrator, a receiver, an agent, a liquidator of a succession, a guardian, a tutor, a curator, a mandatary or an attorney; *("représentant personnel")*

"prescribed" means prescribed by the regulations; *("prescrit")*

"put" means an option transferable by delivery to deliver a specified number or amount of securities at a fixed price within a specified time; *("option de vente")*

"redeemable share" means a share issued by a corporation

   (a) that the corporation may purchase or redeem on the demand of the corporation, or

   (b) that the corporation is required by its articles to purchase or redeem at a specified time or on the demand of a shareholder;

("action rachetable")

"resident Canadian" means an individual who is

(a) a Canadian citizen ordinarily resident in Canada,

(b) a Canadian citizen not ordinarily resident in Canada who is a member of a prescribed class of persons, or

(c) a permanent resident within the meaning of subsection 2(1) of the *Immigration and Refugee Protection Act* and ordinarily resident in Canada, except a permanent resident who has been ordinarily resident in Canada for more than one year after the time at which he or she first became eligible to apply for Canadian citizenship;

("résident canadien")

"security" means a share of any class or series of shares or a debt obligation of a corporation and includes a certificate evidencing such a share or debt obligation; *("valeur mobilière")*

"security interest" means an interest in or charge on property of a corporation to secure payment of a debt or performance of any other obligation of the corporation; *("sûreté")*

"send" includes deliver; *("envoyer")*

"series", in relation to shares, means a division of a class of shares; *("série")*

"special resolution" means a resolution passed by a majority of not less than two-thirds of the votes cast by the shareholders who voted in respect of that resolution or signed by all the shareholders entitled to vote on that resolution; *("résolution spéciale")*

"squeeze-out transaction" means a transaction by a corporation that is not a distributing corporation that would require an amendment to its articles and would, directly or indirectly, result in the interest of a holder of shares of a class of the corporation being terminated without the consent of the holder, and without substituting an interest of equivalent value in shares issued by the corporation, which shares have equal or greater rights and privileges than the shares of the affected class; *("opération d'éviction")*

"unanimous shareholder agreement" means an agreement described in subsection 146(1) or a declaration of a shareholder described in subsection 146(2). *("convention unanime des actionnaires")*

(2) Affilated bodies corporate — For the purposes of this Act,

(a) one body corporate is affilated with another body corporate if one of them is the subsidiary of the other or both are subsidiaries of the same body corporate or each of them is controlled by the same person; and

(b) if two bodies corporate are affilated with the same body corporate at the same time, they are deemed to be affiliated with each other.

(3) Control — For the purposes of this Act, a body corporate is controlled by a person or by two or more bodies corporate if

(a) securities of the body corporate to which are attached more than fifty per cent of the votes that may be cast to elect directors of the body corporate are held, other than by way of security only, by or for the benefit of that person or by or for the benefit of those bodies corporate; and

(b) the votes attached to those securities are sufficient, if exercised, to elect a majority of the directors of the body corporate.

(4) Holding body corporate — A body corporate is the holding body corporate of another if that other body corporate is its subsidiary.

(5) Subsidiary body corporate — A body corporate is a subsidiary of another body corporate if

(a) it is controlled by

(i) that other body corporate,

(ii) that other body corporate and one or more bodies corporate each of which is controlled by that other body corporate, or

(iii) two or more bodies corporate each of which is controlled by that other body corporate; or

(b) it is a subsidiary of a body corporate that is a subsidiary of that other body corporate.

(6) Exemptions — on application by corporation — On the application of a corporation, the Director may determine that the corporation is not or was not a distributing corporation if the Director is satisfied that the determination would not be prejudicial to the public interest.

(7) Exemptions — classes of corporations — The Director may determine that a class of corporations are not or were not distributing corporations if the Director is satisfied that the determination would not be prejudicial to the public interest.

(8) Infants — For the purposes of this Act, the word **"infant"** has the same meaning as in the applicable provincial law and, in the absence of any such law, has the same meaning as the word "child" in the United Nations Convention on the Rights of the Child, adopted in the United Nations General Assembly on November 20, 1989.

R.S.C. 1985, c. 27 (2nd Supp.), s. 10 (Sched., item 5); 1990, c. 17, s. 6; 1992, c. 51, s. 30; 1994, c. 24, s. 2; 1998, c. 30, s. 15(b); 1999, c. 3, s. 16; 2000, c. 12, s. 27; 2001, c. 14, ss. 1(1), (3)–(5), (7), 135 (Sched., s. 1); 2001, c. 27, s. 209; 2002, c. 7, s. 88

Application

3. (1) Application of Act — This Act applies to every corporation incorporated and every body corporate continued as a corporation under this Act that has not been discontinued under this Act.

(2) [Repealed 1991, c. 45, s. 551(1) and 1991, c. 47, s. 719(1).]

(3) Certain Acts do not apply — The following do not apply to a corporation:

(a) the *Canada Corporations Act*, chapter C-32 of the Revised Statutes of Canada, 1970;

(b) the *Winding-up and Restructuring Act*; and

(c) the provisions of a Special Act, as defined in section 87 of the *Canada Transportation Act*, that are inconsistent with this Act.

(4) Limitations on business that may be carried on — No corporation shall carry on the business of

(a) a bank;

(a.1) an association to which the *Cooperative Credit Associations Act* applies;

(b) a company or society to which the *Insurance Companies Act* applies; or

(c) a company to which the *Trust and Loan Companies Act* applies.

(5) Limitations on business that may be carried on — No corporation shall carry on business as a degree-granting educational institution unless expressly authorized to do so by a federal or provincial agent that by law has the power to confer degree-granting authority on an educational institution.

> 1991, c. 45, s. 551; 1991, c. 46, s. 595; 1991, c. 47, s. 719; 1992, c. 1, s. 142 (Sched., item 11); 1994, c. 24, s. 3; 1996, c. 6, s. 167(1)(g); 1996, c. 10, s. 212; 1999, c. 31, s. 63; 2007, c. 6, s. 399

Purposes of Act

4. Purposes — The purposes of this Act are to revise and reform the law applicable to business corporations incorporated to carry on business throughout Canada, to advance the cause of uniformity of business corporation law in Canada and to provide a means of allowing an orderly transference of certain federal companies incorporated under various Acts of Parliament to this Act.

PART II — INCORPORATION

5. (1) Incorporators — One or more individuals not one of whom

(a) is less than eighteen years of age,

(b) is of unsound mind and has been so found by a court in Canada or elsewhere, or

(c) has the status of bankrupt,

may incorporate a corporation by signing articles of incorporation and complying with section 7.

(2) Bodies corporate — One or more bodies corporate may incorporate a corporation by signing articles of incorporation and complying with section 7.

6. (1) Articles of incorporation — Articles of incorporation shall follow the form that the Director fixes and shall set out, in respect of the proposed corporation,

(a) the name of the corporation;

(b) the province in Canada where the registered office is to be situated;

(c) the classes and any maximum number of shares that the corporation is authorized to issue, and

    (i) if there will be two or more classes of shares, the rights, privileges, restrictions and conditions attaching to each class of shares, and

    (ii) if a class of shares may be issued in series, the authority given to the directors to fix the number of shares in, and to determine the designation of, and the rights, privileges, restrictions and conditions attaching to, the shares of each series;

(d) if the issue, transfer or ownership of shares of the corporation is to be restricted, a statement to that effect and a statement as to the nature of such restrictions;

(e) the number of directors or, subject to paragraph 107(a), the minimum and maximum number of directors of the corporation; and

(f) any restrictions on the businesses that the corporation may carry on.

(2) Additional provisions in articles — The articles may set out any provisions permitted by this Act or by law to be set out in the by-laws of the corporation.

(3) Special majorities — Subject to subsection (4), if the articles or a unanimous shareholder agreement require a greater number of votes of directors or shareholders than that required by this Act to effect any action, the provisions of the articles or of the unanimous shareholder agreement prevail.

(4) Idem — The articles may not require a greater number of votes of shareholders to remove a director than the number required by section 109.

2001, c. 14, s. 3

7. Delivery of articles of incorporation — An incorporator shall send to the Director articles of incorporation and the documents required by sections 19 and 106.

8. (1) Certificate of incorporation — Subject to subsection (2), on receipt of articles of incorporation, the Director shall issue a certificate of incorporation in accordance with section 262.

(2) Exception — failure to comply with Act — The Director may refuse to issue the certificate if a notice that is required to be sent under subsection 19(2) or 106(1) indicates that the corporation, if it came into existence, would not be in compliance with this Act.

2001, c. 14, s. 4

9. Effect of certificate — A corporation comes into existence on the date shown in the certificate of incorporation.

10. (1) Name of corporation — The word or expression "Limited", "Limitée", "Incorporated", "Incorporée", "Corporation" or "Société par actions de régime fédéral" or the corresponding abbreviation "Ltd.", "Ltée", "Inc.", "Corp." or "S.A.R.F." shall be part, other than only in a figurative or descriptive sense, of the name of every corporation, but a corporation may use and be legally designated by either the full or the corresponding abbreviated form.

(1.1) Saving for "S.C.C." — Subsection (1) does not apply to a corporation that has a corporate name that, immediately before the day on which this subsection comes into force, included, other than only in a figurative or descriptive sense, the expression "Société commerciale canadienne" or the abbreviation "S.C.C.", and any such corporation may use and be legally designated by either that expression or that abbreviation.

(2) Exemption — The Director may exempt a body corporate continued as a corporation under this Act from the provisions of subsection (1).

(3) Alternate name — Subject to subsection 12(1), the name of a corporation may be set out in its articles in an English form, a French form, an English form and a French form, or a combined English and French form, so long as the combined form meets the prescribed criteria. The corporation may use and may be legally designated by any such form.

(4) Alternative name outside Canada — Subject to subsection 12(1), a corporation may, for use outside Canada, set out its name in its articles in any language form and it may use and may be legally designated by any such form outside Canada.

(5) Publication of name — A corporation shall set out its name in legible characters in all contracts, invoices, negotiable instruments and orders for goods or services issued or made by or on behalf of the corporation.

(6) Other name — Subject to subsections (5) and 12(1), a corporation may carry on business under or identify itself by a name other than its corporate name if that other name does not contain, other than in a figurative or descriptive sense, either the word or expression "Limited", "Limitée", "Incorporated", "Incorporée", "Corporation" or "Société par actions de régime fédéral" or the corresponding abbreviation.

1992, c. 1, s. 53; 1994, c. 24, s. 5; 2001, c. 14, s. 5

11. (1) Reserving name — The Director may, on request, reserve for ninety days a name for an intended corporation or for a corporation about to change its name.

(2) Designating number — If requested to do so by the incorporators or a corporation, the Director shall assign to the corporation as its name a designating number followed by the word "Canada" and a word or expression, or the corresponding abbreviation, referred to in subsection 10(1).

1994, c. 24, s. 6

12. (1) Prohibited names — A corporation shall not be incorporated or continued as a corporation under this Act with, have, carry on business under or identify itself by a name

(a) that is, as prescribed, prohibited or deceptively misdescriptive; or

(b) that is reserved for another corporation or intended corporation under section 11.

(2) Directing change of name — If, through inadvertence or otherwise, a corporation

(a) comes into existence or is continued with a name, or

(b) on an application to change its name, is granted a name

that contravenes this section, the Director may direct the corporation to change its name in accordance with section 173.

(3) [Repealed 1994, c. 24, s. 7(2).]

(4) Idem — If a corporation has a designating number as its name, the Director may direct the corporation to change its name to a name other than a designating number in accordance with section 173.

(4.1) Undertaking to change name — Where a corporation acquires a name as a result of a person undertaking to dissolve or to change names, and the undertaking is not honoured, the Director may direct the corporation to change its name in accordance with section 173, unless the undertaking is honoured within the period specified in subsection (5).

(5) Revoking name — When a corporation has been directed under subsection (2), (4) or (4.1) to change its name and has not within sixty days after the service of the directive to that effect changed its name to a name that complies with this Act, the Director may revoke the name of the corporation and assign a name to it and, until changed in accordance with section 173, the name of the corporation is thereafter the name so assigned.

1994, c. 24, s. 7

13. (1) Certificate of amendment — When a corporation has had its name revoked and a name assigned to it under subsection 12(5), the Director shall issue a certificate of amendment showing the new name of the corporation and shall give notice of the change of name as soon as practicable in a publication generally available to the public.

(2) Effect of certificate — The articles of the corporation are amended accordingly on the date shown in the certificate of amendment.

2001, c. 14, s. 6

14. (1) Personal liability — Subject to this section, a person who enters into, or purports to enter into, a written contract in the name of or on behalf of a corporation before it comes into existence is personally bound by the contract and is entitled to its benefits.

(2) Pre-incorporation and pre-amalgamation contracts — A corporation may, within a reasonable time after it comes into existence, by any action or conduct signifying its intention to be bound thereby, adopt a written contract made before it came into existence in its name or on its behalf, and on such adoption

(a) the corporation is bound by the contract and is entitled to the benefits thereof as if the corporation had been in existence at the date of the contract and had been a party thereto; and

(b) a person who purported to act in the name of or on behalf of the corporation ceases, except as provided in subsection (3), to be bound by or entitled to the benefits of the contract.

(3) Application to court — Subject to subsection (4), whether or not a written contract made before the coming into existence of a corporation is adopted by the corporation, a party to the contract may apply to a court for an order respecting the nature and extent of the obligations and liability under the contract of the corporation and the person who entered into, or purported to enter into, the contract in the name of or on behalf of the corporation. On the application, the court may make any order it thinks fit.

(4) Exemption from personal liability — If expressly so provided in the written contract, a person who purported to act in the name of or on behalf of the corporation before it came into existence is not in any event bound by the contract or entitled to the benefits thereof.

2001, c. 14, s. 7

PART III — CAPACITY AND POWERS

15. (1) Capacity of a corporation — A corporation has the capacity and, subject to this Act, the rights, powers and privileges of a natural person.

(2) Idem — A corporation may carry on business throughout Canada.

(3) Extra-territorial capacity — A corporation has the capacity to carry on its business, conduct its affairs and exercise its powers in any jurisdiction outside Canada to the extent that the laws of such jurisdiction permit.

16. (1) Powers of a corporation — It is not necessary for a by-law to be passed in order to confer any particular power on the corporation or its directors.

(2) Restricted business or powers — A corporation shall not carry on any business or exercise any power that it is restricted by its articles from carrying on or exercising, nor shall the corporation exercise any of its powers in a manner contrary to its articles.

(3) Rights preserved — No act of a corporation, including any transfer of property to or by a corporation, is invalid by reason only that the act or transfer is contrary to its articles or this Act.

17. No constructive notice — No person is affected by or is deemed to have notice or knowledge of the contents of a document concerning a corporation by reason only that the document has been filed by the Director or is available for inspection at an office of the corporation.

18. (1) Authority of directors, officers and agents — No corporation and no guarantor of an obligation of a corporation may assert against a person dealing with the corporation or against a person who acquired rights from the corporation that

(a) the articles, by-laws and any unanimous shareholder agreement have not been complied with;

(b) the persons named in the most recent notice sent to the Director under section 106 or 113 are not the directors of the corporation;

(c) the place named in the most recent notice sent to the Director under section 19 is not the registered office of the corporation;

(d) a person held out by a corporation as a director, an officer or an agent of the corporation has not been duly appointed or has no authority to exercise the powers and perform the duties that are customary in the business of the corporation or usual for a director, officer or agent;

(e) a document issued by any director, officer or agent of a corporation with actual or usual authority to issue the document is not valid or not genuine; or

(f) a sale, lease or exchange of property referred to in subsection 189(3) was not authorized.

(2) Exception — Subsection (1) does not apply in respect of a person who has, or ought to have, knowledge of a situation described in that subsection by virtue of their relationship to the corporation.

2001, c. 14, s. 8

PART IV — REGISTERED OFFICE AND RECORDS

19. (1) Registered office — A corporation shall at all times have a registered office in the province in Canada specified in its articles.

(2) Notice of registered office — A notice of registered office in the form that the Director fixes shall be sent to the Director together with any articles that designate or change the province where the registered office of the corporation is located.

(3) Change of address — The directors of a corporation may change the place and address of the registered office within the province specified in the articles.

(4) Notice of change of address — A corporation shall send to the Director, within fifteen days of any change of address of its registered office, a notice in the form that the Director fixes and the Director shall file it.

2001, c. 14, s. 9

20. (1) Corporate records — A corporation shall prepare and maintain, at its registered office or at any other place in Canada designated by the directors, records containing

(a) the articles and the by-laws, and all amendments thereto, and a copy of any unanimous shareholder agreement;

(b) minutes of meetings and resolutions of shareholders;

(c) copies of all notices required by section 106 or 113; and

(d) a securities register that complies with section 50.

(2) Directors records — In addition to the records described in subsection (1), a corporation shall prepare and maintain adequate accounting records and records containing minutes of meetings and resolutions of the directors and any committee thereof.

(2.1) Retention of accounting records — Subject to any other Act of Parliament and to any Act of the legislature of a province that provides for a longer retention period, a corporation shall retain the accounting records referred to in subsection (2) for a period of six years after the end of the financial year to which the records relate.

(3) Records of continued corporations — For the purposes of paragraph (1)(b) and subsection (2), where a body corporate is continued under this Act, **"records"** includes similar records required by law to be maintained by the body corporate before it was so continued.

(4) Place of directors records — The records described in subsection (2) shall be kept at the registered office of the corporation or at such other place as the directors think fit and shall at all reasonable times be open to inspection by the directors.

(5) Records in Canada — If accounting records of a corporation are kept outside Canada, accounting records adequate to enable the directors to ascertain the financial position of the corporation with reasonable accuracy on a quarterly basis shall be kept at the registered office or any other place in Canada designated by the directors.

(5.1) When records or registers kept outside Canada — Despite subsections (1) and (5), but subject to the *Income Tax Act*, the *Excise Tax Act*, the *Customs Act* and any other Act administered by the Minister of National Revenue, a corporation may keep all or any of its corporate records and accounting records referred to in subsection (1) or (2) at a place outside Canada, if

(a) the records are available for inspection, by means of a computer terminal or other technology, during regular office hours at the registered office or any other place in Canada designated by the directors; and

(b) the corporation provides the technical assistance to facilitate an inspection referred to in paragraph (a).

(6) Offence — A corporation that, without reasonable cause, fails to comply with this section is guilty of an offence and liable on summary conviction to a fine not exceeding five thousand dollars.

1994, c. 24, s. 8; 2001, c. 14, s. 10

21. (1) Access to corporate records — Subject to subsection (1.1), shareholders and creditors of a corporation, their personal representatives and the Director may examine the records described in subsection 20(1) during the usual business hours of the corporation, and may take extracts from the records, free of charge, and, if the corporation is a distributing corporation, any other person may do so on payment of a reasonable fee.

(1.1) Requirement for affidavit — securities register — Any person described in subsection (1) who wishes to examine the securities register of a distributing corporation must first make a request to the corporation or its agent, accompanied by an affidavit referred to in subsection (7). On receipt of the affidavit, the corporation or its agent shall allow the applicant access to the securities register during the corporation's usual business hours, and, on payment of a reasonable fee, provide the applicant with an extract from the securities register.

(2) Copies of corporate records — A shareholder of a corporation is entitled on request and without charge to one copy of the articles and by-laws and of any unanimous shareholder agreement.

(3) Shareholder lists — Shareholders and creditors of a corporation, their personal representatives, the Director and, if the corporation is a distributing corporation, any other person, on payment of a reasonable fee and on sending to a corporation or its agent the affidavit referred to in subsection (7), may on application require the corporation or its agent to furnish within ten days after the receipt of the affidavit a list (in this section referred to as the "basic list") made up to a date not more than ten days before the date of receipt of the affidavit setting out the names of the shareholders of the corporation, the number of shares owned by each shareholder and the address of each shareholder as shown on the records of the corporation.

(4) Supplemental lists — A person requiring a corporation to furnish a basic list may, by stating in the affidavit referred to in subsection (3) that they require supplemental lists, require the corporation or its agent on payment of a reasonable fee to furnish supplemental lists setting out any changes from the basic list in the names or addresses of the shareholders and the number of shares owned by each shareholder for each business day following the date the basic list is made up to.

(5) When supplemental lists to be furnished — The corporation or its agent shall furnish a supplemental list required under subsection (4)

    (a) on the date the basic list is furnished, where the information relates to changes that took place prior to that date; and

    (b) on the business day following the day to which the supplemental list relates, where the information relates to changes that take place on or after the date the basic list is furnished.

(6) Holders of options — A person requiring a corporation to furnish a basic list or a supplemental list may also require the corporation to include in that list the name and address of any known holder of an option or right to acquire shares of the corporation.

(7) Contents of affidavit — The affidavit required under subsection (1.1) or (3) shall state

    (a) the name and address of the applicant;

    (b) the name and address for service of the body corporate, if the applicant is a body corporate; and

    (c) that the basic list and any supplemental lists obtained pursuant to subsection (4) or the information contained in the securities register obtained pursuant to subsection (1.1), as the case may be, will not be used except as permitted under subsection (9).

(8) Idem — If the applicant is a body corporate, the affidavit shall be made by a director or officer of the body corporate.

(9) Use of information or shareholder list — A list of shareholders or information from a securities register obtained under this section shall not be used by any person except in connection with

(a) an effort to influence the voting of shareholders of the corporation;

(b) an offer to acquire securities of the corporation; or

(c) any other matter relating to the affairs of the corporation.

(10) Offence — A person who, without reasonable cause, contravenes this section is guilty of an offence and liable on summary conviction to a fine not exceeding five thousand dollars or to imprisonment for a term not exceeding six months or to both.

2001, c. 14, ss. 11(1)–(3), (5), 135 (Sched., s. 2)

22. (1) Form of records — All registers and other records required by this Act to be prepared and maintained may be in a bound or loose-leaf form or in a photographic film form, or may be entered or recorded by any system of mechanical or electronic data processing or any other information storage device that is capable of reproducing any required information in intelligible written form within a reasonable time.

(2) Precautions — A corporation and its agents shall take reasonable precautions to

(a) prevent loss or destruction of,

(b) prevent falsification of entries in, and

(c) facilitate detection and correction of inaccuracies in

the registers and other records required by this Act to be prepared and maintained.

(3) Offence — A person who, without reasonable cause, contravenes this section is guilty of an offence and liable on summary conviction to a fine not exceeding five thousand dollars or to imprisonment for a term not exceeding six months or to both.

23. (1) Corporate seal — A corporation may, but need not, adopt a corporate seal, and may change a corporate seal that is adopted.

(2) Validity of unsealed documents — A document executed on behalf of a corporation is not invalid merely because a corporate seal is not affixed to it.

2001, c. 14, s. 12

PART V — CORPORATE FINANCE

24. (1) Shares — Shares of a corporation shall be in registered form and shall be without nominal or par value.

(2) Transitional — When a body corporate is continued under this Act, a share with nominal or par value issued by the body corporate before it was so continued is, for the purpose of subsection (1), deemed to be a share without nominal or par value.

(3) Rights attached to shares — Where a corporation has only one class of shares, the rights of the holders thereof are equal in all respects and include the rights

(a) to vote at any meeting of shareholders of the corporation;

(b) to receive any dividend declared by the corporation; and

(c) to receive the remaining property of the corporation on dissolution.

(4) Rights to classes of shares — The articles may provide for more than one class of shares and, if they so provide,

(a) the rights, privileges, restrictions and conditions attaching to the shares of each class shall be set out therein; and

(b) the rights set out in subsection (3) shall be attached to at least one class of shares but all such rights are not required to be attached to one class.

25. (1) Issue of shares — Subject to the articles, the by-laws and any unanimous shareholder agreement and to section 28, shares may be issued at such times and to such persons and for such consideration as the directors may determine.

(2) Shares non-assessable — Shares issued by a corporation are non-assessable and the holders are not liable to the corporation or to its creditors in respect thereof.

(3) Consideration — A share shall not be issued until the consideration for the share is fully paid in money or in property or past services that are not less in value than the fair equivalent of the money that the corporation would have received if the share had been issued for money.

(4) Consideration other than money — In determining whether property or past services are the fair equivalent of a money consideration, the directors may take into account reasonable charges and expenses of organization and reorganization and payments for property and past services reasonably expected to benefit the corporation.

(5) Definition of "property" — For the purposes of this section, **"property"** does not include a promissory note or a promise to pay, that is made by a person to whom a share is issued, or a person who does not deal at arm's length, within the meaning of that expression in the *Income Tax Act*, with a person to whom a share is issued.

2001, c. 14, s. 13

26. (1) Stated capital account — A corporation shall maintain a separate stated capital account for each class and series of shares it issues.

(2) Entries in stated capital account — A corporation shall add to the appropriate stated capital account the full amount of any consideration it receives for any shares it issues.

(3) Exception for non-arm's length transactions — Despite subsection (2), a corporation may, subject to subsection (4), add to the stated capital accounts maintained for the shares of classes or series the whole or any part of the amount of the consideration that it receives in an exchange if the corporation issues shares

(a) in exchange for

(i) property of a person who immediately before the exchange did not deal with the corporation at arm's length within the meaning of that expression in the *Income Tax Act*,

(ii) shares of, or another interest in, a body corporate that immediately before the exchange, or that because of the exchange, did not deal with the corporation at arm's length within the meaning of that expression in the *Income Tax Act*, or

(iii) property of a person who, immediately before the exchange, dealt with the corporation at arm's length within the meaning of that expression in the *Income Tax Act*, if the person, the corporation and all the holders of shares in the class or series of shares so issued consent to the exchange; or

(b) pursuant to an agreement referred to in subsection 182(1) or an arrangement referred to in paragraph 192(1)(b) or (c) or to shareholders of an amalgamating body corporate who receive the shares in addition to or instead of securities of the amalgamated body corporate,

(4) Limit on addition to a stated capital account — On the issue of a share a corporation shall not add to a stated capital account in respect of the share it issues an amount greater than the amount of the consideration it received for the share.

(5) Constraint on addition to a stated capital account — Where a corporation proposes to add any amount to a stated capital account it maintains in respect of a class or series of shares, if

(a) the amount to be added was not received by the corporation as consideration for the issue of shares, and

(b) the corporation has issued any outstanding shares of more than one class or series,

the addition to the stated capital account must be approved by special resolution unless all the issued and outstanding shares are shares of not more than two classes of convertible shares referred to in subsection 39(5).

(6) Other additions to stated capital — When a body corporate is continued under this Act, it may add to a stated capital account any consideration received by it for a share it issued and a corporation at any time may, subject to subsection (5), add to a stated capital account any amount it credited to a retained earnings or other surplus account.

(7) Transitional — When a body corporate is continued under this Act, subsection (2) does not apply to the consideration received by it before it was so continued unless the share in respect of which the consideration is received is issued after the corporation is so continued.

(8) Idem — When a body corporate is continued under this Act, any amount unpaid in respect of a share issued by the body corporate before it was so continued and paid after it was so continued shall be added to the stated capital account maintained for the shares of that class or series.

(9) Transitional — For the purposes of subsection 34(2), sections 38 and 42, and paragraph 185(2)(a), when a body corporate is continued under this Act its stated capital is deemed to include the amount that would have been included in stated capital if the body corporate had been incorporated under this Act.

(10) Restriction — A corporation shall not reduce its stated capital or any stated capital account except in the manner provided in this Act.

(11) Exception for an open-end mutual fund — Subsections (1) to (10) and any other provisions of this Act relating to stated capital do not apply to an open-end mutual fund.

(12) Definition of "open-end mutual fund" — For the purposes of this section, **"open-end mutual fund"** means a distributing corporation that carries on only the business of investing the consideration it receives for the shares it issues, and all or substantially all of those shares are redeemable on the demand of a shareholder.

2001, c. 14, s. 14

27. (1) Shares in series — The articles may authorize, subject to any limitations set out in them, the issue of any class of shares in one or more series and may do either or both of the following:

(a) fix the number of shares in, and determine the designation, rights, privileges, restrictions and conditions attaching to the shares of, each series; or

(b) authorize the directors to fix the number of shares in, and determine the designation, rights, privileges, restrictions and conditions attaching to the shares of, each series.

(2) Series participation — If any cumulative dividends or amounts payable on return of capital in respect of a series of shares are not paid in full, the shares of all series of the same class participate rateably in respect of accumulated dividends and return of capital.

(3) Restrictions on series — No rights, privileges, restrictions or conditions attached to a series of shares authorized under this section shall confer on a series a priority in respect of dividends or return of capital over any other series of shares of the same class that are then outstanding.

(4) Amendment of articles — If the directors exercise their authority under paragraph (1)(b), they shall, before the issue of shares of the series, send, in the form that the Director fixes, articles of amendment to the Director to designate a series of shares.

(5) Certificate of amendment — On receipt of articles of amendment designating a series of shares, the Director shall issue a certificate of amendment in accordance with section 262.

(6) Effect of certificate — The articles of the corporation are amended accordingly on the date shown in the certificate of amendment.

2001, c. 14, s. 15

28. (1) Pre-emptive right — If the articles so provide, no shares of a class shall be issued unless the shares have first been offered to the shareholders holding shares of that class, and those shareholders have a pre-emptive right to acquire the offered shares in proportion to their holdings of the shares of that class, at such price and on such terms as those shares are to be offered to others.

(2) Exception — Notwithstanding that the articles provide the pre-emptive right referred to in subsection (1), shareholders have no pre-emptive right in respect of shares to be issued

(a) for a consideration other than money;

(b) as a share dividend; or

(c) pursuant to the exercise of conversion privileges, options or rights previously granted by the corporation.

29. (1) Options and rights — A corporation may issue certificates, warrants or other evidences of conversion privileges, options or rights to acquire securities of the corporation, and shall set out the conditions thereof

(a) in the certificates, warrants or other evidences; or

(b) in certificates evidencing the securities to which the conversion privileges, options or rights are attached.

(2) Transferable rights — Conversion privileges, options and rights to acquire securities of a corporation may be made transferable or non-transferable, and options and rights to acquire may be made separable or inseparable from any securities to which they are attached.

(3) Reserved shares — Where a corporation has granted privileges to convert any securities issued by the corporation into shares, or into shares of another class or series, or has issued or granted options or rights to acquire shares, if the articles limit the number of authorized shares, the corporation shall reserve and continue to reserve sufficient authorized shares to meet the exercise of such conversion privileges, options and rights.

30. (1) Corporation holding its own shares — Subject to subsection (2) and sections 31 to 36, a corporation

(a) shall not hold shares in itself or in its holding body corporate; and

(b) shall not permit any of its subsidiary bodies corporate to acquire shares of the corporation.

(2) Subsidiary holding shares of its parent — Subject to section 31, a corporation shall cause a subsidiary body corporate of the corporation that holds shares of the corporation to sell or otherwise dispose of those shares within five years from the date

(a) the body corporate became a subsidiary of the corporation; or

(b) the corporation was continued under this Act.

2001, c. 14, s. 17(2)

31. (1) Exception — A corporation may in the capacity of a legal representative hold shares in itself or in its holding body corporate unless it or the holding body corporate or a subsidiary of either of them has a beneficial interest in the shares.

(2) Idem — A corporation may hold shares in itself or in its holding body corporate by way of security for the purposes of a transaction entered into by it in the ordinary course of a business that includes the lending of money.

(3) Exception — subsidiary acquiring shares — A corporation may permit any of its subsidiary bodies corporate to acquire shares of the corporation

(a) in the subsidiary's capacity as a legal representative, unless the subsidiary would have a beneficial interest in the shares; or

(b) by way of security for the purposes of a transaction entered into by the subsidiary in the ordinary course of a business that includes the lending of money.

(4) Exception — conditions precedent — A corporation may permit any of its subsidiary bodies corporate to acquire shares of the corporation through the issuance of those shares by the corporation to the subsidiary body corporate if, before the acquisition takes place, the conditions prescribed for the purposes of this subsection are met.

(5) Conditions subsequent — After an acquisition has taken place under the purported authority of subsection (4), the conditions prescribed for the purposes of this subsection must be met.

(6) Non-compliance with conditions — If

(a) a corporation permits a subsidiary body corporate to acquire shares of the corporation under the purported authority of subsection (4), and

(b) either

> (i) one or more of the conditions prescribed for the purposes of subsection (4) were not met, or

> (ii) one or more of the conditions prescribed for the purposes of subsection (5) are not met or cease to be met,

then, notwithstanding subsections 16(3) and 26(2), the prescribed consequences apply in respect of the acquisition of the shares and their issuance.

2001, c. 14, s. 18(2)

32. (1) Exception relating to Canadian ownership — Subject to subsection 39(8), a corporation may, for the purpose of assisting the corporation or any of its affiliates or associates to qualify under any prescribed law of Canada or a province to receive licences, permits, grants, payments or other benefits by reason of attaining or maintaining a specified level of Canadian ownership or control, hold shares in itself that

> (a) are not constrained for the purpose of assisting the corporation or any of its affiliates or associates to so qualify; or

> (b) are shares into which shares held under paragraph (a) were converted by the corporation that are constrained for the purpose of assisting the corporation to so qualify and that were not previously held by the corporation.

(2) Prohibited transfers — A corporation shall not transfer shares held under subsection (1) to any person unless the corporation is satisfied, on reasonable grounds, that the ownership of the shares as a result of the transfer would assist the corporation or any of its affiliates or associates to achieve the purpose set out in subsection (1).

(3) Offence — A corporation that, without reasonable cause, fails to comply with subsection (2) is guilty of an offence and liable on summary conviction to a fine not exceeding five thousand dollars.

(4) Directors of corporation — Where a corporation commits an offence under subsection (3), any director of the corporation who knowingly authorized, permitted or acquiesced in the commission of the offence is a party to and guilty of the offence and is liable on summary conviction to a fine not exceeding five thousand dollars or to imprisonment for a term not exceeding six months or to both, whether or not the corporation has been prosecuted or convicted.

(5) Where shares are transferred — Where shares held under subsection (1) are transferred by a corporation, subsections 25(1), (3), (4) and (5), paragraph 115(3)(c) and subsection 118(1) apply, with such modifications as the circumstances require, in respect of the transfer as if the transfer were an issue.

(6) Transfer not void — No transfer of shares by a corporation shall be void or voidable solely because the transfer is in contravention of subsection (2).

33. (1) Voting shares — A corporation holding shares in itself or in its holding body corporate shall not vote or permit those shares to be voted unless the corporation

> (a) holds the shares in the capacity of a legal representative; and

> (b) has complied with section 153.

(2) Subsidiary body corporate — A corporation shall not permit any of its subsidiary bodies corporate holding shares in the corporation to vote, or permit those shares to be voted, unless the subsidiary body corporate satisfies the requirements of subsection (1).

2001, c. 14, s. 19

34. (1) Acquisition of corporation's own shares — Subject to subsection (2) and to its articles, a corporation may purchase or otherwise acquire shares issued by it.

(2) Limitation — A corporation shall not make any payment to purchase or otherwise acquire shares issued by it if there are reasonable grounds for believing that

(a) the corporation is, or would after the payment be, unable to pay its liabilities as they become due; or

(b) the realizable value of the corporation's assets would after the payment be less than the aggregate of its liabilities and stated capital of all classes.

35. (1) Alternative acquisition of corporation's own shares — Notwithstanding subsection 34(2), but subject to subsection (3) and to its articles, a corporation may purchase or otherwise acquire shares issued by it to

(a) settle or compromise a debt or claim asserted by or against the corporation;

(b) eliminate fractional shares; or

(c) fulfil the terms of a non-assignable agreement under which the corporation has an option or is obliged to purchase shares owned by a director, an officer or an employee of the corporation.

(2) Idem — Notwithstanding subsection 34(2), a corporation may purchase or otherwise acquire shares issued by it to

(a) satisfy the claim of a shareholder who dissents under section 190; or

(b) comply with an order under section 241.

(3) Limitation — A corporation shall not make any payment to purchase or acquire under subsection (1) shares issued by it if there are reasonable grounds for believing that

(a) the corporation is, or would after the payment be, unable to pay its liabilities as they become due; or

(b) the realizable value of the corporation's assets would after the payment be less than the aggregate of

(i) its liabilities, and

(ii) the amount required for payment on a redemption or in a liquidation of all shares the holders of which have the right to be paid before the holders of the shares to be purchased or acquired, to the extent that the amount has not been included in its liabilities.

2001, c. 14, s. 21(2)

36. (1) Redemption of shares — Notwithstanding subsection 34(2) or 35(3), but subject to subsection (2) and to its articles, a corporation may purchase or redeem any redeemable shares issued by it at prices not exceeding the redemption price thereof stated in the articles or calculated according to a formula stated in the articles.

(2) Limitation — A corporation shall not make any payment to purchase or redeem any redeemable shares issued by it if there are reasonable grounds for believing that

(a) the corporation is, or would after the payment be, unable to pay its liabilities as they become due; or

(b) the realizable value of the corporation's assets would after the payment be less than the aggregate of

(i) its liabilities, and

(ii) the amount that would be required to pay the holders of shares that have a right to be paid, on a redemption or in a liquidation, rateably with or before the holders of the shares to be purchased or redeemed, to the extent that the amount has not been included in its liabilities.

2001, c. 14, s. 22(3)

37. Donated shares — A corporation may accept from any shareholder a share of the corporation surrendered to it as a gift, but may not extinguish or reduce a liability in respect of an amount unpaid on any such share except in accordance with section 38.

38. (1) Other reduction of stated capital — Subject to subsection (3), a corporation may by special resolution reduce its stated capital for any purpose including, without limiting the generality of the foregoing, for the purpose of

(a) extinguishing or reducing a liability in respect of an amount unpaid on any share;

(b) distributing to the holder of an issued share of any class or series of shares an amount not exceeding the stated capital of the class or series; and

(c) declaring its stated capital to be reduced by an amount that is not represented by realizable assets.

(2) Contents of special resolution — A special resolution under this section shall specify the stated capital account or accounts from which the reduction of stated capital effected by the special resolution will be deducted.

(3) Limitation — A corporation shall not reduce its stated capital for any purpose other than the purpose mentioned in paragraph (1)(c) if there are reasonable grounds for believing that

(a) the corporation is, or would after the reduction be, unable to pay its liabilities as they become due; or

(b) the realizable value of the corporation's assets would thereby be less than the aggregate of its liabilities.

(4) Recovery — A creditor of a corporation is entitled to apply to a court for an order compelling a shareholder or other recipient

(a) to pay to the corporation an amount equal to any liability of the shareholder that was extinguished or reduced contrary to this section; or

(b) to pay or deliver to the corporation any money or property that was paid or distributed to the shareholder or other recipient as a consequence of a reduction of capital made contrary to this section.

(5) Limitation — An action to enforce a liability imposed by this section may not be commenced after two years from the date of the act complained of.

(6) [Repealed 2001, c. 14, s. 23.]

2001, c. 14, s. 23

39. (1) Adjustment of stated capital account — On a purchase, redemption or other acquisition by a corporation under section 34, 35, 36, 45 or 190 or paragraph 241(3)(f), of shares or fractions thereof issued by it, the corporation shall deduct from the stated capital account maintained for the class or series of shares of which the shares purchased, redeemed or otherwise acquired form a part an amount equal to the result obtained by multiplying the stated capital of the shares of that class or series by the number of shares of that class or series or fractions thereof purchased, redeemed or otherwise acquired, divided by the number of issued shares of that class or series immediately before the purchase, redemption or other acquisition.

(2) Idem — A corporation shall deduct the amount of a payment made by the corporation to a shareholder under paragraph 241(3)(g) from the stated capital account maintained for the class or series of shares in respect of which the payment was made.

(3) Idem — A corporation shall adjust its stated capital account or accounts in accordance with any special resolution referred to in subsection 38(2).

(4) Idem — On a conversion of issued shares of a corporation into shares of another class or series or a change under section 173, 191 or 241 of issued shares of a corporation into shares of another class or series, the corporation shall

(a) deduct from the stated capital account maintained for the class or series of shares converted or changed an amount equal to the result obtained by multiplying the stated capital of the shares of that class or series by the number of shares of that class or series converted or changed, divided by the number of issued shares of that class or series immediately before the conversion or change; and

(b) add the result obtained under paragraph (a) and any additional consideration received pursuant to the conversion or change to the stated capital account maintained or to be maintained for the class or series of shares into which the shares have been converted or changed.

(5) Stated capital of interconvertible shares — For the purposes of subsection (4) and subject to its articles, where a corporation issues two classes of shares and there is attached to each such class a right to convert a share of the one class into a share of the other class, if a share of one class is converted into a share of the other class, the amount of stated capital attributable to a share in either class is the aggregate of the stated capital of both classes divided by the number of issued shares of both classes immediately before the conversion.

(6) Cancellation or restoration of shares — Shares or fractions thereof of any class or series of shares issued by a corporation and purchased, redeemed or otherwise acquired by it shall be cancelled or, if the articles limit the number of authorized shares, may be restored to the status of authorized but unissued shares of the class.

(7) Exception — For the purposes of this section, a corporation holding shares in itself as permitted by subsections 31(1) and (2) is deemed not to have purchased, redeemed or otherwise acquired such shares.

(8) Idem — For the purposes of this section, a corporation holding shares in itself by paragraph 32(1)(a) is deemed not to have purchased, redeemed or otherwise acquired the shares at the time they were acquired, but

(a) any of those shares that are held by the corporation at the expiration of two years, and

(b) any shares into which any of those shares were converted by the corporation and held under paragraph 32(1)(b) that are held by the corporation at the expiration of two years after the shares from which they were converted were acquired

are deemed to have been acquired at the expiration of the two years.

(9) Conversion or change of shares — Shares issued by a corporation and converted into shares of another class or series or changed under section 173, 191 or 241 into shares of another class or series shall become issued shares of the class or series of shares into which the shares have been converted or changed.

(10) Effect of change of shares on number of unissued shares — Where the articles limit the number of authorized shares of a class of shares of a corporation and issued shares of that class or of a series of shares of that class have become, pursuant to subsection (9), issued shares of another class or series, the number of unissued shares of the first-mentioned class shall, unless the articles otherwise provide, be increased by the number of shares that, pursuant to subsection (9), became shares of another class or series.

(11) Repayment — Debt obligations issued, pledged, hypothecated or deposited by a corporation are not redeemed by reason only that the indebtedness evidenced by the debt obligations or in respect of which the debt obligations are issued, pledged, hypothecated or deposited is repaid.

(12) Acquisition and reissue of debt obligations — Debt obligations issued by a corporation and purchased, redeemed or otherwise acquired by it may be cancelled or, subject to any applicable trust indenture or other agreement, may be reissued, pledged or hypothecated to secure any obligation of the corporation then existing or thereafter incurred, and any such acquisition and reissue, pledge or hypothecation is not a cancellation of the debt obligations.

40. (1) Enforcement of contract to buy shares — A corporation shall fulfil its obligations under a contract to buy shares of the corporation, except if the corporation can prove that enforcement of the contract would put it in breach of any of sections 34 to 36.

(2) Status of contracting party — Until the corporation has fulfilled all its obligations under a contract referred to in subsection (1), the other party retains the status of claimant entitled to be paid as soon as the corporation is lawfully able to do so or, in a liquidation, to be ranked subordinate to the rights of creditors and to the rights of holders of any class of shares whose rights were in priority to the rights given to the holders of the class of shares being purchased, but in priority to the rights of other shareholders.

(3) [Repealed 2001, c. 14, s. 25.]

2001, c. 14, s. 25

41. Commission for sale of shares — The directors may authorize the corporation to pay a reasonable commission to any person in consideration of the person's purchasing or agreeing to purchase shares of the corporation from the corporation or from any other person, or procuring or agreeing to procure purchasers for any such shares.

2001, c. 14, s. 135 (Sched., s. 3)

42. Dividends — A corporation shall not declare or pay a dividend if there are reasonable grounds for believing that

(a) the corporation is, or would after the payment be, unable to pay its liabilities as they become due; or

(b) the realizable value of the corporation's assets would thereby be less than the aggregrate of its liabilities and stated capital of all classes.

43. (1) Form of dividend — A corporation may pay a dividend by issuing fully paid shares of the corporation and, subject to section 42, a corporation may pay a dividend in money or property.

(2) Adjustment of stated capital account — If shares of a corporation are issued in payment of a dividend, the declared amount of the dividend stated as an amount of money shall be added to the stated capital account maintained or to be maintained for the shares of the class or series issued in payment of the dividend.

44. [Repealed 2001, c. 14, s. 26.]

45. (1) Shareholder immunity — The shareholders of a corporation are not, as shareholders, liable for any liability, act or default of the corporation except under subsection 38(4), 118(4) or (5), 146(5) or 226(4) or (5).

(2) Lien on shares — Subject to subsection 49(8), the articles may provide that the corporation has a lien on a share registered in the name of a shareholder or the shareholder's personal representative for a debt of that shareholder to the corporation, including an amount unpaid in respect of a share issued by a body corporate on the date it was continued under this Act.

(3) Enforcement of lien — A corporation may enforce a lien referred to in subsection (2) in accordance with its by-laws.

2001, c. 14, s. 27

PART VI — SALE OF CONSTRAINED SHARES

46. (1) Sale of constrained shares by corporation — A corporation that has constraints on the issue, transfer or ownership of its shares of any class or series may, for any of the purposes referred to in paragraphs (a) to (c), sell, under the conditions and after giving the notice that may be prescribed, as if it were the owner of the shares, any of those constrained shares that are owned, or that the directors determine in the manner that may be prescribed may be owned, contrary to the constraints in order to

(a) assist the corporation or any of its affiliates or associates to qualify under any prescribed law of Canada or a province to receive licences, permits, grants, payments or other benefits by reason of attaining or maintaining a specified level of Canadian ownership or control;

(b) assist the corporation to comply with any prescribed law; or

(c) attain or maintain a level of Canadian ownership specified in its articles.

(2) Obligations of directors in sale — Where shares are to be sold by a corporation under subsection (1), the directors of the corporation shall select the shares for sale in good faith and in a manner that is not unfairly prejudicial to, and does not unfairly disregard the interests of, the holders of the shares in the constrained class or series taken as a whole.

(3) Effect of sale — Where shares are sold by a corporation under subsection (1), the owner of the shares immediately prior to the sale shall by that sale be divested of their interest in the shares, and the person who, but for the sale, would be the registered owner of the shares or a person who satisfies the corporation that, but for the sale, they could properly be treated as the registered owner or registered holder of the shares under section 51 shall, from the time of the sale, be entitled to receive only the net proceeds of the sale, together with any income earned thereon from the beginning of the month next following the date of the receipt by the corporation of the proceeds of the sale, less any taxes thereon and any costs of administration of a trust fund constituted under subsection 47(1) in relation thereto.

(4) Subsections 51(4) to (6) apply — Subsections 51(4) to (6) apply in respect of the person who is entitled under subsection (3) to receive the proceeds of a sale of shares under subsection (1) as if the proceeds were a security and the person were a registered holder or owner of the security.

1991, c. 45, s. 552; 1991, c. 47, s. 720; 2001, c. 14, ss. 28(1), 135 (Sched., s. 4)

47. (1) Proceeds of sale to be trust fund — The proceeds of a sale by a corporation under subsection 46(1) constitute a trust fund in the hands of the corporation for the benefit of the person entitled under subsection 46(3) to receive the proceeds of the sale, and any such trust fund may be commingled by the corporation with other such trust funds and shall be invested in such manner as may be prescribed.

(2) Costs of administration — Reasonable costs of administration of a trust fund referred to in subsection (1) may be deducted from the trust fund and any income earned thereon.

(3) Appointment of trust company — Subject to this section, a corporation may transfer any trust fund referred to in subsection (1), and the administration thereof, to a trust company in Canada registered as such under the laws of Canada or a province, and the corporation is thereupon discharged of all further liability in respect of the trust fund.

(4) Discharge of corporation and trust company — A receipt signed by a person entitled under subsection 46(3) to receive the proceeds of a sale that constitute a trust fund under subsection (1) shall be a complete discharge of the corporation and of any trust company to which a trust fund is transferred under subsection (3), in respect of the trust fund and income earned thereon paid to such person.

(5) Vesting in Crown — A trust fund described in subsection (1), together with any income earned thereon, less any taxes thereon and costs of administration, that has not been claimed by a person entitled under subsection 46(3) to receive the proceeds of a sale that constitute the trust fund for a period of ten years after the date of the sale vests in Her Majesty in right of Canada.

(6) *Escheats Act* applies — Sections 3 to 5 of the *Escheats Act* apply in respect of a trust fund that vests in Her Majesty in right of Canada under subsection (5).

PART VII — SECURITY CERTIFICATES, REGISTERS AND TRANSFERS

Interpretation and General

48. (1) Application of Part — The transfer or transmission of a security shall be governed by this Part.

(2) Definitions — In this Part,

"adverse claim" includes a claim that a transfer was or would be wrongful or that a particular adverse person is the owner of or has an interest in the security; *("opposition")*

"bearer" means the person in possession of a security payable to bearer or endorsed in blank; *("porteur")*

"*bona fide* purchaser" means a purchaser for value in good faith and without notice of any adverse claim who takes delivery of a security in bearer form or order form or of a security in registered form issued or endorsed to the purchaser or endorsed in blank; *("acheteur de bonne foi")*

"broker" means a person who is engaged, whether or not exclusively, in the business of buying and selling securities and who, in the transaction concerned, acts for, or buys a security from, or sells a security to a customer; *("courtier")*

"delivery" means voluntary transfer of possession; *("livraison" ou "remise")*

"fiduciary" means any person acting in a fiduciary capacity and includes a personal representative of a deceased person; *("représentant")*

"fungible", in relation to securities, means securities of which any unit is, by nature or usage of trade, the equivalent of any other like unit; *("fongibles")*

"genuine" means free of forgery or counterfeiting; *("authentique")*

"good faith" means honesty in fact in the conduct of the transaction concerned; *("bonne foi")*

"holder" means a person in possession of a security issued or endorsed to the person or the bearer or in blank; *("détenteur")*

"issuer" includes a corporation

(a) that is required by this Act to maintain a securities register, or

(b) that directly or indirectly creates fractional interests in its rights or property and that issues securities as evidence of such fractional interests;

("émetteur")

"overissue" means the issue of securities in excess of any maximum number of securities that the issuer is authorized by its articles or a trust indenture to issue; *("émission excédentaire")*

"purchaser" means a person who takes an interest in a security by sale, mortgage, hypothec, pledge, issue, reissue, gift or any other voluntary transaction; *("aequéreur")*

"security" or **"security certificate"** means an instrument issued by a corporation that is

(a) in bearer, order or registered form,

(b) of a type commonly dealt in on securities exchanges or markets or commonly recognized in any area in which it is issued or dealt in as a medium for investment,

(c) one of a class or series or by its terms divisible into a class or series of instruments, and

(d) evidence of a share, participation or other interest in or obligation of a corporation; *("valeur mobiliére" ou "certificat de valeur mobiliére")*

"transfer" includes transmission by operation of law; *("transfert")*

"trust indenture" means a trust indenture as defined in section 82; *("act de fiducie")*

"unauthorized", in relation to a signature or an endorsement, means one made without actual, implied or apparent authority and includes a forgery; *("non autorisé")*

"valid" means issued in accordance with the applicable law and the articles of the issuer, or validated under section 52. *("valide")*

(3) Negotiable instruments — Except where its transfer is restricted and noted on a security in accordance with subsection 49(8), a security is a negotiable instrument.

(4) Registered form — A security is in registered form if

(a) it specifies a person entitled to the security or to the rights it evidences, and its transfer is capable of being recorded in a securities register; or

(b) it bears a statement that it is in registered form.

(5) Order form — A debt obligation is in order form where, by its terms, it is payable to the order or assigns of any person therein specified with reasonable certainty or to that person's order.

(6) Bearer form — A security is in bearer form if it is payable to bearer according to its terms and not by reason of any endorsement.

(7) Guarantor for issuer — A guarantor for an issuer is deemed to be an issuer to the extent of the guarantee whether or not the obligation is noted on the security.

2001, c. 14, ss. 29, 135 (Sched., s. 5)

49. (1) Rights of holder — Every security holder is entitled at their option to a security certificate that complies with this Act or a non-transferable written acknowledgement of their right to obtain such a security certificate from a corporation in respect of the securities of that corporation held by them.

(2) Maximum fee for certificate by regulation — A corporation may charge a fee, not exceeding the prescribed amount, for a security certificate issued in respect of a transfer.

(3) Joint holders — A corporation is not required to issue more than one security certificate in respect of securities held jointly by several persons, and delivery of a certificate to one of several joint holders is sufficient delivery to all.

(4) Signatures — A security certificate shall be signed by at least one of the following persons, or the signature shall be printed or otherwise mechanically reproduced on the certificate:

(a) a director or officer of the corporation;

(b) a registrar, transfer agent or branch transfer agent of the corporation, or an individual on their behalf; and

(c) a trustee who certifies it in accordance with a trust indenture.

(5) [Repealed 2001, c. 14, s. 30(2).]

(6) Continuation of signature — If a security certificate contains a printed or mechanically reproduced signature of a person, the corporation may issue the security certificate, notwithstanding that the person has ceased to be a director or an officer of the corporation, and the security certificate is as valid as if the person were a director or an officer at the date of its issue.

(7) Contents of share certificate — There shall be stated on the face of each share certificate issued by a corporation

(a) the name of the corporation;

(b) the words "Incorporated under the *Canada Business Corporations Act*" or "subject to the *Canada Business Corporations Act*";

(c) the name of the person to whom it was issued; and

(d) the number and class of shares and the designation of any series that the certificate represents.

(8) Restrictions — No restriction, charge, agreement or endorsement described in the following paragraphs is effective against a transferee of a security, issued by a corporation or by a body corporate before the body corporate was continued under this Act, who has no actual knowledge of the restriction, charge, agreement or endorsement unless it or a reference to it is noted conspicuously on the security certificate:

(a) a restriction on transfer other than a constraint under section 174;

(b) a charge in favour of the corporation;

(c) a unanimous shareholder agreement; or

(d) an endorsement under subsection 190(10).

(9) Limit on restriction — A distributing corporation, any of the issued shares of which remain outstanding and are held by more than one person, shall not have a restriction on the transfer or ownership of its shares of any class or series except by way of a constraint permitted under section 174.

(10) Notation of constraint — Where the articles of a corporation constrain the issue, transfer or ownership of shares of any class or series in order to assist

(a) the corporation or any of its affiliates or associates to qualify under any prescribed law of Canada or a province to receive licences, permits, grants, payments or other benefits by reason of attaining or maintaining a specified level of Canadian ownership or control, or

(b) the corporation to comply with any prescribed law,

the constraint, or a reference to it, shall be conspicuously noted on every security certificate of the corporation evidencing a share that is subject to the constraint where the security certificate is issued after the day on which the share becomes subject to the constraint under this Act.

(11) Failure to note — The failure to note a constraint or a reference to it pursuant to subsection (10) shall not invalidate any share or security certificate and shall not render a constraint ineffective against an owner, holder or transferee of the share or security certificate.

(12) Transitional — If a body corporate continued under this Act has outstanding security certificates, and if the words "private company" appear on the certificates, those words are deemed to be a notice of a restriction, lien, agreement or endorsement for the purpose of subsection (8).

(13) Particulars of class — There shall be stated legibly on a share certificate issued by a corporation that is authorized to issue shares of more than one class or series

(a) the rights, privileges, restrictions and conditions attached to the shares of each class and series that exists when the share certificate is issued; or

(b) that the class or series of shares that it represents has rights, privileges, restrictions or conditions attached thereto and that the corporation will furnish a shareholder, on demand and without charge, with a full copy of the text of

(i) the rights, privileges, restrictions and conditions attached to each class authorized to be issued and to each series in so far as the same have been fixed by the directors, and

(ii) the authority of the directors to fix the rights, privileges, restrictions and conditions of subsequent series.

(14) Duty — Where a share certificate issued by a corporation contains the statement mentioned in paragraph (13)(b), the corporation shall furnish a shareholder, on demand and without charge, with a full copy of the text of

(a) the rights, privileges, restrictions and conditions attached to each class authorized to be issued and to each series in so far as the same have been fixed by the directors; and

(b) the authority of the directors to fix the rights, privileges, restrictions and conditions of subsequent series.

(15) Fractional share — A corporation may issue a certificate for a fractional share or may issue in place thereof scrip certificates in bearer form that entitle the holder to receive a certificate for a full share by exchanging scrip certificates aggregating a full share.

(16) Scrip certificates — The directors may attach conditions to any scrip certificates issued by a corporation, including conditions that

(a) the scrip certificates become void if not exchanged for a share certificate representing a full share before a specified date; and

(b) any shares for which such scrip certificates are exchangeable may, notwithstanding any pre-emptive right, be issued by the corporation to any person and the proceeds thereof distributed rateably to the holders of the scrip certificates.

(17) Holder of fractional share — A holder of a fractional share issued by a corporation is not entitled to exercise voting rights or to receive a dividend in respect of the fractional share, unless

(a) the fractional share results from a consolidation of shares; or

(b) the articles of the corporation otherwise provide.

(18) Holder of scrip certificate — A holder of a scrip certificate is not entitled to exercise voting rights or to receive a dividend in respect of the scrip certificate.

1991, c. 45, s. 553; 1991, c. 47, s. 721; 2001, c. 14, ss. 30, 135 (Sched., s. 6)

50. (1) Securities records — A corporation shall maintain a securities register in which it records the securities issued by it in registered form, showing with respect to each class or series of securities

(a) the names, alphabetically arranged, and the latest known address of each person who is or has been a security holder;

(b) the number of securities held by each security holder; and

(c) the date and particulars of the issue and transfer of each security.

(2) Central and branch registers — A corporation may appoint an agent to maintain a central securities register and branch securities registers.

(3) Place of register — A central securities register shall be maintained by a corporation at its registered office or at any other place in Canada designated by the directors, and any branch securities registers may be kept at any place in or out of Canada designated by the directors.

(4) Effect of registration — Registration of the issue or transfer of a security in the central securities register or in a branch securities register is complete and valid registration for all purposes.

(5) Branch register — A branch securities register shall only contain particulars of securities issued or transferred at that branch.

(6) Central register — Particulars of each issue or transfer of a security registered in a branch securities register shall also be kept in the corresponding central securities register.

(7) Destruction of certificates — A corporation, its agent or a trustee defined in subsection 82(1) is not required to produce

(a) a cancelled security certificate in registered form, an instrument referred to in subsection 29(1) that is cancelled or a like cancelled instrument in registered form six years after the date of its cancellation;

(b) a cancelled security certificate in bearer form or an instrument referred to in subsecton 29(1) that is cancelled or a like cancelled instrument in bearer form after the date of its cancellation; or

(c) an instrument referred to in subsection 29(1) or a like instrument, irrespective of its form, after the date of its expiration.

51. (1) Dealings with registered holder — A corporation or a trustee defined in subsection 82(1) may, subject to sections 134, 135 and 138, treat the registered owner of a security as the person exclusively entitled to vote, to receive notices, to receive any interest, dividend or other payments in respect of the security, and otherwise to exercise all the rights and powers of an owner of the security.

(2) Constructive registered holder — Notwithstanding subsection (1), a corporation whose articles restrict the right to transfer its securities shall, and any other corporation may, treat a person as a registered security holder entitled to exercise all the rights of the security holder that the person represents, if the person furnishes the corporation with evidence as described in subsection 77(4) that the person is

    (a) the heir of a deceased security holder, or the personal representative of the heirs, or the personal representative of the estate of a deceased security holder;

    (b) a personal representative of a registered security holder who is an infant, an incompetent person or a missing person; or

    (c) a liquidator, of or a trustee in bankruptcy for, a registered security holder.

(3) Permissible registered holder — If a person on whom the ownership of a security devolves by operation of law, other than a person described in subsection (2), furnishes proof of the person's authority to exercise rights or privileges in respect of a security of the corporation that is not registered in the person's name, the corporation shall treat the person as entitled to exercise those rights or privileges.

(4) Immunity of corporation — A corporation is not required to inquire into the existence of, or see to the performance or observance of, any duty owed to a third person by a registered holder of any of its securities or by anyone whom it treats, as permitted or required by this section, as the owner or registered holder thereof.

(5) Persons less than eighteen years of age — If a person who is less than eighteen years of age exercises any rights of ownership in the securities of a corporation, no subsequent repudiation or avoidance is effective against the corporation.

(6) Joint holders — A corporation may treat as owner of a security the survivors of persons to whom the security was issued as joint holders, if it receives proof satisfactory to it of the death of any such joint holder.

(7) Transmission of securities — Subject to any applicable law relating to the collection of taxes, a person referred to in paragraph (2)(a) is entitled to become a registered holder, or to designate a registered holder, if the person deposits with the corporation or its transfer agent

    (a) the original grant of probate or of letters of administration, or a copy thereof certified to be a true copy by

        (i) the court that granted the probate or letters of administration,

        (ii) a trust company incorporated under the laws of Canada or a province, or

        (iii) a lawyer or notary acting on behalf of the person referred to in paragraph (2)(a), or

    (b) in the case of transmission by notarial will in the Province of Quebec, a copy thereof authenticated pursuant to the laws of that Province,

together with

    (c) an affidavit or declaration of transmission made by a person referred to in paragraph (2)(a), stating the particulars of the transmission, and

    (d) the security certificate that was owned by the deceased holder

        (i) in case of a transfer to a person referred to in paragraph (2)(a), with or without the endorsement of that person, and

        (ii) in case of a transfer to any other person, endorsed in accordance with section 65,

and accompanied by any assurance the corporation may require under section 77.

(8) Excepted transmissions — Despite subsection (7), if the laws of the jurisdiction governing the transmission of a security of a deceased holder do not require a grant of probate or of letters of administration in respect of the transmission, a personal representative of the deceased holder is entitled, subject to any applicable law relating to the collection of taxes, to become a registered holder or to designate a registered holder, if the personal representative deposits with the corporation or its transfer agent

(a) the security certificate that was owned by the deceased holder; and

(b) reasonable proof of the governing laws, of the deceased holder's interest in the security and of the right of the personal representative or the person designated by the personal representative to become the registered holder.

(9) Right of corporation — Deposit of the documents required by subsection (7) or (8) empowers a corporation or its transfer agent to record in a securities register the transmission of a security from the deceased holder to a person referred to in paragraph (2)(a) or to such person as the person referred to in that paragraph may designate and, thereafter, to treat the person who thus becomes a registered holder as the owner of those securities.

2001, c. 14, ss. 31, 135 (Sched., s. 7)

52. (1) Overissue — The provisions of this Part that validate a security or compel its issue or reissue do not apply to the extent that validation, issue or reissue would result in overissue, but

(a) if a valid security, similar in all respects to the security involved in the overissue, is reasonably available for purchase, the person entitled to the validation or issue may compel the issuer to purchase and deliver such a security against surrender of the security that the person holds;

(b) if a valid security, similar in all respects to the security involved in the overissue, is not reasonably available for purchase, the person entitled to the validation or issue may recover from the issuer an amount equal to the price the last purchaser for value paid for the invalid security.

(2) Retroactive validation — When an issuer amends its articles or a trust indenture to which it is a party to increase its authorized securities to a number equal to or in excess of the number of securities previously authorized plus the amount of the securities overissued, the securities so overissued are valid from the date of their issue.

(3) Payment not a purchase or redemption — A purchase or payment by an issuer under subsection (1) is not a purchase or payment to which section 34, 35, 36 or 39 applies.

2001, c. 14, s. 135 (Sched., s. 8)

53. Burden of proof — In an action on a security,

(a) unless specifically denied in the pleadings, each signature on the security or in a necessary endorsement is admitted;

(b) a signature on the security is presumed to be genuine and authorized but, if the effectiveness of the signature is put in issue, the burden of establishing that it is genuine and authorized is on the party claiming under the signature;

(c) if a signature is admitted or established, production of the instrument entitles a holder to recover on it unless the defendant establishes a defence or a defect going to the validity of the security; and

(d) if the defendant establishes that a defence or defect exists, the plaintiff has the burden of establishing that the defence or defect is ineffective against the plaintiff or some person under whom the plaintiff claims.

2001, c. 14, s. 135 (Sched., s. 9)

54. Securities fungible — Unless otherwise agreed, and subject to any applicable law, regulation or stock exchange rule, a person required to deliver securities may deliver any security of the specified issue in bearer form or registered in the name of the transferee or endorsed to the transferee or in blank.

2001, c. 14, s. 135 (Sched., s. 10)

Issue — Issuer

55. (1) Notice of defect — Even against a purchaser for value without notice of a defect going to the validity of a security, the terms of the security include those stated on the security and those incorporated therein by reference to another instrument, statute, rule, regulation or order to the extent that the terms so incorporated do not conflict with the stated terms, but such a reference is not of itself notice to a purchaser for value of a defect going to the validity of the security, notwithstanding that the security expressly states that a person accepting it admits such notice.

(2) Purchaser for value — A security is valid in the hands of a purchaser for value without notice of any defect going to its validity.

(3) Lack of genuineness — Subject to section 57, the fact that a security is not genuine is a complete defence even against a purchaser for value without notice.

(4) Ineffective defences — All other defences of an issuer, including non-delivery and conditional delivery of a security, are ineffective against a purchaser for value without notice of the particular defence.

56. Staleness as notice of defect — After an event that creates a right to immediate performance of the principal obligation evidenced by a security, or that sets a date on or after which a security is to be presented or surrendered for redemption or exchange, a purchaser is deemed to have notice of any defect in its issue or of any defence of the issuer,

(a) if the event requires the payment of money or the delivery of securities, or both, on presentation or surrender of the security, and such money or securities are available on the date set for payment or exchange, and the purchaser takes the security more than one year after that date; or

(b) if the purchaser takes the security more than two years after the date set for presentation or surrender or the date on which such performance became due.

2001, c. 14, s. 135 (Sched., s. 11)

57. Unauthorized signature — An unauthorized signature on a security before or in the course of its issue is ineffective, except that the signature is effective in favour of a purchaser for value and without notice of the lack of authority, if the signing has been done by

(a) an authenticating trustee, registrar, transfer agent or other person entrusted by the issuer with the signing of the security, or of similar securities, or their immediate preparation for signing; or

(b) an employee of the issuer or of a person referred to in paragraph (a) who in the ordinary course of their duties handles the security.

2001, c. 14, s. 135 (Sched., s. 12)

58. (1) Completion or alteration — Where a security contains the signatures necessary for its issue or transfer but is incomplete in any other respect,

(a) any person may complete it by filling in the blanks in accordance with their authority; and

(b) notwithstanding that the blanks are incorrectly filled in, the security as completed is enforceable by a purchaser who took it for value and without notice of such incorrectness.

(2) Enforceability — A completed security that has been improperly altered, even if fraudulently altered, remains enforceable but only according to its original terms.

2001, c. 14, s. 135 (Sched., s. 13)

59. (1) Warranties of agents — A person signing a security as authenticating trustee, registrar, transfer agent or other person entrusted by the issuer with the signing of the security warrants to a purchaser for value without notice that

(a) the security is genuine;

(b) the person's acts in connection with the issue of the security are within their authority; and

(c) the person has reasonable grounds for believing that the security is in the form and within the amount the issuer is authorized to issue.

(2) Limitation of liability — Unless otherwise agreed, a person referred to in subsection (1) does not assume any further liability for the validity of a security.

2001, c. 14, s. 135 (Sched., s. 14)

Purchase

60. (1) Title of purchaser — On delivery of a security the purchaser acquires the rights in the security that the transferor had or had authority to convey, except that a purchaser who has been a party to any fraud or illegality affecting the security or who as a prior holder had notice of an adverse claim does not improve their position by taking from a later *bona fide* purchaser.

(2) Title of *bona fide* purchaser — A *bona fide* purchaser, in addition to acquiring the rights of a purchaser, also acquires the security free from any adverse claim.

(3) Limited interest — A purchaser of a limited interest acquires rights only to the extent of the interest purchased.

2001, c. 14, s. 135 (Sched., s. 15)

61. (1) Deemed notice of adverse claim — A purchaser of a security, or any broker for a seller or purchaser, is deemed to have notice of an adverse claim if

(a) the security, whether in bearer or registered form, has been endorsed "for collection" or "for surrender" or for some other purpose not involving transfer; or

(b) the security is in bearer form and has on it a statement that it is the property of a person other than the transferor, except that the mere writing of a name on a security is not such a statement.

(2) **Notice of fiduciary duty** — Notwithstanding that a purchaser, or any broker for a seller or purchaser, has notice that a security is held for a third person or is registered in the name of or endorsed by a fiduciary, they have no duty to inquire into the rightfulness of the transfer and have no notice of an adverse claim, except that where they know that the consideration is to be used for, or that the transaction is for, the personal benefit of the fiduciary or is otherwise in breach of the fiduciary's duty, the purchaser or broker is deemed to have notice of an adverse claim.

2001, c. 14, s. 135 (Sched., s. 16)

62. Staleness as notice of adverse claim — An event that creates a right to immediate performance of the principal obligation evidenced by a security or that sets a date on or after which the security is to be presented or surrendered for redemption or exchange is not of itself notice of an adverse claim, except in the case of a purchase

(a) after one year from any date set for such presentation or surrender for redemption or exchange; or

(b) after six months from any date set for payment of money against presentation or surrender of the security if funds are available for payment on that date.

63. (1) Warranties to issuer — A person who presents a security for registration of transfer or for payment or exchange warrants to the issuer that the person is entitled to the registration, payment or exchange, except that a purchaser for value without notice of an adverse claim who receives a new, reissued or re-registered security on registration of transfer warrants only that the purchaser has no knowledge of any unauthorized signature in a necessary endorsement.

(2) **Warranties to purchaser** — A person by transferring a security to a purchaser for value warrants only that

(a) the transfer is effective and rightful;

(b) the security is genuine and has not been materially altered; and

(c) the person knows of nothing that might impair the validity of the security.

(3) **Warranties of intermediary** — Where a security is delivered by an intermediary known by the purchaser to be entrusted with delivery of the security on behalf of another or with collection of a draft or other claim to be collected against such delivery, the intermediary by such delivery warrants only the intermediary's good faith and authority even if the intermediary has purchased or made advances against the draft or other claim to be collected against the delivery.

(4) **Warranties of pledgee** — A pledgee or other holder for purposes of security who redelivers a security received, or after payment and on order of the debtor delivers that security to a third person, gives only the warranties of an intermediary under subsection (3).

(5) **Warranties of broker** — A broker gives to a customer, to the issuer and to a purchaser, as the case may be, the warranties provided in this section and has the rights and privileges of a purchaser under this section, and those warranties of and in favour of the

broker acting as an agent are in addition to warranties given by the customer and warranties given in favour of the customer.

2001, c. 14, s. 135 (Sched., s. 17)

64. Right to compel endorsement — When a security in registered form is delivered to a purchaser without a necessary endorsement, the purchaser may become a *bona fide* purchaser only as of the time the endorsement is supplied, but against the transferor the transfer is complete on delivery and the purchaser has a specifically enforceable right to have any necessary endorsement supplied.

2001, c. 14, s. 135 (Sched., s. 18)

65. (1) Definition of "appropriate person" — In this section, **"appropriate person"** means

(a) the person specified by the security or by special endorsement to be entitled to the security;

(b) if a person described in paragraph (a) is described as a fiduciary but is no longer serving in the described capacity, either that person or the person's successor;

(c) if the security or endorsement mentioned in paragraph (a) specifies more than one person as fiduciaries and one or more are no longer serving in the described capacity, the remaining fiduciary or fiduciaries, whether or not a successor has been appointed or qualified;

(d) if a person described in paragraph (a) is an individual and is without capacity to act by reason of death, incompetence, minority or other incapacity, the person's fiduciary;

(e) if the security or endorsement mentioned in paragraph (a) specifies more than one person with right of survivorship and by reason of death all cannot sign, the survivor or survivors;

(f) a person having power to sign under applicable law or a power of attorney; or

(g) to the extent that a person described in paragraphs (a) to (f) may act through an agent, the authorized agent.

(2) Determining "appropriate person" — Whether the person signing is an appropriate person is determined as of the time of signing and an endorsement by such a person does not become unauthorized for the purposes of this Part by reason of any subsequent change of circumstances.

(3) Endorsement — An endorsement of a security in registered form is made when an appropriate person signs, either on the security or on a separate document, an assignment or transfer of the security or a power to assign or transfer it, or when the signature of an appropriate person is written without more on the back of the security.

(4) Special or blank — An endorsement may be special or in blank.

(5) Blank endorsement — An endorsement in blank includes an endorsement to bearer.

(6) Special endorsement — A special endorsement specifies the person to whom the security is to be transferred, or who has power to transfer it.

(7) Right of holder — A holder may convert an endorsement in blank into a special endorsement.

(8) Immunity of endorser — Unless otherwise agreed, the endorser assumes no obligation that the security will be honoured by the issuer.

(9) Partial endorsement — An endorsement purporting to be only of part of a security representing units intended by the issuer to be separately transferable is effective to the extent of the endorsement.

(10) Failure of fiduciary to comply — Failure of a fiduciary to comply with a controlling instrument or with the law of the jurisdiction governing the fiduciary relationship, including any law requiring the fiduciary to obtain court approval of a transfer, does not render the fiduciary's endorsement unauthorized for the purposes of this Part.

2001, c. 14, ss. 32, 135 (Sched., s. 19)

66. Effect of endorsement without delivery — An endorsement of a security whether special or in blank does not constitute a transfer until delivery of the security on which it appears or, if the endorsement is on a separate document, until delivery of both the security and that document.

67. Endorsement in bearer form — An endorsement of a security in bearer form may give notice of an adverse claim under section 61 but does not otherwise affect any right to registration that the holder has.

68. (1) Effect of unauthorized endorsement — The owner of a security may assert the ineffectiveness of an endorsement against the issuer or any purchaser, other than a purchaser for value without notice of an adverse claim who has in good faith received a new, reissued or re-registered security on registration of transfer, unless the owner

(a) has ratified an unauthorized endorsement of the security; or

(b) is otherwise precluded from impugning the effectiveness of an unauthorized endorsement.

(2) Liability of issuer — An issuer who registers the transfer of a security on an unauthorized endorsement is liable for improper registration.

69. (1) Warranties of guarantor of signature — A person who guarantees a signature of an endorser of a security warrants that at the time of signing

(a) the signature was genuine;

(b) the signer was an appropriate person as defined in section 65 to endorse; and

(c) the signer had legal capacity to sign.

(2) Limitation of liability — A person who guarantees a signature of an endorser does not otherwise warrant the rightfulness of the particular transfer.

(3) Warranties of guarantor of endorsement — A person who guarantees an endorsement of a security warrants both the signature and the rightfulness of the transfer in all respects, but an issuer may not require a guarantee of endorsement as a condition to registration of transfer.

(4) Extent of liability — The warranties referred to in this section are made to any person taking or dealing with the security relying on the guarantee and the guarantor is liable to such person for any loss resulting from breach of warranty.

70. (1) Constructive delivery of a security — Delivery to a purchaser occurs when

(a) the purchaser or a person designated by the purchaser acquires possession of a security;

(b) the broker of the purchaser acquires possession of a security specially endorsed to or issued in the name of the purchaser;

(c) the broker of the purchaser sends the purchaser confirmation of the purchase and identifies in a record a specific security as belonging to the purchaser; or

(d) with respect to an identified security to be delivered while still in the possession of a third person, that person acknowledges holding it for the purchaser.

(2) Constructive ownership — A purchaser is the owner of a security that a broker holds for the purchaser, but is not a holder except in the cases referred to in paragraphs (1)(b) and (c).

(3) Ownership of part of fungible bulk — If a security is part of a fungible bulk, a purchaser of the security is the owner of a proportionate interest in the fungible bulk.

(4) Notice to broker — Notice of an adverse claim received by a broker or by a purchaser after the broker takes delivery as a holder for value is not effective against the broker or the purchaser, except that, as between the broker and the purchaser, the purchaser may demand delivery of an equivalent security as to which no notice of an adverse claim has been received.

2001, c. 14, s. 135 (Sched., s. 20)

71. (1) Delivery of security — Unless otherwise agreed, if a sale of a security is made on an exchange or otherwise through brokers,

(a) the selling customer fulfils their duty to deliver by delivering the security to the selling broker or to a person designated by the selling broker or by causing an acknowledgement to be made to the selling broker that it is held for the selling broker; and

(b) the selling broker, including a correspondent broker, acting for a selling customer fulfils their duty to deliver by delivering the security or a like security to the buying broker or to a person designated by the buying broker or by effecting clearance of the sale in accordance with the rules of the exchange on which the transaction took place.

(2) Duty to deliver — Subject to this section and unless otherwise agreed, a transferor's duty to deliver a security under a contract of purchase is not fulfilled until the transferor delivers the security in negotiable form to the purchaser or to a person designated by the purchaser, or causes an acknowledgement to be made to the purchaser that the security is held for the purchaser.

(3) Delivery to broker — A sale to a broker purchasing for the broker's own account is subject to subsection (2) and not subsection (1), unless the sale is made on a stock exchange.

2001, c. 14, s. 135 (Sched., s. 21)

72. (1) Right to reclaim possession — A person against whom the transfer of a security is wrongful for any reason, including incapacity, may against anyone except a *bona fide* purchaser reclaim possession of the security or obtain possession of any new security evidencing all or part of the same rights or claim damages.

(2) Recovery if unauthorized endorsement — If the transfer of a security is wrongful by reason of an unauthorized endorsement, the owner may reclaim possession of the security or a new security even from a *bona fide* purchaser if the ineffectiveness of the purported endorsement may be asserted against such purchaser under section 68.

(3) Remedies — The right to reclaim possession of a security may be specifically enforced, its transfer may be restrained and the security may be impounded pending litigation.

2001, c. 14, s. 135 (Sched., s. 22)

73. (1) Right to requisites for registration — Unless otherwise agreed, a transferor shall on demand supply a purchaser with proof of authority to transfer or with any other requisite that is necessary to obtain registration of the transfer of a security, but if the transfer is not for value a transferor need not do so unless the purchaser pays the reasonable and necessary costs of the proof and transfer.

(2) Rescission of transfer — If the transferor fails to comply with a demand under subsection (1) within a reasonable time, the purchaser may reject or rescind the transfer.

2001, c. 14, s. 135 (Sched., s. 23)

74. Seizure of security — No seizure of a security or other interest evidenced thereby is effective until the person making the seizure obtains possession of the security.

75. No conversion if good faith delivery by agent — An agent or bailee who in good faith, including observance of reasonable commercial standards if the agent or bailee is in the business of buying, selling or otherwise dealing with securities of a corporation, has received securities and sold, pledged or delivered them according to the instructions of their principal is not liable for conversion or for participation in breach of fiduciary duty although the principal has no right to dispose of them.

2001, c. 14, s. 135 (Sched., s. 24)

Registration

76. (1) Duty to register transfer — Where a security in registered form is presented for transfer, the issuer shall register the transfer if

(a) the security is endorsed by an appropriate person as defined in section 65;

(b) reasonable assurance is given that that endorsement is genuine and effective;

(c) the issuer has no duty to inquire into adverse claims or has discharged any such duty;

(d) any applicable law relating to the collection of taxes has been complied with;

(e) the transfer is rightful or is to a *bona fide* purchaser; and

(f) any fee referred to in subsection 49(2) has been paid.

(2) Liability for delay — Where an issuer has a duty to register a transfer of a security, the issuer is liable to the person presenting it for registration for loss resulting from any unreasonable delay in registration or from failure or refusal to register the transfer.

77. (1) Assurance that endorsement effective — An issuer may require an assurance that each necessary endorsement on a security is genuine and effective by requiring a guarantee of the signature of the person endorsing, and by requiring

(a) if the endorsement is by an agent, reasonable assurance of authority to sign;

(b) if the endorsement is by a fiduciary, evidence of appointment or incumbency;

(c) if there is more than one fiduciary, reasonable assurance that all who are required to sign have done so; and

(d) in any other case, assurance that corresponds as closely as practicable to the foregoing.

(2) Definition of "guarantee of the signature" — For the purposes of subsection (1), a **"guarantee of the signature"** means a guarantee signed by or on behalf of a person reasonably believed by the issuer to be responsible.

(3) Standards — An issuer may adopt reasonable standards to determine responsible persons for the purpose of subsection (2).

(4) Definition of "evidence of appointment or incumbency" — In paragraph (1)(b), **"evidence of appointment or incumbency"** means

(a) in the case of a fiduciary appointed by a court, a copy of the order certified in accordance with subsection 51(7), and dated not earlier than sixty days before the date a security is presented for transfer; or

(b) in any other case, a copy of a document showing the appointment or other evidence believed by the issuer to be appropriate.

(5) Standards — An issuer may adopt reasonable standards with respect to evidence for the purposes of paragraph (4)(b).

(6) No notice to issuer — An issuer is deemed not to have notice of the contents of any document referred to in subsection (4) except to the extent that the contents relate directly to appointment or incumbency.

(7) Notice from excess documentation — If an issuer demands assurance additional to that specified in this section for a purpose other than that specified in subsection (4) and obtains a copy of a will, trust or partnership agreement, by-law or similar document, the issuer is deemed to have notice of all matters contained therein affecting the transfer.

78. (1) Limited duty of inquiry — An issuer to whom a security is presented for registration has a duty to inquire into adverse claims if

(a) written notice of an adverse claim has been received at a time and in a manner that affords the issuer a reasonable opportunity to act on it before the issue of a new, reissued or re-registered security and the notice discloses the name and address of the claimant, the registered owner and the issue of which the security is a part; or

(b) the issuer is deemed to have notice of an adverse claim from a document that it obtained under subsection 77(7).

(2) Discharge of duty — An issuer may discharge a duty of inquiry by any reasonable means, including notifying an adverse claimant by registered mail sent to the address furnished by the claimant or, if no such address has been furnished, to the claimant's residence or regular place of business, that a security has been presented for registration of transfer by a named person, and that the transfer will be registered unless within thirty days from the date of mailing the notice either

(a) the issuer is served with a restraining order or other order of a court; or

(b) the issuer is provided with an indemnity bond sufficient in the issuer's judgment to protect the issuer and any registrar, transfer agent or other agent of the issuer from any loss that may be incurred by any of them as a result of complying with the adverse claim.

(3) Inquiry into adverse claims — Unless an issuer is deemed to have notice of an adverse claim from a document that is obtained under subsection 77(7) or has received notice of an adverse claim under subsection (1), if a security presented for registration is endorsed by the appropriate person as defined in section 65, the issuer has no duty to inquire into adverse claims, and in particular,

(a) an issuer registering a security in the name of a person who is a fiduciary or who is described as a fiduciary is not bound to inquire into the existence, extent or correct description of the fiduciary relationship and thereafter the issuer may assume without inquiry that the newly registered owner continues to be the fiduciary until the issuer receives written notice that the fiduciary is no longer acting as such with respect to the particular security;

(b) an issuer registering transfer on an endorsement by a fiduciary has no duty to inquire whether the transfer is made in compliance with the document or with the law of the jurisdiction governing the fiduciary relationship; and

(c) an issuer is deemed not to have notice of the contents of any court record or any registered document even if the record or document is in the issuer's possession and even if the transfer is made on the endorsement of a fiduciary to the fiduciary or the fiduciary's nominee.

(4) Duration of notice — A written notice of adverse claim received by an issuer is effective for twelve months from the date when it was received unless the notice is renewed in writing.

2001, c. 14, s. 135 (Sched., s. 25)

79. (1) Limitation of issuer's liability — Subject to any applicable law relating to the collection of taxes, the issuer is not liable to the owner or any other person who incurs a loss as a result of the registration of a transfer of a security if

(a) the necessary endorsements were on or with the security; and

(b) the issuer had no duty to inquire into adverse claims or had discharged any such duty.

(2) Duty of issuer in default — If an issuer has registered a transfer of a security to a person not entitled to it, the issuer shall on demand deliver a like security to the owner unless

(a) subsection (1) applies;

(b) the owner is precluded by subsection 80(1) from asserting any claim; or

(c) the delivery would result in overissue, in which case the issuer's liability is governed by section 52.

80. (1) Notice of lost or stolen security — Where a security has been lost, apparently destroyed or wrongfully taken, and the owner fails to notify the issuer of that fact by giving the issuer written notice of an adverse claim within a reasonable time after discovering the loss, destruction or taking and if the issuer has registered a transfer of the security before receiving such notice, the owner is precluded from asserting against the issuer any claim to a new security.

(2) Duty of issuer to issue a new security — Where the owner of a security claims that the security has been lost, destroyed or wrongfully taken, the issuer shall issue a new security in place of the original security if the owner

(a) so requests before the issuer has notice that the security has been acquired by a *bona fide* purchaser;

(b) furnishes the issuer with a sufficient indemnity bond; and

(c) satisfies any other reasonable requirements imposed by the issuer.

(3) Duty to register transfer — If, after the issue of a new security under subsection (2), a *bona fide* purchaser of the original security presents the original security for registration of transfer, the issuer shall register the transfer unless registration would result in overissue, in which case the issuer's liability is governed by section 52.

(4) Right of issuer to recover — In addition to any rights on an indemnity bond, the issuer may recover a new security issued under subsection (2) from the person to whom it was issued or anyone taking under the person other than a *bona fide* purchaser.

2001, c. 14, s. 135 (Sched., s. 26)

81. (1) Agent's duties, rights, etc. — An authenticating trustee, registrar, transfer agent or other agent of an issuer has, in respect of the issue, registration of transfer and cancellation of a security of the issuer,

(a) a duty to the issuer to exercise good faith and reasonable diligence; and

(b) the same obligations to the holder or owner of a security and the same rights, privileges and immunities as the issuer.

(2) Notice to agent — Notice to an authenticating trustee, registrar, transfer agent or other agent of an issuer is notice to the issuer with respect to the functions performed by the agent.

PART VIII — TRUST INDENTURES

82. (1) Definitions — In this Part,

"event of default" means an event specified in a trust indenture on the occurrence of which

(a) a security interest constituted by the trust indenture becomes enforceable, or

(b) the principal, interest and other moneys payable thereunder become or may be declared to be payable before maturity,

but the event is not an event of default until all conditions prescribed by the trust indenture in connection with such event for the giving of notice or the lapse of time or otherwise have been satisfied; *("cas de défaut")*

"trustee" means any person appointed as trustee under the terms of a trust indenture to which a corporation is a party and includes any successor trustee; *("fiduciaire")*

"trust indenture" means any deed, indenture or other instrument, including any supplement or amendment thereto, made by a corporation after its incorporation or continuance under this Act, under which the corporation issues debt obligations and in which a person is appointed as trustee for the holders of the debt obligations issued thereunder; *("acte de fiducie")*

(2) Application — This Part applies to a trust indenture if the debt obligations issued or to be issued under the trust indenture are part of a distribution to the public.

(3) Exemption — The Director may exempt a trust indenture from this Part if the trust indenture, the debt obligations issued thereunder and the security interest effected thereby are subject to a law of a province or a country other than Canada that is substantially equivalent to this Part.

83. (1) Conflict of interest — No person shall be appointed as trustee if there is a material conflict of interest between their role as trustee and their role in any other capacity.

(2) Eliminating conflict of interest — A trustee shall, within ninety days after becoming aware that a material conflict of interest exists

    (a) eliminate such conflict of interest; or

    (b) resign from office.

(3) Validity — A trust indenture, any debt obligations issued thereunder and a security interest effected thereby are valid notwithstanding a material conflict of interest of the trustee.

(4) Removal of trustee — If a trustee contravenes subsection (1) or (2), any interested person may apply to a court for an order that the trustee be replaced, and the court may make an order on such terms as it thinks fit.

2001, c. 14, s. 135 (Sched., s. 27)

84. Qualification of trustee — A trustee, or at least one of the trustees if more than one is appointed, shall be a body corporate incorporated under the laws of Canada or a province and authorized to carry on the business of a trust company.

85. (1) List of security holders — A holder of debt obligations issued under a trust indenture may, on payment to the trustee of a reasonable fee, require the trustee to furnish, within fifteen days after delivering to the trustee the statutory declaration referred to in subsection (4), a list setting out

    (a) the names and addresses of the registered holders of the outstanding debt obligations,

    (b) the principal amount of outstanding debt obligations owned by each such holder, and

    (c) the aggregate principal amount of debt obligations outstanding

as shown on the records maintained by the trustee on the day that the statutory declaration is delivered to that trustee.

(2) Duty of issuer — On the demand of a trustee, the issuer of debt obligations shall furnish the trustee with the information required to enable the trustee to comply with subsection (1).

(3) Corporate applicant — If the person requiring the trustee to furnish a list under subsection (1) is a body corporate, the statutory declaration required under that subsection shall be made by a director or officer of the body corporate.

(4) Contents of statutory declaration — The statutory declaration required under subsection (1) shall state

(a) the name and address of the person requiring the trustee to furnish the list and, if the person is a body corporate, the address for service thereof; and

(b) that the list will not be used except as permitted under subsection (5).

(5) Use of list — A list obtained under this section shall not be used by any person except in connection with

(a) an effort to influence the voting of the holders of debt obligations;

(b) an offer to acquire debt obligations; or

(c) any other matter relating to the debt obligations or the affairs of the issuer or guarantor thereof.

(6) Offence — A person who, without reasonable cause, contravenes subsection (5) is guilty of an offence and liable on summary conviction to a fine not exceeding five thousand dollars or to imprisonment for a term not exceeding six months or to both.

86. (1) Evidence of compliance — An issuer or a guarantor of debt obligations issued or to be issued under a trust indenture shall, before doing any act under paragraph (a), (b) or (c), furnish the trustee with evidence of compliance with the conditions in the trust indenture relating to

(a) the issue, certification and delivery of debt obligations under the trust indenture;

(b) the release or release and substitution of property subject to a security interest constituted by the trust indenture; or

(c) the satisfaction and discharge of the trust indenture.

(2) Duty of issuer or guarantor — On the demand of a trustee, the issuer or guarantor of debt obligations issued or to be issued under a trust indenture shall furnish the trustee with evidence of compliance with the trust indenture by the issuer or guarantor in respect of any act to be done by the trustee at the request of the issuer or guarantor.

87. Contents of declaration, etc. — Evidence of compliance as required by section 86 shall consist of

(a) a statutory declaration or certificate made by a director or an officer of the issuer or guarantor stating that the conditions referred to in that section have been complied with; and

(b) where the trust indenture requires compliance with conditions that are subject to review

(i) by legal counsel, an opinion of legal counsel that such conditions have been complied with, and

(ii) by an auditor or accountant, an opinion or report of the auditor of the issuer or guarantor, or such other accountant as the trustee may select, that such conditions have been complied with.

88. Further evidence of compliance — The evidence of compliance referred to in section 87 shall include a statement by the person giving the evidence

(a) declaring that they have read and understand the conditions of the trust indenture described in section 86;

(b) describing the nature and scope of the examination or investigation on which the certificate, statement or opinion is based; and

(c) declaring that they have made the examination or investigation that they believe necessary to enable them to make their statements or give their opinions.

2001, c. 14, s. 135 (Sched., s. 28)

89. (1) Trustee may require evidence of compliance — On the demand of a trustee, the issuer or guarantor of debt obligations issued under a trust indenture shall furnish the trustee with evidence in such form as the trustee may require as to compliance with any condition thereto relating to any action required or permitted to be taken by the issuer or guarantor under the trust indenture.

(2) Certificate of compliance — At least once in each twelve month period beginning on the date of the trust indenture and at any other time on the demand of a trustee, the issuer or guarantor of debt obligations issued under a trust indenture shall furnish the trustee with a certificate that the issuer or guarantor has complied with all requirements contained in the trust indenture that, if not complied with, would, with the giving of notice, lapse of time or otherwise, constitute an event of default, or, if there has been failure to so comply, giving particulars thereof.

90. Notice of default — The trustee shall give to the holders of debt obligations issued under a trust indenture, within thirty days after the trustee becomes aware of the occurrence thereof, notice of every event of default arising under the trust indenture and continuing at the time the notice is given, unless the trustee reasonably believes that it is in the best interests of the holders of the debt obligations to withhold such notice and so informs the issuer and guarantor in writing.

91. Duty of care — A trustee in exercising their powers and discharging their duties shall

(a) act honestly and in good faith with a view to the best interests of the holders of the debt obligations issued under the trust indenture; and

(b) exercise the care, diligence and skill of a reasonably prudent trustee.

2001, c. 14, s. 135 (Sched., s. 29)

92. Reliance on statements — Notwithstanding section 91, a trustee is not liable if they rely in good faith on statements contained in a statutory declaration, certificate, opinion or report that complies with this Act or the trust indenture.

2001, c. 14, s. 135 (Sched., s. 30)

93. No exculpation — No term of a trust indenture or of any agreement between a trustee and the holders of debt obligations issued thereunder or between the trustee and the issuer or guarantor shall operate so as to relieve a trustee from the duties imposed on the trustee by section 91.

2001, c. 14, s. 135 (Sched., s. 30)

PART IX — RECEIVERS AND RECEIVER-MANAGERS

94. Functions of receiver — A receiver of any property of a corporation may, subject to the rights of secured creditors, receive the income from the property and pay the liabilities connected with the property and realize the security interest of those on behalf of whom the receiver is appointed, but, except to the extent permitted by a court, the receiver may not carry on the business of the corporation.

2001, c. 14, s. 135 (Sched., s. 31)

95. Functions of receiver-manager — A receiver of a corporation who is also appointed receiver-manager of the corporation may carry on any business of the corporation to protect the security interest of those on behalf of whom the receiver is appointed.

2001, c. 14, s. 135 (Sched., s. 31)

96. Directors' powers cease — If a receiver-manager is appointed by a court or under an instrument, the powers of the directors of the corporation that the receiver-manager is authorized to exercise may not be exercised by the directors until the receiver-manager is discharged.

97. Duty to act — A receiver or receiver-manager appointed by a court shall act in accordance with the directions of the court.

98. Duty under instrument — A receiver or receiver-manager appointed under an instrument shall act in accordance with that instrument and any direction of a court made under section 100.

99. Duty of care — A receiver or receiver-manager of a corporation appointed under an instrument shall

(a) act honestly and in good faith; and

(b) deal with any property of the corporation in their possession or control in a commercially reasonable manner.

2001, c. 14, s. 135 (Sched., s. 32)

100. Directions given by court — On an application by a receiver or receiver-manager, whether appointed by a court or under an instrument, or on an application by any interested person, a court may make any order it thinks fit including, without limiting the generality of the foregoing,

(a) an order appointing, replacing or discharging a receiver or receiver-manager and approving their accounts;

(b) an order determining the notice to be given to any person or dispensing with notice to any person;

(c) an order fixing the remuneration of the receiver or receiver-manager;

(d) an order requiring the receiver or receiver-manager, or a person by or on behalf of whom the receiver or receiver-manager is appointed, to make good any default in connection with the receiver's or receiver-manager's custody or management of the property and business of the corporation, or to relieve any such person from any default on such terms as the court thinks fit, and to confirm any act of the receiver or receiver-manager; and

(e) an order giving directions on any matter relating to the duties of the receiver or receiver-manager.

2001, c. 14, s. 135 (Sched., s. 33)

101. Duties of receiver and receiver-manager — A receiver or receiver-manager shall

(a) immediately notify the Director of their appointment and discharge;

(b) take into their custody and control the property of the corporation in accordance with the court order or instrument under which they are appointed;

(c) open and maintain a bank account in their name as receiver or receiver-manager of the corporation for the moneys of the corporation coming under their control;

(d) keep detailed accounts of all transactions carried out as receiver or receiver-manager;

(e) keep accounts of their administration that shall be available during usual business hours for inspection by the directors of the corporation;

(f) prepare at least once in every six month period after the date of their appointment financial statements of their administration as far as is practicable in the form required by section 155; and

(g) on completion of their duties, render a final account of their administration in the form adopted for interim accounts under paragraph (f).

2001, c. 14, s. 135 (Sched., s. 34)

PART X — DIRECTORS AND OFFICERS

102. (1) Duty to manage or supervise management — Subject to any unanimous shareholder agreement, the directors shall manage, or supervise the management of, the business and affairs of a corporation.

(2) Number of directors — A corporation shall have one or more directors but a distributing corporation, any of the issued securities of which remain outstanding and are held by more than one person, shall have not fewer than three directors, at least two of whom are not officers or employees of the corporation or its affiliates.

2001, c. 14, s. 35

103. (1) By-laws — Unless the articles, by-laws or a unanimous shareholder agreement otherwise provide, the directors may, by resolution, make, amend, or repeal any by-laws that regulate the business or affairs of the corporation.

(2) Shareholder approval — The directors shall submit a by-law, or an amendment or a repeal of a by-law, made under subsection (1) to the shareholders at the next meeting of shareholders, and the shareholders may, by ordinary resolution, confirm, reject or amend the by-law, amendment or repeal.

(3) Effective date — A by-law, or an amendment or a repeal of a by-law, is effective from the date of the resolution of the directors under subsection (1) until it is confirmed, confirmed as amended or rejected by the shareholders under subsection (2) or until it ceases to be effective under subsection (4) and, where the by-law is confirmed or confirmed as amended, it continues in effect in the form in which it was so confirmed.

(4) Idem — If a by-law, an amendment or a repeal is rejected by the shareholders, or if the directors do not submit a by-law, an amendment or a repeal to the shareholders as required under subsection (2), the by-law, amendment or repeal ceases to be effective and no subsequent resolution of the directors to make, amend or repeal a by-law having substantially the same purpose or effect is effective until it is confirmed or confirmed as amended by the shareholders.

(5) Shareholder proposal — A shareholder entitled to vote at an annual meeting of shareholders may, in accordance with section 137, make a proposal to make, amend or repeal a by-law.

104. (1) Organization meeting — After issue of the certificate of incorporation, a meeting of the directors of the corporation shall be held at which the directors may

(a) make by-laws;

(b) adopt forms of security certificates and corporate records;

(c) authorize the issue of securities;

(d) appoint officers;

(e) appoint an auditor to hold office until the first annual meeting of shareholders;

(f) make banking arrangements; and

(g) transact any other business.

(2) Exception — Subsection (1) does not apply to a body corporate to which a certificate of amalgamation has been issued under subsection 185(4) or to which a certificate of continuance has been issued under subsection 187(4).

(3) Calling meeting — An incorporator or a director may call the meeting of directors referred to in subsection (1) by giving not less than five days notice thereof by mail to each director, stating the time and place of the meeting.

105. (1) Qualifications of directors — The following persons are disqualified from being a director of a corporation:

(a) anyone who is less than eighteen years of age;

(b) anyone who is of unsound mind and has been so found by a court in Canada or elsewhere;

(c) a person who is not an individual; or

(d) a person who has the status of bankrupt.

(2) Further qualifications — Unless the articles otherwise provide, a director of a corporation is not required to hold shares issued by the corporation.

(3) Residency — Subject to subsection (3.1), at least twenty-five per cent of the directors of a corporation must be resident Canadians. However, if a corporation has less than four directors, at least one director must be a resident Canadian.

(3.1) Exception — Canadian ownership or control — If a corporation engages in an activity in Canada in a prescribed business sector or if a corporation, by an Act of Parliament or by a regulation made under an Act of Parliament, is required, either individually or in order to engage in an activity in Canada in a particular business sector, to attain or maintain a specified level of Canadian ownership or control, or to restrict, or to comply with a restriction in relation to, the number of voting shares that any one shareholder may hold, own or control, then a majority of the directors of the corporation must be resident Canadians.

(3.2) Clarification — Nothing in subsection (3.1) shall be construed as reducing any requirement for a specified number or percentage of resident Canadian directors that otherwise applies to a corporation referred to in that subsection.

(3.3) If only one or two directors — If a corporation referred to in subsection (3.1) has only one or two directors, that director or one of the two directors, as the case may be, must be a resident Canadian.

(4) Exception for holding corporation — Despite subsection (3.1), not more than one third of the directors of a holding corporation referred to in that subsection need be resident Canadians if the holding corporation earns in Canada directly or through its subsidiaries less than five per cent of the gross revenues of the holding corporation and all of its subsidiary bodies corporate together as shown in

> (a) the most recent consolidated financial statements of the holding corporation referred to in section 157; or

> (b) the most recent financial statements of the holding corporation and its subsidiary bodies corporate as at the end of the last completed financial year of the holding corporation.

2001, c. 14, s. 37

106. (1) Notice of directors — At the time of sending articles of incorporation, the incorporators shall send to the Director a notice of directors in the form that the Director fixes, and the Director shall file the notice.

(2) Term of office — Each director named in the notice referred to in subsection (1) holds office from the issue of the certificate of incorporation until the first meeting of shareholders.

(3) Election of directors — Subject to paragraph 107(b), shareholders of a corporation shall, by ordinary resolution at the first meeting of shareholders and at each succeeding annual meeting at which an election of directors is required, elect directors to hold office for a term expiring not later than the close of the third annual meeting of shareholders following the election.

(4) Staggered terms — It is not necessary that all directors elected at a meeting of shareholders hold office for the same term.

(5) No stated terms — A director not elected for an expressly stated term ceases to hold office at the close of the first annual meeting of shareholders following the director's election.

(6) Incumbent directors — Notwithstanding subsections (2), (3) and (5), if directors are not elected at a meeting of shareholders the incumbent directors continue in office until their successors are elected.

(7) Vacancy among candidates — If a meeting of shareholders fails to elect the number or the minimum number of directors required by the articles by reason of the lack of consent, disqualification, incapacity or death of any candidates, the directors elected at that meeting may exercise all the powers of the directors if the number of directors so elected constitutes a quorum.

(8) Appointment of directors — The directors may, if the articles of the corporation so provide, appoint one or more additional directors, who shall hold office for a term expiring not later than the close of the next annual meeting of shareholders, but the total number of directors so appointed may not exceed one third of the number of directors elected at the previous annual meeting of shareholders.

(9) Election or appointment as director — An individual who is elected or appointed to hold office as a director is not a director and is deemed not to have been elected or appointed to hold office as a director unless

(a) he or she was present at the meeting when the election or appointment took place and he or she did not refuse to hold office as a director; or

(b) he or she was not present at the meeting when the election or appointment took place and

(i) he or she consented to hold office as a director in writing before the election or appointment or within ten days after it, or

(ii) he or she has acted as a director pursuant to the election or appointment.

1994, c. 24, s. 11; 2001, c. 14, ss. 38, 135 (Sched., s. 35)

107. Cumulative voting — Where the articles provide for cumulative voting,

(a) the articles shall require a fixed number and not a minimum and maximum number of directors;

(b) each shareholder entitled to vote at an election of directors has the right to cast a number of votes equal to the number of votes attached to the shares held by the shareholder multiplied by the number of directors to be elected, and may cast all of those votes in favour of one candidate or distribute them among the candidates in any manner;

(c) a separate vote of shareholders shall be taken with respect to each candidate nominated for director unless a resolution is passed unanimously permitting two or more persons to be elected by a single resolution;

(d) if a shareholder has voted for more than one candidate without specifying the distribution of votes, the shareholder is deemed to have distributed the votes equally among those candidates;

(e) if the number of candidates nominated for director exceeds the number of positions to be filled, the candidates who receive the least number of votes shall be eliminated until the number of candidates remaining equals the number of positions to be filled;

(f) each director ceases to hold office at the close of the first annual meeting of shareholders following the director's election;

(g) a director may be removed from office only if the number of votes cast in favour of the director's removal is greater than the product of the number of directors required by the articles and the number of votes cast against the motion; and

(h) the number of directors required by the articles may be decreased only if the votes cast in favour of the motion to decrease the number of directors is greater than the product of the number of directors required by the articles and the number of votes cast against the motion.

2001, c. 14, ss. 39, 135 (Sched., s. 36)

108. (1) Ceasing to hold office — A director of a corporation ceases to hold office when the director

(a) dies or resigns;

(b) is removed in accordance with section 109; or

(c) becomes disqualified under subsection 105(1).

(2) Effective date of resignation — A resignation of a director becomes effective at the time a written resignation is sent to the corporation, or at the time specified in the resignation, whichever is later.

2001, c. 14, s. 135 (Sched., s. 37)

109. (1) Removal of directors — Subject to paragraph 107(g), the shareholders of a corporation may by ordinary resolution at a special meeting remove any director or directors from office.

(2) Exception — Where the holders of any class or series of shares of a corporation have an exclusive right to elect one or more directors, a director so elected may only be removed by an ordinary resolution at a meeting of the shareholders of that class or series.

(3) Vacancy — Subject to paragraphs 107(b) to (e), a vacancy created by the removal of a director may be filled at the meeting of the shareholders at which the director is removed or, if not so filled, may be filled under section 111.

(4) Resignation (or removal) — If all of the directors have resigned or have been removed without replacement, a person who manages or supervises the management of the business and affairs of the corporation is deemed to be a director for the purposes of this Act.

(5) Exception — Subsection (4) does not apply to

(a) an officer who manages the business or affairs of the corporation under the direction or control of a shareholder or other person;

(b) a lawyer, notary, accountant or other professional who participates in the management of the corporation solely for the purpose of providing professional services; or

(c) a trustee in bankruptcy, receiver, receiver-manager or secured creditor who participates in the management of the corporation or exercises control over its property solely for the purpose of the realization of security or the administration of a bankrupt's estate, in the case of a trustee in bankruptcy.

2001, c. 14, s. 40

110. (1) Attendance at meeting — A director of a corporation is entitled to receive notice of and to attend and be heard at every meeting of shareholders.

(2) Statement of director — A director who

(a) resigns,

(b) receives a notice or otherwise learns of a meeting of shareholders called for the purpose of removing the director from office, or

(c) receives a notice or otherwise learns of a meeting of directors or shareholders at which another person is to be appointed or elected to fill the office of director, whether because of the director's resignation or removal or because the director's term of office has expired or is about to expire, is entitled to submit to the corporation a written statement giving reasons for resigning or for opposing any proposed action or resolution.

(3) Circulating statement — A corporation shall forthwith send a copy of the statement referred to in subsection (2) to every shareholder entitled to receive notice of any meeting referred to in subsection (1) and to the Director unless the statement is included in or attached to a management proxy circular required by section 150.

(4) Immunity — No corporation or person acting on its behalf incurs any liability by reason only of circulating a director's statement in compliance with subsection (3).

2001, c. 14, s. 135 (Sched., s. 38)

111. (1) Filling vacancy — Despite subsection 114(3), but subject to subsections (3) and (4), a quorum of directors may fill a vacancy among the directors, except a vacancy resulting from an increase in the number or the minimum or maximum number of directors or a failure to elect the number or minimum number of directors provided for in the articles.

(2) Calling meeting — If there is not a quorum of directors or if there has been a failure to elect the number or minimum number of directors provided for in the articles, the directors then in office shall without delay call a special meeting of shareholders to fill the vacancy and, if they fail to call a meeting or if there are no directors then in office, the meeting may be called by any shareholder.

(3) Class director — If the holders of any class or series of shares of a corporation have an exclusive right to elect one or more directors and a vacancy occurs among those directors,

(a) subject to subsection (4), the remaining directors elected by the holders of that class or series of shares may fill the vacancy except a vacancy resulting from an increase in the number or minimum or maximum number of directors for that class or series or from a failure to elect the number or minimum number of directors provided for in the articles for that class or series; or

(b) if there are no such remaining directors any holder of shares of that class or series may call a meeting of the holders of shares of that class or series for the purpose of filling the vacancy.

(4) Shareholders filling vacancy — The articles may provide that a vacancy among the directors shall only be filled by a vote of the shareholders, or by a vote of the holders of any class or series of shares having an exclusive right to elect one or more directors if the vacancy occurs among the directors elected by that class or series.

(5) Unexpired term — A director appointed or elected to fill a vacancy holds office for the unexpired term of their predecessor.

2001, c. 14, ss. 41, 135 (Sched., s. 39)

112. (1) Number of directors — The shareholders of a corporation may amend the articles to increase or, subject to paragraph 107(h), to decrease the number of directors, or the minimum or maximum number of directors, but no decrease shall shorten the term of an incumbent director.

(2) Election of directors where articles amended — Where the shareholders at a meeting adopt an amendment to the articles of a corporation to increase or, subject to paragraph 107(h) and to subsection (1), decrease the number or minimum or maximum number of directors, the shareholders may, at the meeting, elect the number of directors authorized by the amendment, and for that purpose, notwithstanding subsections 179(1) and 262(3), on

51

the issue of a certificate of amendment the articles are deemed to be amended as of the date the shareholders adopt the amendment.

1994, c. 24, s. 12

113. (1) Notice of change of director or director's address — A corporation shall, within fifteen days after

    (a) a change is made among its directors, or

    (b) it receives a notice of change of address of a director referred to in subsection (1.1),

send to the Director a notice, in the form that the Director fixes, setting out the change, and the Director shall file the notice.

(1.1) Director's change of address — A director shall, within fifteen days after changing his or her address, send the corporation a notice of that change.

(2) Application to court — Any interested person, or the Director, may apply to a court for an order to require a corporation to comply with subsection (1), and the court may so order and make any further order it thinks fit.

2001, c. 14, s. 42

114. (1) Meeting of directors — Unless the articles or by-laws otherwise provide, the directors may meet at any place and on such notice as the by-laws require.

(2) Quorum — Subject to the articles or by-laws, a majority of the number of directors or minimum number of directors required by the articles constitutes a quorum at any meeting of directors, and, notwithstanding any vacancy among the directors, a quorum of directors may exercise all the powers of the directors.

(3) Canadian directors present at meetings — Directors, other than directors of a corporation referred to in subsection 105(4), shall not transact business at a meeting of directors unless,

    (a) if the corporation is subject to subsection 105(3), at least twenty-five per cent of the directors present are resident Canadians or, if the corporation has less than four directors, at least one of the directors present is a resident Canadian; or

    (b) if the corporation is subject to subsection 105(3.1), a majority of directors present are resident Canadians or if the corporation has only two directors, at least one of the directors present is a resident Canadian.

(4) Exception — Despite subsection (3), directors may transact business at a meeting of directors where the number of resident Canadian directors, required under that subsection, is not present if

    (a) a resident Canadian director who is unable to be present approves in writing, or by telephonic, electronic or other communication facility, the business transacted at the meeting; and

    (b) the required number of resident Canadian directors would have been present had that director been present at the meeting.

(5) Notice of meeting — A notice of a meeting of directors shall specify any matter referred to in subsection 115(3) that is to be dealt with at the meeting but, unless the by-laws otherwise provide, need not specify the purpose of or the business to be transacted at the meeting.

(6) Waiver of notice — A director may in any manner waive a notice of a meeting of directors; and attendance of a director at a meeting of directors is a waiver of notice of the meeting, except where a director attends a meeting for the express purpose of objecting to the transaction of any business on the grounds that the meeting is not lawfully called.

(7) Adjournment — Notice of an adjourned meeting of directors is not required to be given if the time and place of the adjourned meeting is announced at the original meeting.

(8) One director meeting — Where a corporation has only one director, that director may constitute a meeting.

(9) Participation — Subject to the by-laws, a director may, in accordance with the regulations, if any, and if all the directors of the corporation consent, participate in a meeting of directors or of a committee of directors by means of a telephonic, electronic or other communication facility that permits all participants to communicate adequately with each other during the meeting. A director participating in such a meeting by such means is deemed for the purposes of this Act to be present at that meeting.

2001, c. 14, s. 43

115. (1) Delegation — Directors of a corporation may appoint from their number a managing director who is a resident Canadian or a committee of directors and delegate to such managing director or committee any of the powers of the directors.

(2) [Repealed 2001, c. 14, s. 44(1).]

(3) Limits on authority — Notwithstanding subsection (1), no managing director and no committee of directors has authority to

(a) submit to the shareholders any question or matter requiring the approval of the shareholders;

(b) fill a vacancy among the directors or in the office of auditor, or appoint additional directors;

(c) issue securities except as authorized by the directors;

(c.1) issue shares of a series under section 27 except as authorized by the directors;

(d) declare dividends;

(e) purchase, redeem or otherwise acquire shares issued by the corporation;

(f) pay a commission referred to in section 41 except as authorized by the directors;

(g) approve a management proxy circular referred to in Part XIII;

(h) approve a take-over bid circular or directors' circular referred to in Part XVII;

(i) approve any financial statements referred to in section 155; or

(j) adopt, amend or repeal by-laws.

2001, c. 14, s. 44

116. Validity of acts of directors and officers — An act of a director or officer is valid notwithstanding an irregularity in their election or appointment or a defect in their qualification.

2001, c. 14, s. 135 (Sched., s. 40)

117. (1) Resolution in lieu of meeting — A resolution in writing, signed by all the directors entitled to vote on that resolution at a meeting of directors or committee of directors, is as valid as if it had been passed at a meeting of directors or committee of directors.

(2) Filing resolution — A copy of every resolution referred to in subsection (1) shall be kept with the minutes of the proceedings of the directors or committee of directors.

(3) Evidence — Unless a ballot is demanded, an entry in the minutes of a meeting to the effect that the chairperson of the meeting declared a resolution to be carried or defeated is, in the absence of evidence to the contrary, proof of the fact without proof of the number or proportion of the votes recorded in favour of or against the resolution.

2001, c. 14, s. 45

118. (1) Directors' liability — Directors of a corporation who vote for or consent to a resolution authorizing the issue of a share under section 25 for a consideration other than money are jointly and severally, or solidarily, liable to the corporation to make good any amount by which the consideration received is less than the fair equivalent of the money that the corporation would have received if the share had been issued for money on the date of the resolution.

(2) Further directors' liabilities — Directors of a corporation who vote for or consent to a resolution authorizing any of the following are jointly and severally, or solidarily, liable to restore to the corporation any amounts so distributed or paid and not otherwise recovered by the corporation:

(a) a purchase, redemption or other acquisition of shares contrary to section 34, 35 or 36;

(b) a commission contrary to section 41;

(c) a payment of a dividend contrary to section 42;

(d) a payment of an indemnity contrary to section 124; or

(e) a payment of a shareholder contrary to section 190 or 241.

(f) [Repealed 2001, c. 14, s. 46(2).]

(3) Contribution — A director who has satisfied a judgment rendered under this section is entitled to contribution from the other directors who voted for or consented to the unlawful act on which the judgment was founded.

(4) Recovery — A director liable under subsection (2) is entitled to apply to a court for an order compelling a shareholder or other recipient to pay or deliver to the director any money or property that was paid or distributed to the shareholder or other recipient contrary to section 34, 35, 36, 41, 42, 124, 190 or 241.

(5) Order of court — In connection with an application under subsection (4) a court may, if it is satisfied that it is equitable to do so,

(a) order a shareholder or other recipient to pay or deliver to a director any money or property that was paid or distributed to the shareholder or other recipient contrary to section 34, 35, 36, 41, 42, 124, 190 or 241;

(b) order a corporation to return or issue shares to a person from whom the corporation has purchased, redeemed or otherwise acquired shares; or

(c) make any further order it thinks fit.

(6) No liability — A director who proves that the director did not know and could not reasonably have known that the share was issued for a consideration less than the fair equivalent of the money that the corporation would have received if the share had been issued for money is not liable under subsection (1).

(7) Limitation — An action to enforce a liability imposed by this section may not be commenced after two years from the date of the resolution authorizing the action complained of.

2001, c. 14, ss. 46, 135 (Sched., s. 41)

119. (1) Liability of directors for wages — Directors of a corporation are jointly and severally, or solidarily, liable to employees of the corporation for all debts not exceeding six months wages payable to each such employee for services performed for the corporation while they are such directors respectively.

(2) Conditions precedent to liability — A director is not liable under subsection (1) unless

(a) the corporation has been sued for the debt within six months after it has become due and execution has been returned unsatisfied in whole or in part;

(b) the corporation has commenced liquidation and dissolution proceedings or has been dissolved and a claim for the debt has been proved within six months after the earlier of the date of commencement of the liquidation and dissolution proceedings and the date of dissolution; or

(c) the corporation has made an assignment or a bankruptcy order has been made against it under the *Bankruptcy and Insolvency Act* and a claim for the debt has been proved within six months after the date of the assignment or bankruptcy order.

(3) Limitation — A director, unless sued for a debt referred to in subsection (1) while a director or within two years after ceasing to be a director, is not liable under this section.

(4) Amount due after execution — Where execution referred to in paragraph (2)(a) has issued, the amount recoverable from a director is the amount remaining unsatisfied after execution.

(5) Subrogation of director — Where a director pays a debt referred to in subsection (1) that is proved in liquidation and dissolution or bankruptcy proceedings, the director is entitled to any preference that the employee would have been entitled to, and where a judgment has been obtained, the director is entitled to an assignment of the judgment.

(6) Contribution — A director who has satisfied a claim under this section is entitled to contribution from the other directors who were liable for the claim.

1992, c. 27, s. 90(1)(h); 2001, c. 14, ss. 47(1), 135 (Sched., s. 42); 2004, c. 25, s. 187

120. (1) Disclosure of interest — A director or an officer of a corporation shall disclose to the corporation, in writing or by requesting to have it entered in the minutes of meetings of directors or of meetings of committees of directors, the nature and extent of any interest that he or she has in a material contract or material transaction, whether made or proposed, with the corporation, if the director or officer

(a) is a party to the contract or transaction;

(b) is a director or an officer, or an individual acting in a similar capacity, of a party to the contract or transaction; or

(c) has a material interest in a party to the contract or transaction.

(2) Time of disclosure for director — The disclosure required by subsection (1) shall be made, in the case of a director,

(a) at the meeting at which a proposed contract or transaction is first considered;

(b) if the director was not, at the time of the meeting referred to in paragraph (a), interested in a proposed contract or transaction, at the first meeting after he or she becomes so interested;

(c) if the director becomes interested after a contract or transaction is made, at the first meeting after he or she becomes so interested; or

(d) if an individual who is interested in a contract or transaction later becomes a director, at the first meeting after he or she becomes a director.

(3) Time of disclosure for officer — The disclosure required by subsection (1) shall be made, in the case of an officer who is not a director,

(a) immediately after he or she becomes aware that the contract, transaction, proposed contract or proposed transaction is to be considered or has been considered at a meeting;

(b) if the officer becomes interested after a contract or transaction is made, immediately after he or she becomes so interested; or

(c) if an individual who is interested in a contract later becomes an officer, immediately after he or she becomes an officer.

(4) Time of disclosure for director or officer — If a material contract or material transaction, whether entered into or proposed, is one that, in the ordinary course of the corporation's business, would not require approval by the directors or shareholders, a director or officer shall disclose, in writing to the corporation or request to have it entered in the minutes of meetings of directors or of meetings of committees of directors, the nature and extent of his or her interest immediately after he or she becomes aware of the contract or transaction.

(5) Voting — A director required to make a disclosure under subsection (1) shall not vote on any resolution to approve the contract or transaction unless the contract or transaction unless the contract or transaction [*sic*]

(a) relates primarily to his or her remuneration as a director, officer, employee or agent of the corporation or an affiliate;

(b) is for indemnity or insurance under section 124; or

(c) is with an affiliate.

(d) [Repealed 2001, c. 14, s. 48.]

(6) Continuing disclosure — For the purposes of this section, a general notice to the directors declaring that a director or an officer is to be regarded as interested, for any of the following reasons, in a contract or transaction made with a party, is a sufficient declaration of interest in relation to the contract or transaction:

(a) the director or officer is a director or officer, or acting in a similar capacity, of a party referred to in paragraph (1)(b) or (c);

(b) the director or officer has a material interest in the party; or

(c) there has been a material change in the nature of the director's or the officer's interest in the party.

(6.1) Access to disclosures — The shareholders of the corporation may examine the portions of any minutes of meetings of directors or of committees of directors that contain disclosures under this section, and any other documents that contain those disclosures, during the usual business hours of the corporation.

(7) Avoidance standards — A contract or transaction for which disclosure is required under subsection (1) is not invalid, and the director or officer is not accountable to the corporation or its shareholders for any profit realized from the contract or transaction, because of the director's or officer's interest in the contract or transaction or because the director was present or was counted to determine whether a quorum existed at the meeting of directors or committee of directors that considered the contract or transaction, if

(a) disclosure of the interest was made in accordance with subsections (1) to (6);

(b) the directors approved the contract or transaction; and

(c) the contract or transaction was reasonable and fair to the corporation when it was approved.

(7.1) Confirmation by shareholders — Even if the conditions of subsection (7) are not met, a director or officer, acting honestly and in good faith, is not accountable to the corporation or to its shareholders for any profit realized from a contract or transaction for which disclosure is required under subsection (1), and the contract or transaction is not invalid by reason only of the interest of the director or officer in the contract or transaction, if

(a) the contract or transaction is approved or confirmed by special resolution at a meeting of the shareholders;

(b) disclosure of the interest was made to the shareholders in a manner sufficient to indicate its nature before the contract or transaction was approved or confirmed; and

(c) the contract or transaction was reasonable and fair to the corporation when it was approved or confirmed.

(8) Application to court — If a director or an officer of a corporation fails to comply with this section, a court may, on application of the corporation or any of its shareholders, set aside the contract or transaction on any terms that it thinks fit, or require the director or officer to account to the corporation for any profit or gain realized on it, or do both those things.

2001, c. 14, s. 48

121. Officers — Subject to the articles, the by-laws or any unanimous shareholder agreement,

(a) the directors may designate the offices of the corporation, appoint as officers persons of full capacity, specify their duties and delegate to them powers to manage the business and affairs of the corporation, except powers to do anything referred to in subsection 115(3);

(b) a director may be appointed to any office of the corporation; and

(c) two or more offices of the corporation may be held by the same person.

122. (1) Duty of care of directors and officers — Every director and officer of a corporation in exercising their powers and discharging their duties shall

(a) act honestly and in good faith with a view to the best interests of the corporation; and

(b) exercise the care, diligence and skill that a reasonably prudent person would exercise in comparable circumstances.

(2) Duty to comply — Every director and officer of a corporation shall comply with this Act, the regulations, articles, by-laws and any unanimous shareholder agreement.

(3) No exculpation — Subject to subsection 146(5), no provision in a contract, the articles, the by-laws or a resolution relieves a director or officer from the duty to act in accordance with this Act or the regulations or relieves them from liability for a breach thereof.

2001, c. 14, s. 135 (Sched., s. 43)

123. (1) Dissent — A director who is present at a meeting of directors or committee of directors is deemed to have consented to any resolution passed or action taken at the meeting unless

(a) the director requests a dissent to be entered in the minutes of the meeting, or the dissent has been entered in the minutes;

(b) the director sends a written dissent to the secretary of the meeting before the meeting is adjourned; or

(c) the director sends a dissent by registered mail or delivers it to the registered office of the corporation immediately after the meeting is adjourned.

(2) Loss of right to dissent — A director who votes for or consents to a resolution is not entitled to dissent under subsection (1).

(3) Dissent of absent director — A director who was not present at a meeting at which a resolution was passed or action taken is deemed to have consented thereto unless within seven days after becoming aware of the resolution, the director

(a) causes a dissent to be placed with the minutes of the meeting; or

(b) sends a dissent by registered mail or delivers it to the registered office of the corporation.

(4) Defence — reasonable diligence — A director is not liable under section 118 or 119, and has complied with his or her duties under subsection 122(2), if the director exercised the care, diligence and skill that a reasonably prudent person would have exercised in comparable circumstances, including reliance in good faith on

(a) financial statements of the corporation represented to the director by an officer of the corporation or in a written report of the auditor of the corporation fairly to reflect the financial condition of the corporation; or

(b) a report of a person whose profession lends credibility to a statement made by the professional person.

(5) Defence — good faith — A director has complied with his or her duties under subsection 122(1) if the director relied in good faith on

(a) financial statements of the corporation represented to the director by an officer of the corporation or in a written report of the auditor of the corporation fairly to reflect the financial condition of the corporation; or

(b) a report of a person whose profession lends credibility to a statement made by the professional person.

2001, c. 14, ss. 50, 135 (Sched., s. 44)

124. (1) Indemnification — A corporation may indemnify a director or officer of the corporation, a former director or officer of the corporation or another individual who acts or acted at the corporation's request as a director or officer, or an individual acting in a similar capacity, of another entity, against all costs, charges and expenses, including an amount paid to settle an action or satisfy a judgment, reasonably incurred by the individual in respect of any civil, criminal, administrative, investigative or other proceeding in which the individual is involved because of that association with the corporation or other entity.

(2) Advance of costs — A corporation may advance moneys to a director, officer or other individual for the costs, charges and expenses of a proceeding referred to in subsection (1). The individual shall repay the moneys if the individual does not fulfil the conditions of subsection (3).

(3) Limitation — A corporation may not indemnify an individual under subsection (1) unless the individual

(a) acted honestly and in good faith with a view to the best interests of the corporation, or, as the case may be, to the best interests of the other entity for which the individual acted as director or officer or in a similar capacity at the corporation's request; and

(b) in the case of a criminal or administrative action or proceeding that is enforced by a monetary penalty, the individual had reasonable grounds for believing that the individual's conduct was lawful.

(4) Indemnification in derivative actions — A corporation may with the approval of a court, indemnify an individual referred to in subsection (1), or advance moneys under subsection (2), in respect of an action by or on behalf of the corporation or other entity to procure a judgment in its favour, to which the individual is made a party because of the individual's association with the corporation or other entity as described in subsection (1) against all costs, charges and expenses reasonably incurred by the individual in connection with such action, if the individual fulfils the conditions set out in subsection (3).

(5) Right to indemnity — Despite subsection (1), an individual referred to in that subsection is entitled to indemnity from the corporation in respect of all costs, charges and expenses reasonably incurred by the individual in connection with the defence of any civil, criminal, administrative, investigative or other proceeding to which the individual is subject because of the individual's association with the corporation or other entity as described in subsection (1), if the individual seeking indemnity

(a) was not judged by the court or other competent authority to have committed any fault or omitted to do anything that the individual ought to have done; and

(b) fulfils the conditions set out in subsection (3).

(6) Insurance — A corporation may purchase and maintain insurance for the benefit of an individual referred to in subsection (1) against any liability incurred by the individual

(a) in the individual's capacity as a director or officer of the corporation; or

(b) in the individual's capacity as a director or officer, or similar capacity, of another entity, if the individual acts or acted in that capacity at the corporation's request.

(7) Application to court — A corporation, an individual or an entity referred to in subsection (1) may apply to a court for an order approving an indemnity under this section and the court may so order and make any further order that it sees fit.

(8) Notice to Director — An applicant under subsection (7) shall give the Director notice of the application and the Director is entitled to appear and be heard in person or by counsel.

(9) Other notice — On an application under subsection (7) the court may order notice to be given to any interested person and the person is entitled to appear and be heard in person or by counsel.

2001, c. 14, s. 51

125. Remuneration — Subject to the articles, the by-laws or any unanimous shareholder agreement, the directors of a corporation may fix the remuneration of the directors, officers and employees of the corporation.

PART XI — INSIDER TRADING

126. (1) Definitions — In this Part,

"business combination" means an acquisition of all or substantially all the property of one body corporate by another, or an amalgamation of two or more bodies corporate, or any similar reorganization between or among two or more bodies corporate; *("regroupement d'entreprises")*

"distributing corporation" [Repealed 2001, c. 14, s. 52(1).]

"insider" means, except in section 131,

(a) a director or officer of a distributing corporation;

(b) a director or officer of a subsidiary of a distributing corporation;

(c) a director or officer of a body corporate that enters into a business combination with a distributing corporation; and

(d) a person employed or retained by a distributing corporation;

("initié")

"officer" means the chairperson of the board of directors, the president, a vice-president, the secretary, the treasurer, the comptroller, the general counsel, the general manager, a managing director, of an entity, or any other individual who performs functions for an entity similar to those normally performed by an individual occupying any of those offices; *("dirigeant")*

"share" means a share carrying voting rights under all circumstances or by reason of the occurrence of an event that has occurred and that is continuing, and includes

(a) a security currently convertible into such a share, and

(b) currently exercisable options and rights to acquire such a share or such a convertible security.

("action")

(2) Further interpretation — For the purposes of this Part,

(a) a director or an officer of a body corporate that beneficially owns, directly or indirectly, shares of a distributing corporation, or that exercises control or direction over shares of the distributing corporation, or that has a combination of any such ownership, control and direction, carrying more than the prescribed percentage of voting rights attached to all of the outstanding shares of the distributing corporation not including shares held by the body corporate as underwriter while those shares are in the course of a distribution to the public is deemed to be an insider of the distributing corporation;

(b) a director or an officer of a body corporate that is a subsidiary is deemed to be an insider of its holding distributing corporation;

(c) a person is deemed to beneficially own shares that are beneficially owned by a body corporate controlled directly or indirectly by the person;

(d) a body corporate is deemed to own beneficially shares beneficially owned by its affiliates; and

(e) the acquisition or disposition by an insider of an option or right to acquire a share is deemed to be a change in the beneficial ownership of the share to which the option or right to acquire relates.

(3) [Repealed 2001, c. 14, s. 52(5).]

(4) [Repealed 2001, c. 14, s. 52(5).]

2001, c. 14, ss. 52, 135 (Sched., s. 45)

127. [Repealed 2001, c. 14, s. 53.]

128. [Repealed 2001, c. 14, s. 53.]

129. [Repealed 2001, c. 14, s. 53.]

130. (1) Prohibition of short sale — An insider shall not knowingly sell, directly or indirectly, a security of a distributing corporation or any of its affiliates if the insider selling the security does not own or has not fully paid for the security to be sold.

(2) Calls and puts — An insider shall not knowingly, directly or indirectly, sell a call or buy a put in respect of a security of the corporation or any of its affiliates.

(3) Exception — Despite subsection (1), an insider may sell a security they do not own if they own another security convertible into the security sold or an option or right to acquire the security sold and, within ten days after the sale, they

(a) exercise the conversion privilege, option or right and deliver the security so acquired to the purchaser; or

(b) transfers the convertible security, option or right to the purchaser.

(4) Offence — An insider who contravenes subsection (1) or (2) is guilty of an offence and liable on summary conviction to a fine not exceeding the greater of one million dollars and three times the profit made, or to imprisonment for a term not exceeding six months or to both.

2001, c. 14, s. 54

131. (1) Definitions — In this section, **"insider"** means, with respect to a corporation,

(a) the corporation;

(b) an affiliate of the corporation;

(c) a director or an officer of the corporation or of any person described in paragraph (b), (d) or (f);

(d) a person who beneficially owns, directly or indirectly, shares of the corporation or who exercises control or direction over shares of the corporation, or who has a combination of any such ownership, control and direction, carrying more than the prescribed percentage of voting rights attached to all of the outstanding shares of the corporation not including shares held by the person as underwriter while those shares are in the course of a distribution to the public;

(e) a person, other than a person described in paragraph (f), employed or retained by the corporation or by a person described in paragraph (f);

(f) a person who engages in or proposes to engage in any business or professional activity with or on behalf of the corporation;

(g) a person who received, while they were a person described in any of paragraphs (a) to (f), material confidential information concerning the corporation;

(h) a person who receives material confidential information from a person described in this subsection or in subsection (3) or (3.1), including a person described in this paragraph, and who knows or who ought reasonably to have known that the person giving the information is a person described in this subsection or in subsection (3) or (3.1), including a person described in this paragraph; and

(i) a prescribed person.

(2) Expanded definition of "security" — For the purposes of this section, the following are deemed to be a security of the corporation:

(a) a put, call, option or other right or obligation to purchase or sell a security of the corporation; and

(b) a security of another entity, the market price of which varies materially with the market price of the securities of the corporation.

(3) Deemed insiders — For the purposes of this section, a person who proposes to make a take-over bid (as defined in the regulations) for securities of a corporation, or to enter into a business combination with a corporation, is an insider of the corporation with respect to material confidential information obtained from the corporation and is an insider of the corporation for the purposes of subsection (6).

(3.1) Deemed insiders — An insider of a person referred to in subsection (3), and an affiliate or associate of such a person, is an insider of the corporation referred to in that subsection. Paragraphs (1)(b) to (i) apply in determining whether a person is such an insider except that references to "corporation" in those paragraphs are to be read as references to "person described in subsection (3)".

(4) Insider trading — compensation to persons — An insider who purchases or sells a security of the corporation with knowledge of confidential information that, if generally known, might reasonably be expected to affect materially the value of any of the securities of the corporation is liable to compensate the seller of the security or the purchaser of the security, as the case may be, for any damages suffered by the seller or purchaser as a result of the purchase or sale, unless the insider establishes that

(a) the insider reasonably believed that the information had been generally disclosed;

(b) the information was known, or ought reasonably to have been known, by the seller or purchaser; or

(c) the purchase or sale of the security took place in the prescribed circumstances.

(5) Insider trading — compensation to corporation — The insider is accountable to the corporation for any benefit or advantage received or receivable by the insider as a result of a purchase or sale described in subsection (4) unless the insider establishes the circumstances described in paragraph (4)(a).

(6) Tipping — compensation to persons — An insider of the corporation who discloses to another person confidential information with respect to the corporation that has not been generally disclosed and that, if generally known, might reasonably be expected to affect materially the value of any of the securities of the corporation is liable to compensate for damages any person who subsequently sells securities of the corporation to, or purchases securities of the corporation from, any person that received the information, unless the insider establishes

(a) that the insider reasonably believed that the information had been generally disclosed;

(b) that the information was known, or ought reasonably to have been known, by the person who alleges to have suffered the damages;

(c) that the disclosure of the information was necessary in the course of the business of the insider, except if the insider is a person described in subsection (3) or (3.1); or

(d) if the insider is a person described in subsection (3) or (3.1), that the disclosure of the information was necessary to effect the take-over bid or the business combination, as the case may be.

(7) Tipping — compensation to corporation — The insider is accountable to the corporation for any benefit or advantage received or receivable by the insider as a result of a disclosure of the information as described in subsection (6) unless the insider establishes the circumstances described in paragraph (6)(a), (c) or (d).

(8) Measure of damages — The court may assess damages under subsection (4) or (6) in accordance with any measure of damages that it considers relevant in the circumstances. However, in assessing damages in a situation involving a security of a distributing corporation, the court must consider the following:

(a) if the plaintiff is a purchaser, the price paid by the plaintiff for the security less the average market price of the security over the twenty trading days immediately following general disclosure of the information; and

(b) if the plaintiff is a seller, the average market price of the security over the twenty trading days immediately following general disclosure of the information, less the price that the plaintiff received for the security.

(9) Liability — If more than one insider is liable under subsection (4) or (6) with respect to the same transaction or series of transactions, their liability is joint and several, or solidary.

(10) Limitation — An action to enforce a right created by subsections (4) to (7) may be commenced only within two years after discovery of the facts that gave rise to the cause of action.

2001, c. 14, s. 54

PART XII — SHAREHOLDERS

132. (1) Place of meetings — Meetings of shareholders of a corporation shall be held at the place within Canada provided in the by-laws or, in the absence of such provision, at the place within Canada that the directors determine.

(2) Meeting outside Canada — Despite subsection (1), a meeting of shareholders of a corporation may be held at a place outside Canada if the place is specified in the articles or all the shareholders entitled to vote at the meeting agree that the meeting is to be held at that place.

(3) Exception — A shareholder who attends a meeting of shareholders held outside Canada is deemed to have agreed to it being held outside Canada except when the shareholder attends the meeting for the express purpose of objecting to the transaction of any business on the grounds that the meeting is not lawfully held.

(4) Participation in meeting by electronic means — Unless the by-laws otherwise provide, any person entitled to attend a meeting of shareholders may participate in the meeting, in accordance with the regulations, if any, by means of a telephonic, electronic or other communication facility that permits all participants to communicate adequately with each other during the meeting, if the corporation makes available such a communication facility. A person participating in a meeting by such means is deemed for the purposes of this Act to be present at the meeting.

(5) Meeting held by electronic means — If the directors or the shareholders of a corporation call a meeting of shareholders pursuant to this Act, those directors or shareholders, as the case may be, may determine that the meeting shall be held, in accordance with the regulations, if any, entirely by means of a telephonic, electronic or other communication facility that permits all participants to communicate adequately with each other during the meeting, if the by-laws so provide.

2001, c. 14, s. 55

133. (1) Calling annual meetings — The directors of a corporation shall call an annual meeting of shareholders

(a) not later than eighteen months after the corporation comes into existence; and

(b) subsequently, not later than fifteen months after holding the last preceding annual meeting but no later than six months after the end of the corporation's preceding financial year.

(2) Calling special meetings — The directors of a corporation may at any time call a special meeting of shareholders.

(3) Order to delay calling of annual meeting — Despite subsection (1), the corporation may apply to the court for an order extending the time for calling an annual meeting.

2001, c. 14, s. 56

134. (1) Fixing record date — The directors may, within the prescribed period, fix in advance a date as the record date for the purpose of determining shareholders

(a) entitled to receive payment of dividend;

(b) entitled to participate in a liquidation distribution;

(c) entitled to receive notice of a meeting of shareholders;

(d) entitled to vote at a meeting of shareholders; or

(e) for any other purpose.

(2) No record date fixed — If no record date is fixed,

(a) the record date for the determination of shareholders entitled to receive notice of a meeting of shareholders shall be

(i) at the close of business on the day immediately preceding the day on which the notice is given, or

(ii) if no notice is given, the day on which the meeting is held; and

(b) the record date for the determination of shareholders for any purpose other than to establish a shareholder's right to receive notice of a meeting or to vote shall be at the close of business on the day on which the directors pass the resolution relating thereto.

(3) When record date fixed — If a record date is fixed, unless notice of the record date is waived in writing by every holder of a share of the class or series affected whose name is set out in the securities register at the close of business on the day the directors fix the record date, notice of the record date must be given within the prescribed period

(a) by advertisement in a newspaper published or distributed in the place where the corporation has its registered office and in each place in Canada where it has a transfer agent or where a transfer of its shares may be recorded; and

(b) by written notice to each stock exchange in Canada on which the shares of the corporation are listed for trading.

2001, c. 14, s. 57

135. (1) Notice of meeting — Notice of the time and place of a meeting of shareholders shall be sent within the prescribed period to

(a) each shareholder entitled to vote at the meeting;

(b) each director; and

(c) the auditor of the corporation.

(1.1) Exception — not a distributing corporation — In the case of a corporation that is not a distributing corporation, the notice may be sent within a shorter period if so specified in the articles or by-laws.

(2) Exception — shareholders not registered — A notice of a meeting is not required to be sent to shareholders who were not registered on the records of the corporation or its transfer agent on the record date determined under paragraph 134(1)(c) or subsection 134(2), but failure to receive a notice does not deprive a shareholder of the right to vote at the meeting.

(3) Adjournment — If a meeting of shareholders is adjourned for less than thirty days it is not necessary, unless the by-laws otherwise provide, to give notice of the adjourned meeting, other than by announcement at the earliest meeting that is adjourned.

(4) Notice of adjourned meeting — If a meeting of shareholders is adjourned by one or more adjournments for an aggregate of thirty days or more, notice of the adjourned meeting shall be given as for an original meeting but, unless the meeting is adjourned by one or more adjournments for an aggregate of more than ninety days, subsection 149(1) does not apply.

(5) Business — All business transacted at a special meeting of shareholders and all business transacted at an annual meeting of shareholders, except consideration of the financial statements, auditor's report, election of directors and re-appointment of the incumbent auditor, is deemed to be special business.

(6) Notice of business — Notice of a meeting of shareholders at which special business is to be transacted shall state

(a) the nature of that business in sufficient detail to permit the shareholder to form a reasoned judgment thereon; and

(b) the text of any special resolution to be submitted to the meeting.

2001, c. 14, s. 58

136. Waiver of notice — A shareholder or any other person entitled to attend a meeting of shareholders may in any manner waive notice of a meeting of shareholders, and their attendance at a meeting of shareholders is a waiver of notice of the meeting, except where they attend a meeting for the express purpose of objecting to the transaction of any business on the grounds that the meeting is not lawfully called.

2001, c. 14, s. 135 (Sched., s. 46)

137. (1) Proposals — Subject to subsections (1.1) and (1.2), a registered holder or beneficial owner of shares that are entitled to be voted at an annual meeting of shareholders may

(a) submit to the corporation notice of any matter that the person proposes to raise at the meeting (a "proposal"); and

(b) discuss at the meeting any matter in respect of which the person would have been entitled to submit a proposal.

(1.1) Persons eligible to make proposals — To be eligible to submit a proposal, a person

(a) must be, for at least the prescribed period, the registered holder or the beneficial owner of at least the prescribed number of outstanding shares of the corporation; or

(b) must have the support of persons who, in the aggregate, and including or not including the person that submits the proposal, have been, for at least the prescribed period, the registered holders, or the beneficial owners of, at least the prescribed number of outstanding shares of the corporation.

(1.2) Information to be provided — A proposal submitted under paragraph (1)(a) must be accompanied by the following information:

(a) the name and address of the person and of the person's supporters, if applicable, and

(b) the number of shares held or owned by the person and the person's supporters, if applicable, and the date the shares were acquired.

(1.3) Information not part of proposal — The information provided under subsection (1.2) does not form part of the proposal or of the supporting statement referred to in subsection (3) and is not included for the purposes of the prescribed maximum word limit set out in subsection (3).

(1.4) Proof may be required — If requested by the corporation within the prescribed period, a person who submits a proposal must provide proof, within the prescribed period, that the person meets the requirements of subsection (1.1).

(2) Information circular — A corporation that solicits proxies shall set out the proposal in the management proxy circular required by section 150 or attach the proposal thereto.

(3) Supporting statement — If so requested by the person who submits a proposal, the corporation shall include in the management proxy circular or attach to it a statement in support of the proposal by the person and the name and address of the person. The statement and the proposal must together not exceed the prescribed maximum number of words.

(4) Nomination for director — A proposal may include nominations for the election of directors if the proposal is signed by one or more holders of shares representing in the aggregate not less than five per cent of the shares or five per cent of the shares of a class of shares of the corporation entitled to vote at the meeting to which the proposal is to be presented, but this subsection does not preclude nominations made at a meeting of shareholders.

(5) Exemptions — A corporation is not required to comply with subsections (2) and (3) if

(a) the proposal is not submitted to the corporation at least the prescribed number of days before the anniversary date of the notice of meeting that was sent to shareholders in connection with the previous annual meeting of shareholders;

(b) it clearly appears that the primary purpose of the proposal is to enforce a personal claim or redress a personal grievance against the corporation or its directors, officers or security holders;

(b.1) it clearly appears that the proposal does not relate in a significant way to the business or affairs of the corporation;

(c) not more than the prescribed period before the receipt of a proposal, a person failed to present, in person or by proxy, at a meeting of shareholders, a proposal that at the person's request, had been included in a management proxy circular relating to the meeting;

(d) substantially the same proposal was submitted to shareholders in a management proxy circular or a dissident's proxy circular relating to a meeting of shareholders held not more than the prescribed period before the receipt of the proposal and did not receive the prescribed minimum amount of support at the meeting; or

(e) the rights conferred by this section are being abused to secure publicity.

(5.1) Corporation may refuse to include proposal — If a person who submits a proposal fails to continue to hold or own the number of shares referred to in subsection (1.1) up to and including the day of the meeting, the corporation is not required to set out in the management proxy circular, or attach to it, any proposal submitted by that person for any meeting held within the prescribed period following the date of the meeting.

(6) Immunity — No corporation or person acting on its behalf incurs any liability by reason only of circulating a proposal or statement in compliance with this section.

(7) Notice of refusal — If a corporation refuses to include a proposal in a management proxy circular, the corporation shall, within the prescribed period after the day on which it receives the proposal or the day on which it receives the proof of ownership under subsection (1.4), as the case may be, notify in writing the person submitting the proposal of its intention to omit the proposal from the management proxy circular and of the reasons for the refusal.

(8) Person may apply to court — On the application of a person submitting a proposal who claims to be aggrieved by a corporation's refusal under subsection (7), a court may restrain the holding of the meeting to which the proposal is sought to be presented and make any further order it thinks fit.

(9) Corporation's application to court — The corporation or any person claiming to be aggrieved by a proposal may apply to a court for an order permitting the corporation to omit the proposal from the management proxy circular, and the court, if it is satisfied that subsection (5) applies, may make such order as it thinks fit.

(10) Director entitled to notice — An applicant under subsection (8) or (9) shall give the Director notice of the application and the Director is entitled to appear and be heard in person or by counsel.

2001, c. 14, s. 59

138. (1) List of shareholders entitled to receive notice — A corporation shall prepare an alphabetical list of its shareholders entitled to receive notice of a meeting, showing the number of shares held by each shareholder,

(a) if a record date is fixed under subsection 134(1)(c), not later than ten days after that date; or

(b) if no record date is fixed, on the record date established under paragraph 134(2)(a).

(2) Voting list — if record date fixed — If a record date for voting is fixed under paragraph 134(1)(d), the corporation shall prepare, no later than ten days after the record date, an alphabetical list of shareholders entitled to vote as of the record date at a meeting of shareholders that shows the number of shares held by each shareholder.

(3) Voting list — if no record date fixed — If a record date for voting is not fixed under paragraph 134(1)(d), the corporation shall prepare, no later than ten days after a record date is fixed under paragraph 134(1)(c) or no later than the record date established under paragraph 134(2)(a), as the case may be, an alphabetical list of shareholders who are entitled to vote as of the record date that shows the number of shares held by each shareholder.

(3.1) Entitlement to vote — A shareholder whose name appears on a list prepared under subsection (2) or (3) is entitled to vote the shares shown opposite their name at the meeting to which the list relates.

(4) Examination of list — A shareholder may examine the list of shareholders

(a) during usual business hours at the registered office of the corporation or at the place where its central securities register is maintained; and

(b) at the meeting of shareholders for which the list was prepared.

2001, c. 14, s. 60

139. (1) Quorum — Unless the by-laws otherwise provide, a quorum of shareholder is present at a meeting of shareholders, irrespective of the number of persons actually present at the meeting, if the holders of a majority of the shares entitled to vote at the meeting are present in person or represented by proxy.

(2) Opening quorum sufficient — If a quorum is present at the opening of a meeting of shareholders, the shareholders present may, unless the by-laws otherwise provide, proceed with the business of the meeting, notwithstanding that a quorum is not present throughout the meeting.

(3) Adjournment — If a quorum is not present at the opening of a meeting of shareholders, the shareholders present may adjourn the meeting to a fixed time and place but may not transact any other business.

(4) One shareholder meeting — If a corporation has only one shareholder, or only one holder of any class or series of shares, the shareholder present in person or by proxy constitutes a meeting.

140. (1) Right to vote — Unless the articles otherwise provide, each share of a corporation entitles the holder thereof to one vote at a meeting of shareholders.

(2) Representative — If a body corporate or association is a shareholder of a corporation, the corporation shall recognize any individual authorized by a resolution of the directors or governing body of the body corporate or association to represent it at meetings of shareholders of the corporation.

(3) Powers of representative — An individual authorized under subsection (2) may exercise on behalf of the body corporate or association all the powers it could exercise if it were an individual shareholder.

(4) Joint shareholders — Unless the by-laws otherwise provide, if two or more persons hold shares jointly, one of those holders present at a meeting of shareholders may in the absence of the others vote the share, but if two or more of those persons who are present, in person or by proxy, vote, they shall vote as one on the shares jointly held by them.

2001, c. 14, s. 135 (Sched., s. 47)

141. (1) Voting — Unless the by-laws otherwise provide, voting at a meeting of shareholders shall be by show of hands except where a ballot is demanded by a shareholder or proxyholder entitled to vote at the meeting.

(2) Ballot — A shareholder or proxyholder may demand a ballot either before or after any vote by show of hands.

(3) Electronic voting — Despite subsection (1), unless the by-laws otherwise provide, any vote referred to in subsection (1) may be held, in accordance with the regulations, if any, entirely by means of a telephonic, electronic or other communication facility, if the corporation makes available such a communication facility.

(4) Voting while participating electronically — Unless the by-laws otherwise provide, any person participating in a meeting of shareholders under subsection 132(4) or (5) and entitled to vote at that meeting may vote, in accordance with the regulations, if any, by means of the telephonic, electronic or other communication facility that the corporation has made available for that purpose.

2001, c. 14, s. 61

142. (1) Resolution in lieu of meeting — Except where a written statement is submitted by a director under subsection 110(2) or by an auditor under subsection 168(5),

    (a) a resolution in writing signed by all the shareholders entitled to vote on that resolution at a meeting of shareholders is as valid as if it had been passed at a meeting of the shareholders; and

    (b) a resolution in writing dealing with all matters required by this Act to be dealt with at a meeting of shareholders, and signed by all the shareholders entitled to vote at that meeting, satisfies all the requirements of this Act relating to meetings of shareholders.

(2) Filing resolution — A copy of every resolution referred to in subsection (1) shall be kept with the minutes of the meeting of shareholders.

(3) Evidence — Unless a ballot is demanded, an entry in the minutes of a meeting to the effect that the chairperson of the meeting declared a resolution to be carried or defeated is, in the absence of evidence to the contrary, proof of the fact without proof of the number or proportion of the votes recorded in favour of or against the resolution.

2001, c. 14, s. 62

143. (1) Requisition of meeting — The holders of not less than five per cent of the issued shares of a corporation that carry the right to vote at a meeting sought to be held may requisition the directors to call a meeting of shareholders for the purposes stated in the requisition.

(2) Form — The requisition referred to in subsection (1), which may consist of several documents of like form each signed by one or more shareholders, shall state the business to be transacted at the meeting and shall be sent to each director and to the registered office of the corporation.

(3) Directors calling meeting — On receiving the requisition referred to in subsection (1), the directors shall call a meeting of shareholders to transact the business stated in the requisition, unless

(a) a record date has been fixed under paragraph 134(1)(c) and notice of it has been given under subsection 134(3);

(b) the directors have called a meeting of shareholders and have given notice thereof under section 135; or

(c) the business of the meeting as stated in the requisition includes matters described in paragraphs 137(5)(b) to (e).

(4) Shareholder calling meeting — If the directors do not within twenty-one days after receiving the requisition referred to in subsection (1) call a meeting, any shareholder who signed the requisition may call the meeting.

(5) Procedure — A meeting called under this section shall be called as nearly as possible in the manner in which meetings are to be called pursuant to the by-laws, this Part and Part XIII.

(6) Reimbursement — Unless the shareholders otherwise resolve at a meeting called under subsection (4), the corporation shall reimburse the shareholders the expenses reasonably incurred by them in requisitioning, calling and holding the meeting.

2001, c. 14, s. 63

144. (1) Meeting called by court — A court, on the application of a director, a shareholder who is entitled to vote at a meeting of shareholders or the Director, may order a meeting of a corporation to be called, held and conducted in the manner that the court directs, if

(a) it is impracticable to call the meeting within the time or in the manner in which those meetings are to be called;

(b) it is impracticable to conduct the meeting in the manner required by this Act or the by-laws; or

(c) the court thinks that the meeting should be called, held and conducted within the time or in the manner it directs for any other reason.

(2) Varying quorum — Without restricting the generality of subsection (1), the court may order that the quorum required by the by-laws or this Act be varied or dispensed with at a meeting called, held and conducted pursuant to this section.

(3) Valid meeting — A meeting called, held and conducted pursuant to this section is for all purposes a meeting of shareholders of the corporation duly called, held and conducted.

2001, c. 14, s. 64

145. (1) Court review of election — A corporation or a shareholder or director may apply to a court to determine any controversy with respect to an election or appointment of a director or auditor of the corporation.

(2) Powers of court — On an application under this section, the court may make any order it thinks fit including, without limiting the generality of the foregoing,

(a) an order restraining a director or auditor whose election or appointment is challenged from acting pending determination of the dispute;

(b) an order declaring the result of the disputed election or appointment;

(c) an order requiring a new election or appointment, and including in the order directions for the management of the business and affairs of the corporation until a new election is held or appointment made; and

(d) an order determining the voting rights of shareholders and of persons claiming to own shares.

145.1 Pooling agreement — A written agreement between two or more shareholders may provide that in exercising voting rights the shares held by them shall be voted as provided in the agreement.

2001, c. 14, s. 66

146. (1) Unanimous shareholder agreement — An otherwise lawful written agreement among all the shareholders of a corporation, or among all the shareholders and one or more persons who are not shareholders, that restricts, in whole or in part, the powers of the directors to manage, or supervise the management of, the business and affairs of the corporation is valid.

(2) Declaration by single shareholder — If a person who is the beneficial owner of all the issued shares of a corporation makes a written declaration that restricts in whole or in part the powers of the directors to manage, or supervise the management of, the business and affairs of the corporation, the declaration is deemed to be a unanimous shareholder agreement.

(3) Constructive party — A purchaser or transferee of shares subject to a unanimous shareholder agreement is deemed to be a party to the agreement.

(4) When no notice given — If notice is not given to a purchaser or transferee of the existence of a unanimous shareholder agreement, in the manner referred to in subsection 49(8) or otherwise, the purchaser or transferee may, no later than 30 days after they become aware of the existence of the unanimous shareholder agreement, rescind the transaction by which they acquired the shares.

(5) Rights of shareholder — To the extent that a unanimous shareholder agreement restricts the powers of the directors to manage, or supervise the management of, the business and affairs of the corporation, parties to the unanimous shareholder agreement who are given that power to manage or supervise the management of the business and affairs of the corporation have all the rights, powers, duties and liabilities of a director of the corporation, whether they arise under this Act or otherwise, including any defences available to the directors, and the directors are relieved of their rights, powers, duties and liabilities, including their liabilities under section 119, to the same extent.

(6) Discretion of shareholders — Nothing in this section prevents shareholders from fettering their discretion when exercising the powers of directors under a unanimous shareholder agreement.

2001, c. 14, s. 66

PART XIII — PROXIES

147. Definitions — In this Part,

"form of proxy" means a written or printed form that, on completion and execution by or on behalf of a shareholder, becomes a proxy; *("formulaire de procuration")*

"intermediary" means a person who holds a security on behalf of another person who is not the registered holder of the security, and includes

(a) a securities broker or dealer required to be registered to trade or deal in securities under the laws of any jurisdiction;

(b) a securities depositary;

(c) a financial institution;

(d) in respect of a clearing agency, a securities dealer, trust company, bank or other person, including another clearing agency, on whose behalf the clearing agency or its nominees hold securities of an issuer;

(e) a trustee or administrator of a self-administered retirement savings plan, retirement income fund, education savings plan or other similar self-administered savings or investment plan registered under the *Income Tax Act*;

(f) a nominee of a person referred to in any of paragraphs (a) to (e); and

(g) a person who carries out functions similar to those carried out by individuals or entities referred to in any of paragraphs (a) to (e) and that holds a security registered in its name, or in the name of its nominee, on behalf of another person who is not the registered holder of the security.

("intermédiaire")

"proxy" means a completed and executed form of proxy by means of which a shareholder appoints a proxyholder to attend and act on the shareholder's behalf at a meeting of shareholders; *("procuration")*

"registrant" [Repealed 2001, c. 14, s. 67(1).]

"solicit" or "solicitation"

(a) includes

(i) a request for a proxy whether or not accompanied by or included in a form of proxy,

(ii) a request to execute or not to execute a form of proxy or to revoke a proxy,

(iii) the sending of a form of proxy or other communication to a shareholder under circumstances reasonably calculated to result in the procurement, withholding or revocation of a proxy, and

(iv) the sending of a form of proxy to a shareholder under section 149; but

(b) does not include

(i) the sending of a form of proxy in response to an unsolicited request made by or on behalf of a shareholder,

(ii) the performance of administrative acts or professional services on behalf of a person soliciting a proxy,

(iii) the sending by an intermediary of the documents referred to in section 153,

(iv) a solicitation by a person in respect of shares of which the person is the beneficial owner,

(v) a public announcement, as prescribed, by a shareholder of how the shareholder intends to vote and the reasons for that decision,

(vi) a communication for the purposes of obtaining the number of shares required for a shareholder proposal under subsection 137(1.1), or

(vii) a communication, other than a solicitation by or on behalf of the management of the corporation, that is made to shareholders, in any circumstances that may be prescribed;

(c) [Repealed 2001, c. 14, s. 67(2).]

(d) [Repealed 2001, c. 14, s. 67(2).]

(e) [Repealed 2001, c. 14, s. 67(2).]

(f) [Repealed 2001, c. 14, s. 67(2).]

(g) [Repealed 2001, c. 14, s. 67(2).]

(h) [Repealed 2001, c. 14, s. 67(2).]

("sollicitation")

"solicitation by or on behalf of the management of a corporation" means a solicitation by any person pursuant to a resolution or instructions of, or with the acquiescence of, the directors or a committee of the directors. *("sollicitation effectuée par la direction ou pour son compte")*

2001, c. 14, ss. 67, 135 (Sched., s. 48)

148. (1) Appointing proxyholder — A shareholder entitled to vote at a meeting of shareholders may by means of a proxy appoint a proxyholder or one or more alternate proxyholders, who are not required to be shareholders, to attend and act at the meeting in the manner and to the extent authorized by the proxy and with the authority conferred by the proxy.

(2) Execution of proxy — A proxy shall be executed by the shareholder or by the shareholder's attorney authorized in writing.

(3) Validity of proxy — A proxy is valid only at the meeting in respect of which it is given or any adjournment thereof.

(4) Revocation of proxy — A shareholder may revoke a proxy

(a) by depositing an instrument in writing executed by the shareholder or by the shareholder's attorney authorized in writing

(i) at the registered office of the corporation at any time up to and including the last business day preceding the day of the meeting, or an adjournment thereof, at which the proxy is to be used, or

(ii) with the chairman of the meeting on the day of the meeting or an adjournment thereof; or

(b) in any other manner permitted by law.

(5) Deposit of proxies — The directors may specify in a notice calling a meeting of shareholders a time not exceeding forty-eight hours, excluding Saturdays and holidays, preceding the meeting or an adjournment thereof before which time proxies to be used at the meeting must be deposited with the corporation or its agent.

2001, c. 14, s. 135 (Sched., s. 49)

149. (1) Mandatory solicitation — Subject to subsection (2), the management of a corporation shall, concurrently with giving notice of a meeting of shareholders, send a form of proxy in prescribed form to each shareholder who is entitled to receive notice of the meeting.

(2) Exception — The management of the corporation is not required to send a form of proxy under subsection (1) if it

(a) is not a distributing corporation; and

(b) has fifty or fewer shareholders entitled to vote at a meeting, two or more joint holders being counted as one shareholder.

(3) Offence — If the management of a corporation fails to comply, without reasonable cause, with subsection (1), the corporation is guilty of an offence and liable on summary conviction to a fine not exceeding five thousand dollars.

(4) Officers, etc., of corporations — Where a corporation commits an offence under subsection (3), any director or officer of the corporation who knowingly authorized, permitted or acquiesced in the commission of the offence is a party to and guilty of the offence and is liable on summary conviction to a fine not exceeding five thousand dollars or to imprisonment for a term not exceeding six months or to both, whether or not the corporation has been prosecuted or convicted.

2001, c. 14, s. 68

150. (1) Soliciting proxies — A person shall not solicit proxies unless

(a) in the case of solicitation by or on behalf of the management of a corporation, a management proxy circular in prescribed form, either as an appendix to or as a separate document accompanying the notice of the meeting, or

(b) in the case of any other solicitation, a dissident's proxy circular in prescribed form stating the purposes of the solicitation

is sent to the auditor of the corporation, to each shareholder whose proxy is solicited, to each director and, if paragraph (b) applies, to the corporation.

(1.1) Exception — solicitation to fifteen or fewer shareholders — Despite subsection (1), a person may solicit proxies, other than by or on behalf of the management of the corporation, without sending a dissident's proxy circular, if the total number of shareholders whose proxies are solicited is fifteen or fewer, two or more joint holders being counted as one shareholder.

(1.2) Exception — solicitation by public broadcast — Despite subsection (1), a person may solicit proxies, other than by or on behalf of the management of the corporation, without sending a dissident's proxy circular, if the solicitation is, in the prescribed circumstances, conveyed by public broadcast, speech or publication.

(2) Copy to Director — A person required to send a management proxy circular or dissident's proxy circular shall send concurrently a copy of it to the Director together with a statement in prescribed form, the form of proxy, any other documents for use in connection with the meeting and, in the case of a management proxy circular, a copy of the notice of meeting.

(3) Offence — A person who fails to comply with subsections (1) and (2) is guilty of an offence and liable on summary conviction to a fine not exceeding five thousand dollars or to imprisonment for a term not exceeding six months or to both, whether or not the body corporate has been prosecuted or convicted.

(4) Officers, etc., of bodies corporate — Where a body corporate commits an offence under subsection (3), any director of the body corporate who knowingly authorized, permitted or acquiesced in the commission of the offence is a party to and guilty of the offence and is liable on summary conviction to a fine not exceeding five thousand dollars or to imprisonment for a term not exceeding six months or to both, whether or not the body corporate has been prosecuted or convicted.

1992, c. 1, s. 54; 1994, c. 24, s. 16; 2001, c. 14, s. 69

151. (1) Exemption — On the application of an interested person, the Director may exempt the person, on any terms that the Director thinks fit, from any of the requirements of section 149 or subsection 150(1), which exemption may have retrospective effect.

(2) Publication — The Director shall set out in a publication generally available to the public the particulars of exemptions granted under this section together with the reasons for the exemptions.

2001, c. 14, s. 70

152. (1) Attendance at meeting — A person who solicits a proxy and is appointed proxyholder shall attend in person or cause an alternate proxyholder to attend the meeting in respect of which the proxy is given and comply with the directions of the shareholder who appointed him.

(2) Right of a proxyholder — A proxyholder or an alternate proxyholder has the same rights as the shareholder by whom they were appointed to speak at a meeting of shareholders in respect of any matter, to vote by way of ballot at the meeting and, except where a proxyholder or an alternate proxyholder has conflicting instructions from more than one shareholder, to vote at such a meeting in respect of any matter by way of any show of hands.

(3) Show of hands — Despite subsections (1) and (2), if the chairperson of a meeting of shareholders declares to the meeting that, if a ballot is conducted, the total number of votes attached to shares represented at the meeting by proxy required to be voted against what to the knowledge of the chairperson will be the decision of the meeting in relation to any matter or group of matters is less than five per cent of all the votes that might be cast by shareholders personally or through proxy at the meeting on the ballot, unless a shareholder or proxyholder demands a ballot,

(a) the chairperson may conduct the vote in respect of that matter or group of matters by a show of hands; and

(b) a proxyholder or alternate proxyholder may vote in respect of that matter or group of matters by a show of hands.

(4) Offence — A proxyholder or alternate proxyholder who without reasonable cause fails to comply with the directions of a shareholder under this section is guilty of an offence and liable on summary conviction to a fine not exceeding five thousand dollars or to imprisonment for a term not exceeding six months or to both.

2001, c. 14, ss. 71, 135 (Sched., s. 50)

153. (1) Duty of intermediary — Shares of a corporation that are registered in the name of an intermediary or their nominee and not beneficially owned by the intermediary must not be voted unless the intermediary, without delay after receipt of the notice of the meeting, financial statements, management proxy circular, dissident's proxy circular and any other documents other than the form of proxy sent to shareholders by or on behalf of any person for use in connection with the meeting, sends a copy of the document to the beneficial owner and, except when the intermediary has received written voting instructions from the beneficial owner, a written request for such instructions.

(2) Restriction on voting — An intermediary, or a proxyholder appointed by an intermediary, may not vote shares that the intermediary does not beneficially own and that are registered in the name of the intermediary or in the name of a nominee of the intermediary unless the intermediary or proxyholder, as the case may be, receives written voting instructions from the beneficial owner.

(3) Copies — A person by or on behalf of whom a solicitation is made shall provide, at the request of an intermediary, without delay, to the intermediary at the person's expense the necessary number of copies of the documents referred to in subsection (1), other than copies of the document requesting voting instructions.

(4) Instructions to intermediary — An intermediary shall vote or appoint a proxyholder to vote any shares referred to in subsection (1) in accordance with any written voting instructions received from the beneficial owner.

(5) Beneficial owner as proxyholder — If a beneficial owner so requests and provides an intermediary with appropriate documentation, the intermediary must appoint the beneficial owner or a nominee of the beneficial owner as proxyholder.

(6) Validity — The failure of an intermediary to comply with this section does not render void any meeting of shareholders or any action taken at the meeting.

(7) Limitation — Nothing in this section gives an intermediary the right to vote shares that the intermediary is otherwise prohibited from voting.

(8) Offence — An intermediary who knowingly fails to comply with this section is guilty of an offence and liable on summary conviction to a fine not exceeding five thousand dollars or to imprisonment for a term not exceeding six months or to both.

(9) Officers, etc., of bodies corporate — If an intermediary that is a body corporate commits an offence under subsection (8), any director or officer of the body corporate who knowingly authorized, permitted or acquiesced in the commission of the offence is a party to and guilty of the offence and is liable on summary conviction to a fine not exceeding five thousand dollars or to imprisonment for a term not exceeding six months or to both, whether or not the body corporate has been prosecuted or convicted.

2001, c. 14, s. 72

154. (1) Restraining order — If a form of proxy, management proxy circular or dissident's proxy circular contains an untrue statement of a material fact or omits to state a material fact required therein or necessary to make a statement contained therein not misleading in the light of the circumstances in which it was made, an interested person or the Director may apply to a court and the court may make any order it thinks fit including, without limiting the generality of the foregoing,

(a) an order restraining the solicitation, the holding of the meeting, or any person from implementing or acting on any resolution passed at the meeting to which the form of proxy, management proxy circular or dissident's proxy circular relates;

(b) an order requiring correction of any form of proxy or proxy circular and a further solicitation; and

(c) an order adjourning the meeting.

(2) Notice to Director — An applicant under this section shall give to the Director notice of the application and the Director is entitled to appear and to be heard in person or by counsel.

PART XIV — FINANCIAL DISCLOSURE

155. (1) Annual financial statements — Subject to section 156, the directors of a corporation shall place before the shareholders at every annual meeting

(a) comparative financial statements as prescribed relating separately to

(i) the period that began on the date the corporation came into existence and ended not more than six months before the annual meeting or, if the corporation has completed a financial year, the period that began immediately after the end of the last completed financial year and ended not more than six months before the annual meeting, and

(ii) the immediately preceding financial year;

(b) the report of the auditor, if any; and

(c) any further information respecting the financial position of the corporation and the results of its operations required by the articles, the by-laws or any unanimous shareholder agreement.

(2) Exception — Notwithstanding paragraph (1)(a), the financial statements referred to in subparagraph (1)(a)(ii) may be omitted if the reason for the omission is set out in the financial statements, or in a note thereto, to be placed before the shareholders at an annual meeting.

156. Exemption — The Director may, on application of a corporation, authorize the corporation to omit from its financial statements any item prescribed, or to dispense with the publication of any particular financial statement prescribed, and the Director may, if the Director reasonably believes that disclosure of the information contained in the statements would be detrimental to the corporation, permit the omission on any reasonable conditions that the Director thinks fit.

2001, c. 14, s. 74

157. (1) Consolidated statements — A corporation shall keep at its registered office a copy of the financial statements of each of its subsidiary bodies corporate and of each body corporate the accounts of which are consolidated in the financial statements of the corporation.

(2) Examination — Shareholders of a corporation and their personal representatives may on request examine the statements referred to in subsection (1) during the usual business hours of the corporation and may make extracts free of charge.

(3) Barring examination — A corporation may, within fifteen days of a request to examine under subsection (2), apply to a court for an order barring the right of any person to so examine, and the court may, if it is satisfied that such examination would be detrimental to the corporation or a subsidiary body corporate, bar such right and make any further order it thinks fit.

(4) Notice to Director — A corporation shall give the Director and the person asking to examine under subsection (2) notice of an application under subsection (3), and the Director and such person may appear and be heard in person or by counsel.

2001, c. 14, s. 75

158. (1) Approval of financial statements — The directors of a corporation shall approve the financial statements referred to in section 155 and the approval shall be evidenced by the manual signature of one or more directors or a facsimile of the signatures reproduced in the statements.

(2) Condition precedent — A corporation shall not issue, publish or circulate copies of the financial statements referred to in section 155 unless the financial statements are

    (a) approved and signed in accordance with subsection (1); and

    (b) accompanied by the report of the auditor of the corporation, if any.

2001, c. 14, s. 76

159. (1) Copies to shareholders — A corporation shall, not less than twenty-one days before each annual meeting of shareholders or before the signing of a resolution under paragraph 142(1)(b) in lieu of the annual meeting, send a copy of the documents referred to in section 155 to each shareholder, except to a shareholder who has informed the corporation in writing that he or she does not want a copy of those documents.

(2) Offence — A corporation that, without reasonable cause, fails to comply with subsection (1) is guilty of an offence and liable on summary conviction to a fine not exceeding five thousand dollars.

2001, c. 14, s. 135 (Sched., s. 51)

160. (1) Copies to Director — A distributing corporation, any of the issued securities of which remain outstanding and are held by more than one person, shall send a copy of the documents referred to in section 155 to the Director

    (a) not less than twenty-one days before each annual meeting of shareholders, or without delay after a resolution referred to in paragraph 142(1)(b) is signed; and

(b) in any event within fifteen months after the last preceding annual meeting should have been held or a resolution in lieu of the meeting should have been signed, but no later than six months after the end of the corporation's preceding financial year.

(2) Subsidiary corporation exemption — A subsidiary corporation is not required to comply with this section if

(a) the financial statements of its holding corporation are in consolidated or combined form and include the accounts of the subsidiary; and

(b) the consolidated or combined financial statements of the holding corporation are included in the documents sent to the Director by the holding corporation in compliance with this section.

(3) Offence — A corporation that fails to comply with this section is guilty of an offence and is liable on summary conviction to a fine not exceeding five thousand dollars.

(4) [Repealed 2001, c. 14, s. 77.]

(5) [Repealed 2001, c. 14, s. 77.]

(6) [Repealed 2001, c. 14, s. 77.]

1992, c. 1, s. 55; 1994, c. 24, s. 17; 2001, c. 14, s. 77

161. (1) Qualification of auditor — Subject to subsection (5), a person is disqualified from being an auditor of a corporation if the person is not independent of the corporation, any of its affiliates, or the directors or officers of any such corporation or its affiliates.

(2) Independence — For the purposes of this section,

(a) independence is a question of fact; and

(b) a person is deemed not to be independent if he or his business partner

(i) is a business partner, a director, an officer or an employee of the corporation or any of its affiliates, or a business partner of any director, officer or employee of any such corporation or any of its affiliates,

(ii) beneficially owns or controls, directly or indirectly, a material interest in the securities of the corporation or any of its affiliates, or

(iii) has been a receiver, receiver-manager, liquidator or trustee in bankruptcy of the corporation or any of its affiliates within two years of his proposed appointment as auditor of the corporation.

(2.1) Business partners — For the purposes of subsection (2), a person's business partner includes a shareholder of that person.

(3) Duty to resign — An auditor who becomes disqualified under this section shall, subject to subsection (5), resign forthwith after becoming aware of the disqualification.

(4) Disqualification order — An interested person may apply to a court for an order declaring an auditor to be disqualified under this section and the office of auditor to be vacant.

(5) Exemption order — An interested person may apply to a court for an order exempting an auditor from disqualification under this section and the court may, if it is satisfied that an exemption would not unfairly prejudice the shareholders, make an exemption order on such terms as it thinks fit, which order may have retrospective effect.

2001, c. 14, ss. 78(1), 135 (Sched., s. 52)

162. (1) Appointment of auditor — Subject to section 163, shareholders of a corporation shall, by ordinary resolution, at the first annual meeting of shareholders and at each succeeding annual meeting, appoint an auditor to hold office until the close of the next annual meeting.

(2) Eligibility — An auditor appointed under section 104 is eligible for appointment under subsection (1).

(3) Incumbent auditor — Notwithstanding subsection (1), if an auditor is not appointed at a meeting of shareholders, the incumbent auditor continues in office until a successor is appointed.

(4) Remuneration — The remuneration of an auditor may be fixed by ordinary resolution of the shareholders or, if not so fixed, may be fixed by the directors.

163. (1) Dispensing with auditor — The shareholders of a corporation that is not a distributing corporation may resolve not to appoint an auditor.

(2) Limitation — A resolution under subsection (1) is valid only until the next succeeding annual meeting of shareholders.

(3) Unanimous consent — A resolution under subsection (1) is not valid unless it is consented to by all the shareholders, including shareholders not otherwise entitled to vote.

(4) [Repealed 1994, c. 24, s. 18]

1992, c. 1, s. 56; 1994, c. 24, s. 18; 2001, c. 14, s. 79

164. (1) Ceasing to hold office — An auditor of a corporation ceases to hold office when the auditor

(a) dies or resigns; or

(b) is removed pursuant to section 165.

(2) Effective date of resignation — A resignation of an auditor becomes effective at the time a written resignation is sent to the corporation, or at the time specified in the resignation, whichever is later.

2001, c. 14, s. 135 (Sched., s. 53)

165. (1) Removal of auditor — The shareholders of a corporation may by ordinary resolution at a special meeting remove from office the auditor other than an auditor appointed by a court under section 167.

(2) Vacancy — A vacancy created by the removal of an auditor may be filled at the meeting at which the auditor is removed or, if not so filled, may be filled under section 166.

166. (1) Filling vacancy — Subject to subsection (3), the directors shall forthwith fill a vacancy in the office of auditor.

(2) Calling meeting — If there is not a quorum of directors, the directors then in office shall, within twenty-one days after a vacancy in the office of auditor occurs, call a special meeting of shareholders to fill the vacancy and, if they fail to call a meeting or if there are no directors, the meeting may be called by any shareholder.

(3) Shareholders filling vacancy — The articles of a corporation may provide that a vacancy in the office of auditor shall only be filled by vote of the shareholders.

(4) Unexpired term — An auditor appointed to fill a vacancy holds office for the unexpired term of the auditor's predecessor.

2001, c. 14, s. 135 (Sched., s. 54)

167. (1) Court appointed auditor — If a corporation does not have an auditor, the court may, on the application of a shareholder or the Director, appoint and fix the remuneration of an auditor who holds office until an auditor is appointed by the shareholders.

(2) Exception — Subsection (1) does not apply if the shareholders have resolved under section 163 not to appoint an auditor.

168. (1) Right to attend meeting — The auditor of a corporation is entitled to receive notice of every meeting of shareholders and, at the expense of the corporation, to attend and be heard thereat on matters relating to the auditor's duties.

(2) Duty to attend — If a director or shareholder of a corporation, whether or not the shareholder is entitled to vote at the meeting, gives written notice not less than ten days before a meeting of shareholders to the auditor or a former auditor of the corporation, the auditor or former auditor shall attend the meeting at the expense of the corporation and answer questions relating to their duties as auditor.

(3) Notice to corporation — A director or shareholder who sends a notice referred to in subsection (2) shall send concurrently a copy of the notice to the corporation.

(4) Offence — An auditor or former auditor of a corporation who fails without reasonable cause to comply with subsection (2) is guilty of an offence and liable on summary conviction to a fine not exceeding five thousand dollars or to imprisonment for a term not exceeding six months or to both.

(5) Statement of auditor — An auditor is entitled to submit to the corporation a written statement giving reasons for resigning or for opposing any proposed action or resolution when the auditor

(a) resigns;

(b) receives a notice or otherwise learns of a meeting of shareholders called for the purpose of removing the auditor from office;

(c) receives a notice or otherwise learns of a meeting of directors or shareholders at which another person is to be appointed to fill the office of auditor, whether because of the resignation or removal of the incumbent auditor or because the auditor's term of office has expired or is about to expire; or

(d) receives a notice or otherwise learns of a meeting of shareholders at which a resolution referred to in section 163 is to be proposed.

(5.1) Other statements — In the case of a proposed replacement of an auditor, whether through removal or at the end of the auditor's term, the following rules apply with respect to other statements:

(a) the corporation shall make a statement on the reasons for the proposed replacement; and

(b) the proposed replacement auditor may make a statement in which he or she comments on the reasons referred to in paragraph (a).

(6) Circulating statement — The corporation shall send a copy of the statements referred to in subsection (5) and (5.1) without delay to every shareholder entitled to receive notice of any meeting referred to in subsection (1) and to the Director, unless the statement is included in or attached to a management proxy circular required by section 150.

(7) Replacing auditor — No person shall accept appointment or consent to be appointed as auditor of a corporation to replace an auditor who has resigned, been removed or whose term of office has expired or is about to expire until the person has requested and received from that auditor a written statement of the circumstances and the reasons, in that auditor's opinion, for their replacement.

(8) Exception — Notwithstanding subsection (7), a person otherwise qualified may accept appointment or consent to be appointed as auditor of a corporation if, within fifteen days after making the request referred to in that subsection, the person does not receive a reply.

(9) Effect of non-compliance — Unless subsection (8) applies, an appointment as auditor of a corporation of a person who has not complied with subsection (7) is void.

2001, c. 14, ss. 80, 135 (Sched., s. 55)

169. (1) Examination — An auditor of a corporation shall make the examination that is in their opinion necessary to enable them to report in the prescribed manner on the financial statements required by this Act to be placed before the shareholders, except such financial statements or part thereof that relate to the period referred to in subparagraph 155(1)(a)(ii).

(2) Reliance on other auditor — Notwithstanding section 170, an auditor of a corporation may reasonably rely on the report of an auditor of a body corporate or an unincorporated business the accounts of which are included in whole or in part in the financial statements of the corporation.

(3) Reasonableness — For the purpose of subsection (2), reasonableness is a question of fact.

(4) Application — Subsection (2) applies whether or not the financial statements of the holding corporation reported on by the auditor are in consolidated form.

2001, c. 14, s. 135 (Sched., s. 56)

170. (1) Right to information — On the demand of an auditor of a corporation, the present or former directors, officers, employees or agents of the corporation shall furnish such

(a) information and explanations, and

(b) access to records, documents, books, accounts and vouchers of the corporation or any of its subsidiaries

as are, in the opinion of the auditor, necessary to enable the auditor to make the examination and report required under section 169 and that the directors, officers, employees or agents are reasonably able to furnish.

(2) Idem — On the demand of the auditor of a corporation, the directors of the corporation shall

(a) obtain from the present or former directors, officers, employees and agents of any subsidiary of the corporation the information and explanations that the present or former directors, officers, employees and agents are reasonably able to furnish and that are, in the opinion of the auditor, necessary to enable the auditor to make the examination and report required under section 169; and

(b) furnish the auditor with the information and explanations so obtained.

(3) No civil liability — A person who in good faith makes an oral or written communication under subsection (1) or (2) is not liable in any civil proceeding arising from having made the communication.

2001, c. 14, ss. 81, 135 (Sched., s. 57)

171. (1) Audit committee — Subject to subsection (2), a corporation described in subsection 102(2) shall, and any other other corporation may, have an audit committee composed of not less than three directors of the corporation, a majority of whom are not officers or employees of the corporation or any of its affiliates.

(2) Exemption — The Director may, on the application of a corporation, authorize the corporation to dispense with an audit committee, and the Director may, if satisfied that the shareholders will not be prejudiced, permit the corporation to dispense with an audit committee on any reasonable conditions that the Director thinks fit.

(3) Duty of committee — An audit committee shall review the financial statements of the corporation before such financial statements are approved under section 158.

(4) Auditor's attendance — The auditor of a corporation is entitled to receive notice of every meeting of the audit committee and, at the expense of the corporation, to attend and be heard thereat; and, if so requested by a member of the audit committee, shall attend every meeting of the committee held during the term of office of the auditor.

(5) Calling meeting — The auditor of a corporation or a member of the audit committee may call a meeting of the committee.

(6) Notice of errors — A director or an officer of a corporation shall forthwith notify the audit committee and the auditor of any error or mis-statement of which the director or officer becomes aware in a financial statement that the auditor or a former auditor has reported on.

(7) Error in financial statements — An auditor or former auditor of a corporation who is notified or becomes aware of an error or mis-statement in a financial statement on which they have reported, if in their opinion the error or mis-statement is material, shall inform each director accordingly.

(8) Duty of directors — When under subsection (7) the auditor or former auditor informs the directors of an error or mis-statement in a financial statement, the directors shall

(a) prepare and issue revised financial statements; or

(b) otherwise inform the shareholders and, if the corporation is one that is required to comply with section 160, it shall inform the Director of the error or mis-statement in the same manner as it informs the shareholders.

(9) Offence — Every director or officer of a corporation who knowingly fails to comply with subsection (6) or (8) is guilty of an offence and liable on summary conviction to a fine not exceeding five thousand dollars or to imprisonment for a term not exceeding six months or to both.

2001, c. 14, ss. 82, 135 (Sched., s. 58)

172. Qualified privilege (defamation) — Any oral or written statement or report made under this Act by the auditor or former auditor of a corporation has qualified privilege.

PART XV — FUNDAMENTAL CHANGES

173. (1) Amendment of articles — Subject to sections 176 and 177, the articles of a corporation may by special resolution be amended to

(a) change its name;

(b) change the province in which its registered office is situated;

(c) add, change or remove any restriction on the business or businesses that the corporation may carry on;

(d) change any maximum number of shares that the corporation is authorized to issue;

(e) create new classes of shares;

(f) reduce or increase its stated capital, if its stated capital is set out in the articles;

(g) change the designation of all or any of its shares, and add, change or remove any rights, privileges, restrictions and conditions, including rights to accrued dividends, in respect of all or any of its shares, whether issued or unissued;

(h) change the shares of any class or series, whether issued or unissued, into a different number of shares of the same class or series or into the same or a different number of shares of other classes or series;

(i) divide a class of shares, whether issued or unissued, into series and fix the number of shares in each series and the rights, privileges, restrictions and conditions thereof;

(j) authorize the directors to divide any class of unissued shares into series and fix the number of shares in each series and the rights, privileges, restrictions and conditions thereof;

(k) authorize the directors to change the rights, privileges, restrictions and conditions attached to unissued shares of any series;

(l) revoke, diminish or enlarge any authority conferred under paragraphs (j) and (k);

(m) increase or decrease the number of directors or the minimum or maximum number of directors, subject to sections 107 and 112;

(n) add, change or remove restrictions on the issue, transfer or ownership of shares; or

(o) add, change or remove any other provision that is permitted by this Act to be set out in the articles.

(2) Termination — The directors of a corporation may, if authorized by the shareholders in the special resolution effecting an amendment under this section, revoke the resolution before it is acted on without further approval of the shareholders.

(3) Amendment of number name — Notwithstanding subsection (1), where a corporation has a designating number as a name, the directors may amend its articles to change that name to a verbal name.

1994, c. 24, s. 19; 2001, c. 14, s. 83(1)

174. (1) Constraints on shares — Subject to sections 176 and 177, a distributing corporation, any of the issued shares of which remain outstanding and are held by more than one person, may by special resolution amend its articles in accordance with the regulations to constrain

(a) the issue or transfer of shares of any class or series to persons who are not resident Canadians;

(b) the issue or transfer of shares of any class or series to enable the corporation or any of its affiliates or associates to qualify under any prescribed law of Canada or a province

(i) to obtain a licence to carry on any business,

(ii) to become a publisher of a Canadian newspaper or periodical, or

(iii) to acquire shares of a financial intermediary as defined in the regulations;

(c) the issue, transfer or ownership of shares of any class or series in order to assist the corporation or any of its affiliates or associates to qualify under any prescribed law of Canada or a province to receive licences, permits, grants, payments or other benefits by reason of attaining or maintaining a specified level of Canadian ownership or control;

(d) the issue, transfer or ownership of shares of any class or series in order to assist the corporation to comply with any prescribed law.

(e) the issue, transfer or ownership of shares of any class or series to enable the corporation to be a registered labour-sponsored venture capital corporation under Part X.3 of the *Income Tax Act*.

(2) Exception in respect of paragraph (1)(c) — Paragraph (1)(c) does not permit a constraint on the issue, transfer or ownership of shares of any class or series of which any shares are outstanding unless

(a) in the case of a constraint in respect of a class, the shares of the class, or

(b) in the case of a constraint in respect of a series, the shares of the series

are already subject to a constraint permitted under that paragraph.

(3) Limitation on ownership of shares — A corporation may, pursuant to paragraph (1)(c), limit the number of shares of that corporation that may be owned, or prohibit the ownership of shares, by any person whose ownership would adversely affect the ability of the corporation or any of its affiliates or associates to attain or maintain a level of Canadian ownership or control specified in its articles that equals or exceeds a specified level referred to in paragraph (1)(c).

(4) Change or removal of constraint — A corporation referred to in subsection (1) may by special resolution amend its articles to change or remove any constraint on the issue, transfer or ownership of its shares.

(5) Termination — The directors of a corporation may, if authorized by the shareholders in the special resolution effecting an amendment under subsection (1) or (4), revoke the resolution before it is acted on without further approval of the shareholders.

(6) Regulations — Subject to subsections 261(2) and (3), the Governor in Council may make regulations with respect to a corporation that constrains the issue, transfer or ownership of its shares prescribing

(a) the disclosure required of the constraints in documents issued or published by the corporation;

(b) the duties and powers of the directors to refuse to issue or register transfers of shares in accordance with the articles of the corporation;

(c) the limitations on voting rights of any shares held contrary to the articles of the corporation;

(d) the powers of the directors to require disclosure of beneficial ownership of shares of the corporation and the right of the corporation and its directors, employees and agents to rely on such disclosure and the effects of such reliance; and

(e) the rights of any person owning shares of the corporation at the time of an amendment to its articles constraining share issues or transfers.

(7) Validity of acts — An issue or a transfer of a share or an act of a corporation is valid notwithstanding any failure to comply with this section or the regulations.

1991, c. 45, s. 554; 1991, c. 47, s. 722; 1994, c. 21, s. 125; 2001, c. 14, s. 84

175. (1) Proposal to amend — Subject to subsection (2), a director or a shareholder who is entitled to vote at an annual meeting of shareholders may, in accordance with section 137, make a proposal to amend the articles.

(2) Notice of amendment — Notice of a meeting of shareholders at which a proposal to amend the articles is to be considered shall set out the proposed amendment and, where applicable, shall state that a dissenting shareholder is entitled to be paid the fair value of their shares in accordance with section 190, but failure to make that statement does not invalidate an amendment.

2001, c. 14, s. 135 (Sched., s. 59)

176. (1) Class vote — The holder of shares of a class or, subject to subsection (4), of a series are, unless the articles otherwise provide in the case of an amendment referred to in paragraphs (a), (b) and (e), entitled to vote separately as a class or series on a proposal to amend the articles to

(a) increase or decrease any maximum number of authorized shares of such class, or increase any maximum number of authorized shares of a class having rights or privileges equal or superior to the shares of such class;

(b) effect an exchange, reclassification or cancellation of all or part of the shares of such class;

(c) add, change or remove the rights, privileges, restrictions or conditions attached to the shares of such class and, without limiting the generality of the foregoing,

(i) remove or change prejudicially rights to accrued dividends or rights to cumulative dividends,

(ii) add, remove or change prejudicially redemption rights,

(iii) reduce or remove a dividend preference or a liquidation preference, or

(iv) add, remove or change prejudicially conversion privileges, options, voting, transfer or pre-emptive rights, or rights to acquire securities of a corporation, or sinking fund provisions;

(d) increase the rights or privileges of any class of shares having rights or privileges equal or superior to the shares of such class;

(e) create a new class of shares equal or superior to the shares of such class;

(f) make any class of shares having rights or privileges inferior to the shares of such class equal or superior to the shares of such class;

(g) effect an exchange or create a right of exchange of all or part of the shares of another class into the shares of such class; or

(h) constrain the issue, transfer or ownership of the shares of such class or change or remove such constraint.

(2) Exception — Subsection (1) does not apply in respect of a proposal to amend the articles to add a right or privilege for a holder to convert shares of a class or series into shares of another class or series that is subject to a constraint permitted under paragraph 174(1)(c) but is otherwise equal to the class or series first mentioned.

(3) Deeming provision — For the purpose of paragraph (1)(e), a new class of shares, the issue, transfer or ownership of which is to be constrained by an amendment to the articles pursuant to paragraph 174(1)(c), that is otherwise equal to an existing class of shares shall be deemed not to be equal or superior to the existing class of shares.

(4) Limitation — The holders of a series of shares of a class are entitled to vote separately as a series under subsection (1) only if such series is affected by an amendment in a manner different from other shares of the same class.

(5) Right to vote — Subsection (1) applies whether or not shares of a class or series otherwise carry the right to vote.

(6) Separate resolutions — A proposed amendment to the articles referred to in subsection (1) is adopted when the holders of the shares of each class or series entitled to vote separately thereon as a class or series have approved such amendment by a special resolution.

177. (1) Delivery of articles — Subject to any revocation under subsection 173(2) or 174(5), after an amendment has been adopted under section 173, 174 or 176 articles of amendment in the form that the Director fixes shall be sent to the Director.

(2) Reduction of stated capital — If an amendment effects or requires a reduction of stated capital, subsections 38(3) and (4) apply.

2001, c. 14, s. 85

178. Certificate of amendment — On receipt of articles of amendment, the Director shall issue a certificate of amendment in accordance with section 262.

179. (1) Effect of certificate — An amendment becomes effective on the date shown in the certificate of amendment and the articles are amended accordingly.

(2) Rights preserved — No amendment to the articles affects an existing cause of action or claim or liability to prosecution in favour of or against the corporation or its directors or officers, or any civil, criminal or administrative action or proceeding to which a corporation or its directors or officers is a party.

180. (1) Restated articles — The directors may at any time, and shall when reasonably so directed by the Director, restate the articles of incorporation.

(2) Delivery of articles — Restated articles of incorporation in the form that the Director fixes shall be sent to the Director.

(3) Restated certificate — On receipt of restated articles of incorporation, the Director shall issue a restated certificate of incorporation in accordance with section 262.

(4) Effect of certificate — Restated articles of incorporation are effective on the date shown in the restated certificate of incorporation and supersede the original articles of incorporation and all amendments thereto.

2001, c. 14, s. 86

181. Amalgamation — Two or more corporations, including holding and subsidiary corporations, may amalgamate and continue as one corporation.

182. (1) Amalgamation agreement — Each corporation proposing to amalgamate shall enter into an agreement setting out the terms and means of effecting the amalgamation and, in particular, setting out

(a) the provisions that are required to be included in articles of incorporation under section 6;

(b) the name and address of each proposed director of the amalgamated corporation;

(c) the manner in which the shares of each amalgamating corporation are to be converted into shares or other securities of the amalgamated corporation;

(d) if any shares of an amalgamating corporation are not to be converted into securities of the amalgamated corporation, the amount of money or securities of any body corporate that the holders of such shares are to receive in addition to or instead of securities of the amalgamated corporation;

(e) the manner of payment of money instead of the issue of fractional shares of the amalgamated corporation or of any other body corporate the securities of which are to be received in the amalgamation;

(f) whether the by-laws of the amalgamated corporation are to be those of one of the amalgamating corporations and, if not, a copy of the proposed by-laws; and

(g) details of any arrangements necessary to perfect the amalgamation and to provide for the subsequent management and operation of the amalgamated corporation.

(2) Cancellation — If shares of one of the amalgamating corporations are held by or on behalf of another of the amalgamating corporations, the amalgamation agreement shall provide for the cancellation of such shares when the amalgamation becomes effective without any repayment of capital in respect thereof, and no provision shall be made in the agreement for the conversion of such shares into shares of the amalgamated corporation.

183. (1) Shareholder approval — The directors of each amalgamating corporation shall submit the amalgamation agreement for approval to a meeting of the holders of shares of the amalgamating corporation of which they are directors and, subject to subsection (4), to the holders of each class or series of such shares.

(2) Notice of meeting — A notice of a meeting of shareholders complying with section 135 shall be sent in accordance with that section to each shareholder of each amalgamating corporation, and shall

(a) include or be accompanied by a copy or summary of the amalgamation agreement; and

(b) state that a dissenting shareholder is entitled to be paid the fair value of their shares in accordance with section 190, but failure to make that statement does not invalidate an amalgamation.

(3) Right to vote — Each share of an amalgamating corporation carries the right to vote in respect of an amalgamation agreement whether or not it otherwise carries the right to vote.

(4) Class vote — The holders of shares of a class or series of shares of each amalgamating corporation are entitled to vote separately as a class or series in respect of an amalgamation agreement if the amalgamation agreement contains a provision that, if contained in a proposed amendment to the articles, would entitle such holders to vote as a class or series under section 176.

(5) Shareholder approval — Subject to subsection (4), an amalgamation agreement is adopted when the shareholders of each amalgamating corporation have approved of the amalgamation by special resolutions.

(6) Termination — An amalgamation agreement may provide that at any time before the issue of a certificate of amalgamation the agreement may be terminated by the directors of an amalgamating corporation, notwithstanding approval of the agreement by the shareholders of all or any of the amalgamating corporations.

2001, c. 14, ss. 87, 135 (Sched., s. 60)

184. (1) Vertical short-form amalgamation — A holding corporation and one or more of its subsidiary corporations may amalgamate and continue as one corporation without complying with sections 182 and 183 if

(a) the amalgamation is approved by a resolution of the directors of each amalgamating corporation;

(a.1) all of the issued shares of each amalgamating subsidiary corporation are held by one or more of the other amalgamating corporations; and

(b) the resolutions provide that

(i) the shares of each amalgamating subsidiary corporation shall be cancelled without any repayment of capital in respect thereof,

(ii) except as may be prescribed, the articles of amalgamation shall be the same as the articles of the amalgamating holding corporation, and

(iii) no securities shall be issued by the amalgamated corporation in connection with the amalgamation and the stated capital of the amalgamated corporation shall be the same as the stated capital of the amalgamating holding corporation.

(2) Horizontal short-form amalgamation — Two or more wholly-owned subsidiary corporations of the same holding body corporate may amalgamate and continue as one corporation without complying with sections 182 and 183 if

(a) the amalgamation is approved by a resolution of the directors of each amalgamating corporation; and

(b) the resolutions provide that

(i) the shares of all but one of the amalgamating subsidiary corporations shall be cancelled without any repayment of capital in respect thereof,

(ii) except as may be prescribed, the articles of amalgamation shall be the same as the articles of the amalgamating subsidiary corporation whose shares are not cancelled, and

(iii) the stated capital of the amalgamating subsidiary corporations whose shares are cancelled shall be added to the stated capital of the amalgamating subsidiary corporation whose shares are not cancelled.

1994, c. 24, s. 20; 2001, c. 14, s. 88

185. (1) Sending of articles — Subject to subsection 183(6), after an amalgamation has been adopted under section 183 or approved under section 184, articles of amalgamation in the form that the Director fixes shall be sent to the Director together with the documents required by sections 19 and 106.

(2) Attached declarations — The articles of amalgamation shall have attached thereto a statutory declaration of a director or an officer of each amalgamating corporation that establishes to the satisfaction of the Director that

(a) there are reasonable grounds for believing that

(i) each amalgamating corporation is and the amalgamated corporation will be able to pay its liabilities as they become due, and

(ii) the realizable value of the amalgamated corporation's assets will not be less than the aggregate of its liabilities and stated capital of all classes; and

(b) there are reasonable grounds for believing that

(i) no creditor will be prejudiced by the amalgamation, or

(ii) adequate notice has been given to all known creditors of the amalgamating corporations and no creditor objects to the amalgamation otherwise than on grounds that are frivolous or vexatious.

(3) Adequate notice — For the purposes of subsection (2), adequate notice is given if

(a) a notice in writing is sent to each known creditor having a claim against the corporation that exceeds one thousand dollars;

(b) a notice is published once in a newspaper published or distributed in the place where the corporation has its registered office and reasonable notice thereof is given in each province where the corporation carries on business; and

(c) each notice states that the corporation intends to amalgamate with one or more specified corporations in accordance with this Act and that a creditor of the corporation may object to the amalgamation within thirty days from the date of the notice.

(4) Certificate of amalgamation — On receipt of articles of amalgamation, the Director shall issue a certificate of amalgamation in accordance with section 262.

2001, c. 14, s. 89

186. Effect of certificate — On the date shown in a certificate of amalgamation

(a) the amalgamation of the amalgamating corporations and their continuance as one corporation become effective;

(b) the property of each amalgamating corporation continues to be the property of the amalgamated corporation;

(c) the amalgamated corporation continues to be liable for the obligations of each amalgamating corporation;

(d) an existing cause of action, claim or liability to prosecution is unaffected;

(e) a civil, criminal or administrative action or proceeding pending by or against an amalgamating corporation may be continued to be prosecuted by or against the amalgamated corporation;

(f) a conviction against, or ruling, order or judgment in favour of or against, an amalgamating corporation may be enforced by or against the amalgamated corporation; and

(g) the articles of amalgamation are deemed to be the articles of incorporation of the amalgamated corporation and the certificate of amalgamation is deemed to be the certificate of incorporation of the amalgamated corporation.

186.1 (1) Amalgamation under other federal Acts — Subject to subsection (2), a corporation may not amalgamate with one or more bodies corporate pursuant to the *Bank Act*, the *Canada Cooperatives Act*, the *Cooperative Credit Associations Act*, the *Insurance Companies Act* or the *Trust and Loan Companies Act* unless the corporation is first authorized to do so by the shareholders in accordance with section 183.

(2) Short-form amalgamations — A corporation may not amalgamate with one or more bodies corporate pursuant to the provisions of one of the Acts referred to in subsection (1) respecting short-form amalgamations unless the corporation is first authorized to do so by the directors in accordance with section 184.

(3) Discontinuance — On receipt of a notice satisfactory to the Director that a corporation has amalgamated pursuant to one of the Acts referred to in subsection (1), the Director shall file the notice and issue a certificate of discontinuance in accordance with section 262.

(4) Notice deemed to be articles — For the purposes of section 262, a notice referred to in subsection (3) is deemed to be articles that are in the form that the Director fixes.

(5) Act ceases to apply — This Act ceases to apply to the corporation on the date shown in the certificate of discontinuance.

(6) Non-application — For greater certainty, section 185 does not apply to a corporation that amalgamates pursuant to one of the Acts referred to in subsection (1).

1994, c. 24, s. 21; 1998, c. 1, s. 380; 2001, c. 14, s. 90

187. (1) Continuance (import) — A body corporate incorporated otherwise than by or under an Act of Parliament may, if so authorized by the laws of the jurisdiction where it is incorporated, apply to the Director for a certificate of continuance.

(2) Amendments in articles of continuance — A body corporate that applies for continuance under subsection (1) may, without so stating in its articles of continuance, effect by those articles any amendment to its Act of incorporation, articles, letters patent or memorandum or articles of association if the amendment is an amendment a corporation incorporated under this Act may make to its articles.

(3) Articles of continuance — Articles of continuance in the form that the Director fixes shall be sent to the Director together with the documents required by sections 19 and 106.

(4) Certificate of continuance — On receipt of articles of continuance, the Director shall issue a certificate of continuance in accordance with section 262.

(5) Effect of certificate — On the date shown in the certificate of continuance

(a) the body corporate becomes a corporation to which this Act applies as if it had been incorporated under this Act;

(b) the articles of continuance are deemed to be the articles of incorporation of the continued corporation; and

(c) the certificate of continuance is deemed to be the certificate of incorporation of the continued corporation.

(6) Copy of certificate — The Director shall forthwith send a copy of the certificate of continuance to the appropriate official or public body in the jurisdiction in which continuance under this Act was authorized.

(7) Rights preserved — When a body corporate is continued as a corporation under this Act,

(a) the property of the body corporate continues to be the property of the corporation;

(b) the corporation continues to be liable for the obligations of the body corporate;

(c) an existing cause of action, claim or liability to prosecution is unaffected;

(d) a civil, criminal or administrative action or proceeding pending by or against the body corporate may be continued to be prosecuted by or against the corporation; and

(e) a conviction against, or ruling, order or judgment in favour of or against, the body corporate may be enforced by or against the corporation.

(8) Issued shares — Subject to subsection 49(8), a share of a body corporate issued before the body corporate was continued under this Act is deemed to have been issued in compliance with this Act and with the provisions of the articles of continuance irrespective of whether the share is fully paid and irrespective of any designation, rights, privileges, restrictions or conditions set out on or referred to in the certificate representing the share; and continuance under this section does not deprive a holder of any right or privilege that the holder claims under, or relieve the holder of any liability in respect of, an issued share.

(9) Exception in case of convertible shares — Where a corporation continued under this Act had, before it was so continued, issued a share certificate in registered form that is convertible to bearer form, the corporation may, if a holder of such a share certificate exercises the conversion privilege attached thereto, issue a share certificate in bearer form for the same number of shares to the holder.

(10) Definition of "share" — For the purposes of subsections (8), and (9), **"share"** includes an instrument referred to in subsection 29(1), a share warrant as defined in the *Canada Corporations Act*, chapter C-32 of the Revised Statutes of Canada, 1970, or a like instrument.

(11) Where continued reference to par value shares permissible — Where the Director determines, on the application of a body corporate, that it is not practicable to change a reference to the nominal or par value of shares of a class or series that the body corporate was authorized to issue before it was continued under this Act, the Director may, notwithstanding subsection 24(1), permit the body corporate to continue to refer in its articles to those shares, whether issued or unissued, as shares having a nominal or par value.

(12) Limitation — A corporation shall set out in its articles the maximum number of shares of a class or series referred to in subsection (11) and may not amend its articles to increase that maximum number of shares or to change the nominal or par value of those shares.

2001, c. 14, ss. 91(1), 135 (Sched., s. 61)

188. (1) Continuance — other jurisdictions — Subject to subsection (10), a corporation may apply to the appropriate official or public body of another jurisdiction requesting that the corporation be continued as if it had been incorporated under the laws of that other jurisdiction if the corporation

(a) is authorized by the shareholders in accordance with this section to make the application; and

(b) establishes to the satisfaction of the Director that its proposed continuance in the other jurisdiction will not adversely affect creditors or shareholders of the corporation.

(2) Continuance — other federal Acts — A corporation that is authorized by the shareholders in accordance with this section may apply to the appropriate Minister for its continuance under the *Bank Act*, the *Canada Cooperatives Act*, the *Cooperative Credit Associations Act*, the *Insurance Companies Act* or the *Trust and Loan Companies Act*.

(2.1) [Repealed 2001, c. 14, s. 92(1).]

(3) Notice of meeting — A notice of a meeting of shareholders complying with section 135 shall be sent in accordance with that section to each shareholder and shall state that a dissenting shareholder is entitled to be paid the fair value of their shares in accordance with section 190, but failure to make that statement does not invalidate a discontinuance under this Act.

(4) Right to vote — Each share of the corporation carries the right to vote in respect of a continuance whether or not it otherwise carries the right to vote.

(5) Shareholder approval — An application for continuance becomes authorized when the shareholders voting thereon have approved of the continuance by a special resolution.

(6) Termination — The directors of a corporation may, if authorized by the shareholders at the time of approving an application for continuance under this section, abandon the application without further approval of the shareholders.

(7) Discontinuance — On receipt of a notice satisfactory to the Director that the corporation has been continued under the laws of another jurisdiction or under one of the Acts referred to in subsection (2.1), the Director shall file the notice and issue a certificate of discontinuance in accordance with section 262.

(8) Notice deemed to be articles — For the purposes of section 262, a notice referred to in subsection (7) is deemed to be articles that are in the form that the Director fixes.

(9) Rights preserved — This Act ceases to apply to the corporation on the date shown in the certificate of discontinuance.

(10) Prohibition — A corporation shall not be continued as a body corporate under the laws of another jurisdiction unless those laws provide in effect that

(a) the property of the corporation continues to be the property of the body corporate;

(b) the body corporate continues to be liable for the obligations of the corporation;

(c) an existing cause of action, claim or liability to prosecution is unaffected;

(d) a civil, criminal or administrative action or proceeding pending by or against the corporation may be continued to be prosecuted by or against the body corporate; and

(e) a conviction against, or ruling, order or judgment in favour of or against, the corporation may be enforced by or against the body corporate.

1991, c. 45, s. 555; 1991, c. 46, s. 596; 1991, c. 47, s. 723; 1994, c. 24, s. 22; 1998, c. 1, s. 381; 2001, c. 14, ss. 92, 135 (Sched., s. 62); 2007, c. 6, s. 400

189. (1) Borrowing powers — Unless the articles or by-laws of or a unanimous shareholder agreement relating to a corporation otherwise provide, the directors of a corporation may, without authorization of the shareholders,

(a) borrow money on the credit of the corporation;

(b) issue, reissue, sell, pledge or hypothecate debt obligations of the corporation;

(c) give a guarantee on behalf of the corporation to secure performance of an obligation of any person; and

(d) mortgage, hypothecate, pledge or otherwise create a security interest in all or any property of the corporation, owned or subsequently acquired, to secure any obligation of the corporation.

(2) Delegation of borrowing powers — Notwithstanding subsection 115(3) and paragraph 121(a), unless the articles or by-laws of or a unanimous shareholder agreement relating to a corporation otherwise provide, the directors may, by resolution, delegate the powers referred to in subsection (1) to a director, a committee of directors or an officer.

(3) Extraordinary sale, lease or exchange — A sale, lease or exchange of all or substantially all the property of a corporation other than in the ordinary course of business of the corporation requires the approval of the shareholders in accordance with subsections (4) to (8).

(4) Notice of meeting — A notice of a meeting of shareholders complying with section 135 shall be sent in accordance with that section to each shareholder and shall

(a) include or be accompanied by a copy or summary of the agreement of sale, lease or exchange; and

(b) state that a dissenting shareholder is entitled to be paid the fair value of their shares in accordance with section 190, but failure to make that statement does not invalidate a sale, lease or exchange referred to in subsection (3).

(5) Shareholder approval — At the meeting referred to in subsection (4) the shareholders may authorize the sale, lease or exchange and may fix or authorize the directors to fix any of the terms and conditions thereof.

(6) Right to vote — Each share of the corporation carries the right to vote in respect of a sale, lease or exchange referred to in subsection (3) whether or not it otherwise carries the right to vote.

(7) Class vote — The holders of shares of a class or series of shares of the corporation are entitled to vote separately as a class or series in respect of a sale, lease or exchange referred to in subsection (3) only if such class or series is affected by the sale, lease or exchange in a manner different from the shares of another class or series.

(8) Shareholder approval — A sale, lease or exchange referred to in subsection (3) is adopted when the holders of each class or series entitled to vote thereon have approved of the sale, lease or exchange by a special resolution.

(9) Termination — The directors of a corporation may, if authorized by the shareholders approving a proposed sale, lease or exchange, and subject to the rights of third parties, abandon the sale, lease or exchange without further approval of the shareholders.

2001, c. 14, ss. 93, 135 (Sched., s. 63)

190. (1) Right to dissent — Subject to sections 191 and 241, a holder of shares of any class of a corporation may dissent if the corporation is subject to an order under paragraph 192(4)(d) that affects the holder or if the corporation resolves to

(a) amend its articles under section 173 or 174 to add, change or remove any provisions restricting or constraining the issue, transfer or ownership of shares of that class;

(b) amend its articles under section 173 to add, change or remove any restriction on the business or businesses that the corporation may carry on;

(c) amalgamate otherwise than under section 184;

(d) be continued under section 188;

(e) sell, lease or exchange all or substantially all its property under subsection 189(3); or

(f) carry out a going-private transaction or a squeeze-out transaction.

(2) Further right — A holder of shares of any class or series of shares entitled to vote under section 176 may dissent if the corporation resolves to amend its articles in a manner described in that section.

(2.1) If one class of shares — The right to dissent described in subsection (2) applies even if there is only one class of shares.

(3) Payment for shares — In addition to any other right the shareholder may have, but subject to subsection (26), a shareholder who complies with this section is entitled, when the action approved by the resolution from which the shareholder dissents or an order made under subsection 192(4) becomes effective, to be paid by the corporation the fair value of the shares in respect of which the shareholder dissents, determined as of the close of business on the day before the resolution was adopted or the order was made.

(4) No partial dissent — A dissenting shareholder may only claim under this section with respect to all the shares of a class held on behalf of any one beneficial owner and registered in the name of the dissenting shareholder.

(5) Objection — A dissenting shareholder shall send to the corporation, at or before any meeting of shareholders at which a resolution referred to in subsection (1) or (2) is to be voted on, a written objection to the resolution, unless the corporation did not give notice to the shareholder of the purpose of the meeting and of their right to dissent.

(6) Notice of resolution — The corporation shall, within ten days after the shareholders adopt the resolution, send to each shareholder who has filed the objection referred to in subsection (5) notice that the resolution has been adopted, but such notice is not required to be sent to any shareholder who voted for the resolution or who has withdrawn their objection.

(7) Demand for payment — A dissenting shareholder shall, within twenty days after receiving a notice under subsection (6) or, if the shareholder does not receive such notice, within twenty days after learning that the resolution has been adopted, send to the corporation a written notice containing

(a) the shareholder's name and address;

(b) the number and class of shares in respect of which the shareholder dissents; and

(c) a demand for payment of the fair value of such shares.

(8) Share certificate — A dissenting shareholder shall, within thirty days after sending a notice under subsection (7), send the certificates representing the shares in respect of which the shareholder dissents to the corporation or its transfer agent.

(9) Forfeiture — A dissenting shareholder who fails to comply with subsection (8) has no right to make a claim under this section.

(10) Endorsing certificate — A corporation or its transfer agent shall endorse on any share certificate received under subsection (8) a notice that the holder is a dissenting shareholder under this section and shall forthwith return the share certificates to the dissenting shareholder.

(11) Suspension of rights — On sending a notice under subsection (7), a dissenting shareholder ceases to have any rights as a shareholder other than to be paid the fair value of their shares as determined under this section except where

(a) the shareholder withdraws that notice before the corporation makes an offer under subsection (12),

(b) the corporation fails to make an offer in accordance with subsection (12) and the shareholder withdraws the notice, or

(c) the directors revoke a resolution to amend the articles under subsection 173(2) or 174(5), terminate an amalgamation agreement under subsection 183(6) or an application for continuance under subsection 188(6), or abandon a sale, lease or exchange under subsection 189(9),

in which case the shareholder's rights are reinstated as of the date the notice was sent.

(12) Offer to pay — A corporation shall, not later than seven days after the later of the day on which the action approved by the resolution is effective or the day the corporation received the notice referred to in subsection (7), send to each dissenting shareholder who has sent such notice

(a) a written offer to pay for their shares in an amount considered by the directors of the corporation to be the fair value, accompanied by a statement showing how the fair value was determined; or

(b) if subsection (26) applies, a notification that it is unable lawfully to pay dissenting shareholders for their shares.

(13) Same terms — Every offer made under subsection (12) for shares of the same class or series shall be on the same terms.

(14) Payment — Subject to subsection (26), a corporation shall pay for the shares of a dissenting shareholder within ten days after an offer made under subsection (12) has been accepted, but any such offer lapses if the corporation does not receive an acceptance thereof within thirty days after the offer has been made.

(15) Corporation may apply to court — Where a corporation fails to make an offer under subsection (12), or if a dissenting shareholder fails to accept an offer, the corporation may, within fifty days after the action approved by the resolution is effective or within such further period as a court may allow, apply to a court to fix a fair value for the shares of any dissenting shareholder.

(16) Shareholder application to court — If a corporation fails to apply to a court under subsection (15), a dissenting shareholder may apply to a court for the same purpose within a further period of twenty days or within such further period as a court may allow.

(17) Venue — An application under subsection (15) or (16) shall be made to a court having jurisdiction in the place where the corporation has its registered office or in the province where the dissenting shareholder resides if the corporation carries on business in that province.

(18) No security for costs — A dissenting shareholder is not required to give security for costs in an application made under subsection (15) or (16).

(19) Parties — On an application to a court under subsection (15) or (16),

(a) all dissenting shareholders whose shares have not been purchased by the corporation shall be joined as parties and are bound by the decision of the court; and

(b) the corporation shall notify each affected dissenting shareholder of the date, place and consequences of the application and of their right to appear and be heard in person or by counsel.

(20) Powers of court — On an application to a court under subsection (15) or (16), the court may determine whether any other person is a dissenting shareholder who should be joined as a party, and the court shall then fix a fair value for the shares of all dissenting shareholders.

(21) Appraisers — A court may in its discretion appoint one or more appraisers to assist the court to fix a fair value for the shares of the dissenting shareholders.

(22) Final order — The final order of a court shall be rendered against the corporation in favour of each dissenting shareholder and for the amount of his shares as fixed by the court.

(23) Interest — A court may in its discretion allow a reasonable rate of interest on the amount payable to each dissenting shareholder from the date the action approved by the resolution is effective until the date of payment.

(24) Notice that subsection (26) applies — If subsection (26) applies, the corporation shall, within ten days after the pronouncement of an order under subsection (22), notify each dissenting shareholder that it is unable lawfully to pay dissenting shareholders for their shares.

(25) Effect where subsection (26) applies — If subsection (26) applies, a dissenting shareholder, by written notice delivered to the corporation within thirty days after receiving a notice under subsection (24), may

(a) withdraw their notice of dissent, in which case the corporation is deemed to consent to the withdrawal and the shareholder is reinstated to their full rights as a shareholder; or

(b) retain a status as a claimant against the corporation, to be paid as soon as the corporation is lawfully able to do so or, in a liquidation, to be ranked subordinate to the rights of creditors of the corporation but in priority to its shareholders.

(26) Limitation — A corporation shall not make a payment to a dissenting shareholder under this section if there are reasonable grounds for believing that

(a) the corporation is or would after the payment be unable to pay its liabilities as they become due; or

(b) the realizable value of the corporation's assets would thereby be less than the aggregate of its liabilities.

1994, c. 24, s. 23; 2001, c. 14, ss. 94(2), (3), 135 (Sched., s. 64)

191. (1) Definition of "reorganization" — In this section, **"reorganization"** means a court order made under

(a) section 241;

(b) the *Bankruptcy and Insolvency Act* approving a proposal; or

(c) any other Act of Parliament that affects the rights among the corporation, its shareholders and creditors.

(2) Powers of court — If a corporation is subject to an order referred to in subsection (1), its articles may be amended by such order to effect any change that might lawfully be made by an amendment under section 173.

(3) Further powers — If a court makes an order referred to in subsection (1), the court may also

(a) authorize the issue of debt obligations of the corporation, whether or not convertible into shares of any class or having attached any rights or options to acquire shares of any class, and fix the terms thereof; and

(b) appoint directors in place of or in addition to all or any of the directors then in office.

(4) Articles of reorganization — After an order referred to in subsection (1) has been made, articles of reorganization in the form that the Director fixes shall be sent to the Director together with the documents required by sections 19 and 113, if applicable.

(5) Certificate of reorganization — On receipt of articles of reorganization, the Director shall issue a certificate of amendment in accordance with section 262.

(6) Effect of certificate — A reorganization becomes effective on the date shown in the certificate of amendment and the articles of incorporation are amended accordingly.

(7) No dissent — A shareholder is not entitled to dissent under section 190 if an amendment to the articles of incorporation is effected under this section.

1992, c. 27, s. 90(1)(h); 2001, c. 14, s. 95

192. (1) Definition of "arrangement" — In this section, **"arrangement"** includes

(a) an amendment to the articles of a corporation;

(b) an amalgamation of two or more corporations;

(c) an amalgamation of a body corporate with a corporation that results in an amalgamated corporation subject to this Act;

(d) a division of the business carried on by a corporation;

(e) a transfer of all or substantially all the property of a corporation to another body corporate in exchange for property, money or securities of the body corporate;

(f) an exchange of securities of a corporation for property, money or other securities of the corporation or property, money or securities of another body corporate;

(f.1) a going-private transaction or a squeeze-out transaction in relation to a corporation;

(g) a liquidation and dissolution of a corporation; and

(h) any combination of the foregoing.

(2) Where corporation insolvent — For the purposes of this section, a corporation is insolvent

(a) where it is unable to pay its liabilities as they become due; or

(b) where the realizable value of the assets of the corporation are less than the aggregate of its liabilities and stated capital of all classes.

(3) Application to court for approval of arrangement — Where it is not practicable for a corporation that is not insolvent to effect a fundamental change in the nature of an arrangement under any other provision of this Act, the corporation may apply to a court for an order approving an arrangement proposed by the corporation.

(4) Powers of court — In connection with an application under this section, the court may make any interim or final order it thinks fit including, without limiting the generality of the foregoing,

(a) an order determining the notice to be given to any interested person or dispensing with notice to any person other than the Director;

(b) an order appointing counsel, at the expense of the corporation, to represent the interests of the shareholders;

(c) an order requiring a corporation to call, hold and conduct a meeting of holders of securities or options or rights to acquire securities in such manner as the court directs;

(d) an order permitting a shareholder to dissent under section 190; and

(e) an order approving an arrangement as proposed by the corporation or as amended in any manner the court may direct.

(5) Notice to Director — An applicant for any interim or final order under this section shall give the Director notice of the application and the Director is entitled to appear and be heard in person or by counsel.

(6) Articles of arrangement — After an order referred to in paragraph (4)(e) has been made, articles of arrangement in the form that the Director fixes shall be sent to the Director together with the documents required by sections 19 and 113, if applicable.

(7) Certificate of arrangement — On receipt of articles of arrangement, the Director shall issue a certificate of arrangement in accordance with section 262.

(8) Effect of certificate — An arrangement becomes effective on the date shown in the certificate of arrangement.

1994, c. 24, s. 24; 2001, c. 14, s. 96(1), (3)

PART XVI — GOING-PRIVATE TRANSACTIONS AND SQUEEZE-OUT TRANSACTIONS

[Heading amended 2001, c. 14, s. 97.]

193. Going-private transactions — A corporation may carry out a going-private transaction. However, if there are any applicable provincial securities laws, a corporation may not carry out a going-private transaction unless the corporation complies with those laws.

2001, c. 14, s. 97

[Heading repealed 2001, c. 14, s. 97.]

194. Squeeze-out transactions — A corporation may not carry out a squeeze-out transaction unless, in addition to any approval by holders of shares required by or under this Act or the articles of the corporation, the transaction is approved by ordinary resolution of the holders of each class of shares that are affected by the transaction, voting separately, whether or not the shares otherwise carry the right to vote. However, the following do not have the right to vote on the resolution:

(a) affiliates of the corporation; and

(b) holders of shares that would, following the squeeze-out transaction, be entitled to consideration of greater value or to superior rights or privileges than those available to other holders of shares of the same class.

2001, c. 14, s. 97

195. [Repealed 2001, c. 14, s. 97.]

196. [Repealed 2001, c. 14, s. 97.]

197. [Repealed 2001, c. 14, s. 97.]

198. [Repealed 2001, c. 14, s. 97.]

199. [Repealed 2001, c. 14, s. 97.]

200. [Repealed 2001, c. 14, s. 97.]

201. [Repealed 2001, c. 14, s. 97.]

202. [Repealed 2001, c. 14, s. 97.]

203. [Repealed 2001, c. 14, s. 97.]

204. [Repealed 2001, c. 14, s. 97.]

205. [Repealed 2001, c. 14, s. 97.]

PART XVII — COMPULSORY AND COMPELLED ACQUISITIONS

[Heading added 2001, c. 14, s. 98.]

206. (1) Definitions — The definitions in this subsection apply in this Part.

"dissenting offeree" means, where a take-over bid is made for all the shares of a class of shares, a holder of a share of that class who does not accept the take-over bid and includes a subsequent holder of that share who acquires it from the first mentioned holder; *("pollicité dissident")*

"offer" includes an invitation to make an offer. *("pollicitation")*

"offeree" means a person to whom a take-over bid is made. *("pollicité")*

"offeree corporation" means a distributing corporation whose shares are the object of a take-over bid. *("société pollicitée")*

"offeror" means a person, other than an agent, who makes a take-over bid, and includes two or more persons who, directly or indirectly,

(a) make take-over bids jointly or in concert; or

(b) intend to exercise jointly or in concert voting rights attached to shares for which a take-over bid is made. *("pollicitant")*

"share" means a share, with or without voting rights, and includes

(a) a security currently convertible into such a share; and

(b) currently exercisable options and rights to acquire such a share or such a convertible security. *("action")*

"take-over bid" means an offer made by an offeror to shareholders of a distributing corporation at approximately the same time to acquire all of the shares of a class of issued shares, and includes an offer made by a distributing corporation to repurchase all of the shares of a class of its shares. *("offre d'achat visant à la mainmise")*

(2) Right to acquire — If within one hundred and twenty days after the date of a take-over bid the bid is accepted by the holders of not less than ninety per cent of the shares of any class of shares to which the take-over bid relates, other than shares held at the date of the take-over bid by or on behalf of the offeror or an affiliate or associate of the offeror, the offeror is entitled, on complying with this section, to acquire the shares held by the dissenting offerees.

(3) Notice — An offeror may acquire shares held by a dissenting offeree by sending by registered mail within sixty days after the date of termination of the take-over bid and in any event within one hundred and eighty days after the date of the take-over bid, an offeror's notice to each dissenting offeree and to the Director stating that

(a) the offerees holding not less than ninety per cent of the shares to which the bid relates accepted the take-over bid;

(b) the offeror is bound to take up and pay for or has taken up and paid for the shares of the offerees who accepted the take-over bid;

(c) a dissenting offeree is required to elect

(i) to transfer their shares to the offeror on the terms on which the offeror acquired the shares of the offerees who accepted the take-over bid, or

(ii) to demand payment of the fair value of the shares in accordance with subsections (9) to (18) by notifying the offeror within twenty days after receiving the offeror's notice;

(d) a dissenting offeree who does not notify the offeror in accordance with subparagraph (5)(b)(ii) is deemed to have elected to transfer the shares to the offeror on the same terms that the offeror acquired the shares from the offerees who accepted the take-over bid; and

(e) a dissenting offeree must send their shares to which the take-over bid relates to the offeree corporation within twenty days after receiving the offeror's notice.

(4) Notice of adverse claim — Concurrently with sending the offeror's notice under subsection (3), the offeror shall send to the offeree corporation a notice of adverse claim in accordance with section 78 with respect to each share held by a dissenting offeree.

(5) Share certificate — A dissenting offeree to whom an offeror's notice is sent under subsection (3) shall, within twenty days after receiving that notice,

> (a) send the share certificates of the class of shares to which the take-over bid relates to the offeree corporation; and

> (b) elect

>> (i) to transfer the shares to the offeror on the terms on which the offeror acquired the shares of the offerees who accepted the take-overbid, or

>> (ii) to demand payment of the fair value of the shares in accordance with subsections (9) to (18) by notifying the offeror within those twenty days.

(5.1) Deemed election — A dissenting offeree who does not notify the offeror in accordance with subparagraph (5)(b)(ii) is deemed to have elected to transfer the shares to the offeror on the same terms on which the offeror acquired the shares from the offerees who accepted the take-over bid.

(6) Payment — Within twenty days after the offeror sends an offeror's notice under subsection (3), the offeror shall pay or transfer to the offeree corporation the amount of money or other consideration that the offeror would have had to pay or transfer to a dissenting offeree if the dissenting offeree had elected to accept the take-over bid under subparagraph (5)(b)(i).

(7) Consideration — The offeree corporation is deemed to hold in trust for the dissenting shareholders the money or other consideration it receives under subsection (6), and the offeree corporation shall deposit the money in a separate account in a bank or other body corporate any of whose deposits are insured by the Canada Deposit Insurance Corporation or guaranteed by the Quebec Deposit Insurance Board, and shall place the other consideration in the custody of a bank or such other body corporate.

(7.1) When corporation is offeror — A corporation that is an offeror making a take-over bid to repurchase all of the shares of a class of its shares is deemed to hold in trust for the dissenting shareholders the money and other consideration that it would have had to pay or transfer to a dissenting offeree if the dissenting offeree had elected to accept the take-over bid under subparagraph (5)(b)(i), and the corporation shall, within twenty days after a notice is sent under subsection (3), deposit the money in a separate account in a bank or other body corporate any of whose deposits are insured by the Canada Deposit Insurance Corporation or guaranteed by the Quebec Deposit Insurance Board, and shall place the other consideration in the custody of a bank or such other body corporate.

(8) Duty of offeree corporation — Within thirty days after the offeror sends a notice under subsection (3), the offeree corporation shall

> (a) if the payment or transfer required by subsection (6) is made, issue to the offeror a share certificate in respect of the shares that were held by dissenting offerees;

> (b) give to each dissenting offeree who elects to accept the take-over bid terms under subparagraph (5)(b)(i) and who sends share certificates as required by paragraph (5)(a), the money or other consideration to which the offeree is entitled, disregarding fractional shares, which may be paid for in money; and

> (c) if the payment or transfer required by subsection (6) is made and the money or other consideration is deposited as required by subsection (7) or (7.1), send to each dissent-

ing shareholder who has not sent share certificates as required by paragraph (5)(a) a notice stating that

> (i) the dissenting shareholder's shares have been cancelled,

> (ii) the offeree corporation or some designated person holds in trust for the dissenting shareholder the money or other consideration to which that shareholder is entitled as payment for or in exchange for the shares, and

> (iii) the offeree corporation will, subject to subsections (9) to (18), send that money or other consideration to that shareholder without delay after receiving the shares.

(9) Application to court — If a dissenting offeree has elected to demand payment of the fair value of the shares under subparagraph (5)(b)(ii), the offeror may, within twenty days after it has paid the money or transferred the other consideration under subsection (6), apply to a court to fix the fair value of the shares of that dissenting offeree.

(10) Idem — If an offeror fails to apply to a court under subsection (9), a dissenting offeree may apply to a court for the same purpose within a further period of twenty days.

(11) Status of dissenter if no court application — Where no application is made to a court under subsection (10) within the period set out in that subsection, a dissenting offeree is deemed to have elected to transfer their shares to the offeror on the same terms that the offeror acquired the shares from the offerees who accepted the take-over bid.

(12) Venue — An application under subsection (9) or (10) shall be made to a court having jurisdiction in the place where the corporation has its registered office or in the province where the dissenting offeree resides if the corporation carries on business in that province.

(13) No security for costs — A dissenting offeree is not required to give security for costs in an application made under subsection (9) or (10).

(14) Parties — On an application under subsection (9) or (10)

> (a) all dissenting offerees referred to in subparagraph (5)(b)(ii) whose shares have not been acquired by the offeror shall be joined as parties and are bound by the decision of the court; and

> (b) the offeror shall notify each affected dissenting offeree of the date, place and consequences of the application and of their right to appear and be heard in person or by counsel.

(15) Powers of court — On an application to a court under subsection (9) or (10), the court may determine whether any other person is a dissenting offeree who should be joined as a party, and the court shall then fix a fair value for the shares of all dissenting offerees.

(16) Appraisers — A court may in its discretion appoint one or more appraisers to assist the court to fix a fair value for the shares of a dissenting offeree.

(17) Final order — The final order of the court shall be made against the offeror in favour of each dissenting offeree and for the amount for the shares as fixed by the court.

(18) Additional powers — In connection with proceedings under this section, a court may make any order it thinks fit and, without limiting the generality of the foregoing, it may

> (a) fix the amount of money or other consideration that is required to be held in trust under subsection (7) or (7.1);

(b) order that that money or other consideration be held in trust by a person other than the offeree corporation;

(c) allow a reasonable rate of interest on the amount payable to each dissenting offeree from the date they send or deliver their share certificates under subsection (5) until the date of payment; and

(d) order that any money payable to a shareholder who cannot be found be paid to the Receiver General and subsection 227(3) applies in respect thereof.

2001, c. 14, ss. 99(1)–(8), (10), (11), 135 (Sched., s. 65)

206.1 (1) Obligation to acquire shares — If a shareholder holding shares of a distributing corporation does not receive an offeror's notice under subsection 206(3), the shareholder may

(a) within ninety days after the date of termination of the take-over bid, or

(b) if the shareholder did not receive an offer pursuant to the take-over bid, within ninety days after the later of

(i) the date of termination of the take-over bid, and

(ii) the date on which the shareholder learned of the take-over bid,

require the offeror to acquire those shares.

(2) Conditions — If a shareholder requires the offeror to acquire shares under subsection (1), the offeror shall acquire the shares on the same terms under which the offeror acquired or will acquire the shares of the offerees who accepted the take-over bid.

2001, c. 14, s. 100

PART XVIII — LIQUIDATION AND DISSOLUTION

207. Definition of "court" — In this Part, **"court"** means a court having jurisdiction in the place where the corporation has its registered office.

208. (1) Application of Part — This Part, other than sections 209 and 212, does not apply to a corporation that is an insolvent person or a bankrupt as those terms are defined in subsection 2(1) of the *Bankruptcy and Insolvency Act*.

(2) Staying proceedings — Any proceedings taken under this Part to dissolve or to liquidate and dissolve a corporation shall be stayed if the corporation is at any time found, in a proceeding under the *Bankruptcy and Insolvency Act*, to be an insolvent person as defined in subsection 2(1) of that Act.

1992, c. 27, s. 90(1)(h); 2001, c. 14, s. 101

209. (1) Revival — Where a body corporate is dissolved under this Part or under section 268 of this Act or section 261 of chapter 33 of the Statutes of Canada, 1974-75-76, any interested person may apply to the Director to have the body corporate revived as a corporation under this Act.

(2) Articles of revival — Articles of revival in the form that the Director fixes shall be sent to the Director.

(3) Certificate of revival — On receipt of articles of revival, the Director shall issue a certificate of revival in accordance with section 262, if

(a) the body corporate has fulfilled all conditions precedent that the Director considers reasonable; and

(b) there is no valid reason for refusing to issue the certificate.

(3.1) Date of revival — A body corporate is revived as a corporation under this Act on the date shown on the certificate of revival.

(4) Rights preserved — Subject to any reasonable terms that may be imposed by the Director, to the rights acquired by any person after its dissolution and to any changes to the internal affairs of the corporation after its dissolution, the revived corporation is, in the same manner and to the same extent as if it had not been dissolved,

(a) restored to its previous position in law, including the restoration of any rights and privileges whether arising before its dissolution or after its dissolution and before its revival; and

(b) liable for the obligations that it would have had if it had not been dissolved whether they arise before its dissolution or after its dissolution and before its revival.

(5) Legal actions — Any legal action respecting the affairs of a revived corporation taken between the time of its dissolution and its revival is valid and effective.

(6) Definition of "interested person" — In this section, **"interested person"** includes

(a) a shareholder, a director, an officer, an employee and a creditor of the dissolved corporation;

(b) a person who has a contractual relationship with the dissolved corporation;

(c) a person who, although at the time of dissolution of the corporation was not a person described in paragraph (a), would be such a person if a certificate of revival is issued under this section; and

(d) a trustee in bankruptcy for the dissolved corporation.

2001, c. 14, s. 102

210. (1) Dissolution before commencing business — A corporation that has not issued any shares may be dissolved at any time by resolution of all the directors.

(2) Dissolution if no property — A corporation that has no property and no liabilities may be dissolved by special resolution of the shareholders or, where it has issued more than one class of shares, by special resolutions of the holders of each class whether or not they are otherwise entitled to vote.

(3) Dissolution where property disposed of — A corporation that has property or liabilities or both may be dissolved by special resolution of the shareholders or, where it has issued more than one class of shares, by special resolutions of the holders of each class whether or not they are otherwise entitled to vote, if

(a) by the special resolution or resolutions the shareholders authorize the directors to cause the corporation to distribute any property and discharge any liabilities; and

(b) the corporation has distributed any property and discharged any liabilities before it sends articles of dissolution to the Director pursuant to subsection (4).

(4) Articles of dissolution — Articles of dissolution in the form that the Director fixes shall be sent to the Director.

(5) Certificate of dissolution — On receipt of articles of dissolution, the Director shall issue a certificate of dissolution in accordance with section 262.

(6) Effect of certificate — The corporation ceases to exist on the date shown in the certificate of dissolution.

2001, c. 14, s. 103(2)

211. (1) Proposing liquidation and dissolution — The directors may propose, or a shareholder who is entitled to vote at an annual meeting of shareholders may, in accordance with section 137, make a proposal for, the voluntary liquidation and dissolution of a corporation.

(2) Notice of meeting — Notice of any meeting of shareholders at which voluntary liquidation and dissolution is to be proposed shall set out the terms thereof.

(3) Shareholders resolution — A corporation may liquidate and dissolve by special resolution of the shareholders or, where the corporation has issued more than one class of shares, by special resolutions of the holders of each class whether or not they are otherwise entitled to vote.

(4) Statement of intent to dissolve — A statement of intent to dissolve in the form that the Director fixes shall be sent to the Director.

(5) Certificate of intent to dissolve — On receipt of a statement of intent to dissolve, the Director shall issue a certificate of intent to dissolve in accordance with section 262.

(6) Effect of certificate — On issue of a certificate of intent to dissolve, the corporation shall cease to carry on business except to the extent necessary for the liquidation, but its corporate existence continues until the Director issues a certificate of dissolution.

(7) Liquidation — After issue of a certificate of intent to dissolve, the corporation shall

(a) immediately cause notice thereof to be sent to each known creditor of the corporation;

(b) without delay take reasonable steps to give notice of it in each province in Canada where the corporation was carrying on business at the time it sent the statement of intent to dissolve to the Director;

(c) proceed to collect its property, to dispose of properties that are not to be distributed in kind to its shareholders, to discharge all its obligations and to do all other acts required to liquidate its business; and

(d) after giving the notice required under paragraphs (a) and (b) and adequately providing for the payment or discharge of all its obligations, distribute its remaining property, either in money or in kind, among its shareholders according to their respective rights.

(8) Supervision by court — The Director or any interested person may, at any time during the liquidation of a corporation, apply to a court for an order that the liquidation be continued under the supervision of the court as provided in this Part, and on such application the court may so order and make any further order it thinks fit.

(9) Notice to Director — An applicant under this section shall give the Director notice of the application, and the Director is entitled to appear and be heard in person or by counsel.

(10) Revocation — At any time after issue of a certificate of intent to dissolve and before issue of a certificate of dissolution, a certificate of intent to dissolve may be revoked by sending to the Director a statement of revocation of intent to dissolve in the form that the Director fixes, if such revocation is approved in the same manner as the resolution under subsection (3).

(11) Certificate of revocation of intent to dissolve — On receipt of a statement of revocation of intent to dissolve, the Director shall issue a certificate of revocation of intent to dissolve in accordance with section 262.

(12) Effect of certificate — On the date shown in the certificate of revocation of intent to dissolve, the revocation is effective and the corporation may continue to carry on its business or businesses.

(13) Right to dissolve — If a certificate of intent to dissolve has not been revoked and the corporation has complied with subsection (7), the corporation shall prepare articles of dissolution.

(14) Articles of dissolution — Articles of dissolution in the form that the Director fixes shall be sent to the Director.

(15) Certificate of dissolution — On receipt of articles of dissolution, the Director shall issue a certificate of dissolution in accordance with section 262.

(16) Effect of certificate — The corporation ceases to exist on the date shown in the certificate of dissolution.

2001, c. 14, s. 104

212. (1) Dissolution by Director — Subject to subsections (2) and (3), the Director may

(a) dissolve a corporation by issuing a certificate of dissolution under this section if the corporation

(i) has not commenced business within three years after the date shown in its certificate of incorporation,

(ii) has not carried on its business for three consecutive years,

(iii) is in default for a period of one year in sending to the Director any fee, notice or document required by this Act, or

(iv) does not have any directors or is in the situation described in subsection 109(4); or

(b) apply to a court for an order dissolving the corporation, in which case section 217 applies.

(c) [Repealed 2001, c. 14, s. 105(1).]

(2) Publication — The Director shall not dissolve a corporation under this section until the Director has

(a) given one hundred and twenty days notice of the decision to dissolve the corporation to the corporation and to each director thereof; and

(b) published notice of that decision in a publication generally available to the public.

(3) Certificate of dissolution — Unless cause to the contrary has been shown or an order has been made by a court under section 246, the Director may, after the expiration of the period referred to in subsection (2), issue a certificate of dissolution in the form that the Director fixes.

(3.1) Exception — non-payment of incorporation fee — Despite anything in this section, the Director may dissolve a corporation by issuing a certificate of dissolution if the required fee for the issuance of a certificate of incorporation has not been paid.

(4) Effect of certificate — The corporation ceases to exist on the date shown in the certificate of dissolution.

1994, c. 24, s. 25; 2001, c. 14, ss. 105, 135 (Sched., s. 66)

213. (1) Grounds for dissolution — The Director or any interested person may apply to a court for an order dissolving a corporation if the corporation has

(a) failed for two or more consecutive years to comply with the requirements of this Act with respect to the holding of annual meetings of shareholders;

(b) contravened subsection 16(2) or section 21, 157 or 159; or

(c) procured any certificate under this Act by misrepresentation.

(2) Notice to Director — An applicant under this section shall give the Director notice of the application, and the Director is entitled to appear and be heard in person or by counsel.

(3) Dissolution order — On an application under this section or section 212, the court may order that the corporation be dissolved or that the corporation be liquidated and dissolved under the supervision of the court, and the court may make any other order it thinks fit.

(4) Certificate — On receipt of an order under this section, section 212 or 214, the Director shall

(a) if the order is to dissolve the corporation, issue a certificate of dissolution in the form that the Director fixes; or

(b) if the order is to liquidate and dissolve the corporation under the supervision of the court, issue a certificate of intent to dissolve in the form that the Director fixes and publish notice of the order in a publication generally available to the public.

(5) Effect of certificate — The corporation ceases to exist on the date shown in the certificate of dissolution.

2001, c. 14, s. 106

214. (1) Further grounds — A court may order the liquidation and dissolution of a corporation or any of its affiliated corporations on the application of a shareholder,

(a) if the court is satisfied that in respect of a corporation or any of its affiliates

(i) any act or omission of the corporation or any of its affiliates effects a result,

(ii) the business or affairs of the corporation or any of its affiliates are or have been carried on or conducted in a manner, or

(iii) the powers of the directors of the corporation or any of its affiliates are or have been exercised in a manner

that is oppressive or unfairly prejudicial to or that unfairly disregards the interests of any security holder, creditor, director or officer; or

(b) if the court is satisfied that

(i) a unanimous shareholder agreement entitles a complaining shareholder to demand dissolution of the corporation after the occurrence of a specified event and that event has occurred, or

(ii) it is just and equitable that the corporation should be liquidated and dissolved.

(2) Alternative order — On an application under this section, a court may make such order under this section or section 241 as it thinks fit.

(3) Application of s. 242 — Section 242 applies to an application under this section.

215. (1) Application for supervision — An application to a court to supervise a voluntary liquidation and dissolution under subsection 211(8) shall state the reasons, verified by an affidavit of the applicant, why the court should supervise the liquidation and dissolution.

(2) Court supervision — If a court makes an order applied for under subsection 211(8), the liquidation and dissolution of the corporation shall continue under the supervision of the court in accordance with this Act.

216. (1) Application to court — An application to a court under subsection 214(1) shall state the reasons, verified by an affidavit of the applicant, why the corporation should be liquidated and dissolved.

(2) Show cause order — On an application under subsection 214(1), the court may make an order requiring the corporation and any person having an interest in the corporation or claim against it to show cause, at a time and place specified in the order, within four weeks after the date of the order, why the corporation should not be liquidated and dissolved.

(3) Powers of court — On an application under subsection 214(1), the court may order the directors and officers of the corporation to furnish the court with all material information known to or reasonably ascertainable by them, including

(a) financial statements of the corporation;

(b) the name and address of each shareholder of the corporation; and

(c) the name and address of each known creditor or claimant, including any creditor or claimant with unliquidated, future or contingent claims, and any person with whom the corporation has a contract.

(4) Publication — A copy of an order made under subsection (2) shall be

(a) published as directed in the order, at least once in each week before the time appointed for the hearing, in a newspaper published or distributed in the place where the corporation has its registered office; and

(b) served on the Director and each person named in the order.

(5) Person responsible — Publication and service of an order under this section shall be effected by the corporation or by such other person and in such manner as the court may order.

1999, c. 31, s. 64

217. Powers of court — In connection with the dissolution or the liquidation and dissolution of a corporation, the court may, if it is satisfied that the corporation is able to pay or adequately provide for the discharge of all its obligations, make any order it thinks fit including, without limiting the generality of the foregoing,

(a) an order to liquidate;

(b) an order appointing a liquidator, with or without security, fixing the liquidator's remuneration and replacing a liquidator;

(c) an order appointing inspectors or referees, specifying their powers, fixing their remuneration and replacing inspectors or referees;

(d) an order determining the notice to be given to any interested person, or dispensing with notice to any person;

(e) an order determining the validity of any claims made against the corporation;

(f) an order, at any stage of the proceedings, restraining the directors and officers from

(i) exercising any of their powers, or

(ii) collecting or receiving any debt or other property of the corporation, and from paying out or transferring any property of the corporation, except as permitted by the court;

(g) an order determining and enforcing the duty or liability of any present or former director, officer or shareholder

(i) to the corporation, or

(ii) for an obligation of the corporation;

(h) an order approving the payment, satisfaction or compromise of claims against the corporation and the retention of assets for such purpose, and determining the adequacy of provisions for the payment or discharge of obligations of the corporation, whether liquidated, unliquidated, future or contingent;

(i) an order disposing of or destroying the documents and records of the corporation;

(j) on the application of a creditor, the inspectors or the liquidator, an order giving directions on any matter arising in the liquidation;

(k) after notice has been given to all interested parties, an order relieving a liquidator from any omission or default on such terms as the court thinks fit and confirming any act of the liquidator;

(l) subject to section 223, an order approving any proposed interim or final distribution to shareholders in money or in property;

(m) an order disposing of any property belonging to creditors or shareholders who cannot be found;

(n) on the application of any director, officer, security holder, creditor or the liquidator,

(i) an order staying the liquidation on such terms and conditions as the court thinks fit,

(ii) an order continuing or discontinuing the liquidation proceedings, or

(iii) an order to the liquidator to restore to the corporation all its remaining property; and

(o) after the liquidator has rendered a final account to the court, an order dissolving the corporation.

2001, c. 14, ss. 108, 135 (Sched., s. 67)

218. Effect of order — The liquidation of a corporation commences when a court makes an order therefor.

219. (1) Cessation of business and powers — If a court makes an order for liquidation of a corporation,

(a) the corporation continues in existence but shall cease to carry on business, except the business that is, in the opinion of the liquidator, required for an orderly liquidation; and

(b) the powers of the directors and shareholders cease and vest in the liquidator, except as specifically authorized by the court.

(2) Delegation by liquidator — The liquidator may delegate any powers vested in the liquidator by paragraph (1)(b) to the directors or shareholders.

2001, c. 14, s. 135 (Sched., s. 68)

220. (1) Appointment of liquidator — When making an order for the liquidation of a corporation or at any time thereafter, the court may appoint any person, including a director, an officer or a shareholder of the corporation or any other body corporate, as liquidator of the corporation.

(2) Vacancy — Where an order for the liquidation of a corporation has been made and the office of liquidator is or becomes vacant, the property of the corporation is under the control of the court until the office of liquidator is filled.

221. Duties of liquidator — A liquidator shall

(a) forthwith after appointment give notice thereof to the Director and to each claimant and creditor known to the liquidator;

(b) without delay publish notice by insertion once a week for two consecutive weeks in a newspaper published or distributed in the place where the corporation has its registered office and take reasonable steps to give notice of the appointment in each province where the corporation carries on business, requiring any person

(i) indebted to the corporation, to render an account and pay to the liquidator at the time and place specified any amount owing,

(ii) possessing property of the corporation, to deliver it to the liquidator at the time and place specified, and

(iii) having a claim against the corporation, whether liquidated, unliquidated, future or contingent, to present particulars thereof in writing to the liquidator not later than two months after the first publication of the notice;

(c) take into custody and control the property of the corporation;

(d) open and maintain a trust account for the moneys of the corporation;

(e) keep accounts of the moneys of the corporation received and paid out by him;

(f) maintain separate lists of the shareholders, creditors and other persons having claims against the corporation;

(g) if at any time the liquidator determines that the corporation is unable to pay or adequately provide for the discharge of its obligations, apply to the court for directions;

(h) deliver to the court and to the Director, at least once in every twelve month period after appointment or more often as the court may require, financial statements of the corporation in the form required by section 155 or in such other form as the liquidator may think proper or as the court may require; and

(i) after the final accounts are approved by the court, distribute any remaining property of the corporation among the shareholders according to their respective rights.

2001, c. 14, ss. 109, 135 (Sched., s. 69)

222. (1) Powers of liquidator — A liquidator may

(a) retain lawyers, accountants, engineers, appraisers and other professional advisers;

(b) bring, defend or take part in any civil, criminal or administrative action or proceeding in the name and on behalf of the corporation;

(c) carry on the business of the corporation as required for an orderly liquidation;

(d) sell by public auction or private sale any property of the corporation;

(e) do all acts and execute any documents in the name and on behalf of the corporation;

(f) borrow money on the security of the property of the corporation;

(g) settle or compromise any claims by or against the corporation; and

(h) do all other things necessary for the liquidation of the corporation and distribution of its property.

(2) Due diligence — A liquidator is not liable if the liquidator exercised the care, diligence and skill that a reasonably prudent person would have exercised in comparable circumstances, including reliance in good faith on

(a) financial statements of the corporation represented to the liquidator by an officer of the corporation or in a written report of the auditor of the corporation fairly to reflect the financial condition of the corporation; or

(b) a report of a person whose profession lends credibility to a statement made by the professional person.

(3) Application for examination — If a liquidator has reason to believe that any person has in their possession or under their control, or has concealed, withheld or misappropriated any property of the corporation, the liquidator may apply to the court for an order requiring that person to appear before the court at the time and place designated in the order and to be examined.

(4) Power of court — If the examination referred to in subsection (3) discloses that a person has concealed, withheld or misappropriated property of the corporation, the court may order that person to restore it or pay compensation to the liquidator.

2001, c. 14, ss. 110, 135 (Sched., s. 70)

223. (1) Costs of liquidation — A liquidator shall pay the costs of liquidation out of the property of the corporation and shall pay or make adequate provision for all claims against the corporation.

(2) Final accounts — Within one year after appointment, and after paying or making adequate provision for all claims against the corporation, the liquidator shall apply to the court

(a) for approval of the final accounts and for an order permitting the liquidator to distribute in money or in kind the remaining property of the corporation to its shareholders according to their respective rights; or

(b) for an extension of time, setting out the reasons therefor.

(3) Shareholder application — If a liquidator fails to make the application required by subsection (2), a shareholder of the corporation may apply to the court for an order for the liquidator to show cause why a final accounting and distribution should not be made.

(4) Publication — A liquidator shall give notice of their intention to make an application under subsection (2) to the Director, to each inspector appointed under section 217, to each shareholder and to any person who provided a security or fidelity bond for the liquidation, and shall publish the notice in a newspaper published or distributed in the place where the corporation has its registered office, or as otherwise directed by the court.

(5) Final order — If the court approves the final accounts rendered by a liquidator, the court shall make an order

(a) directing the Director to issue a certificate of dissolution;

(b) directing the custody or disposal of the documents and records of the corporation; and

(c) subject to subsection (6), discharging the liquidator.

(6) Delivery of order — The liquidator shall forthwith send a certified copy of the order referred to in subsection (5) to the Director.

(7) Certificate of dissolution — On receipt of the order referred to in subsection (5), the Director shall issue a certificate of dissolution in accordance with section 262.

(8) Effect of certificate — The corporation ceases to exist on the date shown in the certificate of dissolution.

2001, c. 14, ss. 111, 135 (Sched., s. 71)

224. (1) Right to distribution in money — If in the course of liquidation of a corporation the shareholders resolve or the liquidator proposes to

(a) exchange all or substantially all the property of the corporation for securities of another body corporate that are to be distributed to the shareholders, or

(b) distribute all or part of the property of the corporation to the shareholders in kind,

a shareholder may apply to the court for an order requiring the distribution of the property of the corporation to be in money.

(2) Powers of court — On an application under subsection (1), the court may order

(a) all the property of the corporation to be converted into and distributed in money; or

(b) the claims of any shareholder applying under this section to be satisfied by a distribution in money, in which case subsections 190(20) to (22) apply.

225. (1) Custody of records — A person who has been granted custody of the documents and records of a dissolved corporation remains liable to produce such documents and records for six years following the date of its dissolution or until the expiration of such other shorter period as may be ordered under subsection 223(5).

(2) Offence — A person who, without reasonable cause, contravenes subsection (1) is guilty of an offence and liable on summary conviction to a fine not exceeding five thousand dollars or to imprisonment for a term not exceeding six months or to both.

226. (1) Definition of "shareholder" — In this section, **"shareholder"** includes the heirs and personal representatives of a shareholder.

(2) Continuation of actions — Notwithstanding the dissolution of a body corporate under this Act,

(a) a civil, criminal or administrative action or proceeding commenced by or against the body corporate before its dissolution may be continued as if the body corporate had not been dissolved;

(b) a civil, criminal or administrative action or proceeding may be brought against the body corporate within two years after its dissolution as if the body corporate had not been dissolved; and

(c) any property that would have been available to satisfy any judgment or order if the body corporate had not been dissolved remains available for such purpose.

(3) Service — Service of a document on a corporation after its dissolution may be effected by serving the document on a person shown in the last notice filed under section 106 or 113.

(3.1) Idem — Service of a document on a company to which the *Canada Corporations Act*, chapter C-32 of the Revised Statutes of Canada, 1970, applied that has been dissolved by subsection 261(8) of the *Canada Business Corporations Act*, chapter 33 of the Statutes of Canada, 1974-75-76 and chapter 9 of the Statutes of Canada, 1978-79, may be effected by serving the document on a person shown as a director in the last annual summary filed by the company pursuant to the *Canada Corporations Act*.

(4) Reimbursement — Notwithstanding the dissolution of a body corporate under this Act, a shareholder to whom any of its property has been distributed is liable to any person claiming under subsection (2) to the extent of the amount received by that shareholder on such distribution, and an action to enforce such liability may be brought within two years after the date of the dissolution of the body corporate.

(5) Representative action — A court may order an action referred to in subsection (4) to be brought against the persons who were shareholders as a class, subject to such conditions as the court thinks fit and, if the plaintiff establishes a claim, the court may refer the proceedings to a referee or other officer of the court who may

(a) add as a party to the proceedings each person who was a shareholder found by the plaintiff;

(b) determine, subject to subsection (4), the amount that each person who was a shareholder shall contribute towards satisfaction of the plaintiff's claim; and

(c) direct payment of the amounts so determined.

1992, c. 1, s. 57; 2001, c. 14, ss. 112, 135 (Sched., s. 72)

227. (1) Unknown claimants — On the dissolution of a body corporate under this Act, the portion of the property distributable to a creditor or shareholder who cannot be found shall be converted into money and paid to the Receiver General.

(2) Constructive satisfaction — A payment under subsection (1) is deemed to be in satisfaction of a debt or claim of such creditor or shareholder.

(3) Recovery — A person who establishes an entitlement to any moneys paid to the Receiver General under this Act shall be paid by the Receiver General an equivalent amount out of the Consolidated Revenue Fund.

2001, c. 14, s. 135 (Sched., s. 73)

228. (1) Vesting in Crown — Subject to subsection 226(2) and section 227, property of a body corporate that has not been disposed of at the date of its dissolution under this Act vests in Her Majesty in right of Canada.

(2) Return of property on revival — If a body corporate is revived as a corporation under section 209, any property, other than money, that vested in Her Majesty pursuant to subsection (1), that has not been disposed of shall be returned to the corporation and there shall be paid to the corporation out of the Consolidated Revenue Fund

(a) an amount equal to any money received by Her Majesty pursuant to subsection (1); and

(b) where property other than money vested in Her Majesty pursuant to subsection (1) and that property has been disposed of, an amount equal to the lesser of

(i) the value of any such property at the date it vested in Her Majesty, and

(ii) the amount realized by Her Majesty from the disposition of that property.

PART XIX — INVESTIGATION

229. (1) Investigation — A security holder or the Director may apply, *ex parte* or on such notice as the court may require, to a court having jurisdiction in the place where the corporation has its registered office for an order directing an investigation to be made of the corporation and any of its affiliated corporations.

(2) Grounds — If, on an application under subsection (1), it appears to the court that

(a) the business of the corporation or any of its affiliates is or has been carried on with intent to defraud any person,

(b) the business or affairs of the corporation or any of its affiliates are or have been carried on or conducted, or the powers of the directors are or have been exercised in a manner that is oppressive or unfairly prejudicial to or that unfairly disregards the interests of a security holder,

(c) the corporation or any of its affiliates was formed for a fraudulent or unlawful purpose or is to be dissolved for a fraudulent or unlawful purpose, or

(d) persons concerned with the formation, business or affairs of the corporation or any of its affiliates have in connection therewith acted fraudulently or dishonestly,

the court may order an investigation to be made of the corporation and any of its affiliated corporations.

(3) Notice to Director — A security holder who makes an application under subsection (1) shall give the Director reasonable notice thereof and the Director is entitled to appear and be heard in person or by counsel.

(4) No security for costs — An applicant under this section is not required to give security for costs.

(5) Hearings *in camera* — An *ex parte* application under this section shall be heard *in camera*.

(6) Consent to publish proceedings required — No person may publish anything relating to *ex parte* proceedings under this section except with the authorization of the court or the written consent of the corporation being investigated.

2001, c. 14, s. 135 (Sched., s. 74)

230. (1) Powers of court — In connection with an investigation under this Part, the court may make any order it thinks fit including, without limiting the generality of the foregoing,

(a) an order to investigate;

(b) an order appointing an inspector, who may be the Director, fixing the remuneration of an inspector, and replacing an inspector;

(c) an order determining the notice to be given to any interested person, or dispensing with notice to any person;

(d) an order authorizing an inspector to enter any premises in which the court is satisfied there might be relevant information, and to examine any thing and make copies of any document or record found on the premises;

(e) an order requiring any person to produce documents or records to the inspector;

(f) an order authorizing an inspector to conduct a hearing, administer oaths, and examine any person on oath, and prescribing rules for the conduct of the hearing;

(g) an order requiring any person to attend a hearing conducted by an inspector and to give evidence on oath;

(h) an order giving directions to an inspector or any interested person on any matter arising in the investigation;

(i) an order requiring an inspector to make an interim or final report to the court;

(j) an order determining whether a report of an inspector should be published and, if so, ordering the Director to publish the report in whole or in part or to send copies to any person the court designates;

(k) an order requiring an inspector to discontinue an investigation;

(l) an order requiring the corporation to pay the costs of the investigation.

(2) Copy of report — An inspector shall send to the Director a copy of every report made by the inspector under this Part.

231. (1) Power of inspector — An inspector under this Part has the powers set out in the order appointing him.

(2) Exchange of information — In addition to the powers set out in the order appointing him, an inspector appointed to investigate a corporation may furnish to, or exchange information and otherwise cooperate with, any public official in Canada or elsewhere who is authorized to exercise investigatory powers and who is investigating, in respect of the corporation, any allegation of improper conduct that is the same as or similar to the conduct described in subsection 229(2).

(3) Court order — An inspector shall on request produce to an interested person a copy of any order made under subsection 230(1).

232. (1) Hearing *in camera* — Any interested person may apply to the court for an order that a hearing conducted by an inspector under this Part be heard *in camera* and for directions on any matter arising in the investigation.

(2) Right to counsel — A person whose conduct is being investigated or who is being examined at a hearing conducted by an inspector under this Part has a right to be represented by counsel.

233. Criminating statements — No person is excused from attending and giving evidence and producing documents and records to an inspector under this Part by reason only that the evidence tends to criminate that person or subject that person to any proceeding or penalty, but no such evidence shall be used or is receivable against that person in any proceeding thereafter instituted against that person under an Act of Parliament, other than a prosecution under section 132 of the *Criminal Code* for perjury in giving the evidence or a prosecution under section 136 of the *Criminal Code* in respect of the evidence.

R.S.C. 1985, c. 27 (1st Supp.), s. 187(Sched. V, item 3)

234. Absolute privilege (defamation) — Any oral or written statement or report made by an inspector or any other person in an investigation under this Part has absolute privilege.

235. (1) Information respecting ownership and control — If the Director is satisfied that, for the purposes of Part XI, XIII or XVII, or for the purposes of enforcing any regulation made under section 174, there is reason to inquire into the ownership or control of a security of a corporation or any of its affiliates, the Director may require any person that the Director reasonably believes has or has had an interest in the security or acts or has acted on behalf of a person with such an interest to report to him or her or to any person the Director designates

(a) information that such person has or can reasonably be expected to obtain as to present and past interests in the security; and

(b) the names and addresses of the persons so interested and of any person who acts or has acted in relation to the security on behalf of the persons so interested.

(2) Constructive interest in securities — For the purposes of subsection (1), a person is deemed to have an interest in a security if

(a) the person has a right to vote or to acquire or dispose of the security or any interest therein;

(b) the person's consent is necessary for the exercise of the rights or privileges of any other person interested in the security; or

(c) any other person interested in the security can be required or is accustomed to exercise rights or privileges attached to the security in accordance with the person's instructions.

(3) Publication — The Director shall publish in a publication generally available to the public the particulars of information obtained by the Director under this section, if the particulars

(a) are required to be disclosed by this Act or the regulations; and

(b) have not previously been so disclosed.

(4) Offence — A person who fails to comply with this section is guilty of an offence and liable on summary conviction to a fine not exceeding five thousand dollars or to imprisonment for a term not exceeding six months or to both.

(5) Officers, etc., of bodies corporate — Where a body corporate commits an offence under subsection (4), any director or officer of the body corporate who knowingly authorized, permitted or acquiesced in the commission of the offence is a party to and guilty of the offence and is liable on summary conviction to a fine not exceeding five thousand dollars or to imprisonment for a term not exceeding six months or to both, whether or not the body corporate has been prosecuted or convicted.

2001, c. 14, ss. 114(2), 135 (Sched., s. 75)

236. Solicitor-client privilege — Nothing in this Part shall be construed as affecting solicitor-client privilege.

2001, c. 14, s. 135 (Sched., s. 76)

237. Inquiries — The Director may make inquiries of any person relating to compliance with this Act.

PART XIX.1 — APPORTIONING AWARD OF DAMAGES
[Heading added 2001, c. 14, s. 115.]

Interpretation and Application
[Heading added 2001, c. 14, s. 115.]

237.1 Definitions — The definitions in this section apply in this Part.

"financial interest", with respect to a corporation, includes

(a) a security;

(b) a title to or an interest in capital, assets, property, profits, earnings or royalties;

(c) an option or other interest in, or a subscription to, a security;

(d) an agreement under which the interest of the purchaser is valued for purposes of conversion or surrender by reference to the value of a proportionate interest in a specified portfolio of assets;

(e) an agreement providing that money received will be repaid or treated as a subscription for shares, units or interests at the option of any person or the corporation;

(f) a profit-sharing agreement or certificate;

(g) a lease, claim or royalty in oil, natural gas or mining, or an interest in the lease, claim or royalty;

(h) an income or annuity contract that is not issued by an insurance company governed by an Act of Parliament or a law of a province;

(i) an investment contract; and

(j) anything that is prescribed to be a financial interest.

("intérêt financier")

"financial loss" means a financial loss arising out of an error, omission or misstatement in financial information concerning a corporation that is required under this Act or the regulations. *("perte financière")*

"third party" includes any subsequent party that is joined in proceedings before a court. *(Version anglaise seulement)*

2001, c. 14, s. 115

237.2 (1) Application of Part — This Part applies to the apportionment of damages awarded to a plaintiff for financial loss after a court has found more than one defendant or third party responsible for the financial loss.

(2) Non-application of Part — This Part does not apply to an award of damages to any of the following plaintiffs:

(a) Her Majesty in right of Canada or of a province;

(b) an agent of Her Majesty in right of Canada or of a province or, a federal or provincial Crown corporation or government agency, unless a substantial part of its activities involves trading, including making investments in, securities or other financial instruments;

(c) a charitable organization, private foundation or public foundation within the meaning of subsection 149.1(1) of the *Income Tax Act*; or

(d) an unsecured creditor in respect of goods or services that the creditor provided to a corporation.

2001, c. 14, s. 115

Apportionment of Damages
[Heading added 2001, c. 14, s. 115.]

237.3 (1) Degree of responsibility — Subject to this section and sections 237.4 to 237.6, every defendant or third party who has been found responsible for a financial loss is liable to the plaintiff only for the portion of the damages that corresponds to their degree of responsibility for the loss.

(2) Uncollectable amounts — If any part of the damages awarded against a responsible defendant or third party is uncollectable, the court may, on the application of the plaintiff, reallocate that amount to the other responsible defendants or third parties, if the application is made within one year after the date that the judgment was made enforceable.

(3) Reallocation — The amount that may be reallocated to each of the other responsible defendants or third parties under subsection (2) is calculated by multiplying the uncollectable amount by the percentage that corresponds to the degree of responsibility of that defendant or third party for the total financial loss.

(4) Maximum amount — The maximum amount determined under subsection (3), in respect of any responsible defendant or third party, may not be more than fifty per cent of the amount originally awarded against that responsible defendant or third party.

2001, c. 14, s. 115

237.4 (1) Exception — fraud — The plaintiff may recover the whole amount of the damages awarded by the court from any defendant or third party who has been held responsible for a financial loss if it was established that the defendant or third party acted fraudulently or dishonestly.

(2) Contribution — The defendant or third party referred to in subsection (1) is entitled to claim contribution from any other defendant or third party who is held responsible for the loss.

2001, c. 14, s. 115

Joint and Several, or Solidary, Liability

[Heading added 2001, c. 14, s. 115.]

237.5 (1) Individual or personal body corporate — Defendants and third parties referred to in subsection 237.2(1) are jointly and severally, or solidarity, liable for the damages awarded to a plaintiff who is an individual or a personal body corporate and who

(a) had a financial interest in a corporation on the day that an error, omission or misstatement in financial information concerning the corporation occurred, or acquired a financial interest in the period between the day that the error, omission or misstatement occurred and the day, as determined by the court, that it was generally disclosed; and

(b) has established that the value of the plaintiff's total financial interest in the corporation was not more than the prescribed amount at the close of business on the day that the error, omission or misstatement occurred or at the close of business on any day that the plaintiff acquired a financial interest in the period referred to in paragraph (a).

(1.1) Exception — Subsection (1) does not apply when the plaintiff brings the action as a member of a partnership or other association or as a trustee in bankruptcy, liquidator or receiver of a body corporate.

(2) Interpretation — For the purposes of this section,

(a) a personal body corporate is a body corporate that is not actively engaged in any financial, commercial or industrial business and that is controlled by an individual, or by a group of individuals who are connected by marriage, common-law partnership or any legal parent-child relationship or are connected indirectly by a combination of those relationships, whether or not the individuals through whom they are connected are members of the group; and

(b) a common-law partnership is a relationship between two persons who are cohabiting with each other in a conjugal relationship and have done so for a period of at least one year.

2001, c. 14, s. 115; 2005, c. 33, s. 5

237.6 (1) Equitable grounds — If the value of the plaintiff's total financial interest referred to in subsection 237.5(1) is greater than the prescribed amount, a court may nevertheless determine that the defendants and third parties are jointly and severally, or solidarily, liable if the court considers that it is just and reasonable to do so.

(2) Factors — The Governor in Council may establish factors that the court shall take into account in deciding whether to hold the defendants and third parties jointly and severally, or solidarily, liable.

(3) Statutory Instruments Act — The *Statutory Instruments Act* does not apply to the factors referred to in subsection (2), but the factors shall be published in Part I of the *Canada Gazette*.

2001, c. 14, s. 115

237.7 (1) Value of security — When, in order to establish the value of the total financial interest referred to in subsection 237.5(1), it is necessary to determine the value of a security that is traded on an organized market, the value of the security is, on the day specified in subsection (3),

(a) the closing price of that class of security;

(b) if no closing price is given, the average of the highest and lowest prices of that class of security; or

(c) if the security was not traded, the average of the bid and ask prices of that class of security.

(2) Court may adjust value — The court may adjust the value of a security that has been determined under subsection (1) when the court considers it reasonable to do so.

(3) Valuation day — The value of the security is to be determined as of the day that the error, omission or misstatement occurred. If the security was acquired in the period between that day and the day, as determined by the court, that the error, omission or misstatement was generally disclosed, the value is to be determined as of the day that it was acquired.

(4) Definition of "organized market" — In this section, **"organized market"** means a recognized exchange for a class of securities or a market that regularly publishes the price of that class of securities in a publication that is generally available to the public.

2001, c. 14, s. 115

237.8 (1) Court determines value — The court shall determine the value of all or any part of a financial interest that is subject to resale restrictions or for which there is no organized market.

(2) Factors — The Governor in Council may establish factors that the court may take into account in determining value under subsection (1).

(3) Statutory Instruments Act — The *Statutory Instruments Act* does not apply to the factors referred to in subsection (2), but the factors shall be published in Part I of the *Canada Gazette*.

2001, c. 14, s. 115

237.9 Application to determine value — The plaintiff may, by application made at any time before or during the course of the proceedings, request the court to determine the value of the plaintiff's financial interest for the purpose of subsection 237.5(1).

2001, c. 14, s. 115

Part XX — Remedies, Offences and Punishment

238. Definitions — In this Part,

"action" means an action under this Act; *("action")*

"complainant" means

(a) a registered holder or beneficial owner, and a former registered holder or beneficial owner, of a security of a corporation or any of its affiliates,

(b) a director or an officer or a former director or officer of a corporation or any of its affiliates,

(c) the Director, or

(d) any other person who, in the discretion of a court, is a proper person to make an application under this Part;

("plaignant")

239. (1) Commencing derivative action — Subject to subsection (2), a complainant may apply to a court for leave to bring an action in the name and on behalf of a corporation or any of its subsidiaries, or intervene in an action to which any such body corporate is a party, for the purpose of prosecuting, defending or discontinuing the action on behalf of the body corporate.

(2) Conditions precedent — No action may be brought and no intervention in an action may be made under subsection (1) unless the court is satisfied that

(a) the complainant has given notice to the directors of the corporation or its subsidiary of the complainant's intention to apply to the court under subsection (1) not less than fourteen days before bringing the application, or as otherwise ordered by the court, if the directors of the corporation or its subsidiary do not bring, diligently prosecute or defend or discontinue the action;

(b) the complainant is acting in good faith; and

(c) it appears to be in the interests of the corporation or its subsidiary that the action be brought, prosecuted, defended or discontinued.

2001, c. 14, s. 116

240. Powers of court — In connection with an action brought or intervened in under section 239, the court may at any time make any order it thinks fit including, without limiting the generality of the foregoing,

(a) an order authorizing the complainant or any other person to control the conduct of the action;

(b) an order giving directions for the conduct of the action;

(c) an order directing that any amount adjudged payable by a defendant in the action shall be paid, in whole or in part, directly to former and present security holders of the corporation or its subsidiary instead of to the corporation or its subsidiary; and

(d) an order requiring the corporation or its subsidiary to pay reasonable legal fees incurred by the complainant in connection with the action.

241. (1) Application to court re oppression — A complainant may apply to a court for an order under this section.

(2) Grounds — If, on an application under subsection (1), the court is satisfied that in respect of a corporation or any of its affiliates

(a) any act or omission of the corporation or any of its affiliates effects a result,

(b) the business or affairs of the corporation or any of its affiliates are or have been carried on or conducted in a manner, or

(c) the powers of the directors of the corporation or any of its affiliates are or have been exercised in a manner

that is oppressive or unfairly prejudicial to or that unfairly disregards the interests of any security holder, creditor, director or officer, the court may make an order to rectify the matters complained of.

(3) Powers of court — In connection with an application under this section, the court may make any interim or final order it thinks fit including, without limiting the generality of the foregoing,

(a) an order restraining the conduct complained of;

(b) an order appointing a receiver or receiver-manager;

(c) an order to regulate a corporation's affairs by amending the articles or by-laws or creating or amending a unanimous shareholder agreement;

(d) an order directing an issue or exchange of securities;

(e) an order appointing directors in place of or in addition to all or any of the directors then in office;

(f) an order directing a corporation, subject to subsection (6), or any other person, to purchase securities of a security holder;

(g) an order directing a corporation, subject to subsection (6), or any other person, to pay to a security holder any part of the monies that the security holder paid for securities;

(h) an order varying or setting aside a transaction or contract to which a corporation is a party and compensating the corporation or any other party to the transaction or contract;

(i) an order requiring a corporation, within a time specified by the court, to produce to the court or an interested person financial statements in the form required by section 155 or an accounting in such other form as the court may determine;

(j) an order compensating an aggrieved person;

(k) an order directing rectification of the registers or other records of a corporation under section 243;

(l) an order liquidating and dissolving the corporation;

(m) an order directing an investigation under Part XIX to be made; and

(n) an order requiring the trial of any issue.

(4) Duty of directors — If an order made under this section directs amendment of the articles or by-laws of a corporation,

(a) the directors shall forthwith comply with subsection 191(4); and

(b) no other amendment to the articles or by-laws shall be made without the consent of the court, until a court otherwise orders.

(5) Exclusion — A shareholder is not entitled to dissent under section 190 if an amendment to the articles is effected under this section.

(6) Limitation — A corporation shall not make a payment to a shareholder under paragraph (3)(f) or (g) if there are reasonable grounds for believing that

(a) the corporation is or would after that payment be unable to pay its liabilities as they become due; or

(b) the realizable value of the corporation's assets would thereby be less than the aggregate of its liabilities.

(7) Alternative order — An applicant under this section may apply in the alternative for an order under section 214.

2001, c. 14, s. 135 (Sched., s. 77)

242. (1) Evidence of shareholder approval not decisive — An application made or an action brought or intervened in under this Part shall not be stayed or dismissed by reason only that it is shown that an alleged breach of a right or duty owed to the corporation or its subsidiary has been or may be approved by the shareholders of such body corporate, but evidence of approval by the shareholders may be taken into account by the court in making an order under section 214, 240 or 241.

(2) Court approval to discontinue — An application made or an action brought or intervened in under this Part shall not be stayed, discontinued, settled or dismissed for want of prosecution without the approval of the court given on such terms as the court thinks fit and, if the court determines that the interests of any complainant may be substantially affected by such stay, discontinuance, settlement or dismissal, the court may order any party to the application or action to give notice to the complainant.

(3) No security for costs — A complainant is not required to give security for costs in any application made or action brought or intervened in under this Part.

(4) Interim costs — In an application made or an action brought or intervened in under this Part, the court may at any time order the corporation or its subsidiary to pay to the complainant interim costs, including legal fees and disbursements, but the complainant may be held accountable for such interim costs on final disposition of the application or action.

243. (1) Application to court to rectify records — If the name of a person is alleged to be or to have been wrongly entered or retained in, or wrongly deleted or omitted from, the registers or other records of a corporation, the corporation, a security holder of the corporation or any aggrieved person may apply to a court for an order that the registers or records be rectified.

(2) Notice to Director — An applicant under this section shall give the Director notice of the application and the Director is entitled to appear and be heard in person or by counsel.

(3) Powers of court — In connection with an application under this section, the court may make any order it thinks fit including, without limiting the generality of the foregoing,

    (a) an order requiring the registers or other records of the corporation to be rectified;

    (b) an order restraining the corporation from calling or holding a meeting of shareholders or paying a dividend before such rectification;

    (c) an order determining the right of a party to the proceedings to have their name entered or retained in, or deleted or omitted from, the registers or records of the corporation, whether the issue arises between two or more security holders or alleged security holders, or between the corporation and any security holders or alleged security holders; and

    (d) an order compensating a party who has incurred a loss.

2001, c. 14, s. 135 (Sched., s. 78)

244. Application for directions — The Director may apply to a court for directions in respect of any matter concerning the Director's duties under this Act, and on such application the court may give such directions and make such further order as it thinks fit.

2001, c. 14, s. 135 (Sched., s. 79)

245. (1) Notice of refusal by Director — If the Director refuses to file any articles or other document that this Act requires the Director to file before the articles or other document become effective, the Director shall, within twenty days after receiving them or twenty days after receiving any approval that may be required under any other Act, whichever is later, give written notice of the refusal to the person who sent the articles or document, giving reasons.

(2) Deemed refusal — If the Director does not file or give written notice of the refusal to file any articles or document within the time limited therefor in subsection (1), the Director is deemed for the purposes of section 246 to have refused to file the articles or document.

2001, c. 14, s. 135 (Sched., s. 80)

246. Appeal from Director's decision — A person who feels aggrieved by a decision of the Director referred to in any of paragraphs (a) to (g) may apply to a court for an order, including an order requiring the Director to change the decision

(a) to refuse to file in the form submitted any articles or other document required by this Act to be filed;

(b) to give a name, to change or revoke a name, or to refuse to reserve, accept, change or revoke a name under section 12;

(c) to grant, or to refuse to grant, an exemption that may be granted under this Act and the regulations;

(d) to refuse under subsection 187(11) to permit a continued reference to shares having a nominal or par value;

(e) to refuse to issue a certificate of discontinuance under section 188 or a certificate attesting that as of a certain date the corporation exists under subsection 263.1(2);

(f) to issue, or to refuse to issue, a certificate or revival under section 209, or the decision with respect to the terms for revival imposed by the Director;

(f.1) to correct, or to refuse to correct, articles, a notice, a certificate or other document under section 265;

(f.2) to cancel, or to refuse to cancel, the articles and related certificate under section 265.1; or

(g) to dissolve a corporation under section 212.

The Court may make any order it thinks fit.

1999, c. 31, s. 65; 2001, c. 14, s. 119

247. Restraining or compliance order — If a corporation or any director, officer, employee, agent, auditor, trustee, receiver, receiver-manager or liquidator of a corporation does not comply with this Act, the regulations, articles, by-laws, or a unanimous shareholder agreement, a complainant or a creditor of the corporation may, in addition to any other right they have, apply to a court for an order directing any such person to comply with, or restraining any such person from acting in breach of, any provisions thereof, and on such application the court may so order and make any further order it thinks fit.

2001, c. 14, s. 135 (Sched., s. 81)

248. Summary application to court — Where this Act states that a person may apply to a court, the application may be made in a summary manner by petition, orginating notice of motion, or otherwise as the rules of the court provide, and subject to any order respecting notice to interested parties or costs, or any other order the court thinks fit.

249. (1) Appeal of final order — An appeal lies to the court of appeal of a province from any final order made by a court of that province under this Act.

(2) Appeal with leave — An appeal lies to the court of appeal of a province from any order other than a final order made by a court of that province, only with leave of the court of appeal in accordance with the rules applicable to that court.

2001, c. 14, s. 120

250. (1) Offences with respect to reports — A person who makes or assists in making a report, return, notice or other document required by this Act or the regulations to be sent to the Director or to any other person that

(a) contains an untrue statement of a material fact, or

(b) omits to state a material fact required therein or necessary to make a statement contained therein not misleading in the light of the circumstances in which it was made

is guilty of an offence and liable on summary conviction to a fine not exceeding five thousand dollars or to imprisonment for a term not exceeding six months or to both.

(2) Officers, etc., of bodies corporate — Where a body corporate commits an offence under subsection (1), any director or officer of the body corporate who knowingly authorized, permitted or acquiesced in the commission of the offence is a party to and guilty of the offence and is liable on summary conviction to a fine not exceeding five thousand dollars or to imprisonment for a term not exceeding six months or to both, whether or not the body corporate has been prosecuted or convicted.

(3) Immunity — No person is guilty of an offence under subsection (1) or (2) if the person did not know, and in the exercise of reasonable diligence could not have known, of the untrue statement or omission.

2001, c. 14, s. 135 (Sched., s. 82)

251. Offence — Every person who, without reasonable cause, contravenes a provision of this Act or the regulations for which no punishment is provided is guilty of an offence punishable on summary conviction.

252. (1) Order to comply — Where a person is guilty of an offence under this Act or the regulations, any court in which proceedings in respect of the offence are taken may, in addition to any punishment it may impose, order that person to comply with the provisions of this Act or the regulations for the contravention of which the person has been convicted.

(2) Limitation period — A prosecution for an offence under this Act may be instituted at any time within but not later than two years after the time when the subject-matter of the complaint arose.

(3) Civil remedy not affected — No civil remedy for an act or omission is suspended or affected by reason that the act or omission is an offence under this Act.

2001, c. 14, s. 135 (Sched., s. 83)

PART XX.1 — DOCUMENTS IN ELECTRONIC OR OTHER FORM

[Heading added 2001, c. 14, s. 121.]

252.1 Definitions — The definitions in this section apply in this Part.

"electronic document" means, except in section 252.6, any form of representation of information or of concepts fixed in any medium in or by electronic, optical or other similar means and that can be read or perceived by a person or by any means. *("document électronique")*

"information system" means a system used to generate, send, receive, store, or otherwise process an electronic document. *("système d'information")*

2001, c. 14, s. 121

252.2 Application — This Part does not apply to a notice, document or other information sent to or issued by the Director pursuant to this Act or to any prescribed notice, document or other information.

2001, c. 14, s. 121

252.3 (1) Use not mandatory — Nothing in this Act or the regulations requires a person to create or provide an electronic document.

(2) Consent and other requirements — Despite anything in this Part, a requirement under this Act or the regulations to provide a person with a notice, document or other information is not satisfied by the provision of an electronic document unless

(a) the addressee has consented, in the manner prescribed, and has designated an information system for the receipt of the electronic document; and

(b) the electronic document is provided to the designated information system, unless otherwise prescribed.

(3) Revocation of consent — An addressee may revoke the consent referred to in paragraph (2)(a) in the manner prescribed.

2001, c. 14, s. 121

252.4 Creation and provision of information — A requirement under this Act or the regulations that a notice, document or other information be created or provided, is satisfied by the creation or provision of an electronic document if

(a) the by-laws or the articles of the corporation do not provide otherwise; and

(b) the regulations, if any, have been complied with.

2001, c. 14, s. 121

252.5 (1) Creation of information in writing — A requirement under this Act or the regulations that a notice, document or other information be created in writing is satisfied by the creation of an electronic document if, in addition to the conditions in section 252.4,

(a) the information in the electronic document is accessible so as to be usable for subsequent reference; and

(b) the regulations pertaining to this subsection, if any, have been complied with.

(2) Provision of information in writing — A requirement under this Act or the regulations that a notice, document or other information be provided in writing is satisfied by the provision of an electronic document if, in addition to the conditions set out in section 252.4,

(a) the information in the electronic document is accessible by the addressee and capable of being retained by the addressee, so as to be usable for subsequent reference; and

(b) the regulations pertaining to this subsection, if any, have been complied with.

(3) Copies — A requirement under this Act or the regulations for one or more copies of a document to be provided to a single addressee at the same time is satisfied by the provision of a single version of the electronic document.

(4) Registered mail — A requirement under this Act or the regulations to provide a document by registered mail is not satisfied by the sending of an electronic document unless prescribed.

2001, c. 14, s. 121

252.6 (1) Statutory declarations and affidavits — A statutory declaration or an affidavit required under this Act or the regulations may be created or provided in an electronic document if

    (a) the person who makes the statutory declaration or affidavit signs it with his or her secure electronic signature;

    (b) the authorized person before whom the statutory declaration or affidavit is made signs it with his or her secure electronic signature; and

    (c) the requirements of sections 252.3 to 252.5 are complied with.

(2) Definitions — For the purposes of this section, **"electronic document"** and **"secure electronic signature"** have the same meaning as in subsection 31(1) of the *Personal Information Protection and Electronic Documents Act*.

(3) Clarification — For the purpose of complying with paragraph (1)(c), the references to an "electronic document" in sections 252.3 to 252.5 are to be read as references to an "electronic document" as defined in subsection 31(1) of the *Personal Information Protection and Electronic Documents Act*.

2001, c. 14, s. 121

252.7 Signatures — A requirement under this Act or the regulations for a signature or for a document to be executed, except with respect to a statutory declaration or an affidavit, is satisfied if, in relation to an electronic document, the prescribed requirements pertaining to this section, if any, are met and if the signature results from the application by a person of a technology or a process that permits the following to be proven:

    (a) the signature resulting from the use by a person of the technology or process is unique to the person;

    (b) the technology or process is used by a person to incorporate, attach or associate the person's signature to the electronic document; and

    (c) the technology or process can be used to identify the person using the technology or process.

2001, c. 14, s. 121

PART XXI — GENERAL

253. (1) Notice to directors and shareholders — A notice or document required by this Act, the regulations, the articles or the by-laws to be sent to a shareholder or director of a corporation may be sent by prepaid mail addressed to, or may be delivered personally to,

    (a) the shareholder at the shareholder's latest address as shown in the records of the corporation or its transfer agent; and

(b) the director at the director's latest address as shown in the records of the corporation or in the last notice filed under section 106 or 113.

(2) Effect of notice — A director named in a notice sent by a corporation to the Director under section 106 or 113 and filed by the Director is presumed for the purposes of this Act to be a director of the corporation referred to in the notice.

(3) Deemed receipt — A notice or document sent in accordance with subsection (1) to a shareholder or director of a corporation is deemed to be received at the time it would be delivered in the ordinary course of mail unless there are reasonable grounds for believing that the shareholder or director did not receive the notice or document at that time or at all.

(4) Undelivered notices — If a corporation sends a notice or document to a shareholder in accordance with subsection (1) and the notice or document is returned on two consecutive occasions because the shareholder cannot be found, the corporation is not required to send any further notices or documents to the shareholder until the shareholder informs the corporation in writing of the shareholder's new address.

2001, c. 14, ss. 122, 135 (Sched., s. 84)

254. Notice to and service on a corporation — A notice or document required to be sent to or served on a corporation may be sent by registered mail to the registered office of the corporation shown in the last notice filed under section 19 and, if so sent, is deemed to be received or served at the time it would be delivered in the ordinary course of mail unless there are reasonable grounds for believing that the corporation did not receive the notice or document at that time or at all.

255. Waiver of notice — Where a notice or document is required by this Act or the regulations to be sent, the sending of the notice or document may be waived or the time for the notice or document may be waived or abridged at any time with the consent in writing of the person entitled thereto.

256. (1) Certificate of Director — Where this Act requires or authorizes the Director to issue a certificate or to certify any fact, the certificate shall be signed by the Director or by a Deputy Director authorized under section 260.

(2) Evidence — Except in a proceeding under section 213 to dissolve a corporation, a certificate referred to in subsection (1) or a certified copy thereof, when introduced as evidence in any civil, criminal or administrative action or proceeding, is conclusive proof of the facts so certified without proof of the signature or official character of the person appearing to have signed the certificate.

257. (1) Certificate of corporation — A certificate issued on behalf of a corporation stating any fact that is set out in the articles, the by-laws, a unanimous shareholder agreement, the minutes of the meetings of the directors, a committee of directors or the shareholders, or in a trust indenture or other contract to which the corporation is a party, may be signed by a director, an officer or a transfer agent of the corporation.

(2) Proof — When introduced as evidence in any civil, criminal or administrative action or proceeding,

(a) a fact stated in a certificate referred to in subsection (1),

(b) a certified extract from a securities register of a corporation, or

(c) a certified copy of minutes or extract from minutes of a meeting of shareholders, directors or a committee of directors of a corporation,

is, in the absence of evidence to the contrary, proof of the facts so certified without proof of the signature or official character of the person appearing to have signed the certificate.

(3) Security certificate — An entry in a securities register of, or a security certificate issued by, a corporation is, in the absence of evidence to the contrary, proof that the person in whose name the security is registered is owner of the securities described in the register or in the certificate.

258. Copies — Where a notice or document is required to be sent to the Director under this Act, the Director may accept a photostatic or photographic copy thereof.

258.1 Content and form of notices and documents — The Director may establish the requirements for the content and fix the form, including electronic or other forms, of notices and documents sent to or issued by the Director pursuant to this Act, including

(a) the notices and documents that may be transmitted in electronic or other form;

(b) the persons or classes of persons who may transmit the notices and documents;

(c) their signature in electronic or other form, or their execution, adoption or authorization in a manner that is to have the same effect for the purposes of this Act as their signature;

(d) the time and circumstances when electronic notices and documents are to be considered to be sent or received, and the place where they are considered to have been sent or received; and

(e) any matter necessary for the purposes of the application of this section.

1994, c. 24, s. 26; 2001, c. 14, s. 124

258.2 Exemption — In the prescribed circumstances, the Director may, on any conditions that the Director considers appropriate, exempt from the application of any provision of this Act requiring notices or documents to be sent to the Director any notices or documents or classes of notices or documents containing information similar to that contained in notices or documents required to be made public pursuant to any other Act of Parliament or to any Act of the legislature of a province as the Director specifies.

1994, c. 24, s. 26; 2001, c. 14, s. 124

259. (1) Proof required by Director — The Director may require that a document or a fact stated in a document required by this Act or the regulations to be sent to the Director shall be verified in accordance with subsection (2).

(2) Form of proof — A document or fact required by this Act or by the Director to be verified may be verified by affidavit or by statutory declaration under the *Canada Evidence Act* before any commissioner for oaths or for taking affidavits.

2001, c. 14, s. 135 (Sched., s. 85)

260. Appointment of Director — The Minister may appoint a Director and one or more Deputy Directors to carry out the duties and exercise the powers of the Director under this Act.

261. (1) Regulations — The Governor in Council may make regulations

(a) prescribing any matter required or authorized by this Act to be prescribed;

(a.1) defining anything that, by this Act, is to be defined by regulation;

(b) requiring the payment of a fee in respect of the filing, examination or copying of any document, or in respect of any action that the Director is required or authorized to take under this Act, and prescribing the amount of the fee or the manner of determining the fee;

(c) respecting the payment of fees, including the time when and the manner in which the fees are to be paid, the additional fees that may be charged for the late payment of fees and the circumstances in which any fees previously paid may be refunded in whole or in part;

(c.1) prescribing, for the purposes of subsection 137(1.1), a manner of determining the number of shares required for a person to be eligible to submit a proposal, including the time and manner of determining a value or percentage of the outstanding shares of the corporation;

(d) prescribing, for the purposes of paragraph 137(5)(d), the minimum amount of support required in relation to the number of times the shareholder has submitted substantially the same, proposal within the prescribed period;

(e) prescribing rules with respect to exemptions permitted by this Act;

(f) prescribing that, for the purpose of paragraph 155(1)(a), the standards as they exist from time to time, of an accounting body named in the regulations shall be followed;

(g) prescribing any matter necessary for the purposes of the application of Part XX.1, including the time and circumstances when an electronic document is to be considered to have been provided or received and the place where it is considered to have been provided or received;

(h) prescribing the manner of, and conditions for, participating in a meeting by means of a telephonic, electronic or other communication facility that permits all participants to communicate adequately with each other during the meeting; and

(i) prescribing, for the purposes of subsection 141(3), the manner of, and conditions for, voting at a meeting of shareholders by means of a telephonic, electronic or other communication facility.

(2) Incorporation by reference — The regulations may incorporate any material by reference regardless of its source and either as it exists on a particular date or as amended from time to time.

(3) Incorporated material is not a regulation — Material does not become a regulation for the purposes of the *Statutory Instruments Act* because it is incorporated by reference.

1994, c. 24, s. 27; 2001, c. 14, s. 125

261.1 Fee to be paid before service performed — The fee in respect of the filing, examination, or copying of any document, or in respect of any action that the Director is required or authorized to take, shall be paid to the Director on the filing, examination, or copying or before the Director takes the action in respect of which the fee is payable.

2001, c. 14, s. 126

262. (1) Definition of "statement" — In this section, **"statement"** means a statement of intent to dissolve and a statement of revocation of intent to dissolve referred to in section 211.

(2) Execution and filing — Where this Act requires that articles or a statement relating to a corporation shall be sent to the Director,

(a) the articles or the statement shall be signed by a director or an officer of the corporation or, in the case of articles of incorporation, by an incorporator; and

(b) on receiving the articles or statement in the form that the Director fixes, any other required documents and the required fees, the Director shall

(i) record the date of the filing,

(ii) issue the appropriate certificate,

(iii) file the certificate and the articles or statement, or a copy, image or photographic, electronic or other reproduction of the certificate and of the articles or statement,

(iv) send the certificate, or a copy, image or photographic, electronic or other reproduction of the certificate, to the corporation or its agent, and

(v) publish a notice of the issuance of the certificate in a publication generally available to the public.

(3) Date of certificate — A certificate referred to in subsection (2) issued by the Director may be dated as of the day the Director receives the articles, statement or court order pursuant to which the certificate is issued or as of any later day specified by the court or person who signed the articles or statement.

(4) [Repealed 1994, c. 24, s. 28(2).]

(5) Date of certificate — Notwithstanding subsection (3), a certificate of discontinuance may be dated as of the day on which the corporation amalgamates pursuant to another Act or is continued.

1994, c. 24, s. 28; 2001, c. 14, ss. 127, 135 (Sched., s. 86)

262.1 (1) Signature — A signature required on a certificate issued by the Director under this Act may be printed or otherwise mechanically reproduced on the certificate or may be in accordance with the regulations made under paragraph 261(1)(c.1).

(2) Authority to sign notices — The notices referred to in subsections 19(2) and (4) and subsections 106(1) and 113(1), and the annual return referred to in section 263, may be signed by any individual who has the relevant knowledge of the corporation and who is authorized to do so by the directors, or, in the case of the notice referred to in subsection 106(1), the incorporators.

(3) Execution of documents — Any articles, notice, resolution, requisition, statement or other document required or permitted to be executed or signed by more than one individual for the purposes of this Act may be executed or signed in several documents of like form, each of which is executed or signed by one or more of the individuals. The documents, when duly executed or signed by all individuals required or permitted, as the case may be, to do so, shall be deemed to constitute one document for the purposes of this Act.

1994, c. 24, s. 29; 2001, c. 14, s. 128

263. Annual return — Every corporation shall, on the prescribed date, send to the Director an annual return in the form that the Director fixes and the Director shall file it.

2001, c. 14, s. 129

263.1 (1) Certificate — The Director may provide any person with a certificate stating that a corporation

(a) has sent to the Director a document required to be sent under this Act;

(b) has paid all required fees; or

(c) exists as of a certain date.

(2) Director may refuse to issue certificate of existence — For greater certainty, the Director may refuse to issue a certificate described in paragraph (1)(c) if the Director has knowledge that the corporation is in default of sending a document required to be sent under this Act or is in default of paying a required fee.

2001, c. 14, s. 129

264. Alteration — The Director may alter a notice or document, other than an affidavit or statutory declaration, if authorized by the person who sent the document or by that person's representative.

2001, c. 14, s. 135 (Sched., s. 87)

265. (1) Corrections at request of Director — If there is an error in articles, a notice, a certificate or other document, the directors or shareholders of the corporation shall, on the request of the Director, pass the resolutions and send to the Director the documents required to comply with this Act, and take such other steps as the Director may reasonably require so that the Director may correct the document.

(2) No prejudice — Before proceeding under subsection (1), the Director must be satisfied that the correction would not prejudice any of the shareholders or creditors of the corporation.

(3) Corrections at the request of the corporation — The Director may, at the request of the corporation or of any other interested person, accept a correction to any of the documents referred to in subsection (1) if

(a) the correction is approved by the directors of the corporation, unless the error is obvious or was made by the Director; and

(b) the Director is satisfied that the correction would not prejudice any of the shareholders or creditors of the corporation and that the correction reflects the original intention of the corporation or the incorporators, as the case may be.

(4) Application to court — If, in the view of the Director, of the corporation or of any interested person who wishes a correction, a correction to any of the documents referred to in subsection (1) would prejudice any of the shareholders or creditors of a corporation, the Director, the corporation or the person, as the case may be, may apply to the court for an order that the document be corrected and for an order determining the rights of the shareholders or creditors.

(5) Notice to Director — An applicant under subsection (4) shall give the Director notice of the application, and the Director is entitled to appear and to be heard in person or by counsel.

(6) Director may require surrender of document — The Director may demand the surrender of the original document, and may issue a corrected certificate or file the corrected articles, notice or other document.

(7) Date of corrected document — A corrected document shall bear the date of the document it replaces unless

(a) the correction is made with respect to the date of the document, in which case the document shall bear the corrected date, or

(b) the court decides otherwise.

(8) Notice — If a corrected certificate materially amends the terms of the original certificate, the Director shall without delay give notice of the correction in a publication generally available to the public.

2001, c. 14, s. 130

265.1 (1) Cancellation of articles by Director — In the prescribed circumstances, the Director may cancel the articles and related certificate of a corporation.

(2) No prejudice — Before proceeding under subsection (1), the Director must be satisfied that the cancellation would not prejudice any of the shareholders or creditors of the corporation.

(3) Request to Director to cancel articles — In the prescribed circumstances, the Director may, at the request of a corporation or of any other interested person, cancel the articles and related certificate of the corporation if

(a) the cancellation is approved by the directors of the corporation; and

(b) the Director is satisfied that the cancellation would not prejudice any of the shareholders or creditors of the corporation and that the cancellation reflects the original intention of the corporation or the incorporators, as the case may be.

(4) Application to court — If, in the view of the Director of the corporation or of any interested person who wishes a cancellation, a cancellation of articles and a related certificate would prejudice any of the shareholders or creditors of a corporation, the Director, the corporation or the person, as the case may be, may apply to the court for an order that the articles and certificate be cancelled and for an order determining the rights of the shareholders or creditors.

(5) Notice to Director — An applicant under subsection (4) shall give the Director notice of the application, and the Director is entitled to appear and to be heard in person or by counsel.

(6) Return of certificate — The Director may demand the surrender of a cancelled certificate.

2001, c. 14, s. 130

266. (1) Inspection — A person who has paid the required fee is entitled during usual business hours to examine a document required by this Act or the regulations to be sent to the Director, except a report sent to the Director under subsection 230(2), and to make copies of or extracts from it.

(2) Copies — The Director shall furnish any person with a copy, extract, certified copy or certifiled extract of a document required by this Act or the regulations to be sent to the Director, except a report sent under subsection 230(2).

2001, c. 14, s. 130

267. (1) Records of Director — Records required by this Act to be maintained by the Director

(a) may be in bound or loose-leaf form or in photographic film form; or

(b) may be entered or recorded by any system of mechanical or electronic data processing or by any other information storage device that is capable of reproducing any required information in intelligible form within a reasonable time.

(2) Obligation to furnish — Where records are maintained by the Director otherwise than in written form,

(a) the Director shall furnish any copy required to be furnished under subsection 266(2) in intelligible form; and

(b) a report reproduced from those records, if it is certified by the Director, is admissible in evidence to the same extent as the original records would have been.

(3) Retention of records — The Director is not required to produce any document, other than a certificate and attached articles or statement filed under section 262, after the expiration of the prescribed period.

1994, c. 24, s. 30; 2001, c. 14, s. 131

267.1 Form of publication — Information or notices required by this Act to be summarized in a publication generally available to the public or published by the Director may be made available to the public or published by any system of mechanical or electronic data processing or by any other information storage device that is capable of reproducing any required information or notice in intelligible form within a reasonable time.

1994, c. 24, s. 31; 2001, c. 14, s. 132

268. (1) Definition of "charter" — In this section, **"charter"** includes

(a) an act of incorporation and any amendments thereto; and

(b) letters patent of incorporation and any letters patent supplementary thereto.

(2) Amendment of charter — special Act — In connection with a continuance under this Act, the shareholders of a body corporate incorporated or continued by or under a special Act of Parliament who are entitled to vote at annual meetings of shareholders may, despite the charter of the body corporate,

(a) by special resolution, authorize the directors of the body corporate to apply under section 187 for a certificate of continuance; and

(b) by the same resolution, make any amendment to the charter of the body corporate that a corporation incorporated under this Act may make to its articles.

(2.1) Amendment of charter — other Act — In connection with a continuance under this Act, the shareholders of a body corporate incorporated or continued by or under an Act of Parliament, other than this Act or a special Act, who are entitled to vote at annual meetings of shareholders may, subject to any other Act of Parliament or the charter of the body corporate,

(a) by special resolution, authorize the directors of the body corporate to apply under section 187 for a certificate of continuance; and

(b) by the same resolution, make any amendment to the charter of the body corporate that a corporation incorporated under this Act may make to its articles.

(3) Change of class rights — Despite subsections (2) and (2.1), the shareholders of a body corporate may not, by a special resolution under any of those subsections, make any change of the nature referred to in subsection 176(1) that affects a class or series of shares, unless

(a) the charter of the body corporate otherwise provides in respect of an amendment of the nature referred to in paragraph 176(1)(a), (b) or (e); or

(b) the holders of the class or series of shares approve the change in accordance with section 176.

(4) Authorizing continuance — Subject to subsections (6) and (7), the directors of a body corporate incorporated or continued by or under a special Act of Parliament may, despite the charter of the body corporate, apply under section 187 for a certificate of continuance if the articles of continuance do not make any amendment to the charter of the body corporate other than an amendment required to conform to this Act.

(4.1) Authorizing continuance — Subject to subsections (6) and (7), the directors of a body corporate incorporated or continued by or under an Act of Parliament, other than this Act or a special Act, may, subject to any other Act of Parliament or the charter of the body corporate, apply under section 187 for a certificate of continuance if the articles of continuance do not make any amendment to the charter of the body corporate other than an amendment required to conform to this Act.

(4.2) Financial institutions — For the purposes of this section, every body corporate that is incorporated or continued under an Act of Parliament and to which the *Bank Act*, the *Cooperative Credit Associations Act*, the *Insurance Companies Act* or the *Trust and Loan Companies Act* applies is deemed to be incorporated or continued by or under an Act of Parliament other than this Act or a special Act.

(5) No dissent — A shareholder is not entitled to dissent under section 190 in respect of an amendment made under subsection (2), (2.1), (3), (4) or (4.1).

(6) Discretionary continuance — The Governor in Council may, by order, require that a body corporate incorporated by or under an Act of Parliament to which Part I or II of the *Canada Corporations Act*, chapter C-32 of the Revised Statutes of Canada, 1970, does not apply, apply for a certificate of continuance under section 187 within any period that may be prescribed except for the following:

(a) a bank;

(a.1) an association to which the *Cooperative Credit Associations Act* applies;

(b) a company or society to which the *Insurance Companies Act* applies; and

(c) a company to which the *Trust and Loan Companies Act* applies.

(7) Discretionary continuance — *Canada Corporations Act* — A body corporate to which Part IV of the *Canada Corporations Act*, chapter C-32 of the Revised Statutes of Canada, 1970, applies, other than a body corporate that carries on a business referred to in any of paragraphs (6)(a.1) to (c), may apply for a certificate of continuance under section 187.

(8) Fees — A body corporate that obtains a certificate of continuance under this section is not required to pay any fees otherwise payable under this Act in respect of such continuance.

(9) Idem — A body corporate referred to in subsection (6) that does not make an application to obtain a certificate of continuance within the period prescribed is dissolved on the expiration of that period.

(10) Continuance prohibited — A body corporate to which Part II or Part III of the *Canada Corporations Act*, chapter C-32 of the Revised Statutes of Canada, 1970, applies or any similar body corporate incorporated otherwise than by or under an Act of Parliament may not apply for a certificate of continuance under section 187.

(11) Exception for railway companies — A body corporate that is incorporated by or under a Special Act, as defined in section 87 of the *Canada Transportation Act*, may apply for a certificate of continuance under section 187.

1991, c. 45, s. 556; 1991, c. 46, s. 597; 1991, c. 47, s. 724; 1992, c. 1, s. 142 (Sched. V, item 12); 1994, c. 24, s. 32; 1996, c. 10, s. 213; 2001, c. 14, s. 133; 2007, c. 6, s. 401

CAN. REG. 2001-512 — CANADA BUSINESS CORPORATIONS REGULATIONS, 2001

made under the *Canada Business Corporations Act*

SOR/2001-512, as am. SOR/2003-317, ss. 1, 2, 3 (Fr.), 4–6; SOR/2005-51; SOR/2006-75.

INTERPRETATION

1. The following definitions apply in these Regulations.

"Act" means the *Canada Business Corporations Act*. *("Loi")*

"end of the taxation year" means the taxation year end as defined in subsection 1104(1) of the Income Tax Regulations and is the equivalent of the financial year end for the purposes of these Regulations. *("fin de l'année d'imposition")*

2. (1) For the purpose of the definition "distributing corporation" in subsection 2(1) of the Act and subject to subsections 2(6) and (7) of the Act and subsection (2) of this section, "distributing corporation" means

(a) a corporation that is a "reporting issuer" under any legislation that is set out in column 2 of an item of Schedule 1; or

(b) in the case of a corporation that is not a "reporting issuer" referred to in paragraph (a), a corporation

(i) that has filed a prospectus or registration statement under provincial legislation or under the laws of a jurisdiction outside Canada,

(ii) any of the securities of which are listed and posted for trading on a stock exchange in or outside Canada, or

(iii) that is involved in, formed for, resulting from or continued after an amalgamation, a reorganization, an arrangement or a statutory procedure, if one of the participating bodies corporate is a corporation to which subparagraph (i) or (ii) applies.

(2) A corporation that is subject to an exemption under provincial securities legislation, or to an order of the relevant provincial securities regulator that provides that the corporation is not a "reporting issuer" for the purposes of the applicable legislation, is not a "distributing corporation" for the purpose of the definition of that expression in subsection (1).

SOR/2003-317, s. 1

3. (1) For the purpose of the definition "going-private transaction" in subsection 2(1) of the Act, "going-private transaction" means an amalgamation, arrangement, consolidation or other transaction involving a distributing corporation, other than an acquisition of shares under section 206 of the Act, that results in the interest of a holder of participating securities of the corporation being terminated without the consent of the holder and without the substitution of an interest of equivalent value in participating securities of the corporation or of a body corporate that succeeds to the business of the corporation, which participating securities have rights and privileges that are equal to or greater than the affected participating securities.

(2) For the purpose of subsection (1), **"participating securities"** means securities of a body corporate that give the holder of the securities a right to share in the earnings of the body corporate and after the liquidation, dissolution or winding up of the body corporate, a right to share in its assets.

PART 1 — GENERAL

Forms

4. Any forms, procedures or policy guidelines that the Director establishes from time to time for the better administration of the Act shall be published in a publication generally available to the public.

5. (1) The annual return referred to in section 263 of the Act shall be sent to the Director within 60 days after the anniversary date of incorporation of the corporation, and shall set out the required information as of the anniversary date.

(2) Despite subsection (1), that annual return shall be sent to the Director within 60 days after the end of the corporation's taxation year, and shall set out the required information as of the date of the taxation year end, if

(a) the corporation has a taxation year end between July 1, 2006 and December 31, 2006; and

(b) the Director has not issued to the corporation a certificate of incorporation, amalgamation or continuance between January 1, 2006 and December 31, 2006.

SOR/2003-317, s. 2; SOR/2006-75, s. 1

Electronic Documents

6. For the purpose of section 252.2 of the Act, the prescribed notices, documents or other information are the notices, documents or other information referred to in sections 48 to 81 of the Act.

7. (1) For the purpose of paragraph 252.3(2)(a) of the Act, the consent shall be in writing.

(2) For the purpose of paragraph 252.3(2)(b) of the Act, an electronic document need not be sent to the designated information system if

(a) the document is posted on or made available through a generally accessible electronic source, such as a web site; and

(b) the addressee is provided with notice in writing of the availability and location of that electronic document.

(3) Subsection (2) does not apply to a notice, document or other information provided under section 10.

8. For the purposes of subsection 252.3(3) of the Act, an addressee shall revoke his or her consent in writing.

9. For the purpose of paragraphs 252.4(b) and 252.5(2)(b) of the Act, when a notice, document or other information is provided to several addressees, the notice, document or other information shall be provided to the addressees concurrently, regardless of the manner of provision.

10. For the purposes of Part XX.1 of the Act, when a notice, document or other information is required under the Act to be sent to a specific place, an electronic document may be sent instead to an information system designated for the receipt of the notice, document or other information.

11. For the purposes of Part XX.1 of the Act, an electronic document is considered to have been provided to a person when it leaves an information system within the control of the originator or another person who provided it on behalf of the originator.

12. For the purposes of Part XX.1 of the Act, an electronic document is considered to have been received

(a) when it enters the information system designated by the addressee; or

(b) if the document is posted on or made available through a generally accessible electronic source, when the notice referred to in paragraph 7(2)(b) is received by the addressee or, if sent electronically, when the notice enters the information system designated by the addressee.

"Resident Canadian" Class of Persons Prescribed

13. For the purpose of paragraph (b) of the definition "resident Canadian" in subsection 2(1) of the Act, the following classes of persons are prescribed:

(a) persons who are full-time employees of the Government of Canada or of a province, of an agency of any of those governments or of a federal or provincial Crown corporation, if the principal reason for their residence outside Canada is to act as employees;

(b) persons who are full-time employees, if the principal reason for their residence outside Canada is to act as employees, of a body corporate

(i) of which more than 50% of the voting shares is beneficially owned, or over which control or direction is exercised, by resident Canadians,

(ii) a majority of the directors of which are resident Canadians, or

(iii) that is a subsidiary of a body corporate described in subparagraph (i) or (ii);

(c) persons who are full-time students at a university or other educational institution recognized by the educational authorities of a majority of the provinces of Canada and who have been resident outside Canada for fewer than 10 consecutive years;

(d) persons who are full-time employees of an international association or organization of which Canada is a member; and

(e) persons who were, at the time of reaching their 60th birthday, ordinarily resident in Canada and who have been resident outside Canada for fewer than 10 consecutive years.

Exemption Circumstances Prescribed

14. For the purpose of section 258.2 of the Act, the prescribed circumstances are that the exemption does not prejudice any of the shareholders or the public interest.

Retention of Records

15. For the purpose of subsection 267(3) of the Act, the prescribed period is six years after the day on which the Director receives the document.

Business Sectors

16. For the purpose of subsection 105(3.1) of the Act, the prescribed business sectors are

(a) uranium mining;

(b) book publishing or distribution; and

(c) book sales, where the sale of books is the primary part of the corporation's business; and

(d) film or video distribution.

PART 2 — CORPORATE NAMES

Interpretation

17. The following definitions apply in this Part.

"confusing", in relation to a corporate name, means a corporate name the use of which causes confusion with a trade-mark, an official mark or a trade-name in the manner described in section 18. *("prête à confusion")*

"corporate name" means the name of a corporation. *("Version anglaise seulement")*

"distinctive", in relation to a trade-name, means a trade-name that distinguishes the business in association with which it is used by its owner from any other business or that is adapted so as to distinguish them from each other. *("distinctive")*

"official mark" means an official mark within the meaning of subparagraph 9(1)(n)(iii) of the *Trade-marks Act*. *("marque officielle")*

"secondary meaning", in relation to a trade-name, means a trade-name that has been used in Canada or elsewhere by an applicant or by their predecessors so as to have become distinctive in Canada as at the date of filing an application for a corporate name. *("sens dérivé")*

"trade-mark" has the same meaning as in section 2 of the *Trade-marks Act*. *("marque de commerce")*

"trade-name" means the name under which a business is carried on, whether it is a corporate name or the name of a body corporate, a trust, a partnership, a sole proprietorship or an individual. *("dénomination commerciale")*

"use" means actual use by a person that carries on business in Canada or elsewhere. *("emploi")*

Confusion of Names

18. A corporate name is confusing with

(a) a trade-mark or an official mark if the use of both the corporate name and either the trade-mark or the official mark, as the case may be, is likely to lead to the inference that the business carried on or intended to be carried on under the corporate name and the business connected with the trade-mark or the official mark, as the case may be, are one business, whether or not the nature of the business of each is generally the same; or

(b) a trade-name if the use of both names is likely to lead to the inference that the business carried on or intended to be carried on under the corporate name and the business carried on under the trade-name are one business, whether or not the nature of the business of each is generally the same.

Consideration of Whole Name

19. When determining whether a trade-name is distinctive, the name as a whole and not only its separate elements shall be considered.

Prohibited Names

20. For the purpose of paragraph 12(1)(a) of the Act, a corporate name is prohibited in respect of a request to reserve a name or in respect of an application for revival under section 209 of the Act, if it is the same as, or is confusing with, a corporate name that has, before the date of the request, been reserved by the Director for another person, unless

(a) written consent has been obtained from the person for whom the corporate name was reserved; or

(b) the 90-day reservation period referred to in subsection 11(1) of the Act has expired without the person for whom the corporate name was reserved having made a renewed request to, reserve the corporate name.

21. For the purpose of paragraph 12(l)(a) of the Act, a corporate name is prohibited if the name contains any of the following elements:

(a) "Air Canada";

(b) "Canada Standard" or "CS";

(c) "cooperative", "coopérative", "co-op" or "pool" when it connotes a cooperative venture;

(d) "Parliament Hill" or "Colline du Parlement";

(e) "Royal Canadian Mounted Police", "Gendarmerie royale du Canada", "RCMP" or "GRC"; or

(f) "United Nations", "Nations Unies", "UN" or "ONU".

22. For the purpose of paragraph 12(1)(a) of the Act, a corporate name is prohibited if it connotes that the corporation

(a) carries on business under royal, vice-regal or governmental patronage, approval or authority, unless the appropriate government department or agency consents in writing to the use of the name;

(b) is sponsored or controlled by or is connected with the Government of Canada, the government of a province, the government of a country other than Canada or a political subdivision or agency of any such government, unless the appropriate government, political subdivision or agency consents in writing to the use of the name;

(c) is sponsored or controlled by or is connected with a university or an association of accountants, architects, engineers, lawyers, physicians or surgeons or another professional association recognized by the laws of Canada or a province, unless the appropriate university or professional association consents in writing to the use of the name; or

(d) carries on the business of a bank, a loan company, an insurance company, a trust company, another financial intermediary or a stock exchange that is regulated by a law of Canada or a province, unless the Superintendent of Financial Institutions or the relevant provincial securities regulator consents in writing to the use of the name.

23. For the purpose of paragraph 12(1)(a) of the Act, a corporate name is prohibited if it contains a word or phrase, or connotes a business, that is obscene.

24. **(1)** For the purpose of paragraph 12(1)(a) of the Act and subject to subsection (2), a corporate name is prohibited if the corporate name is not distinctive because it

(a) is only descriptive, in any language, of the business of the corporation, of the goods and services in which the corporation deals or intends to deal, or of the quality, function or other characteristic of those goods and services;

(b) is primarily or only the name or surname, used alone, of an individual who is living or has died within 30 years before the date of the request to the Director for that name; or

(c) is primarily or only a geographic name, used alone.

(2) Subsection (1) does not apply if a person requesting a corporate name establishes that it has, through use, acquired rights in the name and the name continues at the time of the request to have secondary meaning.

SOR/2003-317, s. 4

25. For the purpose of paragraph 12(1)(a) of the Act, a corporate name is prohibited if it is confusing, having regard to all the circumstances, including

(a) the inherent distinctiveness of the whole or any elements of any trade-mark, official mark or trade-name and the extent to which it has become known;

(b) the length of time the trade-mark, official mark or trade-name has been in use;

(c) the nature of the goods or services associated with a trade-mark or an official mark, or the nature of the business carried on under or associated with a trade-name, including the likelihood of any competition among businesses using such a trade-mark, official mark or trade-name;

(d) the nature of the trade with which a trade-mark, an official mark or a trade-name is associated, including the nature of the products or services and the means by which they are offered or distributed;

(e) the degree of resemblance between the proposed corporate name and a trade-mark, an official mark or a trade-name in appearance or sound or in the ideas suggested by them; and

(f) the territorial area in Canada in which the proposed corporate name or an existing trade-name is likely to be used.

26. For the purpose of paragraph 12(1)(a) of the Act, a corporate name is prohibited if an element of the name is the family name of an individual, whether or not preceded by their given name or initials, unless the individual or their heir or legal representative consents in writing to the use of their name and the individual has or had a material interest in the corporation.

27. For the purpose of paragraph 12(1)(a) of the Act,

(a) a corporate name is prohibited if its use is likely to lead to the inference that the business carried on or intended to be carried on under it and the business of a body corporate that is dissolved are one business, whether or not the nature of their businesses is generally the same; and

(b) the name of a corporation that is revived under section 209 of the Act is prohibited if it is confusing with a name acquired by another corporation during the period beginning on the date of dissolution and ending on the date of revival of the revived corporation.

28. For the purpose of paragraph 12(1)(a) of the Act, a corporate name that is confusing with the name of a body corporate that has not carried on business in the two years immediately before the date of a request for the corporate name is prohibited, unless the body corporate that has that name

(a) consents in writing to the use of the name, and the name is not otherwise prohibited; and

(b) undertakes in writing to dissolve immediately or to change its name before the corporation that proposes to use the name begins to use it, and the name is not otherwise prohibited.

29. For the purpose of paragraph 12(1)(a) of the Act, a corporate name that contains a word that is the same as or similar to the distinctive element of an existing trade-mark, official mark or trade-name and is confusing with one or another of the distinctive elements is prohibited, unless the person who owns the trade-mark, official mark, or trade-name consents in writing to the use of the corporate name, and the name is not otherwise prohibited.

30. (1) For the purpose of paragraph 12(1)(a) of the Act, a corporate name that is confusing with the name of a body corporate is prohibited unless

(a) the corporate name is the name of an existing or a proposed corporation that is the successor to the business of the body corporate and the body corporate has ceased or will, in the immediate future, cease to carry on business under that corporate name and undertakes in writing to dissolve or to change its corporate name before the successor corporation begins carrying on business under that corporate name;

(b) subject to subsection (2), the corporate name of the existing or proposed corporation sets out in numerals the year of incorporation, or the year of the most recent amendment to the corporate name, in parentheses, immediately before the word or expression "Limited", "Limitée", "Incorporated", "Incorporée", "Corporation", "Société par actions de régime fédéral" or "Société commerciale canadienne" or the abbreviation "Ltd.", "Ltée", "Inc.", "Corp.", "S.A.R.F." or "S.C.C."; and

(c) the corporate name is not otherwise prohibited.

(2) The reference in a corporate name to the year of incorporation or the year of the most recent amendment to the corporate name may be deleted two years after its use is introduced, if the corporate name so changed is not confusing.

31. (1) For the purpose of paragraph 12(1)(a) of the Act, if two or more corporations amalgamate, the name of the amalgamated corporation is prohibited if the name is confusing or is otherwise prohibited.

(2) Despite subsection (1), the new corporate name may be the same as the name of one of the amalgamating corporations.

(3) For the purpose of paragraph 12(1)(a) of the Act, if an existing corporation has acquired or will, in the immediate future, acquire all or substantially all of the property of an affiliated body corporate, the use by the corporation of the corporate name of the body corporate is prohibited unless

(a) the body corporate undertakes in writing to dissolve, or to change its name, before the corporation begins using the corporate name; and

(b) the name is not otherwise prohibited.

(4) For the purpose of paragraph 12(1)(a) of the Act, if a proposed corporation will, in the immediate future, acquire all or substantially all of the property of a body corporate that is to be an affiliate of the proposed corporation, the use by the proposed corporation of the name of the affiliated body corporate is prohibited unless

(a) the body corporate undertakes in writing to dissolve, or to change its name, before the proposed corporation begins using the corporate name; and

(b) the name is not otherwise prohibited.

Deceptively Misdescriptive Names

32. For the purpose of paragraph 12(1)(a) of the Act, a corporate name is deceptively misdescriptive if it is likely to mislead the public, in any language, with respect to

(a) the business, goods or services in association with which it is proposed to be used;

(b) the conditions under which the goods or services will be produced or supplied or the persons to be employed in the production or supply of the goods or services; or

(c) the place of origin of the goods or services.

Certain Names Not Prohibited

33. A corporate name is not prohibited only because it contains alphabetic or numeric characters, initials, punctuation marks or any combination of those elements.

Criteria for English and French Forms

34. For the purpose of subsection 10(3) of the Act, a combined English and French form of the name of a corporation shall include only the expression "Inc.".

SOR/2003-317, s. 5

PART 3 — CORPORATE INTERRELATIONSHIPS

Interpretation

35. The following definitions apply in this Part.

"delivery shares" means shares issued by a corporation to a particular subsidiary for the purpose of an acquisition made under subsection 31(4) of the Act. *("actions remises")*

"particular subsidiary" means a subsidiary body corporate referred to in subsection 31(4) of the Act. *("filiale donnée")*

Prescribed Conditions

36. For the purpose of subsection 31(4) of the Act, the prescribed conditions are that

(a) the consideration received by the corporation for the delivery shares is equal to the fair market value of those shares at the time of their issuance;

(b) the class of shares of which the delivery shares are a part is widely held and shares of that class are actively traded on any of the following stock exchanges in Canada, namely,

(i) the Canadian Venture Exchange,

(ii) The Montreal Exchange, or

(iii) the Toronto Stock Exchange;

(c) the sole purpose of effecting the acquisition by the particular subsidiary of delivery shares is to transfer them, as set out in paragraph 37(b), to the shareholders of another body corporate;

(d) immediately before the acquisition of the delivery shares by the particular subsidiary, the other body corporate and its shareholders deal at arm's length, to be determined in accordance with the *Income Tax Act*, with the corporation and the particular subsidiary; and

(e) immediately before the acquisition of the delivery shares by the particular subsidiary, the particular subsidiary and the other body corporate are not resident in Canada, for the purposes of the *Income Tax Act*.

37. For the purposes of subsection 31(5) of the Act, the prescribed conditions are that

(a) the particular subsidiary does not acquire a beneficial interest in the delivery shares as a result of its acquisition of those shares and the beneficial interest is acquired by the shareholders of the other body corporate;

147

(b) the acquisition by the particular subsidiary of the delivery shares is followed immediately by a transfer of the delivery shares by the particular subsidiary to shareholders of the other body corporate;

(c) immediately after the transfer of the delivery shares to the shareholders of the other body corporate, the particular subsidiary and the other body corporate are not resident in Canada, for the purposes of the *Income Tax Act*; and

(d) after the transfer of the delivery shares to the shareholders of the other body corporate, the other body corporate is a subsidiary body corporate of the particular subsidiary.

38. For the purpose of subsection 31(6) of the Act, the prescribed consequences are that within 30 days after one of the conditions described in section 36 or 37 is not met or ceases to be met, the corporation shall

(a) cancel the delivery share, on condition that if the articles of the corporation limit the number of authorized shares, the delivery shares may be restored to the status of authorized but unissued shares;

(b) return the consideration received by the corporation for the delivery shares to the particular subsidiary; and

(c) cancel the entry for the consideration in the corporation's stated capital account.

PART 4 — INSIDER TRADING

39. For the purpose of paragraph 126(2)(a) of the Act, the prescribed percentage of voting rights is 10%.

40. For the purpose of paragraph 131(1)(d) of the Act, the prescribed percentage of voting rights is 10%.

41. For the purpose of subsection 131(3) of the Act, **"take-over bid"** means "take-over bid" under any legislation that is set out in column 2 of an item of Schedule 2.

42. For the purpose of paragraph 131(4)(c) of the Act, the prescribed circumstances are that the insider

(a) entered into the purchase or sale as an agent pursuant to a specific unsolicited order to purchase or sell;

(b) made the purchase or sale pursuant to participation in an automatic dividend reinvestment plan, share purchase plan or other similar automatic plan that the insider entered into before the acquisition of the confidential information;

(c) made the purchase or sale to fulfil a legally binding obligation that the insider entered into before the acquisition of the confidential information; or

(d) purchased or sold the security as agent or trustee in the circumstances described in paragraph (b) or (c).

PART 5 — MEETINGS OF SHAREHOLDERS

Record Date

43. (1) Subject to subsection (3), for the purposes of paragraphs 134(l)(a), (b) and (e) of the Act, the prescribed period for the directors to fix the record date is not more than 60 days before the particular action to be taken.

(2) For the purposes of paragraphs 134(1)(c) and (d) of the Act, the prescribed period for the directors to fix the record date is not less than 21 days and not more than 60 days before the date of the meeting.

(3) For the purpose of subsection 134(3) of the Act, the prescribed period for the directors to provide notice of the record date shall begin not less than seven days before the date fixed.

Notice of Meetings

44. For the purpose of subsection 135(1) of the Act, the prescribed period for the directors to provide notice of the time and place of a meeting of shareholders is not less than 21 days and not more than 60 days before the meeting.

Communication Facilities

45. (1) For the purpose of subsection 141(3) of the Act, when a vote is to be taken at a meeting of shareholders, the voting may be carried out by means of a telephonic, electronic or other communication facility, if the facility

(a) enables the votes to be gathered in a manner that permits their subsequent verification; and

(b) permits the tallied votes to be presented to the corporation without it being possible for the corporation to identify how each shareholder or group of shareholders voted.

(2) For the purpose of subsection 141(4) of the Act, a person who is entitled to vote at a meeting of shareholders may vote by means of a telephonic, electronic or other communication facility, if the facility

(a) enables the vote to be gathered in a manner that permits its subsequent verification; and

(b) permits the tallied vote to be presented to the corporation without it being possible for the corporation to identify how the shareholder voted.

SOR/2003-317, s. 6

PART 6 — SHAREHOLDER PROPOSALS

46. For the purpose of subsection 137(1.1) and paragraph 261(1)(c.1) of the Act,

(a) the prescribed number of shares is the number of voting shares

(i) that is equal to 1% of the total number of the outstanding voting shares of the corporation, as of the day on which the shareholder submits a proposal, or

(ii) whose fair market value, as determined at the close of business on the day before the shareholder submits the proposal to the corporation, is at least $2,000; and

(b) the prescribed period is the six-month period immediately before the day on which the shareholder submits the proposal.

47. For the purpose of subsection 137(1.4) of the Act,

(a) a corporation may request that a shareholder provide the proof referred to in that subsection within 14 days after the corporation receives the shareholder's proposal; and

(b) the shareholder shall provide the proof within 21 days after the corporation's request.

48. For the purpose of subsection 137(3) of the Act, a proposal and a statement in support of it shall together consist of not more than 500 words.

49. For the purpose of paragraph 137(5)(a) of the Act, the prescribed number of days for submitting a proposal to the corporation is at least 90 days before the anniversary date.

50. For the purpose of paragraph 137(5)(c) of the Act, the prescribed period before the receipt of a proposal is two years.

51. (1) For the purpose of paragraph 137(5)(d) of the Act, the prescribed minimum amount of support for a shareholder's proposal is

(a) 3% of the total number of shares voted, if the proposal was introduced at an annual meeting of shareholders;

(b) 6% of the total number of shares voted at its last submission to shareholders, if the proposal was introduced at two annual meetings of shareholders; and

(c) 10% of the total number of shares voted at its last submission to shareholders, if the proposal was introduced at three or more annual meetings of shareholders.

(2) For the purpose of subsection (1), the prescribed period within which an annual meeting of shareholders must be held is five years before the receipt of a proposal.

52. For the purpose of subsection 137(5.1) of the Act, the prescribed period during which the corporation is not required to set out a proposal in a management proxy circular is two years.

53. For the purpose of subsection 137(7) of the Act, the prescribed period for giving notice is 21 days after the receipt by the corporation of the proposal or of proof of ownership under subsection 137(1.4) of the Act, as the case may be.

PART 7 — PROXIES AND PROXY SOLICITATION

Form of Proxy

54. (1) A form of proxy required by subsection 150(2) of the Act to be sent to the Director shall indicate, in bold-face type,

(a) the meeting at which it is to be used; and

(b) whether the proxy is solicited by or on behalf of the management of the corporation.

(2) A form of proxy shall contain a designated blank space for a date and shall state that, if it is not dated in the space, it is deemed to bear the date on which it is mailed by the person making the solicitation.

(3) A form of proxy, an accompanying management proxy circular or a dissident's proxy circular shall state, in bold-face type, that the shareholder may appoint a proxyholder, other than a person designated in the form of proxy, to attend and act on their behalf at the meeting, and shall contain instructions on the manner in which the shareholder may make the appointment.

(4) If a form of proxy designates a person as proxyholder, it shall provide a means for the shareholder to designate some other person as proxyholder.

(5) A form of proxy shall provide a means for the shareholder to specify that the shares registered in their name are to be voted for or against each matter or group of related matters identified in the notice of meeting or in a management proxy circular, dissident's proxy circular or proposal under section 137 of the Act, other than the appointment of an auditor and the election of directors.

(6) A form of proxy may confer authority with respect to matters for which a choice is not provided in accordance with subsection (5) if the form of proxy, the management proxy circular or the dissident's proxy circular states, in bold-face type, how the proxyholder will vote the shares in respect of each matter or group of related matters.

(7) A form of proxy shall provide a means for the shareholder to specify that the shares registered in their name are to be voted or withheld from voting in respect of the appointment of an auditor or the election of directors.

(8) A form of proxy, an accompanying management proxy circular or a dissident's proxy circular shall state that the shares represented by the proxy will be voted or withheld from voting, in accordance with the instructions of the shareholder, on any ballot that may be called for and that, if the shareholder specified a choice under subsection (5) or (7) with respect to any matter to be acted on, the shares will be voted accordingly.

(9) If a document referred to in subsection (1), (3) or (6) is sent in electronic form, the requirement in those subsections that certain information be set out in bold-face type is satisfied if the information in question is set out in some other manner so as to draw the attention of the addressee to the information.

55. A form of proxy may confer discretionary authority in respect of amendments to matters identified in the notice of meeting or other matters that may properly come before the meeting if

(a) the person by whom or on whose behalf the solicitation is made is not aware within a reasonable time before the solicitation that the amendments or other matters are to be presented for action at the meeting; and

(b) the form of proxy, the management proxy circular or the dissident's proxy circular specifically confers discretionary authority.

56. A form of proxy shall not confer authority to vote in respect of the appointment of an auditor or the election of a director unless a *bona fide* proposed nominee for the appointment or election is named in the form of proxy, management proxy circular, dissident's proxy circular or proposal under section 137 of the Act.

Contents of Management Proxy Circular

57. A management proxy circular shall contain the following information:

(a) a statement of the right of the shareholder to revoke a proxy under subsection 148(4) of the Act and of the method by which the shareholder may exercise that right;

(b) a statement that the solicitation is made by or on behalf of the management of the corporation;

(c) the name of any director of the corporation who has informed the management, in writing, that he or she intends to oppose any action intended to be taken by the management and the nature of the action that the director intends to oppose;

(d) the method of solicitation, if otherwise than by mail, and if the solicitation is to be made by specially engaged employees or agents, the material features of any contract or understanding for the solicitation, the parties to the contract or understanding and the cost or anticipated cost of the solicitation;

(e) the name of the person by whom the cost of the solicitation has been or will be borne, directly or indirectly;

(f) the number of shares of each class entitled to be voted at the meeting and the number of votes to which each share is entitled;

(g) the record date as of which the shareholders entitled to vote at the meeting will be determined or particulars as to the closing of the security transfer register, as the case may be, and, if the right to vote is not limited to shareholders of record as at a specified record date, any conditions in respect of that right to vote;

(h) if indemnification under section 124 of the Act is paid or becomes payable in the financial period,

(i) the amount paid or payable,

(ii) the name and title of the individual indemnified or to be indemnified, and

(iii) the circumstances that gave rise to the indemnity,

(i) if insurance referred to in subsection 124(6) of the Act is purchased,

(i) the amount or, if there is a comprehensive liability policy, the approximate amount of premiums paid by the corporation in respect of directors as a group and officers as a group or for both groups on an aggregate basis,

(ii) the aggregate amount of premiums, if any, paid by the individuals in each group,

(iii) the total amount of insurance purchased in respect of each group or for both groups on an aggregate basis, and

(iv) a summary of any deductibility or co-insurance clause or other provision in the insurance contract that exposes the corporation to liability in addition to the payment of the premiums;

(j) the name of each person who, to the knowledge of the directors or officers of the corporation, beneficially owns, directly or indirectly, or exercises control or direction over, shares carrying more than 10% of the votes attached to any class of shares entitled to vote in connection with any matters being proposed for consideration at the meeting, the approximate number of the shares so owned, controlled or directed by each person and the percentage of the class of voting shares represented by the number of shares so owned, controlled or directed;

(k) the percentage of votes required for the approval of any matter that is to be submitted to a vote of shareholders at the meeting, other than the election of directors;

(l) if action is to be taken with respect to the appointment of an auditor, the name of the proposed auditor, the name of each auditor appointed within the preceding five years and the date on which each auditor was first appointed;

(m) if directors are to be elected, a statement of the right of any class of shareholders to elect a specified number of directors or to cumulate their votes and of any conditions precedent to the exercise of the right;

(n) in tabular form, if directors are to be elected, so far as practicable with respect to each person proposed to be nominated by management for election as a director and each director whose term of office will continue after the meeting,

(i) the name of each person, the time when their term of office or the term of office for which they are a proposed nominee will expire and the last major position or office with the corporation or the corporation's holding body corporate held by them, indicating whether the person is a proposed nominee for election as a director at the meeting,

(ii) the present principal occupation or employment of each person, giving the name and principal business of any body corporate or other organization in which the occupation or employment is carried on, and the same information in respect of all principal occupations or employments held by them within the five preceding years, unless the person is now a director and was elected to the present term of office by a vote of shareholders at a meeting the notice of which was accompanied by a proxy circular containing that information,

(iii) if the person is or has been a director of the corporation, the period or periods during which they have so served,

(iv) the number of shares of each class of voting shares of the corporation and the corporation's holding body corporate and any of the corporation's subsidiaries beneficially owned, directly or indirectly, or over which control or direction is exercised, by each person, and

(v) if the voting shares are equal to more than 10% of the votes attached to all voting shares of the corporation, the corporation's holding body corporate or any of the corporation's subsidiaries, the approximate number of each class of shares, and the name of each associate;

(o) whether the corporation has an executive committee of its board of directors or is required to have an audit committee and, if so, the names of the directors who are members of each committee;

(p) the details of any contract or understanding between any proposed management nominee and any other person, except the directors and officers of the corporation acting solely in their capacity as such, under which the nominee is to be elected, including the name of the other person;

(q) the Statement of Executive Remuneration in the form fixed by the Director or, if the corporation is required by the laws of a jurisdiction set out in column 1 of an item of Schedule 3 to file the form or information with respect to executive remuneration that is set out in column 2 of that item, that form or information, when action is to be taken with respect to

(i) the election of directors,

(ii) any bonus, profit-sharing or other plan of remuneration, contract or understanding in which a director or an officer of the corporation will participate,

(iii) any pension or retirement plan of the corporation in which a director or an officer of the corporation will participate, or

(iv) the granting to a director or an officer of the corporation of any option or right to purchase securities, other than rights issued rateably to all shareholders or to all shareholders resident in Canada;

(r) if action is to be taken with respect to any of the matters referred to in subparagraphs (q)(i) to (iv),

(i) a statement setting out the largest aggregate amount of debt, except for indebtedness that has been entirely repaid on or before the date of the management proxy circular and routine indebtedness, that has been outstanding since the beginning of the corporation's last completed financial year, the nature of the indebtedness, the amount of debt that is currently outstanding, details of the transaction in which it was incurred, and the rate of interest paid or charged on it, in respect of the following persons who are or have been indebted to the corporation or any of its subsidiaries since the beginning of the last completed financial year in an aggregate amount that exceeds $25,000, namely,

(A) a director or an officer of the corporation,

(B) a person proposed by management as a nominee for election as a director of the corporation, and

(C) an associate of any person referred to in clause (A) or (B),

and for the purpose of this subparagraph, **"routine indebtedness"** means indebtedness described in any of the following, namely,

(D) if a corporation makes loans to employees of the corporation generally, whether or not in the ordinary course of business, the loans are considered routine indebtedness if made on terms, including those as to interest rate and security, no more favourable to the borrower than the terms on which loans are made by the corporation to employees generally, but the amount of any remaining unpaid loans to any one director, officer or person proposed as a nominee, and their associates, that is considered as routine indebtedness under this clause during the last completed financial year must not exceed $25,000,

(E) whether or not the corporation makes loans in the ordinary course of business, a loan made by it to one of its directors or officers is considered routine indebtedness if

(I) the borrower is a full-time employee of the corporation,

(II) the loan is fully secured against the borrower's residence, and

(III) the amount of the loan does not exceed the borrower's annual salary,

(F) if the corporation makes loans in the ordinary course of business, a loan is considered routine indebtedness if it is made to a person other than a full-time employee of the corporation or to any other body corporate and

(I) is made on substantially the same terms, including those as to interest rate and security, as loans made to other customers of the corporation with comparable credit ratings, and

(II) involves no more than usual risks of collectibility, or

(G) indebtedness arising from purchases made on usual trade terms or from ordinary travel or expense advances, or for similar reasons, is considered routine indebtedness if the repayment provisions are in accordance with usual commercial practice, or

(ii) if the corporation is required by the laws of a jurisdiction set out in column 1 of an item of Schedule 4 to file the form or information with respect to indebtedness of directors and officers that is set out in column 2 of that item, that form or information;

(s) subject to section 58, in any transaction since the beginning of the corporation's last completed financial year or in any proposed transaction that has materially affected or could materially affect the corporation or any of its subsidiaries,

(i) if not previously disclosed, the details, including, when practicable, the approximate amount of any material interest, direct or indirect, of

(A) a director or an officer of the corporation,

(B) a director or an officer of a body corporate that is itself an insider or a subsidiary of the corporation,

(C) a person proposed by management as a nominee for election as a director of the corporation,

(D) a shareholder required to be named under paragraph (j), and

(E) an associate or affiliate of any of the persons referred to in clauses (A) to (D),

(ii) the amounts and other details of transactions that are not required under subparagraph (i) and that involve remuneration paid, directly or indirectly, to any of the persons referred to in clauses (i)(A) to (E) for services in any capacity, unless the interest of the person arises solely from the beneficial ownership, direct or indirect, of less than 10% of any class of voting shares of another body corporate, or one of its subsidiaries, that provides services to the corporation, and

(iii) an interest arising from the ownership of securities of the corporation, if the security holder receives an advantage not shared rateably by all holders of the same class of security or all holders of the same class of security who are resident in Canada;

(t) details of each transaction referred to in paragraph (s), the name and address of each person whose interest in the transaction is disclosed and the nature of the relationship by reason of which the interest is required to be disclosed;

(u) when a transaction referred to in paragraph (s) involves the purchase or sale of assets by the corporation or any of its subsidiaries or holding bodies corporate otherwise than in the ordinary course of business, the cost of the assets to the purchaser and the cost of the assets to the seller, if the assets were acquired by the seller within two years before the transaction;

(v) details of a material underwriting discount or commission with respect to the sale of securities by the corporation if any person referred to in paragraph (s) has contracted or will contract with the corporation in respect of an underwriting or is an associate or affiliate of a person that has so contracted or will so contract;

(w) if a person other than the directors or officers of the corporation or any of its subsidiaries or holding bodies corporate manages the corporation or any of its subsidiaries, subject to the requirements of subparagraph (vi), the following information:

(i) details of the management agreement, including the name and address of every person who is a party to the agreement or who is responsible for its performance,

(ii) the name and full address, or, alternatively, solely the municipality of residence or postal address, of each insider of every body corporate with which the corporation or any of its subsidiaries has a management agreement,

(iii) the amounts paid or payable by the corporation and any of its subsidiaries to each person named under subparagraph (i) since the beginning of the corporation's last completed financial year,

(iv) details of any debt owed to the corporation or any of its subsidiaries by a person referred to in this paragraph, or by that person's associates or affiliates, that was outstanding at any time since the beginning of the corporation's last completed financial year,

(v) details of any transaction, other than one referred to in subparagraphs (i) to (iv), entered into with the corporation or any of its subsidiaries or holding bodies corporate since the beginning of the corporation's last completed financial year, in which a person referred to in subparagraph (i) or (ii) has a material interest that would otherwise be required to be disclosed under subparagraphs (i) to (iv), and

(vi) for the purpose of this paragraph,

(A) details of debt include the largest aggregate amount of debt outstanding at any time during the corporation's last completed financial year, the nature of the indebtedness, details of the transaction in which it was incurred, the amount at present outstanding and the rate of interest paid or charged on it,

(B) an amount owing for purchases, subject to usual trade terms, for ordinary travel and expense advances or for other transactions in the ordinary course of business may be omitted in determining debt, and

(C) any matter that is not material may be omitted;

(x) in any matter to be acted on at the meeting, other than the election of directors or the appointment of an auditor, details of any material interest, direct or indirect, by way of beneficial ownership of securities or otherwise, of

(i) each director or officer of the corporation at any time since the beginning of its last completed financial year,

(ii) each person proposed by management as a nominee for election as a director of the corporation, and

(iii) each affiliate or associate of any of the persons referred to in subparagraph (i) or (ii);

(y) if action is to be taken with respect to the authorization or issue of securities, except to exchange the securities for other securities of the corporation,

(i) the designation and number or amount of securities to be authorized or issued,

(ii) a description of the securities, but

(A) if the terms of securities to be authorized cannot be stated because no issue of securities is contemplated in the immediate future, and if no further authorization by shareholders for their issue is to be obtained, a statement that the terms of the securities to be authorized, including dividend or interest rates, conversion prices, voting rights, redemption prices, maturity dates and other matters will be determined by the directors, and

(B) if the securities are shares of an existing class, the description required, except for a statement of any pre-emptive rights, may be omitted,

(iii) details of the transaction in which the securities are to be issued, including the nature and approximate amount of the consideration received or to be received by the corporation and the purpose for which the consideration has been or is to be used,

(iv) if it is impracticable to furnish the details required under subparagraph (iii), a statement indicating the reason why it is impracticable, the purpose of the authorization and whether shareholders' approval for the issue of the securities will be sought, and

(v) if the securities are to be issued other than in a general public offering for money or other than rateably to all holders of the same class of securities or all holders of the same class of securities who are resident in Canada, the reasons for the proposed authorization or issue and its effect on the rights of present security holders;

(z) if action is to be taken under section 173 or 174 of the Act to modify the rights, privileges, restrictions or conditions attached to any class of securities of the corporation or to authorize or issue securities in order to exchange them for other securities of the corporation,

(i) the designation and number or amount of outstanding securities that are to be modified, and, if securities are to be issued in exchange, the designation and number or amount of securities to be exchanged and the basis of the exchange,

(ii) details of material differences between the outstanding securities and the modified or new securities,

(iii) the reasons for the proposed modification or exchange and the general effect on the rights of existing security holders,

(iv) a brief statement of arrears in dividends or of defaults in principal or interest in respect of the outstanding securities that are to be modified or exchanged, and

(v) all other information material to the proposed modification or exchange, including, if the corporation is a distributing corporation, information required to be included in a prospectus or other similar document under the securities laws of any of the provinces of Canada, unless an exemption from the laws is available or a waiver of the laws or similar relief is granted by the relevant provincial securities regulator;

(z.1) the material features of a plan, including the reasons for it and its general effect on the rights of existing security holders, if action is to be taken with respect to that plan and the plan is for

(i) an amalgamation with another corporation otherwise than under section 184 of the Act,

(ii) a continuance under the laws of another jurisdiction under section 188 of the Act,

(iii) a sale, lease or exchange of all or substantially all of the property of the corporation under subsection 189(3) of the Act, or

(iv) the liquidation or dissolution of the corporation;

(z.2) if action is to be taken with respect to a plan referred to in subparagraph (z.1)(i), a statement that contains, with respect to the corporation and the other body corporate,

(i) a brief description of the business,

(ii) the location and general character of the plants and other important physical properties,

(iii) a brief description of arrears in dividends or defaults in principal or interest in respect of securities of the corporation or body corporate and of the effect of the plan,

(iv) the existing and *pro forma* share and loan capital, in tabular form,

(v) a historical summary of earnings, in tabular form, for each of the last five fiscal years, including per-share amounts of net earnings, dividends declared for each year and book value per share at the end of the most recent fiscal year,

(vi) a combined *pro forma* summary of earnings, in tabular form, for each of the last five fiscal years that indicates the aggregate and per-share earnings for each year and the *pro forma* book value per share at the end of the most recent fiscal year, but if the transaction will establish a new basis of accounting for the assets of the corporation or body corporate, the *pro forma* summary of earnings may be provided only for the most recent fiscal year and interim period and shall reflect appropriate *pro forma* adjustments resulting from the new basis of accounting,

(vii) the high and low sale prices for each quarterly period within the previous two years for each class of securities of the corporation and of the other body corporate that is traded on a stock exchange and that will be materially affected by the plan, and

(viii) an introductory summary, not more than six pages long, of the contents of the proxy circular that highlights the salient features of the transaction, including a summary of the financial information, with appropriate cross-references to the more detailed information in the circular;

(z.3) if action is to be taken with respect to a plan referred to in paragraph (z.1), unless an exemption from the applicable laws is available or a waiver of the laws or similar relief is granted by the relevant securities regulator, the financial statements of the corporation that would be required to be included in a prospectus under the laws of

(i) Ontario,

(ii) Quebec,

(iii) Manitoba,

(iv) British Columbia,

(v) Saskatchewan,

(vi) Alberta, or

(vii) the United States;

(z.4) if action is to be taken as described in paragraph (z.2), unless an exemption from the applicable laws is available or a waiver of the laws or similar relief is granted by the relevant securities regulator, the financial statements of the other corporation that would be required to be included in a prospectus under the laws of

(i) Ontario,

(ii) Quebec,

(iii) Manitoba,

(iv) British Columbia,

(v) Saskatchewan,

(vi) Alberta, or

(vii) the United States;

(z.5) a statement of the right of a shareholder to dissent under section 190 of the Act with respect to any matter to be acted on at the meeting and a brief summary of the procedure to be followed;

(z.6) if action is to be taken with respect to any matter other than the approval of financial statements, including alterations of share capital, amendments to articles, property disposition, amalgamation, arrangements or reorganizations, the substance of each matter or group of related matters, to the extent that it has not been described in paragraphs (a) to (z.5) in sufficient detail to permit shareholders to form a reasoned judgment concerning the matter, and if any of the matters is not required to be submitted to a vote of the shareholders, the reasons for submitting it and the action intended to be taken by management in the event of a negative vote by the shareholders;

(z.7) if the giving of any financial assistance was material to the corporation or any of its affiliates or to the recipient of the assistance, details of that financial assistance by the corporation since the beginning of its last completed financial year in relation to

(i) a shareholder of the corporation or any of its affiliates who is not a director, officer or employee thereof, or to an associate of any such shareholder, or

(ii) any person, in connection with a purchase of shares issued or to be issued by the corporation;

(z.8) a statement, signed by a director or an officer of the corporation, that the contents and the sending of the circular have been approved by the directors; and

(z.9) a statement indicating the final date by which the corporation must receive a proposal for any matter that a person entitled to vote at an annual meeting proposes to raise at the next annual meeting.

58. An interest may be omitted from a management proxy circular if

(a) the rate or charges involved are fixed by law or determined by competitive bids;

(b) the interest of the person in the transaction is solely that of a director of another body corporate that is a party to the transaction;

(c) the transaction involves services as a bank or other depository of funds, transfer agent, registrar or trustee under a trust indenture or other similar services; or

(d) the transaction does not involve, directly or indirectly, remuneration for services and the interest of the person results from the beneficial ownership, direct or indirect, of less than 10% of any class of voting shares of another body corporate that is a party to the transaction, the transaction is in the ordinary course of business of the corporation or one of its subsidiaries and the amount of the transaction or series of transactions is less than 10% of the total sales or purchases, as the case may be, of the corporation and its subsidiaries for their last completed financial year.

59. A management proxy circular sent to the Director shall be submitted with a statement, signed by a director or an officer of the corporation, that a copy of the circular has been sent to each director, each shareholder whose proxy is solicited and the auditor of the corporation.

Dissident's Proxy Circular

60. For the purpose of section 61, **"dissident"** means a person, other than the management of the corporation and its affiliates and associates, by or on behalf of whom a solicitation is made, and includes a committee or group that solicits proxies, any member of the committee or group and any person whether or not named as a member who, acting alone or with one or more other persons, directly or indirectly takes the initiative or engages in organizing, directing or financing the committee or group, except

(a) a person who contributes not more than $250 and who is not otherwise a person by whom or on whose behalf the solicitation is made;

(b) a bank or other lending institution or a broker or dealer that, in the ordinary course of business, lends money or executes orders for the purchase or sale of shares and is not otherwise a person by whom or on whose behalf the solicitation is made;

(c) a person retained or employed by a person by whom or on whose behalf the solicitation is made to solicit proxies and who is not otherwise a person by whom or on whose behalf the solicitation is made;

(d) a person who only transmits proxy soliciting material or performs administrative or clerical duties in connection with the solicitation;

(e) a person employed or retained by a person by whom or on whose behalf the solicitation is made in the capacity of lawyer, accountant, publicity agent or financial or public relations adviser, and whose activities are limited to the performance of duties in the course of the employment or retainment;

(f) a person who is regularly employed as an officer or employee of the corporation or any of its affiliates and who is not otherwise a person by whom or on whose behalf the solicitation is made; and

(g) an officer or a director of, or a person employed by, a person by or on behalf of whom the solicitation is made, if the officer, director or employee is not otherwise a person by whom or on whose behalf the solicitation is made.

Contents of Dissident's Proxy Circular

61. A dissident's proxy circular shall contain the following information:

(a) the name of the corporation to which it relates;

(b) the information required by paragraphs 57(a), (d) and (e);

(c) details of the identity and background of each dissident, including

(i) their name and address,

(ii) their present principal occupation or employment and the name, principal business and address of any body corporate or other person in which the occupation or employment is carried on, and

(iii) all convictions in connection with violations of any corporate or securities laws or criminal convictions in a matter of an economic nature, such as fraud or market manipulation, during the preceding 10 years, for which a pardon has not been granted, and the date and nature of each conviction, the name and location of the court and the sentence imposed;

(d) details of any material interest of the dissident, direct or indirect, by way of beneficial ownership of securities or otherwise, in any matter to be acted on and the interest of the dissident in the securities of the corporation to which the solicitation relates, including

(i) the number of shares in each class of the corporation and of its affiliates and associates that the dissident beneficially owns or over which they exercise control or direction,

(ii) the dates on which securities of the corporation were purchased or sold during the preceding two years, the amount purchased or sold on each date and the price at which they were purchased or sold,

(iii) if any part of the purchase price or market value of any of the securities specified in subparagraph (ii) is represented by funds borrowed or otherwise obtained for the purpose of acquiring or holding the securities, the amount of the indebtedness as of the latest practicable date and a brief description of the transaction, including the names of the parties other than a bank, broker or dealer acting in the transaction in the ordinary course of business,

(iv) whether the dissident is, or was within the preceding year, a party to a contract or an understanding with any person in respect of securities of the corporation, including joint ventures, loans or option provisions, puts or calls, guarantees against loss or guarantees of profit, division of losses or profits and the giving or withholding of proxies and, if so, the names of the parties and the details of the contract or understanding, and

(v) the number of shares in each class of the corporation or one of its affiliates that any associate of the dissident beneficially owns, directly or indirectly, or over which they exercise control or direction, as well as the name and address of each associate;

(e) if directors are to be elected, the information required by paragraphs 57(n), (p), (s) and (x) in respect of each nominee proposed by the dissident for election as a director and in respect of the associates of each nominee;

(f) the information required by paragraphs 57(s) and (x) in respect of each dissident and each dissident's associate; and

(g) the details of any contract or understanding, including the names of the parties, between a dissident or any of the dissident's associates, and any other person with respect to

(i) future employment by the corporation or any of its affiliates, or

(ii) future transactions to which the corporation or any of its affiliates will or may be a party.

62. If a dissident is a partnership, a body corporate, an association or another organization, the information required by paragraphs 61(c) and (d) to be included in a dissident's proxy circular shall be given in respect of each partner, officer and director of, and each person who controls, the dissident but who is not a dissident.

63. Information that is not known to a dissident and that cannot be ascertained by them on reasonable inquiry may be omitted from a dissident's proxy circular, but the circumstances that render the information unavailable shall be disclosed in the proxy circular.

64. (1) A dissident's proxy circular shall contain a statement signed by the dissident or a person authorized by them that the contents and the sending of the circular have been approved by the dissident.

(2) A dissident's proxy circular that is sent to the Director under subsection 150(2) of the Act shall be accompanied by a statement signed by a dissident or a person authorized by them that

(a) the circular complies with these Regulations; and

(b) a copy of the circular has been sent to each director, to each shareholder whose proxy has been solicited and to the auditor of the corporation.

Date of Proxy Circular and Information

65. A proxy circular shall be dated as of a date not more than 30 days before the date on which it is first sent to a shareholder of the corporation and the information, other than financial statements, required to be contained in it shall be given as of the date of the circular.

Financial Statements in Proxy Circular

66. (1) If financial statements accompany or form part of a management proxy circular, the statements shall be prepared in the manner described in Part 8.

(2) The financial statements referred to in subsection (1), if not reported on by the auditor of the corporation, shall be accompanied by a report of the chief financial officer of the corporation stating that the financial statements have not been audited but have been prepared in the manner described in Part 8.

Proxy Circular Exemptions

67. For the purpose of subparagraph (b)(v) of the definition "solicit" or "solicitation" in section 147 of the Act, a solicitation does not include a public announcement that is made by

(a) a speech in a public forum; or

(b) a press release, an opinion, a statement or an advertisement provided through a broadcast medium or by a telephonic, electronic or other communication facility, or appearing in a newspaper, a magazine or other publication generally available to the public.

68. (1) For the purpose of subparagraph (b)(vii) of the definition "solicit" or "solicitation" in section 147 of the Act, the prescribed circumstances are circumstances in which the communication is made to shareholders

(a) by one or more shareholders and concerns the business and affairs of a corporation — including its management or proposals contained in a management proxy circular — and no form of proxy is sent to those shareholders by the shareholder or shareholders making the communication or by a person acting on their behalf;

(b) by one or more shareholders and concerns the organization of a dissident's proxy solicitation, and no form of proxy is sent to those shareholders by the shareholder or shareholders making the communication or by a person acting on their behalf;

(c) as clients, by a person who gives financial, corporate governance or proxy voting advice in the ordinary course of business and concerns proxy voting advice if

(i) the person discloses to the shareholder any significant relationship with the corporation and any of its affiliates or with a shareholder who has submitted a proposal pursuant to subsection 137(1) of the Act and any material interests the person has in relation to a matter on which advice is given,

(ii) the person receives any special commission or remuneration for giving the proxy voting advice only from the shareholder or shareholders receiving the advice, and

(iii) the proxy voting advice is not given on behalf of any person soliciting proxies or on behalf of a nominee for election as a director; or

(d) by a person who does not seek directly or indirectly, the power to act as proxy for a shareholder.

(2) The circumstances described in paragraph (1)(a) are not prescribed circumstances if the communication is made by

(a) a shareholder who is an officer or director of the corporation, or who serves in a similar capacity, if the communication is financed directly or indirectly by the corporation;

(b) a shareholder who is a nominee or who proposes a nominee for election as a director, if the communication relates to the election of directors;

(c) a shareholder whose communication is in opposition to an amalgamation, arrangement, consolidation or other transaction recommended or approved by the board of directors of the corporation and who is proposing or intends to propose an alternative transaction to which the shareholder or an affiliate or associate of the shareholder is a party;

(d) a shareholder who, because of a material interest in the subject-matter to be voted on at a shareholders meeting, is likely to receive a benefit from its approval or non-approval, which benefit would not be shared *pro rata* by all other holders of the same class of shares, unless the benefit arises from the shareholder's employment with the corporation; or

(e) any person acting on behalf of a shareholder described in any of paragraphs (a) to (d).

69. (1) For the purpose of subsection 150(1.2) of the Act, the prescribed circumstances are circumstances in which the solicitation conveyed by public broadcast, speech or publication contains the information required under paragraphs 61(a) to (d) and (f).

(2) A person making a solicitation referred to in subsection (1) shall send the required information and a copy of any related written communication to the Director and to the corporation before soliciting proxies.

PART 8 — FINANCIAL DISCLOSURE

Interpretation
[Heading amended SOR/2005-51, s. 1.]

70. The following definitions apply in this Part.

"Canadian GAAP" means generally accepted accounting principles as set out in the *Handbook of the Canadian Institute of Chartered Accountants*, as amended from time to time. *("PCGR canadiens")*

"Canadian GAAS" means generally accepted auditing standards as set out in the *Handbook of the Canadian Institute of Chartered Accountants*, as amended from time to time. *("PVGR canadiens")*

"NI 52-107" means National Instrument 52-107 of the Canadian Securities Administrators, entitled *Acceptable Accounting Principles, Auditing Standards and Reporting Currency* and published January 16, 2004, as amended from time to time. *("Règlement 52-107")*

"SEC" means the United States Securities and Exchange Commission. *("SEC")*

"SEC registrant" means a corporation that

(a) has securities registered under section 12 of the *Securities Exchange Act of 1934* of the United States, as amended from time to time, or is required to file reports under section 15(d) of that Act; and

(b) is not registered or required to be registered as an investment company under the *Investment Company Act of 1940* of the United States, as amended from time to time.

("société inscrite auprès de la SEC")

"US GAAP" means the generally accepted accounting principles established by the Financial Accounting Standards Board of the United States, as amended from time to time. *("PCGR américains")*

"US GAAS" means the generally accepted auditing standards established by the Public Company Accounting Oversight Board of the United States, as amended from time to time. *("PVGR américains")*

SOR/2005-51, s. 1

Financial Statements
[Heading added SOR/2005-51, s. 1.]

71. (1) Subject to subsection (2), the annual financial statements referred to in paragraph 155(1)(a) of the Act shall be prepared in accordance with Canadian GAAP.

(2) For an SEC registrant, the financial statements may be prepared in accordance with US GAAP.

(3) For the first financial year in which the change from Canadian GAAP to US GAAP takes place, and for the following financial year, the notes to the financial statements shall

(a) explain the material differences between Canadian GAAP and US GAAP that relate to recognition, measurement and presentation;

(b) quantify the effect of the material differences between Canadian GAAP and US GAAP that relate to recognition, measurement and presentation, including a tabular reconciliation between the net income reported in the financial statements and the net income computed in accordance with Canadian GAAP; and

(c) provide information consistent with disclosure requirements of Canadian GAAP to the extent not already reflected in the financial statements.

(4) If the financial statements of an SEC registrant were prepared in accordance with both Canadian GAAP and US GAAP for two years or more before the first financial year in which the statements were prepared in accordance with US GAAP only, for the first financial year in which the change from Canadian GAAP to US GAAP takes place, a note shall accompany the financial statements that

(a) explains the material differences between Canadian GAAP and US GAAP that relate to recognition, measurement and presentation; and

(b) quantifies the effect of the material differences between Canadian GAAP and US GAAP that relate to recognition, measurement and presentation, including a tabular reconciliation between the net income as previously reported in the most recent financial statements, annual or otherwise, prepared in accordance with Canadian GAAP and the net income as restated and presented in accordance with US GAAP.

(5) If the financial statements of an SEC registrant were prepared in accordance with both Canadian GAAP and US GAAP for less than two years before the first financial year in which the statements were prepared in accordance with US GAAP only, for the first financial year in which the change from Canadian GAAP to US GAAP takes place, the following shall be presented with the financial statements:

(a) the financial information as previously reported under provincial securities legislation in the most recent financial statements, annual or otherwise, in accordance with Canadian GAAP;

(b) the financial information referred to in paragraph (a) as restated and presented in accordance with US GAAP; and

(c) an accompanying note supporting the comparative information required under paragraphs (a) and (b) that

(i) explains the material differences between Canadian GAAP and US GAAP that relate to recognition, measurement and presentation, and

(ii) quantifies the effect of the material differences between Canadian GAAP and US GAAP that relate to recognition, measurement and presentation, including a tabular reconciliation between the net income as previously reported in the most recent financial statements, annual or otherwise, prepared in accordance with Canadian GAAP and the net income as restated and presented in accordance with US GAAP.

(6) The comparative information required under paragraphs (5)(a) and (b) shall be presented either on the face of the financial statements or in the note to those statements referred to in paragraph (5)(c).

(7) The financial statements shall contain a note stating whether the statements have been prepared in accordance with Canadian GAAP or US GAAP.

(8) For greater certainty, subsections (3) to (6) do not apply to the financial statements of an SEC registrant that was incorporated after March 15, 2005, and that, since that date, has prepared its financial statements in accordance with US GAAP only.

SOR/2005-51, s. 1

Auditor's Report
[Heading added SOR/2005-51, s. 1.]

71.1 (1) Subject to subsection (2), the auditor's report referred to in section 169 of the Act shall be prepared in accordance with Canadian GAAS.

(2) For an SEC registrant that has prepared its financial statements in accordance with US GAAP and subsections 71(3) to (6), and whose auditors are in compliance with the professional practice standards established or adopted by the Public Company Accounting Oversight Board of the United States, the auditor's report may be prepared in accordance with US GAAS.

(3) If the auditor's report referred to in subsection (2) is prepared in accordance with US GAAS, it shall comply with section 4.2 of NI 52-107, but for the purpose of applying that section,

(a) the expression **"US GAAS"** has the meaning assigned to that expression by section 70 of these Regulations; and

(b) the expression **"SEC issuer"** has the meaning assigned to the expression **"SEC registrant"** by section 70 of these Regulations.

SOR/2005-51, s. 1

Contents of Financial Statements

72. (1) The financial statements referred to in section 155 of the Act shall include at least

(a) a balance sheet;

(b) a statement of retained earnings;

(c) an income statement; and

(d) a statement of changes in financial position.

(2) Financial statements need not be designated by the names set out in paragraphs (l)(a) to (d).

PART 9 — CONSTRAINED SHARE CORPORATIONS

Interpretation

73. The following definitions apply in this Part.

"Canadian" means

(a) a resident Canadian;

(b) a partnership of which a majority of the members are resident Canadians and in which interests representing more than 50% of the total value of the partnership property are owned by resident Canadians;

(c) a trust established by a resident Canadian

(i) a majority of the trustees of which are resident Canadians, or

(ii) in which beneficial interests representing more than 50% of the total value of the trust property are owned by resident Canadians;

(d) Her Majesty in right of Canada or of a province or territory of Canada or a municipal corporation or public board or commission in Canada; or

(e) a body corporate

(i) incorporated under the laws of Canada or a province,

(ii) of which a majority of the directors are resident Canadians, and

(iii) over which persons described in any of paragraphs (a) to (d) or in this paragraph exercise control or direction or of which the persons beneficially own shares or securities currently convertible into shares carrying more than 50% of the voting rights under all circumstances or by reason of the occurrence of an event that has occurred and that is continuing, including currently exercisable options or rights to acquire the shares or convertible securities.

("Canadien")

"constrained class" means the class of persons specified in the articles of a constrained share corporation as being ineligible to hold, as a class, more than the maximum aggregate holdings. *("catégorie restreinte")*

"constrained share corporation" means a corporation that has provisions in its articles imposing a constraint. *("société par actions à participation restreinte")*

"constraint" means a restriction on

(a) the issue or transfer of shares of any class or series to persons who are not resident Canadians;

(b) the issue or transfer of shares of any class or series to enable a corporation or any of its affiliates or associates to qualify under a law referred to in paragraph 87(1)(a)

(i) to obtain a licence to carry on any business,

(ii) to become a publisher of a Canadian newspaper or periodical, or

(iii) to acquire shares of a financial intermediary as defined in paragraph 87(1)(b); or

(c) the issue, transfer or ownership of shares of any class or series in order to assist a corporation or any of its affiliates or associates to qualify under a law referred to in subsection 87(2) to receive licences, permits, grants, payments or other benefits by reason of attaining or maintaining a specified level of Canadian ownership or control.

("restriction")

"control" means control in any manner that results in control in fact, whether directly through the ownership of shares or indirectly through a trust, a contract, the ownership of shares of any other body corporate or otherwise. *("contrôle")*

"maximum aggregate holdings" means the total number of voting shares of a constrained share corporation that may be held by or on behalf of persons in the constrained class and their associates in accordance with the articles of the corporation. *("avoir maximum total")*

"maximum individual holdings" means the total number of voting shares of a constrained share corporation that may be held by or on behalf of any one person in the constrained class and their associates in accordance with the articles of the corporation. *("avoir maximum individuel")*

"voting share" means a share that is subject to a constraint referred to in paragraph (a) or (b) of the definition "constraint" and that carries voting rights under all circumstances or by reason of the occurrence of an event that has occurred and that is continuing, and includes a security currently convertible into such a share and a currently exercisable option or right to acquire such a share or convertible security. *("action avec droit de vote")*

Disclosure Required

74. Each of the following documents issued or published by a constrained share corporation shall indicate conspicuously the general nature of its constrained share provisions:

(a) a certificate representing a voting share;

(b) a management proxy circular; and

(c) a prospectus, statement of material facts, registration statement or similar document.

Powers and Duties of Directors

75. (1) The directors of a constrained share corporation that has provisions in its articles imposing a constraint referred to in paragraph (a) or (b) of the definition "constraint" in section 73 shall refuse to register a transfer of a voting share of the corporation in accordance with the articles if

(a) the total number of voting shares held by or on behalf of persons in the constrained class exceeds the maximum aggregate holdings and the transfer is to a person in the constrained class;

(b) the total number of voting shares held by or on behalf of persons in the constrained class does not exceed the maximum aggregate holdings and the transfer would cause the number of shares held by persons in the constrained class to exceed the maximum aggregate holdings;

(c) the total number of voting shares held by or on behalf of a person in the constrained class exceeds the maximum individual holdings and the transfer is to that person; or

(d) the total number of voting shares held by or on behalf of a person in the constrained class does not exceed the maximum individual holdings and the transfer would cause the number of shares held by that person to exceed the maximum individual holdings.

(2) Despite subsection (1), the directors of a constrained share corporation that is described in that subsection shall register a transfer of a voting share of the corporation to a person in the constrained class if that person establishes that they were the beneficial owner of that share on the day on which the corporation became a constrained share corporation.

(3) The directors of a constrained share corporation that is described in subsection (1) shall not issue a voting share of the corporation to a person in the constrained class if the directors are required by that subsection to refuse to register a transfer of the share.

(4) For the purpose of subsection (3), the directors may count as issued shares the voting shares that the corporation is currently offering to its shareholders or prospective shareholders.

76. The directors of a constrained share corporation that has provisions in its articles imposing a constraint referred to in paragraph (c) of the definition "constraint" in section 73

   (a) shall not issue a share of the corporation to a person

      (i) whose ownership of the share would be contrary to the constraint,

      (ii) who, in respect of the issue of the share, has been requested by the corporation to provide it with information referred to in subsection 80(7) and has not provided the information, or

      (iii) whose ownership of the share the directors have determined, on the basis of information provided to the corporation by that person under a request referred to in subparagraph (ii), may be contrary to the constraint; and

   (b) shall refuse to register a transfer of a share of the corporation if the transfer is to a person

      (i) whose ownership of the share is contrary to the constraint,

      (ii) who, in respect of the registration of the share, has been requested by the corporation to provide it with information referred to in subsection 80(7) and has not provided the information, or

      (iii) whose ownership of the share the directors have determined, on the basis of information provided to the corporation by that person under a request referred to in subparagraph (ii), may be contrary to the constraint.

Limitation on Voting Rights

77. Sections 78 and 79 apply to a constrained share corporation that has provisions in its articles imposing a constraint referred to in paragraph (a) or (b) of the definition "constraint" in section 73.

78. (1) If, on the day on which a corporation becomes a constrained share corporation, the total number of voting shares of the corporation held by or on behalf of a person in the constrained class exceeds the maximum individual holdings, the person or their nominee may only, in person or by proxy, exercise the voting rights attached to the maximum individual holdings so held on that day or on any later day.

(2) After the total number of shares held by or on behalf of the person referred to in subsection (1) is reduced below the maximum individual holdings, they or their nominee may, in person or by proxy, exercise the voting rights attached to shares held.

79. (1) Except as provided in subsection 78(1), if the total number of voting shares of a constrained share corporation held by or on behalf of a person in the constrained class exceeds the maximum individual holdings, no person shall, in person or by proxy, exercise the voting rights attached to those shares.

(2) If it appears from the securities register of a constrained share corporation that the total number of voting shares held by a shareholder is less than the maximum individual holdings, a proxyholder for the shareholder may vote those shares unless the proxyholder has knowledge that the shares beneficially owned by the shareholder exceed the maximum individual holdings.

(3) If, after the day on which a corporation becomes a constrained share corporation, a corporation or trust that was not a person in the constrained class becomes a person in the constrained class, the corporation or trust shall not exercise the voting rights attached to any shares it holds in the constrained share corporation while it is a person in the constrained class.

Sale of Constrained Shares

80. (1) For the purpose of subsection 46(1) of the Act, before a constrained share corporation concludes that shares of the corporation are owned contrary to a constraint referred to in paragraph (c) of the definition "constraint" in section 73 or the directors of the corporation determine that shares of the corporation may be owned contrary to the constraint, the corporation shall send by registered mail a written notice in accordance with subsection (5) to the person shown in the securities register of the corporation as the holder of the shares.

(2) For the purpose of subsection 46(1) of the Act, in determining that shares of a constrained share corporation may be owned contrary to a constraint referred to in paragraph (c) of the definition "constraint" in section 73, the directors of the corporation shall

(a) ascertain whether or not the corporation has received a reply to a request for information referred to in subsection (7) respecting the shares and consider the reply, if any, to the request; and

(b) examine and consider any other records of the corporation that contain information that would indicate whether the shares are owned contrary to the constraint.

(3) For the purpose of subsection 46(1) of the Act, if a constrained share corporation has sent a notice referred to in subsection (1) to a person shown in the securities register of the corporation as the holder of shares and the corporation intends to sell all or some of the shares under subsection 46(1) of the Act, the corporation shall, not less than 90 days but not more than 150 days after sending the notice, send to that person by registered mail a further written notice in accordance with subsection (6) respecting the shares that the corporation intends to sell, if

(a) the corporation has concluded that shares in respect of which the notice was sent are owned contrary to a constraint referred to in paragraph (c) of the definition "constraint" in section 73; or

(b) the directors of the corporation have determined in accordance with subsection (2) that shares in respect of which the notice was sent may be owned contrary to the constraint.

(4) When a corporation sends a notice under subsection (1) or (3), it shall, at the time the notice is sent, enter or cause to be entered in the securities register of the corporation the particulars of the notice, including the date on which it was sent.

(5) The notice referred to in subsection (1) shall contain

(a) the name and address of the holder of the shares as shown in the securities register of the corporation;

(b) a statement that identifies the certificate that represents the shares, by certificate number or otherwise;

(c) a statement that indicates that all or some of the shares may be sold by the corporation under subsection 46(1) of the Act if the shares are owned, or the directors of the corporation determine in accordance with subsection (2) that the shares may be owned, contrary to a constraint referred to in paragraph (c) of the definition "constraint" in section 73;

(d) a statement that indicates that the corporation may conclude that all or some of the shares are owned contrary to a constraint referred to in paragraph (c) of the definition "constraint" in section 73;

(e) a statement that indicates that the directors of the corporation may determine in accordance with subsection (2) that all or some of the shares may be owned contrary to a constraint referred to in paragraph (c) of the definition "constraint" in section 73 and that, for the purpose of making the determination, the directors of the corporation will

(i) consider the reply, if any, to a request for information referred to in subsection (7) respecting the shares, and

(ii) examine and consider any other records of the corporation that contain information that would indicate whether the shares are owned contrary to the constraint;

(f) a statement that indicates that no share in respect of which the notice is sent may be sold under subsection 46(1) of the Act if a transfer of the share is registered in the securities register of the corporation after the notice was sent, unless the corporation again complies with the requirements set out in this Part respecting the sale of the share;

(g) a statement that indicates that no share in respect of which the notice is sent may be sold under subsection 46(1) of the Act unless not less than 60 days but not more than 150 days have elapsed after the day on which a notice referred to in subsection (3) is sent to the holder of the share;

(h) a statement that indicates the earliest date and the latest date on which the corporation may sell the shares, having regard to the requirements of section 82;

(i) a statement that indicates that the shares may be sold on any stock exchange if shares of the corporation are listed and posted for trading or, if shares of the corporation are not listed and posted for trading on a stock exchange, in any other manner that the directors of the corporation determine to be appropriate;

(j) a statement that indicates that, if not all the shares of the holder represented by a certificate are sold under subsection 46(1) of the Act, a certificate that represents the shares that are not sold will be issued on surrender for cancellation of the certificate that represents the shares sold; and

(k) a statement that indicates that, immediately after the sale of the shares under subsection 46(1) of the Act, the corporation will

(i) register the transfer or a notice of the sale of the shares or cause the transfer or a notice of the sale of the shares to be registered in the securities register of the corporation, and

(ii) send a notice of the sale in accordance with paragraph 83(1)(b) to the person shown in the securities register of the corporation as the holder of the shares at the time of sale.

(6) The notice referred to in subsection (3) shall contain

(a) the name and address of the holder of the shares as shown in the securities register of the corporation;

(b) a statement that identifies the certificate that represents the shares, by certificate number or otherwise;

(c) a statement that indicates that all or some of the shares may be sold by the corporation under subsection 46(1) of the Act if the shares are owned, or the directors of the corporation determine in accordance with subsection (2) that the shares may be owned, contrary to a constraint referred to in paragraph (c) of the definition "constraint" in section 73;

(d) a statement that indicates that the corporation has concluded that the shares are owned, or that the directors of the corporation have determined in accordance with subsection (2) that the shares may be owned, contrary to a constraint referred to in paragraph (c) of the definition "constraint" in section 73 and that indicates the reason why the corporation so concluded or the directors so determined, as the case may be;

(e) a statement that indicates that the corporation intends to sell all or a specified number of the shares under subsection 46(1) of the Act;

(f) a statement that indicates that, if before the sale the corporation changes its conclusion that the shares are owned, or the directors of the corporation change their determination made in accordance with subsection (2) that the shares may be owned, contrary to a constraint referred to in paragraph (c) of the definition "constraint" in section 73, or there is a change in the reason for the conclusion or determination, the corporation will send a notice in accordance with subsection 81(1) to the person shown in the securities register of the corporation as the holder of the shares;

(g) a statement that advises that, unless the person shown in the securities register of the corporation as the holder of the shares receives a notice referred to in paragraph (f), the person and all other interested persons should not assume that

(i) the corporation has changed its conclusion that the shares are owned, or the directors of the corporation have changed their determination made in accordance with subsection (2) that the shares may be owned, contrary to a constraint referred to in paragraph (c) of the definition "constraint" in section 73,

(ii) there has been a change in the reason for the conclusion or determination, or

(iii) the corporation no longer intends to sell the shares under subsection 46(1) of the Act;

(h) a statement that indicates that no share in respect of which the notice is sent maybe sold under subsection 46(1) of the Act if a transfer of the share is registered in the securities register of the corporation after the notice referred to in subsection (1) was sent, unless the corporation again complies with the requirements set out in this Part respecting the sale of the share;

(i) a statement that indicates that no share in respect of which the notice is sent may be sold under subsection 46(1) of the Act unless not less than 60 days but not more than 150 days have elapsed from the day on which the notice was sent to the holder of the share; and

(j) a statement that indicates each of the matters referred to in paragraphs (5)(h) to (k).

(7) The notice referred to in subsection (1) shall be accompanied by a request for the information, including a request for the completion of the forms, that would indicate whether the shares are owned contrary to a constraint referred to in paragraph (c) of the definition "constraint" in section 73.

(8) The notice referred to in subsection (3) shall be accompanied by a request for information referred to in subsection (7), unless the corporation has received the requested information before the notice is sent.

(9) A request for information referred to in subsection (7) shall be accompanied by instructions for the provision of the information and the completion of the forms referred to in that subsection and by a sufficient number of copies of the forms.

81. (1) If a constrained share corporation has sent a notice referred to in subsection 80(3) and has not sold, under subsection 46(1) of the Act, any share in respect of which the notice was sent, and if the corporation changes its conclusion referred to in paragraph 80(3)(a) or its directors change their determination referred to in paragraph 80(3)(b) or if there is a change in the reason for the conclusion or determination, the corporation shall immediately send by registered mail to the recipient of that notice a notice of the change to the conclusion, to the determination or to the reason for the conclusion or determination, including the reason for the change.

(2) When a corporation sends a notice under subsection (1), the corporation shall, at the time the notice is sent, enter or cause to be entered in the securities register of the corporation the particulars of the notice, including the date on which it was sent.

82. (1) No share shall be sold by a constrained share corporation under subsection 46(1) of the Act unless

    (a) the corporation has sent the notices referred to in subsections 80(1) and (3) to the person shown in the securities register of the corporation as the holder of the share;

    (b) not less than 150 days but not more than 300 days have elapsed from the day on which the notice referred to in subsection 80(1) was sent to the holder of the share;

    (c) not less than 60 days but not more than 150 days have elapsed from the day on which the notice referred to in subsection 80(3) was sent to the holder of the share;

    (d) the corporation has concluded that the share is owned, or the directors of the corporation have determined in accordance with subsection 80(2) that the share may be owned, contrary to a constraint referred to in paragraph (c) of the definition "constraint" in section 73 and, at the time of sale, the corporation has no reasonable grounds on which to change its conclusion or the directors of the corporation have no reasonable grounds on which to change their determination, as the case may be;

    (e) the sale takes place

        (i) on a stock exchange where shares of the corporation are listed and posted for trading, or

        (ii) if shares of the corporation are not listed and posted for trading on a stock exchange, in any other manner that the directors of the corporation determine to be appropriate; and

    (f) the corporation sells the share with a view to obtaining the best sale price available in the circumstances at the time of sale.

(2) No share in respect of which a notice is sent in accordance with subsection 80(1) shall be sold by a constrained share corporation under subsection 46(1) of the Act if a transfer of the share is registered in the securities register of the corporation after the notice was sent, unless the corporation again complies with the requirements set out in this Part respecting the sale of the share.

83. (1) Immediately after a sale of shares by a constrained share corporation under subsection 46(1) of the Act, the corporation shall

(a) register the transfer or a notice of the sale of the shares or cause the transfer or a notice of the sale of the shares to be registered in the securities register of the corporation; and

(b) send a notice of the sale to the person shown in the securities register of the corporation as the holder of the shares at the time of the sale.

(2) The notice referred to in paragraph (1)(b) shall

(a) state the number of shares sold;

(b) identify the certificate that represents the shares sold, by certificate number or otherwise;

(c) state the date and manner of sale;

(d) state the manner in which the person entitled to receive the net proceeds of the sale under subsection 46(3) of the Act may obtain them;

(e) state that the corporation concluded that the shares were owned, or that the directors determined in accordance with subsection 80(2) that the shares may be owned, contrary to a constraint referred to in paragraph (c) of the definition "constraint" in section 73 and state the reason why the corporation so concluded or the directors so determined, as the case may be; and

(f) contain a statement, if not all of the shares of the holder represented by a certificate were sold, that not all of the shares were sold and that a certificate that represents the shares that were not sold will be issued on surrender for cancellation of the certificate that represents the shares sold.

84. For the purpose of subsection 47(1) of the Act, the proceeds of a sale by a constrained share corporation under subsection 46(1) of the Act shall be deposited in an interest-bearing account with a chartered bank in Canada to which the *Bank Act* applies or a trust company in Canada to which the *Trust and Loan Companies Act* applies.

Disclosure of Beneficial Ownership

85. Section 86 applies to a constrained share corporation that has provisions in its articles imposing a constraint referred to in paragraph (a) or (b) of the definition "constraint" in section 73.

86. (1) Subject to section 103 of the Act, the directors of a constrained share corporation may make, amend or repeal any by-laws required to administer the constrained share provisions set out in the articles of the corporation, including by-laws

(a) to require any person in whose name shares of the corporation are registered to provide a statutory declaration under the *Canada Evidence Act* concerning

(i) whether the shareholder is the beneficial owner of the shares of the corporation or holds them for a beneficial owner,

(ii) whether the shareholder is an associate of any other shareholder,

(iii) whether the shareholder or beneficial owner is a Canadian, and

(iv) any further facts that the directors consider relevant;

(b) to require any person seeking to have a transfer of a voting share registered in their name or to have a voting share issued to them to provide a declaration similar to the declaration a shareholder may be required to provide under paragraph (a); and

(c) to determine the circumstances in which any declarations are required, their form and the times when they are to be provided.

(2) If a person is required to provide a declaration under a by-law made under subsection (1), the directors may refuse to register a transfer of a voting share in their name or to issue a voting share to them until that person has provided the declaration.

(3) In administering the constrained share provisions set out in the articles of a constrained share corporation, the directors of the corporation may rely on

(a) a statement made in a declaration referred to in subsection (1) or (2); and

(b) the knowledge of a director, an officer, an employee or an agent of the corporation.

(4) If the directors are required to determine the total number of voting shares of a constrained share corporation held by or on behalf of persons other than Canadians, the directors may rely on the sum of the voting shares held by every shareholder whose latest address as shown in the securities register is

(a) outside Canada; and

(b) in Canada but who, to the knowledge of a director, an officer, an employee or an agent of the corporation, is not a Canadian.

(5) For the purpose of subsection (4), the directors may rely on the securities register of the constrained share corporation as of any date after the day on which the corporation became a constrained share corporation, but that date shall not be more than four months before the day on which the determination is made.

References and Definitions for the Purpose of Certain Provisions of the Act

87. (1) For the purpose of paragraph 174(1)(b) of the Act,

(a) the following laws are prescribed:

(i) the *Canadian Aviation Regulations* made under the *Aeronautics Act*,

(ii) the *Canada Transportation Act* and any regulations made under it,

(iii) the *Canada Oil and Gas Land Regulations* and the *Canada Oil and Gas Drilling and Production Regulations* made under the *Territorial Lands Act* and *Federal Real Property Act*,

(iv) the *Broadcasting Act*,

(v) the *Northern Mineral Exploration Assistance Regulations* made under *Appropriation Act No. 9, 1966*,

(vi) section 19 of the *Income Tax Act*,

(vii) the *Securities Act* (Ontario), R.S.O. 1990, c. S.5, as amended from time to time, and any regulations made under it,

(viii) the *Securities Act* (Quebec), R.S.Q. c. V-1.1 and any regulations made under it, and

(ix) any other law of Canada or of a province with requirements in relation to Canadian ownership; and

(b) **"financial intermediary"** includes a bank, a trust company, a loan company, an insurance company, an investment company and a body corporate that carries on business as a securities broker, a dealer or an underwriter.

(2) For the purposes of subsection 32(1) and paragraphs 46(1)(a), 49(10)(a) and 174(1)(c) of the Act, the following laws are prescribed:

(a) the *Canada Petroleum Resources Act* and any regulations made under it; and

(b) the *Canada Transportation Act* and any regulations made under it.

(3) For the purpose of paragraphs 46(1)(b), 49(10)(b) and 174(1)(d) of the Act, the following laws are prescribed:

(a) the *Insurance Companies Act* and any regulations made under it; and

(b) the *Trust and Loan Companies Act* and any regulations made under it.

PART 10 — RULES OF PROCEDURE FOR APPLICATIONS FOR EXEMPTIONS

Application

88. This Part applies to every application for an exemption under subsection 2(6), 10(2), 82(3) or 151(1), section 156 or subsection 171(2) or 187(11) of the Act.

Time of Filing Applications

89. (1) An application for an exemption under

(a) subsection 2(6) of the Act may be made at any time;

(b) subsection 10(2) or 187(11) of the Act shall be made before the date of issue of the certificate of continuance referred to in subsection 187(4) of the Act;

(c) subsection 82(3) of the Act shall be made at least 30 days before the corporation is required to comply with Part VIII of the Act;

(d) subsection 151(1) of the Act shall be made before the date of the notice referred to in subsection 149(1) of the Act;

(e) section 156 of the Act shall be made at least 60 days before the documents in respect of which the exemption is requested are to be sent to the Director; and

(f) subsection 171(2) of the Act may be made at any time.

(2) Despite subsection (1), the Director shall extend the time for making an application for an exemption if the applicant establishes that no prejudice will result from the extension.

Notice by Director of Decision

90. The Director shall, within 30 days after receipt of an application for an exemption, grant the exemption requested or send to the applicant written notice of the Director's refusal, together with reasons for the refusal.

General

91. The Director may request that an applicant for an exemption provide the Director with further information or that any other person provide the Director with information in writing that is relevant to the application.

92. The Director shall give the applicant for an exemption a copy of any information received from any other person under section 91 and shall allow the applicant a reasonable opportunity to respond in writing.

93. If an applicant for an exemption or a person from whom the Director has requested information under section 91 does not provide the information within the time specified by the Director, the Director may deal with the application without regard to the information.

94. If the Director does not grant an exemption or send written notice of the Director's refusal within the time specified in section 90, the applicant may exercise their rights under section 246 of the Act as if the Director had refused the exemption.

PART 11 — VALUE OF TOTAL FINANCIAL INTEREST

95. For the purpose of paragraph 237.5(1)(b) of the Act, the prescribed amount of the value of the plaintiff's total financial interest is $20,000.

PART 12 — CANCELLATION OF ARTICLES AND CERTIFICATES

96. (1) For the purpose of subsection 265.1(1) of the Act, the prescribed circumstances are that

(a) the error is obvious;

(b) the error is made by the Director,

(c) the cancellation of the articles and related certificate is ordered by a court; or

(d) the Director lacked the authority to issue the articles and related certificate.

(2) For the purpose of subsection 265.1(3) of the Act, the prescribed circumstances are that

(a) there is no dispute among the directors or shareholders on the circumstances of the request for cancellation; and

(b) the corporation has not used the articles and related certificate, or, if it has, if anyone dealing with the corporation on the basis of the articles and related certificate has consented to the cancellation.

PART 13 — PRESCRIBED FEES

97. (1) The fee in respect of the filing, examination or copying of any document or in respect of any action that the Director is required or authorized to take under the Act, set out in column 1 of an item of Schedule 5,

(a) is the applicable fee set out in column 2 of that item; and

177

(b) shall be paid to the Director on the filing, examination or copying of the document or before the Director takes the action in respect of which the fee is payable.

(2) No fee is payable for the issuance by the Director of

(a) a certificate of amendment issued under section 178 of the Act, if the only purpose of the amendment is to add an English or a French version to a corporation's name, or to replace a corporate name that the Director has directed be changed under subsection 12(2) or (4) of the Act;

(b) a certificate of dissolution issued under subsection 210(5) or 211(15) of the Act;

(c) a certificate of intent to dissolve issued under subsection 211(5) of the Act; or

(d) a corrected certificate issued under subsection 265(6) of the Act when the correction is required solely as the result of an error made by the Director.

(3) For the purpose of subsection 49(2) of the Act, the prescribed maximum fee for the issuance of a security certificate is $3.

Repeal

98. The *Canada Business Corporations Regulations*[1] are repealed.

Coming Into Force

99. These Regulations come into force on November 24, 2001.

SCHEDULE 1 — REPORTING ISSUER
(Subsection 2(1))

Item	Column 1 Jurisdiction	Column 2 Legislation
1.	Ontario	the definition "reporting issuer" in subsection 1(1) of the *Securities Act*, R.S.O. 1990, c. S.5, as amended from time to time
2.	Quebec	the definition "reporting issuer" in sections 5 and 68 of the *Securities Act*, R.S.Q., c. V-1.1, as amended from time to time
3.	Nova Scotia	the definition "reporting issuer" in paragraph 2(1)(ao) of the *Securities Act*, R.S.N.S. 1989, c. 418, as amended from time to time
4.	Manitoba	the definition "reporting issuer" in subsection 80(1) of the *Securities Act*, R.S.M. 1988, c. S50, as amended from time to time

---

[1]SOR/179-316; SOR/189-323

Item	Column 1 Jurisdiction	Column 2 Legislation
5.	British Columbia	the definition "reporting issuer" in subsection 1(1) of the *Securities Act*, R.S.B.C. 1996, c. 418, as amended from time to time
6.	Saskatchewan	the definition "reporting issuer" in paragraph 2(l)(qq) of *The Securities Act, 1988*, S.S. 1988-89, c. S-42.2, as amended from time to time
7.	Alberta	the definition "reporting issuer" in paragraph 1(t.1) and section 117 of the *Securities Act*, S.A. 1981, c. S-6.1, as amended from time to time
8.	Newfoundland	the definition "reporting issuer" in paragraph 2(1)(oo) of the *Securities Act*, R.S.N. 1990, c. S-13, as amended from time to time

SCHEDULE 2 — TAKE-OVER BIDS

(Section 41)

Item	Column 1 Jurisdiction	Column 2 Legislation
1.	Ontario	the definition "take-over bid" in subsection 89(1) of the *Securities Act*, R.S.O. 1990, c. S.5, as amended from time to time
2.	Quebec	the definition "take-over bid" in section 110 of the *Securities Act*, R.S.Q., c. V-1.1, as amended from time to time
3.	Nova Scotia	the definition "take-over bid" in paragraph 95(1)(l) of the *Securities Act*, R.S.N.S. 1989, c. 418, as amended from time to time
4.	Manitoba	the definition "take-over bid" in subsection 80(1) of the *Securities Act*, R.S.M. 1988, c. S50, as amended from time to time
5.	British Columbia	the definition "take-over bid" in subsection 92(1) of the *Securities Act*, R.S.B.C. 1996, c. 418, as amended from time to time
6.	Saskatchewan	the definition "take-over bid" in paragraph 98(l)(j) of *The Securities Act, 1988*, S.S. 1988-89, c. S-42.2, as amended from time to time
7.	Alberta	the definition "take-over bid" in paragraph 131(1)(r) of the *Securities Act*, S.A. 1981, c. S-6.1, as amended from time to time
8.	Newfoundland	the definition "take-over bid" in paragraph 90(1)(l) of the *Securities Act*, R.S.N. 1990, c. S-13, as amended from time to time
9.	Yukon Territory	the definition "take-over bid" in section 196 of the *Business Corporations Act*, R.S.Y. 1986, c. 15, as amended from time to time

Item	Column 1 Jurisdiction	Column 2 Legislation
10.	Northwest Territories	the definition "take-over bid" in section 196 of the *Business Corporations Act*, S.N.W.T. 1996, c. 19, as amended from time to time
11.	Nunavut	the definition "take-over bid" in section 196 of the *Business Corporations Act* (Nunavut) S.N.W.T. 1996, c. 19, as amended from time to time

SCHEDULE 3 — EXECUTIVE REMUNERATION

(Paragraph 57(q))

Item	Column 1 Jurisdiction	Column 2 Form or Information
1.	Ontario	Form 40 of Regulation 1015, as amended from time to time, made under the *Securities Act*, R.S.O. 1990, c. S.5
2.	Quebec	Item 6 of Schedule VIII to the *Securities Regulation*, as amended from time to time, made under the *Securities Act*, R.S.Q., c. V-1.1
3.	Nova Scotia	Form 41 of the *Securities Regulations, 1991*, as amended from time to time, made under the *Securities Act*, R.S.N.S. 1989, c. 418
4.	British Columbia	Form 41 of the *Securities Regulation*, as amended from time to time, made under the *Securities Act*, R.S.B.C. 1996, c. 418
5.	Saskatchewan	Form 38 of *The Securities Regulations*, as amended from time to time, made under The *Securities Act*, 1988, S.S. 1988-89, c. S-42.2
6.	Alberta	Form 40 of the *Securities Regulation*, as amended from time to time, made under the *Securities Act*, S.A. 1981, c. S-6.1
7.	Newfoundland	Form 39 of the *Securities Regulations*, as amended from time to time, made under the *Securities Act*, R.S.N. 1990, c. S-13
8.	United States	Items 402, 403 and 404 of Regulation S-K, as amended from time to time, made under the *Securities Exchange Act of 1934* of the United States

SCHEDULE 4 — INDEBTEDNESS OF DIRECTORS AND OFFICERS

(Subparagraph 57(r)(ii))

Item	Column 1 Jurisdiction	Column 2 Form or Information
1.	Ontario	Item 7 of Form 30 of Regulation 1015, as amended from time to time, made under the *Securities Act*, R.S.O. 1990, c. S.5
2.	Quebec	Item 7 of Schedule VIII to the *Securities Regulation*, as amended from time to time, made under the *Securities Act*, R.S.Q., c. V-1.1
3.	Nova Scotia	Item 7 of Form 30 of the *Securities Regulations, 1991*, as amended from time to time, made under the *Securities Act*, R.S.N.S. 1989, c. 418
4.	British Colum-bia	Item 7 of Form 30 of the *Securities Regulation*, as amended from time to time, made under the *Securities Act*, R.S.B.C. 1996, c. 418
5.	Saskatchewan	Item 7 of Form 28 of *The Securities Regulations*, as amended from time to time, made under *The Securities Act, 1988*, S.S. 1988-89, c. S-42.2
6.	Alberta	Item 7 of Form 30 of the *Securities Regulation*, as amended from time to time, made under the *Securities Act*, S.A. 1981, c. S-6.1
7.	Newfoundland	Item 7 of Form 29 of the *Securities Regulations*, as amended from time to time, made under the *Securities Act*, R.S.N. 1990, c. S-13
8.	United States	Items 402, 403 and 404 of Regulation S-K, as amended from time to time, made under the *Securities Exchange Act of 1934* of the United States

SCHEDULE 5 — FEES

(Subsection 98(1))

Item	Column 1 Filing, Examination or Copying of Documents or Action by the Director under the Act	Column 2 Fee $
1.	Issuance by the Director of	
	(a) a certificate of incorporation under section 8, if the application is made	
	(i) using Industry Canada's online incorporation feature	200
	(ii) using any means other than Industry Canada's online incorporation feature	250
	(b) a certificate of amendment under subsection 27(5), section 178 or subsection 191(5)	200
	(c) a restated certificate of incorporation under subsection 180(3) (unless issued with certificate of amendment)	50
	(d) a certificate of amalgamation under subsection 185(4)	200

Item	Column 1 **Filing, Examination or Copying of Documents or Action by the Director under the Act**	Column 2 **Fee $**
	(e) a certificate of continuance under subsection 187(4) (unless subsection 268(8) applies)	200
	(f) a document evidencing satisfaction of the Director, as required under subsection 188(1)	200
	(g) a certificate of arrangement under subsection 192(7)	200
	(h) a certificate of revival under subsection 209(3)	200
	(i) a certificate of revocation of intent to dissolve under subsection 211(11)	50
	(j) a corrected certificate under subsection 265(1)	200
2.	Sending the annual return to the Director for filing under subsection 263(1)	
	(a) using Industry Canada's online filing feature	20
	(b) using any means other than Industry Canada's online filing feature	40
3.	Examination by the Director of the corporation's file in connection with a request for a certificate under section 263.1	10
4.	Application to the Director for an exemption under subsection 2(6), 10(2), 82(3), 151(1), 171(2) or 187(11)	250
5.	Application to the Director for an exemption under section 156	250
6.	Provision by the Director of uncertified copies of documents under subsection 266(2), per page	1
7.	Provision by the Director of certified copies of documents under subsection 266(2), per certificate	35

CAN. REG. 427 — MINISTER DESIGNATION ORDER (CANADA BUSINESS CORPORATIONS ACT)

made under the *Canada Business Corporations Act*

Order Designating a Member of the Queen's Privy Council for Canada to Act as the Minister for the Purposes of The Canada Business Corporations Act

C.R.C. 1978, c. 427

SHORT TITLE

1. This Order may be cited as the *Minister Designation Order (Canada Business Corporations Act)*.

DESIGNATION

2. The Minister of Consumer and Corporate Affairs is hereby designated as the member of the Queen's Privy Council for Canada to act as the Minister for the purposes of the *Canada Business Corporations Act*.

CBCA FORMS

Form 1 — Articles of Incorporation

■◆■ Industry Canada Industrie Canada	FORM 1	FORMULAIRE 1
Canada Business Loi canadienne sur les	ARTICLES OF INCORPORATION	STATUTS CONSTITUTIFS
Corporations Act sociétés par actions	(SECTION 6)	(ARTICLE 6)

1 -- Name of the Corporation   Dénomination sociale de la société

2 -- The province or territory in Canada where the registered office is situated   La province ou le territoire au Canada où est situé le siège social

3 -- The classes and any maximum number of shares that the   Catégories et le nombre maximal d'actions que la société est autorisée
corporation is authorized to issue   à émettre

4 -- Restrictions, if any, on share transfers   Restrictions sur le transfert des actions, s'il y a lieu

5 -- Number (or minimum and maximum number) of directors   Nombre (ou nombre minimal et maximal) d'administrateurs

6 -- Restrictions, if any, on the business the corporation may carry on   Limites imposées à l'activité commerciale de la société, s'il y a lieu

7 -- Other provisions, if any   Autres dispositions, s'il y a lieu

8 -- Incorporators - Fondateurs

Name(s) - Nom(s)	Address (including postal code) Adresse (inclure le code postal)	Signature	Tel. No. - N° de tél.

FOR DEPARTMENTAL USE ONLY - À L'USAGE DU MINISTÈRE SEULEMENT

IC 3419 (2007/05)

Canada

CBCA Forms

Canada Business Corporations Act

Articles of Incorporation
FORM 1
INSTRUCTIONS

General

If you require more information in order to complete Form 1, you may wish to consult the Incorporation Kit and the Name Granting Compendium or the Name Granting Guidelines.

You can file Form 1 through the Corporations Canada On-line Filing Centre at http://strategis.ic.gc.ca/corporations or you can send or fax the completed documents to the address provided below.

Prescribed Fees

Corporations Canada On-line Filing Centre: $200
By mail or fax: $250

Item 1

Set out the proposed corporate name that complies with sections 10 and 12 of the Act. Articles of incorporation must be accompanied by a Canada-biased NUANS search report dated not more than ninety (90) days prior to the receipt of the articles by the Director. On request, a number name may be assigned under subsection 11(2) of the Act, without a search.

Item 2

Set out the name of the province or territory within Canada where the registered office is to be situated.

Item 3

Set out the details required by paragraph 6(1)(c) of the Act, including details of the rights, privileges, restrictions and conditions attached to each class of shares. All shares must be without nominal or par value and must comply with the provisions of Part V of the Act.

Item 4

If restrictions are to be placed on the right to transfer shares of the corporation, set out a statement to this effect and the nature of such restrictions.

Item 5

State the number of directors. If cumulative voting is permitted, the number of directors must be invariable; otherwise it is mandatory to specify a minimum and maximum number of directors.

Item 6

If restrictions are to be placed on the business the corporation may carry out, set out the restrictions.

Item 7

Set out any provisions, permitted by the Act or Regulations to be set out in the by-laws of the corporation, that are to form part of the articles, including any pre-emptive rights or cumulative voting provisions.

Item 8

Each incorporator must state his or her name and residential address, and affix his or her signature. If an incorporator is a body corporate, that name shall be the name of the body corporate, the address shall be that of its registered office, and the articles shall be signed by a person authorized by the corporation.

Other Documents

The articles must be accompanied by form 2 *'Information Regarding the Registered Office and the Board of Directors'*.

Other Notices

If a proposed corporation is to engage in
a) the construction or operation of a pipeline for the transmission of oil or gas as defined in the *National Energy Board Act*, or
b) the construction or operation of a commodity pipeline as defined in the *Canada Transportation Act*, the incorporator shall inform the Minister of the Department or Agency that regulates such business.

The information you provide in this document is collected under the authority of the *Canada Business Corporations Act* and will be stored in personal information bank number CCA/P-PU-093. Personal information that you provide is protected under the provisions of the *Privacy Act*. However, public disclosure pursuant to section 266 of the *Canada Business Corporations Act* is permitted under the *Privacy Act*.

The completed documents and fees payable to the Receiver General for Canada are to be sent to:

The Director, Canada Business Corporations Act
Jean Edmonds Tower, South
9th Floor
365 Laurier Ave. West
Ottawa, Ontario
K1A 0C8
or by facsimile at: (613) 941-0999
Inquiries: 1-866-333-5556

IC 3419 (2007/01) p.2

Loi canadienne sur les sociétés par actions

Statuts constitutifs
FORMULAIRE 1
INSTRUCTIONS

Généralités

Si vous désirez obtenir de plus amples informations afin de compléter le formulaire 1, veuillez consulter le Recueil d'information sur la constitution, l'Énoncé d'octroi des dénominations ou les Lignes directrices pour l'octroi des dénominations.

Vous pouvez déposer le formulaire 1 par l'entremise du Centre de dépôt des formulaires en ligne de Corporations Canada au http://strategis.ic.gc.ca/corporations ou encore envoyer ou télécopier le document complété à l'adresse indiquée au bas de cette page.

Droits payables

Centre de dépôt des formulaires en ligne : 200 $
Par la poste ou télécopieur : 250 $

Rubrique 1

Indiquer une dénomination sociale qui satisfait aux exigences des articles 10 et 12 de la Loi. Les statuts constitutifs doivent être accompagnés d'un rapport de recherche NUANS couvrant le Canada, dont la date remonte à quatre-vingt-dix (90) jours ou moins avant la date de réception des statuts par le directeur. Si un numéro matricule est demandé, en guise de dénomination sociale, il peut être assigné, sans recherche préalable, en vertu du paragraphe 11(2) de la Loi.

Rubrique 2

Indiquer le nom de la province ou du territoire au Canada où le siège social se situera.

Rubrique 3

Indiquer les détails requis par l'alinéa 6(1)c) de la Loi, y compris les détails des droits, privilèges, restrictions et conditions attachés à chaque catégorie d'actions. Toutes les actions doivent être sans valeur nominale ni sans valeur au pair et doivent être conformes aux dispositions de la partie V de la Loi.

Rubrique 4

Si le droit de transfert des actions de la société doit être restreint, inclure une déclaration à cet effet et indiquer la nature de ces restrictions.

Rubrique 5

Indiquer le nombre d'administrateurs. Si un vote cumulatif est prévu, ce nombre doit être fixe; autrement, il est obligatoire de spécifier un nombre minimal et maximal d'administrateurs.

Rubrique 6

Si des limites doivent être imposées à l'activité commerciale de la société, les indiquer.

Rubrique 7

Indiquer les dispositions que la Loi ou le règlement permet d'énoncer dans les règlements administratifs de la société et qui doivent faire partie des statuts, y compris les dispositions relatives au vote cumulatif ou aux droits de préemption.

Rubrique 8

Chaque fondateur doit donner son nom, son adresse domiciliaire et apposer sa signature. Si un fondateur est une personne morale, le nom doit être celui de la personne morale, l'adresse doit être celle de son siège social et les statuts doivent être signés par une personne autorisée par la société.

Autre documents

Les statuts doivent être accompagnés du formulaire 2 *'Information concernant le siège social et le conseil d'administration'*.

Autres avis

Si la société projetée doit effectuer :
a) la construction ou l'exploitation d'un pipeline pour le transport du pétrole ou du gaz tel que défini par la *Loi sur l'Office national de l'Énergie* ou
b) la construction ou l'exploitation d'un producteduc tel que défini par la *Loi sur les transports au Canada*, les fondateurs doivent informer le ministre responsable du ministère ou de l'agence qui réglemente ces entreprises.

Les renseignements que vous fournissez dans ce document sont recueillis en vertu de la *Loi canadienne sur les sociétés par actions*, et seront emmagasinés dans le fichier de renseignements personnels MCC/P-PU-093. Les renseignements personnels que vous fournissez sont protégés par les dispositions de la *Loi sur la protection des renseignements personnels*. Cependant, la divulgation au public selon les termes de l'article 266 de la *Loi canadienne sur les sociétés par actions* est permise en vertu de la *Loi sur la protection des renseignements personnels*.

Les documents complétés et les droits payables au Receveur général du Canada doivent être envoyés au :

Directeur, Loi canadienne sur les sociétés par actions
Tour Jean Edmonds, sud
9ième étage
365, av. Laurier ouest
Ottawa (Ontario)
K1A 0C8
ou par télécopieur : (613) 941-0999
Renseignements : 1-866-333-5556

Form 2 — Initial Registered Office Address and First Board of Directors

Industry Canada   **Industrie Canada**
Corporations Canada   Corporations Canada

Initial Registered Office Address and First Board of Directors

(To be filed with Articles of Incorporation, Amalgamation and Continuance)

(Sections 19 and 106 of the Canada Business Corporations Act (CBCA))

Form 2

Changes to the registered office or the board of directors are to be made by filing Form 3 — Change of Registered Office Address or Form 6 — Changes Regarding Directors.

Instructions

[4] At least 25 per cent of the directors of a corporation must be Canadian residents. If a corporation has four directors or less, at least one director must be a Canadian resident (subsection 105(3) of the *Canada Business Corporations Act* (CBCA)).

If the corporation is a "distributing" corporation, there must be at least three directors.

However, the board of directors of corporations operating in uranium mining, book publishing and distribution, book sale or film and video distribution must be comprised of a majority of Canadian residents (subsection 105(3.1) of the CBCA). If the space available is insufficient, please attach a schedule to the form.

[5] Declaration

In the case of an incorporation, this form must be signed by the incorporator. In the case of an amalgamation or a continuance, this form must be signed by a director or an officer of the corporation (subsection 262.(2) of the CBCA).

General

The information you provide in this document is collected under the authority of the CBCA and will be stored in personal information bank number IC/PPU-049. Personal information that you provide is protected under the provisions of the *Privacy Act*. However, public disclosure pursuant to section 266 of the CBCA is permitted under the *Privacy Act*.

If you require more information, please consult our website at www.corporationscanada.ic.gc.ca or contact us at 613-941-9042 (Ottawa region), toll-free at 1-866-333-5556 or by email at corporationscanada@ic.gc.ca.

File documents online
(except for Articles of Amalgamation):
Corporations Canada Online Filing Centre:
www.corporationscanada.ic.gc.ca

Or send documents by mail:
Director General,
Corporations Canada
Jean Edmonds Tower South
9th Floor
365 Laurier Ave. West
Ottawa ON K1A 0C8

By Facsimile:
613-941-0999

Canada

---

1   **Corporation name**

2   **Address of registered office** (must be a street address, a P.O. Box is not acceptable)

NUMBER AND STREET NAME

CITY   PROVINCE/TERRITORY   POSTAL CODE

3   **Mailing address (if different from the registered office)**

SAME AS ABOVE ☐

ATTENTION Of

NUMBER AND STREET NAME

CITY   PROVINCE/TERRITORY   POSTAL CODE

4   **Members of the board of directors**

FIRST NAME	LAST NAME	RESIDENTIAL ADDRESS (must be a street address, a P.O. Box is not acceptable)	CANADIAN RESIDENT (Yes/No)

5   **Declaration**

I hereby certify that I have relevant knowledge and that I am authorized to sign and submit this form.

SIGNATURE

( )

PRINT NAME   TELEPHONE NUMBER

Note: Misrepresentation constitutes an offence and, on summary conviction, a person is liable to a fine not exceeding $5000 or to imprisonment for a term not exceeding six months or both (subsection 250(1) of the CBCA).

IC 2904 (2006/12)

CBCA Forms

Form 3 — Change of Registered Office Address

Industry Canada **Industrie Canada**
Corporations Canada Corporations Canada

Form 3

Change of Registered Office Address

(Section 19 of the CBCA)

Subsection 19(4) of the *Canada Business Corporations Act* (CBCA) requires a corporation to send Form 3 to Corporations Canada within 15 days of any change to its registered office address.

INSTRUCTIONS

3 If the registered office address changes to another province, this form must be accompanied by Articles of Amendment (Form 4) and the filing fee of $200 (paragraph 173(1)(b) and subsection 177(1) of the CBCA).

5 Declaration

This form may be signed by any individual who has the relevant knowledge of the corporation and who is authorized by the directors (subsection 262.1(2) of the CBCA).

For example:

- a **director** of the corporation;
- an **authorized officer** of the corporation; or
- an **authorized agent**.

General

If you require more information, please visit the Forms, Policies, Fees and Legislation section of our Web site at **http://corporationscanada.ic.gc.ca** or contact us at (613) 941-9042 or toll-free at 1 866 333-5556.

1 Corporation name

2 Corporation number (as it appears on the certificate)

3 New registered office address (must be a street address)

4 Mailing address (if different from the registered office)

SAME AS ABOVE ☐

File documents online:

Corporations Canada Online Filing Centre:
http://corporationscanada.ic.gc.ca

Or send documents by mail:

Director, Corporations Canada
Jean Edmonds Tower South
9th Floor
365 Laurier Ave. West
Ottawa ON K1A 0C8

By Facsimile:
(613) 941-0999

5 Declaration

I hereby certify that I have the relevant knowledge of the corporation, and that I am authorized to sign and submit this form.

Note: Misrepresentation constitutes an offence and, on summary conviction, a person is liable to a fine not exceeding $5000 or to imprisonment for a term not exceeding six months or both (subsection 250(1) of the CBCA).

IC 3420 (2004/11)

Canadä

188

Form 4 — Articles of Amendment

Industry Canada **Industrie Canada**
Corporations Canada Corporations Canada

Form 4

Articles of Amendment

*(Section 27 or 177 of the **Canada Business Corporations Act (CBCA)**)*

Instructions

3 Any changes in the articles of the corporation must be made in accordance with section 27 or 177 of the CBCA.

A: If an amendment involves a change of corporate name (including the addition of the English or French version of the corporate name), the new name must comply with sections 10 and 12 of the CBCA as well as part 2 of the regulations, and the Articles of Amendment must be accompanied by a Canada-biased NUANS® search report dated not more than ninety (90) days prior to the receipt of the articles by Corporations Canada. A numbered name may be assigned under subsection 11(2) of the CBCA without a NUANS® search.

D: Any other amendments must correspond to the paragraphs and subparagraphs referenced in the articles being amended. If the space available is insufficient, please attach a schedule to the form.

4 Declaration

This form must be signed by a director or an officer of the corporation (subsection 262(2) of the CBCA).

General

The information you provide in this document is collected under the authority of the CBCA and will be stored in personal information bank number IC/PPU-049. Personal information that you provide is protected under the provisions of the *Privacy Act*. However, public disclosure pursuant to section 266 of the CBCA is permitted under the *Privacy Act*.

If you require more information, please consult our website at www.corporationscanada.ic.gc.ca or contact us at 613-941-9042 (Ottawa region), toll-free at 1-866-333-5556 or by email at corporationscanada@ic.gc.ca.

Prescribed Fees

- Corporations Canada Online Filing Centre: $200
- By mail or fax: $200 paid by cheque payable to the Receiver General for Canada or by credit card (American Express®, MasterCard® or Visa®).

Important Reminders

Changes of registered office address and/or mailing address:
Complete and file Change of Registered Office Address (Form 3).

Changes of directors or changes of a director's address:
Complete and file Changes Regarding Directors (Form 6).

These forms can be filed electronically, by mail or by fax free of charge.

File documents online:
Corporations Canada Online Filing Centre:
www.corporationscanada.ic.gc.ca

Or send documents by mail:
Director General,
Corporations Canada
Jean Edmonds Tower South
9th Floor
365 Laurier Ave. West
Ottawa ON K1A 0C8

By Facsimile:
613-941-0999

Canada

IC 3069 (2008/12)

---

1 Corporation name

2 Corporation number

3 The articles are amended as follows:
(Please note that more than one section can be filled out)

A: The corporation changes its name to:

B: The corporation changes the province or territory in Canada where the registered office is situated to:
(Do not indicate the full address)

C: The corporation changes the minimum and/or maximum number of directors to:
(For a fixed number of directors, please indicate the same number in both the minimum and maximum options)

minimum: maximum:

D: Other changes: (e.g., to the classes of shares, to restrictions on share transfers, to restrictions on the businesses of the corporation or to any other provisions that are permitted by the CBCA to be set out in the Articles) **Please specify.**

4 Declaration

I hereby certify that I am a director or an officer of the corporation.

SIGNATURE

(   )

PRINT NAME   TELEPHONE NUMBER

Note: Misrepresentation constitutes an offence and, on summary conviction, a person is liable to a fine not exceeding $5000 or to imprisonment for a term not exceeding six months or both (subsection 250(1) of the CBCA).

189

Form 6 — Changes Regarding Directors

Industry Canada   Industrie Canada
Corporations Canada   Corporations Canada

Changes Regarding Directors

(Sections 106 and 113(1) of the CBCA)

Subsection 113(1) of the *Canada Business Corporations Act* (CBCA) requires a corporation to send Form 6 to Corporations Canada within 15 days of any change involving a director of the corporation.

If the space available at Items [3], [4], [6] and [5] is insufficient, please attach information, on a separate piece of paper, to the form.

INSTRUCTIONS

[5] At least 25 per cent of the directors of a corporation must be Canadian residents. If a corporation has less than four directors, at least one director must be a Canadian resident (subsection 105(3) of the CBCA).

However, the board of directors of corporations operating in uranium mining, book publishing and distribution, book sale or film and video distribution must be comprised of a majority of Canadian residents (subsection 105(3.1) of the CBCA).

If the number of directors is not the same as the number fixed in, or is not within the maximum and minimum number set out in, the corporation's articles, you must also file Articles of Amendment (Form 4) to effect a change. There is a filing fee of $200 for Articles of Amendment (paragraph 173(1)(m) and subsection 177(1) of the CBCA).

[7] **Declaration**

This form may be signed by any individual who has the relevant knowledge of the corporation and who is authorized by the directors (subsection 262.1(2) of the CBCA).

For example:

- a director of the corporation;
- an **authorized officer** of the corporation; or
- an **authorized agent**.

General

A director named in the notice filed by the corporation is presumed for the purposes of the CBCA to be a director of the corporation.

The information you provide in this document is collected under the authority of the CBCA and will be stored in personal information bank number IC/PPU-049. Personal information that you provide is protected under the provisions of the *Privacy Act*. However, public disclosure pursuant to section 266 of the CBCA is permitted under the *Privacy Act*.

If you require more information, please visit the Forms, Policies, Fees and Legislation section of our Web site at **http://corporationscanada.ic.gc.ca** or contact us at (613) 941-9042 or toll-free at 1 866 333-5556.

File documents online:

Corporations Canada Online Filing Centre:
http://corporationscanada.ic.gc.ca

Or send documents by mail:

Director, Corporations Canada
Jean Edmonds Tower South
9th Floor
365 Laurier Ave. West
Ottawa ON K1A 0C8

By Facsimile:
(613) 941-0999

IC 3103 (2004/11)

---

1 Corporation name

2 Corporation number (as it appears on the certificate)

3 The following person(s) is (are) newly appointed director(s)

4 The following person(s) ceased to be director(s)

5 Members of the board of directors (list all board members including newly appointed director(s))

6 Change of address of a director

7 Declaration

I hereby certify that I have the relevant knowledge of the corporation, and that I am authorized to sign and submit this form.

(   )

Note: Misrepresentation constitutes an offence and, on summary conviction, a person is liable to a fine not exceeding $5000 or to imprisonment for a term not exceeding six months or both (subsection 250(1) of the CBCA).

Canada

190

CBCA Forms

Form 7 — Restated Articles of Incorporation

		FORM 7 RESTATED ARTICLES OF INCORPORATION (SECTION 180)	FORMULAIRE 7 STATUTS CONSTITUTIFS MIS À JOUR (ARTICLE 180)
▌◆▌ Industry Canada	Industrie Canada		
Canada Business Corporations Act	Loi canadienne sur les sociétés par actions		

1-- Name of the Corporation - Dénomination sociale de la société	Corporation No. - Nº de la société

2-- The province or territory in Canada where the registered office is situated — La province ou le territoire au Canada où est situé le siège social

3-- The classes and any maximum number of shares that the corporation is authorized to issue — Catégories et tout nombre maximal d'actions que la société est autorisée à émettre

4-- Restrictions, if any, on share transfers — Restrictions sur le transfert des actions, s'il y a lieu

5-- Number (or minimum and maximum number) of directors — Nombre (ou nombre minimal et maximal) d'administrateurs

6-- Restrictions, if any, on business the corporation may carry on — Limites imposées à l'activité commerciale de la société, s'il y a lieu

7-- Other provisions, if any — Autres dispositions, s'il y a lieu

These restated articles of incorporation correctly set out, without substantive change, the corresponding provisions of the articles of incorporation as amended and supersede the original articles of incorporation.

Cette mise à jour des statuts constitutifs démontre exactement, sans changement substantiel, les dispositions correspondantes des statuts constitutifs modifiés qui remplacent les statuts constitutifs originaux.

Signature	Printed Name - Nom en lettres moulées	8 -- Capacity of - En qualité de	9 -- Tel. No. - Nº de tél.

FOR DEPARTMENTAL USE ONLY - À L'USAGE DU MINISTÈRE SEULEMENT

IC 3167 (2003/08)

Canada

191

CBCA Forms

Canada Business Corporations Act

Restated Articles of Incorporation
FORM 7
INSTRUCTIONS

Format
If you require more information in order to complete Form 7, you may wish to consult the Amendment Kit.

You must file Form 7 by sending or faxing the completed documents to the address provided below.

Prescribed Fees
By mail or fax: $50
Free, if issued with the Certificate of Amendment

General
Restated articles of incorporation shall set out without substantive change the Articles of Incorporation as previously amended.

Item 1
Set out the full legal name of the corporation and the corporation number.

Item 2
Set out the name of the province or territory within Canada where the registered office is situated.

Item 3
Set out the details required by paragraph 6(1)(c) of the Act, including details of the rights, privileges, restrictions and conditions attached to each class of shares. All shares must be without nominal or par value and must comply with the provisions of Part V of the Act.

Item 4
If restrictions are to be placed on the right to transfer shares of the corporation, set out a statement to this effect and the nature of such restrictions.

Item 5
State the number of directors. If cumulative voting is permitted, the number of directors must be invariable; otherwise it is permissible to specify a minimum and maximum number of directors.

Item 6
If restrictions are to be placed on the business the corporation may carry on, set out the restrictions.

Item 7
Set out any provisions permitted by the Act or Regulations to be set out in the by-laws of the corporation that are to form part of the article, including any pre-emptive rights or cumulative voting provisions.

Signature

Item 8
Indicate the capacity of the signing person. Form 7 must be signed by one of the following persons:

- a **director** of the corporation
- an **authorized officer** of the corporation

The completed document and fees payable to the Receiver General for Canada are to be sent to:

The Director, Canada Business Corporations Act
Jean Edmonds Towers, South
9th Floor
365 Laurier Ave. West
Ottawa, Ontario
K1A 0C8
or by facsimile at: (613) 941-0999
Inquiries: 1-866-333-5556

IC 3167 (2003/08) p.2

Loi canadienne sur les sociétés par actions

Statuts constitutifs mis à jour
FORMULAIRE 7
INSTRUCTIONS

Présentation
Si vous désirez obtenir de plus amples informations afin de compléter le formulaire 7, veuillez consulter le Recueil d'information sur les modifications.

Vous devez déposer le formulaire 7 en envoyant ou en télécopiant le document complété à l'adresse indiquée au bas de cette page.

Droits payables
Par la poste ou télécopieur : 50 $
Gratuit, s'il est délivré de concert avec un Certificat de modification

Généralités
Les statuts mis à jour doivent indiquer sans modification substantielle les statuts constitutifs modifiés au préalable.

Rubrique 1
Indiquer la dénomination sociale complète de la société et son numéro.

Rubrique 2
Indiquer le nom de la province ou du territoire au Canada où le siège social est situé.

Rubrique 3
Indiquer les détails requis par l'alinéa 6(1)(c) de la Loi, y compris les détails des droits, privilèges, restrictions et conditions assortis à chaque catégorie d'actions. Toutes les actions doivent être sans valeur nominale ou sans valeur au pair et doivent être conformes aux dispositions de la partie V de la Loi.

Rubrique 4
Si le droit de transfert des actions de la société doit être restreint, inclure une déclaration à cet effet et indiquer la nature de ces restrictions.

Rubrique 5
Indiquer le nombre d'administrateurs. Si un vote cumulatif est prévu, ce nombre doit être fixe; autrement, il est permis de spécifier un nombre minimal et maximal d'administrateurs.

Rubrique 6
Si des limites doivent être imposées à l'activité commerciale de la société, les indiquer.

Rubrique 7
Indiquer les dispositions que la Loi ou le règlement permet d'énoncer dans les règlements administratifs de la société et qui doivent faire partie des statuts, y compris les dispositions relatives au vote cumulatif ou aux droits de préemption.

Signature

Rubrique 8
Veuillez indiquer la qualité du signataire. Le formulaire 7 doit être signé par une des personnes suivantes :

- un **administrateur** de la société
- un **dirigeant autorisé** de la société

Le document complété et les droits payables au Receveur général du Canada doivent être envoyés au :

Directeur, Loi canadienne sur les sociétés par actions
Tours Jean Edmonds, sud
9ième étage
365, ave Laurier ouest
Ottawa (Ontario)
K1A 0C8
ou par télécopieur : (613) 941-0999
Renseignements : 1-866-333-5556

Form 9 — Articles of Amalgamation

Industry Canada Industrie Canada Canada Business Corporations Act Loi canadienne sur les sociétés par actions	**FORM 9** **ARTICLES OF AMALGAMATION** **(SECTION 185)**	**FORMULE 9** **STATUTS DE FUSION** **(ARTICLE 185)**

1 – Name of the Amalgamated Corporation — Dénomination sociale de la société issue de la fusion

2 – The province or territory in Canada where the registered office is to be situated — La province ou le territoire au Canada où se situera le siège social

3 – The classes and any maximum number of shares that the corporation is authorized to issue — Catégories et tout nombre maximal d'actions que la société est autorisée à émettre

4 – Restrictions, if any, on share transfers — Restrictions sur le transfert des actions, s'il y a lieu

5 – Number (or minimum and maximum number) of directors — Nombre (ou nombre minimal et maximal) d'administrateurs

6 – Restrictions, if any, on business the corporation may carry on — Limites imposées à l'activité commerciale de la société, s'il y a lieu

7 – Other provisions, if any — Autres dispositions, s'il y a lieu

8 – The amalgamation has been approved pursuant to that section or subsection of the Act which is indicated as follows: — La fusion a été approuvée en accord avec l'article ou le paragraphe de la Loi indiqué ci-après

☐ 183   ☐ 184(1)   ☐ 184(2)

9 – Name of the amalgamating corporations Dénomination sociale des sociétés fusionnantes	Corporation No. N° de la société	Signature	Date	Title Titre	Tel. No. N° de tél.

FOR DEPARTMENTAL USE ONLY - À L'USAGE DU MINISTÈRE SEULEMENT

IC 3190 (2007/06)

Canadä

CBCA Forms

Canada Business Corporations Act	Loi canadienne sur les sociétés par actions

Articles of Amalgamation
FORM 9
INSTRUCTIONS

Statuts de fusion
FORMULAIRE 9
INSTRUCTIONS

General

If you require more information in order to complete Form 9, you may wish to consult the Name Granting Compendium or the Name Granting Guidelines and the Amalgamation Kit.

You must file Form 9 by sending or faxing the completed documents to the address provided below.

Prescribed Fees
By mail or fax: $200

Item 1

Set out the proposed name for the amalgamated corporation that complies with sections 10 and 12 of the Act. If this name is not the same as one of the amalgamating corporations, articles of amalgamation must be accompanied by a Canada-biased NUANS search report dated not more than ninety (90) days prior to the receipt of the articles by the Director. On request, a number name may be assigned under subsection 11(2) of the Act, without a search.

Item 2

Set out the name of the province or territory within Canada where the registered office is to be situated.

Item 3

Set out the details required by paragraph 6(1)(c) of the Act, including details of the rights, privileges, restrictions and conditions attached to each class or series of shares. All shares must be without nominal or par value and must comply with the provisions of Part V of the Act.

Item 4

If restrictions are to be placed on the right to transfer shares of the corporation, set out a statement to this effect and the nature of such restrictions.

Item 5

Set out the number of directors. If cumulative voting is permitted, the number of directors must be invariable; otherwise it is permissible to specify a minimum and maximum number of directors.

Item 6

If restrictions are to be placed on the business the corporation may carry on, set out the restrictions.

Item 7

Set out any provisions, permitted by the Act or Regulations to be set out in the by-laws of the corporation, that are to form part of the articles, including any pre-emptive rights or cumulative voting provisions.

Item 8

Indicate whether the amalgamation is under section 183 or subsection 184(1) or (2) of the Act.

Other Notices and Documents

(1) The Articles must be accompanied by Form 2 *'Information Regarding the Registered Office and the Board of Directors'* and a statutory declaration of a director or authorized officer of each amalgamating corporation in accordance with subsection 185(2) of the Act.
(2) All amalgamating corporations should ensure that all filing requirements contained in the Act have been met.

The completed document and fees payable to the Receiver General for Canada are to be sent to:

The Director, Canada Business Corporations Act
Jean Edmonds Tower, South
9th Floor
365 Laurier Ave. West
Ottawa, Ontario
K1A 0C8
or by facsimile at: (613) 941-0999
Inquiries: 1-866-333-5556

IC 3190 (2004/12) p.2

Généralités

Si vous désirez obtenir de plus amples informations afin de compléter le formulaire 9, veuillez consulter l'Énoncé d'octroi des dénominations ou les lignes directrices pour l'octroi des dénominations ainsi que le Recueil d'information sur les fusions.

Vous devez déposer le formulaire 9 en envoyant ou en télécopiant le document complété à l'adresse indiquée au bas de cette page.

Droits payables
Par la poste ou télécopieur : 200 $

Rubrique 1

Indiquer la dénomination sociale de la société issue de la fusion, laquelle doit satisfaire aux exigences des articles 10 et 12 de la Loi. Si cette dénomination diffère de celle de l'une des sociétés fusionnantes, les statuts de fusion doivent être accompagnés d'un rapport de recherche NUANS couvrant le Canada, dont la date remonte à quatre-vingt-dix (90) jours ou moins avant la date de réception des statuts par le directeur. Si un numéro matricule est demandé en guise de dénomination sociale, il peut être assigné, sans recherche préalable, en vertu du paragraphe 11(2) de la Loi.

Rubrique 2

Indiquer le nom de la province ou du territoire au Canada où le siège social se situera.

Rubrique 3

Indiquer les détails requis par l'alinéa 6(1)c) de la Loi, y compris les détails des droits, privilèges, restrictions et conditions assortis à chaque catégorie ou série d'actions. Toutes les actions doivent être sans valeur nominale ou sans valeur au pair et doivent être conformes aux dispositions de la partie V de la Loi.

Rubrique 4

Si le droit de transfert des actions de la société doit être restreint, inclure une déclaration à cet effet et indiquer la nature de ces restrictions.

Rubrique 5

Indiquer le nombre d'administrateurs. Si un vote cumulatif est prévu, ce nombre doit être fixe; autrement, il est permis de spécifier un nombre minimal et maximal d'administrateurs.

Rubrique 6

Si des limites doivent être imposées à l'activité commerciale de la société, les indiquer.

Rubrique 7

Indiquer les dispositions que la Loi ou le règlement permet d'énoncer dans les règlements administratifs de la société et qui doivent faire partie des statuts, y compris les dispositions relatives au vote cumulatif ou aux droits de préemption.

Rubrique 8

Indiquer si la fusion est faite en vertu de l'article 183 ou du paragraphe 184(1) ou (2) de la Loi.

Autres avis et documents

(1) Les status doivent être accompagnés du formulaire 2 *'Information concernant le siège social et le conseil d'administration'* et d'une déclaration solennelle d'un administrateur ou d'un dirigeant autorisé de chaque société fusionnante conformément au paragraphe 185(2) de la Loi.
(2) Les sociétés fusionnantes doivent s'assurer que toutes les exigences de dépôt contenues dans la Loi ont été remplies.

Le document complété et les droits payables au Receveur général du Canada doivent être envoyés au :

Directeur, Loi canadienne sur les sociétés par actions
Tour Jean Edmonds, sud
9ième étage
365, av. Laurier ouest
Ottawa (Ontario)
K1A 0C8
ou par télécopieur : (613) 941-0999
Renseignements : 1-866-333-5556

194

CBCA Forms

Form 11 — Articles of Continuance

Industry Canada Industrie Canada	FORM 11 ARTICLES OF CONTINUANCE (SECTION 187)	FORMULAIRE 11 CLAUSES DE PROROGATION (ARTICLE 187)
Canada Business Corporations Act Loi canadienne sur les sociétés par actions		

1 -- Name of the Corporation	Dénomination sociale de la société	2 -- Taxation Year End Fin de l'année d'imposition M D - J

3 -- The province or territory in Canada where the registered office is to be situated

La province ou le territoire au Canada où se situera le siège social

4 -- The classes and the maximum number of shares that the corporation is authorized to issue

Catégories et le nombre maximal d'actions que la société est autorisée à émettre

5 -- Restrictions, if any, on share transfers

Restrictions sur le transfert des actions, s'il y a lieu

6 -- Number (or minimum and maximum number) of directors

Nombre (ou nombre minimal et maximal) d'administrateurs

7 -- Restrictions, if any, on business the corporation may carry on

Limites imposées à l'activité commerciale de la société, s'il y a lieu

8 -- (1) If change of name effected, previous name

(1) S'il y a changement de dénomination sociale, indiquer la dénomination sociale antérieure

(2) Details of incorporation

(2) Détails de la constitution

9 -- Other provisions, if any

Autres dispositions, s'il y a lieu

Signature	Printed Name - Nom en lettres moulées	10 -- Capacity of - En qualité de	11 -- Tel. No. - Nº de tél.

FOR DEPARTMENTAL USE ONLY : À L'USAGE DU MINISTÈRE SEULEMENT

IC 3247 (2004/12)

Canada

CBCA Forms

Canada Business Corporations Act

Articles of Continuance
FORM 11
INSTRUCTIONS

General
If you require more information in order to complete Form 11, you may wish to consult the Name Granting Compendium or the Name Granting Guidelines and the Continuance (Import) Kit.

You can file Form 11 through the Corporations Canada On-line Filing Centre at http://strategis.ic.gc.ca/corporations or you can send or fax the completed documents to the address provided below.

Prescribed Fees
Corporations Canada On-line Filing Centre, by mail or fax: $200

Item 1
Set out the full legal name of the corporation which complies with sections 10 and 12 of the Act. Articles of continuance must be accompanied by a Canada-biased NUANS search report dated not more than ninety (90) days prior to the receipt of the articles by the Director. Upon request, a number name may be assigned under subsection 11(2) of the Act, without a search.

Item 2
Set out the taxation year end (day and month) of the corporation. The taxation year must be the same as the taxation year end pursuant to the *Income Tax Act*.

Item 3
Set out the name of the province or territory within Canada where the registered office is to be situated.

Item 4
Set out the details required by paragraph 6(1)(c) of the Act. Unless an exemption is obtained under subsection 187(11) of the Act, all shares must be without nominal or par value and must comply with Part V of the Act. Nominal or par value shares issued by a body corporate before continuance comply with the Act by virtue of subsection 24(2) and 187(8) and (9) of the Act. In the case of the application of subsection 187(11) of the Act, set out the maximum number of shares of a class or series as required by subsection 187(12) of the Act.

Item 5
If restrictions are to be placed on the right to transfer shares of the corporation, set out a statement to this effect and the nature of such restrictions.

Item 6
Set out the number of directors. If cumulative voting is permitted, the number of directors must be invariable; otherwise it is permissible to specify a minimum and maximum number of directors.

Item 7
If restrictions are to be placed on the business the corporation may carry on, set out the restrictions.

Item 8
1) Set out the previous name of the corporate body if a change of name is effected on continuance.
2) Set out the date of incorporation of the body corporate. If the body corporate has been subject to any previous continuance, set out the details of each such continuance, i.e., the date of continuance, any change of name at the time of continuance and the name and provision of the statute under which it was effected.

Item 9
Set out any provisions, permitted by the Act or Regulations that are to form part of the articles, including any pre-emptive rights or cumulative voting provisions.

Item 10
Indicate the capacity of the signing person. Form 11 must be signed by one of the following persons:

- a **director** of the corporation
- an **authorized officer** of the corporation

Other Documents
If the continuance is under subsection 187(1) of the Act, the articles of continuance must be accompanied by:
a) proof of authorization under the laws of the jurisdiction where the body corporate is incorporated; and
b) form 2 *'Information Regarding the Registered Office and the Board of Directors'*.

The completed documents and fees payable to the Receiver General for Canada are to be sent to:

The Director, Canada Business Corporations Act
Jean Edmonds Tower, South
9th Floor
365 Laurier Ave. West
Ottawa, Ontario K1A 0C8
or by facsimile at: (613) 941-0999
Inquiries: 1-866-333-5556

IC 3247 (2004/12) p.2

Loi canadienne sur les sociétés par actions

Clauses de prorogation
FORMULAIRE 11
INSTRUCTIONS

Généralités
Si vous désirez obtenir de plus amples informations afin de compléter le formulaire 11, veuillez consulter l'Énoncé d'octroi des dénominations ou les Lignes directrices pour l'octroi des dénominations ainsi que le Recueil d'information sur la prorogation-importation.

Vous pouvez déposer le formulaire 11 par l'entremise du Centre de dépôt des formulaires en ligne de Corporations Canada au http://strategis.ic.gc.ca/corporations ou encore envoyer ou télécopier le document complété à l'adresse indiquée au bas de cette page.

Droits
Centre de dépôt des formulaires en ligne, par la poste ou télécopieur : 200 $

Rubrique 1
Indiquer la dénomination sociale complète de la société, laquelle doit satisfaire aux exigences des articles 10 et 12 de la Loi. Les clauses de prorogation doivent être accompagnées d'un rapport de recherche NUANS couvrant le Canada, dont la date remonte à quatre-vingt-dix (90) jours ou moins avant la date de réception par le directeur des clauses de prorogation. Si un numéro matricule est demandé en guise de dénomination sociale, il peut être assigné, sans recherche préalable, en vertu du paragraphe 11(2) de la Loi.

Rubrique 2
Indiquer la date (jour et mois) de la fin de l'année d'imposition de la société. La date de fin d'année d'imposition doit être la même que celle en vertu de la *Loi de l'impôt sur le revenu*.

Rubrique 3
Indiquer le nom de la province ou du territoire au Canada où le siège social se situera.

Rubrique 4
Indiquer les détails requis par l'alinéa 6(1)(c) de la Loi. Sauf dans les cas où une dispense est accordée en vertu du paragraphe 187(11) de la Loi, toutes les actions doivent être sans valeur nominale ou sans valeur au pair et doivent se conformer à la partie V de la Loi. Les actions avec valeur au pair ou nominales émises par une personne morale avant sa prorogation sont conformes à la Loi en vertu des paragraphes 24(2) et 187(8) et (9) de la Loi. Si le paragraphe 187(11) de la Loi s'applique, indiquer le nombre maximal des actions d'une série ou catégorie requis par le paragraphe 187(12) de la Loi.

Rubrique 5
Si le droit de transfert des actions de la société doit être restreint, inclure une déclaration à cet effet et indiquer la nature de ces restrictions.

Rubrique 6
Indiquer le nombre des administrateurs. Si un vote cumulatif est prévu, ce nombre doit être fixe; autrement, il est permis de spécifier un nombre minimal et maximal d'administrateurs.

Rubrique 7
Indiquer les limites devant être imposées aux activités commerciales de la société.

Rubrique 8
1) Indiquer la dénomination sociale antérieure de la personne morale si un changement de dénomination sociale est effectué lors de la prorogation.
2) Indiquer la date de constitution de la personne morale. Si la personne morale a fait l'objet de toute prorogation antérieure, indiquer les détails de chacune d'elles, soit la date de prorogation, tout changement de dénomination sociale lors de la prorogation, ainsi que le nom et la disposition du texte de loi en vertu duquel elle a été opérée.

Rubrique 9
Indiquer les dispositions que la Loi ou le règlement permet d'énoncer dans les règlements administratifs de la société et qui doivent faire partie des statuts en incluant les dispositions relatives au vote cumulatif ou aux droits de préemption.

Rubrique 10
Veuillez indiquer la qualité du signataire. Le formulaire 11 doit être signé par une des personnes suivantes :

- un **administrateur** de la société
- un **dirigeant autorisé** de la société

Autres documents
Si la prorogation est effectuée en vertu du paragraphe 187(1) de la Loi, les clauses de prorogation doivent être accompagnées :
a) d'une preuve de l'autorisation en vertu de la Loi sous le régime duquel la personne morale est constituée; et
b) du formulaire 2 *'Information concernant le siège social et le conseil d'administration'*.

Les documents complétés et les droits payables au Receveur général du Canada doivent être envoyés au :

Directeur, Loi canadienne sur les sociétés par actions
Tour Jean Edmonds, sud
9ième étage
365, ave Laurier ouest
Ottawa (Ontario) K1A 0C8
ou par télécopieur : (613) 941-0999
Renseignements : 1-866-333-5556

CBCA Forms

Form 14 — Articles of Reorganization

Industry Canada	Industrie Canada	**FORM 14** **ARTICLES OF REORGANIZATION** **(SECTION 191)**	**FORMULAIRE 14** **CLAUSES DE RÉORGANISATION** **(ARTICLE 191)**
Canada Business Corporations Act	Loi canadienne sur les sociétés par actions		

1 -- Name of Corporation - Dénomination sociale de la société

2 -- Corporation No. - Nº de la société

3 -- In accordance with the order for reorganization, the articles of incorporation are amended as follows:

Conformément à l'ordonnance de réorganisation, les statuts constitutifs sont modifiés comme suit :

Signature	Printed Name - Nom en lettres moulées	4 -- Capacity of - En qualité de	5 -- Tel. No. - Nº de tél.

FOR DEPARTMENTAL USE ONLY - À L'USAGE DU MINISTÈRE SEULEMENT

IC 3409 (2003/06)

Canadä

197

CBCA Forms

Canada Business Corporations Act

Articles of Reorganization
FORM 14
INSTRUCTIONS

Format
You must file Form 14 by sending or faxing the completed documents to the address provided below.

Prescribed Fees
By mail or fax: $200

General
(1) Set out the amendments to the articles of incorporation in accordance with the court order pursuant to section 191 of the Act. If an amendment involves a change of corporate name, the new name must comply with sections 10 and 12 of the Act. Articles of reorganization must be accompanied by a Canada-biased NUANS search report dated not more than ninety (90) days prior to the receipt of the articles by the Director. On request, a number name may be assigned under subsection 11(2) of the Act, without a search.

(2) Any amendment shall conform to and correspond to the paragraph and subparagraph references of the existing articles.

Signature
Indicate the capacity of the signing person. Form 14 must be signed by one of the following:

- a **director** of the corporation
- an **authorized officer** of the corporation, or
- the **court**

Other Documents
The articles must be accompanied by:
(a) a copy of the court order; and
(b) if applicable, a Notice of Change of Registered Office (Form 3) and Notice of Change of Directors (Form 6).

The completed document and fees payable to the Receiver General for Canada are to be sent to:

The Director, Canada Business Corporations Act
Jean Edmonds Tower, South
9th Floor
365 Laurier Ave. West
Ottawa, Ontario
K1A 0C8
or by facsimile at: (613) 941-0999
Inquiries: 1-866-333-5556

Loi canadienne sur les sociétés par actions

Clauses de réorganisation
FORMULAIRE 14
INSTRUCTIONS

Présentation
Vous devez déposer le formulaire 14 en envoyant ou en télécopiant le document complété à l'adresse indiquée au bas de cette page.

Droits payables
Par la poste ou télécopieur : 200 $

Généralités
(1) Indiquer les modifications apportées aux statuts constitutifs en vertu de l'ordonnance rendue par le tribunal conformément à l'article 191 de la Loi. Dans les cas où les modifications comportent un changement de dénomination sociale, la nouvelle dénomination doit satisfaire aux exigences des articles 10 et 12 de la Loi. Les clauses de réorganisation doivent être accompagnées d'un rapport de recherche NUANS couvrant le Canada, dont la date remonte à quatre-vingt-dix (90) jours ou moins avant la date de réception par le directeur des clauses de réorganisation. Si un numéro matricule est demandé en guise de dénomination sociale, il peut être assigné, sans recherche préalable, en vertu du paragraphe 11(2) de la Loi.

(2) Toute modification doit être conforme et correspondre aux renvois des alinéas et sous-alinéas des statuts existants.

Signature
Veuillez indiquer la qualité du signataire. Le formulaire 14 doit être signé par :

- un **administrateur** de la société
- un **dirigeant autorisé** de la société, ou
- par le **tribunal**

Autres documents
Les clauses doivent être accompagnées :
(a) d'un exemplaire de l'ordonnance du tribunal;
(b) s'il y a lieu, d'un avis de changement du siège social (formulaire 3) et d'un avis de changement des administrateurs (formulaire 6).

Le document complété et les droits payables au Receveur général du Canada doivent être envoyés au :

Directeur, Loi canadienne sur les sociétés par actions
Tour Jean Edmonds, sud
9ième étage
365, av. Laurier ouest
Ottawa (Ontario)
K1A 0C8
ou par télécopieur : (613) 941-0999
Renseignements : 1-866-333-5556

IC 3409 (2003/06) p.2

Form 14.1 — Articles of Arrangement

Industry Canada Industrie Canada	FORM 14.1	FORMULAIRE 14.1
Canada Business Loi canadienne sur les Corporations Act sociétés par actions	ARTICLES OF ARRANGEMENT (SECTION 192)	CLAUSES D'ARRANGEMENT (ARTICLE 192)

1 -- Name of the applicant corporation(s) - Dénomination sociale de la(des) requérante(s)	2 -- Corporation No.(s) - Nᵒ(s) de la(des) société(s)

3 -- Name of the corporation(s) the articles of which are amended, if applicable Dénomination sociale de la(des) société(s) dont les statuts sont modifiés, le cas échéant	4 -- Corporation No.(s) - Nᵒ(s) de la(des) société(s)

5 -- Name of the corporation(s) created by amalgamation, if applicable Dénomination sociale de la(des) société(s) issue(s) de la(der) fusion(s), le cas échéant	6 -- Corporation No.(s) - Nᵒ(s) de la(des) société(s)

7 -- Name of the dissolved corporation(s), if applicable Dénomination sociale de la(des) société(s) dissoute(s), le cas échéant	8 -- Corporation No.(s) - Nᵒ(s) de la(des) société(s)

9 -- Name of other corporations involved, if applicable Dénomination sociale des autres sociétés en cause, le cas échéant	10 -- Corporation No.(s) or Jurisdiction of incorporation Nᵒ(s) de la(des) société(s)/ou, loi sous le régime de aquelle elle est constituée

11 -- In accordance with the order approving the arrangement - Conformément aux termes de l'ordonnance approuvant l'arrangement

a. ☐ The articles of the above named corporation(s) are amended in accordance with the attached plan of arrangement
Les statuts de la(des) société(s) susmentionnée(s) sont modifiés en conformité avec le plan d'arrangement ci-joint

The name of _____ is changed to _____

La dénomination sociale de _____ est modifiée pour _____

b. ☐ The following bodies corporate are amalgamated in accordance with the attached plan of arrangement
Les personnes morales suivantes sont fusionnées conformément au plan d'arrangement ci-joint

c. ☐ The above named corporation(s) is(are) liquidated and dissolved in accordance with the attached plan of arrangement
La(les) société(s) susmentionnée(s) est(sont) liquidée(s) et dissoute(s) conformément au plan d'arrangement ci-joint

d. ☐ The plan of arrangement attached hereto, involving the above named body(ies), corporate is hereby effected
Le plan d'arrangement ci-joint portant sur la(les) personne(s) morale(s) susmentionnée(s) prend effet

Signature	Printed Name - Nom en lettres moulées	12 -- Capacity of - En qualité de	13 -- Tel. No. - Nᵒ de tél.

FOR DEPARTMENTAL USE ONLY - À L'USAGE DU MINISTÈRE SEULEMENT

IC 3189 (2003/06)

Canada

CBCA Forms

Canada Business Corporations Act

Articles of Arrangement
FORM 14.1
INSTRUCTIONS

Loi canadienne sur les sociétés par actions

Clauses d'arrangement
FORMULAIRE 14.1
INSTRUCTIONS

General

Format
If you require more information in order to complete Form 14.1, you may wish to consult the Policy of the Director Concerning Arrangements Under Section 192 of the CBCA.

You must file Form 14.1 by sending or faxing the completed documents to the address provided below.

Prescribed Fees
By mail or fax: $200

Items 2, 4, 6, 8 and 10
Insert the corporate number only for the corporations incorporated pursuant to the *Canada Business Corporations Act*.

Item 11
Check the appropriate box or boxes.

In respect of (a), if a corporate name is amended, indicate the new corporate name.

In respect of (b), list the names of all bodies corporate involved in the amalgamation creating the corporation(s) specified in item 5.

In respect of (b), all of the information required by Form 9 (Articles of Amalgamation) should appear clearly in the annexed plan of arrangement or schedule to these articles.

Signature

Item 12
Indicate the capacity of the signing person. Form 14.1 must be signed by one of the following persons:

- a **director** of the corporation
- an **authorized officer** of the corporation

Other Documents
The articles must be accompanied by:

i) a copy of the court order; and

ii) if applicable, a Notice of Change of Registered Office (Form 3) and a Notice of Change of Directors (Form 6) and a Canada-biased NUANS search report dated not more than ninety (90) days prior to the receipt of the articles by the Director.

The completed documents and fees payable to the Receiver General for Canada are to be sent to:

The Director, Canada Business Corporations Act
Jean Edmonds Tower, South
9th Floor
365 Laurier Ave. West
Ottawa, Ontario
K1A 0C8
or by facsimile at: (613) 941-5781
Inquiries: 1-866-333-5556

Généralités

Présentation
Si vous désirez obtenir de plus amples informations afin de compléter le formulaire 14.1, veuillez consulter la Politique concernant les arrangements en vertu de l'article 192 de la LCSA.

Vous devez déposer le formulaire 14.1 en envoyant ou en télécopiant le document complété à l'adresse indiquée au bas de cette page.

Droits payables
Par la poste ou télécopieur : 200 $

Rubriques 2, 4, 6, 8 et 10
Inscrire le numéro de la société dans les seuls cas où les sociétés sont constituées en vertu de la *Loi canadienne sur les sociétés par actions*.

Rubrique 11
Cocher la ou les cases appropriées.

Sous le point (a), si une dénomination sociale est modifiée, indiquez la nouvelle dénomination sociale.

Sous le point (b), énumérer les dénominations de toutes les personnes morales en cause dans la fusion créant la(les) société(s) spécifiée(s) à la rubrique 5.

Sous le point (b), tous les renseignements requis au formulaire 9 (statuts de fusion) doivent apparaître clairement dans le plan d'arrangement ci-joint ou dans une annexe à ces statuts.

Signature

Rubrique 12
Veuillez indiquer la qualité du signataire. Le formulaire 14.1 doit être signé par une des personnes suivantes :

- un **administrateur** de la société
- un **dirigeant autorisé** de la société

Autres documents
Les clauses doivent être accompagnées :

i) d'un exemplaire de l'ordonnance du tribunal

ii) le cas échéant, d'un avis de changement du siège social (formulaire 3) et d'un avis de changement des administrateurs (formulaire 6) et d'un rapport de recherche NUANS couvrant le Canada, dont la date remonte à quatre vingt-dix (90) jours ou moins avant la date de réception par le directeur des clauses d'arrangement.

Les documents complétés et les droits payables au Receveur général du Canada doivent être envoyés au :

Directeur, Loi canadienne sur les sociétés par actions
Tour Jean Edmonds, sud
9ième étage
365, av. Laurier ouest
Ottawa (Ontario)
K1A 0C8
ou par télécopieur : (613) 941-5781
Renseignements : 1-866-333-5556

CBCA Forms

Form 15 — Articles of Revival

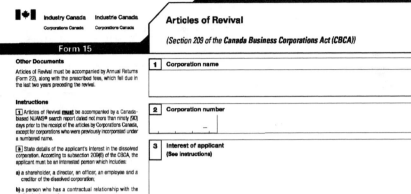

Industry Canada · **Industrie Canada**
Corporations Canada · Corporations Canada

Form 15

Articles of Revival

(Section 209 of the Canada Business Corporations Act (CBCA))

Other Documents

Articles of Revival must be accompanied by Annual Returns (Form 22), along with the prescribed fees, which fell due in the last two years preceding the revival.

Instructions

1 Articles of Revival **must** be accompanied by a Canada-biased NUANS® search report dated not more than ninety (90) days prior to the receipt of the articles by Corporations Canada, except for corporations who were previously incorporated under a numbered name.

3 State details of the applicant's interest in the dissolved corporation. According to subsection 209(6) of the CBCA, the applicant must be an interested person which includes:

a) a shareholder, a director, an officer, an employee and a creditor of the dissolved corporation;

b) a person who has a contractual relationship with the dissolved corporation;

c) a person who was not a person described in paragraph a) at the time of dissolution, but would be such a person if a certificate of revival is issued; and

d) a trustee in bankruptcy for the dissolved corporation.

4 If the applicant is a body corporate, (e.g., a corporation), the name shall be the name of the body corporate, the address shall be that of its registered office, and the articles shall be signed by a person authorized by the body corporate.

General

The information you provide in this document is collected under the authority of the CBCA and will be stored in personal information bank number IC/PPU-049. Personal information that you provide is protected under the provisions of the *Privacy Act.* However, public disclosure pursuant to section 266 of the CBCA is permitted under the *Privacy Act.*

If you require more information, please consult our website at www.corporationscanada.ic.gc.ca or contact us at 613-941-9042 (Ottawa region), toll-free at 1-866-333-5556 or by email at corporationscanada@ic.gc.ca.

Prescribed Fees

- By mail or fax: $200
- Annual Returns: $40 per year
- Fees are payable with a cheque to the Receiver General for Canada or with a credit card (American Express®, Master Card® or Visa®).

Send documents by mail:
**Director General,
Corporations Canada
Jean Edmonds Tower South
9th Floor
365 Laurier Ave. West
Ottawa ON K1A 0C8**

Or by Facsimile:
613-941-0999

1 **Corporation name**

2 **Corporation number**

3 **Interest of applicant**
(See instructions)

WHAT YOU SHOULD KNOW ABOUT REVIVING A CORPORATION

A revived corporation is restored as if it had not been dissolved. Therefore, **the public record will show the articles of the revived corporation exactly as they were on the public record at the time the corporation was dissolved**. Changes made after dissolution will not be reflected.

Reporting Obligations:

If changes have been made to the information contained in the corporation's articles, articles of amendment must be filed.

Changes of registered office address and/or mailing address: Complete and file Change of Registered Office Address (Form 3).

Changes of directors or changes of a director's address: Complete and file Changes Regarding Directors (Form 6).

Remember these changes must be made as soon as possible after the corporation is revived.

4 **Declaration**

I hereby certify that the request for revival of this body corporate is intended for legal purposes, in good faith and in the interest of the applicant.

PRINT NAME

NUMBER AND STREET NAME (a P.O. Box is not acceptable)

CITY — PROVINCE / TERRITORY — POSTAL CODE

( )

SIGNATURE — TELEPHONE NUMBER

Note: Misrepresentation constitutes an offence and, on summary conviction, a person is liable to a fine not exceeding $5000 or to imprisonment for a term not exceeding six months or both (subsection 250(1) of the CBCA).

Canada

IC 3339 (2008/11)

CBCA Forms

Form 17 — Articles of Dissolution

Note: All corporations are to complete Items 1, 2, 3 and 6, and either complete Item 4 or 5.
Nota : Toutes les sociétés doivent remplir les rubriques 1, 2, 3 et 6, ainsi que la rubrique 4 ou 5.

1 -- Name of the Corporation - Dénomination sociale de la société	2 -- Corporation No. - N° de la société

3 -- Is the Corporation bankrupt or insolvent within the meaning of the Bankruptcy and Insolvency Act?
La société est-elle en faillite ou insolvable au sens de la Loi sur la faillite et l'insolvabilité ?

☐ Yes - Oui   ☐ No - Non

Complete either Item 4 or 5, but not both - Remplir la rubrique 4 ou 5, mais non les deux

4 -- Has the corporation previously filed a statement of intent to dissolve (Form 19) under subsection 211(4) of the Act?
La société a-t-elle déjà déposé une déclaration d'intention de dissolution (formulaire 19) en vertu du paragraphe 211(4) de la Loi ?

☐ Yes - Oui   If the answer is negative, please complete only Item 5 - Si la réponse est négative, veuillez remplir seulement la rubrique 5

If yes, has the corporation provided for the payment or discharge of its obligations and distributed its remaining property as required by subsection 211(7) of the Act?
Dans l'affirmative, conformément au paragraphe 211(7) de la Loi, la société a-t-elle constitué une provision pour honorer ses obligations et réparti le reliquat de l'actif ?

☐ Yes - Oui   ☐ No - Non

5 -- Is the Corporation applying for dissolution under section 210 of the Act?
(To apply under section 210, the corporation cannot have previously filed a statement of intent to dissolve (Form 19) under subsection 211(7) of the Act.)

La société dépose-t-elle une demande de dissolution en vertu de l'article 210 de la Loi? (Pour être admissible en vertu de l'article 210, la société ne peut pas avoir déposé une déclaration d'intention de dissolution (formulaire 19) en vertu du paragraphe 211(7) de la Loi.)

☐ Yes - Oui   If the answer is negative, please complete only Item 4 - Si la réponse est négative, veuillez remplir seulement la rubrique 4

If yes, under what subsection of the Act is the corporation applying for dissolution? **(CHECK ONLY ONE ITEM)**
Dans l'affirmative, en vertu de quel paragraphe de la Loi société procède-t-elle ? **(COCHER UNE RUBRIQUE SEULEMENT)**

☐ Subsection 210(1) of the Act applying to a corporation that has not issued any shares.
Paragraphe 210(1) de la Loi applicable à une société qui n'a pas émis d'actions.
or / ou

☐ Subsection 210(2) of the Act applying to a corporation that has no property and no liabilities.
Paragraphe 210(2) de la Loi applicable à une société sans biens ni dettes.
or / ou

☐ Subsection 210(3) of the Act applying to a corporation that has discharged its liabilities and distributed its property.
Paragraphe 210(3) de la Loi applicable à une société qui a réglé ses dettes et réparti ses biens.

6 -- Name, address and occupation of the person keeping the documents and records of the corporation for six years after the date of dissolution.
Nom, adresse et profession de la personne qui garde les documents et livres de la société pour une période de six ans suivant la date de dissolution.

Signature	Printed Name - Nom en lettres moulées	7 -- Capacity of - En qualité de	8 -- Tel. No. - N° de tél.

FOR DEPARTMENTAL USE ONLY - À L'USAGE DU MINISTÈRE SEULEMENT

IC 3317 (2003/06)

Canadä

202

CBCA Forms

Canada Business Corporations Act	**Loi canadienne sur les sociétés par actions**
Articles of Dissolution	**Clauses de dissolution**
FORM 17	**FORMULAIRE 17**
INSTRUCTIONS	**INSTRUCTIONS**

General

If you require more information in order to complete Form 17, you may wish to consult the Dissolution Kit.

You can file Form 17 through the Corporations Canada On-line Filing Centre at http://strategis.ic.gc.ca/corporations or you can send or fax the completed documents to the address provided below.

All corporations must complete Items 1, 2, 3 and 6. All corporations must also complete either Item 4 or 5, but not both.

Item 1
The full legal name of the corporation.

Item 2
The corporation number.

Item 3
It is not possible to dissolve an insolvent or bankrupt corporation under the provisions of the Act.

Item 4
If the corporation is applying for dissolution under Section 211 of the Act and has previously filed a statement of intent to dissolve (Form 19), indicate whether the corporation has provided for payment or discharge of its obligations and distributed its remaining property, as required by subsection 211(7) of the Act.

Item 5
If the corporation is applying for dissolution under Section 210 of the Act, check the appropriate box (check only one). To apply under Section 210, a corporation cannot have previously filed a statement of intent to dissolve (Form 19).

Item 6
The first given name, initials, family name and business address of the person who will be liable to produce the documents and records of the dissolved corporation under Section 225 of the Act.

Item 7
Indicate the capacity of the signing person. Form 17 must be signed by one of the following persons:

- a **director** of the corporation
- an **authorized officer** of the corporation

Caution
This form should not be filed at the same time as a Statement of Intent to Dissolve.

Completed document is to be sent to:

The Director, Canada Business Corporations Act
Jean Edmonds Tower, South
9th Floor
365 Laurier Ave. West
Ottawa, Ontario
K1A 0C8
or by facsimile at: (613) 941-0999
Inquiries: 1-866-333-5556

Généralités

Si vous désirez obtenir de plus amples informations afin de compléter le formulaire 17, veuillez consulter le Recueil d'information sur la dissolution.

Vous pouvez déposer le formulaire 17 par l'entremise du Centre de dépôt des formulaires en ligne de Corporations Canada au http://strategis.ic.gc.ca/corporations ou encore envoyer ou télécopier le document complété à l'adresse indiquée au bas de cette page.

Toutes les sociétés doivent remplir les rubriques 1, 2, 3 et 6. Toutes les sociétés doivent aussi remplir soit la rubrique 4 ou 5, mais non les deux.

Rubrique 1
La dénomination sociale complète de la société.

Rubrique 2
Le numéro de la société.

Rubrique 3
Il n'est pas possible selon les dispositions de la Loi de dissoudre une société insolvable ou en faillite.

Rubrique 4
Si la société veut faire une demande de dissolution en vertu de l'article 211 de la Loi et qu'elle a déjà déposé une déclaration d'intention de dissolution (formulaire 19), indiquer si la société a constitué une provision suffisante pour honorer ses obligations et répartir le reliquat de l'actif, conformément au paragraphe 211(7) de la Loi.

Rubrique 5
Si la société veut faire une demande de dissolution en vertu de l'article 210 de la Loi, cochez la case appropriée (cocher une boîte seulement). Afin de faire une demande en vertu de l'article 210 de la Loi, la société ne doit pas avoir déposé une déclaration d'intention de dissolution (formulaire 19).

Rubrique 6
Le prénom, les initiales, le nom de famille et l'adresse d'affaires de la personne qui peut être tenue de produire, en vertu de l'article 225 de la Loi, les documents et livres de la société dissoute.

Rubrique 7
Veuillez indiquer la qualité du signataire. Le formulaire 17 doit être signé par une des personnes suivantes :

- un **administrateur** de la société
- un **dirigeant autorisé** de la société

Remarque
Ce formulaire ne doit pas être déposé en même temps qu'une déclaration d'intention de dissolution (formulaire 19).

Le document complété doit être envoyé ou :

Directeur, Loi canadienne sur les sociétés par actions
Tour Jean-Edmonds, sud
9ième étage
365, ave Laurier ouest
Ottawa (Ontario)
K1A 0C8
ou par télécopieur : (613) 941-0999
Renseignements : 1-866-333-5556

IC 3317 (2003/06)

Form 19 — Statement of Intent to Dissolve or Revocation of Intent to Dissolve

▌♦▌ Industry Canada	Industrie Canada	**FORM 19**	**FORMULAIRE 19**
Canada Business Corporations Act	Loi canadienne sur les sociétés par actions	**STATEMENT OF INTENT TO DISSOLVE OR REVOCATION OF INTENT TO DISSOLVE (SECTION 211)**	**DÉCLARATION D'INTENTION DE DISSOLUTION OU DE RENONCIATION D'INTENTION DE DISSOLUTION (ARTICLE 211)**

1 — Name of the Corporation - Dénomination sociale de la société

2 — Corporation No. - N° de la société

3 — The Corporation intends to liquidate and dissolve ☐ La société a l'intention de procéder à sa liquidation et à sa dissolution

4 — The Corporation revokes its certificate of intent to dissolve ☐ La société révoque son certificat d'intention de dissolution

Signature	Printed Name - Nom en lettres moulées	5 — Capacity of - En qualité de	6 — Tel. No. - N° de tél.

FOR DEPARTMENTAL USE ONLY - À L'USAGE DU MINISTÈRE SEULEMENT

IC 3344 (2003/09)

Canada

CBCA Forms

Canada Business Corporations Act

Statement of Intent to Dissolve or Statement
of Revocation of Intent to Dissolve
FORM 19
INSTRUCTIONS

Loi canadienne sur les sociétés par actions

Déclaration d'Intention de dissolution ou
déclaration de renonciation d'intention de dissolution
FORMULAIRE 19
INSTRUCTIONS

General
If you require more information in order to complete Form 19, you may wish to consult the Dissolution Kit.

You can file Form 19 through the Corporations Canada On-line Filing Centre at http://strategis.ic.gc.ca/corporations or you can send or fax the completed documents to the address provided below.

Prescribed Fees
Statement of Intent to Dissolve: no fee
Revocation of Intent to Dissolve: $50

Item 1
The full legal name of the corporation.

Item 2
The corporation number.

Item 3
Check item 3 if the corporation intends to liquidate and dissolve under subsection 211(3) of the Act.

Item 4
Check item 4 if the corporation intends to revoke under subsection 211(10) of the Act a certificate of intent to dissolve issued to it under subsection 211(5) of the Act.

Item 5
Indicate the capacity of the signing person. Form 19 must be signed by one of the following persons:

- a **director** of the corporation
- an **authorized officer** of the corporation

Caution
This form should not be filed at the same time as the Articles of Dissolution (Form 17).

The completed document and fees, if applicable, payable to the Receiver General for Canada are to be sent to:

The Director, Canada Business Corporations Act
Jean Edmonds Tower, South
9th Floor
365 Laurier Ave. West
Ottawa, Ontario
K1A 0C8
or by facsimile at: (613) 941-0999
Inquiries: 1-866-333-5556

Généralités
Si vous désirez obtenir de plus amples informations afin de compléter le formulaire 19, veuillez consulter le Recueil d'information sur la dissolution.

Vous pouvez déposer le formulaire 19 par l'entremise du Centre de dépôt des formulaires en ligne de Corporations Canada au http://strategis.ic.gc.ca/corporations ou encore envoyer ou télécopier le document complété à l'adresse indiquée au bas de cette page.

Droits payables
Déclaration d'intention de dissolution : aucun frais
Déclaration de renonciation d'intention de dissolution : 50 $

Rubrique 1
La dénomination sociale complète de la société.

Rubrique 2
Le numéro de la société.

Rubrique 3
Cocher la rubrique 3, si la société envisage de procéder à sa liquidation et à sa dissolution en vertu du paragraphe 211(3) de la Loi.

Rubrique 4
Cocher la rubrique 4, si la société entend révoquer, en vertu du paragraphe 211(10) de la Loi, un certificat d'intention de dissolution délivré en vertu du paragraphe 211(5) de la Loi.

Rubrique 5
Veuillez indiquer la qualité du signataire. Le formulaire 19 doit être signé par une des personnes suivantes :

- un **administrateur** de la société
- un **dirigeant autorisé** de la société

Remarque
Ce formulaire ne peut être déposé en même temps que les clauses de dissolution (formulaire 17).

Le document complété et les droits payables au Receveur général du Canada, s'il y a lieu, doivent être envoyés ou :

Directeur, Loi canadienne sur les sociétés par actions
Tour Jean Edmonds, sud
9ième étage
365, av. Laurier ouest
Ottawa (Ontario)
K1A 0C8
ou par télécopieur : (613) 941-0999
Renseignements : 1-866-333-5556

IC 3344 (2003/09) p.2

Form 22 — Annual Return

Industry Canada   Industrie Canada
Corporations Canada   Corporations Canada

Form 22

Annual Return

(Section 263 of the Canada Business Corporations Act (CBCA))

THIS FORM CAN BE REPRODUCED AS LONG AS THE TITLE, THE QUESTIONS AND THEIR ORDER ARE THE SAME.

Corporations must file an Annual Return (Form 22) along with the prescribed fee. Please be advised that amendments to the *Canada Business Corporations Regulations, 2001* changing the time frames for filing Annual Returns are now in force. For further information, please refer to the Notice from the Director, "How Changes to the Filing Requirements for Annual Returns Affect Your Business", dated May 2, 2006, and available at www.corporationscanada.ic.gc.ca under "What's new".

INSTRUCTIONS

3 Indicate for which taxation year you are filing as well as the taxation year-end as defined in the *Income Tax Act*. For more information, visit the Canada Revenue Agency (CRA) Web site at **www.cra-arc.gc.ca**. Note that a change to the taxation year-end needs the approval of the CRA.

4 Indicate the date of the last annual meeting or the date of the written resolution in lieu of a meeting, signed by all the shareholders entitled to vote. The resolution must deal with at least the following:

* consideration of the financial statements;
* consideration of the auditor's report (if any);
* appointment of the auditor (shareholders of a non-distributing corporation may resolve not to appoint an auditor); and
* election of directors (if applicable).

5 A *non-distributing corporation* is a **private** corporation that is not a reporting issuer under any provincial securities legislation.
A *distributing corporation* is a **public** corporation that is a reporting issuer under provincial securities legislation.

6 Declaration

This form may be signed by any individual who has the relevant knowledge of the corporation and who is authorized by the directors (subsection 262.1(2) of the CBCA).

For example:

* a **director** of the corporation;
* an **authorized officer** of the corporation; or
* an **authorized agent**.

General

The information you provide in this document is collected under the authority of the CBCA and will be stored in personal information bank number IC/PPU-049. Personal information that you provide is protected under the provisions of the *Privacy Act*. However, public disclosure pursuant to section 266 of the CBCA is permitted under the *Privacy Act*.
If you require more information, please consult the Forms, Policies, Fees and Legislation section of our Web site at www.corporationscanada.ic.gc.ca or contact us at (613) 941-9042 or toll-free at 1 866 333-5556 or by email at corporationscanada@ic.gc.ca.

Prescribed Fees

* Corporations Canada Online Filing Centre: $20
* By mail or fax: $40

File documents online:

Corporations Canada Online Filing Centre:
www.corporationscanada.ic.gc.ca

Or send documents by mail:

Director, Corporations Canada
Jean Edmonds Tower South
9th Floor
365 Laurier Ave. West
Ottawa ON K1A 0C8

By Facsimile:
(613) 941-0999

Canada

1 Corporation name

2 Corporation number

3 Year of filing

Year ____ Y ____   Taxation year-end ____ M __ D __

4 Date of last annual meeting of shareholders or date of written resolution in lieu of meeting

Y ____ M ____ D ____

5 Which of the following boxes meets your situation (check only one item)? Please refer to the instructions for definitions

☐ Non-distributing corporation with 50 or fewer shareholders
☐ Non-distributing corporation with more than 50 shareholders
☐ Distributing corporation

IMPORTANT REMINDER

Change of registered office address?
Complete and file a Change of Registered Office Address (Form 3).

Change of directors or change of address of a current director?
Complete and file a Changes Regarding Directors (Form 6).

These changes can be done electronically, free of charge, via Corporations Canada Online Filing Centre at: **www.corporationscanada.ic.gc.ca**

6 Declaration

I hereby certify that I have the relevant knowledge of the corporation, and that I am authorized to sign and submit this form.

SIGNATURE

PRINT NAME   (   )
                              TELEPHONE NUMBER

Note: Misrepresentation constitutes an offence and, on summary conviction, a person is liable to a fine not exceeding $5000 or to imprisonment for a term not exceeding six months or both (subsection 250(1) of the CBCA).

IC 2580 (2006/06)

Notice From The Director: How Changes To The Filing Requirements For Annual Returns Affect Your Business

May 2, 2006

On July 1, 2006, amendments to the *Canada Business Corporations Regulations, 2001* changing the requirements for corporations filing Annual Returns (Form 22) will come into force. The basis for filing will change from the Taxation Year-End to the Anniversary Date. In order to ensure a smooth transition, as well as regulatory compliance for your corporation, we suggest you take the time to review this notice to find out more about how these changes will directly impact the time frames for filing your corporation's Annual Return.

The diagram below illustrates important transition rules that pertain to you and your corporation. Begin by choosing the appropriate date or time span in the left-hand column that includes your corporation's Anniversary Date (i.e., Date of Incorporation, Amalgamation or Continuance). From there, move towards the right to find your Taxation Year-End (TYE), as well as the filing time frame for your 2006 Annual Return and the filing time frame for your 2007 and subsequent Annual Returns. It is important to remember that the information you provide in your Annual Return represents your corporation's situation on the Taxation Year-End or the Anniversary Date, as appropriate.

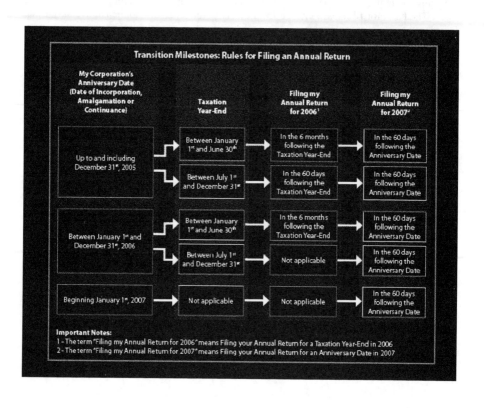

Transition Milestones: Rules for Filing an Annual Return

My Corporation's Anniversary Date (Date of Incorporation, Amalgamation or Continuance)	Taxation Year-End	Filing my Annual Return for 2006[1]	Filing my Annual Return for 2007[2]
Up to and including December 31st, 2005	Between January 1st and June 30th	In the 6 months following the Taxation Year-End	In the 60 days following the Anniversary Date
	Between July 1st and December 31st	In the 60 days following the Taxation Year-End	In the 60 days following the Anniversary Date
Between January 1st and December 31st, 2006	Between January 1st and June 30th	In the 6 months following the Taxation Year-End	In the 60 days following the Anniversary Date
	Between July 1st and December 31st	Not applicable	In the 60 days following the Anniversary Date
Beginning January 1st, 2007	Not applicable	Not applicable	In the 60 days following the Anniversary Date

Important Notes:
1 - The term "Filing my Annual Return for 2006" means Filing your Annual Return for a Taxation Year-End in 2006
2 - The term "Filing my Annual Return for 2007" means Filing your Annual Return for an Anniversary Date in 2007

If you need to confirm your corporation's Anniversary Date, this information is generally found at the bottom, right-hand corner of the Certificate of Incorporation, Amalgamation or Continuance. However, if you are still unable to locate your corporation's Anniversary Date, please visit our website at *www.corporationscanada.ic.gc.ca* and click on "Search for a Federal Corporation" in the left-hand menu of the homepage and enter your corporation number or name in the appropriate box.

You can also use the Annual Return Filing Calculator on the Corporations Canada website to help you to determine the filing timeframe for your Annual Return. To access the Calculator, simply click "Online Filing" on the Corporations Canada website homepage and then "Annual Return Filing Calculator".

If you have any questions about the new regulations or would like to find out more about the Annual Return filing date changes, please visit the Corporations Canada website or contact:

Corporations Canada
Jean Edmonds Towers South
9th Floor
365 Laurier Avenue West
Ottawa, ON K1A 0C8
General Information: (613) 941-9042
Toll-Free: (866) 333-5556
Email: *corporationscanada@ic.gc.ca*
Website: *www.corporationscanada.ic.gc.ca*

Richard G. Shaw
Director General

Form 22A — Change of Taxation Year-End

Form 22-A
(Changes Concerning the Taxation Year-End)

The following form should be used to record changes concerning your corporate taxation year-end. When completed, please attach this form to Corporations Canada Form 22 - Annual Return and return it to:

Corporations Canada
Industry Canada
9th Floor, Jean Edmonds Tower South
Ottawa, Ontario K1A 0C8
Fax: (613) 941-4803

Corporation number: _ _ _ _ _ _ - _
Corporation name:_____
Please check the box describing your situation:

☐ The corporation has received a specific authorization from the Canada Revenue Agency (CRA) allowing it to change its taxation year-end;
From: _____ / _____ to _____ / _____
    Month Day   Month Day

☐ The taxation year-end has been modified by the *Income Tax Act* due to an event, such as a merger of Canadian corporations or takeover of a corporation. (You are responsible for contacting CRA to confirm that these are the circumstances in your case.) The taxation year-end has been modified:
From: _____ / _____ to _____ / _____
    Month Day   Month Day

☐ The corporation ends its taxation year end on a chosen day of the week that is nearest to a certain day of the year (referred to as a 'floating year end'). This is not considered a change in taxation year end by the Canada Revenue Agency and so does not require its approval. For example, the corporation closes its books on the last Saturday in December in every year.

☐ The taxation year-end indicated on a previous Annual Return (Form 22) received by Corporations Canada was erroneously entered; the actual taxation year-end date is:
Date of taxation year-end: _____ / _____
               Month Day

I certify that the above information is consistent with information on file with the Canada Revenue Agency.

_____   _____
Signature   Date

To learn more about the terms and conditions permitting changes concerning your taxation year-end, please consult Policy 10.5.1 - Changes concerning the taxation year-end on Corporations Canada's Website http://corporationscanada.ic.gc.ca under the heading "Forms, Policies, Fees and Legislation/ *Canada Business Corporations Act*/Policies ».

Form 26 — Statement of Executive Remuneration

Canada Business Corporations Act	Loi canadienne sur les sociétés par actions
STATEMENT OF EXECUTIVE REMUNERATION FORM 26 [Section 150 CBCA, Paragraph 57q) of the Regulations]	**DÉCLARATION DE RÉMUNÉRATION DE LA HAUTE DIRECTION FORMULE 26** [article 150 LCSA, alinéa 57q) du Règlement]

Format

The information on Executive Remuneration is required to be disclosed in a management proxy circular in circumstances specified in paragraph 57q) of the *Canada Business Corporations Regulations (2001)*.

Please indicate the following information in the order set out below. The information should be legibly printed.

General

For the purposes of this form, "executive officer" of a corporation means the chairman and any vice-chairman of the board of directors of the corporation, where that chairman or vice-chairman performs the functions of the office on a full-time basis, the president of the corporation, any vice-president in charge of a principal business unit of the corporation, such as sales, finance or production, and any officer of the corporation or of a subsidiary who performs a policy-making function in respect of the corporation, whether or not the officer is also a director of the corporation or its subsidiary.

Remuneration of directors who are not also executive officers is taken into account only as provided in item 5 of this form.

Item 1

Cash

(1) State the number of executive officers of the corporation.

(2) State the aggregate cash remuneration paid to the executive officers of the corporation by the corporation and its subsidiaries for services rendered during the most recently completed financial year.

(3) For the purposes of subsection (2),

    (a) cash remuneration includes salaries, fees, commissions and bonuses and, in addition to amounts actually paid during and for the most recently completed financial year, the following:

        (i) bonuses to be paid for services rendered during the most recently completed financial year, unless these bonuses have not been allocated,

        (ii) bonuses paid during the most recently completed financial year for services rendered in a previous financial year, and

        (iii) any remuneration other than bonuses earned during the most recently completed financial year, the payment of which is deferred;

    (b) remuneration paid to an individual for a period during which the individual was not an executive officer shall not be included in the determination of cash remuneration of executive officers; and,

    (c) remuneration paid during the most recently completed financial year that was disclosed in the filing of a document complying with the requirements of this form or a predecessor thereof in respect of a financial year other than the most recently completed financial year shall not be included.

(4) At the option of the corporation, the cash remuneration figure set out pursuant to subsection (2) may be broken down into categories, such as salaries, fees, commissions and bonuses.

Item 2

Plans

(1) Describe briefly any plan pursuant to which cash or non cash remuneration was paid or distributed to executive officers during the most recently completed financial year, or is proposed to be so paid or distributed in a subsequent year, and include in the description:

    (a) a summary of how the plan operates;

    (b) the criteria used to determine amounts payable;

    (c) the periods during which the benefits will be measured;

    (d) payment schedules;

    (e) any recent material amendments to the plan;

    (f) amounts paid or distributed during the most recently completed financial year; and

    (g) amounts accrued for the group during the most recently completed financial year, inasmuch as the distribution or unconditional vesting of those amounts is not subject to future events.

(2) With respect to any plan involving options to purchase securities granted to executive officers during the most recently completed financial year, set out:

    (a) a summary of how the plan operates;

    (b) the criteria used to determine the number of securities under option;

    (c) the periods during which the benefits will be measured;

    (d) payment schedules;

    (e) any recent material amendments to the plan;

Présentation

Les renseignements concernant la rémunération de la haute direction doivent être divulgués suivant les exigences spécifiées à l'alinéa 57q) du *Règlement sur les sociétés canadiennes par actions (2001)*.

Veuillez fournir les renseignements en suivant l'ordre des rubriques indiqué sur cette formule. Les renseignements doivent être fournis de manière lisible.

Généralités

Aux fins de la présente formule, «haute direction» d'une société désigne le président et les vice-présidents du conseil d'administration qui remplissent aux fonctions à plein temps, le président, les vice-présidents responsables d'un secteur de l'activité principale de la société, notamment es ventes, les finances ou la production, et tout dirigeant de la société ou d'une filiale qui exerce des pouvoirs de décision sur la politique générale de la société, qu'il soit ou non ège en tant administrateur de la société ou de sa filiale.

La rémunération des administrateurs qui ne font pas partie de la haute direction n'est prise en compte qu'aux fins de la rubrique 5 de cette formule.

Rubrique 1

Rémunération en espèces

(1) Indiquer le nombre de personnes composant la haute direction de la société.

(2) Indiquer le montant global de la rémunération en espèces versé à la haute direction de la société par a société et ses filiales en contrepartie des services rendus au cours du dernier exercice.

(3) Aux fins du paragraphe (2) :

    (a) la rémunération en espèces comprend notamment le traitement, les jetons de présence, les commissions et les primes effectivement versés au cours et au titre du dernier exercice, ainsi que :

        (i) les primes à recevoir en contrepartie des services rendus au cours du dernier exercice, à moins qu'elles n'aient pas encore été attribuées,

        (ii) les primes payées au cours du dernier exercice pour des services rendus dans un exercice antérieur,

        (iii) toute rémunération, autre que les primes, gagnée au cours du dernier exercice, mais dont le versement est différé;

    (b) la rémunération versée à un membre de la haute direction pour toute période pendant laquelle il n'était pas membre de la haute direction n'entre pas dans le calcul de la rémunération en espèces de la haute direction;

    (c) la rémunération versée au cours du dernier exercice qui a déjà été déclarée dans un document déposé conformément aux exigences de la présente formule ou d'une formule antérieure relativement à un exercice autre que le dernier exercice n'entre pas dans le calcul de la rémunération en espèces de la haute direction.

(4) Au pré de la société, la rémunération en espèces visée au paragraphe (2) peut être ventilée selon des postes tels que salaires, jetons de présence, commissions et primes.

Rubrique 2

Rémunération sous forme de régimes

(1) Décrire succinctement tout régime en vertu duquel une rémunération, en espèces ou non, a été versée aux membres de la haute direction ou répartie entre eux au cours du dernier exercice ou est censée l'être au cours d'un exercice ultérieur et inclure les renseignements suivants :

    (a) le sommaire du mode de fonctionnement du régime;

    (b) les critères utilisés pour déterminer les sommes à verser;

    (c) les périodes en fonction desquelles les prestations sont déterminées;

    (d) le tableau des versements;

    (e) toute modification importante récemment apportée au régime;

    (f) les sommes versées ou réparties au cours du dernier exercice;

    (g) les sommes portées au compte de la haute direction au cours du dernier exercice, dans la mesure où le versement ou l'acquisition définitive de ces sommes n'est pas subordonné à un événement futur.

(2) À l'égard de tout régime en vertu duquel des options d'achat de valeurs mobilières ont été accordées aux membres de la haute direction au cours du dernier exercice, donner les renseignements suivants :

    (a) le sommaire du mode de fonctionnement du régime;

    (b) les critères utilisés pour déterminer le nombre de valeurs mobilières visées par les options;

    (c) les périodes en fonction desquelles les prestations sont déterminées;

    (d) le tableau des versements;

    (e) toute modification importante récemment apportée au régime;

CBCA Forms

(f) the number of securities optioned during the most recently completed financial year;

(g) the designation and aggregate number of securities under option; and

(h) the average exercise price per security (when options with differing terms are granted, the information should be given for each class or type of option) and, when that price is less than the market price of the security underlying the option on the date the option 's granted, provide the market price on that date.

(3) With respect to options exercised during the most recently completed financial year, provide, with respect to each class or type of option, in addition to the information prescribed by paragraphs (2)(a) to (f), the aggregate net value (market value less exercise price on the date of the exercise) of the securities under option.

(4) For the purposes of this Item:

(a) remuneration pursuant to a plan need ee taken into account only to the extent that the plan discriminates in scope, terms or operation in favour of executive officers and is not available to all full-time employees, other than those covered by a collective agreement;

(b) where an amount paid or distributed pursuant to a plan is disclosed under Item 1, that amount shall not be included under paragraph (1)(f) if a statement 's made under this section confirming that disclosure of the amount was made under Item 1;

(c) amounts paid or distributed that are disclosed under paragraph (1)(f) shall not include amounts paid or distributed that have been disclosed in a previous filing of a document, other than a prospectus, complying with the requirements of this form under paragraph (1)(g) as accrued for the group in respect of a financial year other than the most recently completed financial year;

(d) "options" includes all options, share purchase warrants or rights, other than those issued to all security holders of the same class or to all security holders of the same class resident in Canada on a pro rata basis, and an extension of an option or an option that may be deemed to be the granting of an option;

(e) "plan" includes any plan, contract, authorization or arrangement, whether or not set forth in any forms document, and may be applicable to only one person, but does not include the Canada Pension Plan or a similar government plan.

Item 3

Other Remuneration

(1) Describe all other remuneration not referred to in Items 1 or 2 paid during the most recently completed financial year, including personal benefits and securities or assets properly paid or distributed other than pursuant to a plan referred to in Item 2, which remuneration is not offered on the same terms to all full-time employees, other than those covered by a collective agreement.

(2) For the purposes of describing other remuneration under subsection (1), the value to be given to such remuneration shall be the aggregate incremental cost to the corporation or subsidiary

(3) For the purposes of subsection (2), "incremental cost" is the cost to the corporation or subsidiary of conferring a benefit on an individual, where that cost would not be otherwise incurred by the corporation if the benefit were not so conferred.

(4) Where the aggregate value of the remuneration disclosed under subsection (1) does not exceed the lesser of $10,000 times the number of persons in the group or 10 per cent of the remuneration aimed under section 4, only that fact need be disclosed.

Item 4

Termination of employment or change of control

Describe any plan or arrangement in respect of remuneration received or that may be received by executive officers in the corporation's most recently completed financial year for compensating such officers in the event of termination of employment (as a result of resignation, retirement, change of control, etc.) or a change in responsibilities following a change of control, where the value of such compensation exceeds $60,000 per executive officer.

Item 5

Remuneration of directors

(1) Describe:

(a) any standard arrangements, stating amounts, pursuant to which directors are remunerated by the corporation for their services in their capacity as directors, including any additional amounts payable for committee participation or special assignments; and

(b) any other arrangements, stating amounts, in addition or in lieu of any standard arrangement, pursuant to which directors were remunerated by the corporation in their capacity as directors during the most recently completed financial year.

(2) Where remuneration is not in cash form, state the value of the benefit conferred or, if it is not possible to state the value, describe the benefit conferred.

Completed document should be annexed to the Management Proxy Circular and sent to the auditor of the corporation, to each shareholder whose proxy 's solicited, to each director and to:

The Director,
Canada Business Corporations Act
Jean Edmonds Towers South
9th Floor
365 Laurier Ave. West
Ottawa, Ontario K1A 0C8

(f) le nombre de valeurs mobilières sur lesquelles des options ont été accordées au cours du dernier exercice;

(g) la désignation et le nombre total de valeurs mobilières visées par les options;

(h) le prix moyen de levée d'option par valeur mobilière lorsque des options dont les conditions diffèrent sont accordées, ce renseignement doit être donné pour chaque catégorie ou genre d'option) et, lorsque ce prix est inférieur au cours de la valeur mobilière visée par l'option à la date à laquelle celle-ci est accordée, le cours de la valeur mobilière à cette date.

(3) À l'égard des options levées au cours du dernier exercice de la société, indiquer, pour chaque catégorie ou genre d'option, outre les renseignements prévus aux alinéas (2)(a) à (f), la valeur nette totale des valeurs mobilières visées par les options (le cours moins le prix de levée d'option à la date de la levée d'option).

(4) Aux fins de cette rubrique :

(a) la rémunération versée en vertu d'un régime n'est prise en compte que dans la mesure où le régime n'est pas offert à tous les employés à plein temps non régis par une convention collective et où il favorise les membres de la haute direction par son champ d'application, ses conditions ou son fonctionnement;

(b) lorsqu'une somme versée ou répartie aux termes d'un régime est déclarée en vertu de la rubrique 1, cette somme n'entre pas dans le calcul de la rémunération en espèces visée à l'alinéa (1)(f) si une déclaration faite en vertu du présent article vient confirmer que la somme a été déclarée en vertu de la rubrique 1;

(c) les sommes versées ou réparties qui sont déclarées en vertu de l'alinéa (1)(f) ne comprennent pas celles qui ont déjà été déclarées selon l'alinéa (1)(g) dans un document, autre qu'un prospectus, déposé conformément aux exigences de la présente formule, comme sommes portées au compte du groupe relativement à un exercice autre que le dernier exercice;

(d) le terme «options» désigne les options, les droits ou les bons de souscription d'actions, autres que ceux qui sont attribués aux mêmes conditions ou au prorata à tous les détenteurs de valeurs mobilières de la même catégorie ou à tous ceux d'entre eux qui résident au Canada; la prolongation d'une option est considérée comme l'octroi d'une option;

(e) le terme «régime» désigne tout régime, contrat, autorisation ou arrangement, qu'il soit ou non formulé dans un document officiel et qu'il s'applique à une ou à plusieurs personnes : est exclu d'un régime le Régime de pensions du Canada ou un régime public semblable.

Rubrique 3

Autre rémunération

(1) Décrire toute autre rémunération non mentionnée aux rubriques 1 ou 2 versée au cours du dernier exercice, y compris les avantages personnels et les valeurs mobilières ou biens accordés ou répartis autrement qu'en vertu d'un régime mentionné à la rubrique 2, et qui n'est pas offert aux mêmes conditions à tous les employés à plein temps non régis par une convention collective.

(2) Pour la description des autres formes de rémunération visées au paragraphe (1), la valeur à indiquer est le coût marginal global supporté par la société ou la filiale.

(3) Aux fins du paragraphe (2), «coût marginal» désigne le coût supporté par la société ou la filiale pour accorder un avantage à un particulier, lequel coût ne serait pas par ailleurs engagé si l'avantage n'était pas accordé.

(4) Lorsque la valeur totale de la rémunération déclarée en vertu du paragraphe (1) ne dépasse pas le moins élevé des montants suivants : le produit de 10 000 $ fois le nombre de personnes dans le groupe ou 10% de la rémunération déclarée en vertu de la rubrique 1, il suffit de le mentionner.

Rubrique 4

Cessation d'emploi ou changement de contrôle

Décrire tout régime ou arrangement relatif à la rémunération touchée ou à toucher par les membres de la haute direction au cours du dernier exercice de la société, à titre d'indemnité en cas de cessation d'emploi (démission, retraite, changement de contrôle) ou en cas de changement de fonctions à la suite d'un changement de contrôle, lorsque l'indemnité excède 60 000 $ par personne.

Rubrique 5

Rémunération des administrateurs

(1) Décrire :

(a) le mode normal de rémunération des administrateurs, en indiquant le montant de celle-ci, pour les services rendus en leur qualité d'administrateurs, y compris toute rémunération supplémentaire pour participation aux travaux d'un comité ou pour mission spéciale;

(b) tout autre mode de rémunération des administrateurs, en indiquant le montant de celle-ci, en plus ou à la place du mode normal, pour les services rendus en leur qualité d'administrateurs au cours du dernier exercice.

(2) Dans le cas d'une rémunération autre qu'en espèces, indiquer la valeur de l'avantage accordé ou, s'il cela est impossible, le décrire.

Le document complété doit être joint à la circulaire de procuration de direction et être envoyé au vérificateur, à chacun des administrateurs, aux actionnaires intéressés ainsi qu'au :

Directeur,
Loi canadienne sur les sociétés par actions
Tour Jean Edmonds sud
9ième étage
365, av. Laurier ouest
Ottawa (Ontario) K1A 0C8

IC 3306 (2002/07) p.2

212

Form 27 — Application for Exemption

Industry Canada Industrie Canada Canada Business Loi canadienne sur les Corporations Act sociétés par actions	**FORM 27** **APPLICATION FOR EXEMPTION** (SUBSECTIONS 2(6), 10(2), 82(3), and 151(1), SECTION 156 and SUBSECTIONS 171(2) and 187(11) of the Act and Part 9 of the Regulations)	**FORMULAIRE 27** **DEMANDE DE DISPENSE** (PARAGRAPHES 2(6), 10(2), 82(3), et 151(1), ARTICLE 156 et PARAGRAPHES 171(2) et 187(11) de la Loi et la partie 9 du Règlement)

1 — Name of the Corporation - Dénomination sociale de la société

2 — Corporation No. - Nº de la société

3 — Type of Application for Exemption - Type de la demande de dispense

☐ Distributing Corporation - ss. 2(6)
Société ayant fait appel au public - par. 2(6)

☐ Name of the Corporation - ss. 10(2)
Dénomination sociale de la société - par. 10(2)

☐ Trust Indentures - ss. 82(3)
Acte de fiducie - par. 82(3)

☐ Proxy Solicitation - ss. 151(1)
Sollicitation de procurations - par. 151(1)

☐ Financial Disclosure - s. 156
Divulgation financière - art. 156

☐ Audit committee - ss. 171(2)
Comité de vérification - par. 171(2)

☐ Continued reference to par value - ss. 187(11)
Maintien de la désignation de valeur nominale ou au pair - par. 187(11)

4 — Name and Address of Applicant - Nom et adresse du demandeur

5 — Capacity of Applicant - Qualité du demandeur

6 — List of Documents - Liste des documents

Document No. Nº de document	Description of Documents - Description des documents
1	Description and details of exemption sought Description et détails de la dispense demandée
2	Statement of Facts Exposé des faits
3	Argument Exposé des motifs
4	
5	
6	
7	

The undersigned hereby certifies that the information given in this application and accompanying documents is true and complete in every respect.

Le soussigné certifie que les renseignements donnés dans la présente demande et dans les documents l'accompagnant sont véridiques et complets à tous égards.

Signature of Applicant - Signature du demandeur	Printed Name - Nom en lettres moulées	Tel. No. - Nº de tél.

FOR DEPARTMENTAL USE ONLY - À L'USAGE DU MINISTÈRE SEULEMENT

IC 3080 (2003/06)

Canadä

213

CBCA Forms

Canada Business Corporations Act

Loi canadienne sur les sociétés par actions

Application for Exemption
FORM 27
INSTRUCTIONS

Demande de dispense
FORMULAIRE 27
INSTRUCTIONS

General
If you require more information in order to complete Form 27, you may wish to consult the relevant Exemption Kit.

You must file Form 27 by sending or faxing the completed documents to the address provided below.

Prescribed Fees
By mail or fax: $250

Item 1
Set out the full legal name of the corporation.

Item 2
Set out the corporation number.

Item 3
Check the appropriate box to indicate the provision of the Act to which the requested exemption relates.

Item 4
Set out the full name of the applicant (first name, initial and family name, if an individual) and his/her address, including postal code.

Item 5
State the capacity in which the applicant acts, for example, a director, authorized officer or solicitor of a corporation, or a solicitor or agent of an applicant.

Item 6
Designate by a number each document accompanying the application and complete accordingly the table in Item 6. Each application must be supported by:
a) a description and details of the exemption sought;
b) a statement of facts that states the issue and summarizes briefly the material facts; and
c) an argument that states the legal, economic or other reasons why the application should be granted.

Note
Form 27, any documents attached to Form 27, and any supplemental information obtained by the Director in support of an exemption application are not kept confidential and may be examined by any person once they have been filed with the Director, if the document or information is required in order for the Director to make a decision on the exemption application.

The completed document and fees payable to the Receiver General for Canada are to be sent to:

The Director, Canada Business Corporations Act
Jean Edmonds Tower, South
9th Floor
365 Laurier Ave. West
Ottawa, Ontario K1A 0C8
or by facsimile at: (613) 941-5781
Inquiries: 1-866-333-5556

Généralités
Si vous désirez obtenir de plus amples informations afin de compléter le formulaire 27, veuillez consulter le Recueil d'information pertinent concernant les dispenses.

Vous devez déposer le formulaire 27 en envoyant ou en télécopiant le document complété à l'adresse indiquée au bas de cette page.

Droits
Par la poste ou télécopieur : 250 s

Rubrique 1
Indiquer la dénomination sociale complète de la société.

Rubrique 2
Indiquer le numéro de la société.

Rubrique 3
Cocher la case appropriée pour indiquer la disposition de la Loi à laquelle la demande de dispense se rapporte.

Rubrique 4
Indiquer le nom complet du demandeur (prénom, initiales et nom de famille, s'il s'agit d'un particulier) et son adresse, y compris le code postal.

Rubrique 5
Indiquer à quel titre le demandeur agit, par exemple, administrateur, dirigeant autorisé d'une société, procureur ou mandataire du demandeur.

Rubrique 6
Désigner par un numéro chaque document accompagnant la demande et remplir en conséquence le tableau de la rubrique 6. Chaque demande doit être accompagnée :
a) d'une description et des détails concernant la dispense demandée;
b) d'un exposé des faits énonçant la question et décrivant brièvement les faits importants;
c) d'un exposé énonçant les motifs légaux, économiques ou autres qui justifieraient l'octroi de la dispense.

Note
Le formulaire 27, tous les documents joints au formulaire 27 ainsi que toutes informations supplémentaires obtenues par le directeur appuyant la demande de dispense ne sont pas conservés confidentiels et peuvent être examinés par toute personne une fois qu'ils ont été déposés auprès du directeur si le document ou l'information est requis afin que le directeur prenne une décision quant à la demande de dispense.

Le document complété et les droits payables au Receveur général du Canada doivent être envoyés au :

Directeur, Loi canadienne sur les sociétés par actions
Tour Jean Edmonds, sud
9ième étage
365, ave Laurier ouest
Ottawa (Ontario) K1A 0C8
ou par télécopieur : (613) 941-5781
Renseignements : 1-866-333-5556

IC 3080 (2003/06) p.2

WINDING-UP AND RESTRUCTURING ACT

An Act respecting the winding-up and restructuring of companies

R.S.C. 1985, c. W-11, as am. R.S.C. 1985, c. 27 (2nd Supp.), s. 10 (Sched., item 20); R.S.C. 1985, c. 18 (3rd Supp.), ss. 43–46; R.S.C. 1985, c. 21 (3rd Supp.), s. 55; S.C. 1990, c. 17, ss. 43, 44; 1991, c. 47, ss. 747–752; 1992, c. 1, s. 145 (Sched. VIII, item 32) (Fr.); 1992, c. 26, s. 19; 1992, c. 27, s. 90(1)(o); 1993, c. 28, s. 78 (Sched. III, item 143) [Repealed 1999, c. 3, s. 12 (Sched., item 27).]; 1995, c. 1, s. 62(1)(z); 1996, c. 6, ss. 133–161; 1997, c. 15, s. 411; 1998, c. 30, s. 14(l); 1999, c. 3, s. 85; 1999, c. 28, ss. 76–92; 1999, c. 31, s. 223; 2002, c. 7, s. 251; 2005, c. 3, ss. 17, 18; 2007, c. 6, s. 443–449 [ss. 445, 446(1), 447 not in force at date of publication.]; 2007, c. 29, ss. 113–116.

[Note: The short title of this Act was changed from "Winding-up Act" to "Winding-up and Restructuring Act" by 1996, c. 6, s. 134. The long title of this Act was changed from "An Act respecting the winding-up of insolvent companies" to "An Act respecting the winding-up and restructuring of companies" by 1996, c. 6, s. 133.]

SHORT TITLE

1. Short title — This Act may be cited as the *Winding-up and Restructuring Act*.

1996, c. 6, s. 134

INTERPRETATION

2. (1) Definitions — In this Act,

"aircraft objects" has the same meaning as in subsection 2(1) of the *International Interests in Mobile Equipment (aircraft equipment) Act*; *("biens aéronautiques")*

"assets" means

(a) in respect of a foreign insurance company, the assets in Canada, within the meaning of subsection 2(1) of the *Insurance Companies Act*, of the foreign insurance company together with its other assets held in Canada under the control of its chief agent, within the meaning of section 571 of that Act, including all amounts received or receivable in respect of its insurance business in Canada, and

(b) in respect of an authorized foreign bank, assets within the meaning of section 618 of the *Bank Act*;

("actif" ou "éléments d'actif")

"authorized foreign bank" has the same meaning as in section 2 of the *Bank Act*; *("banque étrangère autorisée")*

"capital stock" includes a capital stock *de jure* or *de facto*; *("capital social")*

"company" includes any corporation subject to this Act; *("compagnie")*

"contributory" means a person liable to contribute to the assets of a company under this Act, and, in all proceedings for determining the persons who are to be deemed contributories and in all proceedings prior to the final determination of those persons, it includes any person alleged to be a contributory; *("contributeur")*

"court" means

(a) in Nova Scotia, British Columbia and Newfoundland, the Supreme Court,

(a.1) in Ontario, the Superior Court of Justice,

(b) in Quebec, the Superior Court,

(c) in New Brunswick, Manitoba, Saskatchewan and Alberta, the Court of Queen's Bench,

(c.1) in the Province of Prince Edward Island, the Trial Division of the Supreme Court, and

(d) in Yukon and the Northwest Territories, the Supreme Court, and in Nunavut, the Nunavut Court of Justice

("tribunal")

"creditor" includes all persons having any claim against a company, present or future, certain, ascertained or contingent, for liquidated or unliquidated damages, and in all proceedings for determining the persons who are to be deemed creditors, it includes any person making any such claim; *("créancier")*

"finanical institution" has the same meaning as in section 3 of the *Office of the Superintendent of Financial Institutions Act*; *("institution financière")*

"foreign insurance company" means an insurance company that is authorized under Part XIII of the *Insurance Companies Act* to insure in Canada risks; *("société étrangère")*

"insurance company" means a company transacting the business of insurance and includes any unincorporated association or reciprocal exchange transacting that business; *("compagnie d'assurance")*

"Minister" [Repealed 1999, c. 28, s. 76(2).]

"official gazette" means the *Canada Gazette* and the gazette published under the authority of the government of the province where the proceedings for the winding-up of the business of a company are carried on, or used as the official means of communication between the lieutenant governor of that province and the people, and if no such gazette is published in the province, any newspaper published in the province and designated by a court for publishing the notices required by this Act; *("gazette officielle")*

"Superintendent" means the Superintendent of Financial Institutions appointed pursuant to subsection 5(1) of the *Office of the Superintendent of Financial Institutions Act* and a reference to the "Office of the Superintendent" shall be construed as a reference to the office established by section 4 of that Act; *("surintendant")*

"trading company" means any company, except a railway or telegraph company, carrying on business similar to that carried on by apothecaries, auctioneers, bankers, brokers, brickmakers, builders, carpenters, carriers, cattle or sheep salesmen, coach proprietors, dyers, fullers, keepers of inns, taverns, hotels, saloons or coffee houses, lime burners, livery stable keepers, market gardeners, millers, miners, packers, printers, quarrymen, sharebrokers, ship-owners, shipwrights, stockbrokers, stock-jobbers, victuallers, warehousemen, wharfingers, persons using the trade of merchandise by way of bargaining, exchange, bartering, commission, consignment or otherwise, in gross or by retail, or by persons who, either for themselves, or as agents or factors for others, seek their living by buying and selling or buying and letting for hire goods or commodities, or by the manufacture, workmanship or the conversion of goods or commodities or trees; *("compagnie de commerce")*

"winding-up order" means an order granted by a court under this Act to wind up the business of a company, and includes any order granted by the court to bring under this Act any company in liquidation or in process of being wound up. *("ordonnance de mise en liquidation")*

(2) Business in Canada — For the purposes of this Act, a reference to the business in Canada of an authorized foreign bank is deemed to be a reference to the business in Canada of the authorized foreign bank under Part XII.1 of the *Bank Act*.

(3) Creditors — For the purposes of this Act, a reference to a creditor in respect of an authorized foreign bank is deemed to be a reference to a creditor of the authorized foreign bank in respect of its business in Canada.

R.S.C. 1985, c. 27 (2nd Supp.), s. 10 (Sched., item 20); 1990, c. 17, s. 43; 1995, c. 1, s. 62(1)(z); 1996, c. 6, s. 135; 1998, c. 30, s. 14(l); 1999, c. 3, s. 85; 1999, c. 28, s. 76; 2002, c. 7, s. 251; 2005, c. 3, s. 17; 2007, c. 6, s. 443

3. When company deemed insolvent — A company is deemed insolvent

(a) if it is unable to pay its debts as they become due;

(b) if it calls a meeting of its creditors for the purpose of compounding with them;

(c) if it exhibits a statement showing its inability to meet its liabilities;

(d) if it has otherwise acknowledged its insolvency;

(e) if it assigns, removes or disposes of, or attempts or is about to assign, remove or dispose of, any of its property, with intent to defraud, defeat or delay its creditors, or any of them;

(f) if, with the intent referred to in paragraph (e), it has procured its money, goods, chattels, land or property to be seized, levied on or taken, under or by any process of execution;

(g) if it has made any general conveyance or assignment of its property for the benefit of its creditors, or if, being unable to meet its liabilities in full, it makes any sale or conveyance of the whole or the main part of its stock in trade or assets without the consent of its creditors or without satisfying their claims;

(h) if it permits any execution issued against it, under which any of its goods, chattels, land or property are seized, levied on or taken in execution, to remain unsatisfied until within four days of the time fixed by the sheriff or other officer for the sale thereof, or for fifteen days after the seizure;

(i) if, in the case of a company that is a federal member institution, within the meaning assigned to that expression by the *Canada Deposit Insurance Corporation Act*, the shares and subordinated debt of which have been vested in the Canada Deposit Insurance Corporation by order of the Governor in Council under paragraph 39.13(1)(a) of that Act, a transaction or series of transactions referred to in subsection 39.2(1) of that

Act is not, in the opinion of the Corporation, substantially completed on or before the date that is not later than

    (i) 60 days after the making of the order vesting the shares and subordinated debt of the federal member institution in the Corporation, or

    (ii) the expiration of any extension of that period; or

(j) if, in the case of a company that is a federal member institution, within the meaning assigned to that expression by the *Canada Deposit Insurance Corporation Act,* in respect of which the Canada Deposit Insurance Corporation has been appointed as receiver by order of the Governor in Council under paragraph 39.13(1)(b) of that Act, a transaction or series of transactions referred to in subsection 39.2(2) of that Act is not, in the opinion of the Corporation, substantially completed on or before the date that is not later than

    (i) 60 days after the making of the order appointing the Corporation as receiver, or

    (ii) the expiration of any extension of that period.

1992, c. 26, s. 19; 2007, c. 6, s. 444

4. Company deemed unable to pay its debts — A company is deemed to be unable to pay its debts as they become due whenever a creditor, to whom the company is indebted in a sum exceeding two hundred dollars then due, has served on the company, in the manner in which process may legally be served on it in the place where service is made, a demand in writing, requiring the company to pay the sum due, and the company has, for sixty days next after the service of the demand, neglected to pay the sum or to secure or compound for the sum to the satisfaction of the creditor.

1999, c. 28, s. 77

5. Commencement of winding-up — The winding-up of the business of a company shall be deemed to commence at the time of the service of the notice of presentation of the petition for winding up.

APPLICATION

6. (1) Application — This Act applies to all corporations incorporated by or under the authority of an Act of Parliament, of the former Province of Canada or of the Province of Nova Scotia, New Brunswick, British Columbia, Prince Edward Island or Newfoundland, and whose incorporation and affairs are subject to the legislative authority of Parliament, and to incorporate banks and savings banks, to authorized foreign banks, and to trust companies, insurance companies, loan companies having borrowing powers, building societies having a capital stock and incorporated trading companies doing business in Canada wherever incorporated where any of those bodies

    (a) is insolvent;

    (b) is in liquidation or in the process of being wound up and, on petition by any of its shareholders or creditors, assignees or liquidators, asks to be brought under this Act; or

    (c) if it is a financial institution, is under the control, or its assets are under the control, of the Superintendent and is the subject of an application for a winding-up order under section 10.1.

(2) Application to authorized foreign banks — In its application to an authorized foreign bank, this Act only applies to the winding-up of its business in Canada and to the liquidation of its assets, and any reference to the winding-up of a company or to the winding-up of the business of a company is deemed, in relation to an authorized foreign bank, to be a reference to the winding-up of the business in Canada of the authorized foreign bank and to include the liquidation of the assets of the authorized foreign bank.

1996, c. 6, s. 136; 1999, c. 28, s. 78

7. Certain corporations excepted — This Act does not apply to building societies that do not have a capital stock or to railway or telegraph companies.

PART I — GENERAL

Limitation of Part

8. Subject to Part II — In their application to authorized foreign banks, the provisions of this Part are subject to the provisions of Part II.

1996, c. 6, s. 137; 1999, c. 28, s. 79

9. Subject to Part III — In the case of insurance companies, the provisions of this Part are subject to the provisions of Part III.

Winding-up Order

10. Cases where winding-up order may be made — A court may make a winding-up order in respect of a company

(a) where the period, if any, fixed for the duration of the company by the Act, charter or instrument of incorporation of the company has expired, or where an event, if any, has occurred, on the occurrence of which it is provided by the Act, charter or instrument of incorporation that the company is to be dissolved;

(b) where the company at a special meeting of shareholders called for the purpose has passed a resolution requiring the company to be wound up;

(c) when the company is insolvent;

(d) when the capital stock of the company is impaired to the extent of twenty-five per cent thereof, and when it is shown to the satisfaction of the court that the lost capital will not likely be restored within one year; or

(e) when the court is of opinion that for any other reason it is just and equitable that the company should be wound up.

10.1 Other winding-up circumstances — Where the Superintendent has taken control of a financial institution or of the assets of a financial institution pursuant to paragraph 648(1)(b) of the *Bank Act*, paragraph 442(1)(b) of the *Cooperative Credit Associations Act*, pararaph 679(1)(b) of the *Insurance Companies Act* or paragraph 510(1)(b) of the *Trust and Loan Companies Act* or, in the case of an authorized foreign bank, has taken control of its assets pursuant to paragraph 619(1)(b) of the *Bank Act* or, in the case of a foreign insurance company, has taken control of its assets under subparagraph 679(1)(b)(i) or (ii) of the *Insurance Companies Act*, a court may make a winding-up order in respect of the financial institution, authorized foreign bank or insurance business in Canada of the foreign insurance company if the court is of the opinion that for any reason it is just and equitable that the financial institution, authorized foreign bank or insurance business in Canada of the foreign insurance company should be wound up or if, in the case of

(a) a bank to which the *Bank Act* applies, the control was taken on a ground referred to in paragraph 648(1.1)(a), (c), (e) or (f) of that Act;

(a.1) an authorized foreign bank, control of its assets was taken on a ground referred to in paragraph 619(2)(a), (b), (d) or (f) of the *Bank Act*;

(b) a company to which the *Trust and Loan Companies Act* applies, the control was taken on a ground referred to in paragraph 510(1.1)(a), (c), (e) or (f) of that Act;

(c) an insurance company to which the *Insurance Companies Act* applies, other than a foreign insurance company, the control was taken on a ground referred to in paragraph 679(1.1)(a), (c), (e) or (f) of that Act;

(d) a foreign insurance company to which the *Insurance Companies Act* applies, the control of its assets was taken on a ground referred to in paragraph 679(1.2)(a), (c) or (e) of that Act; or

(e) an association to which the *Cooperative Credit Associations Act* applies, the control was taken on a ground referred to in paragraph 442(1.1)(a), (c), (e) or (f) of that Act.
1996, c. 6, s. 138; 1999, c. 28, s. 80

Application for Order

11. Application for winding-up order — An application for a winding-up order may

(a) in the cases mentioned in paragraphs 10(a) and (b), be made by the company or by a shareholder of the company;

(b) in the case mentioned in paragraph 10(c), be made by the company or by a creditor of the company for the sum of at least two hundred dollars or, except in the case of banks and insurance corporations, by a shareholder holding shares in the capital stock of the company to the amount of at least five hundred dollars par value, or holding five shares without nominal or par value in the capital stock of the company;

(c) in the cases mentioned in paragraphs 10(d) and (e), be made by a shareholder holding shares in the capital stock of the company to the amount of at least five hundred dollars par value, or holding five shares without nominal or par value in the capital stock of the company; and

(d) in the case mentioned in section 10.1, be made by the Attorney General of Canada.
1996, c. 6, s. 139

12. (1) How and where made — An application for a winding-up order may be made by petition to the court in the province where the head office of the company is situated or in the province where its chief place or one of its chief places of business in Canada is situated.

(2) Notice of application — Except in cases where an application for a winding-up order is made by a company, four days notice of the application shall, unless otherwise directed by a court, be given to the company before the making of the application.
1996, c. 6, s. 140

13. Power of court — A court may, on application for a winding-up order, make the order applied for, dismiss the application with or without costs, adjourn the hearing conditionally or unconditionally or make any interim or other order that it deems just.

14. Proceedings may be adjourned — If a company opposes an application for a winding-up order on the ground that it has not become insolvent, that its suspension or default was only temporary and was not caused by a deficiency in its assets, that its capital stock is not impaired to the extent described in paragraph 10(d), that the impairment does not endanger the capacity of the company to pay its debts in full or that there is a probability that its lost capital will be restored within a year or within a reasonable time thereafter, and shows reasonable cause for believing that its opposition is well founded, the court, in its discretion, may, from time to time, adjourn proceedings on the application, for a time not exceeding six months after the date of the application, and may order an accountant or other person to inquire into the affairs of the company and to report thereon within a period not exceeding thirty days after the date of that order.

15. Duty of company — On the service on the company of an order made under section 14 for an inquiry into the affairs of the company, the president, directors, officers and employees of the company and every other person shall respectively

(a) exhibit to the accountant or other person named for the purpose of making the inquiry the books of account of the company and all inventories, papers and vouchers referring to the business of the company or of any person therewith that are in their possession, custody or control; and

(b) give all such information as is required by the accountant or other person named for the purpose of making the inquiry in order to form a just estimate of the affairs of the company.

16. Power of the court — On receiving the report of the accountant or person ordered to inquire into the affairs of the company under section 14, and after hearing such shareholders or creditors of the company as desire to be heard thereon, the court may either refuse the application or make the winding-up order.

Staying Proceedings

17. Actions against company may be stayed — A court may, on the application of a company, or of any creditor, contributory, liquidator or petitioner for the winding-up order, at any time after the presentation of a petition for the order and before making the order, restrain further proceedings in any action, suit or proceeding against the company, on such terms as the court thinks fit.

1996, c. 6, s. 141

18. Court may stay winding-up proceedings — A court may, on the application of any creditor, contributory, liquidator or petitioner for the winding-up order, at any time after the order is made, and on proof, to the satisfaction of the court, that all proceedings in relation to the winding-up ought to be stayed, make an order staying those proceedings, either altogether or for a limited time, on such terms and subject to such conditions as the court thinks fit.

1996, c. 6, s. 141

Effect of Winding-up Order

19. Company to cease business — A company, from the time of the making of a winding-up order, shall cease to carry on its business, except in so far as is, in the opinion of the liquidator, required for the beneficial winding-up thereof, but the corporate state and all the corporate powers of the company, notwithstanding that it is otherwise provided by the Act, charter or instrument of incorporation of the company, continue until the affairs of the company are wound up.

20. Transfer of shares void — All transfers of shares of a company referred to in section 19, except transfers made to or with the sanction of the liquidator, under the authority of the court, and every alteration in the status of the members of the company, after the commencement of the winding-up, are void.

21. Effect of winding-up order — After a winding-up order is made in respect of a company, no suit, action or other proceeding shall be proceeded with or commenced against the company, except with the leave of the court and subject to such terms as the court imposes.

22. Execution, etc. — Every attachment, sequestration, distress or execution put in force against the estate or effects of a company after the making of a winding-up order is void.

22.1 (1) Permitted actions — Nothing in this Act or an order made under this Act prevents or prohibits the following actions from being taken in accordance with the provisions of an eligible financial contract:

    (a) the termination of the contract;

    (b) the netting or setting off or compensation of obligations between a company in respect of which winding-up proceedings under this Act are commenced and another party to the contract; and

    (c) any dealing with financial collateral including

        (i) the sale or foreclosure or, in the Province of Quebec, the surrender of financial collateral, and

        (ii) the setting off or compensation of financial collateral or the application of the proceeds or value of financial collateral.

(1.01) Net termination values — If the net termination values determined in accordance with the eligible financial contract referred to in subsection (1) are owed by the company to another party to the eligible financial contract, that other party is deemed to be a creditor of the company with a claim provable against the company in respect of the net termination values.

(1.1) Application to authorized foreign banks — In its application to authorized foreign banks, subsection (1) only applies to the eligible financial contracts and obligations between the authorized foreign bank, in respect of its business in Canada, and another party.

(2) Definitions — In subsection (1),

"eligible financial contract" means an agreement of a prescribed kind; *("contrat financier admissible")*

"financial collateral" means any of the following that is subject to an interest, or in the Province of Quebec a right, that secures payment or performance of an obligation in respect of an eligible financial contract or that is subject to a title transfer credit support agreement:

(a) cash or cash equivalents, including negotiable instruments and demand deposits,

(b) securities, a securities account, a securities entitlement or a right to acquire securities, or

(c) a futures agreement or a futures account;

("garantie financière")

"net termination value" means the net amount obtained after setting off the mutual obligations between the parties to an eligible financial contract in accordance with its provisions; *("valeurs nettes")*

"title transfer credit support agreement" means an agreement under which title to property has been provided for the purpose of securing the payment or performance of an obligation in respect of an eligible financial contract; *("accord de transfert de titres pour obtention de crédit")*

(3) Regulations — The Governor in Council may make regulations prescribing kinds of agreements for the purposes of the definition "eligible financial contract" in subsection (2).

1996, c. 6, s. 142; 1999, c. 28, s. 81; 2007, c. 29, s. 113

22.2 Aircraft objects — Nothing in this Act prevents a creditor who holds security on aircraft objects — or a lessor of aircraft objects or a conditional seller of aircraft objects — under an agreement with a company in respect of which an application for a winding-up order is made for the reason set out in paragraph 10(c) from taking possession of the equipment

(a) if, after the commencement of proceedings under this Act, the company defaults in protecting or maintaining the equipment in accordance with the agreement;

(b) sixty days after the commencement of proceedings under this Act unless, during that period, the company

(i) remedied the default of every other obligation under the agreement, other than a default constituted by the commencement of proceedings under this Act or the breach of a provision in the agreement relating to the company's financial condition,

(ii) agreed to perform the obligations under the agreement, other than an obligation not to become insolvent or an obligation relating to the company's financial condition, until the day on which proceedings under this Act end, and

(iii) agreed to perform all the obligations arising under the agreement after the proceedings under this Act end; or

(c) if, during the period that begins on the expiry of the sixty-day period and ends on the day on which proceedings under this Act end, the company defaults in performing an obligation under the agreement, other than an obligation not to become insolvent or an obligation relating to the company's financial condition.

2005, c. 3, s. 18

Appointment of Liquidators

23. (1) Liquidator — A court, in making a winding-up order in respect of a company, may appoint a liquidator or more than one liquidator of the estate and effects of the company.

(2) Trustee under *Bankrutpcy and Insolvency Act* — In the case of a company, except incorporated building societies and railway companies, a court shall not appoint as liquidator any person, other than the Canada Deposit Insurance Corporation, who is not licensed as a trustee under the *Bankruptcy and Insolvency Act*.

(3) Superintendent not to be liquidator — The Superintendent shall not be appointed as a liquidator of a company.

1992, c. 27, s. 90(1)(o); 1996, c. 6, s. 143

24. If more than one liquidator — If more than one liquidator is appointed, a court may

(a) direct whether any act to be done by a liquidator is to be done by all or any one or more of the liquidators; and

(b) allocate responsibilities among the liquidators or permit them to allocate responsibilities among themselves.

1996, c. 6, s. 144; 1999, c. 31, s. 223

25. Additional liquidators — A court may, if it thinks fit, after the appointment of one or more liquidators, appoint an additional liquidator or liquidators.

26. Notice — Except as otherwise ordered by the court, no liquidator shall be appointed under subsection 23(1) unless a previous notice is given to the creditors, contributories and shareholders or members of the company, and the court shall by order direct the manner and form in which the notice shall be given and the length of the notice.

1996, c. 6, s. 145

27. Security — The court shall determine what security shall be given by a liquidator on his appointment.

28. Provisional liquidator — A court may, on the presentation of a petition for a winding-up order or at any time thereafter and before the first appointment of a liquidator, appoint provisionally a liquidator of the estate and effects of the company and may limit and restrict his powers by the order appointing him.

29. Incorporated company — An incorporated company may be appointed liquidator to the goods and effects of a company under this Act, and if an incorporated company is so appointed, it may act through one or more of its principal officers designated by the court.

30. Trust company — Where under the laws of any province a trust company is accepted by the courts of that province and is permitted to act as administrator, assignee or curator without giving security, the trust company may be appointed liquidator of a company under this Act, without giving security.

31. Powers of directors — On the appointment of a liquidator, all the powers of the directors of the company cease, except in so far as the court or the liquidator sanctions the continuance of those powers.

32. Resignation and removal — A liquidator may resign or may be removed by the court on due cause shown, and every vacancy in the office of liquidator shall be filled by the court.

Powers and Duties of Liquidators

33. Duties after appointment — A liquidator, on his appointment, shall take into his custody or under his control all the property, effects and choses in action to which the company is or appears to be entitled, and shall perform such duties with reference to winding-up the business of the company as are imposed by the court or by this Act.

34. Liquidator to prepare statement — A liquidator shall, within 120 days after appointment, prepare a statement of the assets, debts and liabilities of the company and of the value of those assets as shown by the books and records of the company.

1996, c. 6, s. 146

35. (1) Powers — A liquidator may, with the approval of the court, and on such previous notice to the creditors, contributories, shareholders or members of the company as the court orders,

(a) bring or defend any action, suit or prosecution or other legal proceeding, civil or criminal, in his own name as liquidator or in the name or on behalf of the company, as the case may be;

(b) carry on the business of the company so far as is necessary to the beneficial winding-up of the company;

(c) sell the real and personal property, effects and choses in action of the company, by public auction or private contract, and transfer the whole thereof to any person or company, or sell them in parcels for such consideration as may be approved by the court;

(d) do all acts and execute, in the name and on behalf of the company, all deeds, receipts and other documents, and for that purpose use, when necessary, the seal of the company;

(e) prove, rank, claim and draw dividends in the matter of the bankruptcy, insolvency or sequestration of any contributory, for any sum due the company from the contributory, and take and receive dividends in respect of the sum in the matter of the bankruptcy, insolvency or sequestration, as a separate debt due from that contributory and rateably with the other separate creditors;

(f) draw, accept, make and endorse any bill of exchange or promissory note in the name and on behalf of the company;

(g) raise on the security of the assets of the company any requisite sum or sums of money;

(h) do and execute all such other things as are necessary for winding-up the affairs of the company and distributing its assets; and

(i) enter into an agreement with any compensation association designated by order of the Minister of Finance pursuant to section 449 or 591 of the *Insurance Companies Act* in order to facilitate the payment of claims to policyholders and the preservation of the value of the estate.

(1.1) Agreement provisions — An agreement referred to in paragraph (1)(i) may include provisions setting out the priority for repayment to the compensation association of amounts advanced by it to a company in accordance with the agreement.

(2) Company liable — The drawing, accepting, making or endorsing of every bill of exchange or promissory note mentioned in subsection (1), on behalf of the company, has the same effect, with respect to the liability of the company, as if the bill or note had been drawn, accepted, made or endorsed by or on behalf of the company in the course of the carrying on of its business.

(3) No delivery of assets needed — No delivery of the whole or of any part of the assets of the company is necessary to give a lien to any person taking security on the assets of the company.

1996, c. 6, s. 147

35.1 Liquidator not liable — A liquidator is not liable to any person if the liquidator relies in good faith on an opinion, report or statement of a compensation association regarding its financial obligations in relation to an agreement referred to in paragraph 35(1)(i).

1996, c. 6, s. 148

36. Appointment of solicitor — A liquidator may, with the approval of the court, appoint a solicitor or law agent to assist him in the performance of his duties.

37. (1) Debts due to the company — A liquidator may, with the approval of the court, compromise all calls and liabilities to calls, debts and liabilities capable of resulting in debts, and all claims, demands and matters in dispute in any way relating to or affecting the assets of the company or the winding-up of the company, on the receipt of such sums, payable at such times, and generally on such terms, as are agreed on.

(2) Security may be taken — A liquidator may take any security for the discharge of the calls, debts, liabilities, claims, demands or disputed matters referred to in subsection (1), and give a complete discharge in respect of all or any of those calls, debts, liabilities, claims, demands or matters.

38. Creditors may be compromised — A liquidator may, with the approval of the court, make any compromise or arrangements that the liquidator considers appropriate with

(a) in the case of a company other than an authorized foreign bank, creditors or persons claiming to be creditors of the company; and

(b) in the case of an authorized foreign bank, creditors or persons claiming to be creditors of the authorized foreign bank or persons who hold security on its assets.

1999, c. 28, s. 82

39. Court may provide as to powers — A court may provide, by any order subsequent to a winding-up order, that a liquidator may exercise any of the powers conferred on him by this Act, without the sanction or intervention of the court.

40. [Repealed 1996, c. 6, s. 149.]

Appointment of Inspectors

41. Inspectors — A court may appoint, at any time when found advisable, one or more inspectors, whose duty it is to assist and advise a liquidator in the liquidation of a company.

Remuneration of Liquidators and Inspectors

42. (1) Remuneration — A liquidator shall be paid such salary or remuneration, by way of percentage or otherwise, as the court directs, on such notice to the creditors, contributors, shareholders or members as the court orders.

(2) Distribution — If there is more than one liquidator appointed for the liquidation of a company, the remuneration shall be distributed among them in such proportions as the court directs.

43. Remuneration of inspectors — The court shall determine the remuneration, if any is deemed just, of inspectors.

44. [Repealed 1996, c. 6, s. 150, together with previous headings.]

45. [Repealed 1996, c. 6, s. 150, together with previous headings.]

46. [Repealed 1996, c. 6, s. 150, together with previous headings.]

47. [Repealed 1996, c. 6, s. 150, together with previous headings.]

Court Discharging Functions of Liquidator

48. If no liquidator — If at any time no liquidator has been appointed to wind up the business of a company, all the property of the company shall be deemed to be in the custody of the court.

49. (1) Provision for discharge of liquidator — Whenever a company is being wound up and the realization and distribution of its assets has proceeded so far that in the opinion of the court it becomes expedient that the liquidator should be discharged, and that the balance remaining in his hands of the moneys and assets of the company can be better realized and distributed by the court, the court may make an order discharging the liquidator and for payment, delivery and transfer into court, or to such officer or person as the court may direct, of those moneys and assets, and the moneys and assets shall be realized and distributed, by or under the direction of the court, among the persons entitled thereto, in the same way, as nearly as may be, as if the distribution were being made by the liquidator.

(2) Disposal of books and documents — In the case described in subsection (1), the court may make an order directing how the books, accounts and documents of the company and of the liquidator may be disposed of, and may order that they be deposited in court or otherwise dealt with as may be thought fit.

Contributories

50. List of contributories — As soon as possible after the commencement of the winding-up of a company, the court shall settle a list of contributories.

51. Classes distinguished — In the list of contributories referred to in section 50, persons who are contributories in their own right shall be distinguished from persons who are contributories as representatives of or liable for the debts of others.

52. Adding heirs to lists — It is not necessary, where the personal representative of any deceased contributory is placed on a list of contributories, to add the heirs or devisees of the contributory, but the heirs or devisees may be added as and when the court thinks fit.

53. (1) Liability of shareholders — Every shareholder or member of a company or his representative is liable to contribute the amount unpaid on his shares of the capital or on his liability to the company, or to its members or creditors, as the case may be, under the Act, charter or instrument of incorporation of the company, or otherwise.

(2) Liability an asset — The amount that a shareholder is liable to contribute under subsection (1) shall be deemed an asset of the company, and a debt due to the company, payable as directed or appointed under this Act.

54. (1) Liability after transfer of shares — Where a shareholder has transferred his shares under circumstances that do not, by law, free him from liability in respect thereof, or where he is by law liable to the company or its members or creditors, as the case may be, to an amount beyond the amount unpaid on his shares, he shall be deemed a member of the company for the purposes of this Act and is liable to contribute, under subsection 53(1), to the extent of his liabilities to the company or its members or creditors, independently of this Act.

(2) An asset — The amount that a shareholder is liable to contribute under subsection (1) shall be deemed an asset and a debt described in subsection 53(2).

55. Liability of contributory a debt — The liability of any person to contribute to the assets of a company under this Act, in the event of the business of the company being wound up, creates a debt accruing due from that person at the time when his liability commenced, but payable at the time or respective times when calls are made, under this Act, for enforcing that liability.

56. Provable against his estate — In the case of the bankruptcy or insolvency of any contributory, the estimated value of his liability to future calls, as well as calls already made, may be proved against his estate.

57. Handing over money and books — A court may, at any time after making a winding-up order, require any contributory for the time being settled on the list of contributories as trustee, receiver, banker, agent or officer of the company, to pay, deliver, convey, surrender or transfer forthwith, or within such time as the court directs, to or into the hands of the liquidator, any sum or balance, books, papers, estate or effects that are in his hands for the time being, and to which the company appears to be entitled.

58. Payment by contributory — A court may, at any time after making a winding-up order, make an order on any contributory for the time being settled on the list of contributories, directing payment to be made, in the manner mentioned in the order, of any moneys due from him or from the estate of the person whom he represents to the company, exclusive of any moneys that he or the estate of the person whom he represents is liable to contribute by virtue of any call made in pursuance of this Act.

59. Calls on contributories — A court may, at any time after making a winding-up order, and either before or after it has ascertained the sufficiency of the assets of the company, make calls on and order payment thereof by all or any of the contributories for the time being settled on the list of contributories, to the extent of their liability, for payment of all or any sums it deems necessary to satisfy the debts and liabilities of the company, for the costs, charges and expenses of winding-up and for the adjustment of the rights of the contributories among themselves.

60. (1) Consideration of possible failure to pay — A court may, in making a call, take into consideration the probability that some of the contributories on whom the call is made may partly or wholly fail to pay their respective portions of the call.

(2) Maturity of debt — No call compels payment of a debt before the maturity thereof and the extent of the liability of any contributory is not increased by anything in this section.

61. (1) Order for payment — A court may order any contributory, purchaser or other person from whom money is due to the company to pay the money into a bank or Government savings bank, to the account of the court instead of the liquidator.

(2) Enforcement — An order under subsection (1) may be enforced in the same manner as if it had directed payment to the liquidator.

62. Rights of contributories — The court shall adjust the rights of the contributories among themselves.

Meetings of Creditors

63. Meetings — A court may, if it thinks expedient, direct meetings of the creditors, contributories, shareholders or members of a company to be summoned, held and conducted in such manner as the court directs, for the purpose of ascertaining their wishes, and may appoint a person to act as chairman of any of those meetings, and to report the result of those meetings to the court.

64. (1) Votes according to amount of claim — In the case described in section 63, regard shall, with respect to creditors, be had as to the amount of the debt due to each creditor and with respect to shareholders or members, as to the number of votes conferred on each shareholder or member by law or by the regulations of the company.

(2) Preliminary proof — The court may prescribe the mode of preliminary proof of creditors' claims for the purpose of any meeting directed to be held under section 63.

65. Court may summon creditors to consider any proposed compromise — Where any compromise or arrangement is proposed between a company in the course of being wound up under this Act and the creditors of the company, or by and between any of those creditors or any class or classes of those creditors and the company or is proposed by the liquidator, the court, in addition to any other of its powers, may, on the application, in a summary way, of any creditor or of the liquidator, order that a meeting of those creditors or class or classes of creditors shall be summoned in such manner as the court shall direct.

1996, c. 6, s. 151

66. Sanction of compromise — If a majority in number, representing three-fourths in value, of the creditors or class or classes of creditors referred to in section 65, present either in person or by proxy at the meeting summoned under that section, agree to any arrangement or compromise, the arrangement or compromise may be sanctioned by an order of the court, and in such case is binding on all the creditors or on the class or classes of creditors, as the case may be, and also on the liquidator and contributories of the company.

67. Chairman of meeting — In directing meetings of creditors, contributories, shareholders or members of a company to be held as provided in this Act, the court may either appoint a person to act as chairman of the meeting or direct that a chairman be appointed by the persons entitled to be present at the meeting, and, in the event the appointed chairman fails to attend the meeting, the persons present at the meeting may elect a qualified person as chairman who shall perform the duties prescribed by this Act.

68. Voting to be in person or by proxy — No creditor, contributory, shareholder or member of a company shall vote at any meeting unless present personally or represented by a person acting under a written authority, filed with the chairman or liquidator, to act as the representative at the meeting, or generally.

69. [Repealed 1996, c. 6, s. 152, together with previous headings.]

70. [Repealed 1996, c. 6, s. 152, together with previous headings.]

Creditors' Claims

71. (1) What debts may be proved — When the business of a company is being wound up under this Act, all debts and all other claims against the company in existence at the commencement of the winding-up, certain or contingent, matured or not, and liquidated or unliquidated, are admissible to proof against the company and, subject to subsection (2), the amount of any claim admissible to proof is the unpaid debt or other liability of the company outstanding or accrued at the commencement of the winding-up.

(2) Uncertain claims valued — In case of any claim subject to any contingency or for unliquidated damages or which for any other reason does not bear a certain value, the court shall determine the value of the claim and the amount for which it shall rank.

1996, c. 6, s. 153

72. Claims of clerks and employees privileged — Clerks or other persons in, or having been in the employment of, a company, in or about its business or trade, shall be collocated in the dividend sheet by special privilege over other creditors, for any arrears of salary or wages due and unpaid to them at the time of the making of a winding-up order in respect of the company, not exceeding the arrears that have accrued to them during the three months immediately preceding the date of that order.

73. (1) Law of set-off to apply — The law of set-off, as administered by the courts, whether of law or equity, applies to all claims on the estate of a company, and to all proceedings for the recovery of debts due or accruing due to a company at the commencement of the winding-up of the company, in the same manner and to the same extent as if the business of the company was not being wound up under this Act.

(2) Trust money — For greater certainty, where the business of a trust company is being wound up under this Act, the law of set-off applies in respect of all moneys received or held by the company as deposits, without regard to whether those moneys are considered to be received or held by it in a trustee-beneficiary relationship.

1996, c. 6, s. 154

74. Time for sending in claims — A court may, with respect to the winding-up of a company, fix a certain day or certain days on or within which creditors of the company may send in their claims, and may direct notice thereof to be given by the liquidator, and may determine the manner in which notice of the day or days so fixed shall be given by the liquidator to the creditors.

75. (1) Creditors required to prove claims — The liquidator may give notice in writing to creditors who have sent in their claims to him or of whose claims he has notice, and to creditors whose claims he considers should not be allowed without proof, requiring them to attend before the court on a day to be named in the notice and prove their claims to the satisfaction of the court.

(2) Disallowance on default — Where a creditor does not attend in pursuance of the notice given under subsection (1), his claim shall be disallowed, unless the court sees fit to grant further time for the proof thereof.

(3) Disallowance on hearing — Where a creditor attends in pursuance of the notice given under subsection (1), the court may on hearing the matter allow or disallow the claim of that creditor in whole or in part.

76. (1) Distribution of assets — After the notices required by sections 74 and 75 have been given, the respective times specified in the notices have expired and all claims of which proof has been required by due notice in writing by the liquidator in that behalf have been allowed or disallowed by the court in whole or in part, the liquidator may distribute the assets of the company or any part of those assets among the persons entitled to them and without reference to any claim against the company, or, in the case of an authorized foreign bank, against the authorized foreign bank in respect of its business in Canada, that has not then been sent to the liquidator.

(2) Claims not sent in — The liquidator is not liable to any person whose claim has not been sent in at the time of distributing the assets or part thereof under subsection (1) for the assets or part thereof so distributed.

1999, c. 28, s. 83

77. Rank of claims sent in after distribution started — Where any claim or claims are sent in to the liquidator after any partial distribution of the assets of a company, the claim or claims, subject to proof and allowance as required by this Act, shall rank with other claims of creditors in any future distribution of assets of the company.

Secured Claims

78. Duty of creditor holding security — If a creditor holds security on the estate of a company, or, in the case of an authorized foreign bank, a creditor or person holds security on the assets of the authorized foreign bank, the creditor or person shall specify the nature and amount of the security in the claim, and shall, in the claim, on oath, put a specified value on the security.

1999, c. 28, s. 84

79. Option of liquidator — The liquidator, under the authority of the court, may either consent to the retention by the creditor, or, in the case of an authorized foreign bank, by the creditor or person who holds security, of the property and effects constituting the security referred to in section 78 or on which it attaches, at the value specified on the security, property and effects, or may require from the creditor or person an assignment and delivery of the security, property and effects, at the specified value, to be paid by the liquidator out of the estate as soon as the liquidator has realized the security, together with interest on the value from the date of filing the claim until payment.

1999, c. 28, s. 84

80. Ranking of secured creditor — In the event of the retention referred to in section 79, the difference between the value at which the security is retained and the amount of the claim of the creditor shall be the amount for which he may rank in any future distribution of assets.

81. (1) Security by negotiable instrument — If a creditor holds a claim based on negotiable instruments on which the company or, in the case of an authorized foreign bank, the authorized foreign bank in respect of its business in Canada, is only indirectly or secondarily liable and that is not mature or exigible, the creditor is considered to hold security within the meaning of sections 78, 79 and 80, and shall put a value on the liability of the person primarily liable on the security as being the security for the payment of the claim.

(2) Revaluation — After the maturity of the liability referred to in subsection (1) and its non-payment, the creditor is entitled to amend and revalue his claim.

1999, c. 28, s. 85

81.1 Authorized foreign bank — Where a person holds security on the assets of an authorized foreign bank, other than those in respect of its business in Canada

(a) sections 80 and 81 do not apply in relation to the person's claim;

(b) where there is a difference between the value at which the security is retained and the amount of the person's claim, no claim for the difference in value is admissible to proof or may be made under this Act against the assets of the authorized foreign bank; and

(c) the person is not barred from any recourse either in law or in equity against the authorized foreign bank in proceedings outside Canada for the difference referred to in paragraph (b).

1999, c. 28, s. 86

82. Security by mortgage or charge — Where the security consists of a mortgage on ships or shipping or on real property, or of a registered judgment or an execution binding real property that is not by any other provision of this Act invalid for any purpose of creating a lien, claim or privilege on the real or personal property of the company, the property mortgaged or bound by the security shall only be assigned and delivered to the creditor, or, in the case of an authorized foreign bank, to the creditor or person who holds the security

(a) subject to all previous mortgages, judgments, executions, hypothecs and liens on the security, holding rank and priority before the creditor's or person's claim;

(b) on the creditor's or person's assuming and binding themself to pay all of those previous mortgages, judgments, executions, hypothecs and liens; and

(c) on the creditor's or person's securing the estate of the company to the satisfaction of the liquidator against any claim by reason of those previous mortgages, judgments, executions, hypothecs and liens.

1999, c. 28, s. 86

83. In case of subsequent claims — Where there are mortgages, judgments, executions, hypothecs or liens on ships or shipping or real property subsequent to those of a creditor or person referred to in section 82, the creditor or person shall only obtain the property

(a) by consent of the subsequently secured creditors or persons;

(b) on the subsequently secured creditors or persons filing their claims specifying their security on the property as of no value;

(c) on the creditor or person paying the subsequently secured creditors or persons the value by them placed on the property; or

(d) on the creditor or person securing the estate of the company to the satisfaction of the liquidator against any claim by reason of the subsequent mortgages, judgments, executions, hypothecs and liens.

1999, c. 28, s. 86

84. Authority to retain — On a secured claim being filed, with a valuation of the security, the liquidator shall procure the authority of the court to consent to the retention of the security by the creditor or, in the case of an authorized foreign bank, by the creditor or other person who holds the security or shall require from the creditor or person an assignment and delivery of the security.

1999, c. 28, s. 86

Dividend Sheet

85. Preparing dividend sheet — In the preparation of a dividend sheet, due regard shall be had to the rank and privilege of every creditor, but no dividend shall be allotted or paid to any creditor holding security on the estate of the company for his claim until the amount for which he may rank as a creditor on the estate, with respect to dividends therefrom, is established as herein provided.

Liens

86. (1) No lien by execution, etc., after commencement of winding-up — No lien or privilege shall be created

(a) on the real or personal property of the company for the amount of any judgment debt, or of the interest thereon, by the issue or delivery to the sheriff of any writ of execution or by levying on or seizing under that writ the effects or estate of the company, or

(b) on the real or personal property of the company, or on any debts due or accruing or becoming due to the company, by the filing or registering of any memorial or minute of judgment or by the issue or taking out of any attachment or garnishee order or other process or proceeding,

if, before the payment over to the plaintiff of the moneys actually levied, paid or received under the writ, memorial, minute, attachment, garnishee order or other process or proceeding, the winding-up of the business of the company has commenced.

(2) Lien for costs excepted — This section does not affect any lien or privilege for costs that the plaintiff possesses under the law of the province in which the writ, attachment, garnishee order or other process or proceeding was issued or taken out.

Contestation of Claims

87. Claims or dividend may be objected to — Any liquidator, creditor, contributory, shareholder or member of a company or, in the case of an authorized foreign bank, the liquidator, the authorized foreign bank or any creditor, may object to any claim filed with the liquidator or to any dividend declared.

1999, c. 28, s. 87

88. (1) Objections in writing — Where a claim or dividend is objected to under section 87, the objections shall be filed in writing with the liquidator, together with the evidence of the previous service of a copy thereof on the claimant.

(2) Answers and replies — The claimant shall have six days to answer the objections, or such further time as the court allows, and the contestant shall have three days to reply, or such further time as the court allows.

89. Day to be fixed for hearing — On the completion of the issues on the objections filed under section 88, the liquidator shall transmit to the court all necessary papers relating to the contestation, and the court shall, on the application of either party, fix a day for taking evidence on the contestation and hearing and determining the contestation.

90. Costs — The court may make such order as seems proper in respect of the payment of the costs of the contestation referred to in section 89 by either party or out of the estate of the company.

91. Default in answer by claimant — Where, after a claim or dividend has been duly objected to, the claimant does not answer the objections, the court may, on the application of the contestant, make an order barring the claim or correcting the dividend, or may make such other order with reference thereto as appears right.

92. Security for costs — The court may order the person objecting to a claim or dividend to give security for the costs of the contestation within a limited time, and may, in default, dismiss the contestation or stay proceedings thereon on such terms as the court thinks just.

Distribution of Assets

93. Distribution of property — The property of the company shall be applied in satisfaction of its debts and liabilities, and the charges, costs and expenses incurred in winding-up its affairs.

94. Winding-up expenses — All costs, charges and expenses properly incurred in the winding-up of a company, including the remuneration of the liquidator, are payable out of the assets of the company, in priority to all other claims.

95. (1) Distribution of surplus — The court shall distribute among the persons entitled thereto any surplus that remains after the satisfaction of the debts and liabilities of the company and the winding-up charges, costs and expenses, and unless otherwise provided by law or by the Act, charter or instrument of incorporation of the company, any property or assets remaining after the satisfaction shall be distributed among the members or shareholders according to their rights and interests in the company.

(2) Interest from commencement of winding-up — Any surplus referred to in subsection (1) shall first be applied in payment of interest from the commencement of the winding-up at the rate of five per cent per annum on all claims proved in the winding-up and according to their priority.

1996, c. 6, s. 155

Fraudulent Preferences

96. Gratuitous contracts — All gratuitous contracts, or conveyances or contracts without consideration or with a merely nominal consideration, respecting either real or personal property, made by a company in respect of which a winding-up order under this Act is afterwards made, with or to any person whatever, whether a creditor of the company or not, within three months immediately preceding the commencement of the winding-up, or at any time afterwards, shall be presumed to have been made with intent to defraud the creditors of the company.

97. Contracts injuring or obstructing creditors — All contracts by which creditors are injured, obstructed or delayed, made by a company unable to meet its engagements, and in respect of which a winding-up order under this Act is afterwards made, with a person whether a creditor of the company or not, who knows of that inability or has probable cause for believing that inability exists, or after that inability has become public and notorious, shall be presumed to be made with intent to defraud the creditors of the company.

98. When contracts with consideration voidable — A contract or conveyance for consideration, respecting either real or personal property, by which creditors are injured or obstructed, made by a company unable to meet its engagements with a person ignorant of that inability, whether a creditor of the company or not, and before that inability has become public and notorious, but within thirty days next before the commencement of the winding-up of the business of the company under this Act, or at any time afterwards, is voidable, and may be set aside by any court of competent jurisdiction, on such terms with respect to the protection of that person from actual loss or liability by reason of that contract as the court orders.

99. Contracts made with intent to defraud or delay creditors — All contracts or conveyances made and acts done by a company respecting either real or personal property, with intent fraudulently to impede, obstruct or delay the creditors of the company in their remedies against the company, or with intent to defraud the creditors of the company or any of them, and so made, done and intended with the knowledge of the person contracting or acting with the company, whether a creditor of the company or not, and that have the effect of impeding, obstructing or delaying the creditors in their remedies, or of injuring them, or any of them, are void.

100. (1) Sale or transfer in contemplation of insolvency — Where any sale, deposit, pledge or transfer is made of any property, real or personal, by a company in contemplation of insolvency under this Act by way of security for payment to any creditor, or where any property, real or personal, goods, effects or valuable security are given by way of payment by the company to any creditor, whereby that creditor obtains or will obtain an unjust preference over the other creditors, the sale, deposit, pledge, transfer or payment is void, and the subject thereof may be recovered back by the liquidator by suit or action in any court of competent jurisdiction.

(2) Presumption if within thirty days — Where the sale, deposit, pledge or transfer under subsection (1) is made within thirty days next before the commencement of the winding-up of the company under this Act, or at any time afterwards, it shall be presumed to have been so made in contemplation of insolvency, whether or not it was made voluntarily or under presure and evidence of pressure shall not be admissible to support the transaction.

(3) Exception — The presumption referred to in subsection (2) does not apply to a sale, deposit, pledge or transfer of financial collateral made in accordance with the provisions of an eligible financial contract.

1996, c. 6, s. 156; 2007, c. 29, s. 114

101. (1) Payments by company within thirty days — Every payment made within thirty days next before the commencement of the winding-up under this Act by a company unable to meet its engagements in full, to a person who knows of that inability or has probable cause for believing that inability exists, is void, and the amount paid may be recovered back by the liquidator by suit or action in any court of competent jurisdiction.

(2) Restoration of security — Where any valuable security is given in consideration of a payment described in subsection (1), the security or the value thereof shall be restored to the creditor on the return of the payment.

(3) Exception — Subsection (1) does not apply to a payment made in connection with financial collateral in accordance with the provisions of an eligible financial contract.

2007, c. 29, s. 115

101.1 Definitions — In subsections 100(3) and 101(3), **"eligible financial contract"** and **"financial collateral"** have the same meanings as in subsection 22.1(2).

2007, c. 29, s. 116

102. Debts of company transferred to contributories — When a debt due or owing by a company has been transferred within the time and under the circumstances mentioned in section 101, or at any time afterwards, to a contributory, or to any person indebted or liable in any way to the company, who knows or has probable cause for believing the company is unable to meet its engagements, or in contemplation of its insolvency under this Act, for the purpose of enabling that contributory or person to set up, by way of compensation or set-off, the debt so transferred, the debt shall not be set up by way of compensation or set-off against the claim on that contributory or person.

102.1 (1) Inquiry into dividends and redemptions of shares — Where a company that is being wound up under this Act has, within twelve months preceding the commencement of the winding-up, paid a dividend in respect of any share of the company, other than a stock dividend, or redeemed or purchased for cancellation any of the shares of the capital stock of the company, the court may, on the application of the liquidator, inquire into whether the dividend was paid or the shares redeemed or purchased for cancellation at a time when the company was insolvent, or whether the payment of the dividend or the redemption or purchase for cancellation of its shares rendered the company insolvent.

(2) Judgment against directors — The court may give judgment to the liquidator against the directors of the company, jointly and severally, in the amount of the dividend or redemption or purchase price, with interest thereon, as has not been paid to the company when the court finds that

(a) the transaction occurred at a time when the company was insolvent or the transaction rendered the company insolvent; and

(b) the directors did not have reasonable grounds to believe that the transaction was occurring at a time when the company was solvent or the transaction would not render the company insolvent.

(3) Criteria — In making a determination under paragraph (2)(b), the court shall consider whether the directors acted as prudent and diligent persons would have acted in the same circumstances and whether the directors in good faith relied on

(a) financial or other statements of the company represented to them by officers of the company or the auditor of the company, as the case may be, or by written reports of the auditor to fairly reflect the financial condition of the company; or

(b) a report relating to the company's affairs prepared pursuant to a contract with the company by a lawyer, notary, an accountant, engineer or appraiser or other person whose profession gave credibility to the statements made in the report.

(4) Judgment against shareholders — Where a transaction referred to in subsection (1) has occurred and the court makes a finding referred to in paragraph (2)(a), the court may give judgment to the liquidator against a shareholder who is related to one or more directors or to the company or who is a director not liable by reason of paragraph 2(b) or subsection (5) in the amount of the dividend or redemption or purchase price referred to in subsection (1) and the interest thereon, as was received by the shareholder and not repaid to the company.

(5) Directors exonerated by law — A judgment pursuant to subsection (2) shall not be entered against or be binding on a director who had, in accordance with any applicable law governing the operation of the company, protested against the payment of the dividend or the redemption or purchase for cancellation of the shares of the capital stock of the company and had thereby exonerated himself or herself under that law from any liability therefor.

(6) Directors' right to recover — Nothing in this section shall be construed to affect any right, under any applicable law governing the operation of the company, of the directors to recover from a shareholder the whole or any part of any dividend, or any redemption or purchase price, made or paid to the shareholder when the company was insolvent or that rendered the company insolvent.

(7) Onus — For the purposes of an inquiry under this section, the onus of proving

(a) that the company was not insolvent lies on the directors and the shareholders of the company; and

(b) in the case of the directors, that there were reasonable grounds to believe that the company was not insolvent when a dividend was paid or shares were redeemed or purchased for cancellation or that the payment of a dividend or a redemption of shares did not render the company insolvent lies on the directors.

1996, c. 6, s. 157

Appeals

103. Appeals — Any person dissatisfied with an order or decision of the court or a single judge in any proceeding under this Act may,

(a) if the question to be raised on the appeal involves future rights,

(b) if the order or decision is likely to affect other cases of a similar nature in the winding-up proceedings, or

(c) if the amount involved in the appeal exceeds five hundred dollars,

by leave of a judge of the court, or by leave of the court or a judge of the court to which the appeal lies, appeal therefrom.

104. Court of Appeal — An appeal under section 103 lies to the highest court of final resort in or for the province or territory in which the proceeding originated.

105. Practice — All appeals shall be regulated, as far as possible, according to the practice in other cases of the court appealed to, but no appeal hereinbefore authorized shall be entertained unless the appellant has, within fourteen days from the rendering of the order or decision appealed from, or within such further time as the court or judge appealed from allows, taken proceedings therein to perfect his appeal, or unless, within that time, he has made a deposit or given sufficient security according to the practice of the court appealed to that he will duly prosecute the appeal and pay such damages and costs as may be awarded to the respondent.

106. Dismissing appeal — Where an appellant does not proceed with his appeal according to this Act and the rules of practice applicable, the court appealed to, on the application of the respondent, may dismiss the appeal with or without costs.

107. Appeal to Supreme Court of Canada — An appeal, if the amount involved therein exceeds two thousand dollars, lies by leave of the Supreme Court of Canada to that Court from the highest court of final resort in or for the province or territory in which the proceeding originated.

Procedure

108. Describing liquidator — In all proceedings connected with a company, a liquidator shall be described as the "liquidator of the (*name of company*)" or, in the case of an authorized foreign bank, the "liquidator of the business in Canada of the (*name of the authorized foreign bank*)" and not by individual name only.

1999, c. 28, s. 88

109. Similar to ordinary suit — The proceedings under a winding-up order shall be carried on as nearly as may be in the same manner as an ordinary suit, action or proceeding within the jurisdiction of the court.

110. Powers exercised by a single judge — The powers conferred by this Act on a court may, subject to the appeal provided for in this Act, be exercised by a single judge thereof, and the judge may exercise those powers in chambers, either during term or in vacation.

111. Court may refer matters — After a winding-up order is made, the court may, subject to an appeal according to the practice of the court in like cases, as to the court may seem meet, by order of reference, refer and delegate, according to the practice and procedure of the court, to any officer of the court any of the powers conferred on the court by this Act.

112. Service of process out of jurisdiction — A court has the power and jurisdiction to cause or allow the service of process or proceedings under this Act to be made on persons out of the jurisdiction of the court, in the same manner, and with the like effect, as in ordinary actions or suits within the ordinary jurisdiction of the court.

113. Order of court deemed judgment — Every order of a court or judge for the payment of money or costs, charges or expenses made under this Act shall be deemed a judgment of the court, and may be enforced against the person or goods and chattels, lands and tenements of the person ordered to pay in the manner in which judgments or decrees of any superior court obtained in any suit may bind lands or be enforced in the province where the court making the order is situated.

114. Ordinary practice in case of discovery — The practice with respect to the discovery of assets of judgment debtors, in force in the superior courts or in any superior court in the province where any order is made under section 113, is applicable to and may be availed of in like manner for the discovery of the assets of any person who by that order is ordered to pay any money or costs, charges or expenses.

115. Attachment and garnishment — Debts due to any person against whom an order for the payment of money, costs or expenses has been obtained may, in any province where the attachment and garnishment of debts is allowed by law, be attached and garnished in the same manner as debts in that province due to a judgment debtor may be attached and garnished by a judgment creditor.

116. Witnesses attendance — In any action, suit, proceeding or contestation under this Act, the court may order the issue of a writ of *subpoena ad testificandum* or of *subpoena duces tecum*, commanding the attendance, as a witness, of any person who is within Canada.

117. Arrest of absconding contributory, etc. — A court may, at any time before or after it has made a winding-up order, on proof being given that there are reasonable grounds to believe that any contributory or any past or present director, manager, officer or employee of the company is about to quit Canada or otherwise abscond, or to remove or conceal any of his goods or chattels, for the purpose of evading payment of calls or for avoiding examination in respect of the affairs of the company, cause that person to be arrested, his books, papers, moneys, securities for money, goods and chattels to be seized, and that person and property to be safely kept until such time as the court orders.

118. Examination — A court may, after it has made a winding-up order, summon before it or before any person named by it any officer of the company or person known or suspected to have in his possession any of the estate or effects of the company or supposed to be indebted to the company, or any person whom the court deems capable of giving information concerning the trade, dealings, estate or effects of the company.

119. Person summoned refusing to attend — If any person summoned under section 118, after being tendered a reasonable sum for his expenses, refuses, without a lawful excuse, to attend at the time appointed, the court may cause that person to be apprehended and brought up for examination.

120. Production of papers — The court may require any officer or person described in section 118 to produce before the court any book, paper, deed, writing or other document in his custody or power relating to the company.

121. Lien on documents — If any person claims any lien on papers, deeds, writings or documents produced by him, that production is without prejudice to the lien, and the court has jurisdiction in the winding-up to determine all questions relating to the lien.

122. Examination on oath — The court or a person named by it may examine, on oath, either by oral or written interrogatories, any person appearing or brought up in the manner described in section 119, concerning the affairs, dealings, estate or effects of the company, and may reduce to writing the answers of the person and require him to subscribe the answers.

123. (1) Inspection of books and papers — After a winding-up order has been made, the court may make such order for the inspection, by the creditors, contributories, shareholders or members of the company, of its books and papers, as the court thinks just.

(2) Limitation of inspection — Any books and papers in the possession of the company may be inspected in conformity with the order of the court, but not further or otherwise.

124. Officer of company misapplying money — When in the course of the winding-up of the business of a company under this Act it appears that any past or present director, manager, liquidator, receiver, employee or officer of the company has misapplied or retained in his own hands, or become liable or accountable for any moneys of the company, or been guilty of any misfeasance or breach of trust in relation to the company, the court may, on the application of any liquidator or of any creditor or contributory of the company, notwithstanding that the offence is one for which the offender is criminally liable, examine into the conduct of the director, manager, liquidator, receiver, employee or officer and, after that examination, may make an order requiring him to repay any moneys so misapplied or retained, or for which he has become liable or accountable, together with interest at such rate as the court thinks just, or to contribute such sums of money to the assets of the company, by way of compensation in respect of the misapplication, retention, misfeasance or breach of trust, as the court thinks fit.

125. Dispensing with notice — The court may, by any order made after a winding-up order and the appointment of a liquidator, dispense with notice required by this Act to creditors, contributories, shareholders or members of the company or to the authorized foreign bank, its creditors or persons who hold security on its assets, where in its discretion the notice may properly be dispensed with.

1999, c. 28, s. 89

126. Courts and judges auxiliary — The courts of the various provinces, and the judges of those courts respectively, are auxiliary to one another for the purposes of this Act, and the winding-up of the business of a company or any matter or proceeding relating thereto may be transferred from one court to another with the concurrence, or by the order or orders, of the two courts or by an order of the Supreme Court of Canada.

127. Order of one court enforceable by another — When any order made by one court is required to be enforced by another court, an office copy of the order so made, certified by the clerk or other proper officer of the court that made the order, under the seal of that court, shall be produced to the proper officer of the court required to enforce the order.

128. Proceeding on order of another court — The court required to enforce the order mentioned in section 127 shall, on the production of the certified copy of the order, take the same proceedings thereon for enforcing the order as if it were the order of that court.

129. (1) Rules with respect to amendments — The rules of procedure, for the time being, with respect to amendments of pleadings and proceedings in the court, apply, as far as practicable, to all pleadings and proceedings under this Act.

(2) Authority to apply — Any court before which proceedings under this Act are being carried on has full power and authority to apply to those proceedings the appropriate rules of that court with respect to amendments.

130. Irregularity or default — No pleading or proceeding is void by reason of any irregularity or default that may be amended or disregarded, but the pleading or proceeding may be dealt with according to the rules and practice of the court in cases of irregularity or default.

131. Powers conferred are supplementary — Any powers conferred by this Act on a court are in addition to, and not in restriction of, any other powers at law or in equity of instituting proceedings against any contributory or the estate of any contributory, or against any debtor of the company or the estate of any debtor of the company, for the recovery of any call or other sum due from the contributory, debtor or estate, and those proceedings may be instituted accordingly.

132. Wishes of creditors — A court may, with respect to all matters relating to the winding-up of the business of a company, have regard, so far as it deems just, to the wishes of the creditors, contributories, shareholders or members of the company, as proved to it by any sufficient evidence.

133. (1) Solicitors and counsel representing classes of creditors — A court, if satisfied that, with respect to the whole or any portion of the proceedings before it, the interests of creditors, claimants or shareholders can be classified, may, after notice by advertisement or otherwise, nominate and appoint a solicitor and counsel to represent each or any class for the purpose of the proceedings, and all the persons composing any such class are bound by the acts of the solicitor and counsel so appointed.

(2) Service of solicitor — Service on the solicitor appointed to represent a class of notices, orders or other proceedings of which service is required shall for all purposes be, and be deemed to be, good and sufficient service thereof on all the persons composing the class represented by him.

(3) Costs — The court may, by the order appointing a solicitor and counsel for any class, or by subsequent order, provide for the payment of the costs of the solicitor and counsel by the liquidator of the company out of the assets of the company, or out of such portion thereof as to the court seems just and proper.

134. Liquidator subject to summary jurisdiction of court — A liquidator is subject to the summary jurisdiction of the court in the same manner and to the same extent as the ordinary officers of the court are subject to its jurisdiction, and the liquidator may be compelled to perform his duties by order of the court.

135. Remedies obtained by summary order — All remedies sought or demanded for enforcing any claim for a debt, privilege, mortgage, lien or right of property on, in or to any effects or property in the hands, possession or custody of a liquidator may be obtained by an order of the court on summary petition, and not by any action, suit, attachment, seizure or other proceeding of any kind whatever.

Rules, Regulations and Forms

136. (1) Judges may make — A majority of the judges of a court, of which the chief justice shall be one, may, from time to time,

(a) settle the forms and make the rules and regulations to be followed and observed in proceedings under this Act; and

(b) make rules respecting the costs, fees and charges that shall or may be had, taken or paid in those proceedings by or to attorneys, solicitors or counsel, officers of courts, whether for the officers or for the Crown, and sheriffs, or other persons, or for any service performed or work done under this Act.

(2) Ontario and Quebec — In Ontario the judges of the Superior Court of Justice, and in Quebec the judges of the Superior Court, or a majority of those judges, of which the chief justice shall be one, shall settle the forms and make the rules and regulations referred to in subsection (1).

1990, c. 17, s. 44; 1998, c. 30, s. 14(1)

137. Until rules are made, procedure of court to apply — Until the forms, rules and regulations referred to in section 136 are settled or made, the various forms and procedures, including the tariff of costs, fees and charges in cases under this Act shall, unless otherwise specially provided, be the same as nearly as possible as those of the court in other cases.

Unclaimed Deposits

138. (1) Unclaimed dividends — All dividends deposited in a bank and remaining unclaimed at the time of the final winding-up of the business of a company shall be left for three years in the bank where they are deposited, subject to the claim of the persons entitled thereto.

(2) After three years — If the dividends deposited under subsection (1) are unclaimed at the expiration of three years, the bank shall pay them over, with interest accrued on them, to the Minister of Industry.

(3) If afterwards claimed — If the dividends deposited under subsection (1) are afterwards duly claimed, they shall be paid over by the bank, with interest accrued thereon, to the persons entitled thereto.

1999, c. 28, s. 90

139. (1) Money deposited not paid after three years — The money deposited in a bank by a liquidator after the final winding-up of the business of a company shall be left for three years in the bank, subject to be claimed by the persons entitled thereto.

(2) Unclaimed money — Money not paid out pursuant to subsection (1) shall be paid over by the bank, with the interest accrued on it, to the Minister of Industry, and if afterwards claimed shall be paid, with that interest, to the persons entitled to it.

1999, c. 28, s. 91

Offences and Punishment

140. Court may direct criminal proceedings — When a winding-up order is made in respect of a company, if it appears in the course of the winding-up that any past or present director, manager, officer or member of the company is guilty of an offence in relation to the company for which he is criminally liable, the court may, on the application of any person interested in the winding-up, or of its own motion, direct the liquidator to institute and conduct a prosecution or prosecutions for the offence and may order the costs and expenses to be paid out of the assets of the company.

141. Destruction of books or false entry therein — Every person who, with intent to defraud or deceive any person, destroys, mutilates, alters or falsifies any book, paper, writing or security, or makes or is privy to the making of any false or fraudulent entry in any register, book of account or other document belonging to a company, the business of which is being wound up under this Act, is guilty of an indictable offence and liable to imprisonment in the penitentiary for any term not less than two years or to imprisonment in any jail or in any place of confinement other than a penitentiary for any term less than two years, with or without hard labour.

142. (1) Failure to comply with order of court — Any liquidator, director, manager, receiver, officer or employee of a company who fails to comply with the requirements or directions of any order made by a court under this Act is guilty of contempt of court and is subject to all processes and punishments of the court for contempt.

(2) Removal of liquidator — Any liquidator who fails to comply as described in subsection (1) may, in the discretion of the court, be removed from office as liquidator.

143. Refusal by officers of company to give information — Any refusal on the part of the president, directors, officers or employees of a company to give all information possessed by them respectively as to the affairs of the company required by the accountant or other person ordered by a court under this Part to inquire into the affairs of the company and to report thereon is a contempt of court, and the president, directors, officers or employees are subject to all processes and punishments of the court for contempt.

144. [Repealed 1996, c. 6, s. 158.]

145. Refusal of witness to answer or subscribe — Every person who is brought up for examination before a court after the court has made a winding-up order, or appearing before the court for the examination, and who refuses without lawful excuse to answer any question put to him or to subscribe any answer made by him on the examination is guilty of contempt of court and is subject to all processes and punishments of the court for contempt.

Evidence

146. Books to be proof of contents — Where the business of a company is being wound up under this Act, all books of the company and of the liquidators are, as between the contributories of the company, in the absence of evidence to the contrary, proof of the truth of all matters purporting to be therein recorded.

147. Affidavits — Every affidavit, solemn affirmation or declaration required to be sworn or made under or for the purposes of this Act, or to be used in a court in any proceeding under this Act, may be sworn or made

(a) in Canada before a liquidator, judge, notary public, commissioner for taking affidavits or justice of the peace; and

(b) outside Canada, before any judge of a court of record, any commissioner for taking affidavits to be used in any court in Canada, any notary public, the chief municipal officer of any town or city, any British consul or vice-consul or any person authorized by or under any statute of Canada, or of any province, to take affidavits.

148. Judicial notice of seals, stamp or signature — All courts, judges, justices, commissioners and persons acting judicially shall take judicial notice of the seal, stamp or signature, as the case may be, of any court, liquidator, judge, notary public, commissioner, justice, chief municipal officer, consul, vice-consul or other person referred to in section 147, attached, appended or subscribed to any affidavit, solemn affirmation or declaration referred to in that section or to any other document to be used for the purposes of this Act.

149. Copy of order — When any order made by one court is required to be enforced by another court, the production of an office copy of the order so made certified by the clerk or other proper officer of the court that made the order, under the seal of the court, is sufficient evidence of the order having been made.

PART II — AUTHORIZED FOREIGN BANKS
[Heading added 1999, c. 28, s. 92.]

150. Application of Part — This Part applies only to the winding-up of the business in Canada of authorized foreign banks and to the liquidation of their assets.

1996, c. 6, s. 159; 1999, c. 28, s. 92

151. (1) Notice — In their application to an authorized foreign bank, section 26 and subsections 35(1) and 42(1) are to be read as if notice is required to be given to the authorized foreign bank, its creditors and persons who hold security on any of its assets.

(2) Exception — Notice need not be given to persons referred to in subsection (1) who hold security on any of the assets of an authorized foreign bank unless they can be located using information contained in the books and records in Canada of the authorized foreign bank and those books and records are accessible by or under the control of, where section 26 applies, the petitioner for the winding-up order and, where subsection 35(1) or 42(1) applies, the liquidator.

1996, c. 6, s. 160; 1999, c. 28, s. 92

152. Duties after appointment — A liquidator, on appointment in respect of an authorized foreign bank, shall take into custody or under control all the assets of the authorized foreign bank, and shall perform the duties that are imposed by the court or by this Act with reference to

(a) the winding-up of the business in Canada of the authorized foreign bank; and

(b) the liquidation of the assets of the authorized foreign bank.

1996, c. 6, s. 160; 1999, c. 28, s. 92

153. Authorized foreign bank to cease business — From the time of the making of a winding-up order in respect of an authorized foreign bank, it shall cease to carry on its business in Canada or deal in any way with its assets, except in so far as is, in the opinion of the liquidator, required for the beneficial winding-up of its business in Canada and liquidation of its assets.

1996, c. 6, s. 160; 1999, c. 28, s. 92

154. Effect of winding-up order — After a winding-up order is made in respect of an authorized foreign bank, no suit, action or other proceeding may be proceeded with or commenced against the authorized foreign bank in respect of its business in Canada or of its assets, except with the leave of the court and subject to the terms, if any, that the court imposes.

1996, c. 6, s. 160; 1999, c. 28, s. 92

155. Execution, etc. — Every attachment, sequestration, distress or execution put in force against the assets of the authorized foreign bank after the making of a winding-up order in respect of it is void.

1996, c. 6, s. 160; 1999, c. 28, s. 92

156. Liquidator to prepare statement — A liquidator shall, within 120 days after appointment in respect of an authorized foreign bank, prepare a statement of

(a) the assets, debts and liabilities of the authorized foreign bank in respect of its business in Canada and of the value of those assets as shown by the books and records of the authorized foreign bank; and

(b) the assets of the authorized foreign bank, other than those in respect of its business in Canada, and the value of the assets as shown by the books and records of the authorized foreign bank or, where the books and records are not available, an estimated value of the assets.

1996, c. 6, s. 160; 1999, c. 28, s. 92

157. (1) What debts may be proved — When the business in Canada of an authorized foreign bank is being wound up and its assets are being liquidated under this Act, only debts and claims against the authorized foreign bank in respect of its business in Canada in existence at the commencement of the winding-up, certain or contingent, matured or not, and liquidated or unliquidated, are admissible to proof and, subject to subsection (2), the amount of any claim admissible to proof is the unpaid debt or other liability of the authorized foreign bank in respect of its business in Canada outstanding or accrued at the commencement of the winding-up.

(2) Uncertain claims valued — In case of any claim subject to any contingency or for unliquidated damages or which for any other reason does not bear a certain value, the court shall determine the value of the claim and the amount for which it shall rank.

1996, c. 6, s. 160; 1999, c. 28, s. 92

158. Law of set-off to apply — The law of set-off, as administered by the courts, whether of law or equity, applies, in the same manner and to the same extent as if the business in Canada of the authorized foreign bank was not being wound up under this Act, only to

(a) claims by creditors of the authorized foreign bank in respect of its business in Canada; and

(b) proceedings for the recovery of debts due or accruing due to an authorized foreign bank in respect of its business in Canada at the commencement of the winding-up.

1996, c. 6, s. 160; 1999, c. 28, s. 92

158.1 (1) Distribution of property — Where a winding-up order is made in respect of an authorized foreign bank, claims shall be paid in the following order of priority:

(a) charges, costs and expenses, including the remuneration of the liquidator, incurred in the winding-up of the business in Canada of the authorized foreign bank and of the liquidation of its assets;

(b) claims of preferred creditors, specified in section 72; and

(c) debts and liabilities of the authorized foreign bank in respect of its business in Canada in order of priority as set out in sections 625 and 627 of the *Bank Act*.

(2) Distribution and release of surplus assets — Any assets that remain after payment of the claims referred to in paragraphs (1)(a) to (c) are to be applied firstly in payment of interest from the commencement of the winding-up at the rate of five per cent per annum on all claims proved in the winding-up and according to their priority. The liquidator may, with the approval of the court, release to the authorized foreign bank any assets remaining after payment of the interest.

1999, c. 28, s. 92

158.2 Transfer to foreign liquidator — Where an authorized foreign bank is in liquidation in the jurisdiction in which its head office is situated or where it principally carries on business, the Superintendent may, if the Superintendent deems it advisable and in the interests of the creditors of the authorized foreign bank, authorize the liquidator, subject to the approval of the court, to transfer the assets of the authorized foreign bank to the liquidator in that jurisdiction.

1999, c. 28, s. 92

158.3 Right of action not debarred — Subject to this Act, where the assets of an authorized foreign bank are not sufficient to cover in full all claims referred to in paragraphs 158.1(1)(a) to (c), the creditors are not barred from any recourse they have, either in law or equity, except in respect of the share, if any, received in the distribution of the assets.

1999, c. 28, s. 92

PART III — RESTRUCTURING OF INSURANCE COMPANIES

159. Definitions — In this Part,

"company" means an insurance company; *("société")*

"foreign company" means a foreign insurance company; *("Version anglaise seulement")*

"policy" includes, without limiting the generality of its meaning, "policy" as definded in subsection 2(1) of the *Insurance Companies Act. ("police")*

R.S.C. 1985, c. 18 (3rd Supp.), s. 43; 1991, c. 47, s. 747; 1996, c. 6, s. 161

159.1 (1) Application of Part — This Part applies only to insurance companies.

(2) Transitional — This Part applies only in respect of applications for winding-up orders that are made after the date of coming into force of this subsection, and applications for winding-up orders that were made on or before that date shall be dealt with in accordance with the provisions of this Part as they read immediately before that date.

1991, c. 47, s. 747; 1996, c. 6, s. 161

160. Protection of asset orders — The court may, at any time after an application for a winding-up order is made, on the application of the applicant for the winding-up order or of the liquidator, make such order as the court considers appropriate for the protection of the assets of the estate of the company.

1991, c. 47, s. 748; 1996, c. 6, s. 161

161. (1) Order of priority for payment of claims — Subject to this Act, claims shall be paid in the following order of priority:

(a) costs of liquidation and the mortgage insurance and special insurance portions of the expenses described in paragraph 686(1)(a) of the *Insurance Companies Act*;

(b) claims of preferred creditors, specified in section 72;

(c) claims of policyholders of the company ranking as follows:

(i) in the case of policies of life insurance and policies of accident and sickness insurance,

(A) if transfer or reinsurance is not effected as provided in section 162, claims that have arisen under those policies of the company, in accordance with the terms thereof, prior to the date of the filing of the statement of the liquidator in the Office of the Superintendent as provided in subsection 168(1), less any amount previously advanced by the company on the security of those policies, and claims to the value of those policies computed as provided in section 163, or

(B) if transfer or reinsurance is effected as provided in section 162, of all or any of the policies of the company,

(I) in respect of those policies of the company for which transfer or reinsurance is effected, the consideration payable for the transfer or reinsurance of the policies of the company, and

(II) in respect of those policies of the company for which transfer or reinsurance is not effected, claims that have arisen under those policies, in accordance with the terms thereof, prior to the date of the filing of the statement of the liquidator in the Office of the Superintendent as provided in subsection 168(1), less any amount previously advanced by the company on the security of those policies and claims to the value of those policies computed as provided in section 163, and

(ii) in the case of policies of insurance other than policies of life insurance and policies of accident and sickness insurance,

(A) firstly, claims that have arisen under those policies of the company by reason of the occurrence of the event insured against, in accordance with the terms thereof, prior to the date of the filing of the statement of the liquidator in the Office of the Superintendent as provided in subsection 168(1), less any amount previously advanced by the company on the security of those policies, and

(B) secondly, the claims of such policyholders to the value of those policies computed as provided in section 163 or, where transfer or reinsurance is effected as provided in section 162 of all or any of the policies of the company, the consideration payable for the transfer or reinsurance of the policies of the company or, as the case may be, claims that have arisen under those policies of the company by reason of the cancellation of such policies, in accordance with the terms thereof, prior to the date of the filing of the statement of the liquidator in the Office of the Superintendent as provided in subsection 168(1), less any amount previously advanced by the company on the security of the policies so cancelled; and

(d) expenses described in paragraph 686(1)(a) of the *Insurance Companies Act* that were incurred by the Superintendent in respect of the company and assessed against and paid by other companies pursuant to that Act, and interest in respect thereof at such rate as is specified by the Superintendent.

(2) Claims re life companies — No payment on a claim by

(a) a creditor of a company insuring risks under policies referred to in subparagraph 161(1)(c)(i), or

(b) a policyholder of the company claiming a minimum amount that the company has agreed to pay under a policy or in respect of an amount for which a segregated fund is maintained under section 451, subsection 542.03(2) or section 593 of the *Insurance Companies Act* for a deficiency if the assets of the fund are insufficient to satisfy such a claim

shall be made unless the assets of the company are sufficient to pay the claims referred to in subsection (1) and all of the terms of the policies of policyholders referred to in that subsection have been satisfied in full including any interest component of those policies accruing to the date of payment of the claim.

(3) Interest component — For the purposes of subsection (2), the interest component of the claims of policyholders referred to in subparagraph 161(1)(c)(i) shall be treated as part of the claim that has arisen under the policy in accordance with the terms thereof.

(4) Claims re other companies — No payment on a claim by a creditor of a company insuring risks under policies referred to in subparagraph 161(1)(c)(ii) shall be made unless the assets of the company are sufficient to pay the claims referred to in subsection (1).

(5) Subordinated debt holders — Holders of subordinated indebtedness, within the meaning of subsection 2(1) of the *Insurance Companies Act*, of a company and other indebtedness that by their terms rank equally or are subordinate to such indebtedness are entitled to receive payment on their claims only if the assets of the company are sufficient to pay the claims referred to in subsections (2) and (4).

(6) Priority of claims of policyholders in foreign companies — Notwithstanding anything in this Part, but subject to subsection (8), if a company is a foreign company, no claim, after the payment of costs of liquidation and the mortgage insurance and special insurance portions of the expenses described in paragraphs 686(1)(a) of the *Insurance Companies Act*, other than claims of

(a) the preferred creditors referred to in paragraph (1)(b),

(b) holders of policies of a class of insurance specified in the order of the Superintendent under Part XIII of the *Insurance Companies Act*, and

> ### Proposed Amendment — 161(6)(b)
>
> (b) holders of policies of a class of insurance specified in the order of the Superintendent under Part XIII of the *Insurance Companies Act*, other than holders of a policy exempt from Part XIII by virtue of section 572.1 of that Act, and
>
> 2007, c. 6, s. 445 [Not in force at date of publication.]

(c) expenses described in paragraph 686(1)(a) of the *Insurance Companies Act*, that were incurred by the Superintendent in respect of the company and assessed against and paid by other companies pursuant to that Act, and interest in respect thereof at such rate as is specified by the Superintendent,

ranks against the assets, and the balance, if any, of the assets remaining after the claims are paid shall be applied by the liquidator in satisfaction of the claims of any other creditors of the insurance business in Canada of the foreign company in accordance with subsections (2) and (4), but not including policyholders and creditors of the foreign company in respect of a class of insurance not specified in that order.

(7) Definitions — In subsection (8),

"assets in Canada" means assets in Canada, within the meaning of subsection 2(1) of the *Insurance Companies Act*, of a foreign company; *("actif au Canada")*

"assets under the control of the chief agent" means the other assets of the foreign company that are held in Canada under the control of its chief agent, within the meaning of section 571 of the *Insurance Companies Act*, including all amounts received or receivable in respect of its insurance business in Canada. *("actif sous le contrôle de l'agent principal")*

(8) Other foreign company priority provisions — Where a foreign company is authorized to insure in Canada

(a) risks falling within the class of life insurance; and

(b) risks falling within some other class of insurance, other than accident and sickness insurance, accident insurance, personal accident insurance and sickness insurance,

> (i) in the case of
>
> > (A) the costs of liquidation, the mortgage insurance and special insurance portions of the expenses described in paragraph 686(1)(a) of the *Insurance Companies Act*, and
> >
> > (B) the claims of preferred creditors,
>
> the costs, portions of expenses and claims shall be paid from the assets in Canada, maintained for the policies referred to in subparagraphs (ii) and (iii), together with the assets under the control of the chief agent, in such proportion as the court considers fair and equitable,
>
> (ii) in the case of policies falling within the classes of life insurance, accident and sickness insurance, accident insurance, personal accident insurance and sickness insurance, claims shall be paid
>
> > (A) firstly, from the assets in Canada maintained for those policies,
> >
> > (B) secondly, from the assets under the control of the chief agent in such proportion as the court considers fair and equitable, and
> >
> > (C) thirdly, from the balance, if any, of any assets referred to in clauses (iii)(A) and (B) remaining after the claims under subparagraphs (i) and (iii) are paid,
>
> (iii) in the case of policies falling within some other class of insurance, claims shall be paid
>
> > (A) firstly, from the assets in Canada maintained for those policies,
> >
> > (B) secondly, from the assets under the control of the chief agent in such proportion as the court considers fair and equitable, and
> >
> > (C) thirdly, from the balance, if any, of any assets referred to in clauses (ii)(A) and (B) remaining after the claims under subparagraphs (i) and (ii) are paid, and
>
> (iv) in the case of expenses described in paragraph 686(1)(a) of the *Insurance Companies Act* that were incurred by the Superintendent in respect of the foreign company and assessed against and paid by other companies pursuant to that Act, the expenses shall be paid from the balance, if any, of the assets referred to in clauses (ii)(A) and (B) and (iii)(A) and (B) remaining after the claims under subparagraphs (i), (ii) and (iii) are paid.

(9) Priority of costs, etc. — For greater certainty, the costs, claims and expenses referred to in subsections (6) and (8) shall be paid in accordance with the priorities set out in subsection 161(1).

(10) Release of balance of assets to company — The liquidator may, with the approval of the court, release to the foreign company any balance of the assets remaining after payment of claims in the order of priority prescribed by subsection (9).

(11) Payment of liabilities — Notwithstanding anything in this section, the liquidator may, in carrying on the business of the company pursuant to paragraph 35(1)(b), with the approval of the court, pay liabilities relating to the portion of the business being carried on, where the payment is considered desirable for the retention of goodwill and enhancement of value to the estate of the company.

> R.S.C. 1985, c. 18 (3rd Supp.), s. 44; R.S.C. 1985, c. 21 (3rd Supp.), s. 55; 1991, c. 47, s. 749; 1996, c. 6, s. 161; 1997, c. 15, s. 411

162. (1) Transfer and reinsurance of policies by liquidator — The liquidator may, with the approval of the court and without the consent of the policyholders, arrange for the transfer or reinsurance of

(a) all or a portion of the policies of the company, in the case of a company other than a foreign company, or

(b) all or a portion of the policies in Canada of a foreign company

in a company, society, foreign company or provincial company within the meaning of the *Insurance Companies Act* or an insurance company incorporated by or under an Act of a legislature of a province and authorized under the laws of the province to issue policies of the class being transferred or reinsured, where the terms of the transfer or reinsurance are, in the opinion of the court having regard to the priorities set out in this Part, fair and equitable to

(c) the policyholders whose policies are being transferred or reinsured,

(d) the estate of the company as a whole, and

(e) the remaining policyholders of the company.

Proposed Amendment — 162(1)

(1) Transfer and reinsurance of policies by liquidator — The liquidator may, with the approval of the court and without the consent of the policyholders, arrange for the transfer or reinsurance of

(a) all or a portion of the policies of the company, in the case of a company other than a foreign company, or

(b) all or a portion of the policies in respect of a foreign company's insurance business in Canada

in a company, society, foreign company or provincial company within the meaning of subsection 2(1) of the *Insurance Companies Act* or an insurance company incorporated by or under an Act of a legislature of a province and authorized under the laws of the province to issue policies of the class being transferred or reinsured, if the terms of the transfer or reinsurance are, in the opinion of the court having regard to the priorities set out in this Part, fair and equitable to

(c) the policyholders whose policies are being transferred or reinsured,

(d) the estate of the company as a whole, and

(e) the remaining policyholders of the company.

> 2007, c. 6, s. 446(1) [Not in force at date of publication.]

(2) Transfer and reinsurance of policies by liquidator — The liquidator may, with the approval of the court and without the consent of the policyholders, arrange for the transfer or reinsurance of all or a portion of the policies of the company, other than policies in Canada, in any body corporate where the terms of the transfer or reinsurance are, in the opinion of the court, having regard to the priorities set out in this Part, fair and equitable to

    (a) the policyholders whose policies are being transferred or reinsured;

    (b) the estate of the company as a whole; and

    (c) the remaining policyholders of the company.

Proposed Amendment — 162(2)

(2) Transfer and reinsurance of policies by liquidator — The liquidator may, with the approval of the court and without the consent of the policyholders, arrange for the transfer or reinsurance of all or a portion of the policies of the company, other than policies in respect of its insurance business in Canada, in any body corporate if the terms of the transfer or reinsurance are, in the opinion of the court, having regard to the priorities set out in this Part, fair and equitable to

    (a) the policyholders whose policies are being transferred or reinsured;

    (b) the estate of the company as a whole; and

    (c) the remaining policyholders of the company.

> 2007, c. 6, s. 446(1) [Not in force at date of publication.]

(3) Transfer or reinsurance is in lieu of claim on policy — The transfer or reinsurance of policies referred to in subsections (1) and (2) shall be in lieu of the claim for the value of those policies computed as provided in section 163.

(4) Mortgage insurance policies — The liquidator of a company, society or foreign company within the meaning of subsection 2(1) of the *Insurance Companies Act* may, with the approval of the court and the consent of the Canada Mortgage and Housing Corporation, and without the consent of the policyholders, arrange for the transfer to that corporation of all or a portion of the company's, society's or foreign company's policies of mortgage insurance, or arrange for the reinsurance of all or a portion of those policies by that corporation.

> 1991, c. 47, s. 750; 1996, c. 6, s. 161; 2007, c. 6, s. 446(2)

162.1 Partial payment or reinsurance — Where the liquidator estimates that the assets of the company are insufficient to provide for the payment in full of the preferred claims specified in section 72, for the payment in full of claims referred to in subparagraphs 161(1)(c)(i) or (ii) and for the transfer or reinsurance in full of policies of the company, the claims referred to in subparagraphs 161(1)(c)(i) or (ii) may be paid at, and the transfer or reinsurance may be effected at, such percentage of the full amount of the policies as may be approved by the court.

> 1996, c. 6, s. 161

162.2 Modification of policies — The court may, on the application of the liquidator, without the consent of the policyholders concerned but on such notice to them as the court considers appropriate, modify the terms of all or any of the policies of insurance of the company held by those policyholders if the court is satisfied that the modification will have no adverse material impact on the policyholders under the terms of the policies.

1996, c. 6, s. 161

163. (1) Computation of claims — Claims of policyholders of the company to the value of their policies referred to in subparagraphs 161(1)(c)(i) or (ii) shall be computed by the liquidator in accordance with such methods of computation as the Superintendent may deem fair and reasonable, less any amount previously advanced by the company on the security of the policies.

(2) Amendment thereof — The methods of computation established by the Superintendent are binding on all concerned, subject only to modification by the Superintendent.

R.S.C. 1985, c. 18 (3rd Supp.), s. 45; 1996, c. 6, s. 161

164. (1) Transfer of funds and securities to the liquidator — The funds and securities of the company in Canada that may be on deposit with any government in Canada or with trustees or otherwise held for the company or for the protection of the policyholders of the company of the class or classes that are affected by the winding-up order shall, on order of the court having jurisdiction, be transferred to the liquidator.

(2) Assets on deposit outside Canada — Where the company is a Canadian company that has deposited with the government of any state or country outside Canada, or with any trustee or other person in that state or country, any of its funds or securities for the protection of the company's policyholders in that state or country, the liquidator may request that government, trustee or other person to transfer those funds and securities to the liquidator and on the transfer being made, those funds and securities shall be used for the benefit of all the company's policyholders in the same manner as any other assets of the company.

(3) Consequence of non-transfer of assets — Where a government, trustee or other person referred to in subsection (2) does not transfer the funds and securities deposited with it within such period commencing with the date of the liquidator's request therefor as the Court may fix, the policyholders of the company, for whose protection the deposit was made, are deemed to have refused the reinsurance, if any, arranged by the liquidator, and, whether transfer or reinsurance has been arranged or not, to have forfeited all right and claim to any share of the assets of the company other than the funds or securities so deposited for their protection outside Canada.

1996, c. 6, s. 161

165. Transfer to foreign liquidator — Where a foreign company is in liquidation in the country in which its head office is situated, the Superintendent may, if the Superintendent deems it advisable and in the interests of the policyholders in Canada, authorize the liquidator, subject to the approval of the court, to transfer the assets of the foreign company to the liquidator in that country.

Proposed Amendment — 165

165. Transfer to foreign liquidator — If a foreign company is in liquidation in the country in which its head office is situated, the Superintendent may, if the Superintendent considers it advisable and in the interests of policyholders in respect of the foreign company's insurance business in Canada, authorize the liquidator, subject to the approval of the court, to transfer the assets of the foreign company to the liquidator in that country.

2007, c. 6, s. 447 [Not in force at date of publication.]

1991, c. 47, s. 751; 1996, c. 6, s. 161

166. (1) Liquidator to prepare statement of claimants and creditors — The liquidator shall, without the filing of any claim, notice or evidence or the taking of any action by any person, prepare a statement of all the persons appearing by the books and records of the company to be creditors of the company or to be claimants under any policy including any matured, valued or cancelled policy, taking cognizance in that connection of all claims that have arisen in accordance with the terms of the policies of which the liquidator has notice.

(2) Collocation — The statement referred to in subsection (1) shall show the amount, determined as provided in section 161 in respect of policyholders, for which each person is to rank as a claimant or a creditor and every such person shall be collocated and ranked as, and is entitled to the right of, a claimant or a creditor for the amount so ascertained by the liquidator, without filing any claim, notice or evidence, or taking any action.

(3) Objections — Any collocation made pursuant to subsection (2) may be contested by any person interested, and any person who is not collocated, or who is dissatisfied with the amount for which the person is collocated, may file a claim.

(4) Amendment of statement — The liquidator or the court may rectify any statement prepared under subsection (1) on account of omissions or errors therein notified to the liquidator or discovered by the liquidator at any time before the completion of the liquidation, and only the claims appearing in the statement or amended statement shall be regarded in the distribution of the assets.

1996, c. 6, s. 161

167. Right of action not debarred — Where the assets are not sufficient to cover in full all claims appearing in the statement or amended statement described in section 166, the policyholders are not barred from any recourse they have, either in law or equity, against the company issuing the policy or against any shareholder or director thereof, except in respect of the share, if any, received in the distribution of those assets.

1996, c. 6, s. 161

168. (1) Copy of statement filed in Office of the Superintendent — A copy of the statement referred to in subsection 166(1), certified by the liquidator, shall be filed in the Office of the Superintendent, after not less than 30 days' notice of the liquidator's intention to do so has been given by the liquidator by notice in the *Canada Gazette* and in the official gazette of each province, and in two newspapers published at or nearest the place where the head office of the company or the chief agency of the company, as the case may be, is situated.

(2) When policyholder to rank as creditor — Any claim that has arisen under the terms of a policy of which notice is received by the liquidator after the date of the filing of a statement referred to in subsection 166(1) or an amended statement referred to in subsection 166(4) shall rank on the assets only for the value entered in the statement, unless the assets are sufficient to pay all claimants in full, and in that case the policyholder shall rank as a creditor for the balance of the policyholder's claim.

R.S.C. 1985, c. 18 (3rd Supp.), s. 46; 1996, c. 6, s. 161; 2007, c. 6, s. 448

169. Notice of filing — The liquidator shall send by prepaid mail a notice of the filing of the statement under subsection 168(1) to each claimant or creditor named in the statement, addressed to the latest address on record with the company, stating therein the amount for which the creditor or claimant is entitled to rank against the assets of the company.

1996, c. 6, s. 161

170. Report to Superintendent — Where the company is a company, society, foreign company or provincial company within the meaning of subsection 2(1) of the *Insurance Companies Act*, the liquidator shall report to the Superintendent once in every six months, or more often, as the Superintendent may require, on the condition of the affairs of the company, with such particulars as the Superintendent may require.

1991, c. 47, s. 752; 1996, c. 6, s. 161

171. Publication of notice of proceedings — Publication in the *Canada Gazette*, in the official gazette of each province and in two newspapers published at or nearest the place where the head office of the company or chief agency of the company, as the case may be, is situated, of notice of any proceedings of which, under this Act, creditors should be notified, is sufficient notice to holders of policies in respect of which no notice of claim has been received.

1996, c. 6, s. 161; 2007, c. 6, s. 449

172. Priority of certain claims — Nothing in this Part prejudices or affects the priority of any mortgage, lien or charge on the property of the company.

1996, c. 6, s. 161

Transitional Provision

— 2007, c. 29, s. 121:

121. Winding Up and Restructuring Act — An amendment to the *Winding-up and Restructuring Act* made by any of sections 113 to 116 of this Act applies only to companies in respect of which winding up proceedings under that Act are commenced on or after the day on which the amendment comes into force.

POLICY STATEMENTS

CORPORATIONS CANADA POLICY STATEMENTS

Policy Statement 1.1 — Name Granting Compendium

Date: February 11, 2003
Revised: January 2, 2007

This compendium sets out the name granting policy of the Director General, Corporations Canada, of Industry Canada, who is responsible under the *Canada Business Corporations Act* (CBCA) and the *Canada Corporations Act* (CCA) for ensuring that names proposed for Canadian corporations meet the requirements of the Acts and their regulations.

This policy is also available in abridged form called, *Name Granting Guidelines.*

Table of Contents

1. Introduction to Name Policies *4*

    1.1 How Do You Reserve a Corporate Name? 8

    1.2 Previously Existing Reservation by a Person Other Than the Applicant 8

    1.3 Interpretations and Definitions.................................... 8

    1.4 Facts Necessary for a Name Decision 9

    1.5 Voice Information System to Receive Information Orally 11

    1.6 Elements of a Corporate Name — Distinctiveness, Descriptiveness and a Legal Element 11

2. Absolutely Prohibited *12*

3. Qualifiedly Prohibited *13*

    3.1 Names Which Connote Government Sponsorship and Control 13

    3.2 Abbreviations for Government Departments 13

    3.3 Names Connoting a Connection with a University or Professional Association 16

    3.4 Names Connoting a Financial Intermediary........................ 19

4. Obscene Names Prohibited...................................... *23*

5. Lacking Distinctiveness *23*

    5.1 Regulation 17 — Definition of Distinctiveness 23

    5.2 Regulation 24(1)(a) — Only Descriptive 24

    5.3 Regulation 24(1)(b) — Name or surname of individual 25

    5.4 Regulation 26 — Use of family name 27

    5.5 Regulation 24(1)(c) — Use of geographic terms 28

5.6 Regulation 17 — Definition of "secondary meaning" 29

6. Confusion 30

6.1 Factors to Consider in Determining Confusion 31

6.2 Treatment of Existing Names Which are Famous, Highly Distinctive, or Diluted
. . . . 32

6.3 Initials and Confusion 33

6.4 Confusion and the Word "Group" 34

6.5 Revival / Dissolution 35

6.6 Confusion with Corporate Names, Trade Names, Trade-marks, and Official Marks
. . . . 36

6.6.1 Confusion with Trade-marks 36

6.6.2 Confusion with Trade Names 37

6.6.3 Confusion with Official Marks 39

6.7 Overcoming Confusion 39

6.7.1 Regulation 28 — Consent and Undertaking by a Corporation 39

6.7.2 Regulation 29 — Consent to a Distinctive Word 40

6.7.3 Regulation 30 — Successor businesses and Year of Incorporation 42

6.7.4 Amalgamations and Acquisitions 46

6.7.5 Failing to Honour Undertaking 48

6.7.6 Initials and Given Names 48

6.7.7 Bankruptcy 48

6.7.8 Names of Canada, Provinces, and Cities Added to Remove Confusion
. . . . 48

6.7.9 Canadian Subsidiaries 49

7. Deceptively Misdescriptive 50

8. Other Related Policies 51

8.1 Not-for-Profit Organizations 51

8.1.1 Non-Distinctive Names 51

8.1.2 Government Connotation Implied 51

8.1.3 Chamber of Commerce 51

8.1.4 Legal Elements 51

8.1.5 Not-for-profits and Confusion 52

8.2 Regulation 33 (Certain names not prohibited) 52

8.3 Bilingual Names 52

8.3.1 General Rule 52

8.3.2 Guidelines within the General Rule 52

8.3.3 Fee for Articles of Amendment not required 54

8.3.4 Searching each version 54

8.3.5 Legal Element 55

8.3.6 Confusing Descriptive Terms 56

8.3.7 Translation of distinctive element 57

8.3.8 Equivalent name for use outside Canada 57

8.4 Use of the Words "Broadcasting", "Radio", "Television" 57

8.5 USA — Securities and Exchange Commission Names 57

8.6 Number of Corporate Name Search Reports Required 58

8.7 Trade name....................................... 59

8.8 Numbered Name 59

8.9 Microfiche Supplement of Nuans Report for Names with More Than One Distinctive Element 59

8.10 Internet Domain Names as Corporate Name 60

9. Protecting Your Corporate Name *60*

1. — Introduction to Name Policies

The *Canada Business Corporations Act* (CBCA) and the *Canada Corporations Act* (CCA) have almost identical name regulations describing those types of corporate names which are prohibited. Essentially, an applicant cannot have a name that

- lacks distinctiveness

- is likely to cause confusion with other businesses

- is likely to mislead the public

- is reserved for another business

- is obscene, or

- has an unacceptable French or English form

The policies contained in this document are guidelines for interpreting the name regulations. They demonstrate how corporate name regulations will be applied in certain types of fact situations. Since, however, each name decision requires an exercise of judgment, based on the particular facts of that case, and after considering a number of factors, any one particular regulation and guideline may not necessarily determine the decision.

The following checklist should provide assistance in deciding which policies may be important for a particular corporate name:

1. Have you included an ABSOLUTELY PROHIBITED TERM in your name? Check *regulation 21 (see section 2.0 of the Compendium)* prohibiting the use of "Air Canada", "Canada Standard" or "CS", "Cooperative", "Coopérative", "Co-op" or "Pool", "Parliament Hill" or "Colline du Parlement", "Royal Canadian Mounted Police" or "Gendarmerie Royale du Canada", "RCMP" or "GRC", "United Nations" or "Nations Unies", "UN" or "ONU".

2. Where you are using "CANADA" or the name of a province in your name, check *regulation 22(a) and (b) (see 3.1)* which prohibits a name if it connotes government sponsorship and control. Your name should not give the impression of being a government sponsored entity unless the government consents in writing to use of the name.

3. If your corporation will be in a PROFESSIONAL or EDUCATIONAL field, ensure that your name does not mislead or connote affiliation with an existing university or professional association. (*See regulation 22(c)*), (*See 3.3*).

4. If your corporation will have activities of a FINANCIAL nature, make sure the name does not connote carrying on the business of a bank, loan company, insurance company, trust company, other financial intermediary, or stock exchange unless the appropriate federal or provincial regulator consents in writing to the use of the name. (*See regulation 22(d)*), (*see 3.3*).

5. Your name must have some DISTINCTIVENESS to distinguish your business from that of others. You cannot have a name that merely describes the business of a corporation, or its goods and services, or a quality of them, or is merely the name of a person or a geographic location. Check *regulation 24(1)(a), (b)* and *(c)* for details (*see 5.2, 5.3, 5.5* and *5.6*). Keep in mind that the more distinctive your name is, the more protection it will get.

6. If you are using the NAME OF AN INDIVIDUAL in your corporate name, you may be required to file a consent of that individual unless he or she is an incorporator or unless the individual died more than 30 years ago, or unless the name has secondary meaning. (*See regulation 26*) (*see 5.4* and *5.6*).

7. If you are using INITIALS in your proposed corporate name, you should check *section 6.3* for guidelines explaining when names with initials are confusing. If you are proposing the use of initials with surnames, see also *section 6.7.8.*

8. Your corporation should not appear to be the holding corporation of other, unrelated businesses which happen to use the same distinctive element as yours in their names. The use of the word "GROUP" can give this impression. Check *section 6.4* if you are planning to use the word "group".

9. The name you propose will not be found to be available if it seems likely to cause CONFUSION with existing business names (whether or not incorporated), official marks or trade-marks. Confusion can be between names A and B so that A and B are likely to be mistaken for the same company, or it can be between A and B where A misleadingly looks related to B. Both are instances of confusion.

You are required to obtain and file a Newly Upgraded Automated Name Search (NUANS) report that will list business names and trade-marks which look and sound the same as your name. A NUANS report may be obtained in two ways:

1. A NUANS report may be requested from a private company known as a search house. You can find a list of these firms on Strategis at *www.strategis.gc.ca/corporations* by following the links "Online Filing", and "Corporations Directorate Electronic Filing Centre", or in the Yellow Pages of your telephone directory under INCORPORATING COMPANIES, INCORPORATION NAME SEARCH, SEARCHIERS OF RECORDS or TRADE MARK AGENTS — REGISTERED. There is a fee for this service.

2. A NUANS report may be ordered on-line at the Electronic Filing Centre, at *www.strategis.gc.ca/corporations* from the NUANS Real-Time System. The fee is $20 payable by credit card (Visa or Mastercard). The system provides direct access to the NUANS search service but does not provide the professional assistance and recommendations often available from a registered NUANS search house. Applicants should note that a NUANS report that is generated and submitted to the Director may be rejected if the proposed name does not meet the requirements of the CBCA/CCA name regulations.

When you order a NUANS report, that report has a life of 90 days from the date it is requested. Most search houses can advise you whether your proposed name is likely to be accepted by the Director. The final decision, however, always rests with the Director.

Officers of the Branch will examine the NUANS search with certain factors in mind: Do any of the names, trade-marks or official marks which sound alike appear to be in the same business as yours? Would they likely have the same type of client, or territory of operation as yours? How much protection do they deserve?

Officers of the Branch will have the information listed in the paragraph above only if you provide it to them when making your submission. If you have satisfied yourself that your corporation will not create a likelihood of confusion, give the Branch the basis for your conclusions. Chances are it will satisfy the Director. Name submissions must often be rejected for lack of this kind of information. For more details concerning how the Branch determines whether there is a likelihood of confusion, see regulations 18 and 25 (*see 6.1*). For more details about what information to file, *see 1.3*. Failure to provide this information with the first submission of your proposed corporate name will likely result in the rejection of your name request. Approval is often not possible until the information is provided.

10. If you propose to take the name of a corporation which has been DISSOLVED, check *regulation 27 (see 6.5)* For a period of two years after the dissolved corporation ceases operations, the memory of its name is presumed to stay in the public's mind. You will not be able to have the exact same name during that TWO YEAR PERIOD. As explained in item 12 below, you may choose to resolve this problem by adding some distinguishing feature to your name which can be removed after the two year period has expired.

11. If you are REVIVING a corporation that has been dissolved, check *regulation 27 (see 6.5)*. The name may now be prohibited if another corporation was incorporated since your corporation was dissolved.

12. Under certain conditions, you are permitted to have names that appear to be confusing with an existing business name (i.e., appear to be the same business as an existing business, or appear to be affiliated with an existing business). Essentially, the EXISTING BUSINESS must CONSENT in writing to the use of its name, *regulation 29 (see 6.7.2)* or, must CONSENT AND UNDERTAKE TO CHANGE its name. Even then, because of the two-year period referred to in item 10 above, there may still be confusion unless certain other conditions are met. If you wish to use the name of a corporation which has been INACTIVE FOR TWO YEARS, check *regulation 28 (see 6.7.1)*. If you wish to incorporate AN AFFILIATE of an existing corporation, check *regulation 29 (see 6.7.2)*. If you wish to incorporate a corporation which will TAKE OVER THE BUSINESS of an existing corporation, check *regulation 30 (see 6.7.3)*. If you are proposing an AMALGAMATION, check *regulation 31(1) and (2) (see 6.7.5)* for names which are permissible for the amalgamated corporation.

In order to use a name identical to the name of an affiliated corporation whose ASSETS your corporation has or will ACQUIRE, check *regulation 31(3) and 31(4) (see 6.7.5)*. If the existing corporation whose name you wish to take is BANKRUPT, check *section 6.7.9* for the consent that is required.

13. If your proposed name appears to be confusing with a TRADE-MARK, special considerations apply. If a trade-mark has been registered for 5 or more years, the applicant must get the consent of the trade mark owner. If the trade-mark has been registered for less than 5 years this may not be necessary. For information on how to get PROTECTION FROM TRADE-MARKS which may be registered after your incorpo-

ration, check *section 9*. Where a proposed name is confusingly similar to an existing OFFICIAL MARK adopted and used pursuant to the provisions of section 9 of the *Trade-marks Act*, it will be rejected. (For more on trade-marks, official marks and TRADE NAMES, see *section 6.6*).

14. The Branch is reluctant to approve names for profit-making corporations which contain words such as "INSTITUTE" or "CLUM". These words are more commonly used in the names of not-for-profit corporations and may, for that reason, be misleading. (See *section 7.0*).

15. There is no difference between the regulations that apply in respect of the CONTINUANCE of a corporation and the regulations that apply in respect of its incorporation.

16. The legislation and policies with respect to the names of NON-FOR-PROFIT corporations are somewhat different. Generally, it is accepted that not-for-profit names tend to be more general and descriptive. Not-for-profit names are less likely, therefore, to be rejected for being merely descriptive, as set out in item 5 above. (*See 8.1*).

17. If you are proposing a BILINGUAL corporate name, you must ensure that the two language forms are not so different from one another that they appear to be two different corporations. (*See 8.3*).

18. If the name you are proposing is in a COMBINED English and French form, it should only include one legal element. (*See 8.3.5*).

19. If the French and English forms of your corporate name are similar enough, you may not need two NUANS search reports. (*See 8.3.4*).

20. If a corporate name contains a word or phrase, or connotes a business that is obscene, the name is prohibited. (*See 4.0*)

1.1 — How Do You Reserve a Corporate Name?

To reserve your proposed corporate name, you must:

1. obtain a NUANS search on the proposed name, and

2. apply to the Director, CBCA, for determination that the proposed name does not contravene the regulations. In order for the Director to make this determination, the proposed name has to be submitted to Corporations Canada accompanied by the NUANS search report. This can be done before articles are filed if it is important that the articles not be rejected (Save yourself time by using this method!). Otherwise, the Director's decision will be taken when articles of incorporation (and other forms necessary to complete the incorporation) are filed with a proposed name. The articles will be rejected if it is found that the name is not available.

Once the Director has decided that a particular name is approved, that name is automatically reserved for 90 days, retroactive to the date the NUANS search report was requested, i.e. the date appearing in the right-hand column beside the proposed name. Please note that where *two consecutive dates* appear in the right hand column, the reservation will be retroactive to the earlier of the two dates.

1.2 — Previously Existing Reservation by a Person Other Than the Applicant

The Director is not permitted to reserve a corporate name if it is the same as, or is confusing with, a corporate name that has, before the date of the request, been reserved by the Director for another person, unless

(a) written consent has been obtained from the person for whom the corporate name was reserved; or

(b) the 90-day reservation period has expired without the person for whom the corporate name was reserved having incorporated or having made a renewed request to reserve the corporate name.

1.3 — Interpretations and Definitions

The regulations set out the following definitions.

"confusing", in relation to a corporate name, means a corporate name the use of which causes confusion with a trade-mark, official mark or trade name in the manner described in regulation 18. (*prête à confusion*)

"corporate name" means the name of a corporation. (*Version anglaise seulement*)

"distinctive", in relation to a trade name, means a trade name that distinguishes the business in association with which it is used by its owner from any other business or that is adapted so as to distinguish them from each other. (*distinctive*)

"official mark" means an official mark within the meaning of subparagraph 9(1)(n)(iii) of the *Trade-marks Act*. (*marque officielle*)

"secondary meaning", in relation to a trade name, means a trade name that has been used in Canada or elsewhere by an applicant or by their predecessors so as to have become distinctive in Canada as at the date of filing an application for a corporate name. (*sens dérivé*)

"trade-mark" has the same meaning as in section 2 of the *Trade Marks Act*. (*marque de commerce*)

"trade name" means the name under which a business is carried on, whether it is a corporate name or the name of a body corporate, a trust, a partnership, a sole proprietorship or an individual. (*dénomination commerciale*)

"use" means actual use by a person that carries on business in Canada or elsewhere. (*emploi*)

1.4 — Facts Necessary for a Name Decision

To obtain a favourable name decision, you must provide the Director with sufficient information. Even where no confusingly similar names appear on the search report and there is therefore no concern about confusion, the Director cannot properly assess whether a name

- connotes government sponsorship
- connotes the business of trust, loan, insurance or banking
- misdescribes, or merely describes the business of a corporation

unless the Director is given some information about what your business will be.

Where there are names on the search report that look or sound similar to your name, you must provide the type of information listed in section 25 of the Regulations:

- the TYPE OF BUSINESS the proposed company will carry on and how this business is dissimilar to the activities of existing businesses which have similar names.

- WHERE THE PROPOSED COMPANY WILL CARRY ON ITS BUSINESS and whether this territorial area is different from the area in which other businesses with similar names and similar activities are operating.

- with WHAT TYPES OF CLIENTS AND SUPPLIERS the proposed company will do business and whether they are different from the types of clients with whom existing businesses, with similar names and similar activities in a similar territory, will do business — e.g. deal with retailers, computer programmers or the general public.

- the DERVIATION OF THE DISTINCTIVE ELEMENT(S) of the proposed name. If there is a reasonable explanation for why the applicant wants that distinctive element, one is less likely to suspect that the applicant is trying to trade on the goodwill of an existing business with a similar name.

- whether the proposed company will be RELATED TO EXISTING BUSINESS with similar names or trade marks and if so, the written consent of some or all of them.

- whether the proposed company has a FOREIGN PARENT with a similar name which carries on business or is known in Canada. If so, written consent is required and proposed company must add "(Canada)" or "of Canada".

- whether an EARLIER RESERVATION of a similar name which appears on the search report, was made by the same applicant.

- the WRITTEN CONSENT OF AN INDIVIDUAL whose name appears in the corporate name, unless that individual is an incorporator or a director. The consenting individual must indicate that he or she has or had a material interest in the corporation.

If the applicant fails to give us this information, the name must often be rejected because the Director has no basis to be satisfied that the new corporate name will not create a likelihood of confusion with existing similar names appearing on the search report.

Without this information it may appear that the proposed name will likely be confused with an existing name which appears to be in the same business, in the same territory. With the information, it may become clear that the two businesses are, in fact, significantly different, in different territories, dealing with different types of suppliers and customers and therefore confusion is not likely.

Generally speaking, if the applicant has reviewed the search report carefully and is satisfied in his/her own mind that the new corporation is not likely to cause confusion, it is merely a matter of giving to the Director sufficient information to reach the same conclusion. Applicants should always be reasonably cautious in reaching their conclusion however, because the applicant risks being sued by an existing business or being required by the Director to change its corporate name after the Director has been persuaded by an existing business that the new corporate name really does create a likelihood of confusion. Of course, the new corporation would always have the opportunity to state its case before the Director's decision to change its name was taken.

1.5 — Voice Information System to Receive Information Orally

Corporations Canada has implemented a Voice Information System, providing taped answers to commonly asked questions about federal corporate name-granting issues. The system is intended to be an alternate method for explaining, orally, to our applicants how to get a name approval or what to do when their proposed corporate name has been rejected. The system is fully bilingual and accessible by calling either 613-946-0147 or 613-946-0148.

1.6 — Elements of a Corporate Name — Distinctiveness, Descriptiveness and a Legal Element

Generally, a corporate name is composed of three elements:

i) *A distinctive element* which is the unique identifier of the name.

ii) *A descriptive element* which describes the line of business. (Not absolutely required)

iii) *A legal element* which indicates the legal status of the company as an incorporated body.

Example:

distinctive element	descriptive element	legal element
TELFAX	COMMERCIAL COMMUNICATIONS	LTD

To decide whether or not a proposed name is available, several guidelines apply. In accordance with the *Canada Business Corporations Act* and its regulations, the Director must consider if the proposed name is:

I. absolutely prohibited

II. qualifiedly prohibited

III. obscene

IV. lacking distinctiveness

V. confusing

VI. deceptively misdescriptive

Each of the specific *Canada Business Corporations Regulations* is presented in the following pages under these headings with the related policies of the Branch.

2. — Absolutely Prohibited

A corporate name is prohibited, under regulation 21, if the name contains any of the following elements:

a) "Air Canada";

b) "Canada Standard" or "CS";

c) "cooperative", "coopérative", "co-op" or "pool" when it connotes a cooperative venture;

d) "Parliament Hill" or "Colline du Parlement";

e) "Royal Canadian Mounted Police", "Gendarmerie Royale du Canada" "RCMP" or "GRC"; or;

f) "United Nations", "Nations Unies", "UN" or "ONU".

3. — Qualifiedly Prohibited

3.1 — Names Which Connote Government Sponsorship and Control

Reg. 22. A corporate name is prohibited if it connotes that the corporation

(a) carries on business under royal, vice-regal or governmental patronage, approval or authority, unless the appropriate government department or agency consents in writing to the use of the name;

(b) is sponsored or controlled by or is connected with the Government of Canada, the government of a province, the government of a country other than Canada or a political subdivision or agency of any such government, unless the appropriate government, political subdivision or agency consents in writing to the use of the name.

(Canada Business Corporations Regulations, 2001)

Examples of names which connote government patronage or sponsorship and control:

- "SPORTS CANADA"

- "CANADIAN ASSOCIATION OF POSTMASTERS"

- "HEALTH & WELFARE PROGRAMMERS ASSOCIATION"

- "CANADIAN ARMED FORCES"

- "CANADIAN FORCES"

- "CANADIAN LABELLING STANDARDS COUNCIL"

- "ROYAL CANADIAN MINT"

3.2 — Abbreviations for Government Departments

Care should be taken when allowing initials that could connote government sponsorship or control in a proposed name. For example: The abbreviation "IC" for Industry Canada would be available with a descriptive feature like "shoes". The same distinctive element with a descriptive feature like "Corporate Information Services" would be unavailable because it implies government sponsorship and control.

USE OF ALTA, ALBERTA, B.C. or BRITISH COLUMBIA

Use of certain provincial names and abbreviations in federal corporate names is prohibited. At the request of the Alberta and British Columbia Governments, the Director does not allow the use of the terms "ALTA", "ALBERTA", "B.C." or "BRITISH COLUMBIA" in a federal corporate name. This format is reserved for companies incorporated in those two provinces as affiliates of an extra-provincial company of the same or similar name. If an applicant has strong objections, he or she may wish to contact the respective Alberta and British Columbia Companies Branches to try to obtain consent for use.

USE OF ALTA, ALBERTA and OF ALBERTA

The terms "ALTA", "ABLERTA", and "OF ALBERTA" will be available unless they give a government connotation to the name in which case consent of the relevant government authority will be necessary. The Alberta Companies Branch leaves it up to the Director to determine when there is governmental connotation.

Alberta Registries

Corporate Registry
Department of Government Services

18th Floor, Commerce Place

10155-102 Street, Edmonton AB T5J 4L4

Tel: 780-422-7330

Email: *cr@gov.ab.ca* Internet: *www.gov.ab.ca/gs*

USE OF B.C., BRITISH COLUMBIA and OF BRITISH COLUMBIA

The terms "B.C.", "BRITISH COLUMBIA" and "OF BRITISH COLUMBIA" will not be available without the approval of the British Columbia Registrar of Companies. The British Columbia Registrar of Companies wishes all names of this nature to be referred to its office for that determination to be made.

B.C. Registrar of Companies

The Waddington Bldg.

940 Blanshard St., 2nd Floor

Victoria, BC V8W 3E6

Tel: 250-387-7848

Internet: *www.fin.gov.bc.ca/registries/corppg*

USE OF NOVA SCOTIA

"Nova Scotia" cannot be used as the first word in a corporate name without consent from the Nova Scotia Registrar of Joint Stock Companies.

Service Nova Scotia and Municipal Relations

Registrar of Joint Stock Companies

Maritime Centre, 9th floor, Box 1529

1505 Barrington Street

Halifax NS B3J 2Y4

Telephone: 902-424-7770

Fax: 902-424-4633

Email: *joint-stocks@gov.ns.ca*

Internet: *www.gov.ns.ca/snsmr/rjsc/*

USE OF MANITOBA

"Manitoba" cannot be used in the name of a proposed federal company without consent from the Companies Office of Manitoba.

Director

Companies Office

Manitoba Consumer and Corporate Affairs

1010, Woodsworth Building, 10th Floor

405 Broadway Avenue

Winnipeg, MB R3C 3L6

Telephone: 204-945-2500

Fax: 204-945-1459

Email: *companies@cca-gov.mb.ca*

Internet: *www.gov.mb.ca/cca/comp_off/index.html*

USE OF SASK., SASKATCHEWAN (SASK), (SASKATCHEWAN) or coined words such as SASKO

"Sask.", "Saskatchewan", "(Sask.)", "(Saskatchewan)", or any other term which denotes affiliation with the Government of Saskatchewan, may only be used in a name proposed for a federal company with the consent of the Director of Corporations in Saskatchewan. In accordance with the Saskatchewan Justice Name Qualification Policy (www.saskjustice.gov.sk.ca/branches/corporations/forms/name-qualification-policy.pdf), the corporation must agree to:

a) carry on the major portion of its business within Saskatchewan; or

b) have its head office in Saskatchewan, from which it carries on the major portion of its business; AND

c) undertakes to change its name to delete the word "Saskatchewan" from its name, should it cease to carry on its business in Saskatchewan.

Director of Corporations

Corporations Branch

Saskatchewan Justice

2nd floor, 1871 Smith Street

Regina, Saskatchewan S4P 3V7

Telephone: 306-787-2962

Fax: 306-787-8999

Email: *corporations@justice.gov.sk.*

Internet: *www.saskjustice.gov.sk.ca/*

USE OF NEWFOUNDLAND OR NFLD

"Newfoundland" or "Nfld" are not permitted in a name proposed for a federal company without consent from the Registry of Companies of Newfoundland and Labrador.

Registry of Companies

Commercial Registrations Division

P.O. Box 8700, Confederation Building

Ground Floor, East Block

St. John's, NF A1B 4J6

Telephone: 709-729-3317

Fax: 709-729-0232

Email: *ahogan@mail.gov.nf.ca*

Internet: *www.gov.nf.ca/gsl/cca/cr/registry_companies.stm*

USE OF NEW BRUNSWICK

"New Brunswick" cannot be used at the beginning of a corporate name without consent from the Director, Corporate Affairs Registry of New Brunswick.

Director

Corporate Affairs Branch

Service New Brunswick

P.O. Box 1998

Fredericton, NB E3B 5G4

Telephone: 506-453-2703 or 888-832-2762

Fax: 506-453-2613

Email: *snb@snb.ca*

Internet: *www.snb.ca/*

USE OF NAMES OF FOREIGN COUNTRIES

A name such as XYZ (Switzerland) Inc. would be available without consent of the Swiss government.

3.3 — Names Connoting a Connection with a University or Professional Association

> *Reg. 22. For the purpose of paragraph 12(1)(a) of the Act, a corporate name is prohibited if it connotes that the corporation*
>
> > *(c) is sponsored or controlled by or is connected with a university or an association of accountants, architects, engineers, lawyers, physicians, or surgeons or another professional association recognized by the laws of Canada or a province, unless the appropriate university or professional association consents in writing to the use of the name.*
>
> *(Canada Business Corporations Regulations, 2001)*

Professional Associations

The Director does not require the consent of a certain professional organization just because a proposed name makes reference to a member or members of that profession.

The test is whether it could be reasonably assumed that the business is sponsored, controlled by, or connected with the organization.

e.g. *No consent required for:*

- Heritage Lawyers' Association

- John Brown Accounting Services Ltd.

- Black & White Engineers or

- Engineering & Consulting Ltd.

Rather, consent will be required only when the proposed name is confusingly similar with a particular university or professional association.

e.g. *Consent required for:*

- University of Montreal Debating Society

- Upper Canada Lawyers' Debating Society (Law Society of Upper Canada — the professional association)

- Certified General Accountants Debating Society

Since the Director may not be aware of the names of all professional bodies, in each case where a proposed name refers to an existing profession, the applicant should inform us whether this name is likely to be confusing with any existing professional association. The applicant may wish to contact the appropriate authorities for more information before using the name. Please note that the various provincial professional bodies have their own remedies against misuse of their professional titles. Furthermore, a provincial legislature has the power to legislate to prevent a federal professional association from carrying on operations in its province.

Where no professional regulating body exists in a particular field, a body purporting to be such a professional association may be incorporated. The use of the word "professional" in the name is not prohibited.

e.g. North American Professional Shoemakers' Association

Note: We would also incorporate another body purporting to offer the same professional services (i.e. shoemakers' association) providing that the name proposed for that company is not confusing with the existing association name.

e.g.

> North American Professional Shoemakers' Association — existing
>
> Uniso Professional Shoemakers' Society — acceptable

Exception: The name of a professional association bearing the words "Corporation professionnelle du Québec" will be refused, unless it is accompanied by the consent of the Office des professions du Québec, since it connotes an organization approved by the professional code of Quebec.

Use of the term "University"

Where the name of a proposed corporation uses the term "university" in a fashion that suggests that the corporation is a degree-granting institution, the name will be rejected as being misleading unless it can be established that the corporation has been authorized by the relevant federal or provincial authority to grant degrees.

e.g. University Painters Inc. — acceptable

e.g. Northern University Inc. — misleading

Use of terms connoting a degree-granting institution such as "College", "School", or "Adult Education", "Research", "Applied Research"

An applicant's name will be rejected for being misleading where the name of a proposed corporation uses the terms "academy", "college", "school", "institute", "adult education", "research", "applied research" or a like term, and it appears either from the name itself, or from other information we have, that the proposed corporation will grant bachelors, masters or doctorate degrees or a licentiate without the authorization of a relevant authority.

e.g. Sudbury Typing College (Inc) — acceptable, since no bachelors, masters, doctorate degree or licentiate will result

e.g. Northwest Applied Research (Inc) — unacceptable, if it grants degrees without authorization

When an application is received for the incorporation of a post-secondary educational institution, which has the aim of granting a bachelors, masters or doctorate degree or a licentiate (as a university or college), the application will be referred, for comment, to:

Association of Universities and Colleges of Canada

Suite 600

350 Albert St.

Ottawa, Ontario K1R 1B1

Enquiries 613-563-1236 ext. 345

3.4 — Names Connoting a Financial Intermediary

Reg. 22. For the purpose of paragraph 12(1)(a) of the Act, a corporate name is prohibited if it connotes that the corporation

> *(d) carries on the business of a bank, a loan company, an insurance company, a trust company, another financial intermediary or a stock exchange that is regulated by a law of Canada or a province, unless the Superintendent of Financial Institutions or the relevant provincial securities regulator consents in writing to the use of the name.*

(Canada Business Corporations Regulations, 2001)

Related policies

In cases where it is not clear whether a particular proposed corporate name connotes the business of loan, trust, insurance, banking, or stock exchange, the Director will depend on the advice of the Office of the Superintendent of Financial Institutions (OSFI). OSFI staff will provide this advice to applicants. The following are the guidelines that should be followed for these types of corporate names:

A. When a proposed name intended for a CBCA corporation *appears to connote* a loan company, a trust company, an insurance company or a subsidiary of a bank, the applicant should refer to:

Senior Director, Compliance Division
Office of the Superintendent of Financial Institutions (OSFI)

121 King Street West, Toronto, Ontario M5H 3T9

Telephone: 416-973-6117, or Internet: (*http://www.osfi.ca/*)
or Fax: 416-954-3169

For example, the following cases should be referred to OSFI:

where a name uses a descriptive term like "guaranty," "warranty," "surety," "life," "casualty", "assurance" or "indemnity".

When applying to OSFI for a consent to the use of a name, the applicant should provide a description of the proposed business of the applicant corporation in sufficient detail to enable OSFI to understand how the proposed name supports the anticipated activities of the applicant corporation. Where applicable, the applicant should also indicate to OSFI the exemption under the legislation administered by OSFI which, in the opinion of the applicant, permits the applicant corporation to use the descriptive elements contained in the proposed name. Where OSFI requires further information, it will contact the applicant directly.

When OSFI is satisfied that the referred name does not connote a loan, trust or insurance company, a bank or other financial intermediary, it will issue a letter consenting to the use of such name, addressed to the applicant.

B. When a proposed name, intended for a CBCA corporation, *clearly connotes* that the applicant business is a financial intermediary, it will be rejected. Corporations bearing such names may be incorporated only under one of the statutes administered by OSFI or provincial financial regulators. For example, subject to Section C, the following types of descriptive terms clearly connote a financial intermediary:

> i) When a descriptive term like "fiduciary," "trustco," "trust," "loanco," "loan," "savings," "insurance," "annuity" or "lifeco" is used. These terms are reserved for companies incorporated under the *Trust and Loan Companies Act* or the *Insurance Companies Act* administered by OSFI.

> ii) When the descriptive term "mortgage" is used and the corporation is a mortgage lending business and not a mortgage brokerage business (in the latter case, the word "mortgage" would be acceptable).

> iii) When a term like "bank," "banker" or "banking" is used alone or in combination with certain other words (e.g. "bancorp," "banco" or "bankco") in connection with financial activities. These terms are reserved for banks regulated by the *Bank Act* administered by OSFI and are not permitted for CBCA corporations or provincial corporations.

An applicant who intends to incorporate or amend the name of a loan, trust or insurance company or a bank should consult the Registration and Approvals Division of OSFI (For online information, www.osfi.ca):

> For loan and trust companies or banks — 613-990-7251
> For life insurance companies — 613-990-7609
> For property and casualty insurance companies — 613-990-5893

C. When a proposed name *clearly does not connote* a financial intermediary, it does not need to be referred to OSFI. For example, the following situations do not need to be referred:

> i) When any of the terms that normally connote the business of a financial intermediary are used in a fanciful way. Examples are "Once in a Life Time Bridal Boutique Inc." "Piggy Bank Children's Shop Ltd.," "Time Savings Household Cleaner Inc.," "Sam's TrustWorthy Contracting Services Ltd.," "ABC Data Bank Inc."

> ii) When the terms "finance," "acceptance," "credit," "fund," "fidelity" and "underwriters" are used.

> iii) When a term such as "broker," "agent," "agency" or "service(s)" is used in a name in such a way as to connote an insurance or mortgage-related agency or brokerage business, e.g., "Cartier Insurance Brokers Inc."

> iv) When the terms "trust foundation" or "trust society" are used by not-for-profit corporations.

> v) When the term "mortgage investment corporation" is used.

Note 1: Provincial Restrictions on Businesses Offering insurance-Related Services

For the purposes of licensing, some provincial jurisdictions (e.g., Quebec and Ontario) have restrictions on the type of names allowed for companies offering insurance-related services. Since the use of a name granted is subject to the laws of the jurisdiction where the company intends to carry on business, the applicant may wish to contact the appropriate authorities before applying for the proposed name.

In Quebec:

Regarding general insurance: 514-282-8765

Regarding personal insurance: 418-647-2244

In Ontario:

Regarding use of the word "agent": 416-250-7250

Regarding use of the word "broker": 416-365-1900

Note 2: Information Regarding Financial Institution Legislation

For the applicant's information, we are providing the following information regarding the legislation administered by OSFI. This information is for the applicant's interest only and does not directly relate to the operations of Corporations Canada under the regulation set out above. As you will see, however, the legislation administered by Corporations Canada and by OSFI are quite consistent with one another.

The *Insurance Companies Act*, the *Trust and Loan Companies Act*, and the *Bank Act* were amended in June 1996 by Bill C-15 and in June 1997 by Bill C-82. The *Insurance Companies Act*, the *Trust and Loan Companies Act*, and the *Bank Act* contain prohibitions regarding the use of certain words, subject to an exception for non-financial corporations.

Under subsection 47(1) of the *Insurance Companies Act*, subject to certain exceptions, no entity incorporated or formed by or under an Act of Parliament may use the word "assurance," "assurances," "insurance" or "lifeco" in its name. Subsection 47(2) provides that these restrictions do not apply to:

- a company or society (a defined term for an insurance company or fraternal benefit society);
- an entity the business of which is not financial activities;
- an entity that is primarily engaged in insurance brokerage or insurance agency services; or
- an entity that is grandfathered from the provision.

Under subsections 47(1) and (2) of the *Trust and Loan Companies Act*, no entity incorporated or formed by or under an Act of Parliament, other than a trust or loan company, may use the word "fiduciaire," "fiduciary," "fiducie," "trust," "trustco," "loan," "loanco" or "prêt" in its name. However, subsection 47(3) provides that these restrictions do not apply to an entity the business of which is not financial activities.

Under the *Bank Act*, an entity other than a bank is prohibited from adopting a name that includes the word "bank," "banker" or "banking" either alone or in combination with other words or any words of important meaning equivalent to these words, unless the words are used in connection with a business that is not engaged in financial services or that is a subsidiary of a bank. The Minister of Finance's approval is not required for these exceptions. For your information, OSFI considers terms such as "bankcorp," "banc," "bancorp," "bankco" and "banco" to be words that have import equivalent to the words referred to above.

The above note is only a summary of the legislation. Interested persons should refer to the statutes themselves for their specific provisions.

Note 3: Copy to OSFI

At OSFI's request, we will forward to them a copy of a CBCA certificate of incorporation of a subsidiary of an existing bank.

e.g. Bank of Nova Scotia Finance Corporation.

4. — Obscene Names Prohibited

Reg. 23. For the purpose of paragraph 12(1)(a) of the Act, a corporate name is prohibited if it contains a word or phrase, or connotes a business, that is obscene.

(Canada Business Corporations Regulations, 2001)

Because a contravention of this nature arises so rarely, the Director has no guidance to offer here.

5. — Lacking Distinctiveness

5.1 — Regulation 17 — Definition of Distinctiveness

"Distinctive" is defined in section 17 of the regulations as meaning a trade name that actually distinguishes one business from the business of others. Distinctiveness can be inherent or acquired (secondary meaning).

Reg. 19. When determining whether a trade name is distinctive, the name as a whole and not only its separate elements shall be considered.

(Canada Business Corporations Regulations, 2001)

Generally speaking, the most inherently unique names have distinctive features which are composed of letters or figures which have no generic meaning.

e.g.

- XLYK

- DWIDAG

In addition, unusual combinations of generic words can be distinctive.

e.g.

- Jean Junction

Words composed of parts of other words, surnames, family names, initials, numbers, geographic location and arbitrary dictionary words make a less inherently distinctive but acceptable name.

e.g.

- SUNCRAFT Shoes Ltd.

- SMITH Shoes Ltd.

- OTTAWA Shoes Ltd.

- I.I.L. Shoes Ltd.

- STAR Shoes Ltd.

5.2 — Regulation 24(1)(a) — Only Descriptive

Reg. 24.(1) For the purpose of paragraph 12(1)(a) of the Act and subject to subsection (2), a corporate name is prohibited if the corporate name is not distinctive because it

> *(a) is only descriptive, in any language, of the business of the corporation, of the goods and services in which the corporation deals or intends to deal, or of the quality, function or other characteristic of those goods or services;*

(Canada Business Corporations Regulations, 2001)

Related Policies

Examples of names lacking distinctiveness are "Software Inc." and "Car Sales Inc." An acceptable distinctive element would need to be added before such a corporate name could be granted, e.g., "Turner Software Inc." or "Greymark Car Sales Inc."

Some names that are merely suggestive of the industry, product or service, however, would be acceptable. An example of a merely suggestive name is "Tires and Wheels Ltd." for a car sales business. The name "Tires and Wheels Ltd." does not describe the business nor the product produced. It simply suggests the corporation's field of activity. If the corporation manufactured or sold tires and wheels, however, this name would be unacceptable because, in this context, it would be only descriptive.

As a general rule, the Director will not accept names that only describe a quality of the corporation's business or its goods or services, e.g., "Faster Consulting Services Inc."

However, the Director will accept such names when:

- alliteration gives the name an acceptable level of distinctiveness, e.g., "Better Business Boardrooms Inc."

- the NUANS report demonstrates that the word describing a quality is commonly used as a distinctive feature in business names, e.g., "Superior" in "Superior Machinery Ltd." or "Advanced" in "Advanced Technology Solutions Ltd."

- the descriptive word sounds unusual when used to describe the business of the proposed corporation (for example "Endless Furniture Inc." is acceptable, whereas "Long Lasting Furniture Ltd." is not).

Although these names are descriptive of a quality of the business, they are not merely descriptive but have some distinctiveness. By reason of alliteration or being unusual, these names are distinguishable from others. Also, where the NUANS search reports show that a descriptive word is extensively used as a distinctive element, the Director will tend to accept the name.

Please note that the approval of certain words as a corporate name does not necessarily mean that those words would be registrable as a trade-mark.

5.3 — Regulation 24(1)(b) — Name or surname of individual

Reg. 24. (1) For the purpose of paragraph 12(1)(a) of the Act and subject to subsection (2), a corporate name is prohibited if the corporate name is not distinctive because it

    (b) is primarily or only the name or surname, used alone, of an individual who is living or has died within 30 years before the date of the request to the Director for that name;

(Canada Business Corporations Regulations, 2001)

Related Policies

The Director determines whether a name is a surname by asking whether one would reasonably think of this word or words as a name or surname rather than as something else, e.g. a coined word. If it appears to be a name or surname, then that word or words cannot be used alone unless there is secondary meaning.

e.g. *The following proposed corporate names are unacceptable:*

- Legault Inc.

- S. V. Lee Ltd.

- Sarah Legault Inc.

- S & R Wolfe Inc.

Corporate names in which a name or surname (as determined in the paragraph above) is not used alone would be acceptable.

e.g. *The following proposed corporate names are acceptable:*

> (1) Wilson & Myers Ltd. (two names, not one name used alone)
>
> Bob & Carol Harris Inc.
>
> (2) Legault Gardening Enterprises Ltd.
>
> Thomas Construction Inc.

Note: Where the added descriptive word is not specific and gives no indication of the nature of the proposed business[2] the name may be refused for creating a likelihood of confusion with existing similarly named corporations.

e.g. *If Thomas Construction Inc. already exists, then the proposed corporate names are unacceptable:*

> Thomas Enterprises Ltd.
> or G. W. Thomas Enterprises Ltd.

The applicant must either provide information to show that there is in fact no likelihood (based on differences of products, territory, clientele) of confusion with existing companies, or, the applicant should add a more specific descriptive word,

e.g. *The following proposed corporate names are acceptable:*

> Thomas Landscaping Inc. (or, add a more specific name or surname)
> George W. Thomas Enterprises Ltd.

Note: "Associates" or "and Associates" can be used in combination with a name or surname. Although "Associates" is acceptable with a coined word, "and Associates" is not because it could mislead one into assuming that the distinctive element is a surname

e.g. XYLX & Associates — *not acceptable*

Note: The Office of the Superintendent of Bankruptcy prefers that trustees who incorporate use only the name(s) of the principal partner(s) in the corporate name. However, if only one person is involved, then a surname used alone may not be acceptable (see surname formats above). The addition of a descriptive term like "Insolvency Trustee" or "Bankruptcy" would overcome any such objection.

Regulation 26 is being referred to here as a matter of convenience, since it deals with use of a family name. Regulation 26 does not have anything to do with lack of distinctiveness.

5.4 — Regulation 26 — Use of family name

> *Reg. 26. For the purpose of paragraph 12(1)(a) of the Act, a corporate name is prohibited if an element of the name is the family name of an individual, whether or not preceded by their given name or initials, unless the individual or their heir or legal representative consents in writing to the use of their name and the individual has or had a material interest in the corporation.*
>
> *(Canada Business Corporations Regulations, 2001)*

The Regulation appears to state that every word that is in fact a family name of an individual requires a consent in writing regardless of whether the reasonable person would think of it as

---

[2]other such non-specific descriptors are: "agency", "associates", "brothers", "distributions", "enterprises", "industries", "group", "products", "services", "sons", "Canada", "International", etc.

a family name. Any applicant not providing such a consent would be in contravention of this regulation.

For the purpose of ensuring compliance with this regulation however, the Corporations Canada will use the same standard as is used for section 19 of the regulations, i.e. only where a reasonable person would look upon that word as a family name will a consent will be required, otherwise it will not be required.

e.g.

> RAN SHOE INC. — no consent required
> RAN SMITH SHOES INC. — consent of RAN SMITH
> RAN, SMITH SHOES INC. — consent of RAN and consent of SMITH

Punctuation such as a comma (,), ampersand (&) or hyphen (-) is necessary in a proposed name if the use of two surnames could wrongly connote the name of one individual (e.g. "Robert Simpson" should become "Robert, Simpson", "Robert & Simpson", "Robert-Simpson" if two surnames are intended).

A consent is not required where the word is a dictionary word or a Christian name unless it is used in such way as to connote a family name to a reasonable person.

e.g.

- STAR SHOES LTD. — no consent

- STAR, SMITH SHOES LTD. — consents of STAR & SMITH

- STAR SMITH SHOES LTD. — consent of STAR SMITH

- STARSMITH SHOES LTD. — no consent

- STAR ASSOCIATED LTD. — no consent

- STAR & ASSOCIATES LTD. — consent of STAR

- STAR ASSOCIATES LTD. — no consent

- ROSE GREEN'S TOOLS LTD. — consent of ROSE GREEN

Consents are not required where the word or words are obviously the name of an historical person, literary or fictional character.

e.g.

- DORIAN GREY FASHIONS INC. — acceptable

- LADY MACBETH COSMETICS INC. — acceptable

- BONAPARTE SHIRTS INC. — acceptable

- MACKENZIE KING PROMOTIONS INC. — not acceptable since Mr. King lived too recently to be considered a historical figure.

Where the proposed corporate name contains a fictitious name, it will be necessary to file a signed statement of the principal of the proposed company stating that the name in question is a fictitious name and is not the name of a person who is well-known or known to him or her personally.

A consent is not required when the family name is the name of the incorporator or a director of the business applying for the name.

A consent is not required when the family name is the name of a street on which the business is located.

The consenting person must have or must have had a material interest in the corporation as required by section 26 of the regulations.

5.5 — Regulation 24(1)(c) — Use of geographic terms

Reg. 24. (1) For the purpose of paragraph 12(1)(a) of the Act and subject to subsection (2), a corporate name is prohibited if the corporate name is not distinctive because it (c) is primarily or only a geographic name, used alone.

(Canada Business Corporations Regulations, 2001)

Related Policies

e.g.

"Red Lake Inc." is not acceptable because "Red Lake" is primarily or only a geographic name.

There should be no prohibition against the use of a geographic reference in the granting of a corporate name if a descriptive feature is added. Substantiation for the use of a geographic location is not required.

e.g.

"Red Lake Gold Mines Inc." would be acceptable provided that it is not confusing.

A street address used alone is considered primarily a geographic name and is not available unless a descriptive term is added.

e.g.

235 St. Catherine Street Inc. — unacceptable
235 St. Catherine Street Enterprises Inc. — acceptable

5.6 — Regulation 17 — Definition of "secondary meaning"

Reg. 24. (2) Subsection (1) does not apply if a person requesting a corporate name establishes that it has, through use, acquired the name and the name continues at the time of the request to have a secondary meaning.

(Canada Business Corporations Regulations, 2001)

Reg. 17. The following definitions apply in this part.

"secondary meaning", in relation to a trade name, means a trade name that has been used in Canada or elsewhere by any applicant or by their predecessors so as to have become distinctive in Canada as at the date of filing an application for a corporate name.

(Canada Business Corporations Regulations, 2001)

The applicant can escape the prohibitions of paragraphs 24(1)(a), (b), and (c) of the regulations as long as the applicant can show that the trade name has been used in Canada or anywhere else to such an extent that persons in that trade would, on hearing the name, think of the business, rather than the primary meaning of the words in its name.

In order to convince the Director appointed under the CBCA of secondary meaning, the applicant must produce in writing, evidence showing how large and widespread the business is and if necessary, include written statements from others in the trade.

Evidence to support a claim for secondary meaning must be in the form of an affidavit or statutory declaration and must attest to use of the name across Canada, either for significant periods of time or with great intensity.

Note: Reproduced below is a copy of the note which goes out with names rejected due to lack of distinctiveness.

Note — Lacking Distinctiveness

This name has been rejected because it lacks distinctiveness.

If Corporations Canada were to approve names that lacked distinctiveness, the task of preventing confusion among business names would be rendered more difficult. The only way the name attached to business X will not be confused with the name attached to business Y is if there is something in the names to distinguish them. The stronger the distinguishing feature, the less likely confusion will occur.

Based on this reasoning, the corporate name regulations require that corporate names have a distinguishing feature. These regulations also impose rules to indicate where distinctiveness is insufficient or lacking. According to these rules, a name lacks distinctiveness and is therefore unavailable when it is only descriptive, or when it is only an individual's name or a geographic name.

A corporate name that only describes the business of the corporation, industry, goods or services, or the quality or function of those goods and services is unavailable, e.g., "Car Sales Inc." A name will also be unavailable for being "only descriptive" when it merely describes the quality of the corporation's business or its products, e.g., Faster Consulting Services Inc.

A proposed name which appears to lack any distinctiveness may have, in fact, acquired distinctiveness through extensive use. If this distinctiveness is demonstrated in writing, the name will be available.

Otherwise, the best way to overcome the objection of lacking distinctiveness is:

Only descriptive — add a distinctive word

> e.g. a coined word like "Spillex" (Spillex Cleaning Services Corp.)
> e.g. a dictionary word, that does not describe like "Star" (Star Theatres Inc.)
> e.g. an individual's name like "Turner" (Turner Shoes Ltd.)

Primarily a name — add a descriptive word like "Manufacturing"

> e.g. Wilson Manufacturing Ltd.

Primarily a place — add a descriptive word like "Enterprises"

> e.g. Red Lake Enterprises Inc.

6. — Confusion

The proposed corporate name may be found to be confusing with any corporate name, trade name, trade-mark, or official mark appearing on the NUANS® search report.

6.1 — Factors to Consider in Determining Confusion

Reg. 18. A corporate name is confusing with

> *(a) a trade-mark or an official mark if the use of both the corporate name and either the trade-mark or the official mark, as the case may be, is likely to lead to the inference that the business carried on or intended to be carried on under the corporate name and the business connected with the trade-mark or the official mark, as the case may be, are one business, whether or not the nature of the business of each is generally the same; or*

> *(b) a trade name if the use of both names is likely to lead to the inference that the business carried on or intended to be carried on under the corporate name and the business*

carried on under the trade name are one business, whether or not the nature of the business of each is generally the same.

(*Canada Business Corporations Regulations*, 2001)

Reg. 25. For the purposes of paragraph 12(1)(a) of the Act, a corporate name is prohibited if it is confusing, having regard to all the circumstances, including:

(a) the inherent distinctiveness of the whole or any elements of any trade-mark, official mark or trade name and the extent to which it has become known;

(b) the length of time the trade-mark, official mark or trade name has been in use;

(c) the nature of the goods or services associated with a trade-mark or an official mark or the nature of the business carried on under or associated with a trade- mark, official mark or trade name;

(d) the nature of the trade with which a trade-mark, an official mark or trade name is associated, including the nature of the products or services and the means by which they are offered or distributed;

(e) the degree of resemblance between the proposed corporate name and any trade-mark, an official mark or trade name in the appearance or sound or in the ideas suggested by them; and

(f) the territorial area in Canada in which the proposed corporate name or an existing trade name is likely to be used.

(*Canada Business Corporations Regulations*, 2001)

Often, applicants do not supply sufficient information in the name request to properly assess all of the factors under section 25 of the regulations. In these cases the Director can only rely on Regulation 25(a) and (e) to make the name decision. If the applicant should decide to provide more information, the name decision can be re-evaluated in light of the new facts.

A decision of confusing similarity may be based on phonetic similarity alone.

Applicants should note that federal incorporation does not in itself confer to applicants rights over an existing provincial corporate name or trade name.

6.2 — Treatment of Existing Names Which are Famous, Highly Distinctive, or Diluted

The Director's primary concern in enforcing the name regulations is in eliminating confusion. Nowhere do the regulations enshrine the principle that a highly distinctive name should be protected from dilution. In practice, however, the protection principle complements the principle of avoiding confusion. A company may have a highly distinctive name, i.e. unique and imaginative, being a purely arbitrary creation, e.g. DWIDAG FOODS INC. (for a food wholesaler), as opposed to an obviously derived composition, e.g. CORTIVET (for the manufacture of cortisone veterinarian preparation). Granting the highly distinctive element to a second company, e.g. DWIDAG STORES LTD. is more likely to generate confusion because this distinctive element is more likely to linger in the mind of the public. Each case, however, depends on its facts and depending on differences of goods, services, territory and clientele, the Director may or may not feel that there is in fact a likelihood of confusion.

The Director does not assume, for the purposes of name granting policy, that any given existing company with a highly distinctive name will develop into a famous conglomerate, dealing in a variety of products and services.

"Famous" names are a case apart. They may originally have been highly distinctive, e.g. KODAK, or alternatively, very lacking in distinctiveness, e.g. GENERAL MOTORS or INTERNATIONAL BUSINESS MACHINES, but they have acquired high distinctiveness through use. They are generally conglomerates and the Director will not approve any corporate name that uses their distinctive feature.

Some words are so common that they are used as the distinctive element in many business names. Such wide usage dilutes the impact of the business name and gives it a reduced claim to protection. As a general rule, where a distinctive element is highly diluted (low distinctiveness), the same distinctive feature may be used in new corporate names that are only slightly different from the existing names. For instance, a different descriptive word might be all that is needed to distinguish the proposed corporate name from similar existing names, even if the descriptive word describes essentially the same business that is carried on under the existing names.

> *For example*, names such as "Universal Products Inc." or "Universal Bakery Products Inc." would not be prohibited, even though there were existing names like "Universal Food Enterprises Inc.," because the distinctive element "Universal" is highly diluted, and the existing names do not deserve much protection.

Therefore, the guidelines for initial, front-line name decisions (normally without benefit of much detailed information) should be as follows:

Classification	Decision	Considerations
FAMOUS	IBM Draperies Ltd. (Unavailable)	
HIGHLY DISTINCTIVE	1. IGSAC Toys Inc. — *existing* IGSAC Bicylces Ltd. — proposed *(UNAVAILABLE)*	There are circumstances which are not generally known at the time of initial name granting which would make *BICYCLES* available, or *DRAPERY* unavailable on reconsideration or confusion allegation.
	IGSAC Drapery Installation Inc. — proposed (AVAILABLE SUBJECT TO RISK ACCEPTED BY THE APPLICANT IN WRITING)	Upon investigation it may be determined that IGSAC Inc. is in toys, and therefore, on reconsideration, IGSAC Drapery would be available
	2. IGSAC Inc. — *existing* IGSAC Drapery Installation Inc. *(UNAVAILABLE BECAUSE IT IS NOT KNOWN HOW DIFFERENT ITS PRODUCTS & SERVICES ARE)*	

Classification	Decision	Considerations
LOW DISTINCTIVE-NESS/ DILUTION	1. Maple Leaf Toys Inc. — *existing* Maple Leaf Bicycles Ltd. — proposed *(AVAILA-BLE)*	There are circumstances which are not generally known at the time of initial decision which would make *BICYCLES* unavailable on Reconsideration or Confusion Allegation.
	2. Maple Leaf Inc. — existing Maple Leaf Bicycles Inc. — proposed *(AVAILA-BLE)*	

N.B. Of course even the unavailable names would be available if the companies were related and consent was provided.

Detailed information with respect to products, clientele, territory of existing companies must be provided in writing to facilitate the name decision.

6.3 — Initials and Confusion

There is no hard and fast rule with respect to when a name containing initials is likely to cause confusion. Territory of operations and any other relevant information always has to be taken into consideration. What follows is merely a guideline which assumes that the territory of the existing businesses and the proposed business will overlap and that the applicant has produced no other information showing that confusion is unlikely (e.g. totally different clientele, long co-existence, existing company inactive for a long period).

(a) If a distinctive feature is made up of two initials, the proposed name will be considered confusing if:

- the descriptive feature is the same or confusingly similar, and
- the initials are identical and in the same order or if the first initial is the same and the last initial is phonetically similar.

e.g. BN Construction:

- confusing with BM Construction
- confusing with BN Builders
- not confusing with BF Construction

(b) *If three or more* initials make up the distinctive feature of a name, the proposed name will be considered confusing if:

- the descriptive feature is the same or confusingly similar, and
- all of the initials except for the last one are identical, and
- the initials are in the same order as the initials in the existing corporate name.

e.g. ABCD Construction:

- confusing with ABCF Construction
- not confusing with DABC Construction

(c) Initials may be acceptable without a descriptive word if the result is not confusing.

Because it is difficult to develop a general policy which applies to each case that arises, some discretion must be used for cases not strictly covered by these guidelines. For example, a name like "BNND Construction" or "BMND Building" would be considered confusing with "BNMD Construction" because M and N are very similar in sound and appearance. "A & M Construction Inc." would be found to be confusing with "ANM Construction Ltd." because phonetically there is a little difference between the two.

6.4 — Confusion and the Word "Group"

Where there are no other unrelated companies with the same distinctive feature (not very high, not very low distinctiveness) as the proposed corporate name, the proposed name would be available without further requirement.

If there are other companies with the same distinctive feature as the proposed corporate name but unrelated to the corporation for which the name is proposed, the applicant must explain why the proposed corporate name will not misleadingly suggest a grouping of those companies.

Examples of possible responses:

- the business of the proposed corporation and that of the existing *unrelated companies* are too different for them to be confused as being affiliated.

- the proposed corporation will be the umbrella company for *related* companies using that distinctive feature and the proposed name will connote a relationship with them alone.

The addition of a descriptive word (e.g. textile) modifying the word "group" will likely make the proposed name available as long as the descriptive word clearly distinguishes the business of the proposed company from the business of existing companies with the same distinctive element.

Note: Consents of the "grouped" companies will be required unless the existing parent of those companies is requesting a change of name to "Group".

6.5 — Revival/Dissolution

Reg. 27. For the purpose of paragraph 12(1)(a) of the Act,

(a) a corporate name is prohibited if its use is likely to lead to the inference that the business carried on or intended to be carried on under it and the business of a body corporate that is dissolved are one business, whether or not the nature of their businesses is generally the same; and

(b) the name of a corporation that is revived under section 209 of the Act is prohibited if it is confusing with a name acquired by another corporation during the period beginning on the date of dissolution and ending on the date of revival of the revived corporation.

(Canada Business Corporations Regulations, 2001)

DISSOLUTION

A proposed corporate name is prohibited where its use could lead to confusion with the name of a body corporate that is dissolved.

Names identical to those of companies that have dissolved or that have amalgamated under another name or that have changed their name are not available (whether the companies are related or not) for two years after the date of dissolution, amalgamation or amendment. The purpose of this period of non-availability is to allow the public time to disassociate that name from a specific business.

Within the two-year period anyone could, however, incorporate a successor company (i.e. a corporation with the same name but with a year of incorporation in brackets immediately before the legal element of the name), or a company with a slightly varied name (or with an identical name if they meet Reg. 31(3) requirement) as long as the consent of the amalgamated company or the company whose name was amended, is obtained. Because no consent is obtainable from a dissolved company, the applicant for the new corporation must demonstrate that it acquired the rights to the name from the dissolved corporation prior to its dissolution.

After two years, the name becomes available to anyone as long as no successor companies were incorporated within the two years and as long as the original name has not been perpetuated as a registered trade name.

REVIVAL

Where, either before dissolution or in the interval between dissolution and revival of a federal corporation, another company with an *identical* name is incorporated, the federal corporation will not be able to revive in that name as long as the identical name is in existence.

Where, in the above circumstances, the new name is only *confusingly similar*, it is important to know the continuousness of the operation of the applicant for revival. If its operation was continuous during a substantial period of the time that the new company was in operation, this demonstrates that the revival of the federal corporation is unlikely now to cause confusion.

6.6 — Confusion with Corporate Names, Trade Names, Trade-marks, and Official Marks

6.6.1 — Confusion with Trade-marks

(i) In order to approve a name for which there are phonetically similar trade-mark citations, Corporations Canada must know in general terms what the proposed company will do and that all phonetically similar trade-marks are in substantially different products or services in order to determine that there is no likelihood of confusion. *This information must be provided to Corporations Canada in writing.* Where this information is lacking, it will be assumed that the business, products and services associated with the trade-mark are the same as that of the proposed corporation.

(ii) The following guidelines provide guidance in situations where there is an existing trade-mark in substantially the same products or service as the proposed name.

   1. Trade-mark (TM) owned by someone other than applicant (i.e. conflicting trade-mark)

- *TM registered for five years*: Corporate name applicant cannot have the proposed name without consent of TM owner, no matter how long the applicant has used it.

- *TM application, or TM registered for less than five years*: It will be determined who had prior use. If the corporate name applicant files an affidavit that satisfies the Director that the applicant had prior use of a corporate name or a trade name and provides the Director with an undertaking that the applicant will contest the other party's TM application or registration, the applicant will be granted the name.

2. Trade-mark (TM) owned by the applicant (i.e. supporting trade-mark)

- *TM registered for five years*: Even if there is another business name that is confusing, the corporate name applicant will be given the name because the applicant's TM is not likely to be struck from the TM registry.

- *TM application, or TM registered for less than five years*: If there is another business name that is confusing and this business appears to have used the name before the corporate name applicant, the applicant's TM is not sufficient reason to grant the name. The name will not be approved. If, however, the applicant had prior use, the applicant will be allowed to incorporate.

Please note that in these types of trade-mark situations, the important information is:

- the length of time that the TM has been in use

- whether the trade-mark has been registered for five years.

iii. A notice entitled "Protecting Your Corporate Name" is attached at the conclusion of this document. Applicants should be aware that the holder of a corporate name bears the responsibility of ensuring that no new confusing trade-marks are registered by anyone else, after his or her incorporation.

General enquiries concerning trade-marks should be directed to the Canadian Intellectual Property Office at 819-997-1420, or view the website at *www.cipo-opic.gc.ca*.

6.6.2 — Confusion with Trade Names

The Director feels that it could be confusing for a trade name and a confusingly similar corporate name to exist at the same time (even if they are owned by the same person) unless both names form part of the same business.

For this reason, the Director will refuse a proposed corporate name where an individual is carrying on business in that trade name (even if the individual is the applicant for incorporation) unless the Director receives the individual's consent and his or her undertaking to cease carrying on business in that trade name or to transfer the trade name registration to the corporation.

There will, of course, be no need for such a consent and undertaking when

(a) a change of corporate name is proposed by a corporation that has already registered a trade name; and

(b) the proposed name of the corporation will be that trade name.

A copy of the trade name registration showing the corporation as the owner should be filed, however.

Note re Ontario Business Names on the NUANS report: Ontario business names expire after 5 years unless they are renewed. Unrenewed registrations may remain on the NUANS database however. The Director will assume that all Ontario trade name registrations less than 5 $\frac{1}{2}$ years old and appearing on the NUANS report, are active. Any registrations over 5 $\frac{1}{2}$ years old and not renewed, will be disregarded. The $\frac{1}{2}$ year period is a grace period to allow time for renewal after expiry.

Suggested Consent Form from the Owner of an Unincorporated Trade Name

The Director, Corporations Canada

Industry Canada

9th Floor, Jean Edmonds Towers South

365 Laurier Avenue West

Ottawa, Ontario K1A 0C8

Re: Incorporation of a corporation by the name of *INCORPORATING PARTY'S NAME.*

(Consenting party's name), owner of the registered trade name (enter trade name), hereby consents to the incorporation of (name of the proposed corporation).

(Consenting party's name) undertakes to stop carrying on business under the trade name (or to transfer his/her rights in the trade name to the corporation bearing the proposed name) before the corporation proposing to use the name begins to carry on business under the corporate name.

Consent given at (city), this (date) day of (month), (year).

CONSENTING PARTY'S NAME

Per: ....

JANE DOE, President

Note re: Confusion with corporate and trade names for franchised businesses: Because the use of the name of a franchise accrues to the franchisor rather than to the franchisee, the consent of existing business and trade names which are franchisee businesses will not be required for the incorporation of a confusingly similar name. Only the consent of the franchisor will be required. In that consent, the franchisor must identify the existing corporate names as franchisees.

6.6.3 — Confusion with Official Marks

An official mark is "any badge, crest, emblem or mark adopted and used by any public authority, in Canada as an official mark for products or services", as defined in the *Trade-marks Act.*

Where a proposed name is likely to cause confusion with an existing official mark adopted and used pursuant to the provisions of section 9 of the *Trade-marks Act*, it will be rejected.

6.7 — Overcoming Confusion

The regulations suggest various ways to overcome a finding that a proposed corporate name is likely to cause confusion.

6.7.1 — Regulation 28 — Consent and Undertaking by a Corporation

Reg. 28. For the purpose of paragraph 12(1)(a) of the Act, a corporate name that is confusing with the name of a body corporate that has not carried on business in the two years immediately before the date of a request for the corporate name is prohibited, unless the body corporate that has that name

(a) consents in writing to the use of the name, and the name is not otherwise prohibited; and

(b) undertakes in writing to dissolve immediately or to change its name before the corporation that proposes to use the name begins to use it, and the name is not otherwise prohibited.

(*Canada Business Corporations Regulations, 2001*)

This regulation applies only in the situation where the existing business with which the proposed name is confusing, has not carried on business for two years.

Suggested consent form — Regulation 28

> The Director, Corporations Canada
>
> Industry Canada
>
> 9th Floor, Jean Edmonds Towers South
>
> 365 Laurier Avenue West
>
> Ottawa, Ontario K1A 0C8

Re: Incorporation of a corporation by the name of *INCORPORATING PARTY'S NAME*

(Consenting party's name), a body corporate, consents to the incorporation/amendment of (name of the proposed corporation).

(Consenting party's name) undertakes to dissolve immediately or to change its name before the corporation proposing to use that name begins to carry on business under that name.

(Consenting party's name) confirms that it has not carried on business under its corporate name during the past two years.

Consent given at (city), this (date) day of (month), (year).

CONSENTING PARTY'S NAME

Per: ....

JANE DOE, President

Note: The signature of the authorized signing officer must describe him or her as an officer of the consenting corporation.

6.7.2 — Regulation 29 — Consent to a Distinctive Word

> *Reg. 29. For the purpose of paragraph 12(1)(a) of the Act, a corporate name that contains a word that is the same as or similar to the distinctive element of an existing trade-mark, official mark, or trade name and is confusing with one or another of the distinctive elements is prohibited, unless the person who owns the trade-mark, official mark, or trade name consents in writing to the use of the corporate name, and the name is not otherwise prohibited.*
>
> (*Canada Business Corporations Regulations*, 2001)

Note: Such a consent would not be required from a foreign company unless it was known or carrying on business in Canada.

Also, please note the difference between consenting to putting certain distinctive words in a *corporate name* and consent to the use of certain words as a *trade name*. A mere consent to the use of certain words will not be accepted for purposes of regulation 29.

Please note that consents must be unconditional.

Suggested Consent Form — Regulation 29

> The Director, Corporations Canada
>
> Industry Canada
>
> 9th Floor, Jean Edmonds Towers South
>
> 365 Laurier Avenue West
>
> Ottawa, Ontario K1A 0C8

Re: Incorporation of a corporation by the name of *INCORPORATING PARTY'S NAME.*

(Consenting party's name, i.e. the name of an incorporated or unincorporated business or the name of the owner of a trade-mark) consents to the incorporation of (name of the proposed corporation).

Consent given at (city), this (date) day of (month), (year).

CONSENTING PARTY'S NAME

Per: ....

JANE DOE, President

6.7.3 — Regulation 30 — Successor businesses and Year of Incorporation

Reg. 30. (1) For the purpose of paragraph 12(1)(a) of the Act, a corporate name that is confusing with the name of a body corporate is prohibited unless

> *(a) the corporate name is the name of an existing or a proposed corporation that is the successor to the business of the body corporate and the body corporate has ceased or will, in the immediate future, cease to carry on business under that corporate name and undertakes in writing to dissolve or to change its corporate name before the successor corporation begins carrying on business under that corporate name;*

> *(b) subject to subsection (2), the corporate name of the existing or proposed corporation sets out in numerals the year of incorporation, or the year of the most recent amendment to the corporate name, in parentheses, immediately before the word or expression "Limited", "Limitée", "Incorporated", "Incorporée", "Corporation", "Société par actions de régime fédéral" or "Société commerciale canadienne" or the abbreviation "Ltd.", "Ltée", "Inc.", "Corp.", "S.A.R.F." or "S.C.C."; and*

> *(c) the corporate name is not otherwise prohibited.*

(2) The reference in a corporate name to the year of incorporation or the year of the most recent amendment to the corporate name may be deleted two years after its use is introduced, if the corporate name so changed is not confusing.

(Canada Business Corporations Regulations, 2001)

Note: Section 30 may apply both in the case where a corporation changes its name and in the case of a proposed new corporation. In the former case, the date in parenthesis is the date the corporation succeeds to the name and not the date it is incorporated.

Note: Please note that Regulation 30 does not override other applicable regulations. Where, for instance, X1, the body corporate which is consenting and providing an undertaking to the incorporation of X1 (2001), pursuant to regulation 30 was, itself, incorporated pursuant to a consent of X in conformity to regulation 29, the consent of X, pursuant to Regulation 29 will also be required for the incorporation of X1 (2001).

Or, where X is an individual, the requirement to file the consent to use of family name (Reg 26) will still apply.

Note: Where a corporation succeeds to a name of a non-federal body corporate whose name is primarily or only the name of an individual, the corporation will not be able to delete the reference to the year in parentheses after two years, unless secondary meaning can be established. The name without the year in parentheses is prohibited under Regulation 24(1)(b) for being primarily or only the name of an individual. At the time of obtaining the successor company name under Regulation 30, the applicant may wish to add another word, in addition to the year in parentheses, so that the year in parentheses can be deleted after two years pursuant to Regulation 30(2).

Suggested Consent Form — Regulation 30

> The Director, Corporations Canada
> Industry Canada
> 9th Floor, Jean Edmonds Towers South
> 365 Laurier Avenue West

Ottawa, Ontario K1A 0C8

Re: Incorporation of a corporation by the name of *INCORPORATING PARTY'S NAME.*

(Consenting party's name), a body corporate, consents to the incorporation/amendment of (name of the proposed corporation), which is to be a successor corporation and which has the year of incorporation or amendment in parentheses before the legal element.

(Consenting party's name) undertakes to dissolve immediately or to change its name before the corporation proposing to use that name begins to carry on business under that name.

Consent given at (city), this (date) day of (month), (year).

CONSENTING PARTY'S NAME

Per: ....

JANE DOE, President

OTHER USE OF "(2001)" AND SUBSTITUTION OF "(CANADA)" FOR "(2001)"

The regulations do not prohibit the use of numerals indicating the year of incorporation in parentheses e.g. "(2001)", for the incorporation of a non-successor new company. This will be allowed except where the new corporation is going to be the affiliate of an existing corporation which will remain in existence and "(2001)" is proposed as the distinguishing element. This is considered misleading because "(2001)" connotes a successor.

As a general rule, we will not accept "Canada" or any other term as a replacement for "(2001)" in a successor situation unless the successor company is related to the existing company which has undertaken to dissolve or to change its name in which case we are really dealing with regulation 29 not 30.

The chart below provides a clarification of these guidelines.

*

ABC (Canada) or ABC Canada or ABC (2001) or ABC2001* as newco: no existing company, ABC	Approval
ABC (Canada) or ABC Canada as newco related to existing company, ABC which will continue to exist (consent — we assume affiliation)	Approval
ABC (2001) as newco related to existing company, ABC which will continue to exist. (consent — affiliation is assumed)	Rejection (generally not available because it is misleading, however may be permissible where clients of newco are sophisticated enough to know that newco is not the successor to existing co. ABC even though it looks like it is, and ABC consents)

ABC 2001 as a newco related to existing company, ABC, which will continue to exist (consent — we assume affiliation)	Approval
ABC (2001) as newco related or unrelated to existing company, ABC which is dissolving or changing name (consent & undertaking)	Approval
ABC (Canada) or ABC Canada or ABC 2001 as newco related to ABC which is dissolving or changing name (consent)	Approval
ABC (Canada) or ABC Canada or ABC 2001 as newco unrelated to ABC dissolving or changing name	Rejection (as a general rule) (may be permissible where clients of newco are sophisticated enough to know that newco is not related to existing co. ABC even though it looks like it is.)

Notes:

*   as long as the corporation is not to be a successor to an existing company any reasonable date is permissible, unless it is misleading.

e.g. ABC 1884 Ltd. would be misleading for the name of a corporation which has not been in business since 1884.

Exception to Regulation 30(1)(b) Where Existing Company is Inactive

If the existing company has not carried on business for two years preceding the request to use the name, the successor corporation does not need to insert the year of incorporation or amendment but the requirements of Regulation 28 must be met.

Exception to Regulation 30(1)(b) Where Existing Company is a Quebec Company

"DE FACTO" IMPORT CONTINUANCES

The Director will permit a company to incorporate with a name that is identical (i.e. without the year of incorporation) to the name of an existing provincial (e.g. Quebec) company where the federal incorporation is to serve as a "de facto" continuance from that province which does not permit exports to the federal jurisdiction.

The applicant must file with us a written undertaking of the provincial company to dissolve forthwith or to change its name before the corporation proposing to use the name carries on business.

There must be a note on file to indicate that the applicant considers this incorporation to be a "de facto" continuance, i.e., the same shareholders and assets will be involved in the federal company as in the provincial company.

Like other import continuances, the availability of this name will be subject to a name search and approval.

6.7.4 — *Amalgamations and Acquisitions*

Reg. 31.

> *(1) For the purpose of paragraph 12(1)(a) of the Act, if two or more corporations amalgamate, the name of the amalgamated corporation is prohibited if the name is confusing or is otherwise prohibited.*
>
> *(2) Despite subsection (1), the new corporate name may be the same as the name of one of the amalgamating corporations.*
>
> *(3) For the purpose of paragraph 12(1)(a) of the Act, if an existing corporation has acquired or will, in the immediate future, acquire all or substantially all of the property of an affiliated body corporate, the use by the corporation of the corporate name of the body corporate is prohibited unless*
>
> > *(a) the body corporate undertakes in writing to dissolve, or to change its name, before the corporation begins using the corporate name; and*
> >
> > *(b) the name is not otherwise prohibited.*
>
> *(4) For the purpose of paragraph 12(1)(a) of the Act, if a proposed corporation will, in the immediate future, acquire all or substantially all of the property of a body corporate that is to be an affiliate of the proposed corporation, the use by the proposed corporation of the name of the affiliated body corporate is prohibited unless*
>
> > *(a) the body corporate undertakes in writing to dissolve, or to change its name, before the proposed corporation begins using the corporate name; and*
> >
> > *(b) the name is not otherwise prohibited.*

(Canada Business Corporations Regulations, 2001)

Related Policies

Note: Where the name is granted on the understanding that the applicant will, in the immediate future acquire all or substantially all the property of the affiliated body corporate, the applicant should confirm within a few days that substantially all the property *did* transfer from the affiliated body corporate.

Upon incorporation of the proposed corporation, Corporations Canada will keep the file open pending receipt of written confirmation that substantially all property did transfer. If it is not received within a reasonable period, steps will be taken to require the corporation to change its name.

A transfer of all the shares is not considered to be a transfer of property.

Suggested Consent Form — Regulation 31(3)

> The Director, Corporations Canada
>
> Industry Canada
>
> 9th Floor, Jean Edmonds Towers South
>
> 365 Laurier Avenue West
>
> Ottawa, Ontario K1A 0C8

Re: Incorporation of a corporation by the name of *INCORPORATING PARTY'S NAME.*

(Affiliated party's name), a body corporate, consents to the change of name of (Applicant corporation's name) to (proposed corporate name).

(Affiliated party's name) confirms that it is affiliated with (Applicant corporation's name) which (has or will immediately) acquire all or substantially all the property of (Affiliated party's name). (Affiliated party's name) hereby undertakes to dissolve immediately or to change its name before the corporation proposing to use the name begins carrying on business under that name.

AFFILIATED PARTY'S NAME

Per: ....

JANE DOE, President

Suggested Consent Form — Regulation 31(4)

> The Director, Corporations Canada
>
> Industry Canada
> 9th Floor, Jean Edmonds Towers South
>
> 365 Laurier Avenue West
>
> Ottawa, Ontario K1A 0C8

Re: Incorporation of a corporation by the name of *PROPOSED CORPORATION'S NAME.*

(Existing body corporate's name), a body corporate, hereby consents to the incorporation of (name of proposed corporation).

(Existing body corporate's name) confirms that it will be affiliated with (name of proposed corporation) which will immediately acquire substantially all the property of (Existing body corporate's name). (Existing body corporate's name) undertakes to dissolve immediately or to change its name before the corporation proposing to use the name begins to carry on business under that name.

EXISTING BODY CORPORATIVE'S NAME

Per: ....

JANE DOE, President

6.7.5 — Failing to Honour Undertaking

Subsections 12(4.1) and (5) of the Act state that if a corporation acquires a name as a result of a person undertaking to dissolve or to change names, and that undertaking is not honoured, the Director may direct the corporation to change its name in accordance with section 173. The Director may revoke the corporation's name and assign a name unless the undertaking is honoured within 60 days of the Director directing the corporation to change its name.

6.7.6 — Initials and Given Names

The addition of initials to a surname that is otherwise confusing is not sufficient to overcome that confusion.

> e.g. "J.B. SMITH SHOES LTD." would be confusing with "SMITH SHOES INC."

However, adding a given name to a corporate name that contains a surname may be sufficient to overcome confusion.

> e.g "Smith Shoes Ltd." would not be used to refuse "Robert Smith Shoes Ltd." unless we are aware that their territory of operation is the same.

6.7.7 — Bankruptcy

For the purposes of Regulations 28, 29, 30 or 31, a name is available, when it is confusing with the name of a bankrupt corporation, if the trustee in bankruptcy consents.

6.7.8 — Names of Canada, Provinces, and Cities Added to Remove Confusion

The name of a province or city with or without parentheses is not considered a general term and may be added to a corporate name to overcome confusion with the name of an existing related company.

> e.g."Newton Tool Québec Ltd." would not be considered confusingly similar to "Newton Tool Manitoba Ltd." or "Newton Tool (Canada) Ltd."

> "Newton Tool (Canada) Inc." would not be considered confusing with "Newton Tool Inc." (a USA company)

However, the consent of the existing company(ies) would be required under Regulation 29 in order to grant such a similar name. Where there are many existing affiliates, the consent of the geographically closest affiliate or the parent of all the affiliates would be sufficient.

Exception: Use of certain provincial names in federal corporation names. (Refer to section 3.2)

6.7.9 — Canadian Subsidiaries

Where a proposed Canadian subsidiary of a foreign, provincial or federal parent uses the name of that parent, which name is too general or merely descriptive, the proposed company

> a) must add the word "Canada" or equivalent unless there is some other distinguishing feature between parent and subsidiaries and

> b) can overcome the objection of generality by showing that the name has acquired some distinctiveness in Canada, (whether or not it has actually been used in Canada, e.g. the name may have acquired distinctiveness due to advertising which reaches the Canadian market for the product)

> c) will be prohibited if it is confusing with an existing Canadian company or trademark.

Note: A proposed Canadian subsidiary of a foreign parent with the identical name would not be required to add the word "Canada" if it could establish that the foreign company had never carried on business in Canada and is not known in Canada.

Note: Reproduced below is a copy of the note sent out with corporate names which are rejected by reason of their being confusing.

NOTE — HOW TO OVERCOME A REJECTION BASED ON LIKELIHOOD OF CONFUSION

This name has been turned down because, on the basis of the information presented or available, it appears to create a likelihood of confusion with the names indicated on the relevant search report. Please note that corporations dissolved less than 2 years ago are considered to be existing for purposes of confusion.

Corporations Canada will reconsider the decision if other information is presented which demonstrates that, in fact, there is no likelihood of confusion. The kind of information to which this refers is specified in section 25 of the regulations, that is, details concerning the dissimilarity of:

- *the goods and services*

- *territory*

- *clientele*

- *and operations*

of the business to be carried on under the proposed name and the business being carried on under the existing name.

Unless the requirements of Regulation 31(3) have been met, a name which is identical to an existing corporate name will not be approved even with the consent of the existing corporation, unless there are very convincing arguments why no one would be confused, or even if confused, why they could not be harmed thereby.

7. — Deceptively Misdescriptive

Reg. 32. For the purpose of paragraph 12(1)(a) of the Act, a corporate name is deceptively misdescriptive if it is likely to mislead the public, in any language, with respect to

(a) the business, goods or services in association with which it is proposed to be used;

(b) the conditions under which the goods or services will be produced or supplied or the persons to be employed in the production or supply of the goods or services; or

(c) the place of origin of the goods or services.

(Canada Business Corporations Regulations, 2001)

Related Policies

USE OF THE WORD "CLUB" IN CORPORATE NAMES

There is no general restriction on the use of the word "*Club*" in corporate names. The word may be used for business incorporations, but the Director will want to be satisfied that the use of the word does not imply to the public a not-for-profit corporation.

e.g. "Rough Riders Football Club" would be acceptable, as the general public would be aware that such a football club is a profit-making organization.

USE OF WORD "*INSTITUTE*", "*ASSOCIATION*", "*FOUNDATION*" OR OTHER SUCH WORDS

Generally, these terms connote a not-for-profit organization. The Director will, however, consider representations for the use of these words in names of business corporations. The representations should indicate the extent to which the proposed word has been used in the business of the proposed corporation or similar businesses.

USE OF YEAR — "*(2001)*" OR "*2001*" (see 6.7.3)

8. — Other Related Policies

8.1 — Not-for-Profit Organizations

8.1.1 — Non-Distinctive Names

Many not-for-profit corporations use highly descriptive, almost non-distinctive names. Typically, words like "Canadian" or "National" serve to give the name distinctiveness. For this reason, most not-for-profit names do not deserve a lot of protection. See 8.1.5 for amount of protection given.

8.1.2 — Government Connotation Implied

Because of the nature of the names of not-for-profit companies, there may be a greater likelihood of name proposals which connote government sponsorship or control. Regulation 22 will be strictly enforced by the Director.

e.g. "Canadian Association of Postmasters" — is not acceptable

8.1.3 — Chamber of Commerce

The term "Chamber of Commerce" is available for use in the name of a not-for-profit corporation with suitable objects.

8.1.4 — Legal Elements

The only legal elements which are permitted for not-for-profit companies are:

"Incorporated" or "Inc."

"Corporation" or "Corp."

8.1.5 — Not-for-profits and Confusion

Where the name of a proposed not-for-profit corporation includes a geographical distinctive term and an organizational term as well as other descriptors, e.g. "Canada Ultralight Aircraft Association" or "Canada Dance Foundation", and an existing not-for-profit corporation has the same organizational and descriptive terms with a different geographical qualification, e.g. "Calgary Ultralight Aircraft Association" and "Toronto Dance Foundation", the Director requires the consent of the existing corporation. Applicants should note that a slight modification of their proposal would probably make it available, e.g. "Canada Ultralight Aircraft Society" or "Canada Dance Funding Society".

8.2 — Regulation 33 (Certain names not prohibited)

> *Reg. 33. A corporate name is not prohibited only because it contains alphabetic or numeric characters, initials, punctuation marks or any combination of those elements.*
>
> (*Canada Business Corporations Regulations*, 2001)

8.3 — Bilingual Names

8.3.1 — General Rule:

The English and French forms of a corporate name do not have to be literal translations. However, a corporation cannot have French and English forms of a corporate name that are so different as to appear to belong to two different corporations. Where there is concern this may be the case, the proposed name will be rejected.

8.3.2 — Guidelines within the General Rule:

The Director will permit English and French forms of a corporate name in the following situations:

1) The name is made up only of generic words, literally translated. There is no separate distinctive element although the name as a whole is distinctive, e.g., "Think Retail Inc./Pensez Détail Inc."

2) The name consists only of a distinctive element, which is partly translated. The part that is translated is descriptive and the other part is identical in both English and French, e.g., "Techni-Glass (or Techniglass) Inc./Techni-Verre (or Techniverre) Inc."

3) The name consists of both distinctive and descriptive elements, both of which are very literally translated, e.g., "Édition Entre-Nous Inc./Between-Us Publishing Inc."

4) Generally speaking, a corporation with a corporate name whose distinctive feature is an acronym may not have an alternate version of the acronym in the other official language even if the acronym is formed by letters which reflect a translation of the descriptive words of the name.

e.g.

Service Informatique SI Inc.

CS Computer Service Inc.-(not available without proof of acquired secondary meaning in the acronyms)

The name of a not-for-profit corporation in which an acronym (relating to the descriptive words of the name) forms a part, may be available although the acronym is different in the English and French versions of the name. This will occur when the name would be available without the acronym and the acronym forms a non-substantive part of the name.

e.g.

Institut de Recherches Aerospatiale du Canada IRAC

ARIC Aerospace Research Institute of Canada

Note: For corporations operating in Quebec, provincial legislation may require a French form of the corporate name.

Note: When selecting a French form for a corporate name for the purposes of carrying on business in Quebec, it is advisable to check the acceptability of the translation with the Office de la langue française. Where the Office de la langue française (see below for contact information) advises that a rejected French form is the only French form acceptable for use in the Province of Quebec, every effort will be made to find a way to accept that French form.

Note: Only the distinctive part of the name can be in a language which is neither English nor French. Descriptive words, if there are any, must be in English or French. e.g. La Parilla Restaurant Inc. (See 8.3.8 for entire name in another language)

Bilingual Name

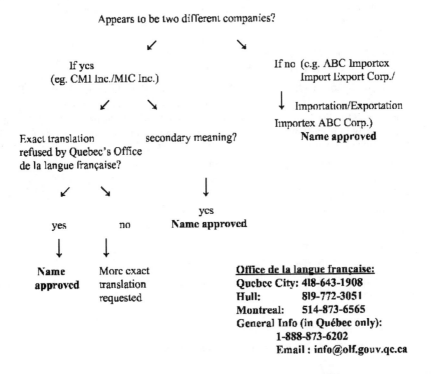

Appears to be two different companies?

If yes
(eg. CM1 Inc./MIC Inc.)

If no (e.g. ABC Importex
Import Export Corp./

↓ Importation/Exportation

Importex ABC Corp.)
Name approved

Exact translation
refused by Quebec's Office
de la langue française?

secondary meaning?

yes
Name approved

yes   no

**Name
approved**

More exact
translation
requested

Office de la langue française:
Quebec City: 418-643-1908
Hull: 819-772-3051
Montreal: 514-873-6565
General Info (in Québec only):
          1-888-873-6202
Email : info@olf.gouv.qc.ca

8.3.3 — Fee for Articles of Amendment not required

a) There is no fee for filing articles of amendment only to add the French or English version of a corporate name.

b) Where articles of amendment are filed requesting that a legal element common to both language versions such as "Inc.", replace the existing legal element, e.g. "Ltd.", the Director will assume that this is to create a French version of the name. The Director will not require the $200.00 filing fee despite the fact that technically the English version is also being amended.

8.3.4 — Searching each version

Articles filed under both linguistic versions are very often accompanied by only one search report. Often two are necessary. Filing only one report results in rejection of the articles by the Corporations Canada. The following criteria should be used to judge whether or not a bilingual name (whether with separate or combined English and French versions) requires two searches:

> 1) identical names require only one search report:
>
>> e.g. AVITEK LTD./AVITEK LTEE
>>
>> e.g. DUBOIS DISTRIBUTIONS LTD./DISTRIBUTIONS DUBOIS LTEE
>
> 2) names which are exact translations with phonetic differences require two searches unless the English and French versions share a substantial, distinctive component and differ only in respect of a minor, ordinary descriptive term, in which case the name can be searched in such a way that one search will suffice.
>
>> e.g. Placements Protar Holdings Inc. — one search
>>
>> e.g. Gestion Quadra Inc./Quadra Management Inc. — one search

In other words, where the bilingual name has a short distinctive part with a long and differing descriptive part, two search reports would be required.

e.g.

> LB Plumbing + Heating Inc.
>
> Tuyauterie et Chauffage LB Inc. — two searches

Similarly, where the descriptive part of a bilingual name is unusual, two search reports would be required.

e.g.

> Collecte de sang Croix Bleue Inc.
>
> Blue Cross Blood Collection Inc. — two searches

8.3.5 — Legal Element

Section 10 of the CBCA states that one of the following legal elements must be part of the name every corporation:

- Limited
- Limitée
- Incorporated
- Incorporée
- Corporation
- Société par actions de régime fédéral
- or the corresponding abbreviation, Ltd., Ltée., Inc., Corp., or S.A.R.F.

A corporate name which, in the English version, has the legal element "Limited", must in the French version use the legal element "Limitée". Similarly "Incorporated" and "Incorporée" go together. Where the legal element in the English version is "Corporation", the French version may have either "Corporation" or "société par actions de régime fédéral" but not "La Corporation" as its legal element. Where the legal element in the English version is "Corp.," the French version may have either "Corp." or "S.A.R.F."

In addition, the legal element for *both* versions must be either in long form *or* in the abbreviated form.

In a combined English and French form of the name, only one legal element, should be included. A legal element such as "Inc." would have the desired bilingual capacity for this purpose.

e.g.

> Coiffures CHICO Hairdressing Inc.
> Avitek Inc.
> Chaussures Chaton/Little Cat Shoes Inc.
> Chauffeur Star/Étoile Inc.
> Techniglass/Techniverre Inc.
> Chauffeur Thompson Inc.

Note: Remember that if a corporation chooses a combined form for its name, it must use and be legally designated by that form. The English and the French forms cannot be used separately.

Note: The Director will reject use of the legal element "S.A.R.F." with the English form of a name.

> e.g. Exeter Shoes S.A.R.F. — unacceptable

8.3.6 — Confusing Descriptive Terms

Because a holding company and an investment company may well be carrying on the same business, i.e. investments, and because applicants are inclined to use the word "Placements" as a translation for both "Holdings" and "Investments", granting names such as those below will likely cause confusion.

The Director will note grant proposed names with the descriptive features of "Holdings", "Placements", "Investments", "Gestion", "Management", "Investissements" when the existing trade names have the same distinctive feature and one of the above descriptive features.

e.g.

> XYZ HOLDING INC. — existing
> XYZ PLACEMENTS INC. — proposed (not acceptable)
> XYZ INVESTMENT INC. — proposed (not acceptable)

Both proposed names are not acceptable because there is a likelihood of confusion with the existing company name.

8.3.7 — Translation of distinctive element

The distinctive element is the only feature in a corporate name which does not require translation for the alternate linguistic version. In addition, the distinctive element is the only element in a corporate name which could be in a foreign language and in this case a descriptive word may be unnecessary if there is no question of confusion. Where the foreign word is a surname, however, a descriptive word may be necessary to satisfy the statutory provisions or Regulation 24.

e.g.

> ETOILE MANUFACTURING LIMITED — acceptable
> INVESTISSEMENTS MAPLE LEAF LIMITEE — acceptable
> VITELLO RESTAURANTS INC. — acceptable

8.3.8 — Equivalent name for use outside Canada

When an applicant proposes a corporate name in English or French or both in its Articles of Incorporation, it can also (in item 7 of Form 1) specify an equivalent name in French or English or any other language for use outside the country. However, it cannot specify *another* name for use outside the country that is other than a translated version of the English or French name under which it has been incorporated. This would mislead the public. To be very clear, where an applicant proposes, for example, an English name under item 1, he or she may insert an Italian or even a French version of that name under item 7 for use outside the country. Please note that English and French forms of the corporate name do not necessarily both have to appear in item 1. This is the applicant's choice. For use in Canada, they would have to appear in item 1.

8.4 — Use of the Words "Broadcasting", "Radio", "Television"...

When must an applicant request consent from the Canadian Radio-Television and Telecommunications Commission (CRTC) for a proposed name using the words "Broadcasting", "Radio" and "Television"?

CBCA gives the Director no authority to deny applicants the right to use these words. However, the CRTC will deny the applicant a licence to operate if the applicant is not qualified.

8.5 — USA — Securities and Exchange Commission Names

NUANS reports may cite corporate names which originate from the Securities & Exchange Commission in the United States. These companies are generally considered to be multi-national corporations doing business in Canada.

It has been the policy of the Director to consider such names in the name-granting process. If a proposed name is refused because it is confusing with a USA-SEC name, the applicant is advised but NOT required to find out from the available sources (see telephone and address below) whether or not the company is doing business in Canada. If the name is not checked, it may be granted with full assumption of risk IN WRITING on the applicant's part.

Public Reference:

> Securities & Exchange Commission
> 450 Fifth Street, NW
> Washington, D.C. 20549
> Telephone: 202-942-8090
> Internet: *http://www.sec.gov*
> Email: *publicinfo@sec.gov*

8.6 — Number of Corporate Name Search Reports Required

There will be cases where one name search will suffice for several different but related name requests.

This is more likely to be the case where the names requested are for proposed affiliated companies distinguished only by the geographical location in brackets.

e.g.

- XYZ TOOLS (OTTAWA) INC.

- XYZ TOOLS (HAMILTON) INC.

- XYZ TOOLS (TORONTO) INC.

At the moment, however, there is no firm rule as to when only a single search report will be required. Each case should be referred to the Manager for individual consideration.

(see also *Bilingual Names (8.3)* for guidelines concerning whether two searches are required for a bilingual name)

WHERE NO COMPLETE NUANS SEARCH REPORT IS REQUIRED

In the case of an application made pursuant to Regulation 30(1) or 31(3), a NUANS *microfiche* search is acceptable in place of a NUANS search but only if the body corporate consenting and undertaking is a federal corporation.

In the case of an application made pursuant to Regulation 30(2), a NUANS database search is acceptable in place of a complete NUANS search.

A complete NUANS search report will not be required where articles of continuance are filed at the same time as articles of amalgamation and where the certificate of amalgamation is to be issued in a name different from the name of the continued corporation and on the same day as the certificate of continuance.

Where articles of continuance are filed at the same time as articles of amalgamation and where the certificate of amalgamation is to be issued in a name different from the name of the continued corporation and within a very short period of time after the certificate of continuance, a NUANS search report will not be required, if the applicant provides a NUANS® database search and undertakes:

- to file a complete NUANS search immediately if the amalgamation does not take effect as planned, and change its name if the Director decides it is necessary

- not to provide a consent under Regulation 31(3) or (4) for another entity to use its continued name, unless that name has been determined to be not confusing by the Branch on the basis of a complete NUANS search report obtained by the entity at that time.

Depending on the length of time between the continuance and the amalgamation, the continued company may also be asked to undertake that it will not carry on business between the date of continuance and the date of amalgamation.

In the case of all other applications, a complete NUANS search is required.

8.7 — Trade name

A corporation may carry on business under, or identify itself by a name other than its corporate name if that other name does not contain, either the word or expression "Limited", "Limitée", "Incorporated", "Incorporée", "Corporation" or "Société par actions de régime fédéral" or the corresponding abbreviation. Provincial law governs the registration of trade names.

8.8 — Numbered name

If requested to do so by the incorporators of a corporation, the Director shall assign to the corporation as its name, a designating number followed by the word "Canada" and a legal element.

8.9 — Microfiche Supplement NUANS Report for Names with More Than One Distinctive Element

Very occasionally, when the corporate name that is searched has more than one distinctive element, the NUANS search report will list business names and trade-marks that are similar to only one of those distinctive features. To spare applicants the time and expense of ordering a second NUANS search on the other distinctive element, Corporations Canada will undertake to carry out a NUANS database search of the other element to see whether there are any confusing names relating to it. The applicant will be asked to accept the risk that the NUANS database search, which, unlike a regular NUANS search, does not list names that are phonetically similar to the one proposed, may not reveal a conflict that later comes to light. The conflicting name which later comes to light could necessitate the Director ordering a change of the applicant's corporate name.

8.10 — Internet Domain Names as CorporateName

Suffixes like ".ca" or ".com" will not be treated as distinctive elements of a corporate name. The name will be treated as if it did not have the suffix. If the name has some distinctiveness without the suffix, e.g., "Doc Systems Inc.," and it is not confusing, it will be approved. If the name has no distinctiveness without the suffix, it will be rejected since the suffix does not add distinctiveness; e.g., "Cars.ca Inc." would not be accepted because the name "Cars Inc." would not be accepted, being merely descriptive of the wares.

9. — Protecting Your Corporate Name

The granting of a corporate name by the Director under the *Canada Business Corporations Act* ("CBCA") generally confers a degree of protection for that corporate name. However, the granting of names under the CBCA does not in itself confer any rights to those names vis-à-vis corporate names or trade names which may have existed at the time of granting but which did not appear on the NUANS search report or which the Director did not, at the time of granting, consider likely to cause confusion. Similarly, the granting of a corporate name may not protect you from earlier or subsequent trade-marks of other parties.

The following gives a succinct overview of the relationship between trade name, corporate name and trade-mark rights and some general guidance as to how you can best protect your corporate name and the goodwill associated with it.

> 1. Before an applicant applies for a corporate name, it is important for him or her to ensure that there are no similar existing corporate names, trade names or trade-marks. A NUANS search report, including trade-marks which are registered or proposed for registration, is required to be filed with articles of incorporation, amendment, etc. and is usually very reliable. Since, however, the NUANS® system is not fool-proof, the applicant remains responsible for any likelihood of confusion.
>
> While a name granted by the Director will appear on future NUANS searches required for incorporation in the federal and most provincial jurisdictions, you may wish to con-

duct your own NUANS searches on a periodic basis after your name has been approved. This would be done in order to ensure, to your own satisfaction, that no confusing corporate or business name has subsequently been approved in the jurisdiction(s) in which you are carrying on business, and to give you up to date information about trade-marks that have been applied for or registered subsequent to the granting of your corporate name.

2. Using a corporate name which is similar to a registered trade-mark may result in liability for infringement of the registered trade-mark even if the trade-mark was registered after the corporate name was granted. This is so because, under trade-marks law, the holder of a corporate name bears the responsibility of ensuring that no new trade-marks are registered which are confusing with that name. Information on registered and advertised trade-marks can be obtained from the Trade-Marks Journal distributed by the Canadian Intellectual Property Office (see *www.cipo.gc.ca*)[*] or by conducting a search of one of the various electronic trade-mark databases[**]. The holder of a corporate name has the right, in certain circumstances, to oppose the registration of a trade-mark or to have a trade-mark registration expunged.

3. Registration of a trade-mark is the best way to obtain the exclusive right to use the mark in all of Canada in association with the products and services for which the registration is obtained. While the Trade-Marks Office[**] can provide basic guidance, it is recommended that a specialist (a trade-mark agent or trade-mark lawyer) be consulted. It should be noted that trade-mark registration is not available for corporate names in all circumstances.

Index

(Please note that numbers are hypertext linked for those using electronic versions of this document)

Abbreviations 13

Absolutely Prohibited 12

ABSOLUTELY PROHIBITED TERM 4

academy 18

---

[*]

Canada Communications Group Publishing
Supply and Services Canada
45 Sacré-Coeur Blvd.
Hull, Quebec
QC K1A 0S9
Tel.: 1-800-635-7943
Fax: 1-819-956-4800

[**]

Trade-Marks Office
Industry Canada
Phase I, Place du Portage
Hull, Quebec
C K1A 0C9
Tel.: 819-953-8098 re on-line databases
Tel.: 819-997-1420 re general enquiries

acceptance 21
accountants 16
Acquisitions 46
acronyms 53
AFFILIATE 6
agency 21
Air Canada 4
Alberta 14
alliteration 24
AMALGAMATION 7, 36
Amalgamations 46
annuity 20
Applied Research 18
architect 16
association 16
Association of Universities and Colleges of Canada 18
bank 19
BANKRUPT 7, 48
BILINGUAL 7, 52
    COMBINED English and French form 7
    may not need two NUANS search reports 7
British Columbia 13
broker 21
CANADA 4
Canada Business Corporations Act (CBCA) 4
Canada Business Corporations Regulations 12
    Reg. 17 29
    Reg. 18 31
    Reg. 19 23
    Reg. 22 13
    Reg. 22(c) 16
    Reg. 22(d) 19
    Reg. 23 23
    Reg. 24(1)(a) 24
    Reg. 24(1)(b) 25
    Reg. 24(1)(c) 28
    Reg. 25 31
    Reg. 26 27
    Reg. 27 35

Reg. 28 39
Reg. 29 40
Reg. 30 42
Reg. 31 46
Reg. 32 50
Reg. 33 52
casualty 19
Chamber of Commerce 51
CLUB 7, 50
coined word 25, 30
Colline du Parlement 4
CONFUSION with existing business names 5
    definitions 8
    making your submission 6
    NUANS search 6
CONSENT 6
    family name of an individual 27
    Office des professions du Québec 17
    Previously Existing Reservation 9
    WRITTEN CONSENT OF AN INDIVIDUAL 10
CONTINUANCE 7
corporate name 10
CRTC 57
descriptive element 11
dilution 32
DISSOLVED 6
distinctive 9, 23
distinctive element 11
DISTINCTIVENESS 5, 23
EDUCATIONAL 4
Famous names 32
Fee 54
fictitious name 28
fidelity 21
fiduciary 22
fiducie 22
FINANCIAL 4
foreign language 57
FOREIGN PARENT 10, 49

foundation 21

Gendarmerie Royale du Canada 4

generic words 23

Gestion 56

Given Names 48

GRC 4

GROUP 5

guaranty 19

holding company 56

Incorporated 59

Incorporée 59

indemnity 19

Initials 34

INITIALS 5

INSTITUTE 7

Insurance Companies Act 20

insurance-related services 21

Internet Domain Names 60

investment 56

language forms 7

lawyers 16

legal element 12, 55

loan company 19

Management 56

mortgage 21

multi-national corporations 57

NAME

    Facts Necessary for a Name Decision 9

    NAME OF AN INDIVIDUAL 5

Nations Unies 4

NEW BRUNSWICK 16

NEWFOUNDLAND OR NFLD 15

NOT-FOR-PROFIT 7, 51

NOVA SCOTIA 14

NUANS 5

    To reserve your proposed corporate name 8

Numbered Name 59

numeric characters 52

Obscene Names 23

Office de la langue française 53
Office of the Superintendent of Financial Institutions 19
    Bankruptcy 26
    Insolvency Trustee 26
    legislation administered by OSFI 21
official mark 5, 9, 39
ONU 4
OSFI 19
Parliament Hill 4
physicians 16
Placements 56
Pool 4
PROFESSIONAL 4
Professional Associations 16
Punctuation 27
Qualifiedly Prohibited 13
    Abbreviations 13
    Abbreviations for Government Departments 13
    Connoting a Financial 60
        Intermediary 19
    names which connote government sponsorship and control 13
    USE OF MANITOBA 15
    USE OF NAMES OF FOREIGN
        COUNTRIES 16
    USE OF NEW BRUNSWICK 16
    USE OF NEWFOUNDLAND OR NFLD 15
    USE OF NOVA SCOTIA 14
    USE OF SASK., SASKATCHEWAN (SASK) 15
    Use of the term University 18
    "College", "School", or "Adult Education", "Research", "Applied Research" . . . 18
Quebec 17
Radio 57
RCMP 4
regulation 21 12
REVIVING 6, 35
S.A.R.F. 42
SASKATCHEWAN 15
School 18
secondary meaning 9

Securities and Exchange Commission 57
Société par actions de régime fédéral 42
surety 19
surgeon 16
surname 48
Television 57
territory 6
TRADE-MARK 7, 9, 37
     phonetically similar 36
trade name 9, 59
     Suggested Consent Form 38
Trust and Loan Companies Act 20
TWO YEAR PERIOD 6
UN 4
underwriter 21
United Nations 4
university 4
Voice Information System 11
warranty 19

Policy Statement 1.1a — Name Granting Guidelines

Date: March 22, 2002

This document is an abridged version of the *Name Granting Compendium*, to access the areas of interest, click on the following headings.

Foreword

This guide is intended for use by businesses requesting to be incorporated under the *Canada Business Corporations Act* (CBCA) or the *Canada Corporations Act* (CCA).

This document sets out the name granting policy of the Director, Corporations Canada, of Industry Canada, who is responsible under the Acts (in the case of the CCA, on behalf of the Minister) for ensuring that names proposed for Canadian corporations meet the requirements of the Acts and their regulations.

The CBCA and the CCA have almost identical regulations in this regard. The CBCA applies to most federally incorporated profit corporations, while the CCA applies only to not-for-profit corporations.

A corporate name proposed under either Act must be distinctive from, and not likely to cause confusion with, any other business name or trade-mark, or official mark registered federally or provincially.

These guidelines are designed to help you select an acceptable corporate name and have it approved. It provides examples of how the CBCA and the CCA name regulations may be interpreted to ensure that proposed names are distinctive and not likely to cause confusion. The more distinctive your proposed name is and the more information in writing you provide to explain your proposed business, clientele, territory of operation and derivation of words used, the more likely it is to be approved by the Director upon your first application.

These guidelines try to demonstrate how certain regulations may be interpreted and applied by the Director in making these decisions in certain types of fact situations. It is a guide only. Each name decision requires an exercise of judgment, based on the particular facts of that case and a number of regulations that may apply. Any one particular regulation or guideline described herein may not necessarily provide the basis for an actual name granting decision.

Note: The corporate names mentioned in this guide are meant to serve as examples only, and not to suggest they are names of real corporations.

Name Granting Process

1.1 — Definitions

"*Articles of incorporation*" are the papers filed with the Director, Corporations Canada, requesting incorporation under the CBCA or the CCA. The term, as used in this guide, should also be taken to refer to related articles pertaining to a name change or name creation effected, for example, by amendment, amalgamation, continuance or revival of a corporation or corporate name.

"*Business Name*" is the term used to denote businesses generally, whether incorporated or unincorporated.

"*Corporate name*" is the name of a corporation incorporated under the CBCA or the CCA, or incorporated in one of the provincial jurisdictions.

"*Official mark*" means a badge, crest, emblem or mark used by Canadian public authorities, as defined in the *Trade-Marks Act*.

"*Trade-mark*" is a mark, picture, symbol or name that identifies a product or service as being produced or sold by a particular company, as defined in the Trade-marks Act.

"*Trade-name*," as used in these guidelines, means the name under which an unincorporated business is carried on.

1.2 — What's in a name?

A corporate name may contain some or all of the following three elements:

- a *distinctive* element, which is a unique identifier that distinguishes this business from all others engaged in the same business activity. It may be a coined word, a dictionary word used in an unusual way, initials or characters, or a name of a person or thing.

- a *descriptive* element, which accurately describes a business activity in which the company is engaged.

- a *legal* element, which indicates the legal status of the company as an incorporated body.

e.g. TELFAX Commercial Communications Ltd.

- TELFAX — distinctive element
- Commercial Communications — descriptive element
- Ltd. — legal element

The terms *Corp., Corporation, Inc., Incorporated, Incorporée, Limited, Limitée, Ltd., Ltée, S.A.R.F.* or *Société par actions de régime fédéral*, except where used in a figurative or descriptive sense, must be part of a CBCA corporate name.

There is no such requirement under the CCA. If a CCA not-for-profit company wants to have a legal element in its name, it should be noted that only the terms *Corp., Corporation, Inc., Incorporated* or *Incorporée* are permitted.

The legal elements of a corporate name having two official language forms must be equivalent. Thus limited in English must be rendered limitée in French, *incorporated* in English must be incorporée in French, and *corporation* in English may be either *corporation* or *société par actions de régime fédéral* in French (but not *la corporation*). Either the full term or its abbreviation may be used, as long as the corresponding full term or abbreviation is used as the legal element in both forms. Thus *Ltd.* in English must be rendered *Ltée* in French, *Inc.* in English must also be *Inc.* in French, and *Corp.* in English may be either *Corp.* or *S.A.R.F.* in French. Note that S.A.R.F. is not acceptable as a legal element in the English form of a corporate name. In the case of a combined English and French form of a name, only one legal element must be used.(The legal element "Inc." would be suitably bilingual for that purpose.)

A corporation may also carry on business under or identify itself by a name other than its corporate name. This is commonly referred to as the corporation's trade-name. It is registered in the province(s) where the corporation will carry on business. A trade-name cannot contain a legal element.

1.3 — When can a name be proposed?

To save yourself time, make a request to the Director to approve your name before you file your articles of incorporation. Otherwise, the Director's decision will be taken when the articles of incorporation and related papers are filed in a certain proposed name. However, if the proposed name is rejected at that time, the articles also will be rejected and returned to you. By whichever method you choose to make your request, do not forget to use the form attached as Annex D, in order to improve your chances of success.

1.4 — What is a NUANS report?

Among other reasons mentioned in the regulations and in this guide, requests for proposed names cannot be granted if they are likely to cause confusion with other business names or trade-marks. A Newly Upgraded Automated Name Search (NUANS) report is a five-page document that includes a list of business names and trade-marks that sound similar to the name you are proposing. The list is drawn from the national data bank of existing and reserved business names as well as trade-marks registered and applied for in Canada.

A NUANS report can be obtained from private businesses known as Search Houses, which are listed under Incorporating Companies, Incorporation — Name Search, Searchers of Records or Trade-mark Agents in the Yellow Pages of your telephone directory. An online list of Search Houses is also available on Strategis, at Corporations Canada Electronic Filing Centre. If similar names do appear in the NUANS report, there are steps you can take to make your name more likely to be accepted by the Director. Many suggestions are given in this guide.

A NUANS report may be ordered online at the *Online Filing Centre* from the NUANS Real-Time System. The fee is $20 payable by credit card (Visa® or Mastercard®). The system provides direct access to the NUANS search service but does not provide the professional assistance and recommendations often available from a registered NUANS search house. Applicants should note that a NUANS report that is generated and submitted to the Director may be rejected if the proposed name does not meet the requirements of the CBCA/CCA name regulations.

A NUANS report must be ordered and submitted to the Director with your name request in almost all cases. You may request the Director to grant your corporation a designating number, followed by the word Canada and a legal element, to serve as your corporate name. For this specific case, no NUANS report is required. Any other kind of proposed name must be supported by a NUANS report.

When you order a NUANS report on your proposed corporate name from a Search House, that report has a life of 90 days from the date the NUANS report was requested. This date appears in the right-hand column beside the proposed name. Where two dates appear in the right-hand column, the earlier of the two dates prevails.

You should submit your proposed name, accompanied by the NUANS report and other information in support of your name request, to the Director for consideration without delay. The Director will examine your request to determine the distinctiveness of your proposed name and assess whether it meets the name granting requirements of the CBCA/CCA and their regulations. The Director will then make a decision to grant or reject it.

If your proposed name and/or articles of incorporation have not been approved before the 90-day period lapses, you must make a renewed request for a name reservation by ordering and submitting a new NUANS report. {see Regulation 20}

Only when the Director makes a decision to approve a particular name is that name automatically reserved. This means that when, during the 90-day period, you do file your articles of incorporation, a certificate of incorporation can be issued to you in the reserved name.

A request to revive (i.e. restore to life after a dissolution) a corporate name of a business that has ceased is subject to the same procedures as for a newly proposed name.

1.5 — How many NUANS reports are required?

One NUANS report may suffice for several name requests. There are no firm rules, but this is more likely to be the case where the names requested are for proposed affiliated companies distinguished only by the geographical location in parentheses.

- *e.g.*

> XYZ Tools (Ottawa) Inc.
> XYZ Tools (Hamilton) Inc.
> XYZ Tools (Toronto) Inc.

A request for a name in both English and French must often be accompanied by two NUANS reports.

The intent behind the need for two search reports is strictly to avoid confusion in names and not for bureaucratic or pecuniary reasons. The following criteria should be used to judge whether or not a bilingual name (whether with separate or combined English and French forms) requires two searches.

Where the English and French forms are phonetically similar, only one search may be necessary.

- *e.g.*

> ABC Distributions Inc. (English form)
> Les Distributions ABC Inc. (French form)

Names that are exact translations but are phonetically different require two searches.

- *e.g.*

> LB Plumbing + Heating Inc. (English form)
> Tuyauterie et Chauffage LB Inc. (French form)

Blue Cross Blood Collection Inc. (English form)
Collecte de sang Croix Bleue Inc. (French form)

Some English and French forms may be phonetically different, but share a substantial distinctive element and differ only in respect of a minor, commonly used descriptive element. In such a situation, a single search is often sufficient because it will turn up both English and French names.

- *e.g.*

Placements Protar Holdings Inc. — substantial distinctive plus minor common descriptive elements

Quadra Management Inc./
Gestion Quadra Inc. — substantial distinctive plus minor common descriptive elements

A NUANS microfiche search may be acceptable in place of a NUANS report when the requesting corporation is a successor to the name of a federal corporation that is ceasing to carry on business or when the proposed corporation is taking over all or substantially all of the property of a federally incorporated affiliate and wishes to keep its name. A NUANS report is required when the ceasing business or the existing affiliate is provincially incorporated. {see Regulations 30(1) and 31 (3) and section 4.3 below for additional requirements}

When a name amendment is requested to delete the year of incorporation from the name of a successor corporation, a NUANS microfiche search is acceptable. {see Regulation 30(2) and section 4.3 below for additional requirements}

Very occasionally, when the corporate name that is searched has more than one distinctive element, the NUANS search report will list business names and trade-marks that are similar to only one of those distinctive features. To spare applicants the time and expense of ordering a second NUANS search on the other distinctive element, Names Officers will undertake to carry out a NUANS microfiche search of the other element to see whether there are any confusing names relating to it. The applicant will be asked to accept the risk that the NUANS microfiche search, which, unlike a regular NUANS search, does not list names that are phonetically similar to the one proposed, may not reveal a conflict and that the Name Officer may fail to find a conflict that later comes to light, causing the name to become disallowed, at the applicant's expense.

Where articles of continuance are filed at the same time as articles of amalgamation and where the certificate of amalgamation is to be issued in a name different from the name of the continued corporation and on the same day as the certificate of continuance, a NUANS search report will not be required.

Where articles of continuance are filed at the same time as articles of amalgamation and where the certificate of amalgamation is to be issued in a name different from the name of the continued corporation and within a very short period of time after the certificate of continuance, a NUANS search report will not be required, if the applicant provides a NUANS microfiche search and undertakes:

- to file a NUANS search immediately if the amalgamation does not take effect as planned, and change its name if the Director decides it is necessary

- not to provide a consent under Regulation 31(3) or (4) for another entity to use its continued name, unless that name has been determined to be not confusing by Corporations Canada on the basis of a NUANS search report obtained by the entity at that time.

Depending on the length of time between the continuance and the amalgamation, the continued company may also be asked to undertake that it will not carry on business between the date of continuance and the date of amalgamation.

1.6 — What facts are necessary for a name decision?

A decision on whether to grant or reject a name request cannot be made without at least some information. Even where no similar names appear on the NUANS report and there is therefore no concern about the likelihood of causing confusion, other issues may be unclear. For example, without some information on what that business will be, the Director cannot properly assess whether a name connotes government sponsorship, connotes a trust, loan, insurance or banking business, misdescribes or merely describes the business of a corporation.

Where the NUANS report reveals several similar names, even more information becomes necessary to help the Director reach a name granting decision. Your name request should describe the following details, where appropriate:

- The type of business the proposed company will carry on and how this business is dissimilar to the activities of existing businesses having similar names.

- Where the proposed company will carry on its business and whether this territory is different from that of other businesses with similar names and similar activities.

- With what types of clients the proposed company will do business and whether they differ from the types of people that existing businesses, with similar names and similar activities in a similar territory, will do business: examples include wholesalers, retailers, computer programmers, the general public, etc.

- The derivation of the distinctive element(s) of the proposed name: if there is a reasonable explanation for why you want a particular distinctive element, the Director is less likely to suspect that you may be trying to trade on the goodwill of an existing business with a similar name.

- Whether the proposed company will be related to existing businesses with similar names or trade-marks and, if so, whether you are submitting the written consent of some or all of them.

- Whether the proposed corporation has a foreign parent with a similar name that carries on business or is known in Canada and, if so, whether you have written consent and intend to add (Canada) or of Canada to your proposed name.

- Whether you had made an earlier reservation of a similar name appearing on the NUANS report.

- Whether you have the written consent of an individual whose name appears in the corporate name and what that individual's material interest in the corporation is (not required if that individual is an incorporator or a director).

Staff of Corporations Canada will have the information listed in the paragraph above only if you provide it to them when making your submission. If you have satisfied yourself that your corporate name is not likely to cause confusion, write a note to the Director outlining the information on which you have based your conclusions. Chances are it will satisfy the Director.

Any information regarding the circumstances of your name choice must be made to the Director in writing

Too often an applicant fails to provide this information. Without it, the name submission must be rejected because the Director does not have an adequate basis on which to determine whether all the requirements of the CBCA and the CCA and their regulations are being respected. See Annex D for a voluntary corporate name information form to assist you in providing the types of information that would help the Director reach a name granting decision.

Should your proposed name be rejected, you are always free to provide more information and submit a request in writing to the Director to reconsider the decision. However, time and money can be saved by including the relevant information with your initial request.

1.7 — What fees are required?

While there is no fee for the name approval itself, fees are required for processing the articles of incorporation, amendment, etc. on which the name will appear.

Where articles of amendment are required simply to add the English or French form of a corporate name, however, no fee is required for that amendment.

Similarly, where a name change application requests simply that a legal element common to both language forms, such as INC., replace the existing legal element, such as Ltd. or Ltée, Corporations Canada will assume that this is to create a form of the name in the other official language. Therefore, no fee will be required, despite the fact that technically the original form of the name is being amended.

Names Must Be Distinctive

To be eligible for incorporation under the CBCA or the CCA, your proposed corporate name must be distinctive.

Distinctive refers to the quality of the name of a business that distinguishes it from all other businesses. A corporate name that is not distinctive is prohibited. The following guidelines may help you choose an appropriate name on which to submit a NUANS search request.

2.1 — Distinctiveness is determined with reference to the name as a whole, and not to its separate elements only. (see *Regulation 19*)

A name that is composed of a unique combination of letters or figures having no generic meaning is inherently highly distinctive. (see *Regulation 33*)

- *e.g.*

  XLYK
  DWIDAG

An unusual combination of generic words or terms may be highly distinctive.

- *e.g.*

  Jean
  Junction

Other names that contain a person's name, initials, a geographical location, etc. are less inherently distinctive because they are more likely to be commonly used.

- *e.g.*

  Smith Shoes Ltd.

Ottawa Shoes Ltd.
I. I. L. Shoes Ltd.
Star Shoes Ltd.

2.2 — A proposed corporate name may acquire distinctiveness through use (secondary meaning). (see *Regulation 24*)

If your proposed name has been and continues to be used as a trade-name in Canada or anywhere else, it may have acquired secondary meaning beyond the ordinary meaning of the component words. This means that persons in the trade readily associate the elements in your proposed name with your particular business above all. If this applies to you, your name request should include an affidavit stating some facts showing how large and widespread your business is and, if necessary, affidavits from others in the trade supporting your claim of secondary meaning.

For example, you may already be incorporated provincially and you wish to transfer your corporation (i.e. continue your corporation) to the federal jurisdiction. Since there are some differences in name granting rules between the two jurisdictions, your existing name may not be deemed acceptable, because it lacks distinctiveness, under the ordinary interpretation of the CBCA regulations.

2.2.1 — Affiliates

Some foreign parent corporations of long standing have names that are too general or merely descriptive. However, they may have acquired secondary meaning.

Such distinctiveness may be claimed for affiliated companies in Canada, whether the name has actually been used in Canada or is merely known through foreign advertising that regularly crosses the border.

- *e.g.*

    General Motors

2.3 — A name lacks distinctiveness if it only describes the business of the corporation, its goods or services or the quality, function or other characteristic of that business or those goods or services. (see *Regulation 24(1)(a)*)

2.3.1 — A name is not acceptable when it is only descriptive of the business of the corporation, its goods or services

- *not acceptable*

    Software Inc.

However, if a distinctive element were added the name would be acceptable.

- *acceptable*

    Turner Software Inc.

Names that are merely suggestive of the type of business, industry, good or service are acceptable. For example, the following for a car sales business may be granted:

- *acceptable*

    Tires and Wheels Ltd. — for a car sales business

This name does not describe the business nor the good produced. It simply suggests the corporation's field of activity. If the corporation manufactured or sold tires and wheels, however, this name would be unacceptable because, it is too general in this context.

- *acceptable*

> Tires and Wheels Ltd. — for a tire and wheel sales business

Please note that the approval of certain words as a corporate name does not necessarily mean that those words would be registrable as a trade-mark.

2.3.2 — As a general rule, a name is not acceptable if it only describes a quality or function of the corporation's business or its goods or services:

- *not acceptable*

> Faster Consulting Services Ltd.

However, such names become acceptable where:

- alliteration gives that name an acceptable level of distinctiveness

> *acceptable*
> Better Business Boardrooms Inc.

- the NUANS report demonstrates that the word describing a quality is commonly used as a distinctive feature in business names

> *acceptable*
> "Superior" in superior Machinery Ltd.
> "Advanced" in Advanced Technology Solutions Ltd.

- the descriptive word sounds unusual when used to describe the business of the proposed corporation

> *acceptable*
> Endless Furniture Inc.

> *not acceptable*
> Long Lasting Furniture Ltd.

Although these names are descriptive of a quality of the business, they are not only descriptive but have some distinctiveness. By reason of alliteration or being unusual, these names are distinguishable from others. Also, where the NUANS search reports show that a descriptive word is extensively used as a distinctive element, we will follow the common practice.

Please note that the approval of certain words as a corporate name does not necessarily mean that those words would be registrable as a trade-mark.

2.4 — A name lacks distinctiveness if it is the name, used alone, of a person who is living or has died within 30 years preceding the date of the request. (see *Regulation 24(1)(b)*)

- *not acceptable*

> Legault Inc.
> S. V. Lee Ltd.
> Sarah Legault Inc.
> S & R Wolfe Inc.

A name in combination with other distinctive or descriptive elements is acceptable.

- *acceptable*

> Wilson & Myers Ltd.
> Bob & Carol Harris Inc.
> Legault Gardening Enterprises Ltd.
> Thomas Construction Inc.

You may use the terms *Associates*, *& Associates* or *and Associates* in combination with a given or family name. You may use Associates with a generic or coined word, but not *and Associates*, because it could suggest the generic or coined word is a family name. Your request should specifically state the origin or meaning of such a word, mentioning whether or not it is a family name.

Bankruptcy administrators in the Bankruptcy Branch of Industry Canada prefer that trustees who incorporate use only the name(s) of the principal partner(s) in the corporate name. If only one person is involved, a personal name used alone is not acceptable. One solution is to add a descriptive term such as *Insolvency Trustee* or *Bankruptcy Trustee*.

2.5 — A name lacks distinctiveness if it is a geographical term used alone. (see *Regulation 24(1)(c)*)

- *not acceptable*

> Red Lake Inc.
> 235 St. Catherine Street Inc.

However, you may use a geographical term in combination with a descriptive term.

- *acceptable*

> Red Lake Gold Mines Inc.

2.6 — A name lacks distinctiveness if the only distinctive element is merely the suffix of an Internet Domain name

Suffixes like ".ca" or ".com" will not be treated as distinctive elements of a corporate name. The name will be treated as if it did not have the suffix. If the name has some distinctiveness without the suffix and it is not confusing, it will be approved.

- *acceptable*

> Doc Systems.ca Inc.

If the name has no distinctiveness without the suffix, it will be rejected, since the suffix does not add distinctiveness.

- *not acceptable*

> Cars.ca Inc.

Since the name "Cars Inc." would not be accepted, being merely descriptive, the name "Cars.ca Inc." is not acceptable.

Names Likely to Cause Confusion Are Not Acceptable

A proposed name that looks, sounds or suggests similar ideas as an existing business name or trade-mark is not eligible for incorporation under the CBCA or the CCA if it is likely to cause confusion with the other business name or trade-mark.

Likely to cause confusion refers to the probability that a similarity between two names could lead the public to believe they are one business, or related businesses, when they are not. Confusion could arise based on phonetic similarity alone.

Your NUANS report may reveal existing names similar to your proposed name. The following guidelines may help you to clarify your name choice, to modify your name choice to overcome confusion or to select another one.

(For information on how to protect your corporate name in Canada, please see Annex C.)

3.1 — Confusion is determined with reference to all circumstances. (see *Regulation 25*)

Your request for approval of a name should include details on the nature of your line of business, your clientele, your means of distribution, the derivation of your name, whether and how long you have already carried on business, and your territory of operation. Such details may show that there is no probability of confusion with an existing business name or trade-mark that looks or sounds similar to yours.

The Director may consider your proposed name not likely to cause confusion with an existing similar one if information you supply can demonstrate that one or more of the following circumstances applies:

- your trade-name has been in use for a significant period of time prior to the date of application for incorporation
- your goods or services differ from those of the existing business
- the nature of your trade or your means of offering or distributing your goods or services differs from those of the existing business
- your business is not likely to operate in the territory in Canada where the other business is likely to operate.

The pertinence of such details to your business should be made clear in your request. Any information regarding the circumstances of your name choice must be made to the Director in writing.

3.2 — A corporate name is likely to cause confusion where its use may suggest that the business is related to a dissolved corporation. (see *Regulations 27* and *28*)

Corporations dissolved less than two years previous to the making of a request for name approval are considered to be existing for purposes of confusion. Their names are not normally available for use by another business that is likely to cause confusion until a two-year period has lapsed. The purpose of such a period of non-use is to allow the public time to dissociate that name from a specific business.

After two years, the name becomes available to anyone, as long as no successor companies were incorporated meanwhile and as long as the original name has not been perpetuated in any way, for example, through use by a successor corporation under *regulation 30*.

3.3 — A corporate name is likely to cause confusion if it is similar to a trade-mark or official mark of an unrelated business. (see *Regulation 18(a)*)

3.3.1 — A proposed name that appears to be likely to cause confusion with a recently registered trade-mark usually is not available. Nevertheless, if you can show that your proposed name has been used prior to the registration of the trade-mark, and therefore you would likely be able to have the trade-mark registration struck out and will try to do so, your proposed name will often be approved. However, once a trade-mark has been registered for five years, it is very difficult to have it struck out. In such circumstances, your proposed name would not be approved

The owner of a trade-mark that has been registered for less than five years, on the other hand, will not be granted a corporate name based on it if another confusing corporate name predates his/her trade-mark registration.

- *e.g.*

> Suncraft Motor Homes — existing corporate name
> Suncraft — trade-mark registered by a different business dealing in the same goods
> Suncraft Travel Machines — unacceptable confusing corporate name requested by the owner of the trade-mark

However, if the trade-mark has been registered for five years or more, the owner of the trade-mark will be given the name because this trade-mark is not likely to be struck out.

3.3.2 — Where a proposed name is likely to cause confusion with an existing official mark adopted and used pursuant to the provisions of section 9 of the Trade-marks Act, the proposed corporate name will be rejected

3.4 — A corporate name is likely to cause confusion if it is similar to a trade-name of an unrelated business. (see *Regulation 18(b)*)

A proposed corporate name may be considered likely to cause confusion with an existing similar trade-name. A likelihood of confusion exists even if they are owned by the same person, unless both names form part of the same business.

On the other hand, a proposed corporate name will not be considered likely to cause confusion with a trade-name if you can show that the businesses offer different goods or services, use different distribution means and/or operate in different geographical areas.

Note re Ontario Business Names on the NUANS report: Ontario Business Names expire after 5 years unless they are renewed. Unrenewed registrations remain on the database however. The Director will assume that all Ontario trade-name registrations less than 5 and 1/2 years old and appearing on the NUANS report, are active. Any registrations over 5 and 1/2 years old and not renewed, will be disregarded. The 1/2 year period is a grace period to allow time for renewal after expiry.

3.5 — Overcoming confusion

Your corporate name must not look, sound or suggest similar ideas as an existing business name. If your NUANS report reveals that names similar to the one you have selected already exist, you may wish to modify your selection to overcome confusion.

A distinctive element made up of two letters or characters is likely to cause confusion with an existing trade-mark, official mark or trade-name in the same business if the initials are identical and in the same order or if the first initials are the same and the second initials are phonetically similar. A variation will often be acceptable.

- *e.g.*

     BN Construction — existing name
     BN Builders — likely to cause confusion
     BM Construction — likely to cause confusion
     BF Construction — acceptable

A distinctive element made up of three or more letters or characters is likely to cause confusion with a similar existing corporate name also. Here, too, a variation will often be acceptable.

- *e.g.*

     ABCD Construction — existing name
     ABCF Construction — likely to cause confusion
     DABC Construction — acceptable

Letters or figures that sound like other letters or words are likely to cause confusion.

- *e.g.*

     BNMD Construction — existing name
     BNND Construction — likely to cause confusion
     BMND Building — likely to cause confusion
     ANM Construction Ltd. — existing name
     A & M Construction Inc. — likely to cause confusion

The addition of initials only to a family name that is otherwise likely to cause confusion is not sufficient to overcome that confusion. A full given name plus a family name is often acceptable.

- *e.g.*

     Smith Shoes Inc. — existing name
     R. E. Smith Shoes Ltd. — likely to cause confusion
     Robert Smith Shoes Ltd. — acceptable

A distinguishing feature must be used to differentiate a new corporation from its provincial, federal or foreign affiliates. A general term may be used for this purpose among affiliated companies. For example, the use of general terms such as *Canada, (Canada), canadian* and *international* would be permissible. Alternatively, some other feature could be added to distinguish between parent and subsidiary, or between subsidiaries. A proposed Canadian subsidiary of a foreign parent with the identical name will not be required to add the word *Canada* if it can establish that the foreign company has never carried on business in Canada and is not known in Canada. (see *section 4.6* for examples)

The name of a province or city with or without parentheses may be added to a corporate name to overcome confusion with the name of an existing affiliated corporation.

- *e.g.*

     Newton Tool Manitoba Ltd. — existing name
     Newton Tool (Canada) Ltd. — acceptable if related
     Newton Tool Québec Ltd. — acceptable if related

However, the consent of the existing corporation would be required in order to grant such a similar name. Where there are many existing affiliates, the consent of the geographically closest affiliate or the parent of the affiliates would be sufficient. Consent of a provincial authority may also be required. (see *section 5.2.3*)

Some common words are used as the distinctive element in many business names. Such wide usage dilutes the impact of the business name, allowing it to be easily borrowed by other businesses with only slight modification. A different descriptive term is all that is needed to distinguish one corporate name from others that sound similar, even if the descriptive words describe essentially the same business.

- *diluted*

> Universal Food Enterprises Inc. — existing name
> Universal Products Inc. — acceptable proposed name
> Universal Bakery Products Inc. — acceptable proposed name

A name that includes a more specific personal or geographical name or coined word is less diluted in impact and more distinctive, deserving more protection. Such a name would require a descriptive term relating to a different business to distinguish it from others that sound similar.

- *less diluted/more distinctive*

> Suncrest Food Enterprises Inc. — existing name
> Suncrest Products Inc. — proposed name likely to cause confusion, unless evidence is provided in writing to show that the nature of the businesses is different
> Suncrest Toys Inc. — acceptable proposed name

Note that no descriptive term at all may be required, if you submit information regarding your likely business activity to the Director with your name request and that business activity is different from that of the existing business.

A unique and imaginative distinctive element in the name of a corporation is more likely to become associated in the public mind with a particular business, and it therefore deserves more protection in order to prevent confusion. In such circumstances, your name may not be accepted, even if it is in a different business from the existing one.

- *e.g.*

> Greenlips Marketing Inc. — existing name
> Greenlips Computer Services Inc. — unacceptable proposed name, because the public could think the new business is related in some way to the existing one

Some of the above names deemed likely to cause confusion or unacceptable could become acceptable if the companies were related and if consent were provided. (see *section 4.2*)

3.6 — Not-for-profit corporations

Not-for-profit corporations are subject to the same regulations as for-profit corporations. However, they may receive a slightly more liberal interpretation in name granting with regard to lack of distinctiveness, because not-for-profit names are typically very general and descriptive.

- *e.g.*

> Canadian Manufacturers' Association

If your proposed name is for a not-for-profit corporation and is similar to that of an existing not-for-profit corporation except for a geographical term, you should submit the consent in writing of the existing corporation.

- *e.g.*

> Calgary Ultralight Aircraft Association — existing name
> Canada Ultralight Aircraft Association — acceptable only with consent

Toronto Dance Foundation — existing name
Canada Dance Foundation — acceptable only with consent

A possible alternative is to modify another word.

- *e.g.*

Calgary Ultralight Aircraft Association — existing name
Canada Ultralight Aircraft Society — acceptable without consent
Toronto Dance Foundation — existing name
Canada Dance Funding Society — acceptable without consent

Terms such as *institute, association* and *foundation* are usually reserved for use by not-for-profit corporations. If you have a strong case for using such a term in the name of a profit-making corporation, you may apply to the Director for a decision, giving your reason in writing.

The term *Chamber of Commerce* is acceptable in the name of a not-for-profit corporation. However, the geographical descriptor must not be a district within Canada alone, but Canada and another nation.

- *e.g.*

Canada-Brazil Chamber of Commerce

The term *club* may be used by profit or not-for-profit corporations. However, the word may not acceptable where the name suggests a not-for-profit membership corporation.

- *e.g.*

Toronto Blue Jays — acceptable, because the general public would be
Baseball Club — aware that such a baseball club is a business corporation

A Consent or Undertaking May Be Necessary

4.1 — A personal name can be used in a corporate name only with consent. (see *Regulation 26*)

A family name of an individual, with or without initials or given names, can form part of a corporate name only if that individual, the heir or legal representative consents in writing to such use, and if that person has or had a material interest in the corporation.

Consent to the use of all personal names in the corporate name should accompany your request. Also indicate the material interest. However, such a consent is not required where the personal name is the name of the incorporator or director of the incorporating company.

In some cases, it may be difficult to determine whether the distinctive element is a person's name or a generic word. Therefore, your request should specifically state the origin or meaning of each word, mentioning whether or not it is a given or family name. Word order, characters and punctuation will often help in determining the difference between a generic word and a personal name.

- *e.g.*

Ran Shoes Inc. — no consent required (appears to be a generic word)
Ran Smith Shoes Inc. — consent of Ran Smith required
Ran, Smith Shoes Inc. — consent of Ran and consent of Smith required
Starsmith Shoes Ltd. — no consent required (coined word)
Star Associates Ltd. — no consent required (generic word)
Star & Associates Ltd. — consent of Star required (personal name)
Rose Green's Tools Ltd. — consent of Rose Green required

Consent is not required when the personal name is the name of the street on which the corporation is located, of an obviously literary character or of an historical person who died more than 30 years before the date of the request. However, your request should clearly identify the origin of the personal name.

- *acceptable*

> Dorian Grey Fashions Inc.
> Lady Macbeth Cosmetics Inc.

Where a fictitious name is used, you should file an affidavit stating that the name in question is a fictitious name and is not the name of a person who is well known or known personally to the principal of the incorporating company.

4.2 — A proposed name that is likely to cause confusion with an existing trade-name, official mark or trade-mark may be acceptable if the existing trade-name holder or official mark or trade-mark owner consents. (see *Regulation 29*)

The consent must be unconditional. It must be signed by a director or officer of the consenting corporation or the owner of the trade-mark or official mark. A trustee in bankruptcy for a corporation may also sign the consent, where appropriate. For a sample consent form, please see *Annex B*.

4.2.1 — Franchises

Use of the name of a franchise accrues to the franchisor rather than to the franchisee. Therefore, the consent of existing business and trade-names that are franchisee businesses is not required for the incorporation of a confusingly similar name proposed for another franchisee. Only the consent of the franchisor will be required. In that consent, the franchisor must identify the existing business names as franchisees.

4.3 — A proposed corporate name that is likely to cause confusion with an existing one may be acceptable if the existing corporation ceases business under that name, and undertakes to dissolve or change its name. (see *Regulations 28, 30* and *31*)

You may wish to take for your corporation the name of a corporation that has recently ceased, or will in the near future cease, to carry on business. You must first obtain an undertaking in writing that the existing corporation will dissolve forthwith or change its corporate name before you commence to use it. The undertaking must be signed by a director or officer of the ceasing business. You must then file this undertaking with Corporations Canada.

Where your proposed name is to be the same as that of a corporation that has been inactive for two years or more, the undertaking of that corporation with its consent is sufficient. (see *Regulation 28*)

Where your proposed name is a successor to the name of a corporation that has ceased, or will in the near future cease, you must set out in numerals the year of incorporation or the year of the most recent amendment to the corporate name, in parentheses, immediately before the legal element. If you wish, you may request a corporate name amendment two years later to delete the reference to the year of incorporation (or the year of the name amendment) from the corporate name, as long as its removal is not likely to cause confusion and will not result in a name that lacks distinctiveness. (see *Regulation 30*)

Where the other corporation has already dissolved, consent is no longer possible. Therefore, to use that name within two years of its ceasing business, you would have to show that you had acquired consent to use the name prior to the dissolution. Alternatively, you could vary the name to remove the likelihood of causing confusion.

Where the ceasing corporation was amalgamated under a different name within the past two years, the consent can be provided by the resulting amalgamated corporation.

Where the ceasing corporation's name includes a personal name whose use was consented to by that person, the heir or legal representative, and that person has or had a material interest in the corporation, the successor corporation also will be required to obtain such consent to use it.

Where the ceasing corporation's name was originally granted based on consent in writing from the owner of an existing trade-mark or official mark for its use, the successor corporation also will be required to obtain such consent to use it. Where your corporation is acquiring all or substantially all of the property (and not just the shares) of an existing corporation that is or will become an affiliate, you may adopt its name, provided that it undertakes in writing to dissolve or to change its corporate name before your corporation commences using it. This condition applies whether your corporation is new or one that is already existing. Until this condition can be met, a name identical to that of an existing corporation will not be approved, even with the latter's consent unless the latter has been inactive for two years as stated above. (see *Regulation 31(3)*)

You should attach confirmation of the transfer of the property with your name request, or send it along to Corporations Canada a few days later. If this transfer is not carried out immediately, you may be required to change the name of your corporation.

4.4 — Failure to honour an undertaking

If your name is granted on the basis of a corporation undertaking to dissolve or to change names, and that undertaking is not honoured, the Director may direct you to change your corporation's name. (see subsections 12(4.1) and 12(5) and section 173 of the CBCA)

4.5 — Amalgamation of corporations

The name you request for an amalgamated corporation may be the existing name of one of the amalgamating corporations, a distinctive combination of both amalgamating names that otherwise is not likely to cause confusion or is prohibited, or a distinctive new name that is not likely to cause confusion. (see *Regulation 31(1)*)

4.6 — Distinguishing your corporate name

You may include the word GROUP in your corporate name if the distinctive element in your proposed name is unique.

Alternatively, you may include the word GROUP in your corporate name if companies using the same distinctive feature are related and consent. The existing parent of such a group of companies may request a change of name to include the word GROUP without consent.

If unrelated corporations use the same distinctive element in its name, your corporation cannot appear to be the holding company for them. Therefore, you must explain why your proposed corporate name will not misleadingly suggest a grouping of the companies. One possible response is that the nature of the businesses is too different to be mistaken for affiliated operations. In this case, you may add a descriptive element to modify the word GROUP.

However, the name must clearly distinguish the business of the proposed company from the unrelated existing companies with the same distinctive element in their names.

A distinguishing feature must be used to differentiate a new corporation from its provincial, federal or foreign affiliates. A general term may be used for this purpose among affiliated companies. For example, the use of general terms such as *Canada, (Canada), canadian* and *international* would be permissible. Alternatively, some other feature could be added to distinguish between parent and subsidiary, or between subsidiaries. A proposed Canadian subsidiary of a foreign parent with the identical name will not be required to add the word *Canada* if it can establish that the foreign company has never carried on business in Canada and is not known in Canada.

Another way to distinguish your corporation is by adding a year or the word Canada, with or without parentheses. Use the following examples to guide you.

- *if there is no existing corporation named ABC*

    ABC Canada, ABC (Canada), ABC 2001, ABC (2001)

    - any one of these variations of a name proposed by a new corporation would be acceptable

- *if there is an existing corporation named ABC*

    ABC Canada, ABC (Canada)

    - acceptable if proposed by an affiliated corporation, with consent in writing

    ABC 2001, ABC (2001)

    - not acceptable if proposed by an affiliated corporation that will continue to exist, because it misleadingly suggests it is a successor to a ceased business rather than an affiliate of one continuing to exist

    - also not acceptable if proposed by an unrelated corporation unless there is a written undertaking by the existing corporation to dissolve or change its name

    - however, if you can show in your request that your clients are sophisticated enough to know that your corporation is not the successor to the existing corporation, and if the existing corporation consents in writing to use of the name, your request may be acceptable

- *if existing corporation ABC is dissolving or changing its name*

    ABC (2001)

    - acceptable with a written undertaking by an existing related or unrelated corporation to dissolve or change its name

    ABC Canada, ABC (Canada), ABC 2001

    - acceptable only if proposed by an affiliated corporation, with consent in writing (however, if you can show in your request that your clients are sophisticated enough to know that your corporation is not affiliated with the existing corporation, your request may be acceptable)

    Except in the case of a successor corporation, any reasonable date is permissible unless it is misleading. For example, ABC 1884 Ltd. would be misleading for the name of a corporation that has not been in business since 1884

Names Containing Certain Terms Are Not Acceptable

5.1 — Names containing the following terms are absolutely prohibited. (see Regulation 21)

not acceptable

- Air Canada
- Canada Standard or CS
- Cooperative, Coopérative, Co-op or Pool when it connotes a cooperative venture
- Parliament Hill or Colline du Parlement
- Royal Canadian Mounted Police, Gendarmerie Royale du Canada, RCMP or GRC
- United Nations, Nations Unies, UN or ONU

5.2 — Names containing terms that may imply Crown patronage, or association, control, sponsorship or affiliation with the federal or provincial governments, their departments or agencies, are qualifiedly prohibited. (see Regulations 22(a) and 22(b))

Names containing such terms are prohibited under most circumstances. A name including part or all of the name of a federal government department or agency, without consent in writing from the appropriate department or agency, is prohibited. A name containing initials the same as those of a federal government department is not acceptable, unless the combination of distinctive element and descriptive element make clear that the business activity is unrelated to government administration.

not acceptable

- Sports Canada Ltd.
- Canadian Association of Postmasters
- Health & Welfare Programmers Association
- Canadian Armed Forces Ltd.
- Canadian Forces Inc.
- Canadian Labelling Standards Council

The use of the word *Canada* preceded by a descriptive word that is within the range of activities in which a client might imagine the federal government to be involved will be rejected.

not acceptable

- Disease Control Canada

5.2.1 — Reference to broadcasting

Broadcasting in Canada is administered by the Canadian Radio-television and Telecommunications Commission (CRTC). A request for a name containing the words *broadcasting, radio* or *television* does not require CRTC consent. However, you should note that the CRTC will deny a licence to operate to a company that is not qualified to broadcast under the CRTC Act.

5.2.2 — Reference to foreign countries

You may use the name of a foreign country in a corporate name without the consent in writing of the foreign government.

acceptable
- XYZ (Switzerland) Inc.

5.2.3 — Reference to Canadian provinces

There are special restrictions regarding the use of names of some provinces, their abbreviations or coined words derived from province names in corporate names.

Alberta

You may not use the terms *(Alta)* or *(Alberta)* in a federal corporate name; they are reserved for companies incorporated in Alberta as affiliates of an extra-provincial company having the same or similar name.

You may use the terms *Alta, Alberta* or *of Alberta* in a corporate name if there is no connotation of association with the Government of Alberta. Where the name does imply an association with the Government of Alberta, you may not use the terms without consent in writing from:

> Alberta Registries
> Corporate Registries
> 18th Floor, Commerce Place
> 10155-102th Street
> Edmonton AB T5J 4L4
> Tel.: (780) 422-7330
> Fax: (780) 422-1091
> Email: *cr@gov.ab.ca*

British Columbia

You may not use the terms (B.C.) or (British Columbia) in a federal corporate name; they are reserved for companies incorporated in British Columbia as affiliates of an extra-provincial company of the same or similar name.

You may not use the terms *B.C., British Columbia* or *of British Columbia* in a corporate name without consent in writing from:

> Registrar of Companies
> Ministry of Finance and Corporate Relations
> Corporate and Personal Property Registries
> 2nd Floor, The Waddington Building
> 940 Blanshard Street
> Victoria BC V8W 3E6
> Tel.: (250) 387-7848
> Fax: (250) 356-9422
> Internet: *Registrar of Companies Website*

Manitoba

You may not use the term *Manitoba* in a corporate name without consent in writing from:

> Director, Companies Office
> Manitoba Consumer and Corporate Affairs
> 10th Floor, 1010 Woodsworth Building
> 405 Broadway Avenue
> Winnipeg MB R3C 3L6

Tel.: (204) 945-2500
Fax: (204) 945-1459
Email: *companies@cca.gov.mb.ca*

New Brunswick

You may not use the term *New Brunswick* at the beginning of a corporate name without consent in writing from:

Director, Corporate Affairs Branch
Service New Brunswick
432 Queen Street
Fredericton NB E3B 1B6
Tel.: (506) 453-2703
Fax: (506) 453-2613
Email: *snb@snb.ca*
Internet: *Corporate Affairs Branch Website*

Newfoundland and Labrador

You may not use the terms *Newfoundland* or *Nfld.* in a corporate name without consent in writing from:

Government of Newfoundland and Labrador
Registrar of Companies
Department of Government Services and Lands
Confederation Building, Ground floor, East Block
P.O. Box 8700
St. John's NF A1B 4J6
Tel.: (709) 729-3317
Fax: (709) 729-0232
Email: *ahogan@mail.gov.nf.ca*

Nova Scotia

You may not use the term *Nova Scotia* at the beginning of a corporate name without consent in writing from:

Service Nova Scotia and Municipal Relations
Registrar of Joint Stock Companies
Maritime Centre, 9th floor, Box 1529
1505 Barrington Street
Halifax NS B3J 2K4
Tel.: (902) 424-7770
Fax: (902) 424-4633
Internet: *Service Nova Scotia and Municipal Relations Website*

Saskatchewan

"Sask.", *"Saskatchewan"*, *"(Sask)"*, *"(Saskatchewan)"* or any other term which denotes affiliation with the Government of Saskatchewan, may only be used in a name proposed for a federal company with the consent of the Director of Corporations in Saskatchewan. In accordance with the *Saskatchewan Justice Name Qualification Policy*, the corporation must agree to carry on the major portion of its business within Saskatchewan; or have its head office in Saskatchewan, from which it carries on the major portion of its business; and undertakes to

change its name to delete the word (Saskatchewan) from its name, should it cease to carry on its business in Saskatchewan.

> Director, Corporations Branch
> Corporation Branch
> Saskatchewan Justice
> 2nd floor,1871 Smith Street
> Regina Saskatchewan S4P 3V7
> Tel.: (306) 787-2962
> Fax: (306) 787-8999
> Email: *corporations@justice.gov.sk.ca*

5.3 — There are restrictions on the reference in names to a university or a professional association. (see *Regulation 22(c)*)

You may not use terms in a corporate name connoting control by or affiliation with a university or professional association of accountants, architects, physicians, engineers, lawyers, surgeons or any other professional association recognized by the laws of Canada or a province without consent in writing from the appropriate body.

consent required

> University of Montreal Debating Society
> Upper Canada Lawyers' Debating Society (connotes a link with the Law Society of Upper Canada)
> Certified General Accountants Debating Society

You may not include the terms *university, academy, college, institute, school, adult education, research, applied research* or a like term in the corporate name of an entity that appears to grant post-secondary degrees unless the corporation is authorized by the relevant federal or provincial authority to grant bachelors, masters or doctoral degrees or licences. Your request should specifically state under which authority your corporation grants degrees. For further information, contact:

> Association of Universities and Colleges of Canada
> 350 Albert Street
> Suite 600
> Ottawa ON K1R 1B1
> Tel: (613) 563-1236
> Fax: (613) 563-9745

The following names are misleading if the entities do not have authority to grant degrees or licences.

not acceptable

- Northern University Inc.
- Northwest Applied Research (Inc.)

Where the context makes it clear that a degree or licence is not granted, you may use such terms.

acceptable

- Sudbury Typing College (Inc.)
- University Painters Inc.

Apart from the above restrictions, you may normally use the name of a profession in a corporate name.

acceptable

- Heritage Lawyers' Association
- John Brown Accounting Services Ltd.
- Black & White Engineers Inc.

However, you should be aware that various provincial professional bodies have their own remedies against misuse of their professional authorities. Moreover, provincial legislation may prevent a federal professional association from carrying on operations in the province. For greater certainty, contact the appropriate professional or provincial authorities for more information before submitting your request. The specific term *"corporation professionnelle du Québec"* is not acceptable without consent in writing from the "Office des Professions du Québec", because it connotes an organization approved by the professional code of Quebec.

5.4 — There are restrictions on the reference in names to financial activity. (see *Regulation 22(d)*)

You should be aware that, to carry on the business of a bank, loan company, insurance company or trust company, you must be incorporated under legislation administered by the Office of the Superintendent of Financial Institutions (OSFI), an agency of the Department of Finance. Proposed names connoting such activity, or the activity of a stock exchange or other financial intermediary, are not acceptable for incorporation under the CBCA.

A proposed name appears to connote a restricted financial activity when it contains descriptive terms like *annuity, assurance, assurances, banc, banco, cancorp, bank, bankco, bankcorp, banker, banking, casualty, fiduciare, fiduciary, fiducie, guaranty, indemnity, insurance, life, loan, loanco, mortgage, prêt, savings, surety, trust, trustco or warranty.*

A proposed name intended for the CBCA incorporation that contains the restricted words in a way that appears to connote a financial activity should be referred to Director of Compliance, OSFI at (tel: (416) 973-6117 fax: (416) 973-8966) for consideration. OSFI may recommend approval of names containing these words if it agrees they do not connote activity as a financial intermediary.

A proposed name intended for CBCA incorporation that uses the restricted terms in a fanciful or other way that clearly does not connote the business of a financial intermediary may be acceptable without reference to OSFI.

e.g.

- Once in a Life Time Bridal Boutique Inc.
- Piggy Bank Children's Shop Ltd.
- Time Savings Household Cleaner Inc.
- Sam's Trust Worthy Contracting Services Ltd.
- ABC Data Bank Inc.

A proposed name containing the terms *acceptance, credit, fidelity, finance, fund or underwriters* in a way that does not connote the business of a financial intermediary may be acceptable without reference to OSFI.

A proposed name that adds a term like *agency, agent, broker or service(s)* along with a term that implies an insurance or mortgage-related service may be acceptable without reference to OSFI.

e.g.

- Cartier Insurance Brokers Inc.

The use of the terms *trust foundation or trust society* in the proposed name of a not-for-profit corporation may be acceptable without reference to OSFI. The term *mortgage investment corporation* may be acceptable in a business corporation. The term "mortgage"may be acceptable without reference to OSFI where it is to be used in connection with a mortgage brokerage business and not a mortgage lending business.

For purposes of licensing, some provincial jurisdictions (for example, Quebec and Ontario) have restrictions on the type of names allowed for companies offering insurance-related services. Since the use of a name granted is subject to the laws of the jurisdiction where the corporation intends to carry on business, you may wish to contact the appropriate provincial authorities for more information before submitting your request. You may find some of the following contacts helpful.

regarding general insurance in Quebec, call

> Tel.: (514) 282-8765

regarding personal insurance in Quebec, call

> Tel.: (418) 647-2244

regarding use of the word agent in Ontario, call

> Tel.: (416) 250-7250

regarding use of the word broker in Ontario, call

> Tel.: (416) 365-1900

At OSFI's request, Corporations Canada will forward to them a copy of a CBCA certificate of incorporation of a subsidiary of an existing bank.

> e.g. Bank of Nova Scotia Finance Corporation

5.5 — Deceptively misdescriptive names are not acceptable. (see *Regulation 32*)

A corporate name is unacceptable if it deceptively misdescribes the business, goods or services, the condition under which the goods or services will be produced or supplied, the persons to be employed, or the place of origin of those goods or services.

5.6 — Obscene names are not acceptable. (see *Regulation 23*)

A name may not contain a word or phrase that is obscene or connotes a business that is obscene.

Names May Be in English or French or Both

You may request your corporate name in an English form only, a French form only, a combined English and French form, or separate English and French forms. Your corporation may use and be legally designated by any such form.(see subsection 10(3) of the CBCA)

A combined English and French form has only one legal element. "Inc." is a suitably bilingual element for this purpose, e.g. Coiffure CHICO Hairdressing Inc. (see *Regulation 34*) If you select a combined English and French form for your name, you must use the full combined form to legally designate your corporation. If your corporate name has separate English and French forms, your business can be legally designated by either of them.

Corporations operating in Quebec may wish to have a French form of the corporate name. When selecting a French name translated from an English name, you may wish to check the accuracy or acceptability of the translation with:

Office de la Langue Française
Quebec — Tel.: (418) 643-1908 or 1-888-873-6202 (in Québec only)
Montreal — Tel.: (514) 873-6565
Email: *info@olf.gouv.qc.ca*

As a general rule, the English and French forms of a corporate name do not have to be literal translations, but a corporation cannot have French and English forms of a corporate name that are so different as to appear to belong to two different corporations. Where there is concern this may be the case, the proposed name will be rejected.

However, Corporations Canada will permit all words contained in English and French forms of a corporate name to be translated in the following situations:

- The name is made only of generic words, literally translated. There is no separate distinctive element although the name as a whole is distinctive.

acceptable

Think retail Inc. (English form)/ Pensez Détail Inc. (French form)

The name consists only of a distinctive element, which is partly translated. The part that is translated is descriptive and the other part is identical in both English and French.

acceptable

Techni-Glass (or Techniglass) Inc. (English)/ Techni-Verre (or Techniverre) Inc. (French)

The name consists of both distinctive and descriptive elements, both of which are very literally translated.

acceptable

Édition Entre-Nous Inc. (French)/ Between-Us Publishing Inc. (English)

Only the distinctive element may be in a foreign language. Descriptive elements (if there are any) must be in either English or French or both.

e.g. La Parilla Restaurant Inc.

The initial letters only of English or French words as the distinctive element are generally not acceptable as alternate name forms. The choice and order of the initials may differ between the languages, even if the words on which they are based are exact translations, and so give the appearance of two unrelated names.

not acceptable

C. M. I. Inc. (English form) / H. I. C. L. Inc. (French form)
CS Computer Services Inc. (English form) / Service Informatique SI Inc. (French form)

However, if you can show that the initials have acquired secondary meaning, the alternate name forms may be acceptable.

And, despite this rule the alternate name forms of a not-for-profit corporation containing the initials of descriptive words may be acceptable, despite differences. The name would have to be available without the initials, and the initials must not form a substantive part of the name.

acceptable

ARIC Aerospace Research Institute of Canada (English form)
Institut de Recherches Aerospatiale du Canada IRAC (French form)

Where a name has been rejected because the French and English forms look like two separate corporations, a possible remedy is to demonstrate that the forms have acquired secondary meaning associating both forms with the same business.

Some descriptive terms may not be acceptable in alternate forms because they are likely to cause confusion in either or both languages. Proposed names containing descriptive terms like *gestion, holdings, investissements, management or placements* are not acceptable when there is an existing name with the same distinctive element and any one of the above terms as the descriptive element. Since holding, management and investment companies may well be carrying on the same type of business, and since the word *placements* is often used as a translation for both *holdings* and *investments*, granting such a new name would be likely to cause confusion, unless the distinctive element were very diluted.

e.g.

XYZ Holdings Inc. — existing name
XYZ Placements Inc. — not acceptable
XYZ Investments Inc. — not acceptable

6.1 — Additional languages

In addition to acceptable names for use in Canada, you may request a name for use outside Canada in English, French or any other language. The names for use outside Canada must be equivalent to the corporate name for use in Canada. A name with a different meaning is not acceptable, as this would likely lead the public to think they were different businesses. The name for use outside Canada is to be stated under "Other Provisions" in the articles of incorporation.

Annexe A — Extracts from the CBCA and its Regs.

From the Canada *Business Corporations Act*

10. (1) **Name of corporation** — The word or expression "Limited", "Limitée", "Incorporated", "Incorporée", "Corporation" or "Société par actions de régime fédéral" or the corresponding abbreviation "Ltd.", "Ltée", "Inc.", "Corp." or "S.A.R.F." shall be part, other than only in a figurative or descriptive sense, of the name of every corporation, but a corporation may use and be legally designated by either the full or the abbreviated form.

(1.1) **Saving for "S.C.C"** — Subsection (1) does not apply to a corporation that has a corporate name that, immediately before the day on which subsection comes into force, included, other than only in a figurative or descriptive sense, the expression "Société commerciale canadienne" or the abbreviation "S.C.C.", and any such corporation may use and be legally designated by either that expression or that abbreviation.

(2) **Exemption** — The Director may exempt a body corporate continued as a corporation under this Act from the provisions of subsection (1).

(3) **Alternate name** — Subject to subsection 12(1), the name of a corporation may be set out in its articles in an English form, a French form, an English form and a French form, or a combined English and French form, so long as the combined form meets the prescribed criteria. The corporation may use and may be legally designated by any such form.

(4) **Alternative name outside Canada** — Subject to subsection 12(1), a corporation may, for use outside Canada, set out its name in its articles in any language form and it may use and may be legally designated by any such form outside Canada.

(5) **Publication of name** — A corporation shall set out its name in legible characters in all contracts, invoices, negotiable instruments and orders for goods or services issued or made by or on behalf of the corporation.

(6) **Other name** — Subject to subsections (5) and 12(1), a corporation may carry on business under or identify itself by a name other than its corporate name if that other name does not contain, other than in a figurative or descriptive sense, either the word or expression "Limited", "Limitée", "Incorporated", "Incorporée", "Corporation" or "Société par actions de régime fédéral" or the corresponding abbreviation.

1992, c. 1, s. 53; 1994, c. 24, s. 5

11. (1) **Reserving name** — The Director may, on request, reserve for ninety days a name for an intended corporation or for a corporation about to change its name.

(2) **Designating number** — f requested to do so by the incorporators or a corporation, the Director shall assign to the corporation as its name a designating number followed by the word "Canada" and a word or expression, or the corresponding abbreviation, referred to in subsection 10(1).

1994, c. 24, s. 6

12. (1) **Prohibited names** — A corporation shall not be incorporated or continued as a corporation under this Act with, have, carry on business under or identify itself by a name

    1. that is, as prescribed, prohibited or deceptively misdescriptive; or

    2. that is reserved for another corporation or intended corporation under section 11.

(2) **Directing change of name** — If, through inadvertence or otherwise, a corporation

    1. comes into existence or is continued with a name, or

    2. on an application to change its name, is granted a name that contravenes this section, the Director may direct the corporation to change its name in accordance with section 173.

(3) Repealed.

(4) **Idem** — If a corporation has a designating number as its name, the Director may direct the corporation to change its name to a name other than a designating number in accordance with section 173.

    (4.1) **Undertaking to change name** — Where a corporation acquires a name as a result of a person undertaking to dissolve or to change names, and the undertaking is not honoured, the Director may direct the corporation to change its name in accordance with section 173, unless the undertaking is honoured within the period specified in subsection (5).

(5) **Revoking name** — When a corporation has been directed under subsection (2), (4) or (4.1) to change its name and has not within sixty days from the service of the directive to that effect changed its name to a name that complies with this Act, the Director may revoke the name of the corporation and assign a name to it and, until changed in accordance with section 173, the name of the corporation is thereafter the name so assigned.

1994, c. 24, s. 7

From the Canada *Business Corporations Regulations*

PART II — CORPORATE NAMES

17. Interpretation — The following definitions apply in this Part.

"confusing" in relation to a corporate name, means a corporate name the use of which causes confusion with a trade-mark, an official mark or a trade-name in the manner described in section 18. *(prête à confusion)*

"corporate name" means the name of a corporation. *(Version anglaise seulement)* "distinctive", in relation to a trade-name, means a trade-name that distinguishes the business in association with which it is used by its owner from any other business or that is adapted so as to distinguish them from each other. *(distinctive)*

"official mark" means an official mark within the meaning of subparagraph 9(1)(n)(iii) of the Trade-marks Act. *(marque officielle)*

"secondary meaning", in relation to a trade-name, means a trade-name that has been used in Canada or elsewhere by an applicant or by their predecessors so as to have become distinctive in Canada as at the date of filing an application for a corporate name. *(sens dérivé)*

"trade-mark" has the same meaning as in section 2 of the Trade-marks Act. *(marque de commerce)*

"trade-name" means the name under which a business is carried on, whether it is a corporate name or the name of a body corporate, a trust, a partnership, a sole proprietorship or an individual. *(dénomination commerciale)*

"use" means actual use by a person that carries on business in Canada or elsewhere. *(emploi)*

18. **Confusion of Names** — A corporate name is confusing with

  1. a trade-mark or an official mark if the use of both the corporate name and either the trade-mark or the official mark, as the case may be, is likely to lead to the inference that the business carried on or intended to be carried on under the corporate name and the business connected with the trade-mark or the official mark, as the case may be, are one business, whether or not the nature of the business of each is generally the same; or

  2. a trade-name if the use of both names is likely to lead to the inference that the business carried on or intended to be carried on under the corporate name and the business carried on under the trade-name are one business, whether or not the nature of the business of each is generally the same.

19. **Consideration of Whole Name** — When determining whether a trade-name is distinctive, the name as a whole and not only its separate elements shall be considered.

20. **Prohibited Names** — For the purpose of paragraph 12(1)(a) of the Act, a corporate name is prohibited in respect of a request to reserve a name or in respect of an application for revival under section 209 of the Act, if it is the same as, or is confusing with, a corporate name that has, before the date of the request, been reserved by the Director for another person, unless

  1. written consent has been obtained from the person for whom the corporate name was reserved; or

  2. the 90-day reservation period referred to in subsection 11(1) of the Act has expired without the person for whom the corporate name was reserved having made a renewed request to reserve the corporate name.

21. For the purpose of paragraph 12(1)(a) of the Act, a corporate name is prohibited if the name contains any of the following elements:

  1. "Air Canada";

  2. "Canada Standard" or "CS";

  3. "cooperative", "coopérative", "co-op" or "pool" when it connotes a cooperative venture;

  4. "Parliament Hill" or "Colline du Parlement";

  5. "Royal Canadian Mounted Police", "Gendarmerie royale du Canada", "RCMP" or "GRC"; or

  6. "United Nations", "Nations Unies", "UN" or "ONU".

22. For the purpose of paragraph 12(1)(a) of the Act, a corporate name is prohibited if it connotes that the corporation

1. carries on business under royal, vice-regal or

2. governmental patronage, approval or authority, unless the appropriate government department or agency consents in writing to the use of the name;

3. is sponsored or controlled by or is connected with

4. the Government of Canada, the government of a province, the government of a country other than Canada or a political subdivision or agency of any such government, unless the appropriate government, political subdivision or agency consents in writing to the use of the name;

5. is sponsored or controlled by or is connected with a

6. university or an association of accountants, architects, engineers, lawyers, physicians or surgeons or another professional association recognized by the laws of Canada or a province, unless the appropriate university or professional association consents in writing to the use of the name; or

7. carries on the business of a bank, a loan company,

8. an insurance company, a trust company, another financial intermediary or a stock exchange that is regulated by a law of Canada or a province, unless the Superintendent of Financial Institutions or the relevant provincial securities regulator consents in writing to the use of the name.

23. For the purpose of paragraph 12(1)(a) of the Act, a corporate name is prohibited if it contains a word or phrase, or connotes a business, that is obscene.

24. (1) For the purpose of paragraph 12(1)(a) of the Act and subject to subsection (2), a corporate name is prohibited if the corporate name is not distinctive because it

1. is only descriptive, in any language, of the business

2. of the corporation, of the goods and services in which the corporation deals or intends to deal, or of the quality, function or other characteristic of those goods and services;

3. is primarily or only the name or surname, used alone,

4. of an individual who is living or has died within 30 years before the date of the request to the Director for that name; or

5. is primarily or only a geographic name, used alone.

(2) Subsection (1) does not apply if a person requesting a corporate name establishes that it has, through use, acquired the name and the name continues at the time of the request to have secondary meaning.

25. For the purpose of paragraph 12(1)(a) of the Act, a corporate name is prohibited if it is confusing, having regard to all the circumstances, including

1. the inherent distinctiveness of the whole or any elements of any trade-mark, official mark or trade-name and the extent to which it has become known;

2. the length of time the trade-mark, official mark or trade-name

3. has been in use;

4. the nature of the goods or services associated with a trade-mark or an official mark, or the nature of the business carried on under or associated with a trade-name, including the likelihood of any competition among businesses using such a trade-mark,

5. official mark or trade-name;

6. the nature of the trade with which a trade-mark, an official mark or a trade-name is associated, including the nature of the products or services and the means by which they are offered or distributed;

7. the degree of resemblance between the proposed corporate name and a trade-mark, an official mark or a trade-name in appearance or sound or in the ideas suggested by them; and

8. the territorial area in Canada in which the proposed corporate name or an existing trade-name is likely to be used.

26. For the purpose of paragraph 12(1)(a) of the Act, a corporate name is prohibited if an element of the name is the family name of an individual, whether or not preceded by their given name or initials, unless the individual or their heir or legal representative consents in writing to the use of their name and the individual has or had a material interest in the corporation.

27. For the purpose of paragraph 12(1)(a) of the Act,

1. a corporate name is prohibited if its use is likely to lead to the inference that the business carried on or intended to be carried on under it and the business of a body corporate that is dissolved are one business, whether or not the nature of their

2. businesses is generally the same; and

3. the name of a corporation that is revived under section 209 of the Act is prohibited if it is confusing with a name acquired by another corporation during the period beginning on the date of dissolution and ending on the date of revival of the revived corporation.

28. For the purpose of paragraph 12(1)(a) of the Act, a corporate name that is confusing with the name of a body corporate that has not carried on business in the two years immediately before the date of a request for the corporate name is prohibited, unless the body corporate that has that name

1. consents in writing to the use of the name, and the name is not otherwise prohibited; and

2. undertakes in writing to dissolve immediately or to change its name before the corporation that proposes to use the name begins to use it, and the name is not otherwise prohibited.

29. For the purpose of paragraph 12(1)(a) of the Act, a corporate name that contains a word that is the same as or similar to the distinctive element of an existing trade-mark, official mark or trade-name and is confusing with one or another of the distinctive elements is prohibited, unless the person who owns the trade-mark, official mark, or trade-name consents in writing to the use of the corporate name, and the name is not otherwise prohibited.

30. (1) For the purpose of paragraph 12(1)(a) of the Act, a corporate name that is confusing with the name of a body corporate is prohibited unless

1. the corporate name is the name of an existing or a proposed corporation that is the successor to the business of the body corporate and the body corporate has ceased or will, in the immediate future, cease to carry on business under that corporate name and undertakes in writing to dissolve or to change its corporate name before the successor corporation begins carrying on business under that corporate name;

2. subject to subsection (2), the corporate name of the existing or proposed corporation sets out in numerals the year of incorporation, or the year of the most recent amendment to the corporate name, in parentheses, immediately before the word or

3. expression "Limited", "Limitée", "Incorporated", "Incorporée", "Corporation", "Société par actions de régime fédéral" or "Société commerciale canadienne" or the abbreviation "Ltd.", "Ltée", "Inc.", "Corp.", "S.A.R.F." or "S.C.C."; and

4. the corporate name is not otherwise prohibited.

(2) The reference in a corporate name to the year of incorporation or the year of the most recent amendment to the corporate name may be deleted two years after its use is introduced, if the corporate name so changed is not confusing.

31. (1) For the purpose of paragraph 12(1)(a) of the Act, if two or more corporations amalgamate, the name of the amalgamated corporation is prohibited if the name is confusing or is otherwise prohibited.

(2) Despite subsection (1), the new corporate name may be the same as the name of one of the amalgamating corporations.

(3) For the purpose of paragraph 12(1)(a) of the Act, if an existing corporation has acquired or will, in the immediate future, acquire all or substantially all of the property of an affiliated body corporate, the use by the corporation of the corporate name of the body corporate is prohibited unless

> 1. the body corporate undertakes in writing to dissolve, or to change its name, before the corporation begins using the corporate name; and
>
> 2. the name is not otherwise prohibited.

(4) For the purpose of paragraph 12(1)(a) of the Act, if a proposed corporation will, in the immediate future, acquire all or substantially all of the property of a body corporate that is to be an affiliate of the proposed corporation, the use by the proposed corporation of the name of the affiliated body corporate is prohibited unless

> 1. the body corporate undertakes in writing to dissolve, or to change its name, before the proposed corporation begins using the corporate name; and
>
> 2. the name is not otherwise prohibited.

32. **Deceptively Misdescriptive Names** — For the purpose of paragraph 12(1)(a) of the Act, a corporate name is deceptively misdescriptive if it is likely to mislead the public, in any language, with respect to

> 1. the business, goods or services in association with which it is proposed to be used;
>
> 2. the conditions under which the goods or services will be produced or supplied or the persons to be employed in the production or supply of the goods or services; or
>
> 3. the place of origin of the goods or services.

33. **Certain Names Not Prohibited** — A corporate name is not prohibited only because it contains alphabetic or numeric characters, initials, punctuation marks or any combination of those elements.

34. **Criteria for English and French Forms** — For the purpose of subsection 10(3) of the Act, a combined English and French form of the name of a proposed corporation shall include only one of the words or expressions listed in subsection 10(1) of the Act.

Annexe B — Sample consent letters

Suggested Consent Form from the Owner of an Unincorporated Trade-name

The Director, Corporations Canada
Industry Canada
9th Floor, Jean Edmonds Towers South
365 Laurier Avenue West
Ottawa ON K1A 0C8

Re: Incorporation of a corporation by the name of

(Incorporating Party's name)

(Consenting party's name), owner of the registered trade-name (enter trade-name), hereby consent to the incorporation of (name of the proposed corporation).

(Consenting party's name) undertakes to stop carrying on business under the trade-name (or to transfer his/her rights in the trade-name to the corporation bearing the proposed name) before the corporation proposing to use the name begins to carry on business under the corporate name.

Consent given at (city), this (date) day of (month), (year).

(Consenting Party's name)

Per: _____

(officer's name), (officer's title)

Note: The signature of the authorized signing officer must describe him/her as an officer of the consenting corporation.

Suggested Consent Form — Regulation 28

The Director, Corporations Canada
Industry Canada
9th Floor, Jean Edmonds Towers South
365 Laurier Avenue West
Ottawa ON K1A 0C8

Re: Incorporation of a corporation by the name of

(Incorporating Party's name)

(Consenting party's name), a body corporate incorporated under the *Canada Business Corporations Act* on the 28th day of June 1990, hereby consents to the incorporation of (name of the proposed corporation).

(Consenting party's name) undertakes to dissolve immediately or to change its name before the corporation proposing to use that name begins to carry on business under that name.

(Consenting party's name) confirms that it has not carried on business under its corporate name during the past two years.

Consent given at (city), this (date) day of (month), (year).

(Consenting Party's name)

Per: _____

(officer's name), (officer's title)

Note: The signature of the authorized signing officer must describe him/her as an officer of the consenting corporation.

Suggested Consent Form — Regulation 29

The Director, Corporations Canada
Industry Canada
9th Floor, Jean Edmonds Towers South
365 Laurier Avenue West
Ottawa ON K1A 0C8

Re: Incorporation of a corporation by the name of

(Incorporating Party's name)

(Consenting party's name, i.e. the name of an incorporated or unincorporated business or the name of the owner of a trade-mark), hereby consents to the incorporation of a corporation in the name of (name of the corporation).

Consent given at (city), this (date) day of (month), (year).

(Consenting Party's name)

Per: _____

(officer's name), (officer's title)

Note: The signature of the authorized signing officer must describe him/her as an officer of the consenting corporation.

Suggested Consent Form — Regulation 30

> The Director, Corporations Canada
> Industry Canada
> 9th Floor, Jean Edmonds Towers South
> 365 Laurier Avenue West
> Ottawa ON K1A 0C8

Re: Incorporation of a corporation by the name of

(Incorporating Party's name)

(Consenting party's name), a body corporate, hereby consents to the incorporation of (name of the proposed corporation), which is to be a successor corporation and which has the year of incorporation in parentheses before the legal element.

(Consenting party's name) undertakes to dissolve immediately or to change its name before the corporation proposing to use that name begins to carry on business under that name.

Consent given at (city), this (date) day of (month), (year).

(Consenting party's name)

Per: _____

(officer's name), (officer's title)

Note: The signature of the authorized signing officer must describe him/her as an officer of the consenting corporation.

Suggested Consent Form — Regulation 31(3)

> The Director, Corporations Canada
> Industry Canada
> 9th Floor, Jean Edmonds Towers South
> 365 Laurier Avenue West
> Ottawa ON K1A 0C8

Re: Incorporation of a corporation by the name of

(Incorporating Party's name)

(Consenting party's name) confirms that the corporation is affiliated to (Consenting party's name) and (has or will immediately) acquire all or substantially all the property of (Consenting party's name). (Consenting party's name) hereby undertakes to dissolve immediately or to change its name before the corporation proposing to use the name begins carrying on business under that name.

Consent given at (city), this (date) day of (month), (year).

(Consenting party's name)

Per: _____

(officer's name), (officer's title)

Note: The signature of the authorized signing officer must describe him/her as an officer of the consenting corporation.

Suggested Consent Form — Regulation 31(4)

The Director, Corporations Canada
Industry Canada
9th Floor, Jean Edmonds Towers South
365 Laurier Avenue West
Ottawa ON K1A 0C8

Re: Incorporation of a corporation by the name of

(Incorporating Party's name)

(Consenting party's name), a body corporate, hereby consents to the incorporation of (name of proposed corporation).

(Consenting party's name) confirms that the proposed corporation will be affiliated to (Consenting party's name) and will immediately acquire substantially all the property of (Consenting party's name). (Consenting party's name) undertakes to dissolve immediately or to change its name before the corporation proposing to use the name begins to carry on business under that name.

Consent given at (city), this (date) day of (month), (year).

(Consenting party's name)

Per: _____

(officer's name), (officer's title)

Note: The signature of the authorized signing officer must describe him/her as an officer of the consenting corporation.

Annexe C — Protecting Your Corporate Name

The granting of a corporate name by the Director under the *Canada Business Corporations Act* (CBCA) generally confers a degree of protection for that corporate name. However, the granting of names under the CBCA does not in itself confer any rights to those names vis-à-vis corporate names or trade-names which may have existed at the time of granting but which did not appear on the NUANS search report or which the Director did not, at the time of granting, consider likely to cause confusion. Similarly, the granting of a corporate name may not protect you from earlier or subsequent trade-marks of other parties.

The following gives a succinct overview of the relationship between trade-name, corporate name and trade-mark rights and some general guidance as to how you can best protect your corporate name and the goodwill associated with it.

1. Before an applicant applies for a corporate name, it is important for him or her to ensure that there are no similar existing corporate names, trade-names or trade-marks. A NUANS search report, including trade-marks which are registered or proposed for registration, is required to be filed with articles of incorporation, amendment, etc. and is usually very reliable. Since, however, the NUANS system is not foolproof, the applicant remains responsible for any likelihood of confusion.

While a name granted by the Director will appear on future NUANS searches required for incorporation in the federal and most provincial jurisdictions, you may wish to conduct your own NUANS searches on a periodic basis after your name has been approved. This would be done in order to ensure, to your own satisfaction, that no confusing corporate or business name has subsequently been approved in the jurisdiction(s) in which you are carrying on business, and to give you up-to-date information about trade-marks that have been applied for or registered subsequent to the granting of your corporate name.

2. Using a corporate name which is similar to a registered trade-mark may result in liability for infringement of the registered trade-mark, even if the trade-mark was registered after the corporate name was granted. This is so because, under trade-marks law, the holder of a corporate name bears the responsibility for ensuring that no new trade-marks are registered which are confusing with that name. Information on registered and advertised trade-marks can be obtained from the *Trade-Marks Journal*, distributed weekly by Supply and Services Canada[3] or by conducting a search of one of the various electronic trade-mark databases. The holder of a corporate name has the right, in certain circumstances, to oppose the registration of a trade-mark or to have a trade-mark registration expunged.

3. Registration of a trade-mark is the best way to obtain the exclusive right to use the mark in all of Canada in association with the wares and services for which the registration is obtained. While the Trade-marks Office[4] can provide basic guidance, it is recommended that a specialist (a trade-mark agent or trade-mark lawyer) be consulted. It should be noted that trade-mark registration is not available for corporate names in all circumstances.

Annexe D — Corporate Name Information Online

For more on name information, see Corporations Canada online through *Corporations Canada Filing Centre*, and click on the section Choosing a name.

Policy Statement 2.1 — Bilingual Form and Bilingualization of Articles

Date: **June 8, 2005**

When filing articles (such as Articles of Incorporation under the *Canada Business Corporations Act*), three linguistic options are available to applicants. Articles may be filed:

1. in a format that uses either official language (i.e., in French or in English);

2. in a format that employs both English and French; or

3. in a fully bilingual format, utilizing both official languages equally.

---

[3]Canada Communications Group — Publishing
45 Sacré-Coeur Blvd.
Hull QC K1A 0S9
Tel.: 1-800-635-7943
Tel.: (819) 956-4800

[4]Trade-Marks Office
Trade-marks Office
Industry Canada
Phase I, Place du Portage
Hull QC K1A 0C9
Tel.: (819) 953-8098 (re: on-line databases)
Tel.: (819) 997-1420 (re: general inquiries)

This means that Form 1 may be submitted:

- in either official language, with the attached schedule(s) in the same language.

- in either official language, with the attached schedule(s) in the other or both official languages.

- in both official languages, with the attached schedule(s) in both official languages.

Note that when a corporate name is being changed to include the name in the other official language, Articles of Amendment must be filed to effect the change. The same linguistic options outlined in the above examples relating to Form 1 are available when filing Articles of Amendment.

In keeping with this policy, applicants wishing to revise their corporate charter by making the articles and schedule(s) available in both official languages may file Restated Articles (Section 180 of the CBCA) at any time. However, if other amendments have already been made to the original Articles of Incorporation, care should be taken to ensure that any amendment(s) is(are) consolidated in the bilingual Restated Articles.

Policy Statement 2.6 — Dating of CBCA Certificates Issued Pursuant to Filing of Articles

Date: September 30, 2002
Revised: January 2, 2007

1. This policy sets out the position of the Director appointed pursuant to the *Canada Business Corporations Act* (CBCA) concerning the dating of CBCA certificates issued pursuant to the filing of articles.

1.1 This policy replaces Director's Policy 2.6 dated September 30, 2002. It reflects the amendments to the CBCA that came into force on November 24, 2001.

1.2 This policy sets out some operating principles and practical guidelines for the purpose of facilitating the application of the provisions related to dating of CBCA certificates pursuant to filing of articles. Although they do not have force of law, these operating principles and guidelines inform the interested parties concerning the relevant provisions. This policy is in no way intended to expand the powers of the Director or of the shareholders or creditors beyond the powers conferred on them under the CBCA. The definitive interpretation of the sections of the CBCA and related provisions is the function of the courts.

1.3 The Director is not bound by this policy in any decision the Director makes in a particular case. Furthermore, this policy cannot substitute for a legal, accounting or commercial opinion or the exercise of professional judgment by legal, accounting and commercial advisors in a particular instance.

1.4 The Director suggests that persons affected by the CBCA provisions concerning dating of CBCA certificates consult legal counsel or other professional advisors.

1.5 It is the Director's opinion that the communication of these operating principles and guidelines to persons affected will help reduce the number of rejected applications and the resulting administrative costs and inconvenience.

1.6 This policy will be amended as needed in light of experience.

2. Pursuant to subsection 262(3), certificates may be dated as of the date of receipt by Corporations Canada or as of any later date specified by the person who signed the articles or statement for which the application is made.

3. *Certificates will not be backdated prior to the original date of receipt of the application.*

   3.1 The only exception that the CBCA permits is for a certificate of discontinuance for an exporting corporation which may be dated as of the day on which the corporation is continued. (CBCA ss. 262(5))

4. The Act does not specify what will be the effective date of the certificate when the original application is *rejected* and *resubmitted*. The policy of the Director is as follows:

   4.1 Where articles must be rejected, the original date of filing will normally be lost.

   4.2 On resubmission of the amended application (articles), the certificate will normally bear the date of resubmission as the effective date, except for an online resubmission, which has a default date of the original filing date.

   4.3 The original filing date cannot be preserved when an application is rejected for being incomplete. In other words, the original effective date is forfeited. An application is incomplete if it does not have all the necessary forms and schedules attached and is not signed. Examples of incomplete applications include Form 2: Initial Registered Office Address and First Board of Directors being missing from an application for incorporation, or item 4 of Form 1: Articles of Incorporation indicating that the information is on Schedule 1 and there is no such schedule. In this case, a notice will be sent to the applicant indicating that the application is incomplete.

   4.4 Where an application is complete, but is rejected for being deficient (e.g., missing a consent for a corporate name), the effective date of the certificate can be the date of receipt of the original application if the applicant expressly requests this date when the application is resubmitted with the deficiency corrected.

5. Since a NUANS® search report is only valid for 90 days from the date of the search report, if a later date is requested and is within the 90 day validity period of the NUANS® search report, or where no NUANS® search report is required to be filed, the certificate may be issued and sent out bearing the later date.

   5.1 If the later date requested is beyond the 90 day validity period of the NUANS® search report, the certificate bearing the requested date will not be issued. The certificate can only be issued when a subsequent NUANS® search report, which has a validity period beyond the effective date, indicates that the proposed name is available. In these cases, any indication of approval by the Director of the application at the time of the request is *SUBJECT TO THE PROPOSED NAME BEING AVAILABLE AT THE EFFECTIVE TIME.*

   5.2 Applicants should note that in the case of an amalgamation the statutory declaration required by subsection 185(2) must be dated less than two weeks before any later effective date requested. In the case of an import continuance from another jurisdiction, please note that an authorization from the exporting jurisdiction, where required, will have to be valid as of the later effective date requested. Some such authorizations have a limited life.

Additional Information and How to reach Corporations Canada

For additional information on Corporations Canada's products and services, please visit Corporations Canada's website or call 1-866-333-5556.

You can also contact Corporations Canada at:

Client Services Section
Corporations Canada
Industry Canada
9th floor, Jean Edmonds Tower South
Ottawa, Ontario K1A 0C8
Fax: 613-941-0601
www.corporationscanada.ic.gc.ca

Policy Statement 2.7 — Requests for Correction of CBCA Certificates

Date: **November 19, 2003**

1. — Introduction and Statement of General Principles

1.1 Corporations Canada often receives requests for the correction of articles and certificates (collectively, the "certificates") that have already been filed or issued. This policy sets out the position of the Director as to these corrections only. The correction of notices and other documents that have already been filed is the subject of a separate policy.

1.2 In order to assist corporations and other interested persons, this policy sets forth certain policy and practice guidelines aimed at facilitating corrections. While this policy and the practice guidelines set out herein do not have the force of law, they do reflect the Director's understanding of the Director's role in correcting certificates. The final interpretation of sub-section 265(3) of the *Canada Business Corporation Act* (the "Act") and related provisions is the function of the courts.

1.3 The Director considers that, by communicating these guidelines to corporations and other interested persons who are considering corrections to a certificate, the instances of rejected requests and the cost and administrative inconvenience thereby encountered can be reduced.

1.4 Nothing in this policy is intended to constitute a binding statement of what position the Director will take with respect to any particular request for a corrected certificate. In addition, this policy is not intended to be a substitute for professional legal, accounting or business advice or for the exercise of professional judgment by legal, accounting and business advisors in any particular instance.

1.5 The Director may also initiate corrections of certificates. In doing so, the Director may require the directors or shareholders of the corporation to pass the necessary resolutions, send to the Director the necessary documents to effect the correction and take such other steps as the Director may reasonably require so that the Director may correct the certificate.

2. — Where the Error is Obvious or the Error was Made Solely Within the Director's Office

2.1 In some cases, an error may be obvious. For example, the certificate does not make sense as it stands and it is evident what was intended, for instance, when a corporate name is misspelled as in "ABC Disbibutors Ltd./Distributeurs ABC Ltée."

In these cases, the Director's intention is to correct the certificate upon receipt of:

a. a written request for correction from the corporation or any other interested person;

b. the original Certificate with replacement pages;

c. (where the error relates to a corporate name), a statutory declaration of a director or officer stating that, to the best of his or her knowledge after diligent enquiry,

- the corporation has not executed any security agreements or other documents using its incorrect name, and

- no filings have been made under any personal property security legislation in Canada, against the incorrect corporate name.

d. the applicable fee, payable to the Receiver General for Canada.

2.2 Errors may also occur solely within the Director's office. In these cases, the Director's intention is to correct the certificate upon receipt of:

a. a written request for correction from the corporation or any other interested person;

b. the original certificate with replacement pages;

c. a declaration to the effect that the certificate has not yet been used or relied on, or (where the error relates to a corporate name), a statutory declaration of a director or officer stating that, to the best of his or her knowledge after diligent enquiry,

- the corporation has not executed any security agreements or other documents using its incorrect name, and

- no filings have been made under any personal property security legislation in Canada, against the incorrect corporate name.

d. (if deemed necessary by the Director), additional documentation, providing assurance that the correction would not prejudice any of the shareholders or creditors of the corporation; and

e. there is no fee when the correction is required solely as the result of an error made by the Director.

3. — Where the Error is Not Obvious From the Certificate Itself or Was Not Made Solely Within the Director's Office

3.1 In these cases, in response to a request for correction, the Director has the sole discretion to correct a certificate. The Director may make the correction but only if:

a. the correction is approved by the directors of the corporation (or the shareholders acting pursuant to a unanimous shareholder agreement or the incorporators where no directors have yet been appointed); and

b. the Director is satisfied that:

i. the correction would not prejudice any of the shareholders or creditors of the corporation; and

ii. the correction reflects the original intention of the corporation or the incorporators, as the case may be.

3.2 In exercising discretion, the Director expects to receive:

a. a written request for correction from the corporation or other interested person;

b. the original certificate together with corrected replacement pages where applicable;

c. a current certified copy of a resolution of the directors (or statutory declaration of the incorporators) which includes recitals or statements of the following:

i. an error was made, and an explanation as to how the error was made;

ii. removal of the error by articles of amendment or other available means would cause undue hardship;

iii. no shareholders or creditors would be adversely affected by the correction and the correction reflects the original intention of the corporation or the incorporators, as the case may be;

iv. information regarding who the shareholders were before (if the correction relates to corporate finance) and after issue of the certificate and the number of shares they held before and after; and

v. (where the correction relates to a corporate name or effective date only), no use has been made of the incorrect name or effective date or, if it has, appending documentary consent to the correction from anyone dealing with the corporation on the basis of the corporate name or effective date;

d. (where the error relates to the corporate name), a statutory declaration of a director or officer stating that, to the best of his or her knowledge after diligent enquiry,

- the corporation has not executed any security agreements or other documents using its incorrect name, and

- no filings have been made under any personal property security legislation in Canada, against the incorrect corporate name.

e. (where the certificate to be corrected was issued over two years prior to the request for correction and only if deemed necessary by the Director), a resolution of shareholders authorizing the correction;

f. a certified copy of the original resolution which authorized the intended amendment (or other fundamental change) incorrectly reflected in the certificate;

g. (if deemed necessary by the Director), additional documentation providing assurance that the correction will not prejudice any of the shareholders or creditors of the corporation, and that the correction reflects the original intention of the corporation or the incorporators, as the case may be;

h. (where the error was made, not by the corporation itself but by its representative to whom it had given correct instructions), the Director may, at the Director's sole discretion, correct the document upon receipt of all documents noted in paragraph 3.2 (a)–(f) above, and:

i. a statutory declaration of the representative indicating the instructions received and the reasons why those instructions were not reflected in the certificate; or

ii. a statutory declaration of an officer of the corporation explaining why it is not possible to obtain (i) above, the instructions given to the representative and why instructions were not reflected in the certificate; and

i. the applicable fee payable to the Receiver General for Canada.

3.3 The Director will review documentation referred to in paragraph 3.2 with a view to determining that neither shareholders nor creditors will be adversely affected by the retroactive correction and that the correction reflects the original intention of the corporation or the incorporators, as the case may be. The Director will not correct errors in judgment but only where the wording used in the articles was not the wording that the applicant, with the advice of any representative, intended to use.

4. — Payment

4.1 Payment of any applicable fee may be made by credit card (Visa™ or MasterCard™ or American Express™), by cheque payable to the Receiver General for Canada, or by a deposit account maintained within Corporations Canada at the time of filing.

4.2 Information on fees for other filing, examination, or copying of documents or action by the Director may be found on Corporation Canada's Web site.

5. — Date of Corrected Certificate

5.1 A corrected Certificate shall bear the date of the document it replaces. However, if a correction is made with respect to the date of the document, the document shall bear the corrected date.

6. — Application to Court and Appeal

6.1 If the Director is not satisfied that a correction will not prejudice any of the shareholders or creditors, the Director, the corporation or any interested person may apply to the court for an order that the certificate be corrected and an order determining the rights of the shareholders or creditors.

6.2 Alternatively, an interested person who feels aggrieved by a decision by the Director to correct or refuse to correct a certificate under section 265, may, pursuant to paragraph 246(f.1) of the Act, apply to a court for an order requiring the Director to change the decision. The court has the power to order a change in the Director's decision.

7. — Notice

7.1 Where a corrected certificate materially amends the terms of the original certificate, the Director will, without delay, give a notice of this correction on Corporation Canada's Web site.

8. — Reference

8.1 CBCA, s. 265

9. — Additional information and how to contact Corporations Canada

9.1 Information on incorporation is available online. You may also contact Corporations Canada at:

> Information Unit
> Corporations Canada
> Industry Canada
> 9th Floor, Jean Edmonds Towers South
> 365, Laurier Avenue West
> Ottawa ON K1A 0C8
> Telephone: (613) 941-9042
> Toll-free: 1 866 333-5556
> Fax: (613) 941-0601

Policy Statement 2.7.1 — Requests for Correction of CBCA Forms 2, 3, 6 and 22

Date: January 26, 2006

1. — Introduction and Statement of General Principles

1.1 Corporations Canada receives requests for the correction of Forms 2, 3, 6 and 22 that have already been filed. This policy sets out the position of the Director on these corrections.

The correction of certificates that have been issued pursuant to articles filed under the Act is the subject of a separate policy.

1.2 In order to assist corporations and other interested persons, this policy sets forth certain policy and practice guidelines aimed at facilitating corrections. While this policy and the practice guidelines set out herein do not have the force of law, they do reflect the Director's understanding of the Director's role in correcting Forms 2, 3, 6 and 22. The final interpretation of the *Canada Business Corporations Act* (the "Act") in respect of such corrections is the function of the courts.

1.3 The Director considers that, by communicating these guidelines to corporations and other interested persons who are considering corrections to Forms 2, 3, 6 and 22, the instances of rejected requests and the cost and administrative inconvenience thereby encountered can be reduced.

1.4 Nothing in this policy is intended to constitute a binding statement of what position the Director will take with respect to any particular request for correction of a Form 2, 3, 6 or 22. In addition, this policy is not intended to be a substitute for professional legal, accounting or business advice or for the exercise of professional judgment by legal, accounting and business advisors in any particular instance.

2. — Policy on Correction of CBCA Certificates Does Not Apply

2.1 The Director's policy on the Correction of CBCA Certificates will not be applied to the correction of Forms 2, 3, 6, and 22. Since certificates are statutory instruments and have legal effect as such, and since the objective of Forms 2, 3, 6 and 22 is to provide information, the practical necessity for section 265 to be used to correct Forms 2, 3, 6 and 22 is much less than the need for it to be used to correct certificates.

3. — Forms 2, 3 and 6

3.1 If the public record incorrectly states a corporation's registered office or directors, the quickest and easiest way to correct the public record is for the corporation to file a new Form 3 or 6 setting out the correct information.

3.2 It is in the interest of the corporation to file another Form 3 or 6. Until the registered office and directors are accurately reflected on the public record, a member of the public will be relying on inaccurate information on the public record.

3.3 All Forms 3 and 6 that are filed are considered to be notices of change of information and not as corrections within the meaning of section 265.

3.4 Where a director has resigned or has been erroneously named on Form 2 or 6 and the corporation refuses to file a new Form 6 with accurate information, the incorrectly listed director has a number of remedies under the Act including obtaining a court order directing the corporation to file a Form 6 under subsection 113(2), a court order correcting the last Form 2 or 6 filed under subsection 265(4), a compliance order under section 247, or an oppression remedy under section 241.

3.5 The Director prefers not to be made a party to applications to court for the rectification of records in respect of directors. The more practical solution would be for the applicant to ask the court for an order directing the corporation to file a new Form 2 or 6 with the Director.

3.6 An individual who takes the position that he or she is not a director of a particular corporation has an opportunity to send a statement to that effect to the Director which will become part of the public record.

4. — Form 22

4.1 Unlike Forms 2, 3 and 6, there is no statutory basis for an outsider to rely on information contained in a filed Form 22. The Director therefore will accept an amended Form 22, identified as an amendment, which serves the purpose of correcting any information set out in a previously filed Form 22. When filing an amended Form 22, no additional fee is required.

5. — Retention of documents

5.1 All Forms 2, 3, 6 and 22 previously filed will not be removed from the corporation's file maintained by Corporations Canada. Please note, however, that the Director is not required to provide any documents which have been filed more than six years before a request for a copy is made.

Additional information regarding Corporations Canada's services is available our website. You may also contact Corporations Canada at:

Enquiries Unit

Corporations Canada

Industry Canada

9th Floor, Jean Edmonds Towers South

365 Laurier Avenue West

Ottawa, Ontario

K1A 0C8

Telephone: (613) 941-9042

Toll free: 1-866-333-5556

Fax: (613) 941-0601

Policy Statement 2.8 — Cancellation of CBCA Certificates and Related Articles

Date: November 19, 2003

1. — Introduction and Statement of General Principles

1.1 Corporations Canada undertakes the cancellation of articles and related certificates from time to time, in response to:

a. administrative errors;

b. cases in which the Director lacked the authority to issue a certificate; and

c. other circumstances such as a cancellation ordered by a court.

1.2 In order to assist corporations and other interested persons, this policy sets forth certain policy and practice guidelines aimed at facilitating cancellations. While the policy and the practice guidelines set out herein do not have the force of law, they do reflect the Director's understanding of the Director's role in cancelling certificates and related articles. The final interpretation of section 265.1 of the *Canada Business Corporations Act* (the "Act") and related provisions is the function of the courts.

1.3 The Director considers that, by communicating these guidelines to corporations and other interested persons who are considering cancelling a certificate and related articles, the instances of rejected requests and the cost and administrative inconvenience thereby encountered can be reduced.

1.4 Nothing in this policy is intended to constitute a binding statement of what position the Director will take with respect to any particular request for a cancellation. In addition, this policy is not intended to be a substitute for professional legal, accounting or business advice or for the exercise of professional judgment by legal, accounting and business advisors in any particular instance.

1.5 The cancellation of a certificate and related articles may be undertaken on the initiative of the Director. In that case, the Director must be satisfied that the cancellation would not prejudice any of the shareholders or creditors of the corporation.

1.6 The cancellation may also be undertaken upon the request of the corporation or any other interested person. In that case:

a. the cancellation must be approved by the directors of the corporation (or the shareholders acting pursuant to a unanimous shareholder agreement); and

b. the Director must be satisfied that the cancellation:

i. would not prejudice any of the shareholders or creditors of the corporation; or

ii. reflects the original intention of the corporation or the incorporators, as the case may be.

1.7 If the applicable requirements in paragraph 5 or 6 above are satisfied, cancellations may be effected as follows:

2. — Cancellation on the Initiative of the Director

2.1 The Act specifically allows the Director to cancel certificates and related articles that have been incorrectly issued. For example, the Director might cancel a certificate that was issued by Corporations Canada to a dissolved corporation or to a financial corporation that is not allowed to be incorporated under the Act.

2.2 The Director may cancel the certificate and related articles of a corporation if:

a. the error is obvious on the face of the articles or certificate;

b. the error was made solely by the Director;

c. the cancellation is ordered by a court; or

d. the Director lacked the authority to issue the certificate.

2.3 In these cases, the Director's intention is to cancel the Certificate upon receipt of:

a. a written acknowledgement of the need for correction from the corporation or any other interested person;

b. the original Certificate with replacement pages;

c. a declaration to the effect that the Certificate has not yet been used or relied on,

or

if deemed necessary by the Director, a statutory declaration of a director or officer stating that, to the best of his or her knowledge, after diligent inquiry, the corporation has not executed any security agreements or other documents using the incorrect name, and no filings have been made under any personal property security legislation in Canada, against the incorrect corporate name.

d. additional documentation, if deemed necessary by the Director, providing assurance that the correction would not prejudice any of the shareholders or creditors of the corporation.

3. — Cancellation at the Request of a Corporation or Other Interested Person

3.1 The cancellation of articles and related certificates may be undertaken at the discretion of the Director upon request of a corporation or any other interested person. The Director expects to receive appropriate documentary evidence including:

    a. a written request for the cancellation from the corporation or other interested person;

    b. a certified copy of a resolution of the directors of the corporation (or the shareholders acting pursuant to a unanimous shareholder agreement, or a statutory declaration of the incorporator(s) where no organizational meeting has been held) approving the cancellation and stating:

        i. that there is no dispute among the directors or shareholders of the corporation about this request;

        ii. if applicable,that the corporation did not authorize the filing of the articles that were filed;

        iii. that the cancellation reflects the original intention of the corporation or the incorporators, as the case may be;

        iv. that the articles were filed in error;

        v. how the error was made;

        vi. if applicable, the effects of cancellation on share ownership by shareholders of the corporation;

        vii. that removal of the error by articles of amendment would cause undue hardship;

        viii. that no shareholders or creditors would be adversely affected by the correction;

        ix. if applicable, information regarding who the directors and shareholders were before and after issue of the certificate and the number of shares they held before and after; and

        x. that the certificate has not yet been used or relied on, or if it has, documentary consent to the cancellation from anyone dealing with the corporation on the basis of the articles and related certificate;

    c. deemed necessary by the Director, a statutory declaration of a director or officer stating that, to the best of his or her knowledge, after diligent inquiry, the corporation has not executed any security agreements or other documents using its incorrect name, and no filings have been made under any personal property security legislation in Canada, against the incorrect corporate name;

    d. the original certificate, attached articles and any certified copies of the original certificate and articles in the possession of the applicant; and:

    e. in cases where the error was made, not by the corporation itself but by its representative to whom it had given correct instructions, the Director will, at her/his discretion, undertake the requested cancellation upon receipt of all documents noted in paragraph section 3 of this policy, and:

        i. a statutory declaration of the representative indicating the instructions received and the reasons why those instructions were not reflected in the articles; or

        ii. a statutory declaration of an officer of the company explaining why it is not possible to obtain (i) above, the instructions given to the representative, and why instructions were not reflected in the articles.

3.2 Each case will be considered on its merits. The Director has discretion to require additional documentation he/she deems necessary.

3.3 The Director will review the documentation referred to in paragraphs 3.1and 3.2 with a view to determining that neither shareholders nor creditors will be adversely affected by the cancellation and that the cancellation reflects the original intention of the corporation or the incorporators, as the case may be.

3.4 The Director has no discretion to authorize a refund of the filing fee for the certificate that has been cancelled.

4. — Application to Court and Appeal

4.1 If cancellation is found to prejudice any of the shareholders or creditors, the Director, the corporation or any interested person may apply to the court for the cancellation and an order determining the rights of the shareholders or creditors.

4.2 Alternatively, an interested person who feels aggrieved by a decision by the Director to cancel, or to refuse to cancel, the articles and related certificate under section 265.1, may, pursuant to paragraph 246(f.2) of the Act, apply to a court for an order requiring the Director to change the decision. The court has the power to order a change in the Director's decision.

5. — References

5.1 CBCA s. 265.1; CBCR s. 90

6. — Additional information

6.1 Information on incorporation is available on-line. You may also contact Corporations Canada at:

Information Unit
Corporations Canada
Industry Canada
9th Floor, Jean Edmonds Towers South
365, Laurier Avenue West
Ottawa ON K1A 0C8
Telephone: (613) 941-9042
Toll-free: 1 866 333-5556
Fax: (613) 941-0601

Policy Statement 3.1 — Incorporation Kit

Date: **May 25, 2006**
Revised: **January 2, 2007**

This kit is intended only as a guide to users; it does not replace or take precedence over the CBCA.

Why use this kit?

The purpose of this kit is to help you submit an application to incorporate a business under the CBCA. By ensuring that you provide all the required information with your initial application, you can help Corporations Canada process your incorporation documents swiftly.

In this kit, you will find:

- general information about the role of Corporations Canada;
- information about what information must be provided to Corporations Canada in order to obtain a Certificate of Incorporation;
- information concerning the various ways that an application can be filed;
- information about choosing a name;
- the forms to use for incorporating and suggestions about how to fill out key parts of Forms 1 and 2.

  Note that all the forms can be obtained at the following address: www.corporationscanada.ic.gc.ca;
- how to reach Corporations Canada.

We suggest that you consult with legal counsel or other professional advisers to consider other features that might be desirable in your corporate structure or to advise you on choosing a name or trade mark for your corporation.

What documents must be filed in order to obtain a Certificate of Incorporation?

An application for a Certificate of Incorporation must include the following documents:

- Form 1: Articles of Incorporation;
- Form 2: Initial Registered Office Address and First Board of Directors;
- If you requested prior approval of your name: the letter from the Director appointed under the CBCA (Director) approving your name (please enclose a copy of the NUANS® report);
- If you did not request prior approval of your name: a NUANS® report not more than 90 days old as well as information pertinent to the name. If you are requesting a numbered name, it is not necessary to file a NUANS® report;
- Payment of the $250 filing fee, *or $200 if the transaction is completed through the Corporations Canada Online Filing Centre.*

There is no requirement that any form of "proof of facts" (such as affidavits) be submitted with Articles of Incorporation. It is the responsibility of the applicant, not the Director, to verify that the contents of the articles meet all requirements of the CBCA.

What does Corporations Canada do?

Corporations Canada will check that your articles are complete and in proper form, and that the proposed name is acceptable. If so, the Director will issue a Certificate of Incorporation showing the date of receipt of your articles as the effective date of incorporation. If you prefer, you may request a later incorporation date instead.

A notice setting out your corporation's name and incorporation date and other information will appear on Corporations Canada's Website.

Please note that Corporations Canada processes applications for incorporation within established timeframes, based on the method by which documents are submitted. For more information on this point, please consult Corporations Canada's Website under the heading "General Information / Services and Contacts".

What happens when an application for incorporation is deficient or incomplete?

Applications for incorporation that are deficient or incomplete will be returned to the applicant with a deficiency notice stating the nature of the deficiency.

The original filing date cannot be preserved when an application is rejected for being incomplete. In other words, the original effective date is forfeited. An application is incomplete if it does not have all the necessary forms and schedules attached and is not signed. Examples of incomplete applications include Form 2: Initial Registered Office Address and First Board of Directors being missing from an application for incorporation, or item 4 of Form 1: Articles of Incorporation indicating that the information is on Schedule 1 and there is no such schedule. In this case, a notice will be sent to the applicant indicating that the application is incomplete.

Where an application is complete, but is rejected for being deficient (e.g., missing a consent for a corporate name), the effective date of the certificate can be the date of receipt of the original application if the applicant expressly requests this date when the application is re-submitted with the deficiency corrected.

The fee will be returned if you advise the Director in writing that you are withdrawing your application.

How to file your Articles of Incorporation and pay the fees

Online Incorporation

You can file the documents needed to incorporate your business on line, at Corporations Canada's Online Filing Centre at *www.corporationscanada.ic.gc.ca*. Please refer to the website for the procedures for incorporation. The fee is $200 payable by credit card (American Express®, MasterCard® or Visa®).

The certificate of Incorporation will be sent to you by e-mail in PDF format.

By Fax

You can also file the Articles of Incorporation and the necessary documents by fax at 613-941-0999. Please note that the forms may be signed by reproducing a hand-written signature or in digital format. The $250 fee must be paid by credit card (American Express®, Master-Card® or Visa®) or deposit to an account opened with Industry Canada.

The Certificate of Incorporation will be sent to you by fax.

By Mail Or Courier

You can file the necessary documents and pay the $250 fee by sending them to the following address:

> Corporations Canada
> Industry Canada
> 9th floor, Jean Edmonds Tower South
> 365 Laurier Avenue West
> Ottawa, Ontario K1A 0C8

The $250 fee must be paid by cheque payable to the Receiver General for Canada, by credit card (American Express®, MasterCard® or Visa®) or by deposit to an account opened with Industry Canada.

The Certificate of Incorporation will be sent to you by mail or by the delivery method requested.

In Person

You may attend in person and file a maximum of 4 applications for incorporation, from Monday to Friday, between 8:30 a.m. and 2:30 p.m., at:

> Corporations Canada
> Industry Canada
> 9th floor, Jean Edmonds Tower South
> 365 Laurier Avenue West
> Ottawa, Ontario K1A 0C8

You must have with you all the necessary documents. The $250 fee must be paid in cash, by cheque payable to the Receiver General for Canada, by credit card (American Express®, MasterCard® or Visa®) or by deposit to an account opened with Industry Canada.

You will be given the Certificate of Incorporation.

Regional Offices

If you have received prior approval for your name, or if you are requesting a numbered name, you can send the necessary documents, with your fee to one of the following regional offices:

> *Toronto*
>
> > Corporations Canada
> > Industry Canada
> > 3rd floor, 151 Yonge Street
> > Toronto, Ontario M5C 2W7
> > Telephone: 416-954-2714
> > Fax: 416-973-8714
>
> *Vancouver*
>
> > Corporations Canada
> > Industry Canada
> > 2000-300 West Georgia Street
> > Vancouver, B.C. V6B 6E1
> > Telephone: 604-666-9875
> > Fax: 604-666-4274
>
> *Montreal*
>
> > Corporations Canada
> > Industry Canada
> > 5 Place Ville-Marie
> > 7th floor, Suite 700
> > Montreal, Quebec H3B 2G2
> > Telephone: 514-496-1797
> > Fax: 514-283-2247

The $250 fee must be paid by cheque payable to the Receiver General for Canada, by credit card (American Express®, MasterCard® or Visa®) or by deposit to an account opened with Industry Canada.

You will be given the Certificate of Incorporation.

The first step for incorporation: Choosing a name

The name that you propose must be approved by the Director. The Director will examine your application to verify that it meets the requirements of the CBCA and the Regulations. The name proposed must be distinctive, must not cause confusion with any existing name or trade-mark used in Canada, and must not be prohibited or misleading.

You may request approval of the name

- before filing the Articles of Incorporation
- when you file the Articles of Incorporation

How to submit an application for a name decision to the Director

Whether you apply for pre-approval or request approval when you file the Articles of Incorporation, you are responsible for providing all of the facts relevant to the name you are proposing, as well as a NUANS® report.

Information Relevant To The Name Proposed

You *must submit* the information relating to the circumstances that led to your choosing the name in question to the Director *in writing*. You can use the *Corporate Name Information Form*, or you can submit a letter to the Director describing your corporation's activities and addressing the following points:

- WHAT TYPE OF BUSINESS will the proposed corporation conduct? How is this dissimilar to the activities of existing businesses with similar names? Even if your NUANS® report does not turn up names that appear to be similar to yours, the Director still needs this information to ensure that your proposed name does not suggest government sponsorship or that the proposed corporation will be carrying on the business of a bank or a trust, loan or insurance company, or merely describe, or misdescribe the business of your corporation.
- WHERE will the proposed corporation carry on its business? You must show that this territory is not the same as that of other businesses with similar names and similar activities.
- WITH WHAT TYPE OF CLIENTS will the proposed corporation conduct business (e.g., retailers, computer programmers, general public)? Indicate whether they are different from the types of people with whom existing businesses with similar names, engaging in similar activities and operating in the same territory will do business.
- What is the DERIVATION OF THE DISTINCTIVE ELEMENT(S) of the proposed name? For example, what is the derivation of the word "Amtech" in the name "Amtech Enterprises Inc."? If you have a valid reason for wanting that distinctive element, the Director is less likely to conclude that you may be trying to trade on the goodwill of an existing business with a similar name.
- Is the proposed corporation RELATED to existing businesses with similar names or trade-marks? If so, you need the consent of their owners in writing.
- Does the proposed corporation have a FOREIGN PARENT with a similar name that carries on business or is known in Canada? If so, you need consent in writing, and you must add (CANADA) or OF CANADA to the proposed name.
- Did you make an EARLIER RESERVATION of a name similar to another name on the NUANS® report? Your request may be denied if it appears that an earlier reservation for the same name has been made by someone else.

- Are you enclosing the CONSENT IN WRITING OF AN INDIVIDUAL WHOSE NAME APPEARS in the corporate name (other than an incorporator of the proposed corporation)? The consenting individual must also indicate that he or she has or had a material interest in the proposed corporation.

If you are satisfied that your corporate name is not likely to cause confusion, outline in your letter to the Director the arguments on which you have based your conclusion.

NUANS® Report

You must provide a search, that is, a NUANS® report under the federal rules for determining whether the name you are proposing is available. A NUANS® report is a five-page document setting out the business names (3 pages) and trade-marks registered in Canada (2 pages) that sound or look similar to the name you are proposing. The list is drawn from a national data bank of existing and reserved trade names as well as trade-marks that have been registered and applied for in Canada.

A NUANS® report may be obtained in two ways:

1. A NUANS® report may be requested from a private company known as a search house. You can find a list of these firms on Corporations Canada's Website at *www.corporationscanada.ic.gc.ca* by following the links "Online Filing" and "Corporations Canada Online Filing Centre", or in the Yellow Pages of your telephone directory under INCORPORATING COMPANIES, INCORPORATION NAME SEARCH, SEARCHERS OF RECORDS or TRADE MARK AGENTS — REGISTERED. There is a fee for this service.

2. A NUANS® report may be ordered on-line at the Corporations Canada Online Filing Centre, at *www.corporationscanada.ic.gc.ca* from the NUANS® Real-Time System. The fee is $20 payable by credit card (American Express®, MasterCard® or Visa®). The system provides direct access to the NUANS® search service but does not provide the professional assistance and recommendations often available from a registered NUANS® search house. Applicants should note that a NUANS® report that is generated may be rejected if the proposed name does not meet the requirements of the CBCA name regulations.

When you order a NUANS® report, that report has a life of 90 days from the date it is requested. A search house can advise you whether your proposed name is likely to be accepted by the Director. The final decision, however, always rests with the Director.

If you intend to do business in the Province of Quebec: Please note that the Province of Quebec does not currently provide corporate name data to NUANS®. It is your responsibility to search the Quebec corporations' database (CIDREQ) to verify that the chosen corporate name is not used in Quebec by another business. You do not have to provide a CIDREQ report with your Articles of Incorporation.

NUANS® Report: Special Cases

Numbered name

Instead of a name, you may ask the Director to assign your proposed corporation a number. Some incorporators do this when they have to incorporate a corporation urgently and do not have enough time to have a name approved. A numbered name must be requested when the Articles of Incorporation are submitted and the applicable fee paid. Obviously you do not submit a NUANS® report.

If you subsequently wish to adopt a trade name, you will have to order a NUANS® report, ask the Director to approve the name and pay a $200 fee for filing Form 4: Articles of Amendment to change the corporation's name.

Bilingual name

If your proposed corporation intends to carry on business in a region or regions where both English and French are spoken, you may wish to consider adopting a bilingual corporate name.

The procedure is the same as for a unilingual name, except that one NUANS® report is required for each name or variation requested. For example, two NUANS® reports must be filed in order to verify that the phonetically dissimilar English and French forms of a name are both distinctive.

Where the English and French forms are phonetically similar except for a legal element (e.g., Ltd./Ltée), only one NUANS® report will be necessary.

Decision of the Director

If your request for pre-approval is accepted, the name in question will be reserved for you for the life of the search report. If the Director has not made a decision within that 90-day period, you will have to submit a fresh request to reserve a name by ordering another NUANS® report.

If you have requested pre-approval and the Director's decision is favourable, your Articles of Incorporation will probably be processed promptly when you file them, provided that all other relevant information is submitted at the same time. Remember to include the letter approving your name when you submit your Articles of Incorporation.

If your proposed name is not available, you can still submit a written request for the Director to reexamine the decision, having regard to the additional information. However, you will save time and money if you include all relevant information in your initial application.

Where to submit a request for approval of a name

A request for pre-approval may be made on-line at Corporations Canada's Online Filing Centre at *www.corporationscanada.ic.gc.ca*. Please refer to the Web site for the procedures.

As well, you can submit your request for pre-approval by fax, mail or in person. Requests for pre-approval may not be obtained from the regional offices.

Please refer to the item HOW TO FILE YOUR ARTICLES OF INCORPORATION AND PAY THE FEES on page 2 of this kit for contact information.

No fee is payable for a request for approval of a name.

How to fill out Form 1: Articles of Incorporation

Please see Form 1 for complete instructions on how to fill out the Articles of Incorporation.

Item 1 — Corporation name

- Write in the proposed name.

If the name has been pre-approved, attach the letter of approval with your Articles of Incorporation. If you are not doing that, or if the name was not examined before you file the Articles of Incorporation, the name will have to be approved when they are filed.

- If you are incorporating under a numbered name to be assigned by the Director, leave a blank space on the left, write in the word "Canada," and add the legal element of your choice, such as Inc., Ltd., Corp., etc.

  Example:

  .... CANADA Inc.

- If you are incorporating under a bilingual name, the English and French forms must be entered here.

  Example:

  CARS ABC Inc.
  AUTOS ABC Inc.

Item 2 — The province or territory in Canada in which the registered office is situated

- Enter only the province or territory in Canada in which the registered office is to be situated. Do not enter to street address of the registered office. The street address is provided using Form 2: Initial Registered Office Address and First Board of Directors.

Item 3 — Description of the classes of shares

The CBCA sets out certain requirements for details regarding shares, including the following:

- All shares must be without nominal or par value.
- The CBCA gives incorporators broad discretion to designate a class of shares as common, preferred or Class A or B shares, or any other designation. Some incorporators designate classes of shares simply as Class A, Class B and "other".
- You do not need to place a limit on the number of shares that the corporation is authorized to issue.
- You do not need to specify a maximum aggregate consideration for the issuance of shares.
- Restrictions may be placed on any class of shares.

Where there is more than one class of shares, the rights, privileges, restrictions and conditions attaching to each class must be specified. At least one class of shares is to be voting, there must be a class that carries the right to receive dividends and one class that carries the right to receive the remaining property of the corporation on dissolution. If only one class of shares is created, that class will carry all those rights.

The Articles of Incorporation may authorize the issuance of certain classes of shares in a series. In that case, the Articles may also fix the number of shares in a class and determine the rights attaching to them, unless, before the shares in a series are issued at a later date, the Director prepares amending clauses specifying the number, rights, privileges and restrictions attaching to the series before it is issued and files those clauses with the Director.

The following sample clauses are often used by incorporators and are acceptable to the Director to cover some very basic kinds of shares. The corporation may choose to issue one class of shares only. If two or more classes of shares are issued, you must specify the rights, privileges, restrictions and conditions attaching to each class.

You may vary the composition and complexity of share structures for particular situations in countless ways. The clauses given here are only examples of the most common kinds of share structures used by many incorporators; and *they are by no means mandatory or exhaustive*. You may wish to seek legal advice if you want to use other clauses to be sure that they are permitted under the CBCA.

Examples

- For a single class of shares:

  The corporation is authorized to issue an unlimited number of shares of one class.

  or

  Unlimited number of shares in a single class.

- For two or more classes of shares:

  The corporation is authorized to issue an unlimited number of Class A and Class B shares. The Class A shareholders shall be entitled to vote at all shareholder meetings, except meetings at which only holders of a specified class of share entitle their holders to vote and to receive such dividend as the board of directors in their discretion shall declare. Subject to the provisions of the *Canada Business Corporations Act*, the Class B shares shall be non-voting. Upon liquidation or dissolution, the holders of Class A and Class B shares shall share equally the remaining property of the corporation.

  or

  The corporation is authorized to issue Class A and Class B shares with the following rights, privileges, restrictions and conditions:

  1. Class A shares, without nominal or par value, the holders of which are entitled:

     (a) to vote at all meetings of shareholders except meetings at which only holders of a specified class of shares are entitled to vote; and

     (b) to receive the remaining property of the corporation upon dissolution.

  2. Class B shares, without nominal or par value, the holders of which are entitled:

     (a) to a dividend as fixed by the board of directors;

     (b) upon the dissolution or liquidation of the corporation, to repayment of the amount paid for such share (plus any declared and unpaid dividends) in priority to the Class A shares, but they shall not confer a right to any further participation in profits or assets.

  3. The holders of Class B shares shall be entitled to vote at all meetings of shareholders.

  or

  The holders of Class B shares shall not, subject to the provisions of the *Canada Business Corporations Act*, be entitled to vote at any meetings of shareholders.

- For shares in a series:

  The directors may authorize the issue of one or more series within each class of shares, and may fix the number of shares in each series, and determine the rights, privileges, restrictions and conditions attaching to the shares of each series subject to the limits provided in the articles.

(As noted earlier, you may create a series of shares immediately in the Articles, rather than waiting until later.)

- Share redemption:

  If a fixed price is not stated, a redemption formula that can be determined in dollars must be used.

  > The said Class X shares or any part thereof shall be redeemable at the option of the corporation without the consent of the holders thereof (at a price of $\_\_$ per share) or (at a price equal to the amount paid per share) plus any declared and unpaid dividend.

Item 4 — Restrictions, if any, on share transfers

Constrained Share Corporations

- Restrictions, if any, on the transfer of shares are normally limited to the consent of the directors and/or shareholders. Exceptions may occur in special cases when the incorporators establish a constrained share corporation, as described in Part IX (Constrained Share Corporations) of the CBCA Regulations.

  Example:

  > No shares of the capital of the corporation shall be transferred without either (a) the sanction of a majority of the directors of the corporation or alternatively (b) the sanction of the majority of the shareholders of the Corporation.

  or

  > No shares of the corporation shall be transferred without the approval of the directors evidenced by a resolution of the board, provided that the approval of any transfer of shares may be given as aforesaid after the said transfer has been effected upon the records of the corporation, in which event, unless the said resolution stipulates otherwise, the said transfer shall be valid and take effect as from the date of its entry upon the books of the corporation.

Non-distributing Corporations

- You may wish to further restrict the transfer of shares or securities to prevent the corporation from becoming a "reporting issuer" under provincial securities legislation and not be designated as a "distributing corporation" under the Act. A corporation is a "distributing corporation" under the definition in subsection 2(1) of the Regulations if the corporation:

  - is a reporting issuer within the meaning of any applicable securities legislation, unless it is subject to an exemption from that legislation;

  - has filed a prospectus or similar document in relation to the public distribution of its shares;

  - has securities that are listed and posted for trading on a stock exchange in or outside Canada;

  - is a distributing corporation that is involved in or results from a statutory procedure, such as an amalgamation or reorganization.

  Under subsections 2(6) and 2(7) of the CBCA, the Director may determine that a corporation is not or was not a distributing corporation if the Director is satisfied that the determination would not be prejudicial to the public interest.

In order to avoid being a reporting issuer under provincial securities legislation, and consequently a "distributing corporation", National Instrument 45-106 requires that:

- The corporation's securities be subject to restrictions on transfer that are contained in the issuer's constating document or security holders' agreements; and

- The corporation's securities, excluding non-convertible debt securities, must be beneficially owned, directly or indirectly, by not more than 50 persons, not including employees and former employees of the issuer or its affiliates, provided that each person is counted as one beneficial owner unless the person is created or used solely to purchase or hold securities of the issuer in which case each beneficial owner or each beneficiary of the person, as the case may be, must be counted as a separate beneficial owner; and

- The corporation's securities be distributed only to persons described in securities legislation or regulations.

To comply with the first requirement, you should make a statement that restricts the transfer of the corporations's shares at *Item 4 — Restrictions, if any, on share transfers* AND a statement that restricts the transfer of the corporation's securities at *Item 7 — Other provisions, if any*:

Example:

Item 4 — Restrictions, if any, on share transfers

No shares of the capital of the corporation shall be transferred without either (a) the sanction of a majority of the directors of the corporation or alternatively (b) the sanction of the majority of the shareholders of the Corporation.

Item 7 — Other provisions, if any

The corporation's securities, other than non-convertible debt securities, shall not be transferred without either (a) the sanction of a majority of the directors of the corporation, or (b) the sanction of the majority of the shareholders of the Corporation, or alternatively (c), if applicable, the restriction contained in security holders' agreements.

There are other exemptions in provincial securities legislation that prevent a corporation from becoming a "reporting issuer", and consequently being designated as "distributing corporation" under the CBCA. You may want to consult with legal counsel or other professional advisers to consider the impact of securities legislation on your corporation.

Item 5 — Minimum and maximum number of directors

- You may specify a minimum and maximum number or a fixed number of directors. However, to permit cumulative voting, the number of directors must be fixed. Moreover, if the corporation is a "distributing" corporation, there must be at least three directors.

Example:

A minimum of 1 and a maximum of 7.

or

Five directors.

Item 6 — Restrictions, if any, on the businesses the corporation may carry on

- A CBCA corporation has all the rights of a natural person, and normally one would not wish to limit this power.

  Example:

  If there are to be no restrictions, simply state "NONE."

- If, however, there are reasons why you wish to restrict the business of the corporation, the following preamble is suggested:

  The business of the corporation shall be limited to the following:...

It should be noted that section 3 of the CBCA itself prohibits CBCA corporations from carrying on the business of a bank or an insurance or trust and loan company, or carry on business as a degree-granting institution.

Item 7 — Other provisions, if any

The CBCA allows you to include a number of additional provisions in the Articles of Incorporation. As well, incorporators occasionally include clauses to satisfy requirements of other legislation or institutions.

The following list illustrates the kinds of wording generally adopted for the most frequently occurring features. The suggested clauses are merely examples of those most commonly used; the listing is not definitive, nor is the wording mandatory. You may wish to seek legal advice if you want to use other clauses to be sure that they are permitted under the CBCA.

- You may want a provision that restricts the transfer of the corporation's securities in order to comply with certain requirements of provincial securities legislation (National Instrument 45-106). *SEE INFORMATION PROVIDED AT ITEM 4 RESTRICTIONS, IF ANY, ON SHARE TRANSFERS.*

- Directors' borrowing power:

  A provision regarding directors' borrowing powers and the delegation of those powers is sometimes used to limit the authority of directors and/or to satisfy lending institutions:

  Example:

  If authorized by a by-law which is duly adopted by the directors and confirmed by ordinary resolution, the directors of the corporation may from time to time:

  (i) borrow money on the credit of the corporation;

  (ii) issue, reissue, sell or pledge debt obligations of the corporation; and

  (iii) mortgage, hypothecate, pledge or otherwise create a security interest in all or any property of the corporation, owned or subsequently acquired, to secure any debt obligation of the corporation.

  Any such by-law may provide for the delegation of such powers by the directors to such officers or directors of the corporation to such extent and in such manner as may be set out in the by-law.

  Nothing herein limits or restricts the borrowing of money by the corporation on bills of exchange or promissory notes made, drawn, accepted or endorsed by or on behalf of the corporation.

- Cumulative voting by directors:

  This clause is allowed only if the number of directors is a fixed number:

Example:

There shall be cumulative voting for directors.

- Increase the majority vote by shareholders:

Example:

In order to effect any (ordinary and/or special) resolution[5] passed at a meeting of shareholders,[6] a majority of not less than ___ per cent of the votes cast by the shareholders who voted in respect of that resolution shall be required.

- Specify the *foreign* form of your corporate name for use *outside Canada*:

Example:

It is hereby provided that the corporation may use and may be equally designated by the following form outside Canada:. ..

(Note: do not use *item 7* to state the *English* or *French* form of the corporate name, for use *inside Canada*; use *item 1*.)

- Specify voting rights on fractional shares:

Example:

A holder of a fractional share shall be entitled to exercise voting rights and to receive dividends in respect of said fractional share.

- Specify that some shareholders have a pre-emptive right:

Example:

It is hereby provided that no shares of a class of shares shall be issued unless the shares have first been offered to the shareholders holding shares of that class, and those shareholders have a pre-emptive right to acquire the offered shares in proportion to their holdings of the shares of that class, at such price and on such terms as those shares are to be offered to others.

- Under the CBCA, directors are not required to own shares of the corporation. However, where incorporators do wish to provide for directors to own shares, the following wording is normally used:

Example:

No person otherwise qualified shall be elected or appointed as a director unless such person beneficially owns at least one share issued by the corporation.

- You may prescribe how shareholders will fill a *vacancy on the board of directors*:

Example:

Any vacancy on the board of directors shall be filled by a vote of the shareholders.

- You may specify a *quorum* of directors:

Example:

The quorum for any meeting of the board of directors shall be ____.

---

[5]The CBCA specifies a simple majority for an ordinary resolution and two-thirds majority for a special resolution. Therefore, any figure set out in the articles must be greater than these statutory majorities.

[6]Other than a resolution to remove a director (see subsection 6(4) of the CBCA).

- You may provide for trust deeds for purposes of the *Quebec Special Corporate Powers Act*, if the corporation intends to carry on business in the Province of Quebec:

    Example:

    > The corporation, through its directors, may, as it deems expedient and notwithstanding the provisions of the *Civil Code*, hypothecate, mortgage or pledge any real or personal property, currently owned or subsequently acquired, of the corporation, to secure the payment of such debentures and other securities, or to provide only a part of these guarantees for the said purposes; and it may constitute the aforesaid hypothec, mortgage or pledge by trust deed, pursuant to sections 23 and 24 of the *Special Corporate Powers Act* (R.S.Q. 1964, c. 275), or in any other manner.

    > The corporation may also hypothecate or mortgage the real property, or pledge or otherwise charge in any manner the personal property of the corporation, or provide these various kinds of guarantees, to secure the payment of loans made otherwise than by the issue of debentures, as well as the payment or performance of other debts, contracts and undertakings of the corporation.

Item 8 — Incorporator's declaration

The Articles of Incorporation must be signed by the incorporators. If the incorporator is a body corporate (i.e. an *existing corporation* acting as the incorporator), the Articles must be signed by a person authorized by the body corporate.

An authorized officer is a person appointed by the directors. The appointment is subject to the Articles, the by-laws, or any unanimous shareholder agreement. The officer may be the chair of the board of directors, the president of the corporation, a vice-president, the secretary, treasurer or comptroller, legal counsel, general manager, a managing director or any other person who performs functions for a corporation similar to those normally performed by a person who holds one of those positions.

Form 1, which is filed with the Director through Corporations Canada's Online Filing Centre or sent by fax, need not necessarily contain the original signatures of the incorporator(s).

However, signed copies of the original documents must be retained in the records of the corporation.

How to fill out Form 2: Initial Registered Office Address and First Board of Directors

Please refer to the form to get complete instructions.

Indicate at *item 1*, the name of the corporation as indicated in Form 1: Articles of Incorporation.

Indicate at *item 2* the address of the registered office. It must be a complete street address within the province or territory specified in the Form 1: Articles of Incorporation . Please indicate at *item 3* the mailing address if it is different from the address of the registered office.

Indicate at *item 4* the name and family name of all directors. The number of directors must correspond with the number indicated in *item 5* of the Form 1: Articles of Incorporation. You must indicate the residential address (a post office or a business address will not be accepted) of each director and indicate if he/she is Canadian resident.

Note that at least 25 per cent of the directors must be Canadian residents. However, some restrictions apply:

- If the corporation has fewer than four directors, at least one of them must be a resident Canadian.
- If the corporation is required by a federal Act or regulations to meet specific requirements respecting Canadian participation or control (e.g., corporations carrying on air transportation or telecommunications businesses), a majority (50% + 1) of its directors must be resident Canadians.
- If the corporation is carrying on one of the following businesses, a majority (50% + 1) of its directors must be resident Canadians:
  - uranium mining
  - book publishing or distribution
  - bookselling, where the sale of books is the primary part of the corporation's business
  - film or video distribution
- However, if a parent corporation belonging to one of those categories (i.e., carrying on a business referred to above, or that must meet requirements respecting Canadian participation or control under a federal Act or regulations) and its subsidiaries earn less than five per cent of their gross revenue in Canada, only one third of the corporation's directors need be resident Canadians.

Form 2 must be signed by one of the incorporators.

Additional Information and How to reach Corporations Canada

For additional information on Corporations Canada's products and services, please visit Corporations Canada's Website or call 1-866-333-5556.

You can also contact Corporations Canada at:

Client Services Section
Corporations Canada
Industry Canada
9th floor, Jean Edmonds Tower South
Ottawa, Ontario K1A 0C8
Fax: 613-941-0601
www.corporationscanada.ic.gc.ca

Checklist

To speed up the processing of your application, please submit a complete application form:

DOCUMENTS REQUIRED	COMPLETED
Form 1: Articles of Incorporation, completed and signed by all incorporators	
Name	
Letter from the Director approving your name if you requested pre-approval or	

DOCUMENTS REQUIRED	COMPLETED
Request for approval of name and NUANS® report	
Form 2: Initial Registered Office Address and First Board of Directors	
$250 fee ($200 if using Corporations Canada's Electronic Filing Centre)	

Policy Statement 3.2 — Registered Office Of The Corporation

Date: July 2, 2002

Revised: January 2, 2007

1. — Statement of general principles

1.1 This policy sets out the position of the Director appointed pursuant to the *Canada Business Corporations Act* (CBCA) concerning the provisions related to the registered office of the corporation.

1.2 This policy replaces the Director's policy dated July 2, 2002 in relation to the place of the registered office of a corporation. It reflects the amendments to the CBCA that came into force on November 24, 2001.

1.3 This policy sets out some operating principles and practical guidelines for the purpose of facilitating the application of the provisions related to the registered office of a corporation. Although they do not have force of law, these operating principles and guidelines inform the interested parties concerning the relevant provisions. This policy is in no way intended to expand the powers of the Director or of the shareholders or creditors beyond the powers conferred on them under the CBCA. The definitive interpretation of the sections of the CBCA and related provisions lies with the courts.

1.4 The Director is not bound by this policy in any decision he makes in a particular case. Furthermore, this policy cannot substitute for a legal, accounting or commercial opinion or the exercise of professional judgment by legal, accounting and commercial advisors in a particular instance.

1.5 The Director suggests that persons affected by the CBCA registered office provisions consult legal counsel or other professional advisors.

1.6 It is the Director's opinion that the communication of these operating principles and guidelines to persons affected by the provisions relating to the registered office of a corporation will help reduce the number of rejected applications and the resulting administrative costs and inconvenience.

1.7 This policy will be amended as needed in light of experience.

2. — Requirements of the *Canada Business Corporations Act*

2.1 Paragraph 6(1)(b) of the CBCA requires that the province where the registered office is to be situated be specified at all times in the corporation's articles.

2.2 Under the *Interpretation Act*, the word "province" also includes a territory.

2.3 Subsection 19(1) of the CBCA requires that the corporation shall at all times have a registered office in Canada situated within the province or territory specified in its articles. Subsection 19(3) allows the directors of a corporation to change the street address of the registered office *within* the province specified in the articles. Subsection 19(4) requires a corporation to send the Director notice of a change in the street address of the registered office within fifteen (15) days of the change.

2.4 Paragraph 173(1)(b) of the CBCA requires a special resolution of shareholders to change the province in which a corporation's registered office is situated. Subsection 177(1) requires articles of amendment to be sent to the Director after any amendment to the articles (i.e., change in the province of the registered office) has been adopted by the shareholders. Section 178 requires the Director to issue a certificate of amendment on receipt of articles of amendment and related fee.

3. — Administrative forms

3.1 For the *province or territory* of the registered office, the applicant shall specify in its articles the province or territory in which the registered office is situated by completing the appropriate form:

- Form 1: Articles of Incorporation (Item 2)
- Form 7: Restated Articles of Incorporation (Item 2)
- Form 9: Articles of Amalgamation (Item 2)
- Form 11: Articles of Continuance (Item 2)

Form 4: Articles of Amendment shall be filed with the Director if the province or territory, in which the registered office is situated, is changed.

3.2 For the *street address* of the registered office, when filing Forms 1, 9 or 11 the applicant shall notify the Director of the street address of the registered office of the corporation by filing a duly-completed Form 2: Initial Registered Office Address and First Board of Directors. The registered office must be located within the province or territory specified in the articles.

When the street address of the registered office of a corporation changes after the corporation becomes subject to the CBCA, the corporation shall notify the Director of the change of address by filing a duly-completed Form 3: Change of Registered Office Address. Form 3 shall be sent to the Director within 15 days following the change of address. The registered office must be located within the province or territory specified in the articles. If the new address is not in the province or territory specified in the articles, Form 3 must be accompanied by Form 4: Articles of Amendment (see para. 5.1 below).

4. — Form 1: Articles of Incorporation

4.1 The incorporator(s), when forming a corporation, shall indicate in Item 2 of Form 1: Articles of Incorporation the province or territory in which the registered office is situated. A duly-completed Form 2: Initial Registered Office Address and First Board of Directors shall be filed at the time of filing of the articles of incorporation.

4.2 *For corporations incorporated prior to November 24, 2001*, it is not necessary to file articles of amendment and to pay the fee of $200 in order to substitute the province or the territory for the place in the articles of incorporation. For example, when the articles of incorporation of a corporation incorporated before November 24, 2001 indicate that the registered office is located in the Montreal Urban Community, it will be assumed that the registered office is located in the province of Quebec. It should be noted that a corporation's articles will continue to indicate the place of the registered office as it was indicated prior to November 24, 2001. Corporations Canada has no authority to unilaterally amend a corporation's articles and change the place to a province or territory. However, a corporation may at any time file articles of amendment under paragraph 173(1)(o) of the CBCA and pay a fee of $200 in order to amend its articles and substitute the province for the place. Alternatively, the corporation may wish to take the opportunity to make the change whenever it has to amend other provisions in its articles.

5. — Form 4: Articles of Amendment

5.1 If the corporation moves the registered office outside of the province or territory specified in its articles, the applicant shall indicate in Item 3 B of Form 4: Articles of Amendment the new province or territory in which the registered office is situated. The applicant shall also pay the $200 fee. In addition to the articles of amendment, the applicant shall file a duly completed Form 3: Change of Registered Office Address.

5.2 It should be noted that the corporation will have to obtain a resolution of the shareholders before filing Form 4: Articles of Amendment and before being able to move the corporation. The shareholders' resolution need not be filed with the articles of amendment.

5.3 When the corporation's registered office is moved within the province or territory specified in the articles, the corporation shall file only Form 3: Change of Registered Office Address within 15 days following the change. No fees apply.

5.4 *For corporations incorporated prior to November 24, 2001*, it is not necessary to file Form 4: Articles of Amendment when the corporation moves its registered office within the province or territory specified in its articles, even if the place originally indicated in the articles changes. For example, it is not necessary to file articles of amendment when the registered office of a corporation moves from Victoria, British Columbia to Vancouver, British Columbia, even though the articles of incorporation before November 24, 2001 indicate that the registered office is located in Victoria. However, the corporation must file Form 3: Change of Registered Office Address with the Director within 15 days of the change of address. It should be noted that a corporation may at any time file Form 4: Articles of Amendment under paragraph 173(1)(o) of the CBCA and pay a fee of $200 in order to amend its articles and substitute the province for the place. Alternatively, the corporation may wish to take the opportunity to make the change whenever it has to amend other provisions in its articles.

6. — Form 7: Restated Articles of Incorporation

6.1 The applicant shall indicate in Item 2 of Form 7: Restated Articles of Incorporation the province or territory in which the registered office of the corporation is situated as specified in the initial articles or subsequent amendments. Under section 180 of the CBCA, the directors may at any time restate the articles of incorporation. This provision applies solely to the restatement of the initial articles with subsequent amendments. Usually, the restatement of articles does not permit amendments to the articles. It is done solely for practical purposes.

6.2 *For articles or amendments prior to November 24, 2001*, the applicant will be allowed to indicate in Item 2 of the Form 7: Restated Articles of Incorporation the province or territory of the place indicated in the articles of incorporation or subsequent amendments thereto. For example, amended articles of incorporation indicate that the registered office of the corporation is located in "Halifax". The applicant may then indicate in Item 2 of the Form 7: Restated Articles of Incorporation that the province of the registered office is Nova Scotia.

6.3 *For corporations with restated articles of incorporation issued prior to November 24, 2001* and whose restated articles specify the place of the registered office, it is not necessary to file articles of amendment and to pay the fee of $200 in order to substitute the province or the territory for the place in the restated articles. For example, when the restated articles of incorporation of a corporation incorporated before November 24, 2001 indicate that the registered office is located in St. John's, it will be assumed that the registered office is located in the province of Newfoundland and Labrador. It should be noted that the corporation's articles will continue to indicate the place of the registered office as it was indicated prior to November 24, 2001. Corporations Canada has no authority to unilaterally amend a corporation's articles and change the place to a province or territory. However, a corporation may file Form 4: Articles of Amendment and pay the fee of $200 in order to amend its articles to substitute the province for the place. Alternatively, the corporation may wish to take the opportunity to make the change whenever it has to amend other provisions in its articles.

7. — Form 9: Articles of Amalgamation

7.1 The applicant shall specify in Item 2 of Form 9: Articles of Amalgamation the province or territory in which the registered office is situated. Subparagraphs 184(1)(b)(ii) and 184(2)(b)(ii) of the CBCA provide that articles of amalgamation must be identical to the articles of the parent corporation in the event of a vertical short-form amalgamation or to those of the subsidiary whose shares are not cancelled in the event of a horizontal short-form amalgamation. For example, the articles of the parent corporation specify that the province of the registered office is "Manitoba" and the articles of the subsidiary specify that the province of the registered office is "Saskatchewan". In the event of a horizontal short-form amalgamation, the applicant shall specify "Saskatchewan" in Item 2 of Form 9: Articles of Amalgamation.

A duly-completed Form 2: Initial Registered Office Address and First Board of Directors shall accompany Form 9: Articles of Amalgamation .

7.2 *For amalgamations involving corporations incorporated prior to November 24, 2001*, the Director will allow the applicant to indicate in Item 2 of Form 9: Articles of Amalgamation the province or the territory of the place indicated in the articles of the parent corporation or of the subsidiary, as appropriate, at the time of the amalgamation. The certificate of amalgamation issued by the Director will indicate the province or territory in which the registered office of the corporation is situated. For example, in the case of a short-form vertical amalgamation, the applicant may specify "Manitoba" in Item 2 of Form 9: Articles of Amalgamation, since the articles of incorporation of the parent corporation indicate "Winnipeg".

7.3 *For corporations amalgamated prior to November 24, 2001* and whose articles of amalgamation specify the place of the registered office, it is not necessary to file articles of amendment and to pay the fee of $200 in order to substitute the province or the territory for the place in the articles of amalgamation. For example, when the articles of amalgamation prior to November 24, 2001 indicate that the registered office is located in Edmonton, it will be assumed that the registered office is located in the province of Alberta. It should be noted that the corporation's articles will continue to specify the place of the registered office as it was specified prior to November 24, 2001. Corporations Canada has no authority to unilaterally amend a corporation's articles and change the place to a province or territory. However, a corporation may at any time, under paragraph 173(1)(o) of the CBCA, file Form 4: Articles of Amendment and pay the fee of $200 in order to amend its articles to substitute the province for the place. Alternatively, the corporation may wish to take the opportunity to make the change whenever it has to amend other provisions in its articles.

8. — Form 11: Articles of Continuance

8.1 The applicant shall specify in Item 2 of Form 11: Articles of Continuance the province or territory in which the registered office of the corporation is situated.

A duly-completed Form 2: Initial Registered Office Address and First Board of Directors shall accompany the articles of continuance.

8.2 *For corporations with articles of continuance issued prior to November 24, 2001* specifying the place of the registered office, it is not necessary to file articles of amendment and to pay the fee of $200 in order to substitute the province or the territory for the place in the articles of continuance. For example, when the articles of continuance prior to November 24, 2001 indicate that the registered office is located in Fredericton, it will be assumed that the registered office is located in the province of New Brunswick. It should be noted that the corporation's articles will continue to specify the place of the registered office as it was specified prior to November 24, 2001. Corporations Canada has no authority to unilaterally amend a corporation's articles and change the place to a province or territory. However, a corporation may at any time, under paragraph 173(1)(o) of the CBCA, file Form 4: Articles of Amendment and pay the fee of $200 in order to amend its articles to substitute the province for the place. Alternatively, the corporation may wish to take the opportunity to make the change whenever it has to amend other provisions in its articles.

9. — Situation in the National Capital Region

9.1 *Before November 24, 2001*, it was possible to indicate the National Capital Region as the place of a registered office. This region straddles two provinces, Ontario and Quebec. Now, the articles must specify the province in which the registered office is situated, and not a place.

9.2 The position of the Director concerning a place straddling two provinces is that the province of the registered office is the province in which the registered office was physically situated on November 24, 2001, as specified in the Notice of Registered Office or Notice of Change of Registered Office. For example, when the corporation indicated the National Capital Region as the place of its registered office and the Notice of Registered Office or Notice of Change of Registered Office indicated that the registered office is located in Gatineau, Quebec, it will be assumed that the registered office is located in the Province of Quebec. It is not necessary to file the Form 4: Articles of Amendment to so notify the Director appointed pursuant to the CBCA. It should be noted that the corporation's articles will continue to indicate the place of the registered office as it was indicated prior to November 24, 2001. Corporations Canada has no authority to unilaterally amend a corporation's articles and change the place to a province or territory. However, a corporation may at any time, under paragraph 173(1)(o) of the CBCA, file articles of amendment and pay the fee of $200 in order to amend its articles to substitute the province for the place. Alternatively, the corporation may wish to take the opportunity to make the change whenever it has to amend other articles.

9.3 For example, if the corporation moves its registered office within the province, for example from Gatineau to Montreal, it will not be necessary to file articles of amendment. Form 3: Change of Registered Office Address shall be filed with the Director, however.

If the corporation moves its office to another province or territory, for example from Gatineau, Quebec to Ottawa, Ontario, the corporation will be required to file articles of amendment. Also, Form 3: Change of Registered Office Address shall be filed with the Director.

Additional Information and How to reach Corporations Canada

For additional information on Corporations Canada's products and services, please visit Corporations Canada's website or call 1-866-333-5556.

You can also contact Corporations Canada at:

Client Services Section
Corporations Canada
Industry Canada
9th floor, Jean Edmonds Tower South
Ottawa, Ontario K1A 0C8
Fax: 613-941-0601
www.corporationscanada.ic.gc.ca

Policy Statement 6.1 — Canada Business Corporations Act Exemption Information Kits Overview

Date: March 19, 2008

1. — Background

The *Canada Business Corporations Act* ("CBCA") provides companies or individuals with relief from some of its requirements through a series of specific exemptions. Corporations or individuals must apply to the Director under the CBCA for these exemptions. To simplify this process, exemption information kits were developed. The available kits are listed in the table below. These kits are intended to meet client needs for information concerning exemption applications. They were conceived as part of a plan to reduce the effort of all parties involved with exemption applications and to explain what the Director and staff consider when deciding whether to grant an exemption. Kits have not been prepared for exemptions that are rarely sought.

Applications to Director — Kits Available

DESCRIPTION OF EXEMPTION	SECTION	STATUS
Distributing Corporation	2(6)	Revised
Trust Indenture	82(3)	Revised
Proxy Solicitation (Management)	151(1)	Revised
Proxy Solicitation (Dissident Shareholder)	151(1)	Revised
Reporting of Financial Statements	156	Revised
Audit Committee	171(2)	Revised

Applications to Director — Kits Not Available

DESCRIPTION OF EXEMPTION	SECTION	STATUS
Name of Corporation	10(2)	Not planned
Where continued reference to par value shares permissible	187(11)	Not planned

Applications to Court — Kits Not Available

DESCRIPTION OF EXEMPTION	SECTION	STATUS
Qualification of Auditor	161(5)	Not planned

2. — Types of Exemptions

(a) — Applications to Director — Kits Available

Distributing Corporation: Certain provisions in the CBCA apply only to distributing corporations and are devised to safeguard the interests of security holders and other stakeholders. However, it is recognized that situations exist where strict adherence to these provisions neither serves the interests of the security holders, nor the corporation, nor any other stakeholder. Subsection 2(6) of the CBCA provides the Director with the authority to determine that a corporation is not, or was not a distributing corporation, if the Director is satisfied that such a determination would not be prejudicial to the public. Circumstances in which the Director is likely to grant such an exemption are listed in the revised subsection 2(6) information kit.

Trust Indenture — Part VIII: Subsection 82(3) of the CBCA states that the Director may exempt a trust indenture if the debt obligations issued and the security interests effected by the indenture are subject to a law of a province or of a foreign country that is substantially equivalent to Part VIII of the CBCA. The major factor in granting an exemption is whether the degree of protection offered to investors is substantially equivalent to the protection that would be given if the trust indenture were subject to the requirements of the CBCA. Typically, exemptions have been granted where the applicant has satisfied the Director that this is the situation and, in the case of foreign offerings, when the debt securities will not be available for sale in Canada. Precedents have been established for the United States.

Proxy solicitation (management and dissident): Subsection 151(1) of the CBCA provides that the Director may exempt a corporation or dissident (usually a shareholder) from any of the requirements of Section 149 or subsection 150(1). Section 149 and subsection 150(1) provide that the management of a distributing corporation must send a "form of proxy" and a "proxy circular" to all shareholders entitled to receive notice of the meeting when the number of shareholders entitled to vote at the meeting is more than 50. Subsection 150(1) also applies to a dissident and provides that a dissident must send a dissident proxy circular. The "form of proxy" and "proxy circular" must contain the information prescribed in Sections 54 to 69 of the Regulations. Corporations and dissidents whose applications provide evidence that shareholders would not be prejudiced by the granting of an exemption are generally successful in receiving either complete or partial exemptions. An information kit is available for the exemption from the requirement to send management proxy solicitation and a separate information kit is available for the exemption from the requirement to send proxy circulars by a dissident.

Reporting of Financial Statements: Section 155 imposes requirements concerning financial statements to be presented to the shareholders at the annual meeting and the frequency with which they must be updated. The content and preparation of financial statements must comply with the requirements of Sections 70 to 72 of the Regulations. These sections require that the financial statements must be prepared in accordance with the provisions of the Canadian Institute of Chartered Accountants' Handbook and must contain a balance sheet, a statement of retained earnings, an income statement and a statement of the change in financial position.

Section 156 states that the Director may authorize a corporation to omit from its financial statements any item prescribed, or to dispense with the publication of any particular financial statement prescribed. The Director will generally permit these omissions, on such reasonable grounds as he thinks fit, if the Director believes that the financial information thus revealed would be detrimental to the corporation. An information kit is available for those corporations requiring an exemption under Section 156.

Audit Committee: Subsection 171(1) of the CBCA states that a distributing corporation must have an audit committee if the corporation's securities are held by more than one person. The audit committee thus established must comprise a minimum of three directors of the corporation where at least two of these directors are neither employees of the corporation nor any of its affiliates Subsection 171(2) states that if the Director is satisfied that the shareholders will not be prejudiced, then an exemption may be issued which exempts the corporation from the requirement to establish an audit committee.

(b) — Applications to Director — Kits Not Available

Name of Corporation: Subsection 10(2) permits the Director to exempt a corporation continuing under the CBCA from the requirements of subsection 10(1): that the name of the corporation include the word or expression "Limited", "Limitée", "Incorporated", "Incorporée", "Corporation", "Société par actions de régime fédéral" or its corresponding abbreviation. There is no kit for this type of exemption as it has been rarely sought. Most exemptions have been granted to corporations incorporated under Special Acts when they were continuing under the CBCA and whose name was already well-known to the Canadian public, for example "Bell Canada".

Where continued reference to par value shares permissible: Where the Director determines, on the application of an importing body corporate, that it is not practicable to change a reference to the nominal or par value of shares of a class or series that the body corporate was authorized to issue before it was continued under the CBCA, subsection 187(11) states that the Director may permit the corporation to refer in its articles to those shares, whether issued or unissued, as shares having a nominal or par value. No kit is available as this exemption is rarely requested.

(c) — Applications to Court — Kits Not Available

Qualification of Auditor: An interested person may apply to a court pursuant to subsection 161(5) for an order exempting an auditor from the need to be independent. For example, the court order would provide that the comptroller of the parent company could act as auditor. Note however that shareholders of all non-distributing corporations may resolve not to appoint an auditor, in which case no exemption application would be necessary. There is no kit for this type of exemption. Note that the CBCA does not require that a notice of application be sent to the Director.

(d) — Single Filing Exemption

Section 258.2 gives the Director, CBCA authority to make a blanket exemption for notices or documents required to be sent to the Director where the information contained in the notice or document is similar to that required to be made public pursuant to another act of Parliament or of a legislature that the Director specifies.

Pursuant to this authority, the Director has issued the Single Filing Exemption providing that proxy materials and financial statements required to be filed with the Director pursuant to Sections 150 and 160 of the CBCA, need not be filed if documents containing similar information have been filed with any of the participating provincial and territorial securities commissions. Corporations do not need to notify the Director in order to rely on this exemption.

3. — The Exemption Application

1. *Format*: Along with a cover letter indicating the name of the applicant corporation, the application must provide information under three distinct headings: description and details of

the exemption sought; statement of facts, and argument. The information kit provides assistance in drafting these applications.

The Director recognizes that in some cases applicants may also be making similar representations under various provincial securities acts. The Director will accept an application made under any provincial securities act providing it contains all relevant information or additional information is attached so as to comply with CBCA requirements. Note, however, that provincial legislation may provide confidentiality protections that do not exist under the CBCA.

2. *The Documents*: Detailed below is a brief description of the three major documents that comprise the submission.

> (i) *Description and Details of the Exemption Sought*: The application must describe the exemption sought and note that it is an application for an exemption under the relevant section of the *Canada Business Corporations Act*, R.S.C. 1985, c. 44.

> (ii) *Statement of Facts*: Information varies depending on the type of exemption sought. The applicant must provide all material facts about the application and describe the circumstances to the degree necessary to allow the Director to make an informed decision on the request.

> (iii) *Argument*: Following the circumstances described, arguments must explain why an exemption is required and, when appropriate, why receiving an exemption would not be prejudicial to the interests of security holders or the public interest. Additional details are provided in the specific information kits.

3. *Effective Date of Exemption*: Exemptions take effect on the date of approval of the application.

4. *Duration*: This varies with the type of exemption sought. Additional details are found in the specific information kits.

5. *Revocation*: Exemptions are only revoked if the facts change and the resulting circumstances dictate that the corporation should no longer be exempt from the particular requirement. Appropriate notice will be provided to ensure the applicant can contest the decision to revoke an exemption decision.

6. *Retrospective Effect*: While the Act may permit exemptions to be granted that have retrospective effect, it is the policy to grant these only when there are valid reasons. Retrospective exemptions will only be considered in situations where the investing public would not be prejudiced and where the corporation would otherwise be prejudiced. Requests for retrospective exemptions will be reviewed on a case-by-case basis.

7. *Fees*: The prescribed fee for this type of application is $250,00.

8. *Number of Copies*: Only one set of documents is required.

9. *Processing of Application*: Section 90 of the Regulations provides the Director 30 days after receipt of an application for an exemption to either grant or refuse the application. If the application contains the necessary information, an exemption is usually issued no later than 15 working days after receipt of the application.

10. *Urgent Cases*: An applicant requiring that the Director review the application on an expedited basis should bring the request immediately to the attention of the Director's staff, providing reasons for the urgency.

11. *Publication*: Issued exemptions are published monthly under the heading "Corporations Canada Monthly Transactions" on its website: http://*corporationscanada.ic.gc.ca*.

12. *Appeal of Director's Decision*: A person who feels aggrieved by a decision of the Director to refuse to grant an exemption may apply to a court for an order requiring the Director to

change his decision, and on such application, the court may so order and make any further order it thinks fit.

13. *Access to Exemption Information Filed*: Pursuant to section 266 of the CBCA, a person who has paid the required fee is entitled to examine, make copies or extracts of any document required by the Act to be sent to the Director. The information filed with the Director in support of an exemption application is not confidential. Such information is required to be filed in order to get an exemption and must therefore be made available to the public.

4. — Additional Information and How to Reach Corporations Canada

For additional information on Corporations Canada's products and services, please visit the Corporations Canada website *www.corporationscanada.ic.gc.ca* or call 1-866-333-5556.

You can also contact Corporations Canada at:

Client Services Section

Corporations Canada

Industry Canada

9th Floor, Jean Edmonds Tower South

Ottawa, Ontario K1A 0C8

Toll free: 1-866-333-5556

Fax: 613-941-0601

www.corporationscanada.ic.gc.ca

Policy Statement 6.2 — Exemption Kit — Application under Subsection 2(6) of the CBCA for a Determination that a Corporation is Not a Distributing Corporation

Date: March 19, 2008

1. — Statement of General Principles

1.01 The September 22, 2004 exemption policy is repealed and replaced with this policy.

1.02 This policy sets out information to facilitate an application to the Director appointed under the CBCA for a determination that the corporation is not or was not a distributing corporation.

1.03 The rules governing distributing corporations in the Act and Regulations are designed to provide safeguards and promote a higher standard of corporate diligence given that securities are distributed to the public on an open market. The Director will only exempt a corporation if satisfied that the determination would not be prejudicial to the public interest

1.04 Nothing in this policy is intended to constitute a binding statement of what position the Director will take with respect to a particular application. This policy is intended to reflect the Director's understanding of the Director's role in processing an application under subsection 2(6) of the CBCA This policy does not address subsection 2(7) and the exemption of classes of corporations.

2. — Legislative Framework

2.01 The term "distributing corporation" is defined in section 2 of the CBCR. According to subsection 2(1) of the CBCR, the term means:

(a) a corporation that is a "reporting issuer" under any legislation that is set out in column 2 of an item of Schedule 1, or

(b) in the case of a corporation that is not a "reporting issuer" referred to in paragraph (a), a corporation

(i) that has filed a prospectus or registration statement under provincial legislation or under the laws of a jurisdiction outside Canada,

(ii) any of the securities of which are listed and posted for trading on a stock exchange in or outside Canada, or

(iii) that is involved in, formed for, resulting from or continued after an amalgamation, a reorganization, an arrangement or a statutory procedure, if one of the participating bodies corporate is a corporation to which subparagraph (i) or (ii) applies.

2.02 The definition seeks to largely harmonize the CBCA with provincial securities legislation. Where a corporation is governed by any securities legislation set out in Schedule 1 of the Regulations and is caught by the definition of "reporting issuer" in that legislation, it then becomes a distributing corporation under the CBCA (see Annex A for a copy of Schedule 1). Alternatively, where a corporation is governed by securities legislation not enumerated in Schedule 1, or where there is no securities legislation in the jurisdiction the corporation operates, paragraph 2(1)(b) then applies Note that where a corporation is subject to an exemption under provincial securities legislation or to an order of the relevant provincial regulator to the effect that the corporation is not a "reporting issuer", that corporation is not a distributing corporation for the purpose of the definition of the term in section 2 and would not have to argue that it is not caught by paragraph 2(1)(b), see 3.02 below.

2.03 The Act and Regulations contain a number of provisions which impose specific requirements for distributing corporations, which include:

- access to securities register under s. 21(1.1);

- access to shareholder lists, ss. 21(3) of the CBCA;

- the definition of open-end mutual fund in ss. 26(12);

- the lack of restrictions on the ownership or transfer of shares under ss. 49(9);

- the number of directors a corporation is required to have, ss. 102(2) of the CBCA;

- the prohibition of short sale for insiders, ss. 130(1) of the CBCA;

- the notice of the time and place of a meeting of shareholders, s. 135 of the CBCA;

- the managment proxy solicitation requirements imposed by s. 149(1) and s. 150(1);

- the obligation to file financial statements with the Director (subject to single filing), s. 160 of the CBCA

- the requirement to have an auditor and audit committee, s. 163 and s. 171 of the CBCA;

- going-private transactions in s. 193; and

- the compulsory and compelled acquisition of shares, s. 206.1 of the CBCA.

The foregoing is a not an exhaustive list

2.04 Subsection 2(6) of the CBCA provides, however, that *on the application of a corporation, the Director may determine that the corporation is not or was not a distributing corporation if the Director is satisfied that the determination would not be prejudicial to the public interest.*

2.05 The Director does not have the power to determine that a corporation is:

a) simultaneously both a distributing corporation and a non-distributing corporation; or

b) a distributing corporation for some purposes under the Act but a non-distributing corporation for other purposes.

2.06 The applicant should determine those provisions of the Act that should no longer apply to the corporation if it ceases to be a distributing corporation and those provisions that should continue to apply notwithstanding that the corporation is no longer a distributing corporation. If the applicant only wants relief from specific obligations imposed on a distributing corporation under the Act and a specific exemption applies (i.e. an exemption under ss. 151(1) from the management proxy solicitation requirements or an exemption under ss. 171(2) from the audit committee requirements), the application should be made under those specific exemptions In other cases, applicants may seek a determination that it is no longer a distributing corporation. In an application under ss. 2(6), the applicant should identify any provisions summarized in s. 2.03 above that should continue to apply to the corporation notwithstanding that it ceases to be a distributing corporation. The Director has the power to determine that a corporation is not a distributing corporation on terms including those whereby the corporation must continue to comply with certain provisions of the Act imposed on distributing corporations notwithstanding the change in the corporation's status.

2.07 A corporation that does not comply with the provisions governing distributing corporations in the Act and Regulations and who fails to obtain an exemption from the Director is in contravention of the Act which can result in civil and/or criminal liability.

3. — Where an Application to the Director Is Not Necessary

3.01 Prior to the 2001 amendments to the Act and Regulations, most applications were made to the Director and exemptions granted on grounds that the applicant did not have or no longer had any securities held by the public (through a going-private transaction or other means)

3.02 Subsection 2(2) of the CBCR now stipulates that *a corporation that is subject to an exemption under provincial securities legislation, or to an order of the relevant provincial regulator that provides that the corporation is not a "reporting issuer" for the purposes of the applicable legislation, is not a "distributing corporation" for the purpose of the definition of that expression in subsection (1).*

3.03 Since the Director cannot grant an exemption under provincial securities legislation, applicants that need both CBCA and provincial exemptions should first obtain the provincial exemption. The provincial exemption will automatically invoke the CBCA exemption However, the CBCA exemption will not automatically invoke any provincial exemption

4. — Guidelines for Making an Application

A. — General Considerations

4.01 The general test used by the Director consists of determining whether the public interest would be prejudiced by such a determination, if an exemption were granted.

B. — The Terms "Prejudice" and "Public Interest"

4.02 There is no definition of the term "prejudice" or "public interest" in the Act or Regulations.

4.03 In reviewing an application under subsection 2(6) of the CBCA, the Director will generally assess the potential for prejudice if the provisions governing distributing corporations in the Act (see 2.03) and Regulations were to no longer apply to the applicant. The Director will consider the interest of the stakeholders who would ordinarily benefit from those provisions from which the applicant would be exempt. Essentially, the question to be asked is "would the exemption cause prejudice to those persons or groups who ordinarily benefit from the provisions for which the applicant would be exempt?"

4.04 Nothing in section 4.03, however, is intended to limit the discretion afforded to the Director under subsection 2(6) of the CBCA especially where the exemption would be incompatible with the interest of the public generally (e.g. investor confidence in capital markets).

C. — Factors Considered in Reviewing an Application

4.05 Based on the statement of facts provided by the applicant (see Annex B, Schedule B for a non-exhaustive list) — e.g. the capital structure of the applicant, the nature of the securities issued or to be issued — the Director attempts to determine if the test is met and, in turn, whether or not to grant the exemption sought.

4.06 An exemption may be granted where particular circumstances, set out in the statement of facts, are argued:

1. the applicant exists solely and for a limited duration to facilitate an exchange of shares (i.e. exchangeco) between two reporting issuers and as a result is deemed a reporting issuer;

2. the applicant is a reporting issuer only due to debt securities that, while held by the public, are governed by an indenture or other agreements that adequately protects the interest of those security holders;

3. the applicant is a wholly-owned subsidiary and is seeking to be exempt from certain provisions;

4. the applicant is a reporting issuer only due to securities held by investors which cannot be found or located but where moneys are held in trust for the repurchase of these securities;

5. the consent of all affected security holders for the exemption has been obtained.

D. — Conditions for Issuing an Exemption

4.07 In granting an exemption to a corporation, the Director may find it appropriate to include one or more conditions in the decision.

4.08 Where the public interest is served, the Director may grant an exemption upon the condition that one or more provisions governing distributing corporations remain in effect, and may find it appropriate to set them out in the decision.

4.09 The Director may require the applicant to forward a copy of the exemption to those security holders affected by the exemption and any securities regulators concerned.

5. — Other Information

A. — Additional Information Required

5.01 The Director may require other information not provided in the application in order to decide whether the public interest will be harmed

5.02 Under section 91 of the CBCR, the Director may also seek additional information from third parties. Section 92 of the CBCR provides however that the applicant shall be given a copy of the information obtained and be given a reasonable opportunity to respond.

5.03 There is no statutory obligation on the Director, however, to seek information at the request of third parties nor to allow third parties to make representations regarding an application

B. — Access to Information Contained in an Application

5.04 Pursuant to section 266 of the CBCA, a person who has paid the required fee is entitled to examine and make copies or extracts of any document required by the CBCA to be sent to the Director. The information filed with the Director in support of an exemption application is not confidential since such information is required to be filed in order to obtain an exemption. Consequently, an application for exemption is public information.

C. — Offences

5.05 Section 250 of the Act creates an offence with respect to documents required by the Act or Regulations to be sent to the Director, or any other person, that contains a false or misleading statement about a material fact or omits to state a material fact

6. — Making the Application

A. — Format

6.01 Along with a cover letter indicating the name of the applicant corporation, the application must provide information under three distinct headings: description and details of the exemption sought, statement of facts, and argument. These are described briefly below with further elaboration contained in the attached Annex B. We recommend the use of Annex B as a model.

B. — The Documents

6.02 Detailed below is a brief description of the three major documents that comprise the submission:

(i) *Description and Details of the Exemption Sought*: The applicant must describe the exemption sought and note that this is an application for an exemption under subsection 2(6) of the *Canada Business Corporations Act* (see attached Annex B, Schedule A)

(ii) *Statement of Facts*: The applicant must include sufficient facts and all material information which might affect the Director's decision (see attached Annex B, Schedule B) The applicant should refer to 4.05 above for a non-exhaustive list of facts that the Director may consider relevant.

(iii) *Argument*: Following the statements of facts, the applicant must provide convincing reasons that the exemption, if granted, will not be prejudicial to the public interest (see attached Annex B, Schedule C). The applicant should refer to 4.07 above for possible arguments and 4.02-4.04 which explain the Director's understanding of the terms "prejudice" and "public interest."

C. — Effective Date of the Exemption

6.03 Pursuant to paragraph 89(1)(a) of the CBCR, an application may be made at any time The exemption will bear the date on which it was granted.

D. — Duration

6.04 The exemption generally takes effect on the date it was granted, unless otherwise indicated on the decision, and remains in effect indefinitely subject to the exemption being modified or revoked

E. — Modification or Revocation

6.05 The Director may, at the Director's discretion, modify or revoke an exemption where the circumstances, for which the decision was granted, have changed (e.g the issuance of securities to the public after the date of the exemption) The exemption will no longer apply if the corporation issues securities to the public or lists and posts any of its securities on a stock exchange after the date of the exemption.

6.06 The Director will generally not revoke an exemption before providing notice to the applicant and the opportunity to respond by submitting new facts and arguments to support the exemption.

6.07 A revoked exemption ceases to have effect from the date of revocation and the corporation must therefore suspend any further action in reliance of the decision

F. — Retrospective Effect

6.08 Subsection 2(6) permits decisions by the Director to have retrospective effect. Requests for retrospective exemptions are reviewed on a case-by-case basis. A retrospective exemption will only be granted where the applicant establishes, beyond the general test, that no prejudice was caused to the public interest during the time prior to the application.

G. — Fees & Number of Copies to File:

6.09 The prescribed fee for an exemption application is $250 00.

6.10 Only one set of documents is required.

H. — Time for Processing an Application

6.11 Section 90 of the CBCR provides that *the Director shall, within 30 days after receipt of an application for an exemption, grant the exemption requested or send to the applicant written notice of the Director's refusal, together with reasons for the refusal.*

6.12 An application duly completed and filed, with no outstanding issue or concern, will usually receive a response from the Director within 15 working days after receipt of the application

6.13 An applicant requiring that the Director review the application on an expedited basis should bring the request immediately to the attention of the Director's staff, providing reasons for the urgency

I. — Publication

6.14 Issued exemptions are published monthly under the heading "Corporations Canada Monthly Transactions" on the following website: *http://corporationscanada.ic.gc.ca.*

J. — Appeal of Director's Decision

6.15 An applicant who feels aggrieved by a decision of the Director to grant, or to refuse to grant, an exemption may apply to the court, pursuant to paragraph 246(c) of the Act, for an order requiring the Director to change the decision.

7. — Additional Information and How to Reach Corporations Canada

7.01 For additional information on Corporations Canada's products and services, please visit the Corporations Canada website *www.corporationscanada.ic.gc.ca* or call 1-866-333-5556

You can also contact Corporations Canada at:

Client Services Section

Corporations Canada

Industry Canada

9th Floor, Jean Edmonds Tower South

Ottawa, Ontario K1A 0C8

Toll free: 1-866-333-5556

Fax: 613-941-0601

www.corporationscanada.ic.qc.ca

Annex A — Schedule 1 of the CBCR Reporting Issuer

Item	Column 1 Jurisdiction	Column 2 Legislation
1.	Ontario	the definition "reporting issuer" in subsection 1(1) of the *Securities Act*, R.S.O., 1990, c. S.5, as amended from time to time
2.	Quebec	the definition "reporting issuer" in sections 5 and 68 of the *Securities Act*, R S Q. c. V-1.1, as amended from time to time
3.	Nova Scotia	the definition "reporting issuer" in paragraph 2(1)(ao) of the *Securities Act*, R.S.N.S. 1989, c. 418, as amended from time to time

	Column 1	Column 2
Item	**Jurisdiction**	**Legislation**
4.	Manitoba	the definition "reporting issuer" in subsection 80(1) of the *Securities Act*, R.S M 1988, c. S50, as amended from time to time
5.	British Columbia	the definition "reporting issuer" in subsection 1(1) of the *Securities Act*, R.S.B.C. 1996, c. 418, as amended from time to time
6.	Saskatchewan	the definition "reporting issuer" in paragraph 2(1)(qq) of *The Securities Act, 1988*, S.S. 1988-89, c S-42.2, as amended from time to time
7.	Alberta	the definition "reporting issuer" in paragraph 1(t.1) and section 117 of the *Securities Act*, S.A. 1981, c. S-6 1, as amended from time to time
8.	Newfoundland and Labrador	the definition "reporting issuer" in paragraph 2(1)(oo) of the *Securities Act*, R.S N 1990, c. S-13, as amended from time to time

Annex B — Sample Documents to Submit When Making an Application under Subsection 2(6) of the CBCA

Schedule A — In the Matter Concerning the Director Appointed under the *Canada Business Corporations Act*

And

The Application Of

(Name of corporation)

(hereinafter called the "Corporation")

Description and Details of the Exemption Sought

1. This application is made under subsection 2(6) *Canada Business Corporations Act* for a determination that the Corporation *("is not" or "was not")* a distributing corporation.

Or

1. This application is made under subsection 2(6) *Canada Business Corporations Act* for a determination that the Corporation *("is not" or "was not")* a distributing corporation, but for the application of: *(indicate which provisions governing distributing corporations in the Act and Regulations that will continue to apply).*

Or

1. This application is made under subsection 2(6) *Canada Business Corporations Act* for a determination that the Corporation *("is not" or "was not")* a distributing corporation with

respect to the application of: *(indicate which provisions governing distributing corporations in the Act and Regulations that will no longer apply).*

Schedule B — Statement of Facts

1. The following statement provides sufficient facts and all material information in order to enable the Director to make an informed decision about the exemption sought:

The following is a non-exhaustive list of facts that may be material:

    1. the capital structure of the applicant:

- *what securities have ever been issued by the applicant;*

- *which securities are currently outstanding on the date of the application;*

- *whether the applicant intends (at the date of the application) to issue securities in the future.*

    2. the nature of the securities issued or to be issued:

- *whether the securities are shares or debt obligations;*

- *what rights/restrictions are attached, or to be attached, to the securities;*

- *whether any trust or other forms of agreements govern the securities.*

    3. who are or will be the holders of each class of securities:

- *the public (in Canada or foreign);*

- *related parties or insiders;*

- *institutional investors.*

    4. whether the corporation is controlled by other CBCA corporations or by corporations governed by foreign legislation.

Schedule C — Arguments

1. This application is made pursuant to subsection 2(6) of the *Canada Business Corporations Act* which empowers the Director to determine that the Corporation is not or was not a distributing corporation, if the Director is satisfied that the determination would not be prejudicial to the public interest.

2. The determination that the Corporation *("is not" or "was not")* a distributing corporation, as described in this application, would not be prejudicial to the public interest.

3. In particular, the exemption should be granted for the following reason(s):

For Instance,

    1. The Corporation exists solely and for a limited duration to facilitate an exchange of shares (i.e.exchangeco) between two reporting issuers and as a result is deemed a reporting issuer.

    2. The Corporation is a reporting issuer only due to debt securities that, while held by the public, are governed by an indenture or other agreements that adequately protects the interest of those security holders.

    3. The Corporation is a wholly-owned subsidiary and is seeking to be exempt from certain provisions.

4. The Corporation is a reporting issuer only due to securities held by investors which cannot be found or located but where moneys are held in trust for the repurchase of these securities

5. The consent of all affected security holders for the exemption has been obtained.

Dated this .... day of ...., 20.........., at the City of ...., Province of ....

.... Signature — Capacity of

Schedule D — Model of a Decision — In the Matter Concerning the Director Appointed under the *Canada Business Corporations Act*

And

The Application Of

(Name of corporation)

(hereinafter called the "Corporation")

For An Exemption Under Subsection 2(6) Of The *Canada Business Corporations Act*

Exemption

UPON APPLICATION BY the Corporation under subsection 2(6) of the *Canada Business Corporations Act* (the "Act"), for a determination that the corporation *("is not" or "was not")* a distributing corporation,

AND UPON reading the application documents and being satisfied that the determination would not be prejudicial to the public interest,

IT IS HEREBY DETERMINED that *(name of the corporation) ("is not" or "was not")* a distributing corporation

DATED, this .... day of ...., 20..........

.... Deputy Director

Examples of Standard or Typical Terms

"THIS DETERMINATION is made subject to the following terms:

1. It ceases to have further effect if, after the date the exemption is granted, the corporation issues any of its securities to the public or lists and posts any of its securities on any stock exchange within or outside Canada.

2. It ceases to have further effect if, after the date the exemption is granted, the Ontario Securities Commission revokes the order made under s. 83 of the *Securities Act* (Ontario) deeming the corporation to have ceased to be a reporting issuer.

3. Notwithstanding that the corporation is not a distributing corporation, the corporation shall:

    (a) provide access to its securities register and shareholders' lists in accordance with s. 21(1.1) and (3);

    (b) have not less than three directors;

    (c) provide not less than, nor more than, the amount of time required for a notice of meeting of shareholders under ss. 135(1) of the Act and s. 44 of the Regulations;

(d) prepare and circulate forms of proxy and a proxy information circular in accordance with ss. 149(1) and ss. 150(1) of the Act and the applicable Regulations;

(e) file financial statements with the Director under s. 160;

(f) have an auditor and an audit committee under s. 163 and s. 171; and

(g) comply with the requirements for compulsory and compelled acquisition of shares under s. 206 and s. 206.1.

Policy Statement 6.3 — Exemption Kit — Application Under Subsection 82(3) of the CBCA to Exempt a Trust Indenture from Part VIII of the CBCA

Date: March 19, 2008

1. — Statement of General Principles

1.01 The September 22, 2004 exemption policy is repealed and replaced with this policy.

1.02 This policy sets out information to facilitate an application to the Director appointed under the CBCA to exempt a trust indenture made by a CBCA corporation from the application of Part VIII of the Act.

1.03 A trust indenture established between a CBCA corporation issuing debt obligations as part of a distribution to the public and a trustee for that debt must comply with Part VIII of the CBCA unless an exemption applies. The rules governing trust indentures in Part VIII are designed to ensure that the terms and conditions of such an agreement provide adequate protection for debt holders. The Director will only exempt a trust indenture from Part VIII of the Act if satisfied that the trust indenture, the debt obligations and any security interests effected are subject to a law of a province or a country other than Canada that affords equivalent protection to Part VIII.

1.04 Nothing in this policy is intended to constitute a binding statement of what position the Director will take with respect to a particular application. This policy is intended to reflect the Director's understanding of the Director's role in processing an application under subsection 82(3) of the CBCA

2. — Legislative Framework

2.01 Subsection 82(1) of the CBCA defines a trust indenture as *any deed, indenture or other instrument, including any supplement or amendment thereto, made by a corporation after its incorporation or continuance under this Act, under which the corporation issues debt obligations and in which a person is appointed as trustee for the holders of the debt obligations issued thereunder.*

2.02 Subsection 82(2) of the CBCA states that Part VIII applies to a trust indenture only *if the debt obligations issued or to be issued under the trust indenture are part of a distribution to the public.*

2.03 Subsection 82(3) of the CBCA provides, however, that the Director may exempt a trust indenture from Part VIII *if the trust indenture, the debt obligations issued thereunder, and the security interest effected thereby are subject to a law of a province or a country other than Canada that is substantially equivalent*

2.04 A corporation and/or a trustee may be held civilly and/or criminally liable where a trust indenture is made in violation of the provisions of Part VIII of the CBCA and where no exemption is granted by the Director

3. — Issuance of Debt Obligations not Part of a Distribution to the Public

3.01 Pursuant to subsection 82(2) of the Act (see 2.02 above), an application is not necessary and the Director will not exempt a trust indenture if the debt obligations issued thereunder are not part of a distribution to the public.

3.02 The debt obligations are part of a distribution to the public where there is a filing of a prospectus, statement of material facts, registration statement or similar document under the laws of Canada, a province or a jurisdiction outside Canada.

4. — Guidelines for Making an Application

A. — General Considerations

4.01 The general test used by the Director consists in determining whether the trust indenture is subject to a law of a province or country other than Canada that offers substantially equivalent protection to Part VIII of the CBCA. The applicant should compare the proposed legislation to the list of requirements set out in the table in Appendix 1 which summarily lists the requirements of Part VIII.

B. — Factors Considered in Reviewing an Application

4.02 Applicants frequently propose a non-Canadian trustee where the debt obligations will be sold outside Canada and it is anticipated that no Canadian will purchase the debt obligations or that only a relatively small number of Canadians will likely purchase the debt obligations under private placement exemptions. Subject to 4.04, the Director may exempt such a trust indenture from Part VIII of the Act if the applicant demonstrates that a law of the jurisdiction in which the debt obligations will be primarily offered has provisions substantially equivalent to Part VIII. Precedents have been established for trust indentures subject to the laws of the following countries which laws are considered substantially equivalent to Part VIII:

> i. *The United States of America: The Trust Indenture Act of 1939 as amended by the Trust Indenture Reform Act of 1990.*

4.03 Note that where the debt obligations will be primarily offered outside Canada, but a portion nevertheless will be sold to the Canadian public, the applicant must address the question of the procedural fairness of the exemption for Canadian debt holders Where no Canadian trustee is appointed or to be appointed and a portion of the debt obligations will be sold to Canadians, the foreign trustee will generally have to appoint an agent for service in Canada and irrevocably submit to at least the non-exclusive jurisdiction of the Canadian courts

C. — Conditions for Issuing an Exemption

4.04 The language used in the exemption must permit a person to identify the specific trust indenture for which the exemption was granted. Typically, the applicant should include the date or the date range (month and year) that the trust indenture is or will be entered into and the identity of the trustee. Where the issuer of the trust indenture does not include a CBCA corporation but one or more CBCA corporations are guarantors of the debt obligations issued under the trust indenture, the description should also name all of the issuers and all of the guarantors that are CBCA corporations.

5. — Other Information

A. — Additional Information Required

5.01 The Director may require other information not provided in the application in order to decide whether or not to exempt a trust indenture made by a corporation from the requirements of Part VIII of the CBCA

5.02 Under s. 89 of the CBCR, an application for an exemption under ss. 82(3) shall be made at least 30 days before the corporation is required to comply with Part VIII of the Act (which runs from the first issuance of debt obligations under the trust indenture) The Director will extend the time for making an application if the applicant establishes that no prejudice will result from the extension.

5.03 Under section 91 of the CBCR, the Director has the authority to seek additional information from the applicant or third parties With respect to information requested from third parties, section 92 of the CBCR provides that the applicant shall be given a copy of the information obtained and be given a reasonable opportunity to respond

5.04 There is no statutory obligation on the Director, however, to seek information at the request of third parties nor to allow third parties to make representations regarding an application.

B. — Access to Information Contained in an Application

5.05 Pursuant to section 266 of the CBCA, a person who has paid the required fee is entitled to examine and make copies or extracts of any document required by the CBCA to be sent to the Director The information filed with the Director in support of an exemption application is not confidential since such information is required to be filed in order to obtain an exemption. Consequently, an application for exemption is public information.

C. — Offences

5.06 Section 250 of the Act creates an offence with respect to documents required by the Act or Regulations to be sent to the Director, or any other person, that contains a false or misleading statement about a material fact or omits to state a material fact

6. — Making the Application

A. — Format

6.01 Along with a cover letter indicating the name of the applicant corporation, the application must provide information under three distinct headings: description and details of the exemption sought, statement of facts, and argument. These are described briefly below with further elaboration contained in the attached Annex A. We recommend the use of Annex A as a model

B. — The Documents

6.02 Detailed below is a brief description of the three major documents that comprise the submission:

(i) *Description and Details of the Exemption Sought*: The application must: state that it is an application for an exemption under subsection 82(3) of the *Canada Business Corporations Act*, indicate the name of the law of a province or country other than Canada that will govern the trust indenture, the debt obligations issued thereunder and, if any, the security interests effected thereby (see attached Annex A, Schedule A).

(ii) *Statement of Facts*: The applicant must include sufficient facts and all material information about the trust indenture, the debt obligations issued thereunder and, if any, the security interests effected thereby, which might affect the Director's decision (see attached Annex A, Schedule B). Where a precedent has not been established (i.e. a jurisdiction other than the U.S.A., see section 4.02 above), the applicant must compare the proposed legislation to Part VIII of the CBCA and demonstrate that the legislation is substantially equivalent to Part VIII.

(iii) *Argument*: Following the Statement of Facts, the applicant must provide convincing reasons that the exemption would not be prejudicial to debt holders or security interests affected thereby (see attached Annex A, Schedule C).

C. — Supplementary Issuance of Debt Obligations

6.03 A separate exemption is not ordinarily required for any supplemental or amending indenture provided that: (a) the exemption for the original trust indenture expressly includes such supplemental or amending indenture; and (b) such supplemental or amending indenture does not negate the basis upon which the original exemption was made. Where a trust indenture has been granted for the issuance of a specific type and/or amount of debt obligations, without reference to any supplemental indenture that might follow, and the applicant now requests an exemption for a supplementary issuance of debt obligations under the same trust indenture, it is not necessary to complete a detailed application. Instead, an applicant may submit a letter referring to the previous exemption and request that the trust indenture be exempt for the supplementary issuance, providing the necessary details about the debt obligations.

D. — Effective Date of the Exemption

6.04 An exemption will bear the date on which it was granted. A separate exemption is ordinarily required for each trust indenture. However, in a given case where there are strong similarities in the applications, it may be administratively convenient to combine several exemption applications into one.

6.05 Pursuant to paragraph 89(1)(c) of the CBCR, an application shall be made at least 30 days before the corporation is required to comply with Part VIII of the Act. Subsection 89(2) provides, however, that the Director shall extend the time for making an exemption application where the applicant establishes that no prejudice will result from the extension.

E. — Duration

6.06 The exemption generally takes effect on the date it was granted, unless otherwise indicated on the decision and remains in effect for the full term of the issuance subject to it being revoked.

F. — Revocation

6.07 The Director will not revoke an exemption before providing notice to the applicant and the opportunity to respond by submitting new facts and arguments to support the exemption

6.08 A revoked exemption ceases to carry effect from the date of revocation.

G. — Fees & Number of Copies of File:

6.09 The prescribed fee for an exemption application is $250 00.

6.10 Only one set of documents is required.

H. — Time for Processing an Application

6.11 Section 90 of the CBCR provides that *the Director shall, within 30 days after receipt of an application for an exemption, grant the exemption requested or send to the applicant written notice of the Director's refusal, together with reasons for the refusal.*

6.12 An application duly completed and filed, with no outstanding issue or concern, will usually receive a response from the Director within 15 working days after receipt of the application

6.13 An applicant requiring that the Director review the application on an expedited basis should bring the request immediately to the attention of the Director's staff, providing reasons for the urgency.

I. — Publication

6.14 Issued exemptions are published monthly under the heading "Corporations Canada Monthly Transactions" on the following website: *http://corporationscanada.ic.gc.ca*

J. — Appeal of Director's Decision

6.15 An applicant who feels aggrieved by a decision of the Director to grant, or to refuse to grant, an exemption may apply to the court, pursuant to paragraph 246(c) of the Act, for an order requiring the Director to change the decision

7. — Additional Information and How to Reach Corporations Canada

7.01 For additional information on Corporations Canada's products and services, please visit the Corporations Canada website *www.corporationscanada.ic.gc.ca* or call 1-866-333-5556

You can also contact Corporations Canada at:

Client Services Section

Corporations Canada

Industry Canada

9th Floor, Jean Edmonds Tower South

Ottawa, Ontario K1A 0C8

Toll free: 1-866-333-5556

Fax: 613-941-0601

www.corporationscanada.ic.gc.ca

Annex A — Example of Documents to Submit When Making an Application under Subsection 82(3) of the CBCA

Schedule A — In the Matter Concerning the Director Appointed under the *Canada Business Corporations Act*

And

The Application Of

(Name of corporation)

(hereinafter called the "Corporation")

Description and Details of the Exemption Sought

1. This application is for an exemption under subsection 82(3) of the *Canada Business Corporations Act* (the "CBCA") to exempt a trust indenture *(made / to be made)* on or about *(date, see 4.04 of the policy)* on between the Corporation and *(name of trustee)*, as trustee, from Part VIII of the CBCA

2. On the date the exemption takes effect:

(i) the trust indenture will be subject to the *(name of legislation and country/province)* which is a law that is substantially equivalent to Part VIII of the CBCA;

(ii) the debt obligation issued under the trust indenture will be subject to the *(name of legislation and country/province)* which is a law that is substantially equivalent to Part VIII of the CBCA;

(iii) any security interest effected by the trust indenture will be subject to the *(name of legislation and country/province)* which is a law that is substantially equivalent to Part VIII of the CBCA.

Schedule B — Statement of Facts

1. The corporation has issued or is proposing to issue debt obligations under a trust indenture *(describe proposed trust indenture: name of trustee, date or date range, etc.; or issued trust indenture; name of trustee, date, type of debt obligations, amount etc.)*

2. The debt obligations will be distributed to the public under a trust indenture *("made" or "to be made")* on or about *(date, see 4.04 of the policy)* between the Corporation and *(name of Trustee)*, as trustee, which is a body corporate authorized to carry on the business of a trust company under the laws of *(identify country/ province/ state)*.

3. Since it is expected that the securities will be primarily issued in *(name geographical area)*, it is imperative that the trustee and the trust indenture be subject to the legislation of *(name of country/ province/ state)*

4. The Corporation does not propose to appoint a trustee which is a body corporate incorporated under the laws of Canada or a province and authorized to carry on the business of a trust company in view of the fact that the debt obligations are intended to be offered for sale outside Canada and it is anticipated that no Canadians will purchase the debt obligations or only a relatively small number of Canadians are likely to purchase the debt obligations under private placement exemptions.

OR

4. The Corporation does not propose to appoint a trustee which is a body corporate incorporated under the laws of Canada or a province and authorized to carry on the business of a trust company in view of the fact that the debt obligations are intended to be offered for sale primarily outside Canada. Nevertheless, it is anticipated that a portion of the debt obligations will be offered for sale to the Canadian public, and therefore the trustee will undertake to appoint an agent for service of process in Canada and attorn to the non-exclusive jurisdiction of courts in a Canadian province *(see 4.03 of the policy)*.

5. The trust indenture, the debt obligations issued, and any security interests affected will be subject to *(name of legislation of country/province)* which contains provisions that are substantially equivalent to those set forth in Part VIII of the CBCA.

6. *Where a precedent has yet to be established* — The table set forth below lists each substantive provision of Part VIII of the CBCA and the corresponding provision of the *(Identify*

legislation) whenever such a corresponding provision exists. To the extent that significant differences in such corresponding provisions have been identified, a brief discussion of those differences has been included in an appendix to the table *(see APPENDIX "1" which provides a proposed format)*

OR

6. *If the trust indenture is governed by the laws of the United States of America* — the Director has concluded that the United States *Trust Indenture Act* of 1939, as amended by the *Trust Indenture Reform Act* of 1990, contains provisions that are substantially equivalent to Part VIII of the CBCA

Schedule C — Arguments

1. This application is made pursuant to subsection 82(3) of the *Canada Business Corporations Act* which empowers the Director to exempt a trust indenture from Part VIII of the CBCA if the trust indenture, the debt obligations issued thereunder and the security interest effected thereby are subject to a law of a province or a country other than Canada that is substantially equivalent to this Part

2. On the date the exemption takes effect, the trust Indenture, the debt obligations issued thereunder, and the security interest effected thereby will be subject to the *(name of legislation of country/province)* that is substantially equivalent to Part VIII of the CBCA

3. The *(name of legislation of country/province)* would not deprive the affected debt holders or security interests of rights that they would be entitled to under Part VIII of the CBCA

Dated this.......... day of.........., 20.........., at the City of ...., Province of ....

.... Signature — Capacity of

Schedule D — Model of a Decision — In the Matter Concerning the Director Appointed under the *Canada Business Corporations Act*

And

The Application Of

(Name of corporation)

(hereinafter called the "Corporation")

For An Exemption Under Subsection 82(3) Of The *Canada Business Corporations Act*

Exemption

UPON APPLICATION OF the Corporation, in accordance with subsection 82(3) of the *Canada Business Corporations Act* (the "Act"), to exempt the trust indenture *("made" or "to be made")* on or about *(date, see 4.04 of the policy)* between the Corporation and *(name of trustee)*, as trustee, for *(details of debt obligations)* to be issued thereunder from the application of Part VIII of the Act,

AND UPON reading the application documents and being satisfied that there is adequate justification for the exemption,

IT IS HEREBY DETERMINED that:

1. the trust indenture made [or to be *made*] on [date] [or *to be made not later than date*] between [*name of the issuer*}, as issuer and [if no CBCA corporation is an issuer, *name of any corporation that is a guarantor*], as guarantor and [*name of trustee*], as trustee, for [*any other available details of the debt obligations*] to be issued thereunder; and

2. any supplemental indenture or amending indenture (including any supplementary issuance of debt obligations under the same trust indenture) that does not negate the basis for this exemption,

is exempt from the application of Part VIII of the Act.

THIS EXEMPTION is made subject to the following terms:

1. (Optional, or subject to modified wording as suits the situation) No debt obligations are issued to a holder residing in any province or territory of Canada.

2. The trust indenture is entered into not later than [date]

3. No supplemental indenture or amending indenture is subsequently entered into that negates the basis for this exemption.

4. The parties to the trust indenture do not amend or waive any provision of the trust indenture, the debt obligations issued thereunder or the security interest, if any, affected thereby that are substantially equivalent to Part VIII of the Act without the written consent of the Director.

DATED, this .... day of ...., 20..........

.... Deputy Director

Appendix "1"

Note: Part VIII of the CBCA should be compared with the provisions of the legislation governing the trust indenture Table 1 summarizes the requirements of Part VIII of the CBCA to which the applicable legislation should be compared.

TABLE 1

PART VIII OF THE CBCA		**LEGISLATION GOVERNING THE TRUST INDENTURE**
83(1)	Conflict of Interest	
83(2)	Eliminating conflict of interest	
83(3)	Validity	
83(4)	Removal of trustee	
84	Qualification of trustee	
85(1)	List of security holders	
85(2)	Duty of issuer	
85(3)	Corporate applicant	
85(4)	Contents of statutory declaration	
85(5)	Use of list	
85(6)	Offence	
86(1)	Evidence of compliance	

TABLE 1

PART VIII OF THE CBCA	**LEGISLATION GOVERNING THE TRUST INDENTURE**
86(2)	Duty of issuer or guarantor
87	Contents of declaration, etc.
88	Further evidence of compliance
89(1)	Trustee may require evidence of compliance
89(2)	Certificate of compliance
90	Notice of default
91	Duty of care
92	Reliance on statements
93	No exculpation

The attached note to this table outlines any significant differences between the provisions of the CBCA and *(name of legislation)* The *(name of legislation)* contains a number of sections that are not found in Part VIII of the CBCA. Certain of these sections provide additional protection to the indenture securities holders which is not offered by Part VIII of the CBCA (Note: Explanations should be provided indicating any material differences that may exist and what is being undertaken to ensure that the security holders are afforded protection that is at least equivalent to Part VIII of the CBCA.)

Policy Statement 6.5 — Exemption Kit — Application Under Subsection 151(1) of the CBCA to Exempt a Dissident from the Proxy Solicitation Requirements

Date: March 19, 2008

1. — Statement of General Principles

1.01 The September 22, 2004 exemption policy is repealed and replaced with this policy.

1.02 This policy sets out information to facilitate an application to the Director appointed under the CBCA to exempt a soliciting dissident from some or all of the requirements of sending a dissident proxy circular in prescribed form.

1.03 The dissident solicitation requirements are designed to ensure that shareholders, whose proxies are solicited, are given sufficient information to form an informed opinion and decide whether or not to grant the dissident proxy authority. The Director will only exempt the dissident if satisfied that the exemption will not deprive solicited shareholders of the information necessary to arrive at an informed decision.

1.04 Nothing in this policy is intended to constitute a binding statement of what position the Director will take with respect to a particular application. This policy is intended to reflect the Director's understanding of the Director's role in processing an application by a dissident under subsection 151(1) of the CBCA.

2. — Legislative Framework

2.01 The term "dissident" in Part XIII of the Act and Part 7 of the Regulations refers to a person who solicits proxies other than management or a person acting on behalf of the management of the corporation (for management solicitation, please consult Policy Statement 6.6).

2.02 Section 147 of the Act defines the term "solicit" or "solicitation," enumerating in paragraph (a) circumstances included in the definition. Paragraph 147(b), however, excludes several circumstances, namely certain communications between shareholders, from the definition of solicitation (see section 3B). Only under circumstances where a dissident is committing an act deemed under the CBCA to be a solicitation will subsection 150(1) apply.

2.03 Subsection 150(1) of the CBCA provides that a dissident shall not solicit proxies unless *a dissident's proxy circular in prescribed form stating the purposes of the solicitation is sent to the auditor of the corporation, to each shareholder whose proxy is solicited, to each director and to the corporation.* The prescribed form of a dissident's proxy circular is set out in sections 60 to 64 of the CBCR.

2.04 Subsection 151(1) of the Act provides however that on the application of a dissident, *the Director may exempt the person, on any terms that the Director thinks fit, from any of the requirements of subsection 150(1), which exemption may have retrospective effect.*

2.05 A dissident who acts in violation of the solicitation requirements and who fails to obtain an exemption by the Director is in contravention of the Act which can result in civil and/or criminal liability.

2.06 Subsection 149(1) requires management of a corporation, concurrently with giving notice of the meeting to shareholders, to send a form of proxy in prescribed form to each shareholder entitled to receive notice of the meeting."

2.07 Sections 54, 55 and 56 of the CBCR specify the requirements for a form of proxy. While these requirements are binding on management, they are not binding on a dissident and, accordingly, subsection 151(1) does not need to confer on the Director the power to grant an exemption in respect of the form of proxy to be used by a dissident. Nevertheless, if a dissident does circulate a form of proxy, subsection 150(2) requires the dissident to send the form of proxy to the Director The Director will take into account the form of proxy and any other documents sent to the shareholders in making a determination as to whether the dissident should be exempt from the proxy solicitation requirements under paragraph 150(1)(b) of the CBCA.

3. — Where an Application to the Director is not Necessary

A. — General

3.01 Following the 2001 amendments to the Act and Regulations, the dissident proxy rules have been relaxed to facilitate communications among shareholders. The Act now provides that under certain conditions a dissident can communicate with shareholders without sending a dissident proxy circular and without having to apply to the Director for an exemption.

3.02 The Director will not issue an exemption in those circumstances

B. — A Dissident Communicating under Circumstances Excluded from the Definition of Solicitation in the Act

3.03 Paragraph 147(b) states that the definition of "solicit" or "solicitation" in the Act does not include:

(i) the sending of a form of proxy in response to an unsolicited request made by or on behalf of a shareholder,

(ii) the performance of administrative acts or professional services on behalf of a person soliciting a proxy,

(iii) the sending by an intermediary of the documents referred to in section 153,

(iv) a solicitation by a person in respect of shares of which the person is the beneficial owner,

(v) a public announcement, as prescribed, by a shareholder of how the shareholder intends to vote and the reasons for that decision,

(vi) a communication for the purposes of obtaining the number of shares required for a shareholder proposal under subsection 137(1.1), or

(vii) a communication, other than a solicitation by or on behalf of the management of the corporation, that is made to shareholders, in any circumstances that may be prescribed,

3.04 The application of subparagraph 147(b)(v) is prescribed in section 67 of the CBCR which describes what types of public announcements are excluded, e.g., a speech made in a public forum, an opinion that is broadcast or in a publication generally available to the public.

3.05 The application of subparagraph 147(b)(vii) is prescribed in section 68 of the CBCR which sets out the conditions under which persons, other than management, can communicate with shareholders without having to produce a dissident proxy circular. For instance, a shareholder, can communicate with shareholders, where no form of proxy is sent, about the business and affairs of the corporation including its management or proposals contained in a management proxy circular (paragraph 68(1)(a)) — or about the organization of a dissident proxy circular (paragraph 68(1)(b))

C. — Solicitation to Fifteen or Fewer Shareholders

3.06 Subsection 150(1.1) of the Act provides that *despite subsection (1), a person may solicit proxies, other than by or on behalf of the management of the corporation, without sending a dissident's proxy circular, if the total number of shareholders whose proxies are solicited is fifteen or fewer, two or more joint holders being counted as one shareholder.* This exception was introduced by the amendments to the Act on November 24, 2001 with a view to harmonizing the CBCA with several provincial securities laws.

D. — Solicitation by Public Broadcast

3.07 Subsection 150 (1.2) of the Act provides *that despite subsection (1), a person may solicit proxies, other than by or on behalf of the management of the corporation, without sending a dissident's proxy circular, if the solicitation is, in the prescribed circumstances, conveyed by public broadcast, speech or publication*

3.08 The application of this exception is prescribed in section 69 of the CBCR which requires the dissident to include certain information in the communication in order to insure that solicited shareholders have been provided sufficient information to make an informed decision. Before soliciting proxies, the person must send the required information and a copy of any related written communication to the Director and the corporation

4. — Guidelines for Making an Application

A. — General Considerations

4.01 The general test used by the Director consists in determining whether solicited share-holders, if the exemption were granted, would, without the prescribed dissident proxy circular, have sufficient information about the dissident and the solicitation to make an informed decision whether or not to grant the dissident proxy authority

B. — Types of Exemption

4.02 A dissident may apply for a full or partial exemption. A partial exemption relieves the dissident from some of the requirements prescribed in sections 60 to 64 of the Regulations. A full exemption relieves the dissident from sending any dissident proxy circular

4.03 Notwithstanding an application for a full exemption, the Director may find that it would be more appropriate to grant a partial exemption in light of the circumstances described in the application

C. — Core Information for a Partial Exemption

4.04 In all cases where a partial exemption is requested, the Director takes the position that shareholders solicited by a dissident should benefit from "core information". The core information is the minimum information deemed sufficient to enable shareholders to make an informed decision on the solicitation While this information may or may not be contained in a circular, it must be disclosed to shareholders at the time of the solicitation The Director will only exempt the dissident if satisfied that the partial exemption will not deprive solicited shareholders of core information

4.05 While the core information may vary from case to case, typically, the minimum information that should be communicated to all solicited shareholders is:

(i) the identity of the corporation and the dissident (paragraphs 61(a) and (c) of the Regulations);

(ii) details of any material interest of the dissident in the securities of the corporation to which the solicitation relates and any material interest of the dissident in the matter to be voted upon (paragragh 61(d) of the Regulations); and

(iii) the right to revoke a proxy, the method of solicitation and the identity of the person bearing the cost of the solicitation (paragragh 61(b) of the Regulations)

D. — Factors Considered in Reviewing an Application

4 06 Based on the statement of facts provided by the applicant (see Annex A, Schedule B for a non-exhaustive list) — eg the nature of the solicitation, the characteristics of solicited shareholders, other sources of information available to shareholders, etc — the Director attempts to determine if the test is met and, in turn, whether or not to grant the exemption sought

4.07 The following lists certain type of exemptions that may be granted where particular circumstances, supported by the statement of facts, are argued:

1. Financial hardship: The financial resources available to the dissident are short of meeting the cost associated with fulfilling the solicitation requirements

Type of exemption granted: A partial exemption may be granted, authorizing an altered form or abridged circular, disclosing at least core information

2. Prejudice to the dissident: This factor goes beyond the issue of financial resources to look at other difficulties. A situation may arise where certain information required to be disclosed in the Regulations has little material value to solicited shareholders and such information is not available or its disclosure would be difficult and prejudicial to the dissident.

Type of exemption granted: A partial exemption may be granted, indicating what information (other than core information) that does not need to be disclosed to shareholders.

3. Securities exemption: The dissident may benefit from an exemption under securities law or an order from a securities regulator

Type of exemption granted: The type of exemption granted varies according to the circumstances filed in support of the securities exemption. Typically, a partial exemption may be granted

4. Proxy-like disclosure: Solicited shareholders are provided with documents (e.g. letter instead of circular) that disclose information substantially equivalent to the information required by the Regulations. Type of exemption granted: A full exemption may be granted from preparing and sending a circular.

5. Solicitation of proxies in support of a shareholder proposal: A shareholder, making a proposal pursuant to section 137 of the Act, may solicit proxies in support of the proposal.

Type of exemption granted: Where the core information is contained in the proposal, a full exemption may be granted with respect to the circular. Otherwise, a partial exemption may be granted.

4.08 In all cases, the Director takes into account the nature of the matters to be discussed at the meeting of shareholders and its potential effect on the corporation, in deciding whether to grant the exemption sought. The Director will review with greater scrutiny proposals calling for a fundamental change, a change of control, or where the dissident stands to receive a material benefit not shared by other shareholders.

D. — Conditions for Issuing a Exemption

4.09 The Director may require the dissident to forward a copy of the exemption directly to the corporation whose shareholders are solicited.

4.10 The Director may require the dissident to make available to interested stakeholders, namely non-solicited shareholders, a copy of the exemption and, if any, materials disclosed to solicited shareholders.

4.11 Where a partial exemption is granted, the Director may find it appropriate to spell out, in the exemption decision, the core information to be included in the document that the dissident will send to solicited shareholders.

5. — Other Information

A. — Additional Information Required

5.01 The Director may require other information not provided in the application in order to decide whether or not to exempt the dissident.

5.02 Under section 91 of the CBCR, the Director has the authority to seek additional information from the applicant or third parties. With respect to information requested from third parties, section 92 of the CBCR provides that the applicant shall be given a copy of the information obtained and be given a reasonable opportunity to respond.

5.03 There is no statutory obligation on the Director, however, to seek information at the request of third parties nor to allow third parties, such as a corporation, to make representations regarding an application made by a dissident.

B. — Access to Information Contained in an Application

5.04 Pursuant to section 266 of the CBCA, a person who has paid the required fee is entitled to examine, make copies or extracts of any document required by the CBCA to be sent to the Director. The information filed with the Director in support of an exemption application is not confidential since such information is required to be filed in order to obtain an exemption. Consequently, an application for exemption is public information.

C. — Offences

5.06 Section 250 in the Act creates an offence with respect to documents required by the Act or Regulations to be sent to the Director, or any other person, that contains a false or misleading statement about material fact or omits to state a material fact.

5.07 Section 250 applies to both the documents filed in support of an exemption application as well as any document/information disclosed in reliance on:an exemption issued by the Director.

6. — Making the Application

A. — Format

6.01 Along with a cover letter indicating the name of the applicant corporation, the application must provide information under three distinct headings: description and details of the exemption sought, statement of facts, and argument. These are described briefly below with further elaboration contained in the attached Annex A. We recommend the use of Annex A as a model.

6.02 The Director recognizes that applicants may also be making similar representations under various provincial securities legislation. The Director will accept an application made under any provincial securities legislation provided it contains all relevant information or additional information is attached so as to comply with the requirements of the CBCA and CBCR. Note however that provincial legislation may provide confidentiality protections that do not exist under the CBCA (See 5-B above)

B. — The Documents

6.03 Detailed below is a brief description of the three major documents that comprise the submission:

(i) Description and Details of the Exemption Sought: The applicant must describe the exemption sought and note that this is an application for an exemption under subsection 151(1) in the *Canada Business Corporations Act* (see attached Annex A, Schedule A). Where a partial exemption is sought, the applicant must indicate the requirements in the Regulations that would not apply or, alternatively, that would apply to the solicitation in question.

(ii) Statement of Facts: The applicant must include sufficient facts and all material information which might effect the Director's decision (see attached Annex A, Schedule B)

(iii) Argument: Following the statements of facts, the applicant must provide convincing reasons that the exemption would not deprive solicited shareholders of sufficient

information to make an informed decision whether or not to grant proxy authority to the dissident (see attached Annex A, Schedule C). The applicant should refer to 4.09 above.

C. — Renewals

6.04 If the applicant seeks to renew an exemption that has been issued previously and the circumstances have not substantially changed, it is not necessary to complete a detailed application. Instead, a letter stating that the applicant is seeking to renew a specific exemption and that the circumstances have not substantially changed will be accepted. Note that if the applicant wishes to change the wording of the exemption, the applicant should refer to the changes and provide reasons for these changes in the letter.

D. — Effective Date of the Exemption

6.05 The exemption will bear the date on which it was granted.

6.06 Pursuant to paragraph 89(1)(d) of the CBCR, an application should be made before the date of notice of meeting referred to in section 149 of the CBCA. Subsection 89(2) provides however that, despite subsection 89(1), the Director shall extend the time for making an exemption application where the applicant establishes that no prejudice will result therefrom.

E. — Duration

6.07 An exemption is only in effect for a specific meeting of shareholders, and any adjournments of that meeting.

F. — Revocation

6.08 The Director will generally not revoke an exemption before providing notice to the dissident and the opportunity to respond by submitting new facts and arguments to support the exemption.

6.09 A revoked exemption ceases to carry effect from the date of revocation.

G. — Retrospective Effect

6.10 Subsection 151(1) permits exemptions by the Director to have retrospective effect. Requests for retrospective exemption are reviewed on a case-by-case basis. A retrospective exemption will only be granted where the applicant establishes that no prejudice was caused to solicited shareholders.

H. — Fees & Number of Copies to File

6.11 The prescribed fee for an exemption application is $250.00

6.12 Only one set of documents is required.

I. — Time for Processing an Application

6.13 Section 90 of the CBCR provides that *the Director shall, within 30 days after receipt of an application for an exemption, grant the exemption requested or send to the applicant written notice of the Director's refusal, together with reasons for the refusal.*

6.14 An application duly completed and filed, with no outstanding issue or concern, will usually receive a response from the Director within 15 working days after receipt of the application

6.15 An applicant requiring that the Director review the application on an expedited basis should bring the request immediately to the attention of the Director's staff, providing reasons for the urgency.

J. — Publication

6.16 Issued exemptions are published monthly under the heading "Corporations Canada Monthly Transactions" on the following website: *http://corporationscanada.ic.gc.ca*.

K. — Appeal of Director's Decision

6.17 An applicant who feels aggrieved by a decision of the Director to grant, or to refuse to grant, an exemption may apply to the court, pursuant to paragraph 246(c) of the Act, for an order requiring the Director to change the decision.

7. — Additional Information and How to Reach Corporations Canada

7.01 For additional information on Corporations Canada's products and services, please visit the Corporations Canada website *www.corporationscanada.ic.gc.ca* or call 1-866-333-5556.

You can also contact Corporations Canada at:

Client Services Section

Corporations Canada

Industry Canada

9th Floor, Jean Edmonds Tower South

Ottawa, Ontario K1A 0C8

Toll free: 1-866-333-5556

Fax: 613-941-0601

www.corporationscanada.ic.gc.ca

Appendix A — Example of Documents for a Dissident to Submit When Making an Application under Subsection 151(1) of the CBCA

Schedule A — In the Matter Concerning the Director Appointed under the *Canada Business Corporations Act*

And

In The Matter Of

(Name of the corporation)

(hereinafter called the "Corporation")

And

The Application Of

(Name of the dissident)

(hereinafter called the "Dissident")

Description and Details of the Exemption Sought

1. This application is made under subsection 151(1) of the *Canada Business Corporations Act* (the "Act") to exempt the Dissident of the Corporation from the requirements of subsection 150(1) of the Act to send the prescribed dissident proxy circular, for the *("annual" or "special" or "annual and special")* meeting of the shareholders to be held on or about the *(date)*.

2. This application is for a *("full" or "partial")* exemption from the requirements of subsection 150(1) of the Act *(for a partial exemption, describe the exemption sought, referring to the provisions of the Regulations)*

Schedule B — Statement of Facts

1. The following statement provides sufficient facts and all material information in order to enable the Director to make an informed decision about the exemption sought:

The following is a non-exhaustive list of facts that may be material:

* *the date of the meeting*;

* *the nature of the meeting (i.e. annual, special or annual and special) and items on the agenda, if known*;

* *the nature of the dissent*;

* *interests of the dissident, if any, in the solicitation*;

* *the proxies solicited (i.e sophistication of solicited shareholders, etc.)*;

* *other sources of information available to shareholders (e.g. press releases, corporate bulletins, management proxy circular, shareholder proposal, etc)*;

* *core and other information/ forms that the Dissident is proposing to disclose, indicating derogations from the requirements of the Regulations (it may be appropriate to include, and the Director may request to review, a copy of the information/ forms that would be sent)*;

* *the method of dissemination of information.*

Schedule C — Arguments

1. This application is made pursuant to subsection 151(1) of the *Canada Business Corporations Act* which empowers the Director to exempt the Dissident from any of the requirements of subsection 150(1) of the Act.

2. The exemption, if granted, will not deprive solicited shareholders of the information necessary to make an informed decision whether or not to grant the Dissident proxy authority

3. In particular, the exemption should be granted for the following reason(s):

For Instance,

1. The financial resources available to the Dissident are short of meeting the cost associated with fulfilling the solicitation requirements

2. The information proposed not to be disclosed would have little material value whereas its disclosure would prejudice the Dissident because *(state cause of prejudice)*.

3. The Dissident is exempt under securities law or has been granted an exemption order from a securities regulator, as follows: *(describe exemption)*

4. Solicited shareholders are provided with *(describe document(s))* that disclose information substantially equivalent to the information required by the Regulations,

5. The Dissident is soliciting proxies in support of a shareholder proposal pursuant to section 137 of the Act and the core information is contained in the proposal.

Dated this .... day of.........., 20.........., at the City of ...., Province of ....,

.... Signature — Capacity of

Schedule D — Model of a Decision — In the Matter Concerning the Director Appointed under the *Canada Business Corporations Act*

And

In The Matter Of

(Name of the corporation)

(hereinafter called the "Corporation")

And

The Application Of

(Name of the dissident)

(hereinafter called the "Dissident")

For An Exemption Under Subsection 151(1) Of The *Canada Business Corporations Act*

Exemption

UPON APPLICATION in accordance with subsection 151(1) of the *Canada Business Corporations Act* (the "Act"), to *("fully" or "partially")* exempt the Dissident of the Corporation from the requirements of subsection 150(1) of the Act to send the prescribed dissident proxy circular, for the *("annual" or "special" or "annual and special")* meeting of shareholders to be held on or about *(date)*.

AND UPON reading the application documents and being satisfied that there is adequate justification for so doing.

IT IS HEREBY DETERMINED that *(name of the dissident)* of *(name of the corporation)* is *("fully" or "partially")* exempt from sending the prescribed dissident proxy circular, for the *("annual" or "special" or "annual and special")* meeting of shareholders to be held on or about *(date)*, with respect to the requirements of subsection 150(1) of the Act, *(For a partial exemption, refer to the provisions of the Regulations)*

DATED, this .... day of ...., 20..........

.... Deputy Director

Policy Statement 6.6 — Exemption Kit — Application Under Subsection 151(1) of the CBCA to Exempt Management from the Proxy Solicitation Requirements

Date: **March 19, 2008**

1. — Statement of General Principles

1.01 The September 22, 2004 exemption policy is repealed and replaced with this policy

1.02 This policy sets out information to facilitate an application to the Director appointed under the CBCA to exempt the management of a corporation from some or all of the management solicitation requirements in the Act and Regulations.

1.03 The management solicitation requirements are designed to enhance the rights of shareholders to participate in decisions of the corporation, at the meeting of shareholders The prescribed form of proxy enables shareholders to exercise their right of vote when they will not be attending the meeting. The prescribed management proxy circular further ensures that shareholders have access to corporate information in a timely manner so they may exercise their vote in an informed way. The Director will only exempt the management if satisfied that the exemption will not deprive shareholders of the capacity to exercise their right to vote or of the information necessary to make an informed decision.

1.04 Nothing in this policy is intended to constitute a binding statement of what position the Director will take with respect to a particular application. This policy is intended to reflect the Director's understanding of the Director's role in processing an application by the management of a corporation under subsection 151(1) of the CBCA.

2. — Legislative Framework

2.01 Management of a distributing corporation and management of a non-distributing corporation having more than 50 shareholders cannot solicit proxies without sending a management proxy circular to the shareholders The term "solicit" or "solicitation" is defined in section 147 of the Act.

2.02 Management is considered to be soliciting when it sends a form of proxy under section 149 of the Act Subsection 149(1) creates a mandatory solicitation requirement that provides that, *subject to subsection (2)* (see section 3 of this policy), *the management of a corporation shall, concurrently with giving notice of a meeting of shareholders, send a form of proxy in prescribed form to each shareholder who is entitled to receive notice of the meeting.* The prescribed form of a proxy form is set out in sections 54 to 56 of the CBCR.

2.03 Subsection 150 (1) of the CBCA provides that management or a person acting on behalf of management shall not solicit proxies unless *a management proxy circular in prescribed form, either as an appendix to or as a separate document accompanying the notice of the meeting is sent to the auditor of the corporation, to each shareholder whose proxy is solicited and to each director.* The prescribed form of a management's proxy circular is set out in sections 57 to 59 of the CBCR.

2.04 Subsection 151 (1) of the Act provides however that *on the application of an interested person, the Director may exempt the person, on any terms that the Director thinks fit, from any of the requirements of section 149 or subsection 150(1), which exemption may have retrospective effect.* Management can apply to be exempt from the requirements of either or both section 149 and subsection 150(1).

2.05 A corporation's management who acts in violation of the mandatory solicitation requirements and who fails to obtain an exemption by the Director is in contravention of the Act which can result in civil and/or criminal liability.

3. — Where an Application to the Director is Not Necessary

3.01 Prior to the 2001 amendments to the Act and Regulations, many exemptions under subsection 151(1) were granted on the grounds that the corporation in question was non-distributing and closely-held, such as family-owned corporations.

3.02 The amendments to the CBCA broadened the exception to the mandatory solicitation requirement. *Under subsection 149(2),* the management of the corporation is not required to send a form of proxy under subsection (1) if it:

(a) is not a distributing corporation; and

(b) has fifty or fewer shareholders entitled to vote at a meeting, two or more joint holders being counted as one shareholder.

3.03 A corporation is not a distributing corporation if the definition in the Regulations does not apply or if it has received an exemption by the Director under subsection 2(6) of the Act (see Policy on making an exemption application under subsection 2(6) of the Act). The term "distributing corporation," as defined in section 2 of the Regulations, encompasses, among other things, the definition of "reporting issuer" found in provincial securities legislation Note that where a corporation is subject to an exemption under provincial securities legislation or to an order of the relevant provincial regulator that provides that the corporation is not a "reporting issuer", the corporation is not a distributing corporation for the purpose of the definition of the term in section 2.

3.04 Where the exception under ss. 149(2) applies, management does not need to send forms of proxy and therefore an application for exemption from such a requirement is not necessary. Note, however, that if management chooses, despite the applicability of subsection 149(2), to send out forms of proxy or otherwise solicit shareholders, management may be caught by the definition in section 147 of the Act since the sending of a form of proxy or other communication to a shareholder under certain circumstances could be reasonably calculated to result in the procurement, withholding or revocation of a proxy. In such cases, management may wish to make an application to the Director to exempt it from some or all of the requirements for sending a prescribed form of proxy and /or management proxy circular.

4. — Guidelines for Making an Application

A. — General Considerations

4.01 With respect to a request for exemption from the prescribed form of proxy, the test used by the Director consists of determining whether shareholders, if the exemption were granted, would have the capacity to exercise their right to vote. With respect to a request for exemption from the prescribed management proxy circular, the test consists of determining whether shareholders would have sufficient information about the business and affairs of the corporation, its management, the solicitation, and the subject matter to be voted upon at the meeting of shareholders to make an informed decision whether or not to grant management proxy authority.

4.02 Under section 89 of the CBCR, an application for an exemption under subsection 151(1) of the Act shall be made before the date of giving the notice of a meeting of shareholders. Nevertheless, the Director will extend the time for making an application if the applicant establishes that no predjudice will result from the extension.

B. — Types of Exemption

4.03 Management may apply for an exemption from any of the requirements of section 149 or subsection 150(1) of the Act for sending the prescribed: (1) management proxy circular or (2) form of proxy and management proxy circular. With respect to each document, management may apply for a partial or full exemption. A partial exemption relieves management from some of the requirements prescribed in the Regulations (sections 54 to 56 for the form of proxy and sections 57 to 59 for the management proxy circular). A full exemption relieves management from sending the document at all

4.04 Notwithstanding an application for a certain type of exemption, the Director may deem that it would be more appropriate to grant another type of exemption in light of the facts and circumstances described in the application.

C. — Factors Considered in Reviewing an Application

4.05 Applicants must demonstrate that all or some of the items to be disclosed in a proxy form or proxy circular are not necessary in the circumstances and that the shareholders would not be prejudiced if the management of the corporation were exempted from any or part of the provisions of section 149 and subsection 150(1) of the CBCA.

4.06 The following are examples where complete or partial exemptions from proxy requirements have been granted:

1. Management intends to provide shareholders with documents that disclose information substantially equivalent to the information required by the Regulations.

Type of exemption granted: A full exemption may be granted with respect to the management proxy circular on condition that the substantially equivalent material is sent.

2. Shareholders have access to or are provided with, on a regular basis, sufficient information, including financial information, to exercise their vote in an informed way This may occur where the corporation periodically issues information to shareholders through information bulletins.

Type of exemption granted: Where what is provided to shareholders generally satisfies the disclosure requirements, a full exemption may be granted with respect to the management proxy circular. Otherwise, a partial exemption may be granted, indicating what information needs to be disclosed to shareholders

3. A majority of the shareholders of the corporation are employees, officers and/or directors of the corporation and the remaining shareholders are either sophisticated investors or former employees, directors and officers of the corporation who routinely have up-to-date and reasonably complete information on the corporation and are able to exercise their right to vote;

Type of exemption granted: A full exemption may be granted with respect to just the management proxy circular or both the management proxy circular and the form of proxy.

4. All shareholders support the exemption.

Type of exemption granted: A full exemption may be granted with respect to just the management proxy circular or both the management proxy circular and the form of proxy

4.07 In all cases, the Director takes into account the nature of the matters to be discussed at the meeting of shareholders and its potential effect on the corporation in deciding whether to grant the exemption sought. The Director will review with greater scrutiny proposals for a fundamental change or a change in control rather than matters of a routine nature.

D. — Conditions for Issuing an exemption

4.08 The Director may require management to make available to interested stakeholders a copy of the exemption as well as all information disclosed or otherwise available to shareholders

4.09 Where the Director exempts management from the mandatory requirement of sending a form of proxy in section 149 of the Act, the Director may nevertheless compel management to send a form of proxy to those shareholders who request one from the corporation.

5. — Other Information

A. — Additional Information Required

5.01 The Director may require other information not provided in the application in order to decide whether or not to exempt management from the solicitation requirements.

5.02 Under section 91 of the CBCR, the Director has the authority to seek additional information from the applicant or third parties. With respect to information requested from third parties, section 92 of the CBCR provides that the applicant shall be given a copy of the information obtained and be given a reasonable opportunity to respond.

5.03 There is no statutory obligation on the Director, however, to seek information at the request of third parties nor to allow third parties, such as a corporation, to make representations regarding an application made by management.

B. — Access to Information Contained in an Application

5.04 Pursuant to section 266 of the CBCA, a person who has paid the required fee is entitled to examine, make copies or extracts of any document required by the CBCA to be sent to the Director. The information filed with the Director in support of an exemption application is not confidential since such information is required to be filed in order to obtain an exemption Consequently, an application for exemption is public information.

C. — Offences

5.05 Applicants are reminded that section 250 in the Act creates an offence with respect to documents required by the Act or Regulations to be sent to the Director, or any other person, that contains a false or misleading statement about material fact or omits to state a material fact.

5.06 Section 250 applies to both the documents filed in support of an exemption application as well as any document/ information disclosed to shareholders in reliance on an exemption issued by the Director

6. — Making the Application

A. — Format

6.01 Along with a cover letter indicating the name of the applicant corporation, the application must provide information under three distinct headings: description and details of the exemption sought, statement of facts, and argument. These are described briefly below with further elaboration contained in the attached Annex A. We recommend the use of Annex A as a model.

6.02 The Director recognizes that, where the applicant is a distributing corporation, it may also be making similar representations under various provincial securities legislation. The Director will accept an application made under any provincial securities legislation provided it contains all relevant information or additional information is attached so as to comply with the requirements of the CBCA and CBCR. Note however, that provincial legislation may provide confidentiality protection that does not exist for exemption documents under the CBCA.

B. — The Documents

6.03 Detailed below is a brief description of the three major documents that comprise the submission:

(i) *Description and Details of the Exemption Sought*: The applicant must describe the type of exemption sought (see 4.05 above) and note that this is an application for an exemption under subsection 151(1) in the *Canada Business Corporations Act* (see attached Annex A, Schedule A). The applicant must indicate whether it seeks to be exempt from the requirements of sending a prescribed (1) management proxy circular or (2) management proxy circular and form of proxy. Where a partial exemption is sought, the applicant must indicate the requirements in the Regulations that would not apply or, alternatively, that would apply to the solicitation in question

(ii) *Statement of Facts*: The applicant must include sufficient facts and all material information which might affect the Director's decision (see attached Annex A, Schedule B).

(iii) *Argument*: Following the statements of facts, the applicant must provide convincing reasons according to the type of exemption sought (i.e form of proxy and/or management proxy circular; partial or total) why the case meets the test(s) set out in 4.01 above. The applicant should refer to 4.05 and 4.06 above.

C. — Renewals

6.04 If the applicant seeks to renew an exemption that has been issued previously and the circumstances have not substantially changed, it is not necessary to complete a detailed application. Instead, a letter stating that the applicant is seeking to renew a specific exemption and that the circumstances have not substantially changed will be accepted. Note that if the applicant wishes to change the wording of the exemption, the applicant should refer to the changes and provide reasons for these changes in the letter.

D. — Effective Date of the Exemption

6.05 An exemption will bear the date on which it was granted.

6.06 Pursuant to paragraph 89(1)(d) of the CBCR, an application shall be made before the date of notice of the meeting referred to in section 149 of the CBCA. Subsection 89(2) provides however that, despite subsection 89(1), the Director shall extend the time for making an exemption application where the applicant establishes that no prejudice will result therefrom.

E. — Duration

6.07 An exemption is only in effect for a specific meeting of shareholders, and any adjournments of that meeting.

F. — Revocation

6.08 The Director will generally not revoke an exemption without providing notice to the applicant and the opportunity to respond by submitting new facts and arguments to support the exemption.

6.09 A revoked exemption ceases to carry effect from the date of revocation

G. — Retrospective Effect

6.10 Subsection 151(1) permits exemptions by the Director to have retrospective effect. Requests for retrospective exemptions are reviewed on a case-by-case basis. A retrospective exemption will only be granted where the applicant establishes that no prejudice was caused to shareholders

H. — Fees & Number of Copies of File:

6.11 The prescribed fee for an exemption application is $250.00.

6.12 Only one set of documents is required.

I. — Time for Processing an Application

6.13 Section 90 of the CBCR provides that *the Director shall, within 30 days after receipt of an application for an exemption, grant the exemption requested or send to the applicant written notice of the Director's refusal, together with reasons for the refusal.*

6.14 An application duly completed and filed, with no outstanding issue or concern, will usually receive a response from the Director within 15 working days after receipt of the application.

6.15 An applicant requiring that the Director review the application on an expedited basis should bring the request immediately to the attention of the Director's staff, providing reasons for the urgency

J. — Publication

6.16 Issued exemptions are published monthly under the heading "Corporations Canada Monthly Transactions" on the following website: *http://corporationscanada.ic.gc.ca*

K. — Appeal of Director's Decision

6.17 An applicant who feels aggrieved by a decision of the Director to grant, or to refuse to grant, an exemption may apply to the court, pursuant to paragraph 246(c) of the Act, for an order requiring the Director to change the decision

7. — Additional Information and How to Reach Corporations Canada

7.01 For additional information on Corporations Canada's products and services, please visit the Corporations Canada website *www.corporationscanada.ic.gc.ca* or call 1-866-333-5556.

You can also contact Corporations Canada at:

> Client Services Section
>
> Corporations Canada
>
> Industry Canada
>
> 9th Floor, Jean Edmonds Tower South
>
> Ottawa, Ontario K1A 0C8

Toll free: 1-866-333-5556

Fax:613-941-0601

www.corporationscanada.ic.gc.ca

Annex A — Example of Documents for Management to Submit When Making an Application under Subsection 151(1) of the CBCA

Schedule A — In the Matter Concerning the Director Appointed under the *Canada Business Corporations Act*

And

The Application Of

(Name of corporation)

(hereinafter called the "Corporation")

Description and Details of the Exemption Sought

1. This application is made under subsection 151(1) of the *Canada Business Corporations Act* (the "Act) to exempt the management of the Corporation from the requirements of *("subsection 150(1) of the Act" or "section 149 and subsection 150(1) of the Act")* to send the prescribed *("management proxy circular" or "form of proxy and management proxy circular")*, for the *("annual" or "special" or "annual and special")* meeting of the shareholders to be held on or about the *(date)*.

2. This application is for a *("full" or "partial")* exemption. *For a partial exemption, describe the exemption sought referring to the provisions of the Regulations).*

Schedule B — Statement of Facts

1. The following statement provides sufficient facts and all material information in order to enable the Director to make an informed decision about the exemption sought:

The following is a non-exhaustive list of facts that may be material:

- *the date of the meeting;*

- *the nature of the meeting (i.e., annual, special, or annual and special) and items on the agenda;*

- *the nature of the solicitation (i.e., mandatory or other);*

- *interest of a member of management, if any, in the action to which the solicitation refers;*

- *whether the applicant is or is not a distributing corporation;*

- *the characteristics of the shareholders (i.e., geographical location, degree of sophistication, etc);*

- *other sources of information available to shareholders generally (e.g. press releases, corporate bulletins, documents disclosed pursuant to securities law, etc);*

- *information/ forms that management is proposing to disclose, indicating derogations from the requirements of the Regulations (it may be appropriate to include, and the Director may request to review a copy of the information/ forms that would be sent);*

- *the method of dissemination of information.*

Schedule C — Arguments

1. This application is made pursuant to subsection 151(1) of the *Canada Business Corporations Act* which empowers the Director to exempt the management of the Corporation from any of the requirements of section 149 and subsection 150(1) of the CBCA.

2. The exemption, if granted, will not deprive shareholders of the capacity to exercise their right to vote or the information necessary to exercise that right.

3. In particular, the exemption should be granted for the following reason(s):

For Instance,

> 1. The shareholders have access to or are provided with, on a regular basis, sufficient information, including financial information, to make an informed decision at the meeting. This may occur where, depending on the circumstances, the Corporation periodically issues information to shareholders through corporate bulletins either voluntarily or in compliance with securities, exchange or market rules.

> 2. Management proposed to provide shareholders with documents that disclose information substantially equivalent to the information required by the Regulations.

> 3. Certain information required to be disclosed under the Regulations has little value to shareholders under the circumstances and that such information is not available or its disclosure would be prejudicial to the Corporation or other persons.

> 4.

>> (a) The majority of shareholders, are employees, officers and directors of the Corporation (or former employees, officers and directors living in the same area of the Corporation); *and*

>> (b) the remaining shareholders are either institutional/sophisticated investors (i e large investors), insiders of the Corporation or other persons closely involved in the business and affairs of the Corporation and able to exercise their right to vote.

> 5. The consent of all shareholders for the exemption has been obtained

Dated this .... day of.........., 20.........., at the City of ...., Province of ....

.... Signature — Capacity of

Schedule D — Model of a Decision — In the Matter Concerning the Director Appointed under the *Canada Business Corporations Act*

And

The Application Of The Management Of

(Name of corporation)

(hereinafter called the "Corporation")

For An Exemption Under Subsection 151(1) Of The *Canada Business Corporations Act*

Exemption

UPON APPLICATION in accordance with subsection 151(1) of the *Canada Business Corporations Act* (the "Act"), to *("fully" or "partially")* exempt the management of the Corporation from the requirements of *("subsection 150(1) of the Act" or "section 149 and subsection 150(1) of the Act")* to send the prescribed *("management proxy circular" or "form of proxy and management proxy circular")*, for the *("annual" or "special" or "annual and special")* meeting of shareholders to be held on or about *(date)*,

AND UPON reading the application documents and being satisfied that there is adequate justification for so doing,

IT IS HEREBY DETERMINED that the management of *(name of the corporation)* is *("fully" or "partially")* exempt from sending the prescribed *("management proxy circular" or "form of proxy and management proxy circular")*, for the *("annual" or "special" or "annual and special")* meeting of shareholders to be held on or about *(date)*, with respect to the requirements of *(for a full exemption refer to the section(s) of the Act stated in paragraph 1; for a partial exemption from the section(s), describe the exemption sought referring to the provisions of the Regulations)*.

DATED, this .... day of ...., 20..........

.... Deputy Director

Examples of standard or typical terms:

> THIS EXEMPTION is made subject to the following terms:
>
> 1. Management provides shareholders with documents as described in the application that disclose information substantially equivalent to the information required by the Regulations
>
> 2 The annual meeting (or annual and special meeting) in respect of which this exemption is made is not held after March 31, 2005.

Policy Statement 6.7 — Exemption Kit — Application Under Section 156 to Exempt a Corporation from the Prescribed Financial Disclosure Requirements

Date: **March 19, 2008**

1. — Statement of General Principles

1.01 The September 22, 2004 exemption policy is repealed and replaced with this policy.

1.02 This policy sets out information to facilitate an application to the Director appointed under the CBCA for an exemption authorizing a corporation to omit prescribed items from, or dispense with publication of, prescribed financial statements.

1.03 The financial disclosure rules prescribed in the Regulations are designed to provide a corporation's shareholders with relevant information about the financial position of the corporation The Director will only grant an exemption if satisfied that disclosure of the prescribed information would be detrimental to the corporation

1.04 Nothing in this policy is intended to constitute a binding statement of what position the Director will take with respect to a particular application This policy is intended to reflect the Director's understanding of the Director's role in processing an application under section 156 of the CBCA.

2. — Legislative Framework

2.01 Section 155 of the Act generally states the obligation of a corporation to present certain financial statements on an annual basis The items and contents of these statements are prescribed in sections 70 and 72 of the Regulations.

2.02 Section 70 of the Regulations stipulates that the *financial statements referred to in paragraph 155(1)(a) of the Act shall, except as otherwise provided by this Part, be prepared in accordance with generally-accepted principles as set out in the Handbook of the Canadian Institute of Chartered Accountants* (CICA).

2.03 Section 72 of the Regulations further stipulates in subsection 72(1) that *the financial statements referred to in section 155 of the Act shall include at least*:

(a) a balance sheet;

(b) a statement of retained earnings;

(c) an income statement; and

(d) a statement of changes in financial position.

2.04 Section 156 of the CBCA provides that the *Director may, on application of a corporation, authorize the corporation to omit from its financial statements any item prescribed, or to dispense with the publication of any particular financial statement prescribed, and the Director may, if the Director reasonably believes that disclosure of the information contained in the statements would be detrimental to the corporation, permit the omission on any reasonable conditions that the Director thinks fit.*

2.05 A corporation that does not comply with the financial disclosure rules prescribed in the Regulations and that fails to obtain an exemption from the Director is in contravention of the CBCA which can result in civil and/or criminal liability

3. — Guidelines for Making an Application

A. — General Considerations

3.01 The general test used by the Director consists in determining whether the disclosure of information would be detrimental to the corporation if the exemption is not granted.

B. — Factors Considered in Reviewing an Application

3.02 In determining whether there would be a detriment to the corporation, the Director may consider the following circumstances, among others:

1. the corporation would be at a disadvantage with suppliers, customers or others;

2. the corporation would be at a disadvantage because it deals only in one line of products or services and its competitors:

i) are not required to make similar disclosure; or

ii) deal in several lines of products or services and disclose information in a form that prevents identification of financial information in respect of any particular product or service;

3. a competitor, who does not disclose, could calculate the profit margin on a specific product or service sold by the corporation and place the latter in a disadvantageous position by reducing its price for this product or service;

4. a supplier could increase the selling price of raw materials sold to the corporation making the disclosure, on the basis of its knowledge of the profitability of a product sold by the latter;

5. an important customer could demand a reduction in the sale price on the basis of its knowledge of the profit made on a product or service by the disclosing corporation;

6. the corporation's only public shares are exchangeable shares whose dividend and dissolution entitlements are determined only by reference to the financial performance of the sole parent corporation and the parent corporation will send to all shareholders of exchangeable shares the same documentation that it sends to its own shareholders, and will make all necessary filings with the appropriate securities regulatory authorities.

3.03 In determining whether the circumstances justify granting an exemption, the Director may weigh the detriment of disclosure to the corporation against the potential prejudice of non-disclosure to shareholders who would otherwise benefit from the information. The Director will look at factors such as:

1 the content of the information;

2. the shareholdings of the corporation (closely-held versus public corporation);

3. whether all the shareholders consent to the exemption;

4. the knowledge the shareholders would have about the financial position of the corporation notwithstanding the lack of exempted information

It should be noted that, except in certain limited circumstances, the fact that the corporation will have to spend a certain amount of money to prepare financial statements cannot be considered a financial detriment caused by the disclosure of information

C. — Conditions for Issuing an Exemption

3.04 In exempting a corporation, the Director may find it appropriate under the circumstances to include one or more conditions in the exemption.

3.05 The Director may also require the applicant to forward a copy of the exemption to shareholders and all securities regulators concerned.

4. — Other Information

A. — Additional Information Required

4.01 The Director may require other information not provided in the application in order to decide whether or not to exempt the corporation

4.02 Under section 91 of the CBCR, the Director has the authority to seek additional information from the applicant or third parties. With respect to information requested from third parties, section 92 of the CBCR provides that the applicant shall be given a copy of the information obtained and be given a reasonable opportunity to respond

4.03 There is no statutory obligation on the Director, however, to seek information at the request of third parties nor to allow third parties to make representations regarding an application.

B. — Access to Information Contained in an Application

4.04 Pursuant to section 266 of the CBCA, a person who has paid the required fee is entitled to examine, make copies or extracts of any document required by the CBCA to be sent to the Director. The information filed with the Director in support of an exemption application is not confidential since such information is required to be filed in order to obtain an exemption Consequently, an application for exemption is public information.

C. — Offences

4.05 Section 250 of the Act creates an offence with respect to documents required by the Act or Regulations to be sent to the Director, or any other person, that contains a false or misleading statement about material fact or omits to state a material fact.

5. — Making the Application

A. — Format

5.01 Along with a cover letter indicating the name of the applicant corporation, the application must provide information under three distinct headings: description and details of the exemption sought, statement of facts, and argument These are described briefly below with further elaboration contained in the attached Annex A. We recommend the use of Annex A as a model.

B. — The Documents

5.02 Detailed below is a brief description of the three major documents that comprise the submission:

(i) *Description and Details of the Exemption Sought*: The applicant must describe the exemption sought and note that this is an application for an exemption under section 156 of the *Canada Business Corporations Act* (see attached Annex A, Schedule A).

(ii) *Statement of Facts*: The applicant must include sufficient facts and all material information which might effect the Director's decision (see attached Annex A, Schedule B). The applicant should specifically speak about the business of the corporation, about the affected shareholders, and about the prescribed items or statements to be excluded (i.e. their function and importance).

(iii) *Argument*: Following the statements of facts, the applicant must provide convincing reasons that the disclosure of the prescribed items or statements in question would be detrimental to the corporation (see attached Annex A, Schedule C).

C. — Renewals

5.03 If the applicant seeks to renew an exemption that has been granted and the circumstances have not substantially changed, it is not necessary to complete a detailed application Instead, a letter identifying the previous exemption, requesting for a renewal of the exemption, and stating that the circumstances have not substantially changed is accepted. Note that if the applicant wishes to change the wording of the decision, the applicant must refer to the changes and provide reasons for these changes in the letter.

D. — Effective Date of the Exemption

5.04 An exemption will bear the date on which it was granted.

5.05 Pursuant to paragraph 89(1)(e) of the CBCR, an application shall be made 60 days before the documents in respect of which the exemption is requested are to be sent to the Director Nevertheless, subsection 89(2) provides that despite subsection (1), the Director shall extend the time for making an application for an exemption if the applicant establishes that no prejudice will result from the extension

E. — Duration

5.06 An exemption generally takes effect on the date it is granted and is applicable for 1 financial year ending on or after the effective date of the exemption.

F. — Revocation

5.07 The Director will generally not revoke an exemption before providing notice to the applicant and the opportunity to respond by submitting new facts and arguments to support the exemption.

5.08 A revoked exemption ceases to carry effect from the date of revocation.

G. — Fees & Number of Copies of File

5.09 The prescribed fee for an exemption application is $250.00

5.10 Only one set of documents is required.

H. — Time for Processing an Application

5.11 Section 90 of the CBCR provides that *the Director shall, within 30 days after receipt of an application for an exemption, grant the exemption requested or send to the applicant written notice of the Director's refusal, together with reasons for the refusal.*

5.12 An application duly completed and filed, with no outstanding issue or concern, will usually receive a response from the Director within 15 working days after receipt of the application

5.13 An applicant requiring that the Director review the application on an expedited basis should bring the request immediately to the attention of the Director's staff, providing reasons for the urgency

I. — Publication

5.14 Issued exemptions are published monthly under the heading "Corporations Canada Monthly Transactions" on the following website: *http://corporationscanada.ic.qc.ca*

J. — Appeal of Director's Decision

5.15 An applicant who feels aggrieved by a decision of the Director to grant, or to refuse to grant, an exemption may apply to the court, pursuant to paragraph 246(c) of the Act, for an order requiring the Director to change the decision.

6. — Additional Information and How to Reach Corporations Canada

6.01 For additional information on Corporations Canada's products and services, please visit the Corporations Canada website *www.corporationscanada.ic.gc.ca* or call 1-866-333-5556. You can also contact Corporations Canada at:

Client Services Section

Corporations Canada

Industry Canada

9th Floor, Jean Edmonds Tower South

Ottawa, Ontario K1A 0C8

Toll free: 1-866-333-5556

Fax: 613-941-0601

www.corporationscanada.ic.qc.ca

Annex A — Example of Documents to Submit When Making an Application under Section 156 of the CBCA

Schedule A — In the Matter Concerning the Director Appointed under the *Canada Business Corporations Act*

And

The Application Of

(Name of the corporation)

(hereinafter called the "Corporation")

Description and Details of the Exemption Sought

1. This application is for an exemption under section 156 of the *Canada Business Corporations Act* authorizing the corporation to omit from its financial statements any item prescribed, or to dispense with the publication of any particular financial statement prescribed, for the financial year ending *(see 5.06 of the policy)*.

2. The item(s) to be omitted or the statement(s) that will not be published are: *(items or statements as prescribed in the Regulations)*

Schedule B — Statement of Facts

1. The following statement provides sufficient facts and all material information in order to enable the Director to make an informed decision about the exemption sought:

    A. Generally,

    where applicable, provide details about:

        (1) the business of the corporation;

        (2) the prescribed items or statements to be excluded (their function, importance);

        (3) the shareholders affected (prejudice if information not disclosed);

    And/Or

    B. Specifically,

    the following list suggests possible facts that, according to the circumstances of the application, may be relevant in determining whether or not there is a detriment of the corporation. Indicate the facts that apply, providing the necessary details:

        1. The names of competitors, customers and suppliers.

        2. The fact that the corporation manufactures and sells only one line of products or services and a description of such products or services.

        3. The estimated value of gross revenues and total assets of the corporation for the financial year that would be covered by the exemption, if granted.

        4. The percentage of the market held by the corporation and each of its competitors.

5. *The name and place of incorporation of each competitor required to disclose the same financial information as the corporation.*

6. *The way in which the competitors can calculate the profitability (profit margin) of a specific product or service sold by the corporation. Give a precise method of calculation.*

7. *The names of customers contributing a substantial proportion (25 per cent or more) of the net profits of the disclosing corporation.*

8. *The percentage of this portion of the profits and details of the impact disclosure would have on sales to this customer and the corresponding effect on the financial situation of the corporation.*

9. *Financial data on which to base an assessment of the economic detriment which would be caused to the corporation.*

Schedule C — Arguments

1. This application is made pursuant to section 156 of the *Canada Business Corporations Act* which empowers the Director to authorize the corporation to omit from its financial statements any item prescribed, or to dispense with the publication of any particular financial statement prescribed, if the Director reasonably believes that their disclosure would be detrimental to the corporation

2. The disclosure of the prescribed item{s) or statement(s) described in this application would be detrimental for the corporation.

3. The exemption would *("not be prejudicial" or "be prejudicial")* to the affected shareholders.

4. The exemption should be granted for the following reason(s):

For instance,

1. the corporation would be at a disadvantage with suppliers, customers or others;

2. the corporation would be at a disadvantage because it deals in only in one line of products or services and its competitors:

i) are not required to make similar disclosure;

ii) deal in several lines of products or services and disclose information in a form that prevents identification on financial information in respect of any particular product or service;

3. a competitor, who does not disclose, could calculate the profit margin on a specific product or service sold by the corporation and place the latter in a disadvantageous position by reducing its price for this product or service;

4. a supplier could increase the selling price of raw materials sold to the corporation making the disclosure, on the basis of its knowledge of the profitability of a product sold by the latter;

5. an important customer could demand a reduction in the sale price on the basis of its knowledge of the profit made on a product or service by the disclosing corporation;

6. the corporation's only public shares are exchangeable shares whose dividend and dissolution entitlements are determined only by reference to the financial performance of the sole parent corporation and the parent corporation will send to all shareholders of

exchangeable shares the same documentation that it sends to its own shareholders, and will make all necessary filings with the appropriate securities regulatory authorities.

Dated this .... day of........., 20........., at the City of ...., Province of ....

.... Signature — Capacity of

Schedule D — Model of a Decision — In the Matter Concerning the Director Appointed under the *Canada Business Corporations Act*

And

The Application Of

(Name of the corporation)

(hereinafter called the "Corporation")

For An Exemption Under Section 156 Of The *Canada Business Corporations Act*

Exemption

UPON APPLICATION BY the Corporation under section 156 of the *Canada Business Corporations Act* (the "Act") to exempt the Corporation from disclosing *(indicate which items or statements prescribed in the Regulations)*, for the financial year ending on or about the *(see 5.07 of the policy)*.

AND UPON reading the application documents and being satisfied that the disclosure of such information would be detrimental to the Corporation;

IT IS HEREBY DETERMINED that *(name of the corporation)* is authorized to *("omit such items from its financial statements" and/or "dispense with the publication of such prescribed statements")*, for the financial year ending on or about the *(see 5.07 of the policy)*.

DATED, this .... day of ...., 20.........

.... Deputy Director

Policy Statement 6.8 — Exemption Kit — Application Under Subsection 171(2) of the CBCA to Exempt a Distributing Corporation from Having an Audit Committee

Date: March 19, 2008

1. — Statement of General Principles

1.01 The September 22, 2004 exemption policy is repealed and replaced with this policy.

1.02 This policy sets out information to facilitate an application to the Director appointed under the CBCA for an exemption authorizing a distributing corporation to dispense with an audit committee.

1.03 The obligation placed on distributing corporations to have an audit committee is designed to enhance the integrity and reliability of the financial statements by providing an oversight function for the benefit of the board of directors and shareholders. The Director will only exempt a distributing corporation if satisfied that the shareholders will not be prejudiced by the absence of an audit committee to review the financial statements

1.04 Nothing in this policy is intended to constitute a binding statement of what position the Director will take with respect to a particular application. This policy is intended to reflect the Director's understanding of the Director's role in processing an application under subsection 171(2) of the CBCA

2. — Legislative Framework

2.01 Subsection 171(1) of the CBCA provides that a distributing corporation shall *have an audit committee composed of not less than three directors of the corporation, a majority of whom are not officers or employees of the corporation or any of its affiliates*

2.02 According to subsection 171(3) of the Act, the audit committee *shall review the financial statements of the corporation* before they are approved by the directors and circulated to shareholders. Subsections 171(4) through 171(9) articulate the role and responsibilities of various parties vis-à-vis the audit committee.

2.03 Subsection 171(2) of the Act provides however that *the Director may, on application of a corporation, authorize the corporation to dispense with an audit committee, and the Director may, if satisfied that the shareholders will not be prejudiced, permit the corporation to dispense with an audit committee on any reasonable conditions that the Director thinks fit.*

2.04 A distributing corporation that circulates financial statements that have not been reviewed by an audit committee and that fails to obtain an exemption by the Director is in contravention of section 171 of the CBCA which can result in civil and/or criminal liability.

3. — Application not Necessary for Non-Distributing Corporations

3.01 The provision in subsection 171(1) of the Act to have an audit committee is not required for non-distributing corporations or corporations that have received an exemption under subsection 2(6) (see Policy on making an application under subsection 2(6) of the Act).

3.02 The term "distributing corporation," defined in section 2 of the Regulations, incorporates by reference the definition of "reporting issuer" found in provincial securities legislation. Note that where a corporation is subject to an exemption under provincial securities legislation or to an order of the relevant provincial regulator to the effect that the corporation is not a "reporting issuer", that corporation is not a distributing corporation for the purpose of the definition of the term in section 2.

3.03 The process of creating or dismantling an audit committee in a non-distributing corporation is purely internal and need not involve the Director. The Director will not grant an exemption in those circumstances

4. — Guidelines for Making an Application

A. — General Considerations

4.01 The general test used by the Director is whether shareholders, if an exemption were granted, would be prejudiced by the lack of an audit committee to review the financial statements. The Director will assess the potential for prejudice by determining whether the integrity of the financial statements would be compromised by the lack of an audit committee

4.02 Audit committees play an important role. The primary function of an audit committee to incite directors to better supervise the work of the corporation's officers for the benefit of shareholders. Consequently, the Director will only grant an exemption in limited circumstances.

B. — Factors Considered in Reviewing an Application

4.03 An applicant must demonstrate to the satisfaction of the Director that the integrity of the corporation's financial statements will not be compromised by the lack of an audit committee.

4.04 The following are circumstances in which an exemption was granted in the past:

> 1. the applicant is a wholly-owned subsidiary and the function of an audit committee is carried out at the level of the parent company during the review of its consolidated financial statements;
>
> 2. the applicant no longer has any shares held by the public;
>
> 3. the applicant is a reporting issuer only due to securities held by investors which cannot be found or located but where moneys are held in trust for the repurchase of these securities;
>
> 4. the applicant is a reporting issuer only due to the issuance of debt obligations;
>
> 5. the consent of all shareholders for the exemption has been obtained

C. — Conditions for Issuing an Exemption

4.05 In exempting a distributing corporation, the Director may find it appropriate under the circumstances to include one or more conditions in the exemption.

4.06 The Director may require the applicant to forward a copy of the exemption to shareholders and any securities regulators concerned.

5. — Other Information

A. — Additional Information Required

5.01 The Director may require other information not provided in the application in order to decide whether or not to exempt a distributing corporation from the audit committee requirements of the Act.

5.02 Under section 91 of the CBCR, the Director has the authority to seek additional information from the applicant or third parties. With respect to information requested from third parties, section 92 of the CBCR provides that the applicant shall be given a copy of the information obtained and be given a reasonable opportunity to respond

5.03 There is no statutory obligation on the Director, however, to seek information at the request of third parties nor to allow third parties to make representations regarding an application

B. — Access to Information Contained in an Application

5.04 Pursuant to section 266 of the CBCA, a person who has paid the required fee is entitled to examine, make copies or extracts of any document required by the CBCA to be sent to the Director. The information filed with the Director in support of an exemption application is not confidential since such information is required to be filed in order to obtain an exemption. Consequently, an application for exemption is public information.

C. — Offences

5.05 Section 250 of the Act creates an offence with respect to documents required by the Act or Regulations to be sent to the Director, or any other person, that contains a false or misleading statement about material fact or omits to state a material fact.

6. — Making the Application

A. — Format

6.01 Along with a cover letter indicating the name of the applicant corporation, the application must provide information under three distinct headings: description and details of the exemption sought, statement of facts, and argument. These are described briefly below with further elaboration contained in the attached Annex A. We recommend the use of Annex A as a model

6.02 The Director recognizes that applicants may also be making similar representations under various provincial securities legislation. The Director will accept an application made under any provincial securities legislation provided it contains all relevant information or additional information is attached so as to comply with the requirements of the CBCA and CBCR. Note, however, that provincial legislation may provide confidentiality protection that does not exist for exemption documents under the CBCA.

B. — The Documents

6.03 Detailed below is a brief description of the three major documents to submit:

(i) *Description and Details of the Exemption Sought*: The applicant must describe the exemption sought and note that this is an application for an exemption under subsection 171(2) in the *Canada Business Corporations Act* (see attached Annex A, Schedule A)

(ii) *Statement of Facts*: The applicant must include sufficient facts and all material information which might affect the Director's decision (see attached Annex A, Schedule B)

(iii) *Argument*: Following the statement of facts, the applicant must provide convincing reasons that the exemption, if granted, will not be prejudicial to shareholders (see attached Annex A, Schedule C).

C. — Renewals

6.04 If the applicant seeks to renew an exemption that has been granted and the circumstances have not substantially changed, it is not necessary to complete a detailed application. Instead, a letter identifying the previous exemption, requesting for a renewal of the exemption, and stating that the circumstances have not substantially changed is accepted. Note that if the applicant wishes to change the wording of the decision, the applicant must refer to the changes and provide reasons for these changes in the letter.

D. — Effective Date of the Exemption

6.05 An exemption will bear the date on which it was granted.

6.06 Pursuant to paragraph 89(1)(f) of the CBCR, an application may be made at any time

E. — Duration

6.07 An exemption generally takes effect on the date it is granted and is applicable for 1 financial year ending on or after the effective date of the exemption.

F. — Revocation

6.08 The Director will generally not revoke an exemption before providing notice to the applicant and the opportunity to respond by submitting new facts and arguments to support the exemption.

6.09 A revoked exemption ceases to carry effect from the date of revocation

G. — Fees & Number of Copies of File

6.10 The prescribed fee for an exemption application is $250.00.

6.11 Only one set of documents is required.

H. — Time for Processing an Application

6.12 Section 90 of the CBCR provides that *the Director shall, within 30 days after receipt of an application for an exemption, grant the exemption requested or send to the applicant written notice of the Director's refusal, together with reasons for the refusal.*

6.13 An application duly completed and filed, with no outstanding issue or concern, will usually receive a response from the Director within 15 working days after receipt of the application

6.14 An applicant requiring that the Director review the application on an expedited basis should bring the request immediately to the attention of the Director's staff, providing reasons for the urgency.

I. — Publication

6.15 Issued exemptions are published monthly under the heading "Corporations Canada Monthly Transactions" on the following website: *http://corporationscanada.ic.gc.ca*

J. — Appeal of Director's Decision

6.16 An applicant who feels aggrieved by a decision of the Director to grant, or to refuse to grant, an exemption may apply to the court, pursuant to paragraph 246(c) of the Act, for an order requiring the Director to change the decision.

7. — Additional Information and How to Reach Corporations Canada

7.01 For additional information on Corporations Canada's products and services, please visit the Corporations Canada website *www.corporationscanada.ic.gc.ca* or call 1-866-333-5556.

You can also contact Corporations Canada at:

Client Services Section

Corporations Canada

Industry Canada

9th Floor, Jean Edmonds Tower South

Ottawa, Ontario K1A 0C8

Toll free: 1-866-333-5556

Fax: 613-941-0601

www.corporationscanada.ic.gc.ca

Annexe A — Example of Documents to Submit When Making an Application under Subsection 171(2) of the CBCA

Schedule A — In the Matter Concerning the Director Appointed under the *Canada Business Corporations Act*

And

The Application Of

(Name of the corporation)

(hereinafter called the "Corporation")

Description and Details of the Exemption Sought

1. This application is for an exemption under subsection 171(2) of the *Canada Business Corporations Act* to exempt the Corporation from the requirement of having an audit committee for the financial year ending *(see 6.07 of the policy)*

Schedule B — Statement of Facts

1. The following statement provides sufficient facts and all material information in order to enable the Director to make an informed decision about the exemption sought:

Schedule C — Arguments

1. This application is made pursuant to subsection 171(2) of the *Canada Business Corporations Act* which empowers the Director to grant an exemption authorizing the Corporation to dispense with an audit committee, if satisfied that the shareholders will not be prejudiced.

2. The Corporation is a distributing corporation *(see section 3 of the policy)*.

3. The decision from the Director authorizing it to dispense with an audit committee would not be prejudicial to the shareholders.

4. The exemption should be granted for the following reason(s):

For instance,

> 1. the Corporation is a wholly-owned subsidiary and the function of an audit committee is carried out at the level of the parent company during the review of its consolidated financial statements.

> 2. the Corporation no longer has any shares held by the public.

> 3. the Corporation is a reporting issuer only due to securities held by investors which cannot be found or located but where moneys are held in trust for the repurchase of these securities.

> 4. the Corporation is a reporting issuer only due to the issuance of debt securities.

> 5. the consent of all shareholders for the exemption has been obtained

Dated this .... day of ...., 20.........., at the City of ...., Province of ....

.... Signature — Capacity of

Schedule D — Model of a Decision — In the Matter Concerning the Director Appointed under the *Canada Business Corporations Act*

And

The Application Of

(Name of the corporation)

(hereinafter called the "Corporation")

For An Exemption Under Subsection 171(2) Of The *Canada Business Corporations Act*

Exemption

UPON APPLICATION BY the Corporation under subsection 171(2) of the *Canada Business Corporations Act* (the "Act") to dispense with the requirement of having an audit committee under section 171 of the Act, for the financial year ending on or about *(see 6.07 of the policy)*,

AND UPON reading the application documents and being satisfied that the shareholders will not be prejudiced,

IT IS HEREBY determined that *(name of the corporation)* is authorized to dispense with an audit committee, for the financial year ending on or about *(see 6.07 of the policy)*.

DATED, this .... day of ...., 20..........

.... Deputy Director

Policy Statement 7.1 — Amendment Kit

Date: **November 25, 2006**
Revised: **January 2, 2007**

This kit is intended only as a guide to users; it does not replace or take precedence over the CBCA.

Why use this kit?

The purpose of this kit is to help you submit an application to amend the articles of a business incorporated under the *Canada Business Corporations Act* (CBCA). By ensuring that you provide all the required information with your initial application, you can help Corporations Canada process your amendment documents swiftly.

In this kit, you will find:

- general information about the role of Corporations Canada;
- information concerning the various ways that an application to amend articles can be filed;
- Form 4: Articles of Amendments and suggestions about how to fill out key parts of Form 4. Note that all the forms can also be obtained at the following address:
  www.corporationscanada.ic.gc.ca;
- how to reach Corporations Canada.

We suggest that you consult with legal counsel or other professional advisers to consider other features that might be desirable in your corporate structure.

What documents must be filed in order to obtain a certificate of amendment?

An application to amend articles must include the following documents:

- Completed Form 4: Articles of Amendment
- Payment of the $200 fee

Depending on the amendments that you wish to make the corporation's articles, you must also send the following documents.

If the amendments relate to the corporation's name

- If you requested prior approval of your name, the letter from the Director appointed under the CBCA approving your name;
- If you did not request prior approval of your name, a NUANS® report not more than 90 days old. If you are requesting a number name, it is not necessary to file a NUANS® report;
- the $200 fee is not required in cases where the amendment's purpose is to add a French or English version to the corporation's name or to replace the existing legal element such as "Ltd." by a legal element common to both language versions, such as "Inc.". Please note that the Corporations Canada Online Filing Centre cannot suppress the fee payable. In such cases, the applicant would be required to send Form 4 by fax or by mail and attach a note indicating the reasons why the applicant is not required to pay the fee.

If the amendments relate to the registered office:

- Form 3: Change of Registered Office Address

There is no requirement that any form of "proof of facts" be submitted with the Articles of Amendment (such as affidavits or resolutions, for example). The Director is not responsible for verifying that the contents of the articles meet all the requirements of the CBCA; it is the responsibility of the applicant.

What does Corporations Canada do?

Corporations Canada will check that your Articles of Amendment are complete and in proper form. If everything meets the requirements of the CBCA, the Director will issue a Certificate of Amendment showing the date of receipt of your articles as the effective date of the amendment. If you prefer, you may request a later effective date.

A notice setting out your corporation's name, the date on which the articles were amended and other information will appear in the Corporations Database on Corporations Canada's Web site.

What happens when an application for amendment of articles is incomplete?

Applications that are deficient or incomplete will be returned to the applicant with a deficiency notice stating the nature of the deficiency.

When deficient or incomplete Articles of Amendment are returned to applicants, the original effective date is forfeited, unless you expressly request the original effective date when you submit your new application. Corporations Canada will retain the fee paid, in anticipation of a further submission of completed articles. The fee will be returned, however, if you advise the Director in writing that you are withdrawing your application.

How to file your articles of amendment
On-line Filing

You can file the documents needed to amend your corporation's articles on-line, at the Corporations Canada Online Filing Centre, at *www:corporationscanada.ic.gc.ca*. Please refer to the Web site for the procedures for filing Articles of Amendment. The fee is $200 payable by credit card (American Express®, MasterCard ® or Visa®).

The Certificate of Amendment will be sent to you by electronic mail in PDF format.

By Fax

You can also amend your articles by sending the necessary documents by fax, at 613-941-0999. Please note that the forms may be signed by reproducing a manual signature, in printed format or digital format. The $200 fee must be paid by credit card (American Express®, MasterCard ® or Visa®) or by deposit to an account opened with Industry Canada.

The Certificate of Amendment will be sent to you by fax.

By Mail Or Courier

You can file the necessary documents and pay the $200 fee by sending them to the following address:

> Corporations Canada
> Industry Canada
> 9th floor, Jean Edmonds Tower South
> 365 Laurier Avenue West
> Ottawa, Ontario K1A 0C8

The $200 fee must be paid by cheque payable to the Receiver General for Canada, by credit card (American Express®, MasterCard ® or Visa®) or by deposit to an account opened with Industry Canada.

The Certificate of Amendment will be sent to you by mail or by the delivery method requested.

In Person

You may attend in person and file a *maximum of 4 applications*, from Monday to Friday, between 8:30 a.m. and 2:30 p.m., at:

> Corporations Canada
> Industry Canada
> 9th floor, Jean Edmonds Tower South
> 365 Laurier Avenue West
> Ottawa, Ontario K1A 0C8

You must have with you all the necessary documents. The $200 fee must be paid in cash, by cheque payable to the Receiver General for Canada, by credit card (American Express®, MasterCard ® or Visa®) or by deposit to an account opened with Industry Canada.

You will be given the Certificate of Amendment.

How to fill out Form 4: Articles of Amendment

Please see Form 4 for complete instructions on how to fill out the Articles of Amendment.

Please note that Form 4 must be signed by an authorized director or officer of the corporation.

Amendments to a corporation's articles

How to change a corporation's name

Please state the proposed name under item 3 A of the Form 4: Articles of Amendment.

- There are a number of reasons why you may wish to change your corporation's name. For example, you may have incorporated under a number name, and you now wish to adopt a word name. Or you may wish to choose a new name, or add a French or English form of the name, or a bilingual or combined form.

  Before filing the Articles of Amendment, please ensure that you have the authorization of the shareholders, by resolution. For a number name, only a directors' resolution is required.

  The name you are proposing must be approved by the Director appointed under the CBCA. The Director will examine your request to determine whether it meets the requirements of the CBCA and the Regulations. The name proposed must be distinctive, must not cause confusion with any existing name or trade mark used in Canada, and must not be prohibited or misleading.

You *may* request approval of the name

- before filing the Articles of Amendment
- when you file the Articles of Amendment

How to submit a request to the Director for a change of name

Whether you apply for pre-approval or request approval when you file the Articles of Amendment, you are responsible for providing all of the facts relevant to the name you are proposing, as well as a NUANS® report.

- Information relevant to the name proposed

You *must submit* the information relating to the circumstances that led to your choosing the name in question to the Director *in writing*. You may use the Corporate Name Information Form, *or* you may submit a letter to the Director describing your corporation's activities and addressing the following points:

- WITH WHAT TYPE OF GOODS OR SERVICES will the proposed corporation be involved? How is this dissimilar to the activities of existing businesses with similar names? Even if your NUANS® report does not turn up names that appear to be similar to yours, the Director still needs this information to ensure that your proposed name does not suggest government sponsorship or that the proposed corporation will be carrying on the business of a bank or a trust, loan or insurance company, or merely describe, or misdescribe the business of your corporation.
- WHERE will the proposed corporation carry on its business? You must show that this territory is not the same as that of other businesses with similar names and similar activities.
- WITH WHAT TYPE OF CLIENTS will the proposed corporation conduct business (e.g., retailers, computer programmers, general public)? Indicate whether they are different from the types of people with whom existing businesses with similar names, involving similar goods or services and operating in a similar territory, will do business.

- What is the DERIVATION OF THE DISTINCTIVE ELEMENT(S) of the proposed name? For example, what is the derivation of the word "Amtech" in the name "Amtech Enterprises Inc."? If you have a valid reason for wanting that distinctive element, the Director is less likely to conclude that you may be trying to trade on the goodwill of an existing business with a similar name.

- Is the proposed corporation RELATED to existing businesses with similar names or trade marks? If so, you need the consent of their owners in writing.

- Does the proposed corporation have a FOREIGN PARENT with a similar name that carries on business or is known in Canada? If so, you need consent in writing, and you must add (CANADA) or OF CANADA to the proposed name.

- Did you make an EARLIER RESERVATION of a name similar to another name on the NUANS® report? Your request may be denied if it appears that an earlier reservation for the same name has been made by someone else.

- Are you enclosing the CONSENT IN WRITING OF AN INDIVIDUAL WHOSE NAME APPEARS in the corporate name (other than an incorporator of the proposed corporation)? The consenting individual must also indicate that he or she has or had a material interest in the proposed corporation.

If you are satisfied that your corporate name is not likely to cause confusion, outline in your letter to the Director the arguments on which you have based your conclusion.

NUANS® Report

- You must provide a search, that is, a NUANS® report under the federal rules for determining whether the name you are proposing is available. A NUANS® report is a five-page document setting out the business names (3 pages) and trade marks registered in Canada (2 pages) that sound or look similar to the name you are proposing. The list is drawn from a national data bank of existing and reserved trade names as well as trade marks that have been registered and applied for in Canada.

- A NUANS® report may be obtained in two ways:

   1. A NUANS® report may be requested from a private company known as a search house. You can find a list of these firms on Corporations Canada's web site by following the links "Online Filing", and "Corporations Canada Online Filing Centre", or in the Yellow Pages of your telephone directory under INCORPORATING COMPANIES, INCORPORATION NAME SEARCH, SEARCHERS OF RECORDS or TRADE MARK AGENTS — REGISTERED. There is a fee for this service.

   2. A NUANS® report may be ordered on-line at the Electronic Filing Centre, from the NUANS® Real-Time System. The fee is $20 payable by credit card (American Express®, MasterCard ® or Visa®). The system provides direct access to the NUANS® search service but does not provide the professional assistance and recommendations often available from a registered NUANS® search house. Applicants should note that a NUANS® report that is generated may be rejected if the proposed name does not meet the requirements of the CBCA name regulations.

When you order a NUANS® report, that report has a life of 90 days from the date it is requested. A search house can advise you whether your proposed name is likely to be accepted by the Director. The final decision, however, always rests with the Director.

NUANS® Report: Special Cases

* Number name

  Instead of a name, the directors may ask the Director to assign a number name. A number name must be requested when the Articles of Amendment are submitted. Obviously you do not submit a NUANS® report.

* Bilingual or combined name

  If your corporation intends to carry on business in a region or regions where both English and French are spoken, you may wish to consider adopting a bilingual corporate name.

  The procedure is the same as for a unilingual name, except that one NUANS® report is required for each name or variation requested. Thus, two NUANS® reports must be filed in order to verify that the phonetically dissimilar English and French forms of a name are both distinctive.

  Where the English and French forms are phonetically similar except for a legal element (e.g., Ltd./Ltée), only one NUANS® report will be necessary.

  Please note that if the change is intended only to add the English or French form to the corporate name, the Certificate of Amendment will be issued free of charge.

Decision of the Director

If your request for pre-approval is accepted, the name in question will be reserved for you for the life of the search report. If the Director has not made a decision within that 90-day period, you will have to submit a fresh request to reserve a name, by ordering another NUANS® report.

If you have requested pre-approval and the Director's decision is favourable, your Articles of Amendment will probably be processed promptly when you file them, provided that all other relevant information is submitted at the same time. Remember to include the letter approving your name when you submit your Articles of Amendment.

If your proposed name is returned to you, you can still submit a written request for the Director to re-examine his decision, having regard to the additional information. However, you will save time and money if you include all relevant information in your initial application.

How to report a change in the province or territory of the registered office

* *When the registered office has moved out of the province or territory shown in the articles,* you must indicate the new province or territory of the registered office under item 3 B of the Form 4: Articles of Amendment. In addition to the Articles of Amendment, you must also file a completed Form 3: Change of Registered Office Address.

  Before filing Form 4, you must obtain, by resolution, the authorization of the shareholders of your corporation. Please note that you must file the Articles of Amendment before the move can be made.

* *When the registered office has moved inside the province or territory shown in the Articles of Incorporation,* no Form 4: Articles of Amendment needs to be filed. However, you must file a Form 3: Change of Registered Office Address with the Director within 15 days of the change of address. No fee is applicable.

How to change the structure of the corporation (classes or maximum number or shares that the corporations is authorized to issue, or restrictions on share transfers)

Please state the nature of the change under item 3 D of the Form 4: Articles of Amendment.

Before filing the Articles of Amendment with the Director, the corporation must obtain a special resolution of the shareholders. By filing Articles of Amendment, the corporation may make the following changes to its structure:

- amend the maximum number of shares that the corporation is authorized to issue;
- create new classes of shares;
- reduce or increase the stated capital, if the stated capital appears in the Articles of Incorporation;
- change the designation of all or any of its shares and add, change or remove any rights, privileges, restrictions and conditions, including rights to accrued dividends, in respect of all or any of its shares, whether issued or unissued;
- change the number of shares, whether issued or unissued, in a class or series, or change the class or series of the shares;
- divide a class of shares, whether issued or unissued, into series and fix the number of shares in each series and the rights, privileges, restrictions and conditions thereof;
- authorize the directors to divide any class of unissued shares into series and fix the number of shares in each series and the rights, privileges, restrictions and conditions thereof;
- authorize the directors to change the rights, privileges, restrictions and conditions attached to unissued shares of any series;
- revoke or change any authority conferred on directors in respect of shares;
- add, change or remove restrictions on the issue, transfer or ownership of shares.

You may vary the composition and complexity of share structures for particular situations in countless ways. The clauses given here are only examples of the most common kinds of share structures used by many incorporators; and *they are by no means mandatory or exhaustive.* You may wish to seek legal advice if you want to use other clauses to be sure that they are permitted under the CBCA.

Examples:

For a single class of shares:

The corporation is authorized to issue an unlimited number of shares of one class.

or

Unlimited number of shares in a single class.

For two or more classes of shares:

The corporation is authorized to issue an unlimited number of Class A and Class B shares. The Class A shares shall be entitled to vote at all meetings of shareholders except meetings at which only holders of a specified class of shares are entitled to vote and to receive such dividend as the board of directors in their discretion shall declare. Subject to the provisions of the *Canada Business Corporations Act*, the Class B shares shall be non-voting. Upon liquidation or dissolution, the holders of Class A and Class B shares shall share equally the remaining property of the corporation.

or

The corporation is authorized to issue Class A and Class B shares with the following rights, privileges, restrictions and conditions:

1. Class A shares, without nominal or par value, the holders of which are entitled:

(a) to vote at all meetings of shareholders except meetings at which only holders of a specified class of shares are entitled to vote; and

(b) to receive the remaining property of the corporation upon dissolution.

2. Class B shares, without nominal or par value, the holders of which are entitled:

(a) to a dividend as fixed by the board of directors;

(b) upon the liquidation or winding-up of the corporation, to repayment of the amount paid for such shares (plus any declared and unpaid dividends) in priority to the Class A shares, but they shall not confer a right to any further participation in profits or assets.

3. The holders of Class B shares shall be entitled to vote at all meetings of shareholders.

or

The holders of Class B shares shall not, subject to the provisions of the *Canada Business Corporations Act*, be entitled to vote at any meetings of shareholders.

For shares in a series:

The directors may authorize the issue of one or more series within each class of shares, and may fix the number of shares in each series, and determine the rights, privileges, restrictions and conditions attaching to the shares of each series subject to the limits provided in the Articles.

(As noted earlier, you may create a series of shares immediately in the Articles, rather than waiting until later.)

Share redemption:

If a fixed price is not stated, a redemption formula that can be determined in dollars must be used.

The said Class X shares or any part thereof shall be redeemable at the option of the corporation without the consent of the holders thereof (at a price of $__ per share) or (at a price equal to the amount paid per share) plus any declared and unpaid dividends.

How to change the number of directors

- Please state the nature of the change under item 3 C of the Form 4: Articles of Amendment.

You may specify a minimum and maximum number or a fixed number of directors. However, to permit cumulative voting, the number of directors must be fixed. Moreover, if the corporation is a "distributing" corporation, there must be at least three directors.

Example:

A minimum of one and a maximum of seven.

or

Five directors.

- You do not need to file Form 4: Articles of Amendment if you are changing the number of directors within the range of minimum and maximum numbers specified in the Articles of Incorporation. However, you must file the completed Form 6: Changes Regarding Directors within 15 days of the change in the composition of the board of directors or receipt of the notice of change of address of a director. No fee is applicable.

- You do not need to file Articles of Amendment when new directors are appointed, vacancies occur on the board of directors or the corporation receives a notice of change of address from a director. However, you must file the Form 6: Changes Regarding Directors within 15 days of the change in the composition of the board of directors or receipt of the notice of change of address of a director. No fee is applicable.

How to change the restrictions on business that the corporation may carry on

- Please state the nature of the changes under item 3 D of the Form 4: Articles of Amendment.

- If it proves necessary to limit the corporation's activities by prohibiting certain kinds of business activity, you may do so by filing Articles of Amendment. Generally, the provision should be worded negatively, that is, it should be a statement of what the corporation *MAY NOT* do, rather than a list of its "objects." The following preamble is suggested:

    The business of the Corporation shall be limited to the following: . . . .

- You may also change or remove any business restrictions that were set out in the existing articles. The following preamble is suggested:

    No limit on the business of the Corporation.

It should be noted that section 3 of the CBCA prohibits CBCA corporations from conducting the business of a bank or an insurance or trust and loan company, or carrying on business as a degree-granting institution.

How to amend the other provisions

The CBCA allows you to include a number of additional provisions in the Articles of Incorporation. These provisions are often included to satisfy requirements of other legislation or institutions.

You may change or delete any extra provisions set out under Item 7 of the Articles of Incorporation by filing Form 4: Articles of Amendment. Please state the nature of the changes under Item 3 D of the Articles of Amendment.

The following list illustrates the kinds of wording generally adopted for the most frequently occurring features. The listing is not definitive, nor is the wording mandatory. You may wish to seek legal advice if you want to use other clauses to be sure that they are permitted under the CBCA.

- Directors' borrowing power:

    A provision regarding directors' borrowing powers and the delegation of those powers is sometimes used to limit the authority of directors and/or to satisfy lending institutions:

    Example:

    If authorized by the by-law which is duly made by the directors and confirmed by ordinary resolution, the directors of the corporation may from time to time:

    (i) borrow money on the credit of the corporation;

    (ii) issue, reissue, sell or pledge debt obligations of the corporation;

    (iii) mortgage, hypothecate, pledge or otherwise create a security interest in all or any property of the corporation, owned or subsequently acquired, to secure any debt obligation of the corporation.

    Any such by-law may provide for the delegation of such powers by the directors to such officers or directors of the corporation to such extent and in such manner as may be set out in the by-law.

    Nothing herein limits or restricts the borrowing of money by the corporation on bills of exchange or promissory notes made, drawn, accepted or endorsed by or on behalf of the corporation.

- Cumulative voting by directors:

    This clause is allowed only if the number of directors is a fixed number:

    Example:

    There shall be cumulative voting for directors.

- Increase the majority vote by shareholders:

    Example:

    In order to effect any (ordinary and/or special) resolution[7] passed at a meeting of shareholders,[8] a majority of not less than ___ per cent of the votes cast by the shareholders who voted in respect of that resolution shall be required.

- Specify the *foreign form* of your corporate name for use *outside Canada*:

    Example:

    It is hereby provided that the corporation may use and may be equally designated by the following form outside Canada: . . ..

    (Note: Do not use item 7 to state the *English* or *French* form of the corporate name, for use *inside Canada*; for that use item 1)

- Specify voting rights on fractional shares:

    Example:

    A holder of a fractional share shall be entitled to exercise voting rights and to receive dividends in respect of said fractional share.

---

[7]The CBCA specifies a simple majority for an ordinary resolution and two-thirds majority for a special resolution. Therefore, any figure set out in the articles must be greater than these statutory majorities.

[8]Other than a resolution to remove a director (see subsection 6(4) of the CBCA).

- Specify that some shareholders have a pre-emptive right:

    Example:

    > It is hereby provided that no shares of a class of shares shall be issued unless the shares have first been offered to the shareholders holding shares of that class, and those shareholders have a pre-emptive right to acquire the offered shares in proportion to their holdings of the shares of that class, at such price and on such terms as those shares are to be offered to others.

- Under the CBCA, directors are not required to own shares of the corporation. However, where incorporators do wish to provide for directors to own shares, the following wording is normally used:

    Example:

    > No person otherwise qualified shall be elected or appointed as a director unless such person beneficially owns at least one share issued by the corporation.

- You may prescribe how shareholders will fill a *vacancy on the board of directors*:

    Example:

    > Any vacancy on the board of directors shall be filled by a vote of the shareholders.

- You may specify a *quorum* of directors:

    Example:

    > The quorum for any meeting of the board of directors shall be _____.

- You may provide for trust deeds for purposes of the Quebec *Special Corporate Powers Act*, if the corporation intends to carry on business in the Province of Quebec.

    Example:

    > The corporation, through its directors, may, as it deems expedient and notwithstanding the provisions of the *Civil Code*, hypothecate, mortgage or pledge any real or personal property, currently owned or subsequently acquired, of the corporation, to secure the payment of such debentures and other securities, or to provide only a part of these guarantees for the said purposes, and it may constitute the aforesaid hypothec, mortgage or pledge by trust deed, pursuant to sections 23 and 24 of the *Special Corporate Powers Act* (R.S.Q. 1964, c. 275), or in any other manner.

    > The corporation may also hypothecate or mortgage the real property, or pledge or otherwise change in any manner the personal property of the corporation, or provide these various kinds of guarantees, to secure the payment of loans made otherwise than by the issue of debentures, as well as the payment or performance of other debts, contracts and undertakings of the corporation.

When should you submit Form 7: Restated Articles of Incorporation?

- When a corporation has effected several amendments to its articles, it may later become desirable to consolidate all the amendments with the original articles in one document, for the sake of convenience or greater clarity. Directors can authorize "restatement" of the articles by completing and filing Form 7: Restated Articles of Incorporation, with the Director. This form should not be used to make substantive changes not already made by filing Form 4: Articles of Amendment.

- The following must be filed:

    - completed Form 7: Restated Articles of Incorporation;

- a $50 filing fee, payable to the Receiver General for Canada. Please note that no fee is payable when Form 7: Restated Articles of Incorporation are filed at the same time as Articles of Amendment.

Additional information and how to reach Corporations Canada

For additional information on Corporations Canada products and services, please visit Corporations Canada's Web site or call 1-866-333-5556.

You can also contact Corporations Canada at:

Client Services Section
Corporations Canada
Industry Canada
9th floor, Jean Edmonds Tower South
Ottawa, Ontario K1A 0C8
Fax: 613-941-0601
www.corporationscanada.ic.gc.ca

Policy Statement 8.1 — Amalgamation Kit

Date: **January 30, 2006**
Revised: **January 2, 2007**

This kit is intended only as a guide to users; it does not replace or take precedence over the CBCA.

Why use this kit?

The purpose of this kit is to help you submit the forms and information required in order for two or more corporations now incorporated under the *Canada Business Corporations Act* (CBCA) to amalgamate and continue as one corporation. By ensuring that you provide all the required information with your initial application, you can help Corporations Canada process your amendment documents swiftly.

In this kit, you will find:

- guidelines on what information must be filed to receive a Certificate of Amalgamation;
- general information about the role of Corporations Canada;
- information on how to file the Articles of Amalgamation and submit the required fee;
- Form 2: Initial Registered Office Address and First Board of Directors and Form 9: Articles of Amalgamation and suggestions on how to fill out key parts. Please note that all the forms can be also obtained at the following address:

   www.corporationscanada.ic.gc.ca;

- information on proof of facts you must submit with the Articles of Amalgamation;
- Sample letter to Corporations Canada enclosing an Application for Amalgamation (Annex A);
- sample Statutory Declaration (Annex B);
- sample fax cover page (Annex C);
- excerpt from the *Canada Business Corporations Act*; the relevant sections of the CBCA, section 181 to section 186, are included in this kit for your convenience (Annex D).

You should note, however, that this kit does not tell you everything you may need to know about amalgamation. You may wish to consult with legal counsel or other professional advisors to consider other features that might be desirable in your corporate structure, or other relevant matters.

CBCA corporations may also seek amalgamation with companies incorporated under the *Bank Act*, the *Canada Cooperatives Act*, the *Cooperative Credit Associations Act*, the *Insurance Companies Act* or the *Trust and Loan Companies Act*. However, the application for amalgamation under one of these statutes must be made to the Office of the Superintendent of Financial Institutions. Upon receipt of a satisfactory notice that a CBCA corporation has been amalgamated with a business incorporated under one of these Acts, a certificate of discontinuance will be issued to the CBCA corporation pursuant to subsection 188(7) of the CBCA, and the CBCA will not apply to the amalgamated entity.

What information must be filed to receive a Certificate of Amalgamation?

A request for a Certificate of Amalgamation must include the following:

- A completed Form 2: Initial Registered Office Address and First Board of Directors;
- A completed Form 9: Articles of Amalgamation
- A statutory declaration of an officer or director of each amalgamating CBCA corporation pursuant to subsection 185(2). The declaration must be signed before a Commissioner of Oaths (see Annex B for a sample of the declaration)
- A NUANS® report (if you wish to adopt a new name for the amalgamated corporation)
- A covering letter to Corporations Canada (see Annex A) for an application for amalgamation. Please make any alterations to this letter to suit your individual circumstances, including whether or not you are enclosing a NUANS® report and the effective date of your Certificate of Amalgamation, if you wish it to be later than the filing date.
- A filing fee of $200.00 payable to the Receiver General for Canada

What proof of facts must you submit with the articles of amalgamation?

The Articles of Amalgamation must be accompanied by a statutory declaration signed by a director or officer of each amalgamating corporation. The statutory declaration included in this kit as Annex B is a suggested model, based on the requirements set out in subsection 185(2) of the CBCA. Note that in addition to both statements (i) and (ii) shown in Annex B, you must also include a third statement that is a choice between subparagraphs 185(2)(b)(i) and (b)(ii), as the case may be (see Annex D for an excerpt of the CBCA). The declarations should be *dated within two weeks of the proposed amalgamation date*, which will be the filing date or any later date you request. Because of the increased volume of applications to be processed by Corporations Canada each December, statutory declarations filed that month may be dated up to four weeks before the proposed amalgamation date.

Where articles of amalgamation are filed with, or very closely after, articles of continuance for one of the amalgamating corporations and where only one meeting of that corporation was called to pass both the resolution to continue and the resolution to amalgamate, the continuing body corporate is expected to comply with the requirements of the CBCA with respect to the calling of that meeting and passing the resolution to approve the amalgamation. Compliance with these requirements is a condition of our processing the amalgamation. Shareholder approval for the amalgamation should be based on the understanding that the amalgamation can take place only upon a certificate of continuance first being issued to the corporation.

What does Corporations Canada do?

Corporations Canada checks that each amalgamating corporations has submitted the last three annual returns with all related fee (unless the corporation has recently continued for the purposes of amalgamation). Corporations Canada reviews the application to ensure that the required documentation is attached and properly completed, that the application fee is enclosed, that there are no pending takeover bids, arrangements or preliminary enquiries involving the amalgamating corporations.

When the Articles of Amalgamation and required documentation are properly completed, the Director issue a Certificate of Amalgamation. A new corporate number is given to the amalgamated corporation.

You will receive a Certificate of Amalgamation with Form 9: Articles of Amalgamation, any annexes and the statutory declarations that you send in duplicate. One copy of Form 2: Initial Registered Office Address and First Board of Directors will be returned to you stamped with the date of processing by Corporations Canada.

What deficiencies should you watch out for?

If your application is deficient in some respect, a notice will be sent to you indicating the nature of the deficiency. Corporations Canada will make every effort to permit you to retain the originally-proposed amalgamation date.

Applications with statutory declarations older than two weeks will be returned to you. Should circumstances require it, you will be asked to complete a new statutory declaration.

Also remember that either a director or authorized officer of the corporation must sign the Articles of Amalgamation. Form 2: Initial Registered Office Address and First Board of Directors can be signed by an individual who has relevant knowledge of the corporation and who is authorized to sign by the directors.

How to file the Articles of Amalgamation and submit the required fee

By fax:

You may submit the forms needed to amalgamate your corporation(s) to Corporations Canada by fax at 613-941-0999. Please note that documents may be accompanied by a fax cover page provided by the Director (See Annex C). The signature can be by reproduction of a manual signature or in digital form. Payment of the $200 fee will have to be made by credit card (American Express®, MasterCard® or Visa®) or by a deposit account maintained at Industry Canada at the time of filing.

The Certificate of Amalgamation will be sent to you by fax.

By mail:

You can submit the Articles of Amalgamation and the required documents by mail to the following address.

Corporations Canada
Industry Canada
9th Floor, Jean Edmonds Towers South
365 Laurier Avenue West

Ottawa, Ontario, K1A 0C8

Payment of the $200 fee, payable to the Receiver General for Canada, may be made by cheque, credit card (American Express®, MasterCard® or Visa®) or by a deposit account maintained at Industry Canada at the time of filing.

The Certificate of Amalgamation will be sent to you by mail or by the method requested.

In person:

You may submit all required documents in person, with the required fee of $200, payable to the Receiver General for Canada as above, Monday to Friday between 8:30 a.m. and 5:00 p.m. at the address noted above.

The Certificate of Amalgamation will be sent to you by mail or by the method requested.

Electronic forms:

The Corporations Canada Online Filing Centre does not process forms for amalgamation.

How to fill out Form 9: Articles of Amalgamation

Please see Form 9 for complete instructions on how to complete the Articles of Amalgamation.

Articles of Amalgamation may be used for either long-form or short-form amalgamation. The difference in the two is explained in item 8 below.

Item 1 — Name of amalgamated corporation

- Write in the name of the amalgamated corporation. A NUANS® report is not required if the new corporation will have a name identical to that of one of the amalgamating corporations. Nor is a NUANS® report needed if the only change is to the legal element.

  If a new name is proposed, or if a French or English version is to be added to the name upon amalgamation, a NUANS® report less than 90 days old is required.

  A NUANS® report may be obtained in two ways:

  1. A NUANS® report may be requested from a private company known as a search house. You can find a list of these firms at *www.corporationscanada.ic.gc.ca* by following the links "Online Filing", and "Corporations Canada Online Filing Centre", or in the Yellow Pages of your telephone directory under INCORPORATING COMPANIES, INCORPORATION NAME SEARCH, SEARCHERS OF RECORDS or TRADE MARK AGENTS — REGISTERED. There is a fee for this service.

  2. A NUANS® report may be ordered on-line at the Electronic Filing Centre, at *www.corporationscanada.ic.gc.ca* from the NUANS® Real-Time System. The fee is $20 payable by credit card (American Express®, MasterCard® or Visa®). The system provides direct access to the NUANS® search service but does not provide the professional assistance and recommendations often available from a registered NUANS® search house. Applicants should note that a NUANS® report that is generated may be rejected if the proposed name does not meet the requirements of the CBCA name regulations.

When you order a NUANS® report, that report has a life of 90 days from the date it is requested. A search house can advise you whether your proposed name is likely to be accepted by the Director. The final decision, however, always rests with the Director.

Pre-approved name

If a proposed new name has been pre-approved, ensure that the letter of approval is enclosed with your articles. If not, or if the name has not been reviewed prior to your filing Articles of Amalgamation, the name will go through the approval process when the articles are filed.

Number Name

If you are incorporating under a number name to be assigned by the Director, leave a blank space on the left hand side, write in the word "Canada", and add the legal element of your choice, such as Inc., Ltd., Corp., etc.

e.g.:

.... CANADA Inc.

Bilingual Name

If you are incorporating under a bilingual name, the English and French forms must be entered here.

e.g.:

CARS ABC Inc.

AUTOS ABC Inc.

Item 2 — Province or territory in Canada in which the registered office is to be situated

The registered office of one of the amalgamating corporations is to be situated in a Canadian province or territory. If the corporation decides to move its registered office within the same province or territory, it will not be necessary to file Articles of Amendment (Form 4) nor to pay the $200.00 filing fee for articles of amendment.

The provisions of the CBCA provide that articles of amalgamation must be identical to the articles of the parent corporation in the event of a vertical short-form amalgamation or to those of the subsidiary whose shares are not cancelled in the event of a horizontal short-form amalgamation. However, prior to November 24, 2001, articles may have specified a place that was not a province, such as "the Greater Metropolitan Toronto". As of November 24, 2001, only the province or territory must be specified. Consequently, Item 2 of the articles of amalgamation (Form 9) must indicate the province or the territory of the place indicated in the articles of the parent corporation or the subsidiary, as appropriate, at the time of the amalgamation. For example, in the event of a vertical short-form amalgamation, where the articles of incorporation of the parent corporation indicated "Winnipeg", the applicant must indicate "Manitoba" in Item 2 of the articles of amalgamation

Item 3 — Classes and any maximum number of shares that the corporation is authorized to issue

The CBCA sets out certain requirements regarding shares as described in Part V of the Act. Although the amalgamated corporation must maintain the existing share structure of one of the amalgamating corporations in a short-form amalgamation, changes can be made in a long-form amalgamation only if covered in the Amalgamation Agreement authorizing the amalgamation. This agreement is not required to be filed. When citing existing share provisions or restructuring new ones, remember to delete all references to "nominal" or "par" value. However, such reference may be used where the Director has given special permission on the basis of a written request for exemption (see subsection 187(11) of the CBCA). Also note:

- The CBCA gives incorporators broad discretion to designate a class of shares as common, preferred or Class A or B shares, or any other designation. Some incorporators designate classes of shares simply as Class A, Class B and "other".
- You do not need to place a limit on the number of shares that the corporation is authorized to issue.
- You do not need to specify the consideration for the issuance of shares.
- Restrictions may be placed on any class of shares.

Where there is more than one class of shares, the rights, privileges, restrictions and conditions attaching to each class must be set out. At least one class must have the right to vote, one class must have the right to receive a dividend, and one class must have the right to receive the remaining property of the corporation on dissolution. Where there is only one class, those rights attach to that one class.

The articles may authorize the issue of certain classes of shares in a series. If so, the same articles may fix the number of shares in, and determine the rights attaching to, a particular series, or, before the shares of a series can be issued at a later time, directors must submit Articles of Amendment with Corporations Canada specifying the number, rights, privileges and restrictions attaching to the series being issued.

Item 4 — Restrictions, if any, on share transfers

- Restrictions, if any, on the transfer of shares are normally limited to requiring the consent of the directors and/or shareholders. Exceptions may occur in special cases when the incorporators establish a constrained share corporation, as described in Part 9 of the *Canada Business Corporations Regulations*.

Item 5 — Number (or minimum and maximum number) of directors

You may specify a range or a fixed number of directors. However, to permit cumulative voting, the number of directors must be fixed. Moreover, if the corporation is a "distributing" corporation, there must be at least three directors.

e.g.:

A minimum of 1 and a maximum of 7.

or

Five directors.

Item 6 — Restrictions, if any, on business the corporation may carry on

- A CBCA corporation has all the rights of a natural person, and normally one would not wish to limit this power.

e.g.:

If there are to be no restrictions, simply state "NONE".

- If, however, there are reasons why you wish to restrict the business of the corporation, the following preamble is suggested:

  The business of the corporation shall be limited to the following: . . ..

It should be noted that section 3 of the CBCA itself prohibits CBCA corporations from carrying on the business of a bank or an insurance or trust and loan company, or carry on business as a degree-granting institution.

Item 7 — Other Provisions, if any

The CBCA allows you to include a number of additional provisions in the Articles of Amalgamation. As well, clauses to satisfy requirements of other legislation or institutions may be included.

Item 8 — Type of amalgamation

You must indicate whether the amalgamation complies with section 183 ("long-form"), subsection 184(1) ("vertical short-form") or subsection 184(2) ("horizontal short form") of the CBCA. In a *"long-form"* amalgamation, each amalgamating corporation signs an amalgamation agreement (as described in subsection 182(1)) and submits it for approval at a meeting of shareholders (as described in subsection 183). The Articles of Amalgamation may contain whatever has been agreed to in the amalgamation agreement. Copies of the amalgamation agreement or shareholder approval should not be filed, but you should ensure that the required meetings take place prior to filing articles.

A *"short-form"* amalgamation is approved by a resolution of the directors and does not require shareholder approval. The resolution of the directors should not be filed.

In a vertical short-form amalgamation between a holding corporation and one or more wholly-owned subsidiaries, the Articles of Amalgamation must be the same as the Articles of the amalgamating holding corporation. However, an exception is made for the name of the amalgamated corporation (Form 9, Item 1) which may be the name of any of the amalgamating corporations.

In a horizontal short-form amalgamation between two or more wholly-owned subsidiaries of the same holding corporation, the Articles of Amalgamation must be the same as the Articles of the amalgamating subsidiary corporation whose share are not cancelled. However, an exception is made for the name of the amalgamated corporation (Form 9, Item 1) which may be the name of any of the amalgamating corporations.

Item 9 — Name of amalgamating corporations and signatures

Write in the name of the amalgamating corporations and their respective corporation numbers. The director or authorized officer of each amalgamating corporation must date and sign their name accordingly.

How to fill out Form 2: Initial Registered Office Address and First Board of Directors

Please refer to the form to get complete instructions.

Indicate at item 1 the name of the corporation as indicated in the Articles of Amalgamation (Form 9).

Indicate at item 2 the address of the registered office. It must be a complete street address within the province or territory specified in the Articles of Incorporation (Form 1). Please indicate at item 3 the mailing address if it is different from the address of the registered office.

Indicate at item 4 the name and family name of all directors. The number of directors must correspond with the number indicated in Item 5 of the Articles of Amalgamation (Form 9). You must indicate the residential address (a post office or a business address won't be accepted) of each director and indicate if he/she is Canadian resident.

Note that at least 25 per cent of the directors must be Canadian residents. However, some restrictions apply:

- If the corporation has fewer than four directors, at least one of them must be a resident Canadian.

- If the corporation is required by a federal Act or regulations to meet specific requirements respecting Canadian participation or control (e.g., corporations carrying on air transportation or telecommunications businesses), a majority (50% + 1) of its directors must be resident Canadians.

- If the corporation is carrying on one of the following businesses, a majority (50% + 1) of its directors must be resident Canadians:
  - uranium mining
  - book publishing or distribution
  - bookselling, where the sale of books is the primary part of the corporation's business
  - film or video distribution

However, if a parent corporation belonging to one of those categories (i.e., carrying on a business referred to above, or that must meet requirements respecting Canadian participation or control under a federal Act or regulations) and its subsidiaries earn less than five per cent of their gross revenue in Canada, only one third of the corporation's directors need be resident Canadians.

Form 2 must be signed by an individual who has relevant knowledge of the corporation and who is authorized to sign by the directors.

Additional information and how to reach Corporations Canada

For additional information on Corporations Canada's products and services, please visit the Corporations Canada website or call 1-866-333-5556.

You can also contact Corporations Canada at:

Client Services Section

Corporations Canada

Industry Canada

9th floor, Jean Edmonds Tower South

Ottawa, Ontario K1A 0C8

Fax: 613-941-0601

www.corporationscanada.ic.gc.ca

Annex A — Sample letter to Corporations Canada enclosing an Application for Amalgamation

Date: ....

Reference: ....

To:

Corporations Canada

Industry Canada

9th floor, Jean Edmonds Tower South

365 Laurier Avenue West

Ottawa, Ontario K1A 0C8

Enclosed herewith are:

1) Form 2: Initial Registered Office Address and First Board of Directors

3) Form 9: Articles of Amalgamation

4) Statutory Declaration of an officer or director of each amalgamating corporation

5) NUANS® search report not more than 90 days old, if applicable

6) Cheque for $200.00 payable to the Receiver General for Canada.

Please be advised that the Certificate of Amalgamation must bear the effective date of .... (a date later than the date of receipt, if a different date is desired) rather than bearing the date of receipt.

Please return the Certificate of Amalgamation to the undersigned according to the following instructions:

❏ Pick-up

❏ Regular Mail

SIGNED: ....

NAME: ....

ADDRESS: ....

TELEPHONE NUMBER: ....

FAX NUMBER: ....

Annex B — In the Matter of The Canada Business Corporations Act And In the Matter of Articles of Amalgamation Filed Pursuant to Section 185 in the Name ....

Statutory Declaration

I, ..., of the City of ....in the Province of ...., DO SOLEMNLY DECLARE that:

1. I am a director or officer of ...., an amalgamating corporation and I have personal knowledge of the matters herein deposed to.

2. I am satisfied that there are reasonable grounds for believing that:

(i) each amalgamating corporation can and the amalgamated corporation will be able to pay its liabilities as they become due; and

(ii) the realizable value of the amalgamated corporation's assets will not be less than the aggregate of its liabilities and stated capital of all classes, and

(iii) there are reasonable grounds for believing that no creditor will be prejudiced by the amalgamation.

AND I make this solemn declaration conscientiously believing it to be true, and knowing that it is of the same force and effect as if made under oath and by virtue of the Canada Evidence Act.

DECLARED before me at the)

City of ....,)
in the Province of ....)
this .... day of ....)
20 ....)   Signature

....
A Commissioner, etc.

Annex C — Cover page for fax transmission

Date submitted: ....
Name of Contact: ....
Address: ....
Telephone Number: ....
Fax Number: ....
E-Mail Address: ....
Corporation name(s) and number(s):

....
....
....
....
....
....

Services Requested

❏ Amalgamation ($200)

❏ Amendment ($200)

❏ Form 2

❏ Annual Return ($40 or $20 if transaction is completed through Corporations Canada's Online Filing Centre — *www.corporationscanada.ic.gc.ca*)

❏ Other

Total: $❏

Method of Payment

Industry Canada Deposit Account Number ....

Credit Card Charges (American Express®, MasterCard® or VISA®)

You have my authorization to charge my credit card for this service:

  Name of cardholder (print) ....

  Account #: .... Exp. Date (YY/MM/DD) ....

Method of Return

Unless otherwise specified, your requested documents will be sent to you by the same means as they were received. Other instructions:

  ....

  ....

  ....

  ....

  ....

Limitation of Liability

Clients should note that the Director is not liable for damages, costs or expenses due to any cause related to the Director's systems for receiving or processing electronic filings. The Director is not responsible for the acts or omissions of electronic filers or third parties such as the suppliers of telecommunications services.

Signature ....

Printed Name ....

Annex D

Excerpt from the *Canada Business Corporations Act*

181. Amalgamation — Two or more corporations, including holding and subsidiary corporations, may amalgamate and continue as one corporation.

182. (1) Amalgamation agreement — Each corporation proposing to amalgamate shall enter into an agreement setting out the terms and means of effecting the amalgamation and, in particular, setting out

  (a) the provisions that are required to be included in articles of incorporation under section 6;

  (b) the name and address of each proposed director of the amalgamated corporation;

  (c) the manner in which the shares of each amalgamating corporation are to be converted into shares or other securities of the amalgamated corporation;

  (d) if any shares of an amalgamating corporation are not to be converted into securities of the amalgamated corporation, the amount of money or securities of any body corporate that the holders of such shares are to receive in addition to or instead of securities of the amalgamated corporation;

  (e) the manner of payment of money instead of the issue of fractional shares of the amalgamated corporation or of any other body corporate the securities of which are to be received in the amalgamation;

(f) whether the by-laws of the amalgamated corporation are to be those of one of the amalgamating corporations and, if not, a copy of the proposed by-laws; and

(g) details of any arrangements necessary to perfect the amalgamation and to provide for the subsequent management and operation of the amalgamated corporation.

(2) **Cancellation** — If shares of one of the amalgamating corporations are held by or on behalf of another of the amalgamating corporations, the amalgamation agreement shall provide for the cancellation of such shares when the amalgamation becomes effective without any repayment of capital in respect thereof, and no provision shall be made in the agreement for the conversion of such shares into shares of the amalgamated corporation.

183. (1) **Shareholder approval** — The directors of each amalgamating corporation shall submit the amalgamation agreement for approval to a meeting of the holders of shares of the amalgamating corporation of which they are directors and, subject to subsection (4), to the holders of each class or series of such shares.

(2) **Notice of meeting** — A notice of a meeting of shareholders complying with section 135 shall be sent in accordance with that section to each shareholder of each amalgamating corporation, and shall

(a) include or be accompanied by a copy or summary of the amalgamation agreement; and

(b) state that a dissenting shareholder is entitled to be paid the fair value of their shares in accordance with section 190, but failure to make that statement does not invalidate an amalgamation.

(3) **Right to vote** — Each share of an amalgamating corporation carries the right to vote in respect of an amalgamation agreement whether or not it otherwise carries the right to vote.

(4) **Class vote** — The holders of shares of a class or series of shares of each amalgamating corporation are entitled to vote separately as a class or series in respect of an amalgamation agreement if the amalgamation agreement contains a provision that, if contained in a proposed amendment to the articles, would entitle such holders to vote as a class or series under section 176.

(5) **Shareholder approval** — Subject to subsection (4), an amalgamation agreement is adopted when the shareholders of each amalgamating corporation have approved of the amalgamation by special resolutions.

(6) **Termination** — An amalgamation agreement may provide that at any time before the issue of a certificate of amalgamation the agreement may be terminated by the directors of an amalgamating corporation, notwithstanding approval of the agreement by the shareholders of all or any of the amalgamating corporations.

184. (1) **Vertical short-form amalgamation** — A holding corporation and one or more of its subsidiary corporations may amalgamate and continue as one corporation without complying with sections 182 and 183 if

(a) the amalgamation is approved by a resolution of the directors of each amalgamating corporation;

(a.1) all of the issued shares of each amalgamating subsidiary corporation are held by one or more of the other amalgamating corporations; and

(b) the resolutions provide that

(i) the shares of each amalgamating subsidiary corporation shall be cancelled without any repayment of capital in respect thereof,

(ii) except as may be prescribed, the articles of amalgamation shall be the same as the articles of the amalgamating holding corporation, and

(iii) no securities shall be issued by the amalgamated corporation in connection with the amalgamation and the stated capital of the amalgamated corporation shall be the same as the stated capital of the amalgamating holding corporation.

(2) **Horizontal short-form amalgamation** — Two or more wholly-owned subsidiary corporations of the same holding body corporate may amalgamate and continue as one corporation without complying with sections 182 and 183 if

(a) the amalgamation is approved by a resolution of the directors of each amalgamating corporation; and

(b) the resolutions provide that

(i) the shares of all but one of the amalgamating subsidiary corporations shall be cancelled without any repayment of capital in respect thereof,

(ii) except as may be prescribed, the articles of amalgamation shall be the same as the articles of the amalgamating subsidiary corporation whose shares are not cancelled, and

(iii) the stated capital of the amalgamating subsidiary corporations whose shares are cancelled shall be added to the stated capital of the amalgamating subsidiary corporation whose shares are not cancelled.

185. (1) **Sending of articles** — Subject to subsection 183(6), after an amalgamation has been adopted under section 183 or approved under section 184, articles of amalgamation in the form that the Director fixes shall be sent to the Director together with the documents required by sections 19 and 106.

(2) **Attached declarations** — The articles of amalgamation shall have attached thereto a statutory declaration of a director or an officer of each amalgamating corporation that establishes to the satisfaction of the Director that

(a) here are reasonable grounds for believing that

(i) each amalgamating corporation is and the amalgamated corporation will be able to pay its liabilities as they become due, and

(ii) the realizable value of the amalgamated corporation's assets will not be less than the aggregate of its liabilities and stated capital of all classes; and

(b) there are reasonable grounds for believing that

(i) no creditor will be prejudiced by the amalgamation, or

(ii) adequate notice has been given to all known creditors of the amalgamating corporations and no creditor objects to the amalgamation otherwise than on grounds that are frivolous or vexatious.

(3) **Adequate notice** — For the purposes of subsection (2), adequate notice is given if

(a) a notice in writing is sent to each known creditor having a claim against the corporation that exceeds one thousand dollars;

(b) a notice is published once in a newspaper published or distributed in the place where the corporation has its registered office and reasonable notice thereof is given in each province where the corporation carries on business; and

(c) each notice states that the corporation intends to amalgamate with one or more specified corporations in accordance with this Act and that a creditor of the corporation may object to the amalgamation within thirty days from the date of the notice.

(4) **Certificate of amalgamation** — On receipt of articles of amalgamation, the Director shall issue a certificate of amalgamation in accordance with section 262.

186. **Effect of certificate** — On the date shown in a certificate of amalgamation

(a) the amalgamation of the amalgamating corporations and their continuance as one corporation become effective;

449

(b) the property of each amalgamating corporation continues to be the property of the amalgamated corporation;

(c) the amalgamated corporation continues to be liable for the obligations of each amalgamating corporation;

(d) an existing cause of action, claim or liability to prosecution is unaffected;

(e) a civil, criminal or administrative action or proceeding pending by or against an amalgamating corporation may be continued to be prosecuted by or against the amalgamated corporation;

(f) a conviction against, or ruling, order of judgment in favour of or against, an amalgamating corporation may be enforced by or against the amalgamated corporation;

(g) the articles of amalgamation are deemed to be the articles of incorporation of the amalgamated corporation and the certificate of amalgamation is deemed to be the certificate of incorporation of the amalgamated corporation.

186.1 (1) Amalgamation under other federal Acts — Subject to subsection (2), a corporation may not amalgamate with one or more bodies corporate pursuant to the *Bank Act*, the *Canada Cooperatives Act*, the *Cooperative Credit Associations Act*, the *Insurance Companies Act* or the *Trust and Loan Companies Act* unless the corporation is first authorized to do so by the shareholders in accordance with section 183.

(2) Short-form amalgamations — A corporation may not amalgamate with one or more bodies corporate pursuant to the provisions of one of the Acts referred to in subsection (1) respecting short-form amalgamations unless the corporation is first authorized to do so by the directors in accordance with section 184.

(3) Discontinuance — On receipt of a notice satisfactory to the Director that a corporation has amalgamated pursuant to one of the Acts referred to in subsection (1), the Director shall file the notice and issue a certificate of discontinuance in accordance with section 262.

(4) Notice deemed to be articles — For the purposes of section 262, a notice referred to in subsection (3) is deemed to be articles that are in the form the Director fixes.

(5) Act ceases to apply — This Act ceases to apply to the corporation on the date shown in the certificate of discontinuance.

(6) Non-application — For greater certainty, section 185 does not apply to a corporation that amalgamates pursuant to one of the Acts referred to in subsection (1).

Excerpt from the *Canada Business Corporations Regulations*

31. (1) For the purpose of paragraph 12(1)(a), if two or more corporations amalgamate, the name of the amalgamated corporation is prohibited if the name is confusing or is otherwise not prohibited.

(2) Despite subsection (1), the new corporate name may be the same as the name of one of the amalgamating corporations.

Policy Statement 9.1 — Continuance (Import) Kit

Date: November 22, 2004
Revised: January 2, 2007

This kit is intended only as a guide to users; it does not replace or take precedence over the CBCA.

Why use this kit?

The purpose of this kit is to guide you in filing Form 11: Articles of Continuance to continue, under the provisions of the *Canada Business Corporations Act* (CBCA), a business that has been incorporated under other legislation. By providing all the required information with your initial application, you can help Corporations Canada process your continuance documents swiftly.

In this kit, you will find:

- general information about continuance under the provisions of the CBCA;
- general information about the role of Corporations Canada;
- information about the information you must provide Corporations Canada to obtain Form 11: Articles of Continuance;
- information concerning the various ways that an application can be filed;
- Forms 2 and 11 and suggestions about how to fill out key parts of Form 11. Note that all the forms can also be obtained at the following address: *http://corporations.canada.ic.gc.ca*;
- how to reach Corporations Canada.

We suggest that you consult with legal counsel or other professional advisers in order to obtain additional information on opportunities to continue your corporation or on the consequences of continuance.

What corporations can continue under the provisions of the Canada Business Corporations Act?

The continuance of a corporation is regulated by sections 187 and 268 of the CBCA.

- The continuance of a body corporate incorporated otherwise than by a federal law, such as a provincial, a state or a foreign country's law, is regulated by section 187 of the CBCA. The Director can continue this corporation provided continuance is permitted by the corporate law by which it is governed. If required by the law of the other jurisdiction, the request for continuance must include a document approving the continuance (often referred to as an "authorization") from that jurisdiction.

  A copy of the relevant sections of the corporate statute governing the corporation must normally be provided with the request. The Director has already approved requests for continuance of corporations constituted in different Canadian jurisdictions; it is not necessary to provide a copy of the Act for such jurisdictions. In Annex 1 of this document, you will find the list of Canadian jurisdictions previously approved by the Director appointed under the CBCA.

- For corporations governed by a federal corporate statute other than the CBCA, continuance under the CBCA is regulated by section 268 of the CBCA; a letter of approval is not normally required unless it is required by the Act under which the corporation is presently governed. Please consult section 268 of the CBCA for specific details concerning the continuance of your corporation.

What documents must be filed to obtain a certificate of continuance?

An application for a Certificate of Continuance must include the following documents:

- Form 11: Articles of Continuance, properly completed;

- Form 2: Initial Registered Office Address and First Board of Directors, properly completed;
- Authorization from the exporting jurisdiction, if applicable;
- If you requested prior approval of your name: the letter from the Director appointed under the CBCA approving your name (please enclose a copy of the NUANS® report). If you did not request prior approval of your name: a NUANS® report not more than 90 days old as well as information pertinent to the name. If you are requesting a number name, it is not necessary to file a NUANS® report;
- A copy of the relevant parts of the Act by virtue of which the body corporate is actually constituted, unless the jurisdiction has been approved previously (see Annex 1) or unless the body corporate has been constituted by virtue of a federal Act;
- A filing fee of $200.00, payable to the Receiver General for Canada. Please note that no fee is applicable for corporations requesting continuance under section 268 of the CBCA.
- Where the import is from a non-federal jurisdiction not listed in Annex I, a legal opinion addressed to the Director, CBCA, from counsel qualified to provide opinions on the law of the non-federal jurisdiction ("foreign law") stating 1) that the foreign law permits export to the CBCA in such a manner that once the corporation is continued under the CBCA, the foreign law will cease to apply, and, 2) where the foreign law does not require any authorization to be issued by the foreign jurisdiction, that the corporation has met all requirements for export under the foreign law.

There is no requirement that any form of "proof of facts" (such as affidavits or resolutions) be submitted with the request for continuance. It is the responsibility of the applicant, not the Director, to verify that the contents of the articles meet all requirements of the CBCA.

What does Corporations Canada do?

Corporations Canada will check that your request is complete and in proper form and that the proposed name is acceptable. The analysts will determine whether laws of the non-federal jurisdiction under which your corporation is incorporated authorize it to change jurisdictions or, alternatively, whether the continuance of your federal corporation under the CBCA is authorized according to section 268 of the CBCA.

When a body corporate is incorporated under a jurisdiction that is not pre-approved by the Director, the Act under the body corporate is actually incorporated will be examined by the Department of Justice. They would determine if the continuance may be authorized, as when continued, the Act of the jurisdiction where the body corporate is incorporated does not apply any more to the corporation. They would also determined if other requirements are needed before authorizing the continuance.

Once the continuance is approved, the Director will issue a Certificate of Continuance showing the date of receipt of your request as the effective date. If you prefer, you may request a later incorporation date instead. Please note that the CBCA applies as of the date shown on the Certificate of Continuance.

One copy of the Certificate of Continuance will be sent to the authority in the other jurisdiction that has issued an authorization to export. A notice setting out your corporation's name and the effective date of the continuance will appear on Corporations Canada's web site.

What happens when an application for continuance is deficient or incomplete?

Applications for continuance that are deficient or incomplete will be returned to the applicant with a deficiency notice stating the nature of the deficiency.

When a deficient or incomplete application is returned, the original effective date is forfeited, unless you expressly request the original effective date when you submit your new application. Corporations Canada will retain the fee paid, in anticipation of a further request for continuance. The fee will be returned, however, if you advise the Director in writing that you are withdrawing your application.

How to file your Form 11: Articles of Continuance and pay the fees

On-line Filing

You can file the documents needed to continue your business on line at Corporations Canada Online Filing Centre, at *http://corporationscanada.ic.gc.ca*. Please refer to this web site for the procedures for filing your Form 11: Articles of Continuance. The fee is $200 payable by credit card (American Express®, MasterCard® or Visa®).

The Certificate of Continuance will be sent to you by electronic mail in PDF format.

By Fax

You can also file Form 11: Articles of Continuance by fax at 613-941-0999. Please note that the forms may be signed by reproducing a hand-written signature or in digital format. The $200 fee must be paid by credit card (American Express®, MasterCard® or Visa®) or by deposit to an account opened with Industry Canada.

The Certificate of Continuance will be sent to you by fax.

By Mail Or Courier

You can file the necessary documents and pay the $200 fee by sending them to the following address:

Corporations Canada
Industry Canada
9th floor, Jean Edmonds Tower South
365 Laurier Avenue West
Ottawa, Ontario K1A 0C8

The $200 fee must be paid by cheque payable to the Receiver General for Canada, by credit card (American Express®, MasterCard® or Visa®) or by deposit to an account opened with Industry Canada.

The Certificate of Continuance will be sent to you by mail or by the delivery method requested.

How to fill out Form 11: Articles of Continuance

Please see Form 11 for complete instructions on how to fill out the Articles of Continuance.

Item 1 — Name of Corporation

- Write in the proposed name.
    - If the name has been pre-approved, ensure that the letter of approval is enclosed with your request together with a copy of the NUANS® report.

- If the name has not been reviewed prior to your filing Form 11: Articles of Continuance, the name will go through the approval process when the articles are filed.

- If you are continuing under a number name, which will be assigned by the Director, you need only leave a blank space on the left hand side, write in the word Canada and add the legal element of your choice, such as Inc., Ltd., Corp., etc.

  Example:

  .... CANADA Inc.

- If you are continuing under a bilingual name, both English and French forms of the name should appear here.

What Corporate Name Should Be Used?

A body corporate can continue with its current name, if available, or it can change its name in its Form 11: Articles of Continuance. The rules for searching the availability of a proposed corporate name and obtaining approval from the Director are the same for a continuing corporation as for a newly-incorporating corporation.

Your proposed corporate name must be approved by the Director appointed under the CBCA. The Director will examine your application to verify that it meets the requirements of the CBCA and the Regulations. The name proposed must be distinctive, must not cause confusion with any existing name or trade mark used in Canada, and must not be prohibited or misleading.

You may request approval of the name

- before filing the Form 11: Articles of Continuance
- when you file the Form 11: Articles of Continuance

How to submit an application for a name to the Director

Whether you apply for pre-approval or request approval when you file Form 11: Articles of Continuance, you are responsible for providing all of the facts relevant to the name you are proposing, as well as a NUANS® report.

Information Relevant To The Proposed Name

You *must submit* the information relating to the circumstances that led to your choosing the name in question to the Director *in writing*. You can use the Corporate Name Information Form, *or* you can submit a letter to the Director describing your corporation's activities and addressing the following points:

- WHAT TYPE OF BUSINESS will the proposed corporation conduct? How is this dissimilar to the activities of existing businesses with similar names? Even if your NUANS® report does not turn up names that appear to be similar to yours, the Director still needs this information to ensure that your proposed name does not suggest government sponsorship or that the proposed corporation will be carrying on the business of a bank or a trust, loan or insurance company, or merely describe, or misdescribe the business of your corporation.

- WHERE will the proposed corporation carry on its business? You must show that this territory is not the same as that of other businesses with similar names and similar activities.

- WITH WHAT TYPE OF CLIENTS will the proposed corporation conduct business (e.g., retailers, computer programmers, general public)? Indicate whether they are different from the types of people with whom existing businesses with similar names, engaging in similar activities and operating in the same territory will do business.

- What is the DERIVATION OF THE DISTINCTIVE ELEMENT(S) of the proposed name? For example, what is the derivation of the word "Amtech" in the name "Amtech Enterprises Inc."? If you have a valid reason for wanting that distinctive element, the Director is less likely to conclude that you may be trying to trade on the goodwill of an existing business with a similar name.

- Is the proposed corporation RELATED to existing businesses with similar names or trade marks? If so, you need the consent of their owners in writing.

- Does the proposed corporation have a FOREIGN PARENT with a similar name that carries on business or is known in Canada? If so, you need consent in writing, and you must add (CANADA) or OF CANADA to the proposed name.

- Did you make an EARLIER RESERVATION of a name similar to another name on the NUANS® report? Your request may be denied if it appears that an earlier reservation for the same name has been made by someone else.

- Are you enclosing the CONSENT IN WRITING OF AN INDIVIDUAL WHOSE NAME APPEARS in the corporate name (other than an incorporator of the proposed corporation)? The consenting individual must also indicate that he or she has or had a material interest in the proposed corporation.

If you are satisfied that your corporate name is not likely to cause confusion, outline in your letter to the Director the arguments on which you have based your conclusion.

NUANS® Report

You must provide a search, that is, a NUANS® report under the federal rules for determining whether the name you are proposing is available. A NUANS® report is a five-page document setting out the business names (3 pages) and trade marks registered in Canada (2 pages) that sound or look similar to the name you are proposing. The list is drawn from a national data bank of existing and reserved trade names as well as trade marks that have been registered and applied for in Canada.

A NUANS® report may be obtained in two ways:

1. A NUANS® report may be requested from a private company known as a search house. You can find a list of these firms on Corporations Canada's web site at *www.corporationscanada.ic.gc.ca* by following the links "Online Filing", and "Corporations Canada Online Filing Centre", or in the Yellow Pages of your telephone directory under INCORPORATING COMPANIES, INCORPORATION NAME SEARCH, SEARCHERS OF RECORDS or TRADE MARK AGENTS — REGISTERED. There is a fee for this service.

2. A NUANS® report may be ordered on-line at the Electronic Filing Centre at *www.corporationscanada.ic.gc.ca* from the NUANS® Real-Time System. The fee is $20 payable by credit card (American Express®, MasterCard® or Visa®). The system provides direct access to the NUANS® search service but does not provide the professional assistance and recommendations often available from a registered NUANS® search house. Applicants should note that a NUANS® report that is generated may be rejected if the proposed name does not meet the requirements of the CBCA name regulations.

When you order a NUANS® report, that report has a life of 90 days from the date it is requested. A search house can advise you whether your proposed name is likely to be accepted by the Director. The final decision, however, always rests with the Director.

NUANS® Report: Special Cases

Number name

Instead of a name, you may ask the Director to assign your proposed corporation a number. Some incorporators do this when they have to incorporate a corporation urgently and do not have enough time to have a name approved. A number name must be requested when the Articles of Incorporation are submitted and the applicable fee paid. Obviously you do not submit a NUANS® report.

If you subsequently wish to adopt a trade name, you will have to order a NUANS® report, ask the Director to approve the name and pay a $200 fee for filing Articles of Amendment (Form 4) to change the corporation's name.

Bilingual name

If your proposed corporation intends to carry on business in a region or regions where both English and French are spoken, you may wish to consider adopting a bilingual corporate name.

The procedure is the same as for a unilingual name, except that one NUANS® report is required for each name or variation requested. For example, two NUANS® reports must be filed in order to verify that the phonetically dissimilar English and French forms of a name are both distinctive.

Where the English and French forms are phonetically similar except for a legal element (e.g., Ltd./Ltée), only one NUANS® report will be necessary.

Decision of the Director

If your request for pre-approval is accepted, the name in question will be reserved for you for the life of the search report. If the Director has not made a decision within that 90-day period, you will have to submit a fresh request to reserve a name by ordering another NUANS® report.

If you have requested pre-approval and the Director's decision is favourable, your Form 11: Articles of Continuance will probably be processed promptly when you file them, provided that all other relevant information is submitted at the same time. Remember to include the letter approving your name when you submit your Articles of Incorporation.

If your proposed name is returned to you, you can still submit a written request for the Director to re-examine his decision, having regard to the additional information. However, you will save time and money if you include all relevant information in your initial application.

Where to submit a request for approval of a name

A request for pre-approval may be made on-line at Corporations Canada Online Filing Centre, at *www.corporationscanada.ic.gc.ca*. Please refer to Corporations Canada's web site for the procedures.

As well, you can submit your request for pre-approval by fax, mail or in person at Corporations Canada.

Please refer to the item *"How to file your Form 11: Articles of Continuance and pay the fees"* on page 2 of this kit for contact information.

No fee is payable for a request for approval of a name.

Item 2 — Place of Registered Office

Indicate the province or territory in Canada in which the registered office is to be situated.

Item 3 — Classes and Maximum Number of Shares the Corporation May Issue

Although most continuing corporate entities maintain their existing share structure, changes can be made if covered in the Special Resolution authorizing continuance.

The CBCA sets out certain requirements for details regarding shares, including the following:

- All shares must be without nominal or par value;
- The CBCA gives incorporators broad discretion to designate a class of shares as common, preferred or Class A or B shares, or any other designation. Some incorporators designate classes of shares simply as Class A, Class B and other;
- You do not need to place a limit on the number of shares that the corporation is authorized to issue.
- You do not need to specify a maximum aggregate consideration for the issuance of shares.
- Restrictions may be placed on any class of shares.
- Where there is more than one class of shares, the rights, privileges, restrictions and conditions attaching to each class must be specified. At least one class of shares is to be voting, there must be a class that carries the right to receive dividends and one class that carries the right to receive the remaining property of the corporation on dissolution. If only one class of shares is created, that class will carry all those rights.
- If you cite the existing provisions of the shares or restructure new shares, remember to eliminate all references to "nominal" or "par" value. Such references can, however, be used if the Director has granted special permission based on a written request for exemption (see subsection 187(11) of the CBCA).
- The following sample clauses are often used by incorporators and are acceptable to the Director to cover some very basic kinds of shares. The corporation may choose to issue one class of shares only. If two or more classes of shares are issued, you must specify the rights, privileges, restrictions and conditions attaching to each class.
- You may vary the composition and complexity of share structures for particular situations in countless ways. The clauses given here are only examples of the most common kinds of share structures used by many incorporators; and *they are by no means mandatory or exhaustive*. You may wish to seek legal advice if you want to use other clauses to be sure that they are permitted under the CBCA.

Examples:

For a single class of shares:

The corporation is authorized to issue an unlimited number of shares of one class.

or

Unlimited number of shares in a single class.

For two or more classes of shares:

> The corporation is authorized to issue an unlimited number of Class A and Class B shares. The Class A shareholders shall be entitled to vote at all shareholder meetings, except meetings at which only holders of a specified class of share entitle their holders to vote and to receive such dividend as the board of directors in their discretion shall declare. Subject to the provisions of the *Canada Business Corporations Act*, the Class B shares shall be non-voting. Upon liquidation or dissolution, the holders of Class A and Class B shares shall share equally the remaining property of the corporation.

or

> The corporation is authorized to issue Class A and Class B shares with the following rights, privileges, restrictions and conditions:
>
> > 1. Class A shares, without nominal or par value, the holders of which are entitled:
> >
> > > (a) to vote at all meetings of shareholders except meetings at which only holders of a specified class of shares are entitled to vote; and
> > >
> > > (b) to receive the remaining property of the corporation upon dissolution.
> >
> > 2. Class B shares, without nominal or par value, the holders of which are entitled:
> >
> > > (a) to a dividend as fixed by the board of directors;
> > >
> > > (b) upon the dissolution or liquidation of the corporation, to re-payment of the amount paid for such share (plus any declared and unpaid dividends) in priority to the Class A shares, but they shall not confer a right to any further participation in profits or assets.
> >
> > 3. The holders of Class B shares shall be entitled to vote at all meetings of shareholders.

or

> The holders of Class B shares shall not, subject to the provisions of the *Canada Business Corporations Act*, be entitled to vote at any meetings of shareholders.

For shares in a series:

> The directors may authorize the issue of one or more series within each class of shares, and may fix the number of shares in each series, and determine the rights, privileges, restrictions and conditions attaching to the shares of each series subject to the limits provided in the articles.

(As noted earlier, you may create a series of shares immediately in the Articles, rather than waiting until later.)

Share redemption:

> If a fixed price is not stated, a redemption formula that can be determined in dollars must be used.
>
> > The said Class X shares or any part thereof shall be redeemable at the option of the corporation without the consent of the holders thereof (at a price of $__ per share) or (at a price equal to the amount paid per share) plus any declared and unpaid dividend.

Item 4 — Restrictions on Share Transfers

- Restrictions, if any, on the transfer of shares are normally limited to the consent of the directors and/or shareholders. Exceptions may occur in special cases when the incorporators establish a constrained share corporation, as described in Part IX (Constrained Share Corporations) of the CBCA Regulations.

    Example:

    > No shares of the capital of the Corporation shall be transferred without either (a) the sanction of a majority of the directors of the corporation or alternatively (b) the sanction of the majority of the shareholders of the corporation.

    or

    > No shares of the corporation shall be transferred without the approval of the directors evidenced by resolution of the board, provided that approval of any transfer of shares may be given as aforesaid after the said transfer has been effected upon the records of the corporation, in which event, unless the said resolution stipulates otherwise, the said transfer shall be valid and shall take effect as from the date of its entry upon the books of the corporation.

- You may wish to further restrict the transfer of shares by designating the corporation as "non-distributing" or "distributing." If you expressly wish the corporation to remain "non-distributing," then you should, in addition to the statements referred to above, make the following statement:

    Example:

    > The corporation shall not make a distribution to the public of any of its securities.

- You may add the following clause to clarify your corporation's status as "non-distributing" for the purposes of provincial securities regulations:

    > The number of shareholders is limited to fifty, not including persons who are in the employment of the corporation and persons who, having been formerly in the employment of the corporation, were, while in that employment, and have continued after the termination of that employment, to be shareholders of the corporation, two or more persons holding one or more shares jointly being counted as a single shareholder.

Adding these clauses will prevent the corporation from becoming an issuer that is required, under provincial securities legislation, to file a prospectus or register shares on a stock exchange.

In fact, your corporation will be a "non-distributing" corporation unless, under the definition in subsection 2(1) of the Regulations, the corporation:

(i) is a reporting issuer within the meaning of any applicable securities legislation, unless it is subject to an exemption from that legislation;

(ii) has filed a prospectus or similar document in relation to the public distribution of its shares;

(iii) has securities that are listed and posted for trading on a stock exchange in or outside Canada;

(iv) is a distributing corporation that is involved in or results from a statutory procedure, such as an amalgamation or reorganization.

Under subsections 2(6) and 2(7) of the CBCA, the Director may also determine that a corporation is not or was not a distributing corporation if the Director is satisfied that the determination would not be prejudicial to the public interest.

Item 5 — Number of Directors

You may specify a minimum and maximum number or a fixed number of directors. However, to permit cumulative voting, the number of directors must be fixed. Moreover, if the corporation is a "distributing" corporation, there must be at least three directors.

Example:

A minimum of 1 and a maximum of 7.

or

Five directors.

Item 6 — Restrictions on Business

- A CBCA corporation has all the rights of a natural person, and normally one would not wish to limit this power.

  Example:

  If there are to be no restrictions, simply state "NONE."

- If, however, for any reason you wish to restrict the business of the corporation, the following preamble is suggested:

  The business of the corporation shall be limited to the following:. ...

It should be noted that section 3 of the CBCA itself prohibits CBCA corporations from carrying on the business of a bank or an insurance or trust and loan company, or carry on business as a degree-granting institution.

Item 7 — Previous Name and Details

Please indicate the previous name of your corporation under the exporting jurisdiction, if a change was effected upon continuance. Also give details such as the date of the previous incorporation and the exporting jurisdiction.

Item 8 — Other Provisions

The CBCA allows you to include a number of additional provisions in Form 11: Articles of Continuance. This item is frequently used to include clauses to meet the requirements of other laws or institutions.

The following list illustrates the kind of wording generally adopted for the more frequently occurring features. This listing is not complete and the wording is only a suggestion.

- Borrowing Power of Directors:

  A provision regarding directors' borrowing powers and their delegation is sometimes used to limit the authority of directors and/or to satisfy lending institutions:

  Example:

  If authorized by by-law which is duly made by the directors and confirmed by ordinary resolution, the directors of the corporation may from time to time:

  i) borrow money upon the credit of the corporation;

  ii) issue, reissue, sell or pledge debt obligations of the corporation; and

iii) mortgage, hypothecate, pledge or otherwise create a security interest in all or any property of the corporation, owned or subsequently acquired to secure any debt obligation of the corporation.

Any such by-law may provide for the delegation of such powers by the directors to such officers or directors of the corporation to such extent and in such manner as may be set out in the by-law.

Nothing herein limits or restricts the borrowing of money by the corporation on bills of exchange or promissory notes made, drawn, accepted or endorsed by or on behalf of the corporation.

- Cumulative Voting for Directors:

    You may include provision for cumulative voting for directors, but only if the number of directors is a fixed number:

    Example:

    There shall be cumulative voting for directors.

- Increasing the Majority Vote by Shareholders:

    You may insert wording similar to the following to increase the majority vote by shareholders:

    Example:

    In order to effect any (ordinary and/or special)[9] resolution passed at a meeting of shareholders[10], a majority of not less than __ per cent of the votes cast by the shareholders who voted in respect of that resolution shall be required.

- Specifying the *foreign* version of your corporate name for use *outside* Canada:

    Example:

    It is hereby provided that the corporation may use and may be equally designated by the following form outside Canada:.. ..

    (Note: do not use item 8 to state the *French* or *English* form of the corporate name for use *inside* Canada — use item 1)

- Specifying voting rights on fractional shares:

    Example:

    A holder of a fractional share shall be entitled to exercise voting rights and to receive dividends in respect of said fractional share.

- Specifying that some shareholders have a pre-emptive right:

    Example:

    It is hereby provided that no shares of a class of shares shall be issued unless the shares have first been offered to the shareholders holding shares of that class, and those shareholders have a pre-emptive right to acquire the offered shares in proportion to their holdings of the shares of that class, at such price and on such terms as those shares are to be offered to others.

---

[9]The CBCA specifies a simple majority for an ordinary resolution and two-thirds majority for a special resolution. Therefore, any figure set out in the articles must be greater than these statutory majorities.

[10]Other than a resolution to remove a director (see subsection 6(4) of the CBCA).

- Under the CBCA, directors are not required to own shares of the corporation. However, where you do wish to provide for directors to own shares, the following wording is normally used.

  Example:

  > No person otherwise qualified shall be elected or appointed as a director unless such person beneficially owns at least one share issued by the corporation.

- Prescribing how shareholders will fill a *vacancy on the board of directors*:

  Example:

  > Any vacancy among the directors shall be filled by a vote of the shareholders.

- Specifying a *quorum* of directors:

  Example:

  > The quorum for any meeting of the board of directors shall be ___.

- You may provide for trust deeds for purposes of the Quebec *Special Corporate Powers Act*, if the corporation intends to carry on business in the Province of Quebec:

  Example:

  > The corporation, through its directors, may, as it deems expedient and notwithstanding the provisions of the *Civil Code*, hypothecate, mortgage or pledge any real or personal property, currently owned or subsequently acquired, of the corporation, to secure the payment of such debentures and other securities, or to provide only a part of these guarantees for the said purposes; and it may constitute the aforesaid hypothec, mortgage or pledge by trust deed, pursuant to sections 23 and 24 of the *Special Corporate Powers Act* (R.S.Q. 1964, c 275), or in any other manner.

  > The corporation may also hypothecate or mortgage the real property, or pledge or otherwise charge in any manner the personal property of the corporation, or provide these various kinds of guarantee, to secure the payment of loans made otherwise than by the issue of debentures, as well as the payment or performance of other debts, contracts and undertakings of the corporation.

Signing of Form 11

Form 11: Articles of Continuance must be signed by a director or an authorized officer of the company.

An authorized officer is a person appointed by the directors. The appointment is subject to the Articles, the by-laws, or any unanimous shareholder agreement. The officer may be the chair of the board of directors, the president of the corporation, a vice-president, the secretary, treasurer or comptroller, legal counsel, general manager, a managing director or any other person who performs functions for a corporation similar to those normally performed by a person who holds one of those positions.

Form 11, which is filed with the Director through the Corporations Canada Online Filing Centre or sent by fax, need not necessarily contain the original signatures of the incorporator(s). However, signed copies of the original documents must be retained in the records of the corporation.

How to fill Form 2: Initial Registered Office Address and First Board of Directors

Please, refer to the form to get complete instructions.

Indicate at item 1 the name of the corporation as indicated in Form 11: Articles of Continuance.

Indicate at item 2 the address of the registered office. It must be a complete street address within the province or territory specified in Form 11: Articles of Continuance. Please indicate at item 3 the mailing address if it is different from the address of the registered office.

Indicate at item 4 the name and family name of all directors. The number of directors must correspond with the number indicated in item 6 of Form 11: Articles of Continuance. You must indicate the residential address (a post office or a business address won't be accepted) of each director and indicate if he/she is Canadian resident.

Note that at least 25 per cent of the directors must be Canadians residents. However, some restrictions apply:

- If the corporation has fewer than four directors, at least one of them must be a resident Canadian.
- If the corporation is required by a federal Act or regulations to meet specific requirements respecting Canadian participation or control (e.g., corporations carrying on air transportation or telecommunications businesses), a majority (50% + 1) of its directors must be resident Canadians.
- If the corporation is carrying on one of the following businesses, a majority (50% + 1) of its directors must be resident Canadians:
  - uranium mining
  - book publishing or distribution
  - bookselling, where the sale of books is the primary part of the corporation's business
  - film or video distribution

However, if a parent corporation belonging to one of those categories (i.e., carrying on a business referred to above, or that must meet requirements respecting Canadian participation or control under a federal Act or regulations) and its subsidiaries earn less than five per cent of their gross revenue in Canada, only one third of the corporation's directors need be resident Canadians.

Form 2 must be signed by an individual who has relevant knowledge of the corporation and who is authorized to sign by the directors.

Additional information and how to reach Corporations Canada

For additional information on Corporations Canada products and services, please visit Corporations Canada's Web site or call 1-866-333-5556.

You can also contact Corporations Canada at:

Client Services Section
Corporations Canada
Industry Canada
9th floor, Jean Edmonds Tower South
Ottawa, Ontario K1A 0C8
Fax: 613-941-0601
www.corporationscanada.ic.gc.ca

Annex 1 — List of Jurisdictions Previously Approved by the Director Appointed Under the CBCA

The Director has received and approved applications for import from the following Canadian jurisdictions. The documentation required may vary with the provisions of the exporting jurisdictions legislation. Should that legislation be amended, the filing requirements listed below might change. It is the responsibility of the applicant to ensure that the request filed with the Director satisfies the requirements of the legislation where the body corporate is actually incorporated as well as the CBCA.

Jurisdiction	Requested Documents
Alberta	- Name search report - Forms 2 and 11 properly completed - fee of $200 - Letter of Approval from the Alberta Corporate Registry
British Columbia	- Name search report - Forms 2 and 11 properly completed - Fee of $200 - Letter of Authorization from the British Columbia Corporate Registry
Manitoba	- Name search report - Forms 2 and 11 properly completed - Fee of $200 - An endorsed "Application for approval to continue in another jurisdiction" from the Manitoba Companies Office
New Brunswick	- Name search report - Forms 2 and 11 properly completed - Fee of $200 - Letter of Satisfaction from the New Brunswick Corporate Affairs Registry
Newfoundland and Labrador	- Name search report - Forms 2 and 11 properly completed - Fee of $200 - Letter of Satisfaction from the Newfoundland and Labrador Registry of Companies
Northwest Territories	- Name search report - Forms 2 and 11 properly completed - Fee of $200 - Continue-Out Letter from the Northwest Territories Corporate Registries
Nova Scotia	- Name search report - Forms 2 and 11 properly completed - Fee of $200

Jurisdiction	Requested Documents
	- Letter of Non-objection from the Nova Scotia Registry of Joint Stock Companies
Nunavut	- Name search report - Forms 2 and 11 properly completed - Fee of $200 - Letter of Approval from the Legal Registries Division, Government of Nunavut
Ontario	- Name search report - Forms 2 and 11 properly completed - Fee of $200 - An endorsed "Application for authorization to continue in another jurisdiction" (Form 7) from the Ontario Companies and Personal Property Security Branch
Prince Edward Island	- Name search report - Forms 2 and 11 properly completed - Fee of $200 - Letter of Satisfaction from the Prince Edward Island Consumer, Corporate and Insurance Division
Saskatchewan	- Name search report - Forms 2 and 11 properly completed - Fee of $200 - Certificate of Authorization from the Saskatchewan Corporations Branch
Yukon	- Name search report - Forms 2 and 11 properly completed - Fee of $200 - Letter of Approval from the Yukon Corporate Registry

Policy Statement 9.2 — Policy on Import Continuance

Date: November 22, 2004

We have received and approved applications for import from the following Canadian jurisdictions. The documentation required may vary with the provisions of the exporting jurisdictions legislation. Should that legislation be amended, the filing requirements listed below might change. It is the responsibility of the applicant to ensure that the request filed with the Director appointed under the Canada Business Corporations Act (CBCA) satisfies the requirements of the legislation where the body corporate is actually incorporated as well as the CBCA.

Jurisdiction	Requested Documents
Alberta	- Name search report - Forms 2 and 11 properly completed - Fee of $200

Jurisdiction	Requested Documents
	- Letter of Approval from the Alberta Corporate Registry
British Columbia	- Name search report - Forms 2 and 11 properly completed - Fee of $200 - Letter of Authorization from the British Columbia Corporate Registry
Manitoba	- Name search report - Forms 2 and 11 properly completed - Fee of $200 - An endorsed "Application for approval to continue in another jurisdiction" from the Manitoba Companies Office
New Brunswick	- Name search report - Forms 2 and 11 properly completed - Fee of $200 - Letter of Satisfaction from the New Brunswick Corporate Affairs Registry
Newfoundland and Labrador	- Name search report - Forms 2 and 11 properly completed - Fee of $200 - Letter of Satisfaction from the Newfoundland and Labrador Registry of Companies
Northwest Territories	- Name search report - Forms 2 and 11 properly completed - Fee of $200 - Continue-Out Letter from the Northwest Territories Corporate Registries
Nova Scotia	- Name search report - Forms 2 and 11 properly completed - Fee of $200 - Letter of Non-objection from the Nova Scotia Registry of Joint Stock Companies
Nunavut	- Name search report - Forms 2 and 11 properly completed - Fee of $200 - Letter of Approval from the Legal Registries Division, Government of Nunavut
Ontario	- Name search report - Forms 2 and 11 properly completed - Fee of $200

Jurisdiction	Requested Documents
	- An endorsed "Application for authorization to continue in another jurisdiction" (Form 7) from the Ontario Companies and Personal Property Security Branch
Prince Edward Island	- Name search report - Forms 2 and 11 properly completed - Fee of $200 - Letter of Satisfaction from the Prince Edward Island Consumer, Corporate and Insurance Division
Saskatchewan	- Name search report - Forms 2 and 11 properly completed - Fee of $200 - Certificate of Authorization from the Saskatchewan Corporations Branch
Yukon	- Name search report - Forms 2 and 11 properly completed - Fee of $200 - Letter of Approval from the Yukon Corporate Registry

Where we receive a request for import from a jurisdiction which does not appear in the above list, the applicant will file a copy of the relevant parts of the current legislation of the exporting jurisdiction and forms 2 and 11, $200 and a name search or name pre-approval. The applicant must also file a legal opinion addressed to the Director, CBCA, from counsel qualified to provide opinions on the law of this jurisdiction ("foreign law") stating 1) that the foreign law permits export to the CBCA in such a manner that once the corporation is continued under the CBCA, the foreign law will cease to apply, and, 2) where the foreign law does not require any authorization to be issued by the foreign jurisdiction, that the corporation has met all requirements for export under the foreign law.

Policy Statement 9.3 — Export Policy

Date: **October 25, 2007**

Introduction

This policy sets out the position of the Director appointed under the *Canada Business Corporations Act* (CBCA) concerning "export" transactions. An export transaction, or a continuance (export), results in a corporation moving to another federal corporate statute, or another corporate statute of a Canadian province or of another country. The transaction will result in the corporation being governed by that statute and no longer subject to the provisions of the CBCA.

This policy states the main principles and provides practical guidance intended to facilitate export transactions. Although they do not have the force of law, these principles and guidelines provide information on how the Director reviews these transactions in relation to the Director's responsibilities under the CBCA. The policy is not intended to expand the Director's powers in any way. Nor is it intended to expand the powers of shareholders or creditors, beyond those given to them under the CBCA. The Director believes that by communicating the main principles and guidelines to persons intending to carry out export transactions, there will be fewer rejected requests as well as less cost and administrative inconvenience. In the end, however, the final interpretation of the CBCA and its related provisions is the responsibility of the courts.

The Director is not bound by this policy as regards the position taken in a particular case. This policy is not intended to replace legal advice. Accordingly, you may want to consult with legal counsel or other professional advisors prior to making an application for continuance (export).

For more detailed information on how to apply for an export under section 188, please see "Steps to Follow for an Export Transaction Policy" on the Corporations Canada website *www.corporationscanada.ic.gc.ca*.

Scope of Policy

This policy concerns transactions under which persons with a security or debt interest in a CBCA corporation have their interest changed to a corresponding interest in a non-CBCA entity.

Although it is not exhaustive, the following list describes, in general, the type of export transactions that can be performed:

- An export continuance under section 188 of the CBCA, when a CBCA corporation becomes a non-CBCA body corporate;

- An export amalgamation under section 182 of the CBCA involving a "three-cornered amalgamation" (e.g., two corporations amalgamate, with the shareholders of those corporations receiving shares of a third corporation affiliated with one of the amalgamating corporations as part of the amalgamation); and

- An export arrangement under section 192 of the CBCA may result in a CBCA corporation continuing into another jurisdiction, or may leave a CBCA corporation in existence but transfer some of its investors to a non-CBCA body corporate (e.g., holders of equity and debt securities might be transferred, while trade creditors remain as creditors of a CBCA corporation).

The Director believes that situations in which persons with a security or debt interest in a CBCA corporation become holders of a similar interest in a non-CBCA entity (whether or not it is a body corporate) warrant attention in the application of the disclosure and other requirements of the CBCA. Accordingly, the following description of the principles to be followed applies in any situation where persons with a security or debt interest (the "Affected Persons") in a CBCA corporation (the "exporting CBCA corporation") have had their interest replaced by a similar interest in a non-CBCA entity (the "non-CBCA successor").

Affected Persons will normally be security holders, but in some cases might include others (e.g., a court might give a trade creditor or other stakeholder status as a "complainant" under paragraph (d) in the definition of that word in section 238 of the CBCA. In addition, relief may be granted under subsection 241(2) if conduct is found to be oppressive to any "security holder, creditor, director or officer").

General Considerations

Director's Responsibilities

The Director recognizes that an export transaction may be in the best interests of a CBCA corporation. It may facilitate completion of some larger corporate restructuring or be desirable for some other business reason. If shareholders are given full disclosure and the transaction is carried out in full accordance with the CBCA, which requires shareholder approval for most types of export transactions, then the Director will become involved only to perform administrative responsibilities and carry out the Director's other statutory responsibilities. The Director is given specific responsibilities depending on the export transactions, such as the requirement in:

- subsection 188(1), that the Director be satisfied that creditors and shareholders are not adversely affected if the export transaction is effected by continuance;
- subsection 185(2), that the Director be satisfied as to the solvency of the corporations if the export transaction is effected by amalgamation; and
- subsection 192(5), that the Director be given notice of an application for interim and final order and be satisfied as to the application if the export transaction is to be effected by arrangement.

More generally, the Director will consider intervening if the Director is of the view that the transaction may not be adequately disclosed or that it may be oppressive to Affected Persons who did not give their specific consent. The "Varity" case (Re *Canada Business Corporations Act* (1991) 3 O.R. 3d (Ont. C.A.) 336) makes clear that the "adversely affect" test in subsection 188(1) does not apply to other "non-188" types of export transactions. However, a number of CBCA provisions give the Director the authority to act if the Director believes that there may be inadequate disclosure or oppressive conduct. Some of these provisions enable the Director to act on an administrative basis while others require the Director to make a court application.

Disclosure

If a shareholders' meeting is necessary to approve an export transaction, then the information accompanying, or provided, in the notice of meeting must give sufficient detail to enable the shareholders to form a reasoned decision to support or reject the transaction. While the degree of detail required may vary between a corporation that has fewer than 50 shareholders and the one that has more than 50 shareholders, such disclosure should at least include:

a. a description of any significant differences between protections available to security holders (e.g., derivative action, oppression, dissent and appraisal rights or equivalent protections) under the CBCA and the law applicable after the export transaction;

b. a description of a subsequent transaction if the exporting CBCA corporation knows that such a transaction may have a material impact upon Affected Persons and could not have been effected under the CBCA without affording all the shareholder rights under the CBCA. This disclosure should be made whether or not the ability to effect the proposed subsequent transaction is a major motivating influence for the export transaction, and whether or not a legal commitment has been made to effect the proposed subsequent transaction after completion of the export transaction. Examples of such subsequent transactions include:

  - a non-CBCA successor effecting a corporate transaction that would not be permissible for a CBCA corporation or would be permissible only in modified form; and
  - a non-CBCA successor effecting a corporate transaction without a dissenting shareholder's appraisal remedy that, if effected under the CBCA, would require such dissent rights.

c. the business reasons for the export transaction;

d. the level of shareholder approval required for the export transaction (e.g., a two-thirds approval requirement if a special resolution is necessary), whether a dissenting shareholder's appraisal remedy is available and whether a requirement of a relevant securities law requires a shareholder meeting or dictates the requisite level of approval; and

e. any other material considerations.

Certain Canadian Provinces

The Director recognizes that the corporate statutes of British Columbia, Alberta, Saskatchewan, Manitoba, Ontario, Nova Scotia, New Brunswick, Newfoundland and Labrador and the Yukon contain derivative action, oppression, dissent and appraisal rights sufficiently similar to those in the CBCA that disclosure of the differences should not be necessary.

Disclosure to Other Affected Persons

Shareholders are not the only Affected Persons. Other Affected Persons may well feel they have an interest in an export transaction. The Director cannot require that Affected Persons other than shareholders be given notice of an export transaction if the CBCA does not require that notice be given to them. However, the Director considers that it is good corporate practice for a CBCA corporation to advise such non-shareholder Affected Persons of an export transaction if it has the potential to detract from their position or from the legal protection to which they are entitled. If such a notice is appropriate, a news release may well be adequate.

Action by the Director

The Director has the following authority to take action with respect to an export transaction:

- under section 188, if the Director is of the view that the export will adversely affect shareholders or creditors who did not give their specific consent, the Director has the authority, without reference to a court, to reject the application;
- under subsection 185, if the Director is not satisfied with respect to the requirements of subsection 185(2) (e.g., as to the solvency of the corporations or that creditors will not be prejudiced or have not been given adequate notice of the amalgamation), the Director has the authority, without reference to a court, to reject an application for a "three-cornered" amalgamation;
- under section 192, the Director has the right to appear and be heard in court, and may well choose to argue lack of fairness in an arrangement application;
- under section 241, if the Director concludes that an export transaction involves oppressive elements, the Director has the authority to appear before the court as a complainant and may be prepared to exercise that authority;
- under subsection 154(1), the Director may take action if circumstances warrant; and
- under section 247, the Director may take action if circumstances warrant.

In verifying compliance with the solvency requirements of subsection 185(2) and the "will not adversely affect" requirement of subsection 188(1), the Director usually obtains all the necessary information through the required affidavits supplemented as necessary, for example by undertakings and legal opinions.

Complaints

In practice, the Director relies primarily on complaints received from Affected Persons to determine whether or not to take action. The reason for this is that, although Corporations Canada reviews all documents relating to export transactions to ensure that they comply with the views expressed in this policy statement, such reviews do not always bring to light the factual evidence needed to support an allegation of inadequate disclosure or of oppression. This is not to suggest, however, that the Director will take action on all complaints of inadequate disclosure or oppressive conduct; especially if legal remedies are available that do not require action by the Director.

In deciding whether to act on a complaint, the Director will consider not only the merits of the complaint, but also:

- the adequacy of the legal remedies available;
- the resources and access to legal remedies available to the Affected Person;
- the nature of the public interest involved;
- the available resources of Corporations Canada; and
- other relevant factors.[11]

The Director will not initiate a non-disclosure related oppression application on behalf of a person who has specifically consented, by vote or otherwise, to that transaction. The Director is sensitive to the fact that export transactions may need to happen very quickly, within a narrow window of opportunity. Because the Director does not want to unduly delay such transactions, complainants must act quickly, ensuring that their initial representations are well documented and reflect the number of persons affected by the complained-of action. The Director will not consider complaints that lack these elements.

If an Affected Person provides credible evidence or analysis that raises doubts about the accuracy or completeness of the information contained in an affidavit filed with the Director concerning matters specified in subsection 185(2) or 188(1), the Director will ask the exporting CBCA corporation to explain the issues raised. In such cases, the Director may require that the issues raised be resolved before the export proceeds.

In both of these situations and in those where another concern has been raised, specifically as to adequate disclosure or oppressive conduct, the Director may request or require a reasonable delay in the export transaction to permit an adequate review of the matter. If the doubt relates to the matters specified in subsection 185(2) or 188(1), the Director has the authority to require that the export be delayed until the doubt is resolved. In other situations, if a request for delay is not granted, the Director will consider what other measures are available, including the possibility of initiating (or supporting an Affected Person in initiating) an application to require a delay under section 154 or 241.

The Director's Review

The Director's review will be conducted expeditiously and will consider all relevant facts. Three that are frequently relevant merit particular reference:

1. Adequacy of disclosure. If a transaction is approved by the required majority of affected shareholders after full and meaningful disclosure of its implications, special circumstances such as an oppressive impact on another class of Affected Persons would ordinarily be necessary before the Director will intervene;

2. Availability of a dissenting shareholder's appraisal remedy. The cost, uncertainty and delay which may be involved in the enforcement of this remedy (whether it arises

---

[11]The Director has developed a policy to set out more clearly the circumstances which would prompt the Director to initiate or intervene in a court action respecting alleged oppressive conduct.

under subsection 190(1) or in some other way) will be taken into account in determining to what extent it adequately protects shareholders; and

3.   The quality of protection under the laws applicable to the non-CBCA successor is of direct relevance.

Other factors, such as the use of a majority of the minority approval requirement, may also be relevant in appropriate situations.

Ongoing Concerns

If the Director's concerns persist after this review, the Director will determine how to proceed. If a dispute exists as to an issue arising under subsection 185(2) or 188(1), or as to a disclosure or oppression issue in which the Director should be involved, the Director will seek an efficient way to resolve it. Procedures open to the Director in appropriate cases are to initiate, or to support an Affected Person in initiating, an oppression application under section 241, or an application for a restraining order under subsection 154(1), or a compliance order under section 247, or, if the discretion exists, the Director may refuse to accept a document for filing unless ordered to do so by the court.

If appropriate in a section 188 application, having regard to the time constraints of the transaction, the Director will explore with interested and affected parties, alternative methods of dispute resolution such as mediation and arbitration. The Director's decision will be made only after appropriate consultation and will reflect a balancing of the issues discussed in this policy statement.

Action by Affected Persons

Besides possible actions by the Director, Affected Persons who feel aggrieved by an export transaction may apply to a court under the CBCA. A court would have wide discretion to design an appropriate remedy for an Affected Person. Available options include:

- the "oppression remedy" under section 241;
- if the export transaction takes the form of an arrangement, the aggrieved person may challenge it before the court under section 192;
- an application to the court for the calling of a shareholders' meeting under subsection 144(1);
- an application under subsection 154(1) to restrain the holding of a meeting; or
- an application under section 247 for a restraining or compliance order.

Additional information and how to reach Corporations Canada

For additional information on Corporations Canada's products and services, please visit the Corporations Canada website *www.corporationscanada.ic.gc.ca* or call our toll free number 1-866-333-5556.

You can also contact Corporations Canada at:

Client Services Section
Corporations Canada
Industry Canada
9th floor, Jean Edmonds Tower South
Ottawa, Ontario K1A 0C8
Toll free: 1-866-333-5556
Fax: 613-941-0601

www.corporationscanada.ic.gc.ca

Policy Statement 9.4 — Steps to Follow for an Export Transaction

Date: October 25, 2007

Introduction

The purpose of this policy is to help you obtain approval to "export" your corporation either to another federal statute or to the statute of another jurisdiction. This will result in your corporation being removed from the jurisdiction of the *Canada Business Corporations Act* (CBCA). Corporations may be exported to another federal corporate statute; to a corporate statute of a Canadian province; or to the corporate statute of another country. The procedure varies slightly depending on the statute or jurisdiction. More information on export transactions is available in the "Export Policy" on the Corporations Canada website *www.corporationscanada.ic.gc.ca*.

Non-Federal Jurisdiction (i.e., to a Canadian province or another country)

In order for a CBCA corporation to be exported to a non-federal jurisdiction, whether a Canadian province or another country, you must follow a three-step process:

1. You must obtain a Letter of Satisfaction from Corporations Canada that you will then submit to the authority of the importing jurisdiction (see subsection 188(1) of the CBCA) together with any continuance documents that may be required under the importing jurisdiction's laws. This letter states that the Director appointed under the CBCA is satisfied that the continuance will not adversely affect creditors or shareholders of the corporation. The Letter of Satisfaction is valid for 90 days.

2. If the authorities at the importing jurisdiction accept your application for continuance, they will issue you some kind of documentation (e.g., Certificate of Continuance) indicating that your corporation is duly continued under that legislation (i.e., as if it had been incorporated in that jurisdiction).

3. Finally, you must then give evidence of this continuance to the Director (i.e., a copy of the documentation issued by the importing jurisdiction), in order for the Director to issue a Certificate of Discontinuance (see subsection 188(7) of the CBCA). This completes the export process. If a certificate of discontinuance is not issued, the corporation continues to be governed by the CBCA.

Letters of Satisfaction

Letters of Satisfaction are issued at the discretion of the Director. The principal concerns of the Director regarding an export transaction are whether:

- the export is legally possible;
- the export has been duly authorized by the corporation;
- the export will not adversely affect creditors or shareholders of the corporation; and
- the corporation wishing to export is in good standing under the CBCA (e.g., the corporation is up to date with filings of annual returns and financial statements, if applicable, and it is not the subject of a current investigation for non-compliance).

Unless the Director receives a complaint from a person who claims to be adversely affected or oppressed by the transaction, a Letter of Satisfaction will normally be issued upon receipt of your written request accompanied by the following documents, as applicable:

1. If the corporation intends to export to the corporate law statute of one of the provinces or territories listed below, a representative of the corporation must send a letter to the Director stating that a special resolution of the shareholders authorizing the export has been passed as required by subsection 188(5) of the CBCA:

   Alberta
   Manitoba
   Nova Scotia
   Saskatchewan
   Yukon
   British Columbia
   New Brunswick
   Ontario
   Newfoundland and Labrador

2. For other Canadian provinces or another country, the Director must receive:

   a. a copy of the relevant continuance provisions of the legislation of the importing jurisdiction;

   b. an opinion from counsel qualified to provide opinions on the law of the importing jurisdiction that the law of that jurisdiction:
      - permits import of a CBCA corporation, and
      - provides for the rights set out in subsection 188(10) of the CBCA;

   c. an affidavit of an authorized director or officer stating that:
      - shareholders have been given full disclosure of the effect of export on their rights and interests;
      - the export has been authorized by special resolution of the shareholders of the corporation, and
      - shareholders and creditors will not be adversely affected; and

   d. if there are any dissenters, a statement of a director or officer that the corporation:
      - will undertake to honour the dissent right granted by section 190 and, if necessary, turn to the Canadian courts for that purpose, and
      - has sufficient funds to pay dissenting shareholders and that arrangements have been made to ensure that those funds will be available to satisfy that claim.

The filing fee for a Letter of Satisfaction is $200.00, payable to the Receiver General for Canada.

Obtaining a Certificate of Discontinuance

If the authority of the importing jurisdiction accepts your application for continuance, they will issue you a document (e.g., a Certificate of Continuance) as proof that the corporation has been continued into their (importing) jurisdiction. You must then submit a copy of the document to the Director who in turn will issue a Certificate of Discontinuance.

Please note that certain jurisdictions will send a copy of the document certifying continuance directly to the Director. However, the onus is on you to ensure that the Director receives confirmation of the continuance by one means or another.

Upon receiving such document or notice, the Director will issue a Certificate of Discontinuance dated retroactively to the effective date of the importing jurisdiction's Certificate of Continuance. The CBCA ceases to apply to the corporation as of that date.

There is no fee for the issuance of a Certificate of Discontinuance.

A notice of the discontinuance will be published on our website in the section "Corporations Canada's Monthly Transactions."

Filing documents with the Director and paying fees?

By Fax

You can submit the completed application by fax to (613) 941-0999. The $200 fee for the Letter of Satisfaction must be paid by credit card (American Express7®, MasterCard® or Visa®) or from a deposit account with Industry Canada.

The Letter of Satisfaction and the Certificate of Discontinuance will be sent to you by fax.

By Email

You may send the completed application by email to corporationscanada.ic.gc.ca. Signatures can be a reproduction of a handwritten signature. You must keep the original signed copy with your corporate records. The $200 fee for the Letter of Satisfaction must be paid by credit card (American Express®, MasterCard® or Visa®) or from a deposit account with Industry Canada.

The Letter of Satisfaction and the Certificate of Discontinuance will be emailed to you.

By Mail or Courier

You can file the necessary documents by sending them to the following address:

> Corporations Canada
> Industry Canada
> 9th floor, Jean Edmonds Tower South
> 365, Laurier Avenue West
> Ottawa, Ontario K1A 0C8

The $200 fee for the Letter of Satisfaction must be paid by cheque payable to the Receiver General for Canada, by credit card (American Express®, MasterCard® or Visa®) or from a deposit account with Industry Canada.

The Letter of Satisfaction and the Certificate of Discontinuance will be sent to you by mail or by the delivery method requested.

In Person

You may attend in person and file an export application, from Monday to Friday, between 8:30 a.m. and 5:00 p.m., at:

> Corporations Canada
> Industry Canada
> 9th floor, Jean Edmonds Tower South
> 365 Laurier Avenue West
> Ottawa, Ontario K1A 0C8

You must have with you all the necessary documents. The $200 fee must be paid in cash, by cheque payable to the Receiver General for Canada, by credit card (American Express®, MasterCard® or Visa®) or by deposit to an account opened with Industry Canada.

You will be given the Letter of Satisfaction or the Certificate of Discontinuance.

Bank Act, Insurance Companies Act and Trust and Loan Companies Act

The *Bank Act*, the *Insurance Companies Act* and the *Trust and Loan Companies Act*, are administered by the Office of the Superintendent of Financial Institutions Canada (OSFI). If a corporation wishes to export to any of these statutes, there is a five-step process:

1. The shareholders of the corporation must authorize the export in a special resolution.

2. An application for continuance must be made directly to OSFI at:

> Office of the Superintendent of Financial Institutions Canada
> Kent Square
> 255 Albert Street
> Ottawa, Ontario K1A 0H2
> Tel.: (613) 990-7788
> Toll free: 1-800-358-3980
> Fax: (613) 952-8219

3. OSFI will provide notice of the application to the Director under the CBCA. This will permit the Director to bring any matter the Director considers relevant or important to the attention of OFSI before the continuance is approved.

4. If the application is satisfactory, OSFI will issue Letters Patent of Continuance and send a copy of them to the Director, indicating that a continuance under OSFI legislation occurred on a specific date.

5. Upon receipt of the OSFI documents, the Director will file the notice and issue a Certificate of Discontinuance to the CBCA corporation, dated the effective date of the continuance.

A notice of the discontinuance will be published on our website in the section "Corporations Canada's Monthly Transactions".

Canada Cooperatives Act

If a corporation wishes to export to the *Canada Cooperatives Act* (Co-op Act), there is a three-step process:

1. The shareholders of the corporation must authorize the export in a special resolution.

2. An application for continuance under the Co-op Act must be made directly to the Director under the Co-op Act, who is also the Director under the CBCA. More information on continuance under the Co-op Act is available in the "Canada Cooperatives Act Continuance Policy".

3. If the application is satisfactory, the Director will issue a Certificate of Continuance under the Co-op Act dated the effective date of the continuance. A copy of the certificate will be sent to the applicant.

A notice of the continuance under the Co-op Act and the discontinuance from the CBCA will be published on our website in the section "Corporations Canada's Monthly Transactions".

Additional information and how to reach Corporations Canada

For additional information on Corporations Canada's products and services, please visit the Corporations Canada website *www.corporationscanada.ic.gc.ca* or call our toll free number 1-866-333-5556.

You can also contact Corporations Canada at:

Client Services Section
Corporations Canada
Industry Canada
9th floor, Jean Edmonds Tower South
Ottawa, Ontario K1A 0C8
Toll free: 1-866-333-5556
Fax: 613-941-0601
www.corporationscanada.ic.gc.ca

Policy Statement 10.1 — Canada Business Corporations Act Dissolution Kit

Date: May 30, 2002

This policy statement replaces policy 10.1, Dissolution Kit, dated August 19, 1999. This policy statement reflects the amendments to the *Canada Business Corporation Act* and the *Canada Business Corporations Regulations (2001)* that came into effect on November 24, 2001.

This kit is intended only as a guide to users; it does not replace or take precedence over the CBCA

Why Use This Kit?

The purpose of this kit is to help you submit the information required for obtaining approval for a corporation's dissolution under the *Canada Business Corporations Act* (CBCA). By ensuring that you provide all the required information with your initial application, you can help Corporations Canada process your documents swiftly.

Please note that only voluntary dissolutions are covered in this kit. The CBCA also provides for involuntary dissolutions in certain circumstances, for example, failure to file annual returns.

In this kit, you will find:

- details on what information must be filed in order to obtain a Certificate of Dissolution;
- general information about the role of Corporations Canada;
- information on what happens when an application for dissolution is deficient;
- information concerning the various ways to file the dissolution documents;
- information about how a corporation is dissolved;
- suggestions about how to fill out key parts of Form 17 and Form 19;
- the forms to use for dissolution; (Please note that forms are available online under "Information Kits and Administrative Forms" on the Corporations Canada website, and
- contact information for Corporations Canada.

You should note that this kit does not tell you everything you may need to know about dissolution. You may wish to consult with legal counsel or other professional advisors on this or other relevant matters.

What Information Must Be Filed?

To receive a Certificate of Dissolution, a Certificate of Intent to Dissolve or a Certificate of Revocation of Intent to Dissolve, you must send some or all of the following supporting materials, duly completed, as may be applicable to the circumstances of your corporation to the Director under the CBCA (the "Director"), whose address appears at the end of this kit:

- completed Form 17, Articles of Dissolution OR a completed Form 19, Statement of Intent to Dissolve or Revocation of Intent to Dissolve

- a filing fee of $50.00, payable to the Receiver General for Canada, when submitting a Revocation of Intent to Dissolve only.

Instructions for completing the forms are given on the reverse side of each document. Forms must be signed by a director or authorized officer of the corporation.

There is no requirement that any form of "proof of facts" (such as affidavits) be submitted with Articles of Dissolution. It is the responsibility of the applicant, not the Director, to verify that the contents of the articles meet all requirements of the CBCA.

What Does Corporations Canada Do?

Corporations Canada will check that your Articles of Dissolution (Form 17) are complete and in proper form. If so, the Director will issue a Certificate of Dissolution showing the date of receipt of your articles as the effective date of dissolution.

For corporations submitting a Statement of Intent to Dissolve (Form 19), Corporations Canada will check that documents are received by the Director in complete and proper form. The Director will issue a Certificate of Intent to Dissolve.

For corporations submitting a Statement of Revocation of Intent to Dissolve (Form 19), Corporations Canada will ensure documents are complete and in proper form and the applicable fee of $50 is submitted, after which a Certificate of Revocation of Intent to Dissolve will be issued to the corporation, which will then be able to continue operating in normal fashion.

In each case, a notice will be published on the Corporations Canada website.

What Happens When an Application for Dissolution is Deficient?

Applications bearing deficiencies will be returned to the applicant with a "Deficiency Notice" indicating the nature of the deficiency. When deficient articles are returned to applicants, the original effective date is forfeited.

How to File the Dissolution Documents

Note that there is no fee required for filing dissolution documents, except in the case of filing a Revocation of Intent to Dissolve, which requires payment of a $50 fee payable by cheque payable to the Receiver General for Canada, credit card (Visa or MasterCard) or a deposit account maintained with Industry Canada at the time of filing.

Electronic forms:

An electronic Form 17 or electronic Form 19 can be filed on-line at Corporations Canada Electronic Filing Centre.

By fax:

You may submit forms to Corporations Canada by fax at (613) 941-0999. The signature can be by reproduction of a manual signature, in printed form or in digital form. On receipt of documents duly completed, a Certificate will be issued and sent to you by fax.

By mail or courier:

You can submit the required documents by sending them to:

Corporations Canada
Industry Canada
9th Floor, Jean Edmonds Towers South
365 Laurier Avenue West
Ottawa ON K1A 0C8

On receipt of documents duly completed, a Certificate will be issued and sent to you by the method requested.

In person:

You may submit all required documents in person, Monday to Friday between 8:30 a.m. and 2:30 p.m. at the address noted above. After examination of duly-completed documents, a Certificate will be issued and sent to you by mail or by the method requested.

How Do You Dissolve Before Commencing Business or Where There is No Property or Where Property Has Been Disposed of?

It sometimes happens that a corporate structure is never actively used after the granting of a Certificate of Incorporation. Perhaps the corporation's expected financial backing never materialized, or the business environment changed, or any number of other contingencies may have occurred. If the incorporators do not envisage ever operating actively, they may simply decide that it is desirable to terminate the corporation's existence and avoid the annual filing requirements under the CBCA.

You may complete and file Form 17, Articles of Dissolution, and send them to the Director, at the address appearing at the end of this kit, if your corporation fits any or all of the following criteria:

- no shares of the corporation have been issued
- your corporation has shareholders, but no property and no liabilities
- the shareholder or shareholders of a closely-held corporation with few creditors have authorized the distribution of property and the discharging of liabilities of the corporation, and such distribution and discharging have been completed.

No fee is applicable.

Where no shares have been issued, the dissolution can be authorized by the directors. In all other cases, a special resolution of two-thirds vote of the shareholders is required. Note that where more than one class of shares has been issued, the holders of each such class are entitled to vote separately as a class, whether or not they are otherwise entitled to vote.

If your articles are received by the Director complete and in proper form (i.e. correctly completed), the Director will issue a Certificate of Dissolution. A notice will be published on the Corporations Canada website.

How to Fill Out Form 17, Articles of Dissolution

Please see the back of Form 17 for complete instructions on how to fill out the Articles of Dissolution.

Items 1 and 2, Name of Corporation and Corporation Number.

Write in the full legal name of the corporation and the corporation number for items 1 and 2, respectively.

Item 3, Is the Corporation bankrupt or insolvent?

Indicate "No" if the corporation is not bankrupt or insolvent.

Indicate "Yes" if the corporation is bankrupt, or is for any reason unable to meet its obligations as they generally become due, or has ceased paying current obligations in the ordinary course of business as they generally become due, or if the aggregate of the corporation's property is not, at a fair valuation, sufficient, or, if disposed of at a fairly conducted sale under legal process, would not be sufficient to enable payment of all obligations, due and accruing due.

Item 4, Has the corporation provided for the payment or discharge of its obligations and distributed its remaining property?

Respond to this item *only* if the corporation has previously filed a Statement of Intent to Dissolve (Form 19) and has already received a Certificate of Intent to Dissolve.

Item 5, If the Corporation is applying for dissolution under section 210, indicate the subsection under which the corporation is applying for dissolution.

Respond to this item *only* if the corporation is applying under section 210, as a corporation that has not issued any shares (ss. 210(1)), or as a corporation that has no property and no liabilities (ss.210(2)), or as a corporation that has discharged its liabilities and distributed its property before it sends articles of dissolution to the Director (ss. 210(3)).

Item 6, Contact details for person keeping documents and records.

Indicate name, address and occupation of the person keeping the documents and records of the corporation. Please note that a post office box address alone is insufficient.

A corporation may be designated to keep the documents and records.

A person who has been granted custody of the documents and records of a dissolved corporation remains liable to produce such documents and records for six years following the date of its dissolution or until the expiration of a shorter period ordered by a court.

Item 7, Capacity of signing person.

Indicate either director or authorized officer of the corporation.

How Do You Liquidate and Dissolve a Corporation That Has Been Active and Has Property?

The directors or any shareholder of a corporation may propose its voluntary liquidation and dissolution. Such a proposal must be voted on at a shareholders' meeting. Note that where more than one class of shares has been issued, the holders of each such class are entitled to vote separately as a class, whether or not they are otherwise entitled to vote.

Prior to obtaining a Certificate of Dissolution, you must comply with several steps, as described under section 211 of the CBCA.

- The first step is to submit Form 19, Statement of Intent to Dissolve, duly completed. No fee is applicable. If your document is received by the Director complete and in proper form, the Director will issue a Certificate of Intent to Dissolve, showing the date of receipt of your articles as the effective date. A notice will be published on the Corporations Canada website.

- When the Certificate of Intent to Dissolve is issued, the corporation must cease carrying on business except to the extent necessary for the liquidation. Its corporate existence continues until the Director issues a Certificate of Dissolution.

- The corporation must notify creditors of its intent to dissolve and give notice in each province in Canada where the corporation was carrying on business at the time it sent the Statement of Intent to Dissolve to the Director.

- Once the corporation has complied with subsection 211(7) of the CBCA relating to giving notice of its dissolution, collecting its property and discharging its obligations, and if the Certificate of Intent to Dissolve has not been revoked (see next paragraph), you may prepare and submit Form 17, Articles of Dissolution, duly completed. No fee is applicable.

- If your articles are received by the Director complete and in proper form, the Director will issue a Certificate of Dissolution, showing the date of receipt of your articles as the effective date of dissolution. If you prefer, you may request a later dissolution date instead. Public notice of the dissolution will be published on the Corporations Canada website.

- If at any time after the issuance of the Certificate of Intent to Dissolve and before the issuance of a Certificate of Dissolution you decide, for any reason, to revoke the Certificate of Intent to Dissolve, you may do so by filing Form 19, Statement of Revocation of Intent to Dissolve, duly completed, with the Director. The prescribed filing fee is $50.00, payable to the Receiver General for Canada. Please note that where more than one class of shares has been issued, the holders of each such class are entitled to vote separately as a class, whether or not they are otherwise entitled to vote. A Certificate of Revocation of Intent to Dissolve will be issued to the corporation, which will then be able to continue operating in normal fashion. Notice of the withdrawal of the dissolution application will be published on the Corporations Canada website.

How to Fill Out Form 19, Statement of Intent to Dissolve or Revocation of Intent to Dissolve

Please see the back of Form 19 for complete instructions on how to fill out the Form.

- For items 1 and 2, respectively, write in the full legal name of the corporation and the corporation number.

- Indicate by checking the box in item 3 if the corporation intends to liquidate and dissolve.

- Indicate by checking the box in item 4 in cases where a corporation that has already filed a Statement of Intent to Dissolve (Form 19) and, prior to the issuance of a Certificate of Dissolution, decides not to dissolve. In such cases, a fee of $50 will apply as noted above.

- In item 5, indicate either director or authorized officer of the corporation.

Additional Information and Contacts for Corporations Canada

If you wish to obtain more information on dissolution, consult the Federal Incorporation section of Industry Canada's Strategis web site. You may request the following documents and kits, under "Information Kits and Administrative Forms" on Corporations Canada website:

Amalgamation Kit
Amendment Kit
Continuance (Import) Kit
Continuance (Export) Kit
Dissolution Kit
Exemptions Kit
Name-granting Guidelines

You may also contact Corporations Canada at the following address:

Publications and Information Unit
Corporations Canada
Industry Canada
9th Floor, Jean Edmonds Towers South
365 Laurier Avenue West
Ottawa, Ontario K1A 0C8
Tel.: (613) 941-9042
Fax: (613) 941-0601

Policy Statement 10.5 — Annual Returns

Date: July 1, 2006
Revised: January 2, 2007

1. — Statement of general principles

This policy outlines the position of the Director appointed under the *Canada Business Corporations Act* (CBCA) with respect to certain provisions pertaining to the filing of a corporation's Annual Return.

This policy is designed to assist corporations in filing their Annual Returns, as well as to reduce the number of rejected Annual Returns. It does not in any way expand the powers of the Director, the corporation or its shareholders or creditors, beyond those powers that are conferred under the CBCA.

Note also that this policy summarizes requirements under the CBCA and the regulations. Where there is a conflict, the provisions in the CBCA and the regulations prevail. As with all statutes, the courts are responsible for the final interpretation of the CBCA and its related provisions.

The Director believes that communication of these guidelines will reduce the number of Annual Returns that are rejected and, consequently, reduce the resulting costs and administrative burden.

2. — CBCA requirements

Form 22: Annual Return is the form fixed by the Director for meeting the CBCA requirement for an Annual Return (Section 263). Form 22 provides up-to-date information about your corporation. It allows Corporations Canada to ensure that the corporation complies with certain requirements of the CBCA. Investors, consumers, financial institutions and many others also rely on this information. The Director may dissolve a corporation that fails to file its Annual Return (Section 212).

3. — For the year 2007 and all subsequent years: Deadline for filing Form 22: Annual Return

Form 22: Annual Return must be sent to the Director within the 60 days following a corporation's anniversary date (Section 5 of the Regulations). The anniversary date is the date the corporation was created or the date the corporation first came under CBCA (e.g. the date of incorporation, continuance or amalgamation). The date is generally found at the bottom, right-hand corner of the corporation's Certificate of Incorporation, Amalgamation or Continuance. You can also find your anniversary date on Corporations Canada's website at *www.corporationscanada.ic.gc.ca* (click on "Search for a Federal Corporation" in the left-hand menu on the homepage and enter your corporation number or name in the appropriate box).

For Form 22: Annual Return information must reflect the corporation's situation on the anniversary date.

4. — For the year 2006: Deadline for filing Form 22: Annual Return

If the taxation year-end is *between January 1st and June 30th*	The Annual Return must be filed within the *six months* following the corporation's taxation year-end
If the taxation year-end is *between July 1st and December 31st*	The Annual Return must be filed within the *60 days* folowing the corporation's taxation year-end

The taxation year-end is the end of the corporation's fiscal year as defined in the *Income Tax Act* (Section 1 of the CBCA Regulations and paragraph 1104 (1) of the *Income Tax Regulations* (ITR)). The taxation year-end is not necessarily the same as the calendar year-end. For the purposes of Form 22: Annual Return, the taxation year-end consists of the month and day of the month.

The Annual Return always pertains to a completed taxation year rather than to the taxation year in progress. Information appearing in the Annual Return must reflect the corporation's situation on the day of the financial year-end.

Important

From January 1st 2007, all corporations must file an annual return within the 60 days following its anniversary date.

Please note, from January 1st, 2007, all corporations must file their annual returns within the 60 days following their anniversary date. The anniversary date is the date the corporation was created or the date the corporation first came under the jurisdiction of the Canada Business Corporations Act (i.e., the date of incorporation, amalgamation or continuance).

The date is generally found at the bottom, right-hand corner of the corporation's Certificate of Incorporation, Amalgamation or Continuance. You can also find your anniversary date on the Corporations Canada website at *www.corporationscanada.ic.gc.ca*, click on "Search for a Federal Corporation" in the left-hand menu on the homepage and enter your corporation number or name in the appropriate box. Please consult the diagram below to know the transition rules that apply to your corporation.

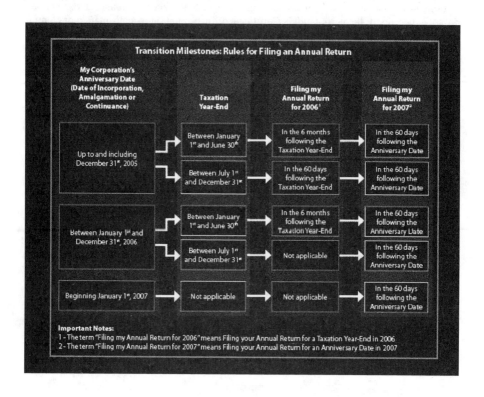

5. — Where to obtain Form 22: Annual Return, how to send it and the filing fees

Form 22: Annual Return may be sent to the Director via Corporations Canada's Online Filing Centre at corporationscanada.ic.gc.ca. Instructions for completing the online Annual Return appear on the website. Filing fees are $20 (Appendix 5 of the Regulations). This amount may be paid by credit card (American Express®, MasterCard® or VISA®).

Form 22: Annual Return is also available on Corporations Canada's website under the "Forms, policies, fees and legislation" heading or it may be obtained by calling the Client Services Unit at 1-866-333-5556. Instructions appear on the form. Filing fees are $40 for forms that are faxed or mailed (Schedule 5 of the Regulations). Fees for Annual Returns that are mailed may be paid by a cheque made out to the Receiver General for Canada or by credit card (American Express®, MasterCard® or VISA®). Payment for Annual Returns that are faxed may be made by credit card (American Express®, MasterCard® or VISA®).

Please note that the option of filing the Annual Return at the same time that the T-2 return is filed to the Canada Revenue Agency is no longer available.

6. — Notice of receipt

If Form 22: Annual Return is filed using Corporations Canada's Online Filing Centre, an electronic notice of receipt is automatically sent by email.

If Form 22: Annual Return is faxed or mailed, no notice of receipt is sent to the sender. You may, however, check on Corporations Canada's website *www.corporationscanada.ic.gc.ca* (click on "Search for a Federal Corporation" in the left-hand menu on the homepage and enter your corporation number or name in the appropriate box) to ensure that the corporate data has been updated.

7. — Compliance

If a corporation fails to file its Annual Return within the required time period, fails to pay the required fees and/or submits an incomplete return, the corporation is deemed non-compliant with the CBCA. The corporation's good standing will only be restored when the missing Annual Return has been filed and/or fees have been paid, even if the corporation has filed the Annual Return and paid the fees for a subsequent year.

A corporation that is non-compliant will be sent a default notice advising that it has failed to comply with the provisions of the CBCA (Section 263). The default notice stipulates what measures may be taken if the corporation fails to rectify the default.

This default notice will be sent to the most recent address appearing on Form 3: Change of Registered Office Address. The default notice is presumed to have been received by the corporation unless there are reasonable grounds to believe that the corporation has not received it.

No certificate of compliance shall be issued for a corporation that is non-compliant.

8. — Dissolution for failure to file Form 22: Annual Return

Under subparagraph 212(1)(a)(iii) of the CBCA, the Director may dissolve any corporation that has failed for a period of at least one year to send fees, notices or documents required pursuant to the CBCA .

Corporations Canada will send a further notice to the corporation and its directors advising them of the Director's intention to dissolve the corporation. In the absence of a response or justifiable opposition, the Director will issue a certificate of dissolution following the expiration of the deadline stated in that notice.

9. — Additional information

For additional information on Corporations Canada's products and services, please visit the Corporations Canada website or call 1-866-333-5556.

You can also contact Corporations Canada at:

> Client Services Unit
> Corporations Canada
> Industry Canada
> 9th floor, Jean Edmonds Tower South
> Ottawa, Ontario K1A 0C8
> Fax: 613- 941-0601
> *www.corporationscanada.ic.gc.ca*

Policy Statement 10.5.1 — Changes concerning the taxation year-end

Date: July 1, 2006

1. — Statement of general principles

This policy outlines the position of the Director appointed under the *Canada Business Corporations Act* (CBCA) (Director) with respect to changes concerning the taxation year-end.

Although these guidelines do not have the force of law, they are aimed to inform the public on procedures relating to changes concerning the taxation year-end. This policy is not designed to expand the powers of the Director in any manner nor those of the corporation or its shareholders or creditors, beyond those powers that are conferred upon them under the CBCA. The courts are responsible for the final interpretation of the CBCA and its related provisions.

The Director believes that communication of these guidelines will reduce the number of annual returns that are rejected and, consequently, reduce the resulting costs and administrative burden.

2. — CBCA requirements

Form 22 is the form fixed by the Director for meeting the *Canada Business Corporations Act* requirement for an annual return.

Important

On July 1st 2006, amendments to the *Canada Business Corporations Regulations, 2001* changing the requirements for corporations filing Annual Returns (Form 22) came into force. Please consult the Annual Return Policy (10.5) to obtain pertinent information concerning your corporation.

3. — Corporation seeking to change its taxation year-end

A corporation seeking to change its taxation year-end must ensure that this change is permitted under the *Income Tax Act Act* (ITA) or pursuant to Canada Revenue Agency (CRA) rules and procedures. Such a change may be specifically authorized by CRA or the taxation year-end may be modified pursuant to the ITA in cases such as a merger of corporations or takeover of a corporation. A corporation is responsible for verifying with CRA if such a situation applies.

If a change is permitted under the ITA or CRA rules and procedures, the corporation must also advise Corporations Canada at the time that it files its annual return by specifying the new taxation year-end (month and day of the month) on item 3 of Form 22 — Annual Return and by attaching Form 22-A, duly completed. This form may be downloaded from the Corporations Canada's website.

Although a corporation may modify its taxation year-end, it is still required to send an annual return for a period of no more than 53 weeks. If the change of the taxation year-end results in an interval of more than 53 weeks between the former and new taxation year-end, an interim annual return must be sent to the Director. This means completing Form 22 — Annual Return, entering the change of date and paying the filing fees.

For example:

A corporation having December 31 as its taxation year-end decides, in 2002, to change (with CRA authorization) this date to July 31. It must submit an annual return for each of the following periods:

Annual Return	End of taxation year-end	Period to send the annual return to the Director
For the period from January, 2001 to December 31, 2001	December 31	Between January 1, 2002 and June 30, 2002
In 2002, the corporation changes its taxation year-end to July 31		
For the period from January 1, 2002 to July 31, 2002 (interim return)	July 31	Between August 1, 2002 and January 1, 2003
For the period from Augustnbsp;1, 2002 to July 31, 2003	July 31	Between August 1, 2003 and January 1, 2004

4. — Corporation seeking to revise its taxation year-end

When a corporation has erroneously indicated the date of the taxation year on a previous annual return filed with Corporations Canada, the corporation must advise Corporations Canada at the time that it files its annual return by specifying the actual taxation year-end (month and day of the month) on item 3 of Form 22 — Annual Return and by attaching Form 22-A, duly completed. This form may be downloaded from the Corporations Canada's website.

5. — Where to obtain Form 22, how to send it to the Director and filing fees

Forms 22 and 22-A are available on Corporations Canada's website under the heading "Forms, Policies, Fees and Legislation" or they may be obtained by calling the Client Services Unit at 1-866-333-5556. Instructions appear on the forms. Forms 22 and 22-A must be sent by fax or by mail to:

Corporations Canada
Industry Canada
9th Floor, Jean Edmonds Tower South
Ottawa, Ontario K1A OC8
Fax: 613-941-0601

Filing fees are $40 for forms that are faxed or mailed (Schedule 5 of the Regulations). Payment for returns may be made by credit card (American Express®, MasterCard® or VISA®).

6. — Notice of receipt

No notice of receipt is sent to the sender. You may, however, check on the Corporations Canada's website (search for a Federal Corporation) to ensure that the corporate data has been updated.

7. — Additional information

For additional information on Corporations Canada's products and services, please visit the Corporations Canada website or call 1-866-333-5556.

You can also contact Corporations Canada at:

Client Services Unit
Corporations Canada
Industry Canada
9th floor, Jean Edmonds Tower South
Ottawa, Ontario K1A 0C8
Fax: 613-941-0601

Policy Statement 10.6 — Revival Policy

Date: October 25, 2007

Introduction

This policy sets out the position of the Director appointed under the *Canada Business Corporations Act* (CBCA) concerning a revival of a corporation dissolved under the provisions of the CBCA. The final interpretation of the CBCA is a function of the courts.

Nothing in this policy is intended to constitute a binding statement of the position the Director will take with respect to a particular revival. In addition, this policy is not intended to be a substitute for professional, legal, accounting, commercial or business advice in specific cases. Corporations Canada recommends that you consult a legal advisor or other professional advisors who will assess your specific case and the possible impacts of revival as well as determine what you need to include in your application for revival.

Information on the steps to follow to revive a dissolved corporation is available in the CBCA policy "Steps to Follow to Revive a Corporation" on the Corporations Canada website *www.corporationscanada.ic.gc.ca*.

What is a revival?

Revival allows a dissolved corporation to be restored to its previous legal position in the same manner and to the same extent as if it had not been dissolved. A revival retroactively validates the business and affairs of the corporation during the time of its dissolution. A dissolved corporation that is insolvent or bankrupt within the meaning of subsection 2(1) of the *Bankruptcy and Insolvency Act* may be revived. A corporation is deemed to be revived on the date appearing on the certificate of revival[12].

---

[12]Subsection 209(3.1) of the CBCA.

What are the impacts of revival on the corporation?

Retroactivity

The CBCA provides for the retroactivity of the revival[13]. The corporation can benefit from, is bound to and is liable for, all acts of the corporation taken while the corporation was dissolved. Also, any changes to the internal affairs of the corporation are deemed valid. The revived corporation is liable for the contracts and torts/faults occurring between dissolution and revival. Rights, liabilities and obligations arising before and after the dissolution are restored to the revived corporation.

Any legal action[14] respecting the internal affairs of a revived corporation taken between the time of its dissolution and its revival is valid.

Corporation's Articles

Since no filings can be made while a corporation is dissolved, the articles of a revived corporation are exactly as they were at the moment of its dissolution. Therefore, if changes were made to the information contained in the articles of the corporation, you are required to update this information by first reviving the corporation and then filing Form 4: Articles of Amendment. Please see the Amendment Policy for more information.

With respect to the corporation's name, the revived corporation must apply for the revival using the same corporation name it had at the time of its dissolution. At the time of the revival, the corporation's name is subject to a name decision by Corporations Canada. If Corporations Canada does not approve the name because it is prohibited (e.g., if it is likely to be confused with a corporate name acquired by another corporation between the date of the dissolution and the date of revival), the Director will assign a numbered name to the revived corporation. If this is the case, once the Certificate of Revival is issued, the revived corporation may request a new corporate name by filing Form 4: Articles of Amendment.

Corporation number

The revived corporation's number is the same number it had at the time of its dissolution. This number can be found on the certificate of incorporation, amalgamation, or continuance, as applicable. It can also be found on the Corporations Canada website under "Search for Federal Corporation".

Directors

The public record will show the directors of a revived corporation exactly as they were at the moment of its dissolution. Therefore, if changes have been made to the board of directors of the revived corporation, you are required to update this information by filing Form 6: Changes Regarding Directors with the revival application.

Anniversary Date

The anniversary date of the corporation is relevant for filing annual returns (i.e. the corporation must file its annual return within the 60 days following its Anniversary Date). The Anniversary Date of a revived corporation is the date of its incorporation, amalgamation, or continuance, as applicable, and not the revival date. The Anniversary Date is generally found on

---

[13]Subsection 209(4) of the CBCA.

[14]Subsection 209(5) of the CBCA.

the certificate of incorporation, amalgamation or continuance issued before the dissolution or on the Corporations Canada website under "Search for Federal Corporation". Please consult the Annual Return Policy for more information on filing annual returns.

Property that vested in Her Majesty in Right of Canada as a result of the dissolution

On the date of the corporation's dissolution, property that had not been disposed of (e.g., money and moveable and real property) vested in Her Majesty in Right of Canada[15]. Upon revival of the corporation, property that vested in Her Majesty in Right of Canada will be returned to the corporation[16]. However, if some or all of the property received on dissolution under subsection 228(1) has been disposed of by the Crown, the corporation will receive an amount equal to the lesser of:

- the value of the property at the date it vested in the Crown, and
- the amount realized by the Crown from the disposition of the property[17].

If you believe that money or property should be returned to the revived corporation, you may attach a letter to the application for revival requesting its return. Please note that the request for the return of property or money may be made after the revival of the corporation. The letter must include a description of the property in question and any supporting evidence that it was owned by the corporation at the time of its dissolution. In the case of money or moveable property, state whether actual possession of it was ever transferred to Her Majesty in Right of Canada. It must also enclose a statutory declaration by the applicant stating that:

1. the applicant is authorized to request the return of the property;
2. the property was owned by the corporation at the moment of the dissolution;
3. no other person has rights to claim against the property; and
4. the revived corporation has the right to receive the whole or a part of the property.

If the application is for money, Corporations Canada will review the application and determine whether the money should be returned to the revived corporation. If moveable property is involved, Corporations Canada will contact the relevant government department in order to initiate a process for returning any property. The revived corporation is responsible for following up with the appropriate departments.

According to the *Department of Public Works and Government Services Act* (S.C. 1996, c. 16), the Minister of Public Works and Government Services administers all federal real property and, accordingly, has the authority to return real property to the revived corporation. A request for reconveyance should be made to the Director, attaching evidence that establishes that the land was owned by the corporation at the time of its dissolution and has not been disposed of by Her Majesty or otherwise. The Director will ask Public Works and Government Services to arrange for the appropriate document reconveying the property to the revived corporation.

In situations where it is preferred that the property be restored to a third party (i.e. not to the dissolved corporation), the *Escheats Act* (R.S.C. 1985, c. E-13) may be of assistance. The third party must be claiming rights to the property through the dissolved corporation.

---

[15]Subsection 228(1) of the CBCA.

[16]Subsection 228(2) of the CBCA.

[17]Subsection 228(2) of the CBCA.

Note that there can be no return of property where possession by Her Majesty was never taken. Instead, Corporations Canada will send you a letter waiving any rights over the personal property in question.

Other Considerations

Who can apply for a revival?

Any interested person may apply for the revival of a dissolved corporation. An interested person is:

- a shareholder, director, officer, employee or creditor of the dissolved corporation, or anyone who, although not one of the foregoing at the time of dissolution, would be such a person if the corporation were revived;
- any person having a contractual relationship with the dissolved corporation; and
- any person with a valid reason for applying for a revival, for example, a trustee in bankruptcy or a liquidator.

Corporation in compliance upon revival

With the application for revival, the dissolved corporation is required to file its outstanding annual returns with Corporations Canada and pay all prescribed fees. Normally, only the annual returns for the two years immediately preceding the revival are required. However, the Director reserves the right to require the corporation to file all outstanding annual returns for periods both before and after the dissolution of the corporation.

In certain situations, the Director may agree that the annual returns can be filed after the corporation has been revived, particularly if the person reviving the corporation is not a director or officer. Such situations will be determined by the Director on a case-by-case basis.

Date of the Revival

The corporation is revived as of the date on the Certificate of Revival. Normally, this is the date on which Form 15: Articles of Revival is received by Corporations Canada. When making your application for revival, you may request a later revival date than the date on which Form 15: Articles of Revival is received by Corporations Canada.

Conditions on revival

Corporations Canada may, under the appropriate conditions, revive dissolved corporations that will not, upon revival, be in compliance with the CBCA, especially if the applicant is not a director, shareholder or officer of the dissolved corporation. In such cases, Corporations Canada may impose certain conditions in issuing a Certificate of Revival, such as the requirement that the corporation correct any deficiencies within a reasonable time frame following its revival. If the conditions are not observed, the revived corporation may be dissolved again. Examples of conditions are:

- that reasonable measures be taken to inform directors, officers or shareholders of the corporation's revival;
- that all annual returns falling due since the dissolution of the corporation be filed within a reasonable time frame (usually sixty days) or that reasonable measures be taken to ensure they are filed; if the corporation does not meet its obligation to file annual returns, it may be subject to dissolution procedures 120 days following its revival;

- that the Certificate of Revival be sent to a director or an officer of the corporation; or
- that measures be taken to inform the corporation of the filing requirements it must observe.

Appeal of the Director's decision

If you are dissatisfied with a decision made by Corporations Canada, you may ask that the decision be reviewed. You will need to provide a letter with new information and your reasons. Once your application has been re-examined and if you continue to feel you have been aggrieved by the decision to reject the application or to impose conditions on the revival, you may ask the court to review the decision under section 246 of the CBCA.

Copy of the articles of the corporation

You may obtain a copy of the articles of the corporation as they exist at the moment of dissolution by asking Corporations Canada. Your request must be made in writing and be accompanied by the required fees, which are $1 a page for uncertified copies or $35 for a certified copy of a document[18]. While Corporations Canada normally provides documents requested on the day following the request, the time frame increases to six business days when the corporation involved is dissolved. Requests for copies must be sent by mail, e-mail or by fax to:

> Database Integrity Unit
> Corporations Canada
> 9th Floor, Jean Edmonds Tower South
> 365 Laurier Avenue West
> Ottawa, Ontario K1A 0C8
> Toll free: 1-877-568-9922
> Fax: 613-941-5789
> E-mail: corporationscanada.ic.gc.ca

Additional information and how to reach Corporations Canada

For additional information on Corporations Canada's products and services, please visit the Corporations Canada website *corporationscanada.ic.gc.ca* or call our toll free number 1-866-333-5556.

You can also contact Corporations Canada at:

> Client Services Section
> Corporations Canada
> Industry Canada
> 9th floor, Jean Edmonds Tower South
> Ottawa, Ontario K1A 0C8
> Toll free: 1-866-333-5556
> Fax: 613-941-0601
> *www.corporationscanada.ic.gc.ca*

---

[18]Schedule 5 of the *Canada Business Corporations Regulations (2001)*.

Policy Statement 10.8 — Steps to Follow to Revive a Corporation

Date: October 25, 2007

Introduction

The purpose of this policy is to help you submit the information required to obtain approval to revive your corporation. Revival allows a corporation dissolved under the *Canada Business Corporations Act* (CBCA) to be restored to its previous legal position in the same manner and to the same extent as if it had never been dissolved. A revival retroactively validates the business and affairs of a corporation during the time of its dissolution. More detailed information on the consequences of reviving a corporation is available in the Corporations Canada "Revival Policy" on the Corporations Canada website *www.corporationscanada.ic.gc.ca*.

Revival Procedure

Reviving a corporation that has been dissolved under the CBCA is a three-step process:

1. The applicant submits an application to Corporations Canada with all the required information.

2. Corporations Canada reviews the application to determine if:

    a.   the corporation would be in compliance with the CBCA[19] if revived, and

    b.   the application is complete and not deficient.

3. If everything is in order, Corporations Canada will issue a Certificate of Revival; or if there are any problems with the application, a deficiency letter will be issued.

An application for a certificate of revival must include the following:

❑   Form 15: Articles of Revival;

❑   If the corporation has a corporate name, a Canada-biased NUANS® report not more than 90 days old. (If the corporation has a numbered name, a NUANS® report is not needed.);

❑   Any outstanding annual returns that would have fallen due in the two-year period immediately preceding the revival;

❑   Form 3: Change of Registered Office Address (if applicable);

❑   Form 6: Changes Regarding Directors (if applicable);

❑ $40 for each annual return attached to the application; and

❑ $200 for the application itself.

What happens when an application for revival is deficient or incomplete?

Applications for revival that are deficient or incomplete will be returned to the applicant with a notice stating the nature of the deficiency.

---

[19]The corporate name is available for approval and annual returns have been filed.

How do I complete the Form 15: Articles of Revival?

Item 1: Corporation Name

State the corporation name as it appears in the corporation's articles on the date of its dissolution. If the corporation name is not a numbered name (e.g., 1234567 Canada Inc.), you must also include a Canada-biased NUANS® report not more than 90 days old. This report is not needed for a numbered name (e.g., 1234567 Canada Inc.).

Item 2: Corporation number

Please indicate the corporation number. The corporation number must be identical to that of the dissolved corporation. The number is located on the certificate of incorporation, amalgamation or continuance, as applicable. You can also find it on the Corporations Canada website under "Search for a Federal Corporation."

Item 3: Interest of applicant

Please state in what capacity the applicant is submitting the Form 15: Articles of Revival. Examples are:

— shareholder;
— director;
— officer;
— employee;
— creditor;
— person with a contractual relationship with the dissolved corporation;
— trustee in bankruptcy; or
— liquidator.

Please note that professionals must meet the definition of "interested person" to be an applicant and sign the articles of revival[20] (e.g., be a shareholder, director, officer, or have a contractual relationship with the dissolved corporation). A professional representing a shareholder, director, officer, etc. cannot sign the articles of revival. Please identify clearly that interest.

Signature

Form 15: Articles of Revival must be signed by the interested person. If the interested person is a body corporate (i.e. another corporation), the name must be that of the body corporate and the address must be that of its registered office. Form 15: Articles of Revival must be signed by an individual authorized by that body corporate.

Annual Returns

Outstanding annual returns for the two years immediately preceding the revival must be sent to Corporations Canada with the application for revival. Please note that the information on an Annual Return of a corporation must be as of its Anniversary Date for the year covered. For example, if a corporation's Anniversary Date is January 31, its Annual Return for the year 2007 would provide information as of January 31, 2007.

---

[20]Sections 209, 262 and 262.1 of the CBCA.

It is important to remember that the rules for sending Annual Returns changed on January 1, 2007. The information on an Annual Return for a year prior to 2007 is the information as of the corporation's Taxation Year-End for that year. For example, if the corporation's Taxation Year-End is October 31, the information on the 2005 Annual Return is the information as of October 31, 2005, even if the Annual Return is sent in 2007. Consult Corporations Canada's Annual Return Policy for more information (see contact section below).

In certain situations, Corporations Canada may agree that the required Annual Returns can be sent after the corporation has been revived, particularly if the person reviving the corporation is not a director or officer of the corporation. Such situations will be determined by Corporations Canada on a case-by-case basis. If this is your situation, please provide the necessary information in a covering letter.

Change of Registered Office Address[21]

Change of registered office address within the province or territory stated in the Articles at the time of dissolution

If there has been a change in the registered office address to a place within the province or territory in the Articles, you must file Form 3: Change of Registered Office Address with the application for revival. Corporations Canada will not allow Form 3: Change of Registered Office Address to be filed while the corporation is dissolved (i.e., before the corporation is revived). The form must be signed by an authorized director or officer, or by an individual who has sufficient knowledge of the corporation and who has been authorized by the directors.

Change of registered office address to a province other than that stated in the Articles at the time of dissolution

Please note that if the registered office address has changed to a province or territory other than the one specified in the Articles at the time of dissolution, you must revive the corporation first and then update the articles by filing Form 4: Articles of Amendment with the required $200 fee. Once the articles are amended, you must provide the new address by filing Form 3: Change of Registered Office Address. Please see the Amendment Policy for more information (see contact section below).

Changes Regarding Directors[22]

If there has been a change in the directors, you must file Form 6: Changes Regarding Directors with the application for revival. Corporations Canada will not allow Form 6: Changes Regarding Directors to be filed while the corporation is dissolved (i.e., before the corporation is revived). The form must be signed by an authorized director or officer, or by an individual who has sufficient knowledge of the corporation and who has been authorized by the directors.

Please note that if the minimum/maximum number of directors specified in the articles has changed, you must revive the corporation first and then update the articles by filing Form 4: Articles of Amendment with the required $200 fee. Once the articles are amended, you must then file Form 6: Changes Regarding Directors.

---

[21]If there has been no change in the registered office address, you do not need to file Form 3: Change of registered Office Address.

[22]If there has been no change in the directors, you do not need to file Form 6: Changes Regarding Directors.

Please see the Amendment Policy for more information (see contact section below).

Articles of Amendment

Form 4: Articles of Amendment may only be considered by Corporations Canada after a corporation has been revived. However, the completed applications for both revival and amendment of articles may be filed together, along with the appropriate fees. In such cases, Corporations Canada will process the revival first and then the articles of amendment.

Filing the application and paying the applicable fees

By Fax

You may send the completed application by fax to 613-941-0999. Signatures can be a reproduction of a handwritten signature. You must keep the original signed copy with your corporate records. The $200 fee for filing Form 15: Articles of Revival and the $40 fee per Annual Return must be paid by credit card (American Express®, MasterCard® or Visa®) or from a deposit account with Industry Canada.

The Certificate of Revival will be faxed to you.

By Email

You may send the completed application by email to corporationscanada.ic.gc.ca. Signatures can be a reproduction of a handwritten signature. You must keep the original signed copy with your corporate records. The $200 fee for filing Form 15: Articles of Revival and the $40 fee per Annual Return must be paid by credit card (American Express®, MasterCard® or Visa®) or from a deposit account with Industry Canada.

The Certificate of Revival will be emailed to you.

By Mail or Courier

You may send the completed application to the following address:

Corporations Canada
Industry Canada
9th Floor, Jean Edmonds Tower South
365 Laurier Avenue West
Ottawa, Ontario K1A 0C8

The $200 fee for filing Form 15: Articles of Revival and the $40 fee per Annual Return must be paid by cheque payable to the Receiver General for Canada, by credit card (American Express®, MasterCard® or Visa®) or from a deposit account with Industry Canada.

The Certificate of Revival will be sent to you by mail or courier, at your choice.

In Person

You may attend in person and file an application for revival, from Monday to Friday, between 8:30 a.m. and 5:00 p.m., at:

Corporations Canada
Industry Canada
9th floor, Jean Edmonds Tower South
365 Laurier Avenue West
Ottawa, Ontario K1A 0C8

You must have with you all the necessary documents. The $200 fee must be paid in cash, by cheque payable to the Receiver General for Canada, by credit card (American Express®, MasterCard® or Visa®) or by deposit to an account opened with Industry Canada.

You will be given the Certificate of Revival.

Online Filing

Applications for revival, and associated annual returns, cannot be filed online.

Obligations of a Revived Corporation

Once a corporation is revived, you now have an obligation to ensure that your corporation's public information is up-to-date. Keeping your corporation's public information up-to-date is required by law and failure to file required information can result in your corporation being dissolved again.

If you have changed:

- the name of the corporation;
- any provision related to its share structure;
- the province or territory in which the registered office is situated;
- the minimum and/or maximum number of directors;
- any restrictions on share transfers;
- any restrictions on the business the corporation may carry on; and/or
- any other provisions that are permitted by the CBCA to be set out in the articles,

you are required to file Form 4: Articles of Amendment and the required $200 fee. Please note that these changes are not legally effective until you receive a certificate of amendment from Corporations Canada.

If you have changed your registered office address, you must file Form 3: Change of Registered Office. This form can be filed free of charge.

If you have made any changes to the members of the board of directors or if any of the current directors have changed their residential address, you must file Form 6: Changes Regarding Directors. This form can be filed free of charge.

For more information on filing any of these forms, contact Corporations Canada.

Additional information and how to reach Corporations Canada

For additional information on Corporations Canada's products and services, please visit the Corporations Canada website *www.corporationscanada.ic.gc.ca* or call our toll free number 1-866-333-5556.

You can also contact Corporations Canada at:

Client Services Section
Corporations Canada
Industry Canada
9th floor, Jean Edmonds Tower South
Ottawa, Ontario K1A 0C8
Toll free: 1-866-333-5556
Fax: 613-941-0601
www.corporationscanada.ic.gc.ca

Policy Statement 11.2 — Policy Related to the Certificate of Existence and to the Certificate of Compliance

Date: June 1, 2005

1. — Introduction and Statement of General Principles

1.1 This policy replaces the Director's policy dated August 29, 2002, concerning certificates of compliance. It reflects amendments to the *Canada Business Corporations Act* (CBCA) that came into force on November 24, 2001.

1.2 In order to assist corporations and other interested persons, this policy sets out certain policy and practice guidelines aimed at facilitating the application for a certificate of existence or a certificate of compliance. However, these policy and practice guidelines do not have the force of law, and are not intended to give shareholders, creditors or the Director any powers broader than those conferred to them by the CBCA. The final interpretation of section 263.1 of the CBCA and related provisions is the function of the courts.

1.3 The Director considers that, by communicating these guidelines to corporations and other interested persons, the instances of rejected requests and the cost and administrative inconvenience thereby encountered can be reduced.

1.4 Nothing in this policy is intended to constitute a binding statement of what position the Director will take with respect to any particular request for a certificate of existence or certificate of compliance. In addition, this policy is not intended to be a substitute for professional legal, accounting or business advice or for the exercise of professional judgment by legal, accounting and business advisors in any particular instance.

2. — Certificate of Compliance and Certificate of Existence

2.1 Under subsection 263.1(1) of the CBCA, the Director appointed under the Act may provide any person with a certificate stating that a corporation has sent to the Director a document required to be sent under the Act, has paid the required fees, or exists as of a certain date.

2.2 Certificate of Compliance

The Director may issue a certificate of compliance to anyone who requests one. It certifies that a company:

- has not been dissolved,

- has sent to the Director the annual return required under section 263 of the CBCA, and

- has paid all required fees.

2.3 Certificate of Existence

The Director may issue a certificate of existence in respect of a corporation to anyone who requests such a certificate. It certifies that a corporation has not been dissolved as of the specified date. Also, the Director can issue a certificate of existence for a specific period if the corporation has not been dissolved or discontinued during the specific period and the corporation has not changed its structure in such a way as to cause a change to its corporate number.

A certificate of existence does not certify whether a corporation has sent all the required documents to the Director or has paid all required fees.

Examples:

Here are a few examples to illustrate when a certificate of existence would be issued. Assume that the request is made on the present date.

ABC Inc.	incorporated on April 1, 2001 (corporate number: 123)	request for a certificate of existence for April 1, 2002.	certificate issued
ABC Inc.	incorporated on April 1, 2001 (corporate number: 123) corporation dissolved on March 1, 2002.	request for a certificate of existence for April 1, 2002.	request refused as the corporation was dissolved on the requested date.
ABC Inc.	incorporated on April 1, 2001 (corporate number: 123)	request for a certificate of existence for the period of April 1, 2001 to April 1, 2002.	certificate issued
ABC Inc.	incorporated on April 1, 2001 (corporate number: 123)	request for a certificate of existence for the period of April 1, 2000 to April 1, 2002.	request refused as the corporation was not in existence at a certain time during the specific period requested. i.e. before April 1st, 2001.
ABC Inc.	incorporated on April 1, 2001 (corporate number: 123) the corporation changed its name to DEF Inc. on January 1, 2002 (corporate number: 123)	request for a certificate of existence for the period of April 1, 2001 to April 1, 2002.	certificate issued as the name change did not require a change in the corporate number.
ABC Inc. *XYZ Inc.*	incorporated on April 1, 2001 (corporate number: 123) incorporated on January 1, 2002 (corporate number: 345)	request for a certificate of existence for ABCXYZ Inc. for the period of April 1, 2001 to April 1, 2002.	request refused as the amalgamation between both corporations required a change in the corporate number.

ABC Inc. and XYZ Inc. have been amalgamated on March 1, 2002. The name of the new corporation is ABCXYZ Inc. (corporate number: 678)		

3. — Fees

3.1 A fee of $10 is charged for each application for a certificate of compliance or certificate of existence and for each additional copy requested. Please note that a certificate cannot be issued if the fees are not paid.

3.2 If the request for a certificate of compliance or existence is rejected, Corporations Canada will not refund the fee.

4. — How do I obtain a certificate of compliance or a certificate of existence?

4.1 You must submit a request to Corporations Canada containing all of the following information:

- The type of certificate you are requesting, i.e.
  - a certificate of compliance, or
  - a certificate of existence.
- The corporate name of the corporation for which the certificate is being requested.
- The corporate number for which the certificate is being requested.
- If you are requesting a certificate of existence, please state the exact date or period for which you would like the Director to certify that the corporation existed. The date or period must be prior to the date of the request.
  - Example: May 31, 2002; or from December 1, 2001 to May 31, 2002.
- The name and telephone number of the applicant.
- The address or fax number to which Corporations Canada should send the certificate.

You must also enclose the applicable fee of $10 per application for a certificate. (See section 3 for the other applicable fees.)

5. — How do I request a certificate and pay the fee?

• Online

You may make your request for a certificate online through Corporations Canada *Online Filing Centre*. Please visit our website for an explanation of the procedures. Please visit the website for an explanation of the procedures. The $10 fee is payable by credit card (American Express®, MasterCard® or Visa®).

The certificate of compliance or certificate of existence will be e-mailed to you in PDF format.

• By fax

You may also fax your request to (613) 941-5789. The $10 fee per certificate must be paid by credit card (American Express®, MasterCard® or Visa®) or from an Industry Canada's Deposit Account.

If you choose this method, the certificate of existence or certificate of compliance will be sent to you by fax or by such other method as you request.

• By mail or messenger

You may send your request for a certificate, along with the fee, to the following address:

> Corporations Canada
>
> Industry Canada
>
> 9th Floor, Jean Edmonds Towers South
>
> 365 Laurier Avenue West
>
> Ottawa, ON K1A 0C8

The fee must be paid by cheque payable to the Receiver General for Canada, by credit card (American Express®, MasterCard® or Visa®) or from an Industry Canada Deposit Account.

The certificate of compliance or certificate of existence will be sent to you by mail or by such other method as you request.

• In person

You may make the request in person from Monday to Friday between 8:30 a.m. and 2:30 p.m. at:

> Corporations Canada
>
> Industry Canada
>
> 9th Floor, Jean Edmonds Towers South
>
> 365 Laurier Avenue West
>
> Ottawa, ON K1A 0C8

The $10 fee may be paid in cash, by cheque payable to the Receiver General for Canada, by credit card (American Express®, MasterCard® or Visa®) or from an Industry Canada Deposit Account.

The certificate of compliance or certificate of existence will be issued to you on the premises.

• Regional offices

You may send your request for a certificate of compliance along with your payment to one of the following regional offices. Please note that the regional offices do not issue certificates of existence.

Toronto

> Corporations Canada
>
> Industry Canada
>
> 3rd Floor, 151 Yonge Street
>
> Toronto ON M5C 2W7

Telephone: (416) 954-2714

Fax: (416) 973-8714

Vancouver

Corporations Canada

Industry Canada

2000-300 West Georgia Street

Vancouver BC V6B 6E1

Telephone: (604) 666-9875

Fax: (604) 666-4274

Montréal

Corporations Canada

Industry Canada

5 Place Ville-Marie

7th Floor, Suite 700

Montreal QC H3B 2G2

Telephone: (514) 496-1797

Fax: (514) 283-2247

The $10 fee per certificate may be paid by cheque payable to the Receiver General for Canada, by credit card (American Express®, MasterCard® or Visa®) or from an Industry Canada Deposit Account.

The certificate of compliance will be issued to you on the premises.

6 — On what grounds may the Director refuse to issue a certificate?

6.1 The Director may reject a request for a *certificate of compliance* for any of the following reasons:

- one of the two last annual returns has not been filed

- the fees for filing the annual returns were not paid

- the corporate name of the corporation for which the certificate is requested does not exist or is incorrect

- the corporation number provided does not exist or is incorrect

- the corporation has been dissolved

- the fee was not enclosed

6.2 The Director may reject a request for a *certificate of existence* for any of the following reasons:

- the corporate name of the corporation for which the certificate is requested does not exist or is incorrect

- the corporation number provided does not exist or is incorrect

- on or during the date or period specified in the request, the corporation made changes to its structure that caused its corporate number to change

- the date or period for which the certificate is requested is later than the date of the request

- the corporation was dissolved on or during the specified date or period, or is dissolved during the specified period

- the corporation had discontinued on or during the specified date or period, or discontinued during the specified period

- in exceptional circumstances, the corporation, to the Director's knowledge, failed to send a document required to be sent under the CBCA or pay an applicable fee

- the fee was not enclosed

6.3 If your request is rejected, Corporations Canada will send you a notice specifying the reasons.

7. — Additional information and how to contact Corporations Canada

Additional information on incorporation is available on the *Corporations Canada's website*

You may also contact Corporations Canada:

Client Services Unit

Corporations Canada

Industry Canada

9th Floor, Jean Edmonds Towers South

365 Laurier Avenue West

Ottawa, ON K1A 0C8

Telephone: (613) 941-9042

Fax: (613) 941-0601

Email: *Corporations Canada*

Policy Statement 11.4 — Notice of Acknowledgment For Forms Filed Under the *Canada Business Corporations Act*

Date: February 16, 2004

Revised: January 2, 2007

No notice of acknowledgment for forms submitted by mail or fax

Corporations Canada does not acknowledge receipt of Form 22: Annual Returns, Form 3: Change of Registered Office Address and Form 6: Changes Regarding Directors filed by mail or fax.

Corporations Canada does not send out copies of the filed form, even if a duplicate of the form has been submitted with a self-addressed stamped envelope.

Notice of acknowledgment for forms submitted online

An automatic acknowledgment by e-mail is sent when a form is submitted through the Corporations Canada Online Filing Centre.

Information on the website

On receipt of Form 3, 6 or 22, Corporations Canada will process the information and update the website. Usually, the updated information will appear on our website within five days of the date of receipt of the form. To confirm that your form has been processed, you can access the website at *www.corporationscanada.ic.gc.ca* and click "Search for a Federal Corporation" to verify if the information shown reflects the information you submitted.

Request for copies of documents filed with Corporations Canada

Requests for copies of submissions must be sent in writing or by fax to:

> Database Integrity Unit
> Corporations Canada
> 9th Floor, Jean Edmonds Tower South
> 365 Laurier Avenue West
> Ottawa, Ontario K1A 0C8
> Tel: 613-941-6631
> Fax: 613-941-5789

A fee of $1 (one dollar) per page will be charged. (Section 6 of Schedule 5 of the *Canada Business Corporations Regulations, (2001)*).

Additional information

For additional information on Corporations Canada's products and services, please visit Corporations Canada's website or call toll free 1-866-333-5556.

You can also contact Corporations Canada at:

> Client Services Section
> Corporations Canada
> Industry Canada
> 9th Floor, Jean Edmonds Tower South
> Ottawa, Ontario K1A OC8
> Fax: 613-941-0601
> *www.corporationscanada.ic.gc.ca*

Policy Statement 11.20 — Criteria for complaints to be considered by Corporations Canada

Date: June 13, 2005

In order for a complaint concerning an alleged contravention of the *Canada Business Corporations Act*, the *Canada Corporations Act* — Part II or the *Canada Cooperatives Act* to be considered by Corporations Canada, it must meet the following criteria:

- it must be *in writing*;

- it must be addressed to the administrator of the acts, the Director General, Corporations Canada, at the address set out below (please note that any complaints sent to the Minister or Deputy Minister of Industry Canada will be forwarded to the Director General, Corporations Canada in accordance with this Policy); and

- it must contain sufficient information to substantiate the complaint (including, but not limited to the name and address of the complainant, the name of the corporation and specific details of the alleged contravention).

Please send complaints to:

Director General

Corporations Canada

Industry Canada

9th Floor, Jean Edmonds Towers South

365 Laurier Avenue West

Ottawa, Ontario

K1A 0C8

Fax: (613) 941-0601

Email: *Corporations Canada*

Policy Statement 11.28.1 — Exemption from the Filing of Certain Documents (Single Filing Exemption)

Date: **May 31, 2002**
Revised: **January 2, 2007**

The attached single filing exemption provides that proxy materials and financial statements required to be filed with Corporations Canada, pursuant to sections 150 and 160 of the *Canada Business Corporations Act* (CBCA), need not be filed if documents containing similar information have been filed with any of the participating provincial and territorial securities commissions.

It is necessary for corporations relying on a single filing order to determine that the filing they make with an identified regulatory body contains similar information to that in the document required to be filed by the CBCA. Given the similarity in requirements between the CBCA and provincial and territorial securities legislation, this will in most cases enable the corporation to determine that the filing does contain similar information.

There is no need for a CBCA corporation to apply for an exemption, or to notify the office of the Director, in order to rely on this single filing exemption.

Exemption No. 1, 2002 (Sending of Notices and Documents)

Exemptions

1. A person who is required to send a notice or document set out in column I of an item of Part A of the schedule by the provision of the *Canada Business Corporations Act* set out in column II of that item is exempt from the application of that provision where:

(a) the person is required by any provincial legislation set out in Part B of the schedule to file a notice or document containing information that is similar to the information contained in the notice or document set out in column I of that item of Part A of the schedule;

(b) the notice or document has been filed in accordance with the provincial legislation set out in Part B of the schedule; and

(c) the notice and document is made available to the public.

Schedule (Section 1)
Notices And Documents Exempted Under Section 258.2 of the
Canada Business Corporations Act (CBCA)

Part A

Notices, Documents And Provisions

	Column I	Column II
Item	Notice or Document	CBCA Provision
1.	Proxy material	section 150
2.	Financial statements	section 160

Part B

Provincial Legislation

Securities Act, R.S.O. 1990, c. S-5 (Ontario)

Securities Act, R.S.Q., c. V-1.1 (Quebec)

Securities Act, R.S.N.S. 1989, c. 418 (Nova Scotia)

Security Frauds Prevention Act, R.S.N.B. 1973, c. S-6 (New Brunswick)

The Securities Act, R.S.M. 1988, c. S50 (Manitoba)

The Securities Act, R.S.B.C. 1996, c. 418 (British Columbia)

Securities Act, R.S.P.E.I. 1988, c. S-3 (Prince Edward Island)

The Securities Act, S.S. 1988-89, c. S-42.2 (Saskatchewan)

Securities Act, S.A. 1981, c. S-6.1 (Alberta)

Securities Act, R.S.N. 1990, c. S-13 (Newfoundland)

Securities Act, R.S.Y. 1986, c. 15 (Yukon)

Securities Act, S.N.W.T. 1996, c. 19 (Northwest Territories)

Policy Statement 11.30 — Oppression Remedy Guidelines
Date: June 8, 2005

Introduction

Section 241 of the CBCA gives a "complainant" the right to bring a court action against a corporation where conduct has occurred which is oppressive, unfairly prejudicial or which unfairly disregards the interests of a shareholder, creditor, director or officer. This right is commonly referred to as the "oppression remedy". The oppression remedy has been interpreted by courts and commentators as imposing a general standard of "fair" conduct on each CBCA corporation and its management. When this standard has been breached, complainants may apply to court for an order rectifying the oppressive conduct. The court may make any order it thinks fit, including awarding money damages, appointing a receiver, dissolving the corporation, forcing the acquisition of securities and amending charter documents.

Potential complainants under the oppression remedy are shareholders (present and past), directors and officers of a CBCA corporation or its affiliates, the Director appointed under the CBCA and any other person the court decides may properly make an application.

Purpose of Guidelines

These guidelines are intended to clarify the limited circumstances in which the Director may decide to participate in an oppression action. Persons considering asking for the Director's assistance should use these guidelines both as an indicator of whether or not their situation is an appropriate case to present to the Director, and as a tool for determining what information the Director's staff will need to receive in order to determine if the complaint warrants further review. This document is limited to a discussion of when the Director may be inclined to make an application to court; it does not purport to define what constitutes oppressive conduct on the part of a corporation or its management.

Background to Guidelines

In March of 1995, the Director released and consulted upon a discussion paper on the Director's potential role in oppression cases. Although extremes of opinion were expressed on many of the issues raised in that paper, consensus was reached on two critical points.

First, consultation confirmed and supported the Director's past practice of only infrequently becoming involved in the affairs of a corporation or its management through a section 241 action, and generally only participating in extraordinary cases. This infrequency is primarily a result of the self-enforcing philosophy behind the CBCA.

Second, because the Director's involvement in an oppression case is always discretionary and must not be restricted in any way, there was agreement that it would be inappropriate and inadvisable to set out precise criteria which, when satisfied, might seem to require the Director to become involved in a section 241 action.

Although the Director's discretion will not be constrained in any manner, it is recognized that a listing of the factors that are taken into account in deciding on the Director's involvement in section 241 proceedings may be of use to persons who are considering asking for assistance.

Research and consultation have identified a number of these factors, some of which are listed below. While there is no formula to weight the relative importance of these factors, it is acknowledged that certain criteria may be more compelling than others. It is also important to note that the factors set out in these guidelines will rarely exist independently of each other. However, in the final analysis, the Director's decision on whether or not to become involved in an oppression action will be based on an analysis of all relevant factors, including those discussed below.

Factors Relevant to Director's Decision to Exercise Discretion

When attempting to determine whether the Director may decide to exercise the discretion available under section 241 of the CBCA, it is important to remember that the definition of "complainant" in that section is extremely broad and includes "any interested person". This is consistent with the primarily self-enforcing nature of the statute. In an oppression action, all complainants have all of the procedural rights available to the Director. In general, therefore, the Director will only become involved where the person complaining of oppressive conduct has, for good reason, not accessed those rights and the proceedings are, in the Director's opinion, justified on the basis of factors such as those set out below.

1. *Seriousness of Conduct.* The degree to which the interests of shareholders or other interested parties appear to have been unfairly disregarded, or to which provisions of the CBCA have been breached, will influence the Director's determination of whether or not to intervene under the oppression remedy.

2. *Deterrence.* In cases where the Director's intervention may attract media attention and public notice, thereby helping to deter the conduct that is the subject of complaint, the Director will be more inclined to act. This is a significant factor in cases where the Director is aware of actual or suspected widespread infringement of the statute.

3. *Clarification of Case Law.* Where the involvement of the Director could help to clarify unresolved corporate law issues, the Director will be more inclined to act.

4. *Availability of Other Law Remedies.* While not necessarily favouring shareholders over other classes of complainants, the Director will likely be less inclined to act where other corporate or non-corporate law remedies are available, such as proceedings to enforce the contractual rights of a complainant.

5. *Availability of Alternate Resolutions.* The Director will consider, both for a private and a public company, whether a simple exit through the sale of shares would be a more efficient and fair manner of dispute resolution than costly litigation. Where a market offering fair value for the shares exists, but the party complaining of the oppressive action chooses not to access it, the Director may be less inclined to act. On the other hand, the existence of such a market will not, in and of itself, necessarily dissuade the Director from taking action. Similarly, where other procedural means are available to assist a complainant, the Director may decline to become involved. For example, where a jurisdiction allows class action suits and/or contingency fees for legal advisors, the general ability of potential plaintiffs to commence litigation is increased and the Director's intervention may be less necessary. Conversely, where procedural hurdles make pursuing a claim more difficult, the Director may be more willing to act.

6. *Absence of or Actions by Other Parties.* The Director will consider whether other persons involved with the same corporation or management have joined forces in order to prosecute or resolve their dispute. Where a concerted effort is already underway to address the conduct that is the subject of the complaint, the Director may suggest that complainants join that effort.

7. *Economic Consequences.* The Director may or may not be influenced by the value of the investment that a complainant alleges is at risk. While the amount of money involved may be significant to a particular corporate participant, the Director is not likely to be persuaded by this factor in the absence of other compelling circumstances. At the same time, however, where an aggrieved party does not have sufficient means to initiate proceedings (such as in the case of a cash-rich corporation whose investors are faced with losing what is, to them, a substantial sum of money but who do not individually, or even collectively, have sufficient funds to pursue litigation), the Director may be more inclined to intervene.

Initiation Versus Intervention

Complainants occasionally ask the Director to intervene in an ongoing proceeding, either in favour of the complainant making the request, or as a friend of the court. However, most of these requests are for the Director to initiate an action. In other words, the request is for the Director to act as plaintiff. Regardless of the nature of the request, however, the Director may decide to seek only the right to intervene in an action. In this way, the Director's evidence or submissions can be strictly limited to issues that are considered compelling. Since intervention can be a cost-effective way in which to address such key issues, the Director will tend to favour this approach, where it is available. In such cases, individuals seeking the Director's help would bring an action as plaintiff and the Director would seek to intervene in that action.

Conclusion

Although the presence or absence of any or all of the above factors may be persuasive, it is important to remember that this alone will not determine how the Director will exercise the discretion available under section 241. It is also worth noting that the Director only infrequently becomes involved in section 241 oppression actions. Despite these cautionary notes, individuals who are seeking the Director's assistance should continue to be mindful of the importance of these factors to the Director's deliberations and provide information addressing those that are directly applicable to their complaint.

Formal requests for assistance under section 241 must be presented, in writing, either to the Director or to the Deputy Directors. Requests must contain a complete and comprehensive description of the alleged oppressive conduct, and must be accompanied by any available supporting evidence.

Note that these guidelines are not intended to substitute for professional legal, accounting or business advice, nor for the exercise of professional judgment by legal, accounting or business advisors. This document may be amended from time to time to reflect experience with its application and new developments in the law.

For further information, please contact:

Cheryl Ringor

Deputy Director, *Canada Business Corporations Act*

Corporations Canada

9th Floor, Jean Edmonds Tower South

365 Laurier Avenue West

Ottawa, Ontario

K1A 0C8

Tel.: (613) 941-5756

Fax: (613) 941-5781

Policy Statement 15.1 — Policy of the Director concerning Arrangements Under Section 192 of the CBCA

Date: November 7, 2003

1. — Introduction and Statement of General Principle

1.01 This policy sets out the position of the Director appointed under the *Canada Business Corporations Act* (the "Act") as to the permissible use of and appropriate procedural safeguards and substantive requirements applicable to arrangements under section 192 of the Act.

1.02 The Director endorses the position that the arrangement provisions of the Act are intended to be facilitative and should not be construed narrowly. This position is subject to the express limitations in the Act and to the proviso that any proposed arrangement transaction must satisfy requirements of procedural and substantive fairness.

1.03 In order to assist applicant corporations, this policy also sets forth certain policy and practice guidelines aimed at facilitating the Director's review of proposed arrangements. While such policy and practice guidelines do not necessarily have the force of law, the Director believes that the policies and practices outlined represent appropriate conduct on the part of corporations proposing to enter into arrangement transactions. The Director takes the position that any proposed departures from such policies and practices should be discussed in advance with the Director or the Director's staff. The Director may appear before the court pursuant to section 192(5) of the Act to oppose the proposed arrangement at an interim or final court hearing if the Director believes that departures from the following guidelines are not warranted in the particular case.

1.04 The Director believes that by communicating these guidelines to security holders and corporations which are considering entering into arrangement transactions, the instances in which the Director finds it necessary to actively intervene in arrangement proceedings can be reduced. However, nothing in this policy is intended to constitute a binding statement of how the Director will respond to any particular arrangement transaction. Moreover, this policy is not intended to be a substitute for professional legal, accounting and business advice or for the exercise of professional judgment by legal, accounting and business advisers in any particular case.

2. — Scope of Permissible Use of Arrangement Provisions

2.01 The Director endorses the view that the arrangement provisions of the Act are intended to be facilitative and notes that the arrangement provisions of the Act have been utilized by corporations to effect a wide range of different types of transactions, such as "spin-offs" of business enterprises, combinations of business enterprises, continuances of corporations to or from other jurisdictions and so-called "going-private" transactions.

2.02 The applicant under the arrangement provisions of the Act must be a "corporation". The Director also notes that there are certain additional jurisdictional limitations embodied in section 192 of the Act. These include the requirements that (a) the applicant must not be insolvent (as defined in subsection 192(2) of the Act), (b) it not be practicable for the corporation to carry out the arrangement under any other provision or provisions of the Act, and (c) the arrangement provisions of the Act may only be utilized by a corporation to effect a fundamental change in the nature of an arrangement. The limitation that any exchange of securities must not constitute a take-over bid, as defined was removed in the recent amendment, to the Act. The following sets forth in more detail the Director's views with respect to certain aspects of each of the following limitations.

(a) — Solvency Limitations

2.03 The applicant corporation must not be insolvent within the meaning of subsection 192(2) of the Act. The Director is aware that the arrangement provisions of the Act have been utilized in circumstances where the total business enterprise affected by the arrangement was not solvent (at least as of the date of the interim hearing). Such plans have proceeded on two bases. The first is on the basis that the applicant, while insolvent at the interim hearing date, is solvent at the date of the final order. See, for example, *Re Computel Systems Ltd.*, where the applicant corporation, while insolvent (as defined in subsection 192(2) of the Act but solvent under applicable insolvency legislation) at the interim hearing date, reduced its stated capital by special resolution in order to satisfy the solvency requirement prior to the date the court was asked to grant final approval of the arrangement. Notwithstanding *Computel Systems Ltd.* and other precedents for plans proceeding on this basis, the Director is unaware of a court expressly determining that the solvency requirement must only be met at the final order stage. The second basis is where the applicant corporation is solvent but one of the principal corporate entities involved in the overall arrangement transaction is not solvent. This was the case in *Savage v. Amoco Acquisition Co.* where the court ruled that use of the arrangement provisions of the Act is not limited to cases where none of the corporations involved is insolvent provided that the arrangement, as proposed, is not a sham. More recently, in *Re St. Lawrence & Hudson Railway Co.* the court described the solvency requirement in subsection 192(2) of the Act as requiring only that at least one of the corporate applicants under the plan of arrangement must not be insolvent (as defined in subsection 192(2) of the Act).

2.04 The Director acknowledges that certain other corporate statutes do not impose a solvency limitation on arrangements, but believes that so long as the Act contains such a limitation, applicants should be prepared to demonstrate compliance with this limitation, as interpreted by the courts, both before the court and in the materials provided to the Director with notice of the interim hearing. Where it is not apparent from the affidavit materials provided with notice of the interim hearing that there is compliance with the solvency limitation, the Director may request additional financial information demonstrating compliance. Where the Director is not satisfied that compliance with the solvency limitation has been demonstrated, the Director may intervene.

2.05 The use of the term "security holder", rather than "shareholder", in section 192 of the Act clearly allows courts to entertain proposed arrangement transactions which alter debtholders' rights. (The Director believes that ordinary unsecured creditors, such as trade creditors, do not properly fall within the definition of security holders,[23] and has concerns about the use of the arrangement procedure to adversely affect or to compromise contingent claims or any other type of claim that is not a claim of a security holder, as was attempted in *Re Enron Canada Corp.*). The Director, mindful of the solvency limitations, is of the opinion that transactions involving principally the compromise of debtholder claims against insolvent business enterprises may be more appropriately carried out under the provisions of applicable insolvency law. Nonetheless, the Director recognizes that it may be appropriate to utilize the arrangement provision under the CBCA to effect transactions affecting debtholders, provided the statutory requirements are met. While insolvency legislation may provide guidance as to appropriate procedural safeguards, the Director believes that the applicant should provide, at a minimum, the safeguards set out in paragraphs 3.06, 3.08, 3.09, and 4.03 of this Policy, for arrangements contemplating the possible compromise of debt. Specifically, these provisions address disclosure, voting requirements, and independent opinion reports. These safeguards are not only strongly endorsed in arrangements involving debtholder claims against an insolvent corporation but also in arrangements involving debtholder claims against a corporation that, while not insolvent, is near insolvency. To determine whether a corporation involved in the arrangement is near insolvency, the Director will look to available financial and operating indicators. Presence of one or more of the following may indicate that a corporation is near insolvency:

- The arrangement contemplates a compromise of debt
- A note to the corporation's audited financial statements warning the reader of the potential inappropriateness of the use of generally accepted accounting principles that are applicable to a going concern because there is significant doubt about the appropriateness of the assumption.

---

[23]While "security holder" is not defined in the Act, the term "security" means a share of any class or series of shares or a debt obligation of a corporation. "Debt obligation" is defined to mean a bond, debenture, note or other evidence of indebtedness or guarantee of a corporation, whether secured or unsecured. A "holder" as defined in Part VII of the CBCA, which governs the transfer or transmission of a security, means a person in possession of a security issued or endorsed to him or her or to bearer or in blank. Given these definitions and relying on the ejusdem generis principle of interpretation, the Director's position is that the term "security holder" would include debtholders such as debenture and bond holders but not ordinary unsecured creditors.

- An action by a bond rating service that may indicate a solvency problem. These actions include a rating suspension, a rating downgrade from investment grade to non-investment grade, or a lower rating if the corporation is already in the non-investment grade range, and an issuance of a press release indicating that the corporation is on a credit watch with negative implications or that the rating outlook has changed from stable to negative in cases where a negative outcome may suggest a solvency problem.

- Where the corporation's shares are listed, a trading suspension has been ordered by a stock exchange because the corporation's financial condition does not meet the requirements for continued trading.

- The resignation of all or substantially all of the directors of the corporation within the year immediately preceding a court application for approval of an arrangement.

(b) — Impracticability Requirement

2.07 The Director endorses the view that the impracticability requirement means something less than "impossible" and, generally, that the test would be satisfied by demonstrating that it would be inconvenient or less advantageous to the corporation to proceed under other provisions of the Act. The Director endorses this view subject to a concern that the arrangement provisions of the Act not be utilized to subvert the procedural or substantive safeguards applicable to other sorts of transactions possible under the Act.

(c) — Fundamental Change

2.08 Subsection 192(3) of the Act allows the arrangement provisions of the Act to be used only in circumstances where the corporation proposes to effect a fundamental change in the nature of an arrangement. The Director recognizes that the term arrangement is not exhaustively defined in subsection 192(1) of the Act and believes that use of the arrangement provisions of the Act is not necessarily limited to arrangement transactions involving one or more of the types of transactions provided for under other provisions of Part XV — "Fundamental Changes" of the Act. There must, however, be a proposed fundamental change in the nature of an arrangement to the applicant in order to proceed under section 192 of the Act and the Director has concerns with respect to the use of the arrangement as a procedural tool to affect stakeholders' rights in the absence of a proposal to effect a fundamental change to the applicant. The Director is also of the view that subsection 192(3) of the Act requires that the applicant corporation itself undergo a fundamental change and that it is not sufficient that another body corporate involved in the arrangement transaction undergoes a fundamental change. The Director notes, however, that this requirement will be satisfied if the applicant corporation itself undergoes any one or more of the transactions specifically enumerated in subsection 192(1) of the Act. For example, in the case of an arrangement consisting of an exchange of securities within the meaning of paragraph (f) of subsection 192(1) of the Act, as it is the corporation whose securities are being acquired rather than the issuer of the securities, that is effecting the arrangement, it is the former corporation that would be the proper applicant.

3. — Procedural Guidelines

(a) — Interim Orders

3.01 A practice has developed in arrangement transactions whereby a corporation proposing to carry out an arrangement will apply to court seeking an interim order governing various procedural matters prior to the calling of any security holder meetings to approve the proposed arrangement. The Director endorses this practice and believes that ordinarily it would be appropriate for a corporation proposing an arrangement to apply for an interim order which addresses the following general matters:

i. information and notice requirements for the calling of meetings of shareholders and other security holders;

ii. class voting requirements, if applicable;

iii. quorum requirements;

iv. the levels of approval required of each class of security holder (including any appropriate "majority of minority" approval requirements);

v. dissent and appraisal rights of shareholders; and

vi. notice requirements in connection with the final hearing to approve the arrangement.

This is not intended to be an exhaustive list of the matters that may be appropriate for the court to deal with in the interim order, but only to illustrate those matters which the Director believes would ordinarily be appropriate for applicants to seek to have the court address at an interim hearing.

(b) — Notice to the Director

3.02 Subsection 192(5) of the Act requires the applicant to give notice of the application to the Director and entitles the Director to appear and be heard in person or by counsel. Section 192 specifically requires that notice be given of both the interim and final application proceedings. While as a matter of law, the required notice to the Director is a combined function of applicable rules of civil procedure and judicial discretion, the Director believes that as a matter of practice it is desirable to establish minimum notice requirements. The Director regards the following notice requirements as the minimum notice sufficient to enable the Director to determine whether to appear and make submissions at any interim or final court hearing in cases where the applicant has strictly complied with the requirements of this policy. Where the applicant is not complying strictly with the policy, there is a greater likelihood that the Director may choose to be represented in court, and in this situation, the minimum notice might not be sufficient. In this case, the applicant would be well advised to provide the Director with the full notice provided under applicable rules of procedure, in order to avoid the necessity of the Director requesting a postponement of the court hearing.

3.03 With respect to interim hearings, the Director believes that ordinarily the applicant should provide a minimum of five working days' of the date of the initial interim hearing. The notice should be accompanied by materials sufficient to allow the Director to make a proper determination of compliance with statutory requirements and as to whether minimum standards of procedural fairness are being observed. Ordinarily, this would consist of the following:

i. affidavit materials being filed with the court (in final, or final draft form), and specifically including affidavit and other materials demonstrating that the corporation is not insolvent within the meaning of subsection 192(2) of the Act and an explanation as to why it is not practicable for the corporation to achieve the objective of the proposed arrangement under other provisions of the Act;

ii. draft form of notices of meeting to shareholders and other security holders;

iii. draft management proxy circular describing the proposed arrangement (in reasonably final form and including a description of the plan of arrangement and the holdings of significant security holders);

iv. draft form of proxy;

v. draft plan of arrangement;

vi. draft interim order; and

vii. the most recent financial statements of the applicant corporation, if they are not part of the information circular.

3.04 With respect to the final hearing, ordinarily the Director should be provided with affidavit materials (in draft form where necessary) being filed or to be filed with the court at least three working days' prior to the date of the final hearing. Such affidavit materials should specifically include the following:

i. report on attendance and quorum at each meeting;

ii. report of the results of ballots of each meeting to approve the arrangement (including separate tabulation of voting demonstrating any required "majority of minority" approvals);

iii. issued interim order; and

iv. draft final order. (Note that where the arrangement involves an amalgamation of a body corporate with a corporation, it may be prudent for the final order to contain a clause directing the relevant authority of the jurisdiction governing the body corporate to amend its records to recognize that amalgamation as of the time it becomes effective pursuant to the arrangement.)

As soon as practicable thereafter, final copies of all affidavit and other materials filed with the court should be filed with the Director.

3.05 In setting forth these guidelines, the Director recognizes that it may not be appropriate or practicable to comply strictly with these requirements in every case, but believes that applicant corporations should be in a position to justify departures from the foregoing guidelines and to provide the Director with sufficient information in a timely manner to allow the Director to determine whether intervention is appropriate. Applicants who do not afford the Director the opportunity to review the necessary information sufficiently in advance of any interim or final hearing are inviting the Director to appear in order to seek an adjournment of the hearing on this basis. Where the Director does not intend to seek an adjournment or to intervene, the Director will send to the applicant, by fax, a letter of non-appearance prior to the court hearing.

(c) — Information and Notice Requirements to Affected Constituencies

3.06 Generally, the Director believes that notice should be given to those security holders entitled to vote in respect of a plan and that all security holders affected by a plan (see discussion in paragraph 3.07 below) should be entitled to vote in respect of that plan. The general principle governing information and notice requirements should be that shareholders and other security holders voting on a proposed arrangement receive sufficient information to allow them to form a reasoned judgment as to whether to support or to vote against the proposal. In determining what specific disclosure is appropriate, corporations should, at a minimum, provide all disclosure required by the regulations under the Act which would otherwise be applicable to the various elements of an arrangement otherwise specifically provided for in the Act (e.g. amalgamations, amendments to articles, etc.). In addition, where an arrangement transaction effects a result which is in substance the same as another type of transaction specifically provided for in the Act (e.g. an amalgamation), the issuer should provide to security holders any additional material disclosure which would be required to be provided under the Act in connection with the substantively equivalent transaction. Where the plan of arrangement contemplates a possible compromise of debt (see discussion in paragraph 2.05), the Act and regulations, however, provide no assistance. The Director's position, in these circumstances, is that disclosure should be made of known security holders (who are debtholders) (1) who are "related persons", as defined in section 4 of the *Bankruptcy and Insolvency Act*,[24] with respect to the debtor-corporation, (2) who hold a significant proportion (33% or more) of the total debt held by their voting class, or (3) who are entitled to vote in more than one class of securities. Recognizing that there may be difficulties in determining who all the security holders are, the Director requires, at a minimum, the corporation to obtain the information on a "best efforts" basis. The corporation must be able to satisfy the Director that such an undertaking was done.

(d) — Dissemination of Information

3.07 The Director believes that meeting materials should generally be provided to security holders only through a method expressly permitted under the Act. In particular, the information circular sent to security holders in connection with the meeting to approve the plan of arrangement should, absent unusual circumstances, only be transmitted electronically to those security holders who have consented to receive materials in that form. A practice has evolved of providing portions of the meeting materials in paper form and providing other parts of the materials on CD ROM, sending them electronically or advising security holders that they are available electronically or in paper form upon request. Although the Director believes that all of the meeting materials should generally be provided to security holders in paper form (unless they have otherwise consented), the Director will not generally object to exhibits or schedules to the information circular being provided by the various methods described above, so long as the information circular (together with the plan of arrangement documents and shareholder resolution thereto) are provided through a method expressly permitted under the Act and so long as the applicant confirms in the affidavit materials to be filed in connection with the interim hearing, that such method of dissemination is in compliance with applicable Securities Law Requirements (as defined in paragraph 3.10 below).

(e) — Voting Requirements

3.08 Section 192 of the Act does not require security holder approval as a pre-condition to a court order approving an arrangement. However, the Director is of the view that, at a minimum, all security holders whose legal rights are affected by a proposed arrangement are entitled to vote on the arrangement. The Director is also of the view that, notwithstanding that a proposed arrangement may not affect the legal rights of holders of securities of a particular class, it may nevertheless be appropriate in cases where a proposed arrangement fundamentally alters the security holders' investment, whether economically or otherwise, that the right to vote on the arrangement should be provided to these security holders. For example, in an arrangement involving a divestiture of significant assets, the Director will review the financial statements, looking at such factors as the percentage of assets being "dividended-out", credit ratings and the rights of participation of any preferred shareholder classes. At the same time, the Director recognizes that in determining whether debt security holders should be provided with voting and approval rights, the trust indenture or other contractual instrument creating such securities should ordinarily be determinative absent extraordinary circumstances.

---

[24]See Annex A for the provisions of Section 4 of the *Bankrupcy and Insolvency Act,* R.S.C., 1985, c. B-1, as amended.

3.09 While the type and levels of approval which a court will require before approving any proposed arrangement are ultimately a matter of judicial discretion, the Director believes that normally class voting and voting approval requirements should be determined with reference to the class voting rules and levels of approval that would apply if the various elements of the transactions comprising the arrangement were carried out separately under the provisions of the Act. In this respect, the Director believes that the fundamental objective of class voting requirements is to ensure that security holders having a sufficient commonality of interest are grouped together for voting purposes and security holders without a sufficient commonality of interest be allowed a separate vote. The Director believes that where the applicant proposes at the interim hearing stage that different classes of security holders be grouped together for voting purposes, the burden of persuasion rests with the applicant to justify why such an arrangement is consistent with procedural fairness. In arrangements contemplating the possible compromise of debt (see discussion in paragraph 2.05), the Director also believes that grouping security holders who are debtholders based on commonality of interest is appropriate. For example, because the debtor-corporation involved in the arrangement is at risk of becoming insolvent resulting in little or no economic value in equity, the Director accepts that the grouping together of common and preferred shareholders for voting purposes will usually be appropriate. Where common and preferred shareholders are grouped into one class, the Director, however, believes a separate tabulation of votes should be kept. Among other reasons, a separate tabulation would serve as a safeguard against the possibility of a subsequent determination that separate votes should have been taken. In the Director's opinion, the appropriate voting level for debtholders is two thirds in value of the total debt held by all the debtholders of each class present, personally or by proxy.

3.10 The Director believes that in certain circumstances it may be appropriate to require that security holder approval be demonstrated to have been obtained on a disinterested basis (i.e. by those security holders in a class who do not have any collateral interest in the approval of the arrangement). Ordinarily, it will be sufficient for such purposes if the applicant adheres to the requirements for "majority of minority" approval of transactions imposed under applicable securities laws (such as Ontario Securities Commission Rule 61-501 and Quebec Securities Commission Policy Statement Q-27) and of relevant Canadian stock exchanges (collectively, "Securities Law Requirements") with respect to related party or non-arm's length transactions. Where the arrangement will effect a going-private transaction (as defined in the regulations under the Act), the affidavit materials to be filed in connection with the interim hearing should include express confirmation that the arrangement will comply with, if applicable, the majority of minority approval and other requirements of "applicable provincial securities laws", as contemplated under section 193 of the Act. Where the arrangement will effect a squeeze-out transaction (as defined in the Act), the affidavit materials to be filed in connection with the interim hearing application should include express confirmation that the arrangement will comply with the "majority of minority" requirements of section 194 of the Act. For other arrangements, and where Securities Law Requirements are not applicable to the arrangement, the Director nevertheless believes that ordinarily the principles established by such Securities Law Requirements relating to "majority of minority" security holder approval requirements should be followed by applicant corporations. In arrangement transactions contemplating a possible compromise of debt (see discussion in paragraph 2.05), the Director believes that the principles underlying the "majority of minority" voting requirements are applicable. In particular, the Director strongly endorses a "majority of minority" approval where the security holder who is a debtholder is related to the debtor corporation. A "related person" is one who falls within the definition of "related persons" as set out in section 4 of the *Bankruptcy and Insolvency Act*.[25] Where the debtholder is related to the debtor corporation, the Director accepts as an alternative to the "majority of minority" voting, a voting scheme that prohibits a related debtholder from voting for but not against the plan of arrangement.

(f) — Final Order

3.11 At the hearing of the application for the final order, the court will consider whether there has been compliance with the terms of the interim order and will make its final determination as to the fairness of the arrangement. The Director will also have an opportunity to consider the arrangement in final form in determining the position that will be taken at the hearing. Although the Director will endeavour to raise, prior to the interim hearing, at the interim hearing, or otherwise as soon as practicable, any objections the Director may have to a proposed arrangement (provided there has been compliance with the requirements respecting notice to the Director), the Director will not be bound at the final hearing by any position the Director has taken with respect to the apparent fairness of the arrangement in connection with the interim hearing.

(g)

3.12 Certain plans of arrangement are drafted to permit amendments to the plan. While the Director does not object to such provisions being included in a plan of arrangement, certain procedural safeguards should be provided for and followed by the applicant corporation. The Director should be notified of any amendment to a plan of arrangement. If an amendment occurs before the meeting of security holders to approve the plan, then the amendment should be expressly brought to the attention of security holders before the vote on the plan. Depending on the nature of the amendment, consideration will have to be given to the need to amend the information circular and send to security holders the amended information circular or supplemental information circular. Any amendment made after the security holder vote and before the fairness hearing should be expressly brought to the attention of the judge at the hearing for the final order. No amendments, except with court approval, should be made to a plan of arrangement after the final order is granted.

(h)

3.13 In order to facilitate future dealings relating to the corporation resulting from the arrangement, the Director recommends that article provisions of the corporation resulting from the arrangement be set out in the articles of arrangement in a manner which closely parallels the format utilized for articles of incorporation. The Director notes that the instructions to Form 14.1, Articles of Arrangement, effectively requires such presentation for arrangement transactions involving an amalgamation. The Director's experience is that this can be best achieved by attaching a form as an annex to the articles of arrangement, following the format of articles of incorporation, setting out these provisions. The Director believes that this is particularly important since the name which will appear on the certificate of arrangement will often not be the same as the name of the resulting corporation (since the name(s) of the applicant(s) are recorded on the certificate of arrangement). The Director is also of the view that where one of the elements of an arrangement is an amalgamation, the effect of the arrangement on the corporation continuing from such amalgamation should be the same as if

---

[25]See Annex A for the provisions of Section 4 of the *Bankrupcy and Insolvency Act,* R.S.C., 1985, c. B-1, as amended.

the amalgamation were carried out under the provisions of sections 180 to 186 of the Act. Accordingly, the Director strongly recommends that the plan of arrangement (contained in the articles of arrangement) in such cases contain express provisions to the same effect as is set forth in section 186 of the Act.

4. — Substantive Fairness

4.01 The Director believes that in addition to demonstrating compliance with jurisdictional requirements (discussed above in Section 2) and statutory and court-ordered procedural requirements (including those designed to ensure procedural fairness), there rests with the applicant proposing an arrangement an onus to demonstrate that the proposed arrangement is fair from the perspective of the security holder constituencies whose rights are affected by the arrangement.

4.02 Although the substantive fairness of a proposed arrangement is a determination ultimately to be made by the court in each particular case, the Director also will consider the fairness of the proposed arrangement. In the Director's fairness review, the Director will consider the materials provided in connection with the interim hearing application and, in particular, overall financial statements and the overall financial position of the corporation and other bodies corporate involved in the arrangement both before and after giving effect to the proposed arrangement. In addition, certain practices have developed in the context of arrangement transactions with respect to the use of fairness opinions and the extension of dissent and appraisal rights to shareholders and, as these are considered by the Director in the review of the application, the Director believes that it would be appropriate for him to comment on such practices.

(a) — Fairness Opinions

4.03 A practice has developed whereby corporations proposing to carry out an arrangement will typically commission and provide to affected security holder constituencies an opinion of a financial adviser to support the conclusion that the proposed arrangement is "fair and reasonable" to relevant security holder constituencies. While fairness opinions are not required under the Act, the Director strongly endorses the practice of obtaining fairness opinions as a means of providing objective evidence that a proposed arrangement is fair. Ideally, fairness opinions should be provided by financial advisers who are independent from all parties involved in the arrangement. However, the Director recognizes that providers of opinions are not always independent as that term is interpreted under applicable Securities Law Requirements. Accordingly, the Director requires, at a minimum, disclosure of any relationship the providers of the fairness opinion may have with any party involved in the arrangement and whether their compensation is, in any way, contingent on the consummation of the transaction on which they have expressed an opinion and confirmation that the provider of the fairness opinion has represented that notwithstanding such relationships or arrangements it believes it is independent. The Director recognizes that there will be circumstances in which an applicant will believe that a fairness opinion is not necessary (such as where the arrangement is inherently fair to all security holders). An applicant who does not intend to obtain a fairness opinion should be prepared to justify its position to the Director. Where the plan of arrangement contemplates a possible compromise of debt (see discussion in paragraph 2.05), the Director's position is that an opinion report of an independent financial adviser be provided to all security holders, setting out reasons why the plan of arrangement is advantageous to them. The report should demonstrate that each class of security holders would be in a better position under the arrangement than if the corporation were liquidated. A financial adviser, in these circumstances, should generally be an accountant or person with a financial background who has experience in assessing liquidation values.

4.04 Without attempting to limit or dictate the considerations which are appropriate for an independent financial adviser to consider in opining as to the fairness of any proposed arrangement, the Director believes that, ordinarily, for the fairness opinion to be meaningful, the person providing the opinion must be in a position to state that the arrangement is fair to each class of security holders affected by the arrangement. In the Director's view, a fairness opinion addressed only to selected classes of security holders and which does not address fairness from an inter-security holder class perspective (i.e. fairness among security holders), provides only limited evidence as to the fairness of any proposed arrangement and invites inquiry as to the fairness of the arrangement to classes of security holders to whom the opinion is not addressed.

(b) — Dissent and Appraisal Rights

4.05 Although the provisions of paragraph 192(4)(d) of the Act (under which a court may order that shareholders are entitled to dissent under section 190 of the Act) are drafted in permissive rather than mandatory terms, the Director believes that ordinarily shareholders should be permitted to dissent in respect of proposed arrangements. Accordingly, in cases where an arrangement is proposed under which shareholders will not be afforded dissent and appraisal rights, the Director will examine carefully the reasons for not permitting shareholders to dissent. In this respect, the Director believes that the applicant corporation should be prepared to justify (in both the materials submitted to the Director with notice of the interim hearing and before the court) why it would not be appropriate in the particular case to extend dissent and appraisal rights to shareholders. In the absence of a satisfactory justification, the Director may determine that it is appropriate to intervene before the court at any interim or final hearing to object to a proposed arrangement on this basis.

5. — Miscellaneous

5.01 The Director and the staff of Corporations Canada are available for consultation with interested persons as to the interpretation and application of this policy in particular situations. If significant issues may be involved, the consultation should be initiated at the earliest possible date.

5.02 From time to time this policy will be amended to address developments in the law, experience with the application of this policy and experience with transactions to which this policy applies.

5.03 The Director welcomes any comments or questions which corporations, security holders, counsel or others may have with respect to this policy. For the purpose of consultation, comments or questions, please contact the Compliance Branch, Corporations Canada, at 1-866-333-5556, fax number 613-941-5781, or write to the following address:

Compliance & Policy Directorate
Corporations Canada
Industry Canada
9th floor, Jean Edmonds Tower South
365 Laurier Avenue West
Ottawa ON
K1A 0C8
Telecopier: (613) 941-5781

Annex A — Bankruptcy and Insolvency Act, Section 4

(1) In this section,

"related group" means a group of persons each member of which is related to every other member of the group;

"unrelated group" means a group of persons that is not a related group.

(2) For the purposes of this Act, persons are related to each other and are "related persons" if they are

  a. individuals connected by blood relationship, marriage or adoption;

  b. a corporation and

      i. a person who controls the corporation, if it is controlled by one person,

      ii. a person who is a member of a related group that controls the corporation, or

      iii. any person connected in the manner set out in paragraph (a) to a person described in subparagraph (i) or (ii); or

  c. two corporations

      i. controlled by the same person or group of persons,

      ii. each of which is controlled by one person and the person who controls one of the corporations is related to the person who controls the other corporation,

      iii. one of which is controlled by one person and that person is related to any member of a related group that controls the other corporation,

      iv. one of which is controlled by one person and that person is related to each member of an unrelated group that controls the other corporation,

      v. one of which is controlled by a related group a member of which is related to each member of an unrelated group that controls the other corporation, or

      vi. one of which is controlled by an unrelated group each member of which is related to at least one member of an unrelated group that controls the other corporation.

(3) [Relationships] For the purposes of this section,

  a. where two corporations are related to the same corporation within the meaning of subsection (2), they shall be deemed to be related to each other;

  b. where a related group is in a position to control a corporation, it shall be deemed to be a related group that controls the corporation whether or not it is part of a larger group by whom the corporation is in fact controlled;

  c. a person who has a right under a contract, in equity or otherwise, either immediately or in the future and either absolutely or contingently, to, or to acquire, shares in a corporation, or to control the voting rights of shares in a corporation, shall, except where the contract provides that the right is not exercisable until the death of an individual designated therein, be deemed to have the same position in relation to the control of the corporation as if he owned the shares;

  d. where a person owns shares in two or more corporations, he shall, as shareholder of one of the corporations, be deemed to be related to himself as shareholder of each of the other corporations;

  e. persons are connected by blood relationship if one is the child or other descendant of the other or one is the brother or sister of the other;

f. persons are connected by marriage if one is married to the other or to a person who is connected by blood relationship to the other;

f.1 persons are connected by common-law partnership if one is in a common-law partnership with the other or with a person who is connected by blood relationship or adoption to the other; and

g. persons are connected by adoption if one has been adopted, either legally or in fact, as the child of the other or as the child of a person who is connected by blood relationship, otherwise than as a brother or sister, to the other.

CAN. REG. 2001-512 — CANADA BUSINESS CORPORATIONS REGULATIONS, 2001

made under the *Canada Business Corporations Act*

SOR/2001-512, as am. SOR/2003-317, ss. 1, 2, 3 (Fr.), 4–6; SOR/2005-51; SOR/2006-75.

. . . . .

. . . . .

SCHEDULE 5 — FEES

(Subsection 98(1))

Item	Column 1 Filing, Examination or Copying of Documents or Action by the Director under the Act	Column 2 Fee $
1.	Issuance by the Director of	
	(a) a certificate of incorporation under section 8, if the application is made	
	(i) using Industry Canada's online incorporation feature	200
	(ii) using any means other than Industry Canada's online incorporation feature	250
	(b) a certificate of amendment under subsection 27(5), section 178 or subsection 191(5)	200
	(c) a restated certificate of incorporation under subsection 180(3) (unless issued with certificate of amendment)	50
	(d) a certificate of amalgamation under subsection 185(4)	200
	(e) a certificate of continuance under subsection 187(4) (unless subsection 268(8) applies)	200
	(f) a document evidencing satisfaction of the Director, as required under subsection 188(1)	200
	(g) a certificate of arrangement under subsection 192(7)	200
	(h) a certificate of revival under subsection 209(3)	200
	(i) a certificate of revocation of intent to dissolve under subsection 211(11)	50
	(j) a corrected certificate under subsection 265(1)	200
2.	Sending the annual return to the Director for filing under subsection 263(1)	
	(a) using Industry Canada's online filing feature	20
	(b) using any means other than Industry Canada's online filing feature	40

Item	Column 1 **Filing, Examination or Copying of Documents or Action by the Director under the Act**	Column 2 **Fee $**
3.	Examination by the Director of the corporation's file in connection with a request for a certificate under section 263.1	10
4.	Application to the Director for an exemption under subsection 2(6), 10(2), 82(3), 151(1), 171(2) or 187(11)	250
5.	Application to the Director for an exemption under section 156	250
6.	Provision by the Director of uncertified copies of documents under subsection 266(2), per page	1
7.	Provision by the Director of certified copies of documents under subsection 266(2), per certificate	35

LEGISLATIVE INDEX

All references are to section numbers of the legislation. The following abbreviations have been used in this Index:

CBCA — *Canada Business Corporations Act, R.S.C. 1985, c. C-44, as amended*
CBCR — *Canada Business Corporations Regulations, 2001*
MDO — *Minister Designation Order (Canada Business Corporations Act), C.R.C., c. 427*
WA — *Winding-up and Restructuring Act, R.S.C. 1985, c. W-11, as amended*

Canada Business Corporations Act

Actions
- continuation on dissolution, CBCA 226(2)

Affiliated corporations
- defined, CBCA 2(2)

Amalgamation
- agreement
- • general, CBCA 182
- • termination of, CBCA 183(6)
- articles, *see* Articles
- cancellation of shares, CBCA 182(2)
- certificate, *see* Certificate
- declarations in support, CBCA 185(2)
- discontinuance of corporation upon, CBCA 186.1(3)–(4)
- horizontal short-form, CBCA 184(2)
- shareholder approval, CBCA 183, 186.1(1), *see also* Meetings
- vertical short-form, CBCA 184(1), 186.1(2)

Amendments
- articles, *see* Articles
- certificate, *see* Certificate
- constraint on shares, CBCA 174, *see also* Constrained share corporation

- general, CBCA 173(1)
- shareholder proposals
- • class vote, when entitled to, CBCA 176
- • general, CBCA 175
- termination of authorizing resolution, CBCA 173(2)

Annual return
- sending to Director under CBCA, CBCA 263(1); CBCR 4

Arrangement
- articles, *see* Articles
- court approval, CBCA 192(3)–(4)
- defined, CBCA 192(1)
- effective date, CBCA 192(8)
- notice to Director under CBCA, CBCA 192(5)

Articles
- amalgamation
- • form, Form 9
- • sending, CBCA 185(1)
- amendment
- • delivery, CBCA 177(1)
- • form, Form 4
- arrangement
- • form, Form 14.1
- • sending, CBCA 192(6)

525

Articles *(cont'd)*

- cancellation, CBCA 265.1; CBCR 96; PS 2.8
- continuance
- • form, Form 11
- • sending, CBCA 187(3)
- dissolution
- • form, Form 17
- • sending, CBCA 210(4), 211(14)
- • execution and filing, CBCA 262
- incorporation
- • contents, CBCA 6
- • delivery, CBCA 7
- • form, Form 1
- reorganization
- • form, Form 14
- • sending, CBCA 191(4)
- restated
- • delivery, CBCA 180(2)
- • form, Form 7
- revival
- • form, Form 15
- • sending, CBCA 209(2)

Audit committee

- duties, CBCA 171(3)
- exemption, CBCA 171(2); CBCR Part 10
- meetings, CBCA 171(5)
- requirement, CBCA 171(1)

Auditors

- appointment, CBCA 162(1)
- attendance at meetings, CBCA 168
- ceasing to hold office, CBCA 164
- court appointed, CBCA 167
- defined, CBCA 2(1)
- dispensing with, CBCA 163
- examination, CBCA 169
- proxy re appointment, CBCR 56
- qualifications, CBCA 161
- reliance on others, CBCA 169(2)
- removal, CBCA 165(1)
- replacement, CBCA 168(5.1)–(8)
- report, CBCR 71.1
- right to information, CBCA 170
- statement of, CBCA 168(5)
- vacancies, CBCA 165(2), 166(1), 166(3)

Ballot

- shareholder's right on, CBCA 141

Bankruptcy and Insolvency Act

- insolvency under, effect on dissolution proceedings, CBCA 208

Body corporate

- holding, CBCA 2(4)
- incorporation, CBCA 5(2)
- subsidiary of, CBCA 2(5)

By-laws

- directors, power to make, CBCA 103(1)
- making at organizational meeting, CBCA 104(1)(a)
- shareholder approval, CBCA 103(2)
- shareholder proposal to amend, CBCA 103(5), *see also* Proposals

Canada Business Corporations Act

- application, CBCA 3(1)
- purposes, CBCA 4

Canada Gazette

- publication in
- • certificate, correction, CBCA 265
- • certificate, issuance of, CBCA 262(b)(v)
- • claimants, search for, CBCA 221(b)
- • dissolution, CBCA 212(2)(b), 213(4)(b)
- • name change, CBCA 13(1)
- • regulations, CBCA 261(2)

Certificate

- amalgamation
- • effect, CBCA 186

Certificate *(cont'd)*
- • form, CBCA Form 14.2
- • issuance, CBCA 185(4)
- amendment
- • issuance, CBCA 13, 27(5), 177(3), 191(5), 192(7)
- arrangement
- • form, CBCA Form 14.2
- • issuance, CBCA 192(7)
- continuance
- • as means of amending original articles, CBCA 187(3)
- • effect, CBCA 187(5)
- • form, Form 12
- • issuance, CBCA 187(4)
- discontinuance
- • date, CBCA 262(5)
- • issuance, CBCA 188(7)
- dissolution
- • effect, CBCA 210(6), 211(6), 212(4), 213(5), 223(8)
- • issuance, CBCA 210(5), 211(5), 212(3), 213(4), 223(7)
- incorporation
- • effect, CBCA 9
- • issuance, CBCA 8
- intent to dissolve
- • effect, CBCA 211(6)
- • issuance, CBCA 211(5)
- restated
- • effect, CBCA 180(4)
- • issuance, CBCA 180(3)
- revival
- • effect, CBCA 209(4)
- • issuance, CBCA 209(3)
- revocation of intent to dissolve
- • effect, CBCA 211(12)
- • issuance, CBCA 211(11)
- signatures on
- • mechanical reproductions allowed, CBCA 262.1

Compulsory and Compelled Acquisitions, CBCA 206–206.1

Constrained share corporation
- amendment of articles, CBCA 174; CBCR 86
- definitions
- • Canadian, CBCR 73
- • constrained class, CBCR 73
- • constrained share corporation, CBCR 73
- • constraint, CBCR 73
- • control, CBCR 73
- • maximum aggregate holdings, CBCR 73
- • maximum individual holdings, CBCR 73
- • voting share, CBCR 73
- disclosure, CBCR 74
- issuance of shares, refusal, CBCR 76
- limitation on voting rights, CBCR 77–79
- registration of share, refusal, CBCR 75
- sale of shares
- • director's duties, re, CBCA 46(2)
- • effect on previous owner, CBCA 46(3)
- • general, CBCA 46(1); CBCR 82–83
- • notice, CBCR 80–81, 83(1)(b)
- • proceeds, CBCA 47; CBCR 84

Continuance
- articles, *see* Articles
- certificate, *see* Certificate
- charter companies and, CBCA 268
- exporting of company
- • effect of, CBCA 188(9)
- • general, CBCA 188(1)
- • prohibition, CBCA 188(10)
- • shareholder approval, CBCA 183(3)–(5)
- importing of company
- • effect of, CBCA 187(8)–(12)

Continuance *(cont'd)*
- • shares, CBCA 187(8)–(12)
- under legislation other than CBCA, CBCA 188(2.1)

Contracts
- directors
- • avoidance standards, CBCA 120(7)
- • disclosure, CBCA 120(7)
- pre-amalgamation, CBCA 14(2)
- pre-incorporation, CBCA 14(2)
- share purchase
- • burden of proof, re, CBCA 40(2)
- • enforceability against corporation, CBCA 40(1)
- status of contracting party, CBCA 40(3)

Control
- defined, CBCA 2(3); CBCR 73

Corporate seal
- not required, CBCA 23

Corporations
- capacity
- • extra-territorial, CBCA 15(3)
- • general, CBCA 15(1)–(2)
- defences, limitations, CBCA 18
- immunity, CBCA 51(4)
- limits on activities of, CBCA 3(4)–(5)
- names, *see* Names
- proposals, *see* Proposals
- records, *see* Records

Costs
- security not required
- • dissenting shareholder, CBCA 190(18)
- • investigations, CBCA 229(4)
- • remedies, CBCA 242(3)
- • take-over bids, CBCA 206(14)

Court
- defined, CBCA 2(2)
- powers

- • compliance order, CBCA 247
- • contracts, setting aside, CBCA 119(8)
- • decisions of Director under CBCA, appeals, CBCA 246
- • derivative action, CBCA 240
- • dissolution, CBCA 212–219
- • election of directors and auditors, CBCA 145
- • investigations, CBCA 229–230
- • liquidation, distribution of money, CBCA 224
- • liquidation, examinations, CBCA 222(3)–(4)
- • liquidation, final account, CBCA 223(2)–(6)
- • liquidation, supervision, CBCA 211(8)
- • meetings, CBCA 144
- • oppression remedy, CBCA 241
- • payments to corporations, CBCA 97, 100
- • pre-incorporation contracts, CBCA 14(3)
- • proposals, CBCA 137(8)–(9)
- • proxies, CBCA 154
- • receivers and receiver-managers, CBCA 97, 100
- • take-over bids, CBCA 205(3)
- • valuation of dissenter's shares, CBCA 190(15)–(23), 206(9)–(17)

Criminal Code
- perjury charges under, CBCA 233

Damages
- apportionment of, CBCA 237.2–237.9
- definitions, CBCA 237.1
- liability, CBCA 237.5–237.9; CBCR 95

Debt obligations
- acquisitions and reissue, CBCA 39(12)
- defined, CBCA 2(1)
- repayment, CBCA 39(11)

Definitions, *see also specific headings*

- adverse claim, CBCA 48(2)
- affairs, CBCA 2(1)
- affiliate, CBCA 2(1)
- appropriate persons, CBCA 65(1)–(2)
- articles, CBCA 2(1)
- associate, CBCA 2(1)
- auditor, CBCA 2(1)
- bearer, CBCA 48(1)
- beneficial interest, CBCA 2(1)
- beneficial ownership, CBCA 2(1)
- body corporate, CBCA 2(1)
- bona fide purchaser, CBCA 48(2)
- broker, CBCA 48(1)
- business combination, CBCA 126(1)
- call, CBCA 2(1)
- Canadian GAAP, CBCR 70
- Canadian GAAS, CBCR 70
- confusing, CBCR 17
- corporate name, CBCR 17
- corporation, CBCA 2(1)
- court, CBCA 2(1), 207
- court of appeal, CBCA 2(1)
- debt obligation, CBCA 2(1)
- delivery, CBCA 48(2)
- Director, CBCA 2(1)
- director, CBCA 2(1)
- distinctive, CBCR 17
- distributing corporation, CBCA 2(1); CBCR 2
- distribution to the public, CBCA 2(7)
- entity, CBCA 2(1)
- fiduciary, CBCA 48(1)
- financial collateral, WA 22.1(2)
- fungible, CBCA 48(2)
- genuine, CBCA 48(2)
- going-private transactions, CBCA 2(1); CBCR 3
- good faith, CBCA 48(2)
- holder, CBCA 48(2)
- incorporator, CBCA 2(1)
- individual, CBCA 2(1)
- liability, CBCA 2(1)
- Minister, CBCA 2(1)
- offer, CBCA 206(1)
- offeree, CBCA 206(1)
- offeree corporation, CBCA 206(1)
- offeror, CBCA 206(1)
- officer, CBCA 2(1)
- ordinary resolution, CBCA 2(1)
- person, CBCA 2(1)
- personal representative, CBCA 2(1)
- prescribed, CBCA 2(1)
- put, CBCA 2(1)
- redeemable share, CBCA 2(1)
- resident Canadian, CBCA 2(1); CBCR 13
- SEC, CBCR 70
- SEC registrant, CBCR 70
- security, CBCA 2(1)
- send, CBCA 2(1)
- series, CBCA 2(1)
- share, CBCA 206(1)
- special resolution, CBCA 2(1)
- squeeze-out transaction, CBCA 2(1)
- take-over bid, CBCA 206(1)
- title transfer credit support agreement, WA 22.1(2)
- transfer, CBCA 48(1)
- US GAAP, CBCR 70
- US GAAS, CBCR 70
- unanimous shareholder agreement, CBCA 2(1)
- use, CBCR 17
- valid, CBCA 48(2)

Derivative action

- commencement
  - • conditions precedent, CBCA 239(2)
  - • general, CBCA 239(1)
- definitions

Derivative action *(cont'd)*
- - action, CBCA 238(1)
- - complainant, CBCA 238(1)
- powers of court, CBCA 240

Director under CBCA
- appealing decisions of, CBCA 246
- appointment, CBCA 260
- powers
- - derivative action, commencing, CBCA 238, 239(1)
- - dissolution of corporation, CBCA 212
- - exemptions, CBCA 2(8), 10(2), 82(3), 151(1), 156, 160(3)–(4), 171(2), 187(11)
- - financial statement's approval, CBCA 158(1)
- - investigation, ordering, CBCA 229
- - name change, ordering, CBCA 10(2); CBCR Part 10
- - ownership enquiries, CBCA 235(1)
- records, CBCA 267

Directors
- appointment, CBCA 106(8) 110(1)
- attendance at shareholder meetings, CBCA 110(1)
- board of, information re, Form 2
- ceasing to hold office, CBCA 108(1)
- class director, CBCA 111(3)
- contracts
- - disclosure requirements, CBCA 120
- definition, CBCA 2(1)
- delegation of authority
- - general, CBCA 115(1)
- - limitation, CBCA 115(3)
- dissent
- - procedure, CBCA 123
- duty
- - audit, re, CBCA 171(8)
- - court-ordered amendment of articles and/or by-laws, CBCA 103
- - general, CBCA 122

- election
- - cumulative voting, CBCA 107
- - general, CBCA 106(3)
- - term, CBCA 106(2), (4)–(6), 111(5)
- form re,, Form 6
- indemnification, CBCA 124
- liabilities
- - corporation holding shares in itself, CBCA 32(4)
- - effect of reliance on third parties, CBCA 123(4)
- - general, CBCA 118
- - limitations upon, CBCA 118(6), 119(2)–(4)
- - proxies, CBCA 150(4)
- - registrants, CBCA 153(9)
- - wages, CBCA 119(1)
- meetings, *see* Meetings
- notice of change, CBCA 113; Form 6
- number, CBCA 102(2), 112
- powers
- - bind company, CBCA 18(d)–(e)
- - by-laws, pass, CBCA 103
- - general, CBCA 102(1)
- - organizational meeting, CBCA 104
- qualifications
- - general, CBCA 105(1)
- - residency, CBCA 105(3)
- records, CBCA 19(2)
- removal
- - by shareholders, CBCA 109
- - right to be heard, CBCA 110(2)
- remuneration, CBCA 125
- resignation
- - effective date, CBCA 108(2)
- - statement of reasons, CBCA 110(2)
- vacancy, filling, CBCA 108(3), 109(4), 111(1)
- validity of acts, CBCA 116

Director's circular, *see* Take-over bid

Discontinuance, *see also* **Certificate** *and* **Continuance**

- upon amalgamation, CBCA 186.1(3)–(6)

Dissolution

- actions, effect upon, CBCA 226
- articles, *see* Articles
- before commencing business, CBCA 210(1)
- certificate, *see* Certificate
- court application
- • grounds, CBCA 213(1), 214(1)
- • orders, effect, CBCA 218, 219
- • orders, general, CBCA 213(3), 214(2)
- • powers of court, CBCA 216(3), 217
- Director under CBCA, by
- • grounds, CBCA 212(1)
- • publication of notice, CBCA 212(2)
- liquidation
- • distribution of property in money, CBCA 224
- • general, CBCA 211(7)
- • payment of costs, CBCA 223(1)
- • supervision by court, CBCA 211(8), 215
- • unknown claimants, CBCA 227(1)
- liquidator, *see* Liquidator
- procedure, voluntary
- • before commencing business, CBCA 210(1)
- • no corporate property, CBCA 210(2)
- • property disposed of, CBCA 210(3)
- property vesting in Crown, CBCA 228(1), *see also* Revival
- service of documents after, CBCA 226(3)
- shareholder approval, CBCA 211(1)–(3), *see also* Meetings
- statement of intent to dissolve
- • filing with Director under CBCA, CBCA 211(4), 262(2)
- • form, Form 19

Dividends

- form, CBCA 43(1)
- restrictions on payment, CBCA 42

Documents

- Director under CBCA and
- • acceptance of photostat, CBCA 258
- • copies, CBCA 266(2)
- • corrections, CBCA 265
- • electronic filing, CBCA 258.1
- • fees payable to Director in respect of, CBCA 261.1; CBCR 97, CBCR Schedule 5
- • verification, CBCA 259
- electronic
- • affidavits, CBCA 252.6
- • consent, CBCA 252.3; CBCR 7–8
- • defined, CBCA 252.1
- • information system, CBCA 252.1
- • requirements, CBCA 252.4–252.5; CBCR 9
- • signature, CBCA 252.7
- • statutory declaration, CBCA 252.6
- • use, CBCA 252.3(1)
- inspection of, CBCA 266(1)
- signatures, CBCA 262.1

Donated shares

- acceptance, CBCA 37

Electronic Filing

- documents and notices, CBCA 258.1

Exemptions

- audit committee, dispensing, CBCA 171(2)
- disclosure requirements, CBCA 156; CBCR Part 10
- distribution to public, CBCA 2(8)
- financial statements, delivery to Director under CBCA, CBCA 160(5)
- financial statements, non-disclosure, CBCA 156; CBCR Part 10
- information kits

Exemptions *(cont'd)*
- insider report, CBCA 127(8)
- name, use of "Limited", CBCA 10(1)
- proxy solicitation, CBCA 151(1); CBCR Part 10
- rules of procedure, application, CBCR 88–94, Form 27
- security not part of distribution to public, CBCA 2(8)
- shares, nominal value in, CBCA 187(11); CBCR Part 10
- trust indentures, CBCA 82(3)

Fees
- prescribed, CBCR 97
- security certificate, CBCA 49(2)

Financial statements
- annual, CBCA 155
- contents, CBCR 72
- delivery
- • Director under CBCA, CBCA 160
- • shareholders, CBCA 159(1)
- director's approval, CBCA 158
- examination, CBCA 157(2)–(4)
- exemptions, *see* Exemptions
- records, CBCA 157(1)
- regulation re,, CBCR 71

Forms
- prescribed by Regulations, CBCR 4

Funds
- takeover bids
- • arrangement, CBCA 199

Going private transactions
- general, CBCA 193

Guarantee, *see* Loans and guarantees

Guarantor
- when deemed, CBCA 48(7)

Incorporators
- definition, CBCA 2
- qualifications

- • bodies corporate, CBCA 5(2)
- • individuals, CBCA 5(1)

Infants
- rights re securities, CBCA 51(5)

Information circular, *see* Proxies

Information kits, *see* Policy statements

Insider
- civil liability for use of confidential information, CBCA 131(4)–(5)
- definition, *see* Insider Trading
- prohibited activities
- • purchasing of calls or puts, CBCA 130(2)
- • short selling, CBCA 130(1)
- • use of confidential information, CBCA 131(4)

Insider trading
- definitions, *see also* Definitions
- • business combination, CBCA 131(3)
- • distributing corporation, CBCA 126(1)
- • insider, CBCA 126(1)–(3), 131(1)–(2)
- • officer, CBCA 126(1)
- • share, CBCA 126(1)
- report
- • exemption, CBCA 127(8)

Investigations
- application for
- • grounds, CBCA 229(2)
- • hearings in camera, CBCA 229(5)
- • publications of proceedings, prohibition, CBCA 229(6)
- • who may apply, CBCA 229(1)
- costs, *see also* Costs
- • Director under CBCA
- • compliance with Act, CBCA 237
- • inquiry into ownership of securities, CBCA 235(1)

Investigations *(cont'd)*

- • investigator's report, right to, CBCA 230(2)
- • notice of application, entitlement, CBCA 229(3)
- • publication of results, CBCA 235(3)
- • investigator
- • appointment, CBCA 230(1)
- • hearings in camera, CBCA 232(1)
- • powers, CBCA 230–231
- • right to counsel, at hearing before, CBCA 232(2)
- • statements, privilege, CBCA 234–235
- • solicitor-client privilege, CBCA 236

Issuer

- • defined, CBCA 48(2)
- • security
- • liability for unauthorized endorsements, CBCA 68(2)
- • limitation of liability, CBCA 68(2)
- • warranties, CBCA 69(3)

Liens

- • enforcement, CBCA 45(3)
- • provision in articles, CBCA 45(2)

Liquidator, *see also* **Dissolution**

- • appointment, CBCA 220(1)
- • duties, CBCA 221
- • final account
- • application for approval, CBCA 223(2)
- • notice, application, CBCA 223(4)
- • shareholder application, CBCA 223(3)
- • powers
- • application to examine parties, CBCA 222(3)–(4)
- • delegation of powers, CBCA 219(2)
- • general, CBCA 221(1)
- • reliance on third parties, CBCA 222(2)

Meetings, *see also* **Notice, Resolutions**

- • directors
- • adjournment, CBCA 114(7)
- • Canadian majority rules, CBCA 114(3)–(4)
- • general, CBCA 114(1)
- • notice, CBCA 114(5)–(6)
- • participation by phone, CBCA 114(9)
- • quorum, CBCA 114(2)
- • resolution in lieu of, CBCA 117
- • where only one director, CBCA 114(8)
- • organizational, *see* Directors
- • proposals, *see* Proposals
- • shareholders, *see also* Shareholders list
- • annual, CBCA 133(a)
- • court ordered, CBCA 144
- • directors' entitlement to attend, CBCA 110(1)
- • location, CBCA 132(1)
- • notice, CBCA 135–136; CBCR 44
- • quorum, CBCA 139
- • requisition for calling, CBCA 143
- • resolution in lieu of, CBCA 142
- • special, CBCA 133(b)

Minister of Consumer and Corporate Affairs, MDO 2

Names

- • change of
- • amending of articles, by, CBCA 173(1)
- • designating number, from, CBCA 12(4)
- • order by Director under CBCA, CBCA 12(2)
- • undertaking to, CBCA 12(4.1)
- • designating number
- • order to change from, CBCA 12(4)
- • request for, CBCA 11(2)
- • French or English format, CBCA 10(3)

Names *(cont'd)*
- indication of incorporation
- • abbreviations, CBCA 10(1)
- • exemption from requirement, CBCA 10(1.1)–10(2)
- • general, CBCA 10(1)
- other than corporate name
- • use of, CBCA 10(6)
- outside of Canada, CBCA 10(4)
- prohibition
- • confusing, CBCR 17, 18, 25
- • deceptively misdescriptive, CBCR 32
- • exceptions, CBCR 28–31, 33
- • family name, CBCR 26
- • general, CBCA 12(1)(a); CBCR 19–21, 27
- • not distinctive, CBCR 16, 24
- • reserved name, CBCA 12(1)(b)
- • scandalous, obscene or immoral, CBCR 23
- • secondary meaning, CBCR 15, 22
- publication, CBCA 10(5)
- reservation of
- • right to, CBCA 11(1)
- revocation, CBCA 12(5)

Notice, *see also* **Meetings**
- corporation, service procedure, CBCA 254
- directors and shareholders, delivery procedure, CBCA 253
- waiver, by director, CBCA 114(6)
- waiver, by Director under CBCA, CBCA 258.2; CBCR 14
- waiver, by shareholder, CBCA 136
- waiver, general, CBCA 255

Offences
- auditor, failure to attend meeting, CBCA 168(4)
- corporation holding shares in itself, CBCA 32(3)
- dissolved company, failure to maintain records, CBCA 225(2)
- financial statements, director's failure to correct, CBCA 171(9)
- financial statements, failure to deliver to Directors under CBCA, CBCA 160(3)
- insider's report, failure to file, CBCA 127(9)
- investigation, failure to comply with order of Director under CBCA, CBCA 235(4)
- proxy, failure to circulate, CBCA 149(3)
- proxy, failure to send to shareholder, CBCA 149(3)
- proxy circular, failure to send, CBCA 150(3)
- proxyholder, failure to obey orders, CBCA 150(4)
- publications under
- • format, CBCA 267.1
- purposes, CBCA 4
- records, destruction, CBCA 22(3)
- records, failure to maintain, CBCA 20(6)
- records, failure to safeguard, CBCA 20(3), 225(2)
- security holders' list, misuse, CBCA 85(6)
- shareholders' list, misuse, CBCA 21(9)

Office, *see* **Registered office**

Officers
- appointment, CBCA 104(1), 121
- duty of care, CBCA 122
- indemnification, CBCA 124
- renumeration, CBCA 125
- validity of acts, CBCA 116

Oppression remedy
- costs, *see* Costs
- grounds, CBCA 241(2)
- limitations on remedy, CBCA 241(6)
- powers of court

Oppression remedy *(cont'd)*
- • approval to discontinue action, CBCA 242(2)
- • general, CBCA 241(3)

Proposals
- by-laws, re, CBCA 103(5)
- court's power, re, CBCA 137(8)–(10)
- director's nomination, CBCA 137(4)
- general, CBCA 137(1)–(1.4); CBCR 46–47
- prohibitions, CBCA 137(5)–(5.1); CBCR 48–52
- refusal to allow, CBCA 137(7); CBCR 53
- inclusion in management proxy circular, CBCA 137(2)

Proxies, *see also* **Proxy circular, Proxyholder**
- appointment, CBCA 148(1)
- definitions
- • dissident, CBCR 60
- • form of proxy, CBCA 147
- • proxy, CBCA 147
- • registrant, CBCA 147
- • solicit or solicitation, CBCA 147; CBCR 67–68
- • solicitation by or on behalf of the management of a corporation, CBCA 147
- execution, CBCA 148(2)
- exemption, CBCA 151(1)
- form, CBCR 54–56
- management proxy
- • exceptions, CBCA 149(2); CBCR 58
- • mandatory solicitation, CBCA 149; CBCR 59
- offences, *see* Offences
- remedies, re, CBCA 154
- solicitation, CBCA 150; CBCR 69
- revocation, CBCA 148(4)

Proxy circular
- date, CBCR 65
- Director under CBCA, entitled to copy, CBCA 150(2)
- exemption, CBCA 151(1)
- form
- • dissident, CBCR 61
- • management, CBCR 57
- mandatory, CBCA 150
- offences, *see* Offences
- remedies, re, CBCA 154

Proxyholder
- beneficial owner, appointment as, CBCA 153(5)
- intermediary
- • duties, CBCA 153(1), (4)
- • offences, CBCA 153(8)–(9)
- • rights, CBCA 152(2)–(3)
- meetings, mandatory attendance, CBCA 152(1)
- offences, *see* Offences

Receiver
- appointment, effect on directors' powers, CBCA 96
- courts, powers re, CBCA 100
- duties, CBCA 97–99
- functions
- • receiver, CBCA 94, 101
- • receiver-manager, CBCA 95, 101

Receiver-manager, *see* **Receiver**

Record date, *see also* **Shareholders' list**
- fixing and purposes, CBCA 134(1)–(2)

Records
- accounting
- • retention period, CBCA 20(2.1)
- corporate
- • access, CBCA 21
- • contents, CBCA 20(1)
- • form, CBCA 22(1)

Records *(cont'd)*
- • location, CBCA 20(1), (5)
- Director under CBCA's, CBCA 267; CBCR 15
- directors
- • general, CBCA 20(2)
- • location, CBCA 20(2)
- dissolution, custody upon, CBCA 225
- offences, *see* Offences
- duty to safeguard, CBCA 22(2)
- rectification, CBCA 243

Registered office
- change of address, CBCA 19(3)
- change of place, CBCA 173(1)(b)
- form, Form 3
- general, CBCA 19(1)
- information re, Form 2
- notice, CBCA 19(2), (4)

Registrant, *see* **Proxyholder**

Regulations
- power of Governor-in-Council to make, CBCA 261(1)
- publication, CBCA 261(2)–(3)

Reorganization
- articles, CBCA 191(2), *see also* Articles
- certificate, *see* Certificate
- definition, CBCA 191(1)

Resolution
- definition
- • special resolution, CBCA 2(1)
- in lieu of meetings, CBCA 117, 142

Revival
- articles, *see* Articles
- certificate, *see* Certificate
- general, CBCA 209(1)
- preservation of rights, CBCA 209(4)

Securities
- actions

- • burden of proof, CBCA 53
- • defences, CBCA 55(3)–(4)
- bearer form, CBCA 48(6)
- certificate
- • destruction upon cancellation, CBCA 51(7)
- • fee for issuance, CBCA 49(2)
- • right to, CBCA 49(1), (3)
- • signature, CBCA 49(4)–(6)
- definition, CBCA 2(1), 48(2)
- endorsement
- • effect of without delivery, CBCA 66
- • general, CBCA 65
- • unauthorized, effect of, CBCA 68
- options to acquire, CBCA 29
- order form, CBCA 48(5)
- overissue
- • defined, CBCA 48(1)
- • prohibition, CBCA 52
- purchaser
- • adverse claim, notice of, CBCA 61, 62, 67
- • defect, notice of, CBCA 55(1), 56
- • delivery, CBCA 70–71
- • title, CBCA 55(2), 60
- • wrongful transfer, reclaiming possession, CBCA 72
- registered form, CBCA 48(4)
- registration
- • duty to register transfer, CBCA 76–79
- • security holder
- • corporation's rights re, CBCA 51(1)
- • loss, duty to notify, CBCA 80
- securities register
- • contents, CBCA 50(1)
- • branch and central, CBCA 50(2), (5), (6)
- • location, CBCA 50(3)
- share certificates, *see* Share Certificates

Securities *(cont'd)*
- transmission
  - parties entitled, CBCA 51(2), (3)
  - rights of corporation upon, CBCA 51(9)
  - supporting documentation, CBCA 51(7)–(8)
- warranties
  - agents, CBCA 59
  - broker, CBCA 63(5)
  - guarantor of endorsement, CBCA 69
  - intermediary, CBCA 63(3)
  - issuer, CBCA 63(1)
  - pledgee, CBCA 63(4)

Share certificates

- contents
  - class particulars, CBCA 49(13)
  - general, CBCA 49(7)
  - notation of constraint, CBCA 49(10)
- dissenting shareholder, return of, CBCA 190(8)
- fractional shares, CBCA 49(15), (17)
- scrip certificate, CBCA 49(16), (18)

Shareholders, *see also* **Meetings, Proposals, Voting**

- approval, when required
  - amalgamation, CBCA 183
  - articles, amendment of, CBCA 173–176
  - by-laws, CBCA 103(2)
  - continuance, CBCA 188(5)
  - directors, election, CBCA 106(3)
  - sale of property, CBCA 189(5)
- dissent
  - disposal of shares, CBCA 190(3)–(4), (7)–(26)
  - procedure, CBCA 190(5)
  - when available, CBCA 190(1)–(2)
- pre-emptive right to new issuance, CBCA 28
- voting
  - class, CBCA 176, 182(4)
  - general, CBCA 141

Shareholders' list, *see also* **Record date**

- access, CBCA 21(4)
- offences, *see* Offences
- preparation of for meeting
  - effect, CBCA 138(2)–(3)
  - examination, CBCA 138(4)
  - general, CBCA 138(1)
- supplemental lists, CBCA 21(4)–(5)
- use, CBCA 21(9)

Shares

- acquisition by corporation
  - limitations, CBCA 34(2), 35(3)
  - when available, CBCA 34(1), 35(1)–(2)
- acquisition by subsidiary, CBCA 31(3)–(5)
- cancellation, CBCA 39(6)
- classes, CBCA 24(4)
- commission on sale, CBCA 41
- constrained, *see* Constrained share corporation
- conversion, CBCA 39(9)
- corporation holding own
  - exceptions, CBCA 31–32
  - prohibition, CBCA 30
- donated, CBCA 37
- general, CBCA 24(1)–(2)
- issuance
  - consideration, CBCA 25(3)–(4)
  - dividend, as form of, CBCA 43(1)
  - general, CBCA 25(1)–(2), 27
  - non-assessment, CBCA 25(2)
- redemption, CBCA 36
- reserved, CBCA 29(3)
- rights attached to, CBCA 24(3)

Squeeze-out transactions, CBCA 194

Stated capital account
- additions, CBCA 26(2)–(6)
- adjustments, CBCA 39(1)–(4), 43(2)
- maintenance, CBCA 26
- reductions, CBCA 38

Taxation
- year-end
- • form, Form 22

Trust indentures
- definitions
- • event of default, CBCA 82(1)
- • trustee, CBCA 82(1)
- exemption, CBCA 82(3), PS 6.3
- evidence of compliance, CBCA 86–89
- notice of default, CBCA 90
- offences, *see* Offences
- security holders
- • list, furnishing, CBCA 85(1)
- • list, use, CBCA 85(5)
- trustee
- • conflict of interest, CBCA 83(1)–(2)
- • duty of care, CBCA 91
- • qualifications, CBCA 84
- • removal, CBCA 83(4)

Unanimous shareholders agreement
- definitions, CBCA 2(1), 146(3)
- validity, CBCA 146(2)

Voting
- class vote
- • when available, CBCA 176
- electronic, CBCA 141(3)–(4); CBCR 45
- pooling agreement, CBCA 146(1)
- shareholders' rights, CBCA 140(1)

Wages, *see* **Directors, Liabilities**

Winding-up and Restructuring Act

Appeals, WA 103–107

Applications for winding-up order
- adjournment, WA 14
- cases where order may be made, WA 10, 10.1
- duty of company, WA 15
- how and where made, WA 12
- notice, WA 12(2)
- power of court, WA 13, 16
- who may apply, WA 11

Application of Act, WA 6, 7

Application of Act (Part I), WA 9

Authorized Foreign Banks
- application of Act, WA 6(2), 8
- application of Part III, WA 150
- ceasing business, WA 153
- distribution of property, WA 158.1
- execution, WA 155
- liquidator
- • duties of, WA 158.2
- • preparation of statement, WA 156
- • transfer to foreign, WA 158.2
- notice, WA 151
- right of action, WA 158.3
- secured claims, WA 81.1
- set-off, WA 158
- winding-up order
- • effect of, WA 154

Commencement of winding-up, WA 5

Contestation of claims, WA 87–92

Contributories
- absconding, arrest of, WA 117
- bankruptcy of, WA 56
- classics, WA 51
- liability of shareholders, WA 53–54
- list, WA 50, 52
- powers of court, WA 57–62

Creditors' claims
- debts of company, WA 71

Creditors' claims *(cont'd)*
- distribution of assets, WA 76–77
- employee claims privileged, WA 72
- notice, WA 74
- proof of claim, WA 75
- secured claims
- • authorized foreign bank assets of, WA 81.1
- • duty of creditor, WA 78
- • mortgage, WA 82–83
- • negotiable instrument, WA 81(1)
- • option of liquidator, WA 79
- • ranking, WA 80
- • retention of security, WA 84
- • revaluation, WA 81(2)
- set-off, WA 73
- valuation of, WA 21(2)

Definitions, WA 2

Distribution of assets
- distribution by liquidator, WA 76–77
- expenses, WA 94
- property, WA 93
- surplus, WA 95

Dividend sheet, WA 85

Evidence, WA 146–150

Examination, WA 118–119, 122

Fraudulent preferences
- contracts obstructing creditors, WA 97
- debts of company, WA 102
- dividend, WA 102.1
- gratuitous contracts, WA 96
- intent to defraud, WA 99
- redemption of shares, WA 102.1
- sale/transfer in contemplation of insolvency, WA 100
- void payments, WA 101, 101.1
- voidable contracts, WA 98

General
- limitation of Part I, WA 8, 9

Insolvent company, WA 3

Inspectors
- appointment of, WA 41

Liability of officers, WA 124

Liens, WA 86

Liquidators
- appointment of, WA 23–30
- appointment of solicitor, WA 36
- authorized foreign bank, WA 152
- court discharging functions of liquidator, WA 48–49
- creditors, arrangements, WA 38
- debts due to company, WA 37
- distribution of assets, WA 76–77
- notice of appointment, WA 26
- powers of directors, WA 31
- powers and duties of, WA 33–39
- provisional liquidator, WA 28
- removal, WA 32

Meetings of creditors
- compromise, sanction of, WA 66
- powers of court, WA 63, 64(2), 65, 67
- voting, WA 64, 68

Offences and punishment
- books, destruction of false entry, WA 141
- criminal proceedings, WA 140
- failure to comply with order, WA 142
- refusal to answer, WA 145
- refusal to give information, WA 143

Procedure, WA 108–137

Production of documents, WA 120–121, 123

Remuneration
- inspectors, WA 43
- liquidators, WA 42

Rules and regulations, WA 136–137

Service

• outside jurisdiction, WA 112

Stay of proceedings, WA 17, 18

Unclaimed deposits, WA 138–139

Winding-up order

• effect of order, WA 19–22.2, 154

• where order may be made, WA 10

Winding-up — Restructuring of Insurance Companies

• aircraft objects, WA 22.2

• application of Act (Part III), WA 159.1

• computation of claims, WA 163

• definitions, WA 159

• notice of proceeding, publication, WA 171

• permitted actions, WA 22.1

• policies

• • modification, WA 162.2

• • partial payment, WA 162.1

• • reinsurance, WA 162, 162.1

• • transfer, WA 162

• priority, payment of claims, WA 161, 172

• protection of asset orders, WA 160

• report to Superintendent, WA 170

• right of action, WA 167

• statement of claimants/creditors

• • filing, WA 168

• • notice of filing, WA 169

• • objections, WA 166(3)

• • preparation, WA 166

• transfer of funds to liquidator, WA 164, 165